D0087943

LATIN AMERICA

LATIN AMERICA

History, Politics, and U.S. Policy

Second Edition

James D. Cockcroft

Empire State College
State University of New York

Nelson-Hall Publishers

Chicago

Project Editor: Dorothy Anderson
Photo Researcher: Nicholas Communications
Typesetter: E.T. Lowe
Printer: Capital City Press
Cover Painting: Hector Giuffre, *"Buenos Aires Birthday"*

Library of Congress Cataloging–in–Publication Data

Cockcroft, James D.
    Latin America : history, politics, and U.S. policy / James D.
Cockcroft. — 2nd ed.
        p.   cm.
    Rev. ed. of: Neighbors in turmoil. ©1989.
    Includes bibliographical references and index.
    ISBN 0-8304-1398-7
    1. Latin America—History—20th century.   2. Latin America-
-History—1830–1898.   3. United States—Relations—Latin America.
4. Latin America—Relations—United States.   I. Cockcroft, James D.
F1414.C6   1995
980.03'3—dc20   94-40030
                                                            CIP

Manufactured in the United States of America

10   9   8   7   6   5   4   3   2   1

 The paper used in this book meets the minimum requirements of American National Standard for Information Sciences—Permanence of Paper for Printed Library Materials, ANSI Z39.48-1984.

Contents

About the Author

Three-time Fulbright scholar and 1988 University of California Regents Lecturer, Dr. James D. Cockcroft (Ph.D., Stanford University, 1966) is a pioneering scholar of "dependency" historical analysis and "cooptation/control" political theory. A long time resident of Latin America, he has written and taught widely in the fields of history, political science, sociology, Latin American and Caribbean Studies, and Mexican American Studies. This is his twentieth book and the first one on *all* of Latin America and U.S-Latin American relations since his pathbreaking co-authored *Dependence and Underdevelopment: Latin America's Political Economy* (1972).

Preface to Second Edition

This is a substantially revised and updated version of the original edition, with a new title: *Latin America: History, Politics, and U.S. Policy*. It takes into account the demise of Stalinism in the former Soviet Union and Eastern Europe and addresses the question of U.S. policy in a "post–Cold War" world. The fall of the Soviet Union has shifted U.S. policymakers' attention away from Central America, at least momentarily, and focused it on Cuba—so I have added policy debate materials on Cuba in the Documents section and reduced the Central American materials there.

Readers of the original edition who found the book useful for U.S. foreign policy and international relations courses will find this revised edition equally helpful. Select reading in the Overview, Introductions to the three parts, Conclusion, and Documents section, together with a couple of case studies (for example, in the chapters on Chile, Cuba, Panama, Nicaragua, and El Salvador), can generate excellent discussions on policy-making debates. "Anatomy of a coup," a very special and intriguing subject involving a subtle mix of national and international factors, can be found in almost every chapter, but the reader might benefit by starting with either the 1964 coup in Brazil or the 1973 coup in Chile.

Using the contents and index, the reader can quickly locate all the key issues, including such "hot" topics as NAFTA (and other recent trade agreements), narcotrafficking, and the environment. Based on feedback from the first edition, it is clear that the select bibliographies are a very good starting point for anyone doing a research paper. Numerous teachers have said that it has saved them and their students time.

In the preparation of that first edition, through an editorial oversight the names of two friends were left out of the list of individuals who lent especially valuable help. I thank them here: Michel Mill and Bruce Clark, who provided insights into Nicaragua and Cuba, respectively. In similar fashion two colleagues' names were omitted and I thank them: Charlie Gillespie, who provided some materials for the Uruguay chapter and the Southern Cone, and E. Bradford Burns, who offered invaluable suggestions for the film/video lists.

For the 1994 edition I wish to thank friend and colleague Emelio Betances for his suggestions on the Dominican Republic, as well as Eugene Miller for his help on Costa Rica. I also want to extend a very special thanks to the librarians and staff at SUNY-Albany Library and at Crandall Library (Glens Falls, New York). Finally, I want to express deep gratitude to Nelson-Hall editors Richard Meade and Dorothy Anderson and all the Nelson-Hall editorial and production people who made this edition such an attractive one; to Bill Culver for providing additional research materials; and to Hedda Garza, prize-winning indexer and author, for a superb index, making it a remarkably helpful guide.

James D. Cockcroft

Preface to First Edition

After living and teaching more than a quarter of my adult life in Latin America and writing nearly a dozen books on themes related to that area of the world or to U.S. foreign policy, I was concerned in the mid-1980s by the apparent ignorance of so many U.S. citizens about developments "south of the border," some of which threatened to plunge them into war. A *New York Times*/CBS news poll indicated that only a third of Americans knew where Nicaragua was; another third said they did not know; and yet another third shockingly placed Nicaragua in South America, the Middle East, Africa, or Asia (near Vietnam, according to some). Moreover, as rising, sometimes violent, social movements in Latin America with heavy anti-U.S. overtones escalated, other polls showed the U.S. public's optimism about the nation's future slipping, reaching an uneasiness unmatched since the most troubled days of the Vietnam War. As the 1980s drew to a close, concerned students hungrily sought information, and enrollments in college courses on Latin America (and Vietnam) increased dramatically. The boards of education of the nation's public schools were asked to overhaul their curricula in order to introduce more materials about Latin America.

To try to explain the historical context and to shed some light on this rapidly developing situation, I decided to write an analytical textbook for both students and the general public that would be exciting to read, informative, and up-to-date. Such a text, I realized, would be the first in two decades to bring under single authorship a separate treatment of every Latin American country. It would also be among the first to incorporate recent trends in scholarship and events in history like Latin America's "new politics," the "debt crisis," the rise of the "national security state," "re-democratization," the central role of "drug czars," shifting "class alliances," the "Arias Peace Plan," and "Iran-contragate." Harper & Row editors were enthusiastic about the idea as well, and we agreed to produce this text.

The result, this book, introduces students and the public to modern Latin American politics and history, with a generous sprinkling of important cultural and geographical factors contributing to national or regional heritages. Wherever possible, it presents Latin American–U.S. relations.

Hence, the title is not "Troubled Latin America" but "Neighbors in Turmoil"— for we are neighbors, and the turmoil is not limited to Latin America. A fierce debate on U.S. foreign policy in Latin America has raged throughout the Western Hemisphere since widespread disillusionment with the exaggerated optimism connected with the 1959 Cuban Revolution and the Alliance for Progress. Contending policy positions and actions not only in Latin America but inside the United States are highlighted here.

Often, three distinct perspectives are presented: first, official U.S. position; second, typical nationalist responses from the Latin American country in question; and third, different views expressed by U.S. citizens or groups opposed to the official U.S. position. By presenting this range of viewpoints and the basic facts, I hope to leave the reader better equipped to deal with the issues. The advantages of this approach in place of the more ordinary "author's opinion" or "expert authority" approach are self-evident. A "Documents" section at the end of the book offers a unique opportunity to examine several contrasting perspectives.

The book opens with an Overview to emphasize the differences among Latin American countries while pointing out their commonalities. It is advisable to read this first because it explains fundamental concepts and controversies affecting any discussion of Latin America and U.S.–Latin American relations. As throughout the text, conflicting points of view on highly controversial issues are summarized (including conceptual debates dealing with "modernization," "dependence," "underdevelopment," "reform or revolution," "corporativism," "bureaucratic authoritarianism," and so on).

The Overview explains some of the new (and old) trends and themes shaping today's Latin America—forces which reappear in almost every chapter. These include: the historic impact of attempted revolutions in Bolivia,

Chile, Cuba, Guatemala, Mexico, and Nicaragua; competing versions of nationalism; the ongoing important roles of elite families and one or two dominant export commodities; issues of human rights and the two-decade-long "dark night of state-sponsored terror"; the "new Marxism" and "theology of liberation"; military and civilian forms of "populism"; the growing gap between rich and poor; student, slumdweller, peasant, minority rights, and other social movements; U.S. aid programs and acts of interventionism (including an historical record from the Monroe Doctrine to the present).

Introductions to the book's three parts, divided by geographical region, further flesh out these and related themes, adding to the flexibility of the book's use for more specialized courses or for comparative analysis. Each country chapter starts with a dramatized scene vivifying a particularly striking or controversial issue that makes the country and its people immediately palpable to the reader. It then presents the historical background and contemporary narrative, infusing each with information on population, ethnicity, urbanization, economics, politics, and international relations.

Reflecting the widely held view among Latin Americanists that "Latin" America consists of the former colonies of Spain and Portugal, I have chosen to include a chapter on Puerto Rico (absent from most textbooks on Latin America) but to omit chapters on the former possessions or present dependencies of France, England, or the Netherlands. Readers interested in these last-named areas will find convenient summaries in the Introduction to part Two (or for Belize, Part One). On Haiti and Grenada, there is a more thorough discussion because of the recent revolutionary upheavals there (some of Haiti's history, of course, appears in the chapter on the Dominican Republic as well).

In order to enrich our understanding of Latin America's current turmoil in all its complexity, this book emphasizes the particularities of each Latin American country and the region's diverse historical experiences. Primarily a nineteenth- and twentieth-century history and political science textbook, it does not pretend to be a complete text on colonial or pre-colonial history. In this sense, it is a text on what historians call "the modern period." At the same time, it describes the accomplishments, limitations, and legacies of the pre-colonial societies and "the colonial period." It explains the violent eruption and impact of the nineteenth-century wars of independence (the Overview points out which chapters contain the more detailed discussions of these earlier historical periods, usually the chapters covering the nations most commonly studied). In sum, this book's presentation of history illustrates how events of the past have given rise to many of the problems and conflicts of contemporary Latin America.

The annotated select references to representative books, articles, films, and videotapes at the end of each chapter (or Overview and Introductions) do not substitute for more complete bibliographies. They are intended to assist readers in locating additional materials on topics commonly emphasized in classrooms or professional circles. The short-list and annotation method (where titles are self-explanatory, no further annotation is offered) seems more practical than a long unannotated list that can overwhelm an uninformed reader. Naturally, any knowledgeable reader will notice the omission of a significant work here or there. The line for inclusion or omission has been drawn in favor of recent works, liveliness, accuracy, balance, and illustration of major themes or controversies.

This book can be used in a variety of ways, depending upon the reader's interest or the subject emphasized (lands and peoples, politics, history, economics, sociology, anthropology, urban geography, Latin American or Caribbean Studies, international relations, U.S. foreign policy, etc.). For teachers, judicious choice of chapters or regions can make the text useful over a two-semester period, while a one-semester use is also perfectly feasible. One does not have to read every country chapter, of course, and either a "country sampling" or a "regional" approach will work. Naturally, a comparative approach (economic development, revolutions, military dictatorships, types of political systems, etc.) is possible if one reads the Overview and Introductions and carefully selects chapters.

An approach favored in some circles is initial examination of Argentina, Brazil, Chile, Cuba, and Mexico, because of their geographical diversity, historical importance, significant industrialization or economic growth, and influential political or cultural heritages (Colombia and Venezuela should probably be added to this group of countries, however, in light of their recent industrial advances and developing political complexity). Another approach gaining in popularity is to read up on the "hot spots" by looking at the pertinent Introduction and country chapter. For example, to learn about the "Noriega affair" of the late 1980s, be sure to look at the Introduction to Part One and the Panama chapter.

Yet another approach, often challenging for advanced students, is to address the question "How is U.S. policy made and is it in the best interests of the American people?" (creating American jobs, improving the U.S. image abroad, etc.). Then read the chapters on U.S. interventions in Guatemala (1954), Cuba (1961), the Dominican Republic (1965), Chile (1973), Nicaragua (1980s). Finally, read the materials on U.S. foreign policy in the Overview, Introductions, and Documents sections and outline an alternative scenario—for example, What if the U.S. government had supported the post-dictatorship reformist governments in the Caribbean Basin and the elected "socialist" government in Chile? In sum, a wide range of approaches is possible.

Although I have written the book in part to satisfy the public's interest in learning more about Latin America and the debates shaping U.S. foreign policy there, I have also tailored it for college classroom use. In my own teaching experience, I have found that focusing on controversy is an effective method of instruction, as this text in fact reflects. I have tried to summarize here opposing viewpoints on major controversial issues, enabling teachers and students to pursue any number of debates in class or through individual or group research projects. An example may help.

Let us take the issue of "aid to the contras." There exist two clearly opposed viewpoints: aid, or no aid. Examination of the pros and cons entails a look at the 1979 Nicaraguan revolution, the situation before and after its occurrence, who the contras are, the Soviet and Cuban presence, and the revolution's post-1979 accomplishments and failures. Additional viewpoints are bound to surface, including criticisms of the revolution from the left and the right (provided in chapter 5). The undeniable debate issue, however, remains aid to the contras or not. ("Humanitarian aid," however defined or practiced, is still aid, although attempts at compromise are often made in the U.S. Congress through granting "humanitarian aid" instead of "military aid.") Some students and teachers may be made uncomfortable by the tension and conflict that this kind of debate generates, but most welcome it since they realize that, in everyday life, conflict—not consensus or "yes'ism"—is what generates most learning in actual fact.

I have found this "conflictual" pedagogical approach extremely fruitful for developing both critical thinking and a knowledge base. It obligates people to look at two sides of a question, that is, *to think* and to confront an opposing viewpoint. A research paper or an oral report that merely parrots the teacher (or an encyclopedia or other author's work!) rarely educates a person as well. On the other hand, a paper or report that delves into controversy and then chooses a position on the basis of critical thought and research can be both educating and exciting.

A variant of this approach is the "commission of inquiry" method. Each "team" of students—up to half a dozen—looks into a particular controversy chosen from a list of topics provided by the teacher and presents its findings to the class, carefully delineating a few questions for a class-wide vote. The teacher, after briefly "cross- examining" the team, moderates the class's "cross-examination" of the team members. The class then votes on the issues raised. The class is thus the "hearing body" to which the "commission of inquiry" team reports; it is, if you like, the Congress, U.N., Senate Committee, or World Court. One of the incidental benefits of this approach is that each student leans from another student's research (on the other hand, rarely do students read one another's research papers). Other side benefits include practice in speaking in public and in preparing reports on unknown subjects, tasks that students are often assigned in the early years of their postgraduate careers.

An example illustrates the method. Recently, in both my history and political science classes, "commissions of inquiry" looked into the Bay of Pigs and Missile Crises in Cuba. They presented dramatic skits in which the students acted the roles of Castro, Kennedy, and Khrushchev, as well as "typical" Cubans commenting on their revolution (including a sugarcane cutter and an ex-prostitute who liked the changes the revolution had produced and a businessman and journalist who did not). After cross- examination, each class had to vote on whether the Bay of Pigs invasion should have been undertaken or not, on whether it should have succeeded or not, on whether the revolution had materially helped or harmed most Cubans, and so on. Votes on equally challenging questions had to be taken on the Missile Crisis. Each team then had to announce its considered judgment on these questions, with minority reports allowed.

Often, unexpected contradictions and thought provocations surface with such a methodology, and students usually participate with surprising gusto. Naturally, written work accompanies the "commission of inquiry" approach and can be tailored to the level of study (written summations, full-length papers, arguments with evidence, annotated bibliographies, and so on, often divided up among team members according to subtopics relating to the controversy being investigated). The individual work involved allows for grading the work on both a team *and* an individual basis (students not willing to "'risk" even part of their grade through team involvement can write a standard term paper instead).

Without digressing from the weight of evidence or the thematic narrative I have tried in this book to provide sufficient controversy to stimulate discussion whether or not the "commission of inquiry" method is used. Statistics introduced have a certain margin of error but are those most commonly accepted and widely reported. Special terms or foreign-language expressions are explained in the text as they occur.

The words "'terror" and "terrorism" do, however, merit specific comment. They are emotionally laden terms and real phenomena. U.S. citizens should know that their government is perceived in many circles as complicitous in terrorism, or even practicing it. This book explains why. Guerrilla groups, too, are often perceived as "terrorist." This book sets all the acts of violence in Latin America, along with all the issues of human rights, in as fair and accurate a perspective as possible, pointing out to readers what "conventional wisdom" says and how different groups or individuals strongly disagree.

In brief, by highlighting central themes and issues in Latin American politics and history, along with key factors in each country's evolution, I have sought to provide a quick, easy-to-use source of up-to-date information and policy choices for all readers of whatever background. Hopefully, the result helps to fill a gap in the existing literature on a critically important area of the world.

I would like to dedicate this book to those who have most educated me (and others) on Latin America. Too numerous to name individually, they include all those colleagues of LASA (Latin American Studies Association, the professional organization of Latin Americanists in the United States) who have worked so hard to educate a public that still remains too much "in the dark" about our neighbors to the south. Even more significantly, they include all those Latin Americans—particularly people most victimized by poverty and human rights violations—who have drawn me (and the world) into their orbit of humanity and "new politics." To these several key "political actors," then, in both parts of the Western Hemisphere, I would like to dedicate this work, with all its shortcomings for which I alone bear responsibility.

A number of individuals went out of their way to make this book possible. First and foremost is my life companion and best friend, Hedda Garza, to whom I express my affectionate thanks. Our many long and heated discussions on the subjects raised here (and related ones affecting people's lives throughout the world) helped me sort out the significant from the insignificant. She helped me understand core issues with ever greater clarity. Hedda Garza's critical commentary and editorial services throughout the preparation of this work have sharpened my analyses considerably.

Other colleagues commented on individual chapters, showing a sense of mutual aid many U.S.-based Latin Americanists cherish. I thank them here: Jane Canning, William Culver, Ronald Ernest, Astrid Fischel, Sheldon Liss, Jose Moreno, and June Nash, among others.

Historical Overview: Latin America's New Politics and the Challenge for U.S. Policymakers

The United States appear to be destined by Providence to plague America with misery in the name of liberty.—*Simón Bolívar (1829)*

The enemy is the Communist system itself—implacable, insatiable, unceasing in its drive for world domination. . . .Those who make pacific revolution impossible make violent revolution inevitable.—*President John F. Kennedy (1960)*

They [Communists, Marxists] are the focus of evil in the modern world.—*President Ronald Reagan (1983)*

"Armed aggression" and "violation of another country's sovereignty" were the charges. Nicaragua was the accuser, the United States the accused. The World Court in the Hague had conducted its hearings for more than two years.

The judges were accustomed to being patient in these matters. Ever since the end of World War II, the World Court had served as the internationally recognized authority on matters not resolved at lower levels of the post–World War II system of international law. In fact, after very lengthy deliberations, the Court recently had ruled in favor of the United States in the matter of the 1979 seizure of the U.S. Embassy in Teheran and the holding of U.S. hostages by Iranians. Then the United States, after answering the Nicaraguan charges with its own claims of Nicaraguan aggression against El Salvador, had withdrawn as a member of the Court on the grounds that it would not receive a fair hearing.

Now, on June 6, 1986 the Court issued its ruling (see Documents).

"Guilty!" screamed the newspaper headlines in the Hague.

The Court censured the United States on fifteen counts of international law for acts of aggression against Nicaragua, including attacks on Nicaraguan oil installations, ports and shipping in 1983 and 1984, the mining of Nicaraguan

1

ports and harbors in 1984, and the dissemination of a CIA (Central Intelligence Agency) manual to contra forces instructing them in antihumanitarian and illegal acts. The Court called for an immediate halt to these aggressive acts and the "training, arming, equipping, financing and supplying the contra forces" and encouraging "the commission by them of acts contrary to general principles of humanitarian law." The Court further condemned the 1985 U.S. trade embargo against Nicaragua as a violation of the 1956 treaty of friendship between the two countries (see Documents).

The contras were a group of mercenaries commanded by the CIA and officers of the defunct Nicaraguan National Guard, the armed forces of longtime dictator Anastasio "Tachito" Somoza, overthrown in Nicaragua's popular revolution of 1979 (see chapter 5). U.S. President Ronald Reagan denied the contras were mercenaries, claiming instead that they were "freedom fighters" and "the moral equivalent of our Founding Fathers," worthy of U.S. aid.

The Court also found that Nicaragua had sent a small amount of aid to Salvadoran rebels in 1980 and 1981. However, it ruled that this did not constitute an "armed attack" under international law.

. . .

The Iran and Nicaragua cases before the Court had nothing to do with one another. Yet they indirectly symbolized a curious "mix" of U.S. policy-making about two nations having little in common except that their peoples had overthrown detested U.S.-backed dictatorships in 1979. Ironically, not long after the World Court's censure of U.S. aggression, the "Iran-contragate" scandal erupted (see Introduction to Part One). The result of investigations into that affair, so far as U.S. policymakers were concerned, was that U.S. credibility was gravely undermined throughout the world, especially in Latin America and the Middle East.

The U.S. government's credibility was also damaged at home, where details began leaking out about U.S. combat deaths in Nicaragua, U.S. "secret armies" fighting in Central America, U.S. plots on the lives of the presidents of Central American nations, and alleged U.S. drug trafficking using planes that flew arms to the contras and returned with cocaine to land at U.S. military airfields in Florida. Plans to suspend the U.S. Constitution and to use already constructed "concentration camps" to crush U.S. citizen protests against a possible invasion of Nicaragua caused further alarm (see Introduction to Part One).

In the midst of these shocking developments, a new peace plan for Central America was endorsed by the presidents of Costa Rica, El Salvador, Guatemala, Honduras, and Nicaragua. Known as the "Arias Peace Plan" (because of the role of Costa Rican President Oscar Arias in its preparation—see Documents), its call for demilitarization of Central America marked a startling departure by four presidents from earlier cooperation with the United States on the contra aid issue. It eventually became the guiding outline for internationally monitored peace settlements in Nicaragua, El Salvador, and Guatemala.

Serious as these challenges were for U.S. policymakers, there were even more problems surfacing in Latin America as a whole. The worst economic depression since the 1930s was stirring the embers of social despair and popular revolt just when most Latin American nations were trying to consolidate new limited democracies introduced after a twenty-year "long, dark night" of military dictatorships and state terrorism. Because Latin America experienced a *per capita* GDP (Gross Domestic Product) growth rate of minus 1.2 percent in the 1980s, the entire decade became known as "the lost decade." UN estimates showed 40 percent of all Latin Americans living below the poverty line.

But Latin America's "democratic transition," as it was called, stirred new hopes and was cited by President Reagan in his 1988 State of the Union address: "Today, over 90 percent of Latin Americans live in nations committed to democratic principles." Reagan's Republican party administration, like the preceding Democratic party one of President Jimmy Carter, had long sought to take credit for the modest gains in human rights and democratic representation being achieved by Latin America's political activists. Knowledgeable people, however, like Thomas Carothers, a former Reagan appointee who worked for the U.S. Agency for International Development (AID) in the mid-1980s, gave "a qualified no" to the question of whether any of the credit should go to the United States (see Selected Bibliography).

Indeed, in the eyes of many Latin Americans, the U.S. government, because of its military and police aid programs, was part of the problem rather than part of the solution. The actions of Latin American military and police officers had introduced new terms like "death squads" and "disappearances" into the world's political vocabulary. Their grisly regimes of recent decades had usually been installed and sustained with generous U.S. assistance. Many of the military and police were U.S.-trained. Estimates of the number of Latin Americans who "disappeared," that is, were kidnapped and murdered, during the military's long, dark night of state terror, ranged higher than 150,000. Several civilian governments of the 1980s and early 1990s (Guatemala, El Salvador, Colombia) gained the reputation of being "death-squad democracies."

When the dictatorships went on borrowing sprees, and U.S. and other banks rushed in with huge loans, the monies were spent on lavish projects of benefit to a few corporations or military officers. The dance of the dollars in the candlelight of the long, dark night left each nation with a foreign debt thirty times its original level. Latin America's debt in 1993 surpassed $440 billion (the United States' debt surpassed $4.4 *trillion*).

As Latin America's "credit worthiness" declined, so did new loans, most of which went to pay off the interest on old ones. Wealthy individuals and cor-

3

porations aggravated the region's scarcity of capital by sending billions of dollars abroad to more lucrative markets. More than half of Latin America's borrowings went unaccounted for and were probably sent to foreign banking accounts or for the purchase of overseas assets. From 1977 to 1987, according to the Morgan Guaranty Trust Company, "capital flight" from only Mexico, Venezuela, Argentina, and Brazil (in order of amounts) surpassed $200 billion. Latin America's economies became rollercoasters of speculation, and by the late 1980s major U.S. banks were posting "losses" and "writing down" their Latin American debts to offset loans that clearly could never be paid back. In addition, they offered "debt for nature" swaps to help protect Latin America's disappearing rain forests (and assure access to them for foreign capital), as well as other debt-reduction schemes aimed at offsetting bank losses with more favorable conditions for foreign investment.

Just to meet interest payments on the debt, most Latin American countries became more dependent on single-commodity export trade than ever before (Ecuador, Venezuela, and Mexico on oil, Bolivia on legal tin and illegal cocaine, Chile on copper, the Caribbean and Central America on sugar, coffee, or tropical fruits). In most cases the prices of Latin America's legal exports dropped, forcing yet more production for export to keep up with the debt payment schedule or simply to pay for the machinery and raw materials necessary to keep production going. In fact, while the region grew poorer in the 1980s, production for export actually increased.

Starting in the late 1970s, recessions elsewhere became depressions in Latin America. Combined unemployment and underemployment approached or surpassed half the workforce in almost every Latin American country. Despite anti-inflationary measures imposed by the IMF (International Monetary Fund) and enforced by "national security states" or their successors, prices kept skyrocketing while wages fell further behind. A region with 16 percent of the world's cultivable land and under 8 percent of its population (432 million in 1990), Latin America had more hungry people than India, Pakistan, and Bangladesh. One out of every five people suffered severe malnutrition; three thousand children under five years of age died every day. As sanitation and health care conditions deteriorated, previously eliminated diseases appeared. In 1991, a cholera epidemic broke out in Peru and began spreading to the rest of Latin America, affecting hundreds of thousands of people and killing thousands. By the early 1990s, 73 percent of all Latin Americans lived in cities of over 100,000, most in wretched slums.

In the midst of this holocaust of human despair the tightening of the debt noose created a crisis of Latin American state management and a widespread fear of U.S. interventionism. U.S. policies in the region were increasingly perceived as contributing to a strangulation of local economies and the ability of the state to govern. As Mexican President José López Portillo stated in his 1979 "state of the nation" address:

> When stabilization programs, justified by transitory conditions, are perpetuated, greater injustices result than those supposedly being corrected. Fatally, salaried workers' wages are restricted; capital centralizes; and the state's room for maneuver is reduced. The state's capacity to resolve conflicts is annulled, its possibility of governing cancelled.

Some spoke bitterly of Latin America's new fledgling "democracies" as "stateless democracies."

Only a minority of Latin Americans shared the prevalent U.S. view of an "East-West" (Communist-capitalist) conflict shaping their destinies. Most Latin Americans, including new civilian presidents taking office during the 1980s, believed the main axis of conflict, as well as of wealth and poverty, was "North-South" (rich-poor). The collapse of the Soviet Union strengthened this view.

Sharing much of the prevailing Latin American perspective on U.S. policies was a majority of scholars of Latin America in the United States and a growing number of U.S. citizens opposed to U.S. interventionism. Some were critical of Washington's Latin American policies under both Republicans and Democrats (see Documents). Critical and innovative thinking about U.S. foreign policy was surfacing among all major political currents. The U.S. government and U.S.-based TNCs (transnational corporations)[1] were often being singled out for careful analysis and severe criticism. At the same time, growing numbers of U.S. governmental and corporate policymakers were beginning to appreciate, or at least to consider, much of the new thinking. For example, AID official Carothers later acknowledged "the continuing tensions between U.S. anti-Communist concerns and prodemocracy goals." (The withdrawal of Soviet and Eastern European aid to Latin America in the early 1990s, however, was not reciprocated by the United States.)

For their part, Latin Americans were reexamining their tendency to blame the United States for all of Latin America's ills. Venezuelan President Carlos Andrés Pérez claimed in 1988: "The whole culture of anti-Americanism has fortunately receded." This marked a change from the preceding long, dark night of state-sponsored terrorism when anti-Americanism had flourished as a modern-day kind of "black legend."[2] Anti-Americanism had deep historical roots dating back to Teddy Roosevelt's "taking" of Panama and U.S. gunboat diplomacy. Since the 1954 CIA-engineered overthrow of Guatemala's first-ever democracy and the 1959 Cuban Revolution, overt and covert U.S. interventions in the name of anticommunism had escalated: "Bay of Pigs" Cuba (1961); Brazil (1964); the Dominican Republic (1965); Chile (1973);

5

Argentina (1976); Grenada (1983); Bolivia (1986); Honduras (1988); Panama (1989); and Nicaragua and El Salvador (1980s).

The original black legend went back to colonial times. Numerous writers traditionally had blamed most of Latin America's colonial ills on Spain or Portugal, whose monarchies presumably could do no good. Historians Lesley Byrd Simpson and Lewis Hanke, among others, viewed this as a black legend, suggesting that Spaniards and Portuguese had been unfairly criticized. Spain's or Portugal's looting, killing and subjugating of other peoples—colonialism—was no worse than that of other European powers. Indeed, in some respects, it was better.

They pointed out, for example, that the treatment of Indians and African slaves in Latin America was not so abusive as it was in "North America" (as Latin Americans preferred to call the non-Latin part of the Western Hemisphere, since back in Columbus's time it was all known as "America"). Slavery was outlawed in most of Latin America before it was in the United States—usually during wars of national independence, in which slaves often were key participants. Similarly, although Latin America's Indians were abused and the vast majority of them did die, most of the deaths were from diseases spread by European settlers or slaves (especially smallpox, but also typhoid, malaria, measles, yellow fever, diphtheria, and mumps).

Defenders of Spain and Portugal pointed to the strong influences the "mother countries" asserted over Latin American culture, many of which were positive—whether in architecture, the arts, education, or manners. Detractors emphasized unequal power relationships and the destruction of equally meritorious cultural and architectural wonders of numerous Indian civilizations (see chapters 1 and 14). Several historians pointed out that the black legend applied to all colonial powers.

Both the Crown and the Roman Catholic Church periodically issued pronouncements defending Indian human rights, and in 1550 the Spanish monarchy actually ordered the conquest to cease until the government could decide whether or not it was "just." The writings and testimonies of Bishop Bartolomé de Las Cases in defense of Indian human rights (see chapter 1) helped bring about this decision. After Las Casas's death the Standard Law of 1573 replaced the word "conquest" with "pacification" and urged the Spaniards to moderate their use of force.[2]

Whatever the merits or demerits of the original black legend, one reality stood out long after the departure of the Spaniards and Portuguese as colonial rulers of Latin America. Among the region's Indians and *castas* (mixed races), a deep distrust of white people, the government, and the Church hierarchy persisted. During the postindependence part of the nineteenth century Latin America's landed oligarchy, high Church officials, and merchant elites asserted their control over darker-skinned underclasses more ruthlessly than ever before, reinforcing the colonial heritage. To be sure, both then and on into the twentieth century an occasional Indian or mulatto became president (e.g., Juárez in Mexico, Batista in Cuba); and other nonwhites joined the middle and even the upper classes. But this tempering of racial differentiation was based on class and/or military power.

Not surprisingly, peasants of whatever racial or ethnic derivation were still described in many countries as "Indians." Among other colonial traditions perpetuated to the present were the following: influential roles of the Church and military officer corps in politics; *personalismo* (reliance on an individual for governance or access to jobs, power, or status); patriarchical and macho norms of family and social organization; *continuismo* (perpetuation of an individual or political part in power); "monoculture" (reliance on one or two commodities for export and sustenance of the domestic economy); clientelism (patron–client relations, often overlapping with godfather relations, linking the powerless to the powerful); and a strong central state, or authoritarianism. (Reviews of the colonial and independence periods and their legacies are more fully developed in chapters 1, 2, 8 to 11, 14, 18, and 20.)

A kind of subliminal anti-wealthy "collective historical consciousness" persisted among Latin America's toiling masses during the nineteenth and twentieth centuries that psychologically reinforced the black legend. It was this consciousness, together with the inflammatory rhetoric of Latin American intellectuals and nationalists, that made it easy for many Latin Americans to transfer their hatred of colonialism to the new foreign powers that economically dominated their region after independence: first Great Britain, and increasingly, after 1898, the United States.

Most North Americans in the last third of the twentieth century were genuinely bewildered by the intense anti-U.S. emotional tide sweeping not only Latin America but much of the so-called Third World (the "first" world being either the most industrialized or "capitalist"; the second being also industrialized and "socialist/Communist"; the third being the poorest, least industrialized and either capitalist or socialist/Communist). The explanation for anti-U.S. feelings was fairly obvious in Latin America, where people resented being viewed as *anyone's* "backyard." Historically, they had seen U.S. warships, U.S. Marines, and what the conservative Mexican philosopher José Vasconcelos once called U.S. "Proconsuls" (ambassadors) repeatedly interfere in their lives (see the introductions to Part One and Part Two).

Yet during the 1970s Latin Americans began to sharply criticize the familiar position of placing the blame for all problems on the U.S. government or U.S. corporations ("anti-imperialism"). For instance, in his book *The Latin Americans: Their Love-hate Relationship with the United States*, Venezuelan author Carlos Rangel denounced the new black legend, criticizing Latin American leftists for their instinctive carping at U.S. policy, or what he called their

7

reliance on myth. Uruguayan writer Eduardo Galeano did not see U.S. interventionism as a myth, but he did upbraid his fellow Latin Americans on the title page of his best-selling *Open Veins of Latin America* by quoting an 1809 revolutionary proclamation issued in La Paz (then Peru, today Bolivia): "We have maintained a silence closely resembling stupidity." His book lambasted Latin America's ruling classes and not just greedy foreign powers.

Actually, Latin Americans had long written about faults within their own cultures and politics. For example, Mexican poet-statesman Octavio Paz, in *Labyrinths of Solitude*, poignantly portrayed the complex psychology of death and violence inside the very "soul" of Mexican culture. And several other writers had recounted the foibles of Latin Americans from all social or ethnic backgrounds. Indeed, starting in the 1960s a veritable "boom" in Latin American literature occurred, bringing the region a number of international literary prizes. The names of novelists like Amado, Borges, Carpentier, Cortazar, Fuentes, García Márquez, and Vargas Llosa became known worldwide. The long, dark night only partially silenced Latin America's literary innovativeness.

Also stating in the 1960s, a "new politics" began to sweep Latin America, one that challenged many standard conceptualizations and practices. It was marked by revolutionary priests fighting as guerrillas or joining governments and challenging the orders of the Pope (see chapters 3, 5, 12, and 20); slum dwellers throwing down the gauntlet to the IMF (see chapters 1, 4, 10, 14, and 15); U.S.-trained military personnel becoming anti-U.S. guerillas or nationalist reformist presidents (see chapters 2, 7, 13 to 15, and 20); women moving to the forefront of human rights struggles (see chapters 1, 2, 7, 15, 18, and 20); Indians leading revolutionary upheavals or organizing across regional barriers (see chapters 1, 2, 11 to 16, and 20); rank-and-file workers challenging labor union bossism (see almost any chapter); old political enemies forming "broad front" political alliances (see especially Part One and Part Three); Christians and Marxists working together instead of at cross-purposes (see chapters 3, 5, 12, and 20).

In part a result of the new politics, in part its cause, a fresh, multiangled debate began affecting a region long seen in simple and often negative terms by the rest of the world. At the same time, Latin America became a major player on the world stage of politics—and people had to examine more closely its history and politics.

Roots of Turmoil: Standard Concepts and Interpretations

Something new was going on in Latin America, and its roots were to be found in two watersheds of contemporary Latin American history: first, the Cuban Revolution and Alliance for Progress of the early 1960s; and second, the long, dark night of violence and extremism that descended over most of Latin America from the mid-1960s to the mid-1980s. The first watershed raised new hopes; the second, new fears. Both introduced sudden changes and accelerated earlier ones in the economy and politics of the region. Both were interrelated. Both dealt with the persistent problems of widespread poverty for many; fabulous wealth for a handful of elite families (known as "the oligarchy" or "bourgeoisie"); middle-class, working-class, and peasant discontents; and how to handle revolutionary ferment.

The revolutions shaking Cuba and Vietnam had a profound effect in U.S. policy-making circles in the 1960s. Cuba's 26th of July movement showed that the U.S. backyard could no longer easily be patrolled by gunboats or declarations of good neighborliness. Vietnam showed how easy it was for the United States to be drawn into a war being fought by highly motivated nationalists, an apparently unwinnable war in spite of superior U.S. technology.

As these nationalist revolutions, each with Communist or Communist-oriented leaderships, moved to the world's center stage, in Washington it was decided that strong action reforming archaic structures and facilitating economic "modernization" was required. *Modernization* was a concept that roughly meant industrialization and the incorporation of "less-developed" countries into the "modern" world. It implied a mix of modern methods of economic production with modern political forms—in brief, capitalist democracy. (*Capitalism* is that economic system guided by the individual profit motive where the major banks, factories, farms, and mines are owned by the big capitalists, or bourgeoisie; under capitalism, there exist different degrees of state intervention in the economy and many forms of the state or government, democratic or otherwise.)

A "diffusionist" branch of modernization theory had long postulated that a "diffusion" into Latin America of Western industrialized nations' capital, technology, and "know-how," imbued with the "Protestant work ethic," would conquer economic "backwardness." In Latin America capitalist agriculture would have to replace the traditional ways of *hacendado* agriculture (based on low-wage or debt-peon labor on large estates, or *haciendas*) and the skewed land structure of *latifundismo* (huge estates controlling most of the land, much of which lay idle) and *minifundismo* (tiny peasant parcels of land too small to produce a surplus).

A new president, John F. Kennedy, a Democrat, proclaimed what the outgoing Republican president had proposed—an "Alliance for Progress." It promised increased U.S. economic aid on the condition that Latin American nations initiate land-reform programs. "Those who make pacific revolution impossible," Kennedy intoned, "make violent revolution inevitable."

The Cuban Revolution and construction of the Western Hemisphere's first Socialist state and the Alliance for Progress posed two clear-cut alternatives: revolution or reform. (*Socialism* is that economic system where the major banks, factories, farms, and mines are owned collectively by the state, not the bourgeoisie; under socialism individuals can still own property and there exist many forms of the state, democratic or otherwise.)

The question for U.S. policymakers became what to do if reforms ignited too great a threat to U.S. economic interests or those of local elites, including the *hacendados* and *latifundistas*, with whom the United States had long cultivated cordial relations. Kennedy gave the answer during his brief presidency (1961–1964), cut short by his assassination.

He introduced a new program of "counterinsurgency" training for Latin American and U.S. military officers. It updated the weaponry and skills of Latin America's security forces to check any possible advances of guerrilla warfare or urban insurrection. Leading U.S. scholars declared Latin America's "modernized" militaries a "democratic" force.[3] At the same time, a spate of U.S.-backed antireformist military coups showed that, under the Alliance for Progress, the "stick" carried more weight than the "carrot." From the counterinsurgency programs of the early 1960s evolved Latin America's several "national security states" and the long, dark night of state terror. From 1961 to 1975 the U.S. government trained more than 70,000 Latin American military personnel (of whom eight became dictators) and sent $2.5 billion worth of weapons to the region.

Simultaneously, the CIA dispatched labor "reformers" to build anti-left labor unions in Latin America. CIA labor organizers operated first in the 1950s through the ORIT (Inter-American Regional Organization of Workers) and then, in the 1960s, through the AIFLD (American Institute for Free Labor Development). The AIFLD was chaired by J. Peter Grace, president of W. R. Grace and Co. and a director of First National City Bank (both corporations with large stakes in Latin America). The U.S. AID funded nearly 90 percent of AIFLD's declared income, while the CIA and U.S. trade- union dues financed the rest.

The carriers of this carrot of U.S. foreign policy occasionally suffered the consequences of their "free-trade unionism" rhetoric at the hands of those who wielded the stick. For instance, in 1982 a right-wing death squad killed one of AIFLD's operatives in El Salvador. Noted Salvadoran death-squad leader Treasury Police Chief Carranza was on the CIA payroll at the time (see chapter 3).

To understand these matters we need first to review standard concepts and interpretations used in all discussions of the historical evolution of Latin America and U.S. policy-making—notions that became central to the changes shaking the continent. The language of "*caudillismo*," "underdevelopment," "modernization," "dependence," and "imperialism" permeated the entire era before, during, and after the watersheds of the 1960s.

Underdevelopment was the concept used to describe the less industrial-ized nations of the world. They were said to be characterized by economic "backwardness," extremes of wealth and poverty, the absence of a large mid-dle class, and usually "traditionalist" (or old-fashioned) forms of social orga-nization and behavior. In Latin America the "underdeveloped" nations were said to be either predominantly rural or else marked by a "dual society"—a countryside that was feudalistic or traditional and an urban landscape that was capitalistic or modern. Politically, underdeveloped countries were usually ruled by traditional means such as military dictatorship, one-man rule, *caciques* (regional or local bosses), and *caudillos* ("strong men on horse-back").

A central issue in the post–World War II period of Latin American his-tory was that of "development." *Development* meant not just industrialization, but also the introduction of more humane forms of social interaction based on more equitable distribution of economic means and opportunities. Thus, the United Nations (UN) began to collect data on not just GDP growth rates but "quality of life" as measured by health, education, life expectancy, individual purchasing power, and availability of different "life choices." On that "human development" scale, a giant semi-industrialized economy like Brazil's ranked seventieth in 1993 (Mexico ranked fifty-third, the United States, sixth).

Numerous contending schools of thought contested over how best to "develop" Latin America. Modernization theorists advocated rapid industrial-ization and an overhaul of traditional agriculture with the assistance of the UN, the World Bank, and the private investment resources of the "advanced" in-dustrialized countries. Since this meant the diffusion of capitalism, a modern-ization approach was the prevalent one in U.S. policy-making circles. Its first appearance in agriculture occurred during the 1940s in Mexico with the intro-duction of the "Green Revolution," which increased crop yields but also dis-placed peasants from their lands and favored big agribusiness (see chapter 1).

Dependence theorists maintained that the modernization approach was ethnocentric and possibly racist, since it assumed Western superiority. If im-plemented, it would only perpetuate an economic system that historically had left Latin America underdeveloped and overdependent on more industrialized countries. Western banks and corporations would deepen and modernize their hold over Latin America, these theorists argued. The old "enclave economies" in Latin America for the export of raw materials like oil or agricultural prod-ucts like bananas would simply become more diversified and generalized with the rise of TNCs.

The dependence thesis of André Gunder Frank and others[4] was that capi-talism added to economic growth in the metropolitan centers through the ap-propriation of the economic surplus of the satellites, thereby accentuating a skewed division of wealth internationally and leaving the peripheral nations economically unable to compete and underdeveloped. Industrialization would continue to occur in Latin America with increased foreign investment, but it would be dependent and would not cure the region's socioeconomic ills. By 1965 nearly one-third of returned income on all U.S. direct investments overseas came from Latin America, where the rate of profit was exceptionally high.

Numerous writers in the dependence camp, and several in the modernization camp as well, spoke of a "new international division of labor," in which low-wage labor forces in the Third World provided raw materials and agricultural products and assembled parts for the more industrialized nations of "the North." The North's employers in turn grew wealthier, while reducing the average wage levels of their own work forces through "runaway plants" (to the Third World) and the importation of cheap labor (see chapter 1 and Conclusion).

Both modernization and dependence schools of thought had a wide range of subschools that led to left-wing, centrist, or right-wing political approaches in their proposed solutions. For example, the "Chicago Boys"—advocates of free-market capitalism named after Nobel Prize winner Milton Friedman of the University of Chicago—had their right-wing version of modernization that was widely applied in Latin America during the long, dark night. They were directly called upon to plan the economy of post-1973 Chile (see chapter 17), one of Latin America's few countries to show a declining level of industrial output between 1950 and 1985. Critics of the Chicago Boys' free-market approach—one usually reinforced by the credit and development policies of the IMF and World Bank—claimed it "deindustrialized" Latin America (in the sense of denationalizing Latin American industries on behalf of foreign capital—see Part Three.)

A moderate and procapitalist subschool of thought, one of the first to enunciate the dependence notion, was that of the UN's ECLA (Economic Commission on Latin America). It felt that Latin America had to become less economically dependent on outside capital. One way to accomplish this was through the building up of local manufacture. A "national bourgeoisie" of progressive capitalists could be nourished by capitalist states practicing "import-substitution" policies favorable to locally owned industry.

Since the 1930s and increasingly during the next two decades most Latin American nations *did* attempt a policy known as *import substitution*. This policy created protective tariffs on industrial imports in order to favor domestic manufacturers and thereby industrialize without so great a dependence on foreign investors and bankers. The champions of this "national capitalist" road to development in the 1950s and 1960s were Latin American economists and technocrats, many of whom had ECLA experience.

Import substitution proved expensive, however, and failed. Latin America's foreign debt rose as it borrowed to pay for the machinery imports necessary for industrialization. The region's manufacturers were unable to penetrate

12

export markets dominated by others and unable or unwilling to offer sufficiently high wages to generate more than a limited internal market. Increasing amounts of equipment, spare parts, and raw materials had to be imported to keep the new industries going. Licensing fees had to be paid. Import substitution became import-intensive. Unemployment persisted and economic conditions worsened. Traditional exports of primary products (coffee, bananas, copper, oil, etc.) were again overemphasized to help pay the costs.

TNCs found optimal conditions for exporting equipment, extending new loans, and setting up assembly plants and even entire factories in Latin America. They raised most of their initial capital by buying out local firms unable to compete and by obtaining local loans. The more that import substitution failed, the more the TNCs moved in to take advantage of failing firms, low-priced labor, and tax-free "industrial parks" offered by host governments. Import substitution contributed to industrialization but made it more dependent on foreign capital, not less.

As an alternative to import substitution, the idea of a common market took hold. Latin American countries would trade with one another, thereby breaking their overdependence on trade with the United States and other industrial giants. The LAFTA (Latin American Free Trade Association), CACM (Central American Common Market), and the Andean Pact all rose and fell with little lasting success. Indeed, since common markets tended to lower or eliminate tariff barriers and free trade was the banner of the TNCs, many of which operated *within* the participating nations of the common markets, the U.S. government usually supported these common market attempts.

Decision 24 of the Andean Pact, however, which gave foreign firms up to twenty years to transform their holdings into "joint ventures" with the host country's private investors or state, drew the wrath of Washington, as did limitations on the repatriation of profits by foreign-based TNCs to their home countries. The rise of right-wing state terrorist regimes broke the back of whatever economically nationalist potential the common markets had. Numerous policymakers and scholars began enunciating notions of "managed interdependence," arguing that governments could regulate "the terms of dependence" and that decisions about foreign capital had potential "trade-offs."

Increasingly the "trade-offs" approach gave way to the "privatization" approach. Latin America's governments began selling off state enterprises to private investors in hopes of attracting fresh influxes of foreign capital to jump-start their sagging economies. Even Cuba began to welcome foreign private investment, especially after the Soviet Union cut off its aid. By the 1990s, privatization prevailed and there was talk about an eventual hemispheric common market modelled after NAFTA, the North American Free Trade Agreement between Canada, the United States, and Mexico (see chapter 1).

Some dependence thinkers, nationalists, and Marxists remained leary of

13

what they called the "capitalist triumphalism" that helped consolidate the privatization agenda after the fall of the Soviet Union. They pointed to the recessions that swept across the industrialized world in the early 1990s, seemingly with no possibility of sustained recovery short of some new major war or series of localized wars. They also noted the failure of Latin America's escalated privatization efforts to overcome the underlying structural problems of poverty and dependence. Instead, these critics emphasized either a return to a "trade-offs" approach or even sharper breaks with the capitalist "centers" and the introduction of "mixed" or socialist economies based more on local or regional resources.

Several Marxists, however, criticized all these approaches for underestimating the importance of *internal* factors of class oppression. These critics argued that "class warfare" operated with or without the presence of foreign business firms, "mixed" economies, or "socialist" governments. They doubted the possibilities of a "mixed" economy and pointed to Nicaragua's economic failures during the Sandinista revolution in the 1980s as an example of how inadequate such an approach could be (see chapter 5). In their eyes, a "mixed" economy was an illusion.

These Marxists, like many non-Marxist political scientists, noted that a political system is not the same as an economic system. Capitalism does not necessarily entail democracy, as Latin American and European history confirmed (frequent instances of military dictatorship and fascist authoritarianism). An economic system, on the other hand, is either capitalist, that is, dominated by the profit motive, or socialist. If some say it is "mixed," then in reality it is capitalist or state-capitalist since the profit motive remains dominant. If it is socialist, then the profit motive is not allowed to prevail even if numerous market forces go on functioning or are given new impetus. Under socialism, this line of thinking concludes, people produce goods primarily for use instead of profit. A socialist economy, of course, just like a capitalist one, can exist under different political systems with varying degrees of authoritarianism or democracy—running the gamut from Soviet Union Stalinist-type dictatorship to a more participatory "workers' democracy." Ideally, according to the Marxist vision, socialism will one day lead to communism, where there will be enough goods for everybody and the state can "wither away." Many Marxists pointed to Cuba as an example of a socialist economy based on market forces, although even there privatization augured a possible future "mixed" economy opening the doors to a capitalist restoration, a prospect encouraged by new U.S. pressures to topple Cuban leader Fidel Castro (see chapter 8).

Anti-Marxists, of course, claimed that Socialist and Communist parties usually opened the doors to arbitrary state behavior and the creation of a new ruling "bureaucratic class." Socialism, they asserted, discouraged hard and creative work through excessive state social programs that left workers unmo-

14

tivated and deprived people of "freedom of choice." The anti-Communists illustrated their points by referring to Stalinism in the Soviet Union (the time of rule by Joseph Stalin, when many heinous abuses did in fact occur). Some claimed that Stalinism was being reproduced in Cuba and the Sandinistas' Nicaragua of the 1980s.

Anti-Stalinist Marxists answered these critics by saying that communist *political* (not economic) systems come in many varieties, even as capitalist ones do. They pointed to the conquests made by different kinds of socialism against starvation, malnutrition, bad health, illiteracy, and inadequate housing. Democracy of a few in a society of hunger for the many was meaningless, they asserted. Socialist democracy differed from capitalist democracy precisely because it gave people usually excluded from the power system a voice in changing society.

According to Marxists, *imperialism,* not dependence, was the more appropriate theory. Modern imperialism had long been recognized by both Marxists and non-Marxists as the rise of monopoly capitalism, the appearance of cartels, trusts, and holding companies, and the export of surplus capital overseas. These changes in capitalism, most of which occurred at the end of the nineteenth century, led to aggressive, expansionist behavior by modern capitalist states and corporations.

Thus, according to many Marxists, only a sharp break with the capitalist economic system—socialism—could lead to Latin America's economic independence. Since no single country could achieve this without suffering renewed military aggression from outside, new alliances would have to be formed to preserve any socialist revolution. This type of thinking moved Cuba into the Soviet bloc in the early 1960s, at the same time it later caused Cuba to strengthen its ties to the rest of Latin America, China, and the capitalist world, and to encourage Nicaragua *not* to break its trade relations with the United States (see chapters 5 and 8). In a predominantly capitalist world economy, isolation spelled death for either socialism or a "mixed economy" revolution.

Marxists too had sharp cleavages of opinion. Some argued (along lines long spelled out by the old pro-Moscow Communist parties) that a revolution had to proceed by stages—first a bourgeois democratic stage to eradicate feudalism or feudalistic remnants, and then a Socialist stage to end capitalism. Many Maoists agreed with this "stage-by-stage" approach. Trotskyists disagreed, claiming that the revolution had to be "permanent" in both the sense of proceeding directly to socialism and the sense of spreading internationally (see chapters 14 and 15).

In Latin America a "new Marxism" incorporated tendencies from many schools of Marxist thought and introduced peculiarly Latin American features. The new Marxism found an influential group of allies among advocates of the "theology of liberation" (see later section on "Theology of Liberation and 'New Marxism.'")

In contending with all these schools of thought, those who governed Latin America—usually members of elite families or generals or both, heavily sprinkled with upwardly mobile middle-class professionals and "technocrats"—increasingly used their language. Even presidents from Conservative parties spoke of "imperialism" (see chapter 12).

By the 1990s, a new approach to economic development became fashionable, especially in Europe and among environmentalists: *sustainable development*. As the world's forests disappeared and nuclear and other toxic waste disposal problems worsened, a clarion call went out to "develop" Third World countries in an environmentally "sustainable" manner. In Rio de Janeiro, Brazil, a world conference on saving the environment took place in 1992—the UN Conference on Environment and Development, or "Earth Summit." A majority of Nobel Prize scientists and over 1,500 members of science academies from sixty-eight nations, including the nineteen largest economic powers, issued a "Warning to Humanity" that called for "a great change in our stewardship of the earth . . . if vast human misery is to be avoided and our global home on this planet is not to be irretrievably mutilated." It called for better resource management, reduction and eventual elimination of poverty, voluntary family planning, and "sexual equality guaranteeing women control over their own reproductive decisions." Recognizing that "the developed nations are the largest polluters in the world," it called for "a great reduction in violence and war" so that the industrialized world might finance environmental protection.

Meanwhile, reacting to charges of "abetting environmental destruction and ethnocide," the World Bank was forced to condition its megabuck loans for huge dam, forestry, and agribusiness projects on a receiving government's provision of "environmental impact assessment" statements and protection measures for displaced indigenous peoples (often to no avail—see chapters 1, 16, and 20). Investigative journalist William J. Weinberg discovered that the United States was engaging in mass dumping of its industrial and urban wastes in Central America, leading to the poisoning of the environment—and people (see Selected Bibliography).

Some Latin American governments criticized the sustainable development approach for its "double standard." Now that it was "their turn" to industrialize, they were expected to honor far stricter environmental standards than the countries of the North had ever faced. Other critics noted the interest of large pharmaceutical and biotechnology companies in gaining control of the world's last major remaining source of unexplored and diverse species, plants, and "gene pools": the rainforests. They urged a "biodiversity agreement" on the world community that would modify (but not seriously threaten) the near monopoly of knowledge, patents, and ownership enjoyed by these companies (see chapter 20, and Documents.)

Even as in the discussions about economic development and the environment, so too in political science there appeared new emphases and fashions in vocabulary. Words like *populism, corporativism, bureaucratic authoritarianism,* and *nationalism* peppered the political science landscape. The old ideological language of *liberalism* and *conservatism* was largely relegated to nineteenth-century history textbooks. (*Neo-liberalism,* however, was introduced to characterize the economic ideology of free enterprise capitalist development, privatization of state industries, reduced social spending, and "free market" solutions to social problems.)

Even in the nineteenth century, scholars pointed out, the differences between liberalism and conservatism that had generated so many civil wars were, in the long run, less severe than their commonalities in practice (see, for example, chapters 1, 5, and 12). Back then, *Conservatives* championed a strong central state and were pro-Church, whereas, the *Liberals* wanted more local democracy and were anticlerical. In practice, however, regional *caudillos* (leaders, or "strong men") used these ideological banners in their contests for state power, shifting sides like chameleons. Although an occasional theocratic state appeared on the scene (see, for example, chapter 13), there were few lasting consequences of these Liberal-Conservative wars other than continued economic underdevelopment. Even in a country as ideologically polarized as Colombia, Liberal and Conservative leaders repeatedly joined forces to make sure the quarreling elite families would not be toppled by the angry masses whose services they called upon to fight their wars (see chapter 12).

Twentieth-century presidents and governments often used the techniques of populism, corporativism, and nationalism to establish a semblance of political stability over Latin America's contending class forces. As an ideology, *populism* promised something for everyone and appeared to be in the interests of the masses. Most politicians and several military officers, priests, and political agitators preached a populist message.

But a populist program practiced as governmental policy usually occurred only at certain historical moments and led either to socialism (Cuba, 1959–1960), or a restructured or successfully defended capitalism (Brazil and Mexico, 1930s; Argentina, 1940s), or a right-wing overthrow of the populist government (several countries in the 1960s and 1970s). The final outcome depended on which class, class fraction, or set of classes gained the upper hand. (A *class,* as conceived by Max Weber, is a group or set of groups having similar income and social status, or, as Karl Marx defined it, an aggregate of people who share a similar position in relation to the major means of economic production—"owners" and "workers," broadly speaking; a *class fraction* is a branch or section of a class, such as the "national industrial bourgeoisie" as opposed to the "comprador bourgeoisie," or junior partners of foreign capitalists.) The historical moment of the rise of a populist government always was one in which no single class or class fraction could assert clear-cut hegemony.

17

Under populist governments, the role of the state in the economy always noticeably increased.

"Corporativism" was less ideological than populism, although it too
promised something for everyone. More an authoritarian capitalist type of political structure than a political program, corporativism was introduced in several Latin American countries as a means to perpetuate capitalist rule (see, for
example, chapters 1, 15, 18, and 20). *Corporativism* "incorporated" entire
classes or "interest groups" into the structure of the state, which in turn set the
capitalist "rules of the game" and guided the corporate organizations of these
groups under its umbrella. Anyone outside the corporative organizational
structures was a kind of "nonperson," and only mass organizations were "persons." Since the corporate organizations were state-run or state-regulated,
most people were politically excluded from having an actual voice in running
their own affairs.

Often compared to types of fascism, corporativism in Latin America in
fact had its own special characteristics depending on the country. Moreover, unlike fascism, which always had a mass base of some kind, Latin American corporativism often lacked a mass base except in its early stages and always evolved into a form of political exclusion of immense segments of the
population.

Some political scientists came to view corporativism either as too vague
a concept or too deflective of attention from the key question of "who rules
and for whom?" to be worth much attention. Some tried to apply corporativism as an analytical tool for understanding socialist Cuba, but there the
change in economic system seemed far more important than any resemblance
of the political changes to corporativism (see chapter 8).

The "national security states" of the generals and admirals in the last
third of the twentieth century were, like corporativist states, capitalist-authori-
tarian forms of the state. Argentine political scientist Guillermo O'Donnell,
among others, categorized them as "bureaucratic authoritarian states." O'Donnell's concept took into account both the power of the military officers and the
influence of the bureaucrats—often civilian technocrats with advanced training in economics. O'Donnell's approach was criticized, however, for omitting
as much as it included.

National security states were highly repressive. They demobilized and
moved to the margins of the political scene not only workers, peasants, and
students, but also the political parties of the elites. They banned democracy
and trade unions, while usually siding with foreign capital and building up the
economic power of the military and police. Assisted by the United States, they
set up internal security agencies that still existed in the 1990s and often had
links with organized crime and drug traffickers (for more on the narcotics

question and U.S. policy, see introductions to Part One and Part Three and specific chapters).

Nationalism, like corporativism and populism, meant many things to many people. The rulers of the national security states genuinely believed they were saving "the nation" from the evils of Communists, "red priests," and Zionists. (*Zionists* are advocates of a Jewish national or religious community and state in Palestine, today's Israel; not all Jews are Zionists.) The national security state commanders' nationalism sometimes seemed like an attack on the nation, since so many people of the nation were harmed, directly or indirectly, by their state-terror campaigns and economic austerity programs.

Most nationalists in Latin America, whether of the Left or Right, shared one thing in common: a tendency to escalate their anti-U.S. rhetoric during politically difficult times. Easy though it was for many North Americans to make fun of this sometimes exaggerated "anti-Yanqui" nationalism, everyone knew it was based on a certain historical reality. How else could one explain the widespread continental popular appeal of the democratic "revolution" in Guatemala in the early 1950s or the revolutions of Cuba and Nicaragua later? The strength of Latin American nationalism was the single most important dimension of the many challenges the region posed for policymakers in Washington.

Latin American nationalism had both divisive and unifying characteristics. Each country cultivated its own "national" image and mythology, thus helping to keep the continent carved up into several republics, some of which seemed economically unviable (particularly in the Caribbean Basin, a region defined as including all states bordering on the Caribbean, including those in South America and Central America). Yet almost every famous Latin American nationalist spoke of unifying the region, from Simón Bolívar's dream of a single America that led to the calling of the aborted Panama Congress in 1826 to José Martí's notion of *"nuestra América"* (our America) to Fidel Castro's convoking of Latin American leaders in Havana for an international conference on how to handle the area's insurmountable debt structure (see chapters 7, 8, and 11).

Commonalities and Differences

All these concepts and interpretations had one thing in common: they tended to emphasize Latin America's commonalities instead of its differences. Yet in reality the differences were probably more important than the commonalities, even within single countries—and almost every scholar knew it. Immersion in the study of one country, or a set of countries, offered the advantage of detecting the differences *and* highlighting critical commonalities (this book does both).

Five differences stood out. First, there were the obvious differences in geography, language, race, ethnicity, and culture. Majestic mountains, rivers, and deserts laced much of Latin America, leading to national barriers to national or transnational unity. Part of Latin America's *patria chica* (little fatherland) syndrome of loyalty to one's hometown or region derived from the natural borders thrown up by mountains or rivers. Geography thus served to reinforce the regionalism favored by foreign powers ("divide and rule") or local power figures.

Brazilians spoke Portuguese, whereas the other nineteen republics spoke Spanish—heavily accented with Italian in Argentina and Uruguay or with such distinct multilingual Caribbean accents among the *costeños* (coastal peoples) of Andean America that often citizens of highland capitals like Bogotá or Quito had difficulty understanding them! Some nations were predominantly Euro-Caucasian (e.g., Argentina, Chile, Costa Rica, Uruguay), whereas others had strong concentrations of Indian peoples (Bolivia, Guatemala, Ecuador, Peru) or descendants of African slaves (the Caribbean and coasts of Central and South America); others were largely Euro-Amerindian, or mestizo (Honduras, Mexico, Nicaragua, Venezuela). Degrees of Europeanization and Westernization also varied.

Second, there were differences in degrees of industrialization and wealth among nations, including amounts of natural resources capable of generating full-scale industrialization. Semi-industrialized or rapidly industrializing nations like Argentina, Brazil, Chile, Colombia, Mexico, Peru, Puerto Rico, Uruguay, and Venezuela (even to a degree Costa Rica, Cuba, or El Salvador) clearly eclipsed the impoverished nations of Bolivia, Haiti, Honduras, and Nicaragua. Some authorities even spoke of a "fourth world" of underdevelopment (extreme poverty and absence of industrialization) to characterize the poorest countries. Other nations had special features in the ways they handled their economies—for instance, socialist Cuba, canal-dependent and offshore banking Panama, the "operation bootstrap" colony of Puerto Rico, narcotic-exporting Bolivia, Peru, and Colombia.

The debt crisis further complicated this web of economic differentiation. Authorities viewed a relatively well-off country like Costa Rica, whose Central American neighbors lacked the extent of industrialization, democracy, or rural health its people enjoyed, as a "fourth-world nation" when it came to the question of its burdensome foreign debt that propelled its decline to forty-second on the UN "human development" scale in 1993.

Third, Latin American nations differed in their actual forms of governance, whether dictatorial or democratic. There were various types of one-man dictatorship (Stroessner in Paraguay, Pinochet in Chile) and distinct types of one-party rule (Cuba's Communist party, Mexico's PRI [Institutional Revolutionary party]). Socialist "democracy" in Cuba obviously differed from a rich variety of other Latin American democracies—from the limited ones of Argentina, Brazil, El Salvador, Guatemala, Honduras, and Uruguay in the early 1990s, where the militaries retained a virtual veto power, to the "two-party" systems in both their more democratic forms (Costa Rica, Venezuela) and their less democratic ones (Dominican Republic, Colombia).

Military regimes also varied, at least during the long, dark night—from military reformist regimes like Velasco's in Peru, Torres's in Bolivia, and Torrijos's in Panama, to national security states with a civilian façade like Uruguay's or those with direct military rule like Brazil's. The national security states also differed in the degree of sophistication of their practices of state terror and economic planning, from the highly refined Brazilian model with its carefully worked out national economic and political program to more irrational ones convinced that the "Third World War" had already started, like Argentina's, Chile's, and Uruguay's (the "war" presumably pitted Christian civilization against communism and Zionism).

Political scientists include under the rubric "governance" a medley of special interest groups and social classes or other popular organizations. Latin America had a rich mix of groups, from chambers of commerce to peasant leagues, in many different forms and combinations. As contrasted to North America, it also sported a long tradition of student political involvement (see chapters 11 and 18). Yet here too differences abounded—with Christian Democrats showing more pre-1980s strength among students in some countries (El Salvador) and Marxists more in others (Argentina, Venezuela).

Fourth, although nationalism was usually known as a commonality among Latin American countries, the differences in their approaches or selection of national "enemies" cannot be emphasized enough. Right-wing regimes saw their mission to be a nationalist one of saving the world from communism and preserving "Christian civilization." Socialist Cuba, pluralistic mixed economy Nicaragua, leftist groups of either Christian or Marxist persuasion, and many centrist and even some right-of-center groups saw their mission as one of carving out an independent space to "free" their peoples from "capitalist oppression" and/or U.S. domination. Their nationalist goal was a second Latin American revolution—the economic one to meet basic human needs (the first one having been the anticolonial one for political independence). Internationally they advocated "nonalignment."

Argentina (Malvinas/Falkland Islands) and Guatemala (Belize) had long nationalist conflicts with Great Britain, honored by the Left and Right alike! Chile, Mexico, and Puerto Rico, even though under quite different forms of government, had a special relationship with the United States that mixed close relations with hostile rejection.

Fifth, there were major differences in political traditions and values even *within* regions. Costa Rica's and Uruguay's "Swiss democracy" traditions blossomed in the unlikely midst of the militaristic dictatorships of Central America and the southern cone of South America. Similarly, in the Caribbean, there evolved many political contrasts among Cuba, the Dominican Republic, and Puerto Rico.

Because of such country-specific differences, many analysts stumbled badly when attempting to generalize about Latin America. There existed a long tradition of viewing Latin America as a single region, apart from the rest of the world or linked only to a few major powers (Spain, Portugal, Britain, the United States). In spite of widespread recognition of the important differences within Latin America, both supporters of the status quo and advocates of social change long tended to view the area as having a more or less single, continuous history and a common set of choices for economic and political development. Yet everything indicated that "imitating" a given path of development, or attempting to spread it, did not work in Latin America.

The historical record of failed models dotted the Latin American landscape. The "Mexican road to revolution" was championed by many in the 1920s and 1930s, yet its influences did not last. The *Aprista* (see chapter 14) road to anti-Communist democratic reform in the post–World War II period was advocated by Peru's Raúl Haya de la Torre, Venezuela's Rómulo Betancourt, Costa Rica's José "Pepe" Figueres, and the Dominican Republic's Juan Bosch, among others. But, except in Costa Rica it ran up against repeated military coups or coup attempts and then new obstacles like the 1965 U.S. invasion of the Dominican Republic.

New strategies challenging those old roads also faltered along the way. The Castroite/Guevarist guerrilla road to power (the so-called foco theory of an armed insurrection triggering a societywide revolution) failed in Venezuela (see chapter 11) and everywhere else except in parts of Central America. There it took two decades and underwent a series of transformations that made it unrecognizable as a foco approach. Moreover, once in power its practitioners were less Marxist-Leninist or socialist than Castro ever was, as witness the mixed economy of the Sandinistas' Nicaragua.

The World Bank development loans of the 1950s and 1960s and the Alliance for Progress peaceful road to social change gave way to the economic austerity, antireform "rules of the game" established by the IMF, counterreform by bayonet, and debt burdens that made real reform economically unfeasible. Latin America's few nationalist, populist, and so-called revolutionary military governments of the 1970s did not last, although they did add to the many differences shaping the continent's future. The longer-lasting military state-terror national security regimes, far from bringing prosperity to the region, left nations bankrupt and the torture-tainted officer corps in disrepute. The "reprivatization of the economy" endeavors of the IMF and the "Reagan revolution" of the 1970s and 1980s added to corporate profits but left most

Latin Americans impoverished and their governments gravely weakened. Foreign investor confidence rose and fell, as foreign investments approached $10 billion a year in the 1970s and zero in 1987 (at 1988 prices).

There emerged three highly publicized elements of Latin America's politics in the last third of the twentieth century. First, there were the violence and state terrorism of strong right-wing governments or the armed violence of their guerrilla opponents (whose occasional acts of terrorism, although highly publicized, were dwarfed by those of the rightist military regimes, as this book's country chapters reveal). Second, there were the human rights and peace movements, leading to Nobel Peace Prizes for Latin Americans like Costa Rican President Arias (1987) and Guatemala's Indian peasant activist, Rigoberta Menchúe (1992). Third, there was the "theology of liberation" and its curious alliance with the new Marxism (examined in the next section).

But here too the differences stood out. For example, in the case of the human rights movements, they did not become very generalized into the broad populace of Latin America. Most individual Latin Americans, however much frightened from time to time, did not view themselves as directly affected by either state torturers or guerrillas. They went about their daily lives in a vague unconscious haze of anticommunism, which was increasingly generalized throughout the popular culture by powerful right-wing states and the mass media. The communications industry in Latin America remained controlled largely by Western television and wire services or similarly oriented monopolies at the local level. Consequently, for most Latin Americans sudden imprisonment or torture was for Communists, not themselves. Similarly, a sudden guerrilla attack affected a banker, a foreign diplomat, a Supreme Court judge, or a military officer—again, not themselves.

The human rights movements took many years to gain the attention of everyday citizens, even when coming from amidst their very ranks as in the case of Argentina's "Mothers and Grandmothers of the Plaza de Mayo" (see chapter 18) whose weekly silent processions to protest thousands of disappearances later drew worldwide attention. Eventually, combined with other forces affecting society such as the devastating economic depression of the late 1970s and early 1980s, the human rights activists did succeed in initiating a "democratic transition." Several of them "disappeared" or were assassinated along the way.

While Latin America's heterogeneity made it difficult to generalize, there *were* a number of commonalities (although even then not true for every country). Some, such as the long dark night of state-sponsored terror and violence, have already been mentioned. But others were as important.

For example, a common theme in Latin American history remained the reliance on one or two dominant export commodities—so-called monoculture. Similarly, there was the ongoing important role and changing contours of elite families (incorporating drug magnates in many countries today, e.g., Colombia—see chapter 12). Also, the prevalent twentieth-century economic trends continued to be the semi-industrialization of more and more countries. Coinciding with this trend since World War II was an expanded impact of loans and investments by foreign-based TNCs and a recurrent drive for common markets. Common economic factors included the foreign debt burden; the austerity programs recommended by the IMF and World Bank (freezing wages while allowing prices to rise, devaluating currencies, lowering tariffs, and other measures presumed to combat inflation); the attempted "privatizing" of the economies; the growing gap between the rich and poor; and the economic pinch being felt by Latin America's expanded middle classes.

Also, while the extent varied from place to place, every Latin American nation found itself enmeshed in a complex web of dependence on outside powers, usually the United States. Decisions in the boardrooms of corporate giants like Standard Oil, United Brands (formerly United Fruit), and Citibank, or in office buildings of Washington, London, Rome, Berlin, Paris, Tokyo, or Moscow sometimes affected Latin Americans more than those made by their own governments. The IMF's role in regulating Latin America's economies was so powerful that in Costa Rica they had a saying: "Here Mr. Fondo [Mr. Fund, the IMF] rules."

Although each country had its own special flavor, all of Latin America was rocked by competing versions of nationalism. Similarly, many forces contested for control over labor unions and peasant organizations. Even the role of the Catholic Church, long a mediating one and in colonial times a major economic one as well, had undergone drastic changes. No longer could a dictator take Church support for granted, as Paraguay's Stroessner and Chile's Pinochet learned to their dismay when prelates condemned their human rights violations and helped ease them out of office (see chapters 16 and 17).

Another commonality was the stepped-up militarization of Latin America, including countries with decades of stable civilian rule (e.g., Chile, Mexico, Panama, Uruguay, and, to a lesser degree, Costa Rica—see chapters 1, 6, 7, 17, and 19). After the Brazilian military coup of 1964, there emerged an increasing coordination of military coups and repression throughout Latin America (see chapters 2–5, 10, 13–20). This coordination continued even during the transitions from military to civilian rule and yet perpetuation of military influence.

The Middle Classes and the Falling Away of the Political Center

A critical commonality was the falling away of the much acclaimed "political center" in Latin America. The Alliance for Progress and increased state role in local economies initially helped many individuals in the middle classes (or "intermediate classes" as some analysts called them, since they were located in an intermediate position between the owners of the productive forces and those who worked them). Ever since their first major emergence on the political scene in the early twentieth century the middle classes had been important political actors in Latin America. The idea of the Alliance for Progress was that these elements would build a middle-of-the- road polity, immune from the threats of the Right and Left. But the hard choices among revolution, reform, or repression that had faced Latin Americans for generations soon drove most middle-class people to side with either revolution or repression.

To succeed, reforms had to overcome structural obstacles presented by uneven land and income distribution and powerful monopolies, sometimes foreign owned. When the owners of great wealth balked at having their privileges reduced by reforms, the reformers had to decide whether to proceed to a stage of revolution, insist on maintaining the attempts at reform, or pull back and accept the status quo. Those who insisted on continuing with reform were usually overthrown by military coup d'état. In some cases, like the 1960s' Christian Democratic period in Chile, reforms sped up the demands for revolutionary change. In Chile, people elected a socialist president, Salvador Allende, whose administration was destabilized by powerful foreign and domestic interests and in 1973 toppled by a military coup (see chapter 17). Whether in the Dominican Republic, Chile, or El Salvador and several other nations in the 1960s and 1970s, the defeat of the reformers by forces to their right spelled doom for the political center.

While some intermediate-class elements became nouveau riche industrialists and businesspeople, most remained caught in the middle between society's main political polarities: capitalists and landlords, on the one hand, workers and peasants on the other. Several commentators talked about a new political class—one of technocrats, government officials, political leader-administrators, professional politicians. This influential group had grown in number and influence under the triple impact of the Cuban Revolution, the Alliance for Progress, and the stepped-up industrialization of Latin America.

According to a 1987 report of the IDB (Interamerican Development Bank), Latin America's output in both industry and services increased sixfold between 1950 and 1980, while agricultural production was trebling. Services overtook agriculture as the main sector of employment, while industry was not far behind, having tripled its workforce to 30 million. The numbers of women in the workforce tripled, compared with only a doubling of the numbers of men working. More than a quarter of the labor force was female, and women's share of employment continued rising in the 1980s and 1990s.

Education still trailed far behind that of the industrialized nations of the world, but more people were learning how to read and write. School enrollments doubled in the 1950s and again in the 1960s, before tapering off.

By 1985 three-quarters of Latin America's population aged six to eighteen was enrolled. The number of postsecondary enrollments rose from a quarter of a million in 1950 to 5.6 million in 1985 (of whom 45 percent were women). Yet at the same time gains were made in college enrollments, malnutrition and functional illiteracy became so widespread that the World Bank warned that the world's eighth largest economy, Brazil's, might soon collapse because the economy was being deprived of "a skilled and productive labor force."

The changes in higher education swelled the ranks of the middle classes, which still rarely surpassed 25 percent of any nation's population. Many middle-class people prospered during periods of rapid economic growth. But when hard times came, they felt frustrated or blocked from further advance. Some moved to the Right, supporting the right-wing offensive against state intervention in the economy and against the labor unions. Others rallied to Left-nationalist calls for completing a revolution for economic independence and a more equitable distribution of wealth.

By the time of Latin America's severe economic downturn of the late 1970s only a small percentage of the politically active remained in the center of the political spectrum. Previously well-off technocrats felt the economic crunch. The dual-career family bred of economic necessity blossomed in societies where women had been expected to stay at home and raise their children (with the help of lower-class women servants). A middle-class woman's incorporation into the wage labor force heightened her political awareness and reduced the macho male's ability to keep her in her place. Some of Latin America's middle-class women, who in many instances had supported counterrevolutionary movements or been apolitical prior to the late 1970s, began joining leftist-led movements.

Many in the post-1970s' generation of politically influential middle-class people began digging in for the long haul—whether as students, employees, politicians, bureaucrats, guerrillas, or technocrats, professionals, and paraprofessionals. They were seeking to master the new technologies of computers, macroeconomic planning, public health, and education (nationwide literacy campaigns appealed to some). Few of them could strongly identify with the disappearing political center.

The center's attempt at recovery in South America under moderate-to-conservative civilian governments in the late 1980s and early 1990s faced a difficult road ahead. In off-year elections the governing parties usually suffered serious defeats. New political candidates often marginal to mainstream political parties drew large vote counts from disillusioned electorates, winning an occasional presidency (for example, Peru—see chapter 14). Venezuela's President Pérez, a one-time populist reformer who (like Latin America's other populist reformers) had moved far to the right, became so corrupt he was impeached and had to resign in 1993. As economic conditions worsened and political instability intensified, middle-class people who could raise the money flooded South America's airports, carrying extra luggage in an apparent flight of the middle class to the United States as "tourists." The military began reasserting itself as the only force capable of controlling South America's social unrest.

Theology of Liberation and the "New Marxism"

Of all the many efforts at reform in Latin America, those of the theology of liberation achieved the most success in actually reaching large numbers of Latin Americans and not just intellectuals, politicians, or professionals interested in human rights. (Liberation theology overlapped, of course, with the human rights movements.)

The intellectual roots of Latin America's theology of liberation went far back. In colonial times Las Casas was an early precursor; Jesuit missions in Brazil and Paraguay often harbored people fleeing slaverunners. Europe's twentieth-century worker-priests also influenced liberation theology. But the first official articulation of its premises came from the papacy in Rome during Vatican II (Second Ecumenical Council, 1962–1965).

Vatican II expanded the definition of "sin" to include any contribution to social injustice. It mandated a "preferential option for the poor." The 1967 papal encyclical "Populorum Progressio" further developed these ideas. Then, in 1968 the CELAM (General Conference of Latin American Bishops) was held in Medellín, Colombia. The bishops issued their own program for a liberating theology. They called for a radical redistribution of wealth in all Latin America and blamed the rich industrialized nations for much of the area's underdevelopment. By 1984 Pope John Paul II was denouncing "imperialistic monopoly," declaring that "this poor south will judge the rich north."

The fact that the Roman Catholic Church issued such radical pronouncements reflected the changes taking place in Latin America, particularly the challenges presented by the Cuban Revolution and its moral appeal for helping the downtrodden—an appeal that reached and influenced millions of younger Latin Americans in the 1960s. The Catholic Church had a reactionary reputation in Latin America. In colonial times Latin America's riches in gold, silver, and other items produced by slave labor, wage labor, and debt-ridden workers became the economic pillar for the Church in most of Europe. Dissenting priests who became revolutionists advocating the rights of the poor were sometimes defrocked and executed—for example, Hidalgo and Morelos during Mexico's war of independence (see chapter 1). Over the centuries the Catholic Church allied itself with wealthy elite families that dominated Latin America's politics. It "blessed" a long list of unsavory military dictators.

27

By the 1960s Latin America's people were the largest single bloc of Roman Catholics in the world. But they were no longer a captive audience, and many were not deeply religious. Once the appeal of revolutionism erupted on the scene with the Cuban Revolution, and once the Vatican defined sin in terms of social injustice, the Church had to make some hard choices: to side with Latin America's elites, as in the past, or to take the road of revolution or reform.

Moreover, the Catholic Church faced challenges from pro–right-wing forces encouraged by the Evangelicals, Pentecostals, and "Moonies" spreading their "gospel" into Latin America. In parts of Central America these Protestant rivals of the Catholic Church (not all of whom were Conservative) were winning over as much as 20 percent of the population and sometimes succeeding in heavily influencing governments, such as the bloodthirsty dictatorships of General Ríos Montt in Guatemala and General Alvarez in Honduras (see chapters 2, 4, and 7).

Other believers in Protestantism gained strength by championing liberation theology. The World Council of Churches secretary-general, an Uruguayan, said of Catholic liberation theologians "Their struggle is my struggle."

Buffeted by the forces of change and reaction, the Catholic Church attempted to adapt to both. In Latin America's new Marxism it found a particularly strong and widespread challenge—one that attracted countless bishops, priests, and nuns. The young Marxists who joined Fidel Castro in the guerrilla war against U.S.-imposed dictator Fulgencio Batista were the first successful representatives of Latin America's new Marxism. They emphasized armed action in the face of injustice; they wished to assist other nation's revolutions with material aid (internationalism). They emphasized moral issues and no compromise with capitalist firms that refused to treat workers decently—rather than cautious revolution by stages and other subtle doctrinal distinctions long championed by Soviet-influenced communism. The Argentine-born revolutionary Ernesto "Che" Guevara, Cuba's minister of industries, was the foremost representative of the new Marxism, proclaiming that a revolutionary was motivated "by profound feelings of love" (see chapters 8 and 15).

As the new Marxism evolved, it emphasized a mix of humanist and moralistic values. It chose not to believe in God but to engage in historical-materialist analysis instead of spiritual interpretation. As it united with the forces of the theology of liberation during the late 1960s and throughout the 1970s, the new Marxism became even more flexible, most notably in Nicaragua's and El Salvador's revolutionary upheavals (see chapters 3 and 5).

Both Marxists and Christians began searching for new answers and new political alliances. Castro himself abandoned the guerrilla foco approach and encouraged broad alliances. The Sermon on the Mount, he said, could have been written by Karl Marx. The Cuban Communist party removed the word *atheism* from its party program and proscribed offending people's religious sentiments.

In the search for new solutions many Christians and some Jews and Muslims welcomed an exploration of Marxism. They accepted Marxist analyses of society while rejecting materialist philosophy. Marxist analysis logically led to revolution against oppression and foreign interventionism.

As early as 1966 Colombian sociologist-priest Camilo Torres (see chapter 12) took up the gun to fight with a guerrilla army opposed to that country's ruling elites. He cited the Vatican's own pronouncements on the legitimacy of violent revolution to combat oppression when all other means fail. In 1973 Gustavo Gutiérrez of Peru wrote his book *A Theology of Liberation*, in which he recognized class struggle and called it "a will to build a socialist society." Two years later Uruguay's Juan Luis Segunda wrote *Liberation of Theology*, describing Jesus Christ as a "dangerous political adversary" to established religion. The Pope told Latin America's bishops in 1979 that Jesus was not a "political activist." Friar Leonardo Boff of Brazil, in his 1981 work *Church: Charisma and Power*, likened the Catholic Church to a capitalist institution in which clerics produced religious values to be consumed by believers.

By then it was too late to stop the tide of new political activism among Catholics all over the world. In 1980 Archbishop Romero was assassinated in El Salvador; not long afterward four U.S. Catholic nuns and lay workers were kidnapped and killed there (see chapter 3). In the United States an ecumenical "sanctuary movement" numbering 100,000 activists gave refuge to Central Americans fleeing violent dictatorships. In Brazil some 80,000 revolution-oriented, Bible-studying Christian base communities flourished with the blessing of a majority of Brazilian bishops. In November 1987 U.S. Catholic bishops condemned President Reagan's interventionist policies in Nicaragua as "morally flawed."

Increasingly, Pope John Paul II criticized the embrace of Marxism by many of Latin America's advocates of liberation theology. He took disciplinary action against a number of radical priests, nuns, and theologians who saw in the Marxist method of historical-materialist analysis the most scientific way to, in Marx's words, "understand society in order to change it."

The relative success of the theology of liberation only confirmed that to surmount the great diversities separating Latin Americans and their twenty republics it was useful to have a firmly entrenched transnational organizational structure like the Roman Catholic Church. Although by no means limited to Catholics, the main thrust of the theology of liberation in Latin America came out of the Catholic Church, an institution supremely skilled at organizing and diffusing its doctrines. While some clerics prophesied a split in the Church and the creation of two churches—conceivably, a leftist one based in Latin America—most priests and nuns agreed that the differences generated by Latin America's liberation theology were likely to remain internal to the Church and decided to continue to help it adapt to the "new politics" shaking the continent.

Besides the Church, there existed other skilled organizational structures—at least in the 1960s—such as the Communists' Moscow-based Third International, the Trotskyists' Fourth International, Western Europe's Socialist International and Christian Democratic International, or Havana's OLAS (Organization of Latin American Solidarity). But each of these lacked the historical entrenchment inside Latin America that the Catholic Church enjoyed. Consequently, when followers of these other transnational forces politically split into many factions and Latin America's long, dark night of military state terrorism shrouded their mutilated bodies, they were unable to sustain even a successful "defensive" battle against the forces of reaction and repression. While a number of radical bishops and priests also fell before the hail of the state's bullets and electrified torture tables, most did not.

The Catholic radical leaders had the protection of a strong institution within whose hallowed chambers they carried out most of their faction fighting. Thus their message reached and affected more and more people. In El Salvador their success elicited the reactionary slogan "Be a patriot, kill a priest."

Ironically, President Reagan and some other U.S. observers of Latin America equated the radical Catholics with the Marxist-Leninists. In fact these traditional God-fearing and God-denying rivals were setting aside their philosophical differences to form new alliances, new unities against "greater enemies." If there existed an "evil empire," it was not, in their eyes, the Soviet Union, but the North. The real curse was not communism, but poverty, ignorance, oppression. If the revolutionary governments of Cuba and Nicaragua earned UN accolades for their health and literacy campaigns that improved people's lives—and that was communism—then it sounded correct and righteous to those who preached "love thy neighbor."

After the collapse of communism in Easter Europe, the appeal of Marxism suffered a tailspin. But its method of economic and class analysis continued to influence Latin America's "new politics," as did its preoccupation with the well being of everyday working people.

The "New Politics"

The most striking and original commonality of all in Latin America was the *new politics*. Talk of a new politics was not uncommon in Latin American history. For a long time many had seen post–World War II developments in Latin America as a new politics—the upsurge in democratic revolutions against dictatorships, the rise to political power of reformist political parties like

Venezuela's AD (Democratic Action), the stepped-up introduction of import-substitution programs, the increased role in the economy for the state.

Latin America's more traditional "political culture" of paternalism, authoritarianism, hierarchical client-patron systems, personalism, corporativism, and corruption both changed and, in many instances, became updated in form. By the 1960s much of the new politics described for the 1940s and 1950s had become the "old politics." Even the new politics of the 1960s in some ways began to look "old."

For example, guerrilla warfare strategies changed, as new unities were forged between Marxists and radical Christians and broad civilian political fronts became the "political arms" of guerrilla armies. Nicaragua's Sandinista revolution was the first to incorporate priests into the government's top leadership. And soon even Premier Castro was seen walking in Havana political demonstrations arm-in-arm with the archbishop. For the first time guerrilla armies ran candidates in national elections (Colombia, 1986; Venezuela, 1983 and 1988). Peru's "Shining Path" guerrillas were the only exception (see chapter 14).

The impetus for Latin America's politics gradually shifted from the military officers' clubs, the Catholic Church, the foreign embassies and corporate offices, the salons of the ruling elite families, and the old political class, to the streets and homes of so-called average citizens. During the long dark night, the new politics emerged as a bottom-up challenge to military national security states and/or civilian bureaucratic authoritarian or corporativist states dominated by one or two political parties. The new politics represented an attempt to establish popular democracy. (*Popular* is the term used in Latin America to describe all working people and an equitable distribution of basic goods and rights.)

The new politics was particularly strong in the eight semi-industrialized giants that accounted for nearly nine-tenths of Latin America's gross domestic product: Brazil, Mexico, Argentina, Colombia, Venezuela, Chile, Uruguay, and Peru (listed here in approximate order of degree of industrialization, gross national product, trade, and population). Large U.S. economic stakes were involved, and mass poverty was a central issue.

Independently created on the basis of self-help, the new politics' social movements were unaccountable to traditional political parties or state organizations. Their peaceful street demonstrations, general strikes, land grabs, sit-ins, and other forms of protest defied conventional wisdom. The poor were *not* too busy struggling to survive to rebel. Better-paid industrial workers did *not* shun joint actions with unemployed shantytown dwellers. Complete elimination of democracy by state-terrorist regimes (or modest concessions by civilian ones) did *not* permanently deter popular mobilization for change.

By the 1990s, the social movements of the new politics tended to bypass

31

the standard political options of electing to office nationalist/populists or neo-liberal rightists and moderates or opting for military rule as too much like politics as usual. Even during the earlier transitions to civilian rule, they realized that right-wing forces "remained in control" (the phrasing is from political scientist Douglas A. Chalmer's introduction to a 1992 book on the Right—see Selected Bibliography). The amazing perseverance of the new politics reshaped people's expectations of government and social decency and radicalized the rhetoric of even conservative political leaders. For example, the well financed, right-wing-backed presidential campaigns of Brazil's Fernando Collor de Mello and Peru's Mario Vargas Llosa in 1989–90 were based on populist appeals to the urban poor against advocates of the new politics known to have a decent chance of winning.

Indeed, despite their successes in ending Latin America's long, dark night, practitioners of the new politics still faced the obstacle of the radical Right's reconsolidation. By the 1990s, "disappearances" were again on the rise in Brazil and the southern cone. New right-wing death squads proliferated in Peru and Columbia. Highly respected journalists and leaders of the new politics were being assassinated in Brazil, Chile, Peru, Colombia, and Mexico. When drug "hit squads" were involved, even judges and archbishops fell before the bullets (see chapters 1 and 12). Fascists and neofascists, professional anti-Communists and anti-Semites, and key military, police, and intelligence officers sought to slam the door on Latin America's limited democratic openings in order to crush the new politics the way they had crushed the leftists and liberals of the 1960s.

What were some of the major features of this new politics, besides their being organized from the bottom-up and merging different ideologies like Marxism and the theology of liberation? To what degree did they incorporate characteristics of the old politics but nonetheless remain uniquely new and important? Several things stood out.

First the new politics superseded or restructured the fading old politics as in the cases just mentioned or others—such as the transmutations in Argentina's Peronism or the revitalization of *Aprismo* in Peru and the evermore populist PAN (National Action party) in Mexico (see chapters 1, 14, and 18). Even the old politics of military coups and repression assumed new dimensions: the technification of torture, the widespread use of high-tech communications and weaponry, the practice of disappearances, the tieing into international drug trafficking. A new concept reflecting a new reality was introduced in Bolivia in 1980—the "cocaine coup"—when drug czars and their military allies took over the government (see chapter 15).

A second feature of the new politics was its idealism and firm commitment to democracy. The experience of dictatorship left the majority of Latin Americans extraordinarily desirous of free speech and a chance to be heard. In the face of terroristic methods of state repression the human rights movement tapped hidden reservoirs of human courage and democratic dreams. Activists called for no amnesty for violators of human rights, including those "just following orders." (Amnesty was usually granted as part of a deal between the military and its opponents during negotiations for the democratic transition.) The "Nuremberg principle" of bringing state-sponsored torturers and murderers to justice, introduced against the Nazis after World War II and incorporated into international law, was being severely tested in Latin America.

The use of repression by civilian regimes in the late 1980s and early 1990s only sharpened the demands of the new politics for a genuine popular democracy as the only lasting remedy against Latin America's traditional malady of military coups. Even though many citizens initially welcomed the new-style do-it-yourself coup in Peru (an elected president decreeing an end to democracy while allowing the military to rule unimpeded), most Peruvians soon realized a coup is still a coup (see chapter 14). For new politics advocates, a democratic state had to be one that not only delivered on its promises of social reform but also eliminated bureaucratic corruption. Brazilians and Venezuelans illustrated this in 1992–93 when they reacted favorably to the constitutional removal from office of presidents Collor de Mello and Pérez.

A third feature of the new politics was the emergence during Latin America's long, dark night of new, surprisingly broad alliances linking previously conflicting groups. Back in the early 1960s Marxist revolutionists and Catholic radicals had usually found themselves at each other's throats. Then they formed *frentes amplias,* or broad fronts, incorporating as many political parties and groups as possible, including conflicting ones like Liberals and Conservatives, bosses and workers, bankers and peasants. These fronts demanded human rights and the replacement of authoritarian military rule with democratic civilian governance. They helped bring about democratic transitions, most notably in Argentina, Bolivia, Brazil, Ecuador, Guatemala, Nicaragua, Peru, and Uruguay. Some conservative currents in Christianity resisted the broad-front trend, as in El Salvador. There, after the majority of the PDC (Christian Democratic party) went over to the guerrillas or their political arm the FDR (Democratic Revolutionary Front), a stubborn conservative minority held on, with more than a million dollars a day of U.S. aid, to share the 1980s' Duarte government with the military.

A fourth feature of the new politics was the emergence of the urban poor as key political actors. After World War II, Latin America had become one of the world's most urbanized areas. Urbanization was commonly attributed to increased industrialization and the displacement of peasants from their lands by the rise of modern agribusiness. Slum dwellers' mass movements, starting in the 1970s, gradually broadened the notion of citizenship to include a fair share of social wealth and services (health, housing, potable drinking water, nutrition, education, sanitation, etc.). Their movements were unusual in that they pitted residents armed only with stones against modernized military assault forces that often shot to kill. This happened even in "democratic" Venezuela, where in 1989 troops gunned down people protesting price hikes on basic food and cooking items (leaving a reported thousand or more dead).

Slum dwellers had risen up before in spontaneous outpourings of rage variously described as "tumultos" (in colonial times) or "social vomiting" (as the 1948 Bogotazo in Colombia was once described—see chapter 12). Contemporary mobilizations were completely different, however. While political leaders mouthed abstract generalities like New International Economic Order or Debt Moratorium, people in the slums began taking direct action. They seized vacant lots, created relatively self- governing neighborhoods, and eventually showed the political class a less abstract way to politicize the debt problem.

During the 1970s in Peru's *pueblos jóvenes* (young towns), the urban poor of Lima for the first time anywhere in the world challenged the legitimacy of the IMF by marching through the streets denouncing its influence on the nation's rising prices and frozen wages. Linking their demands to those of industrial workers, they soon earned Peru the nickname, "the IMF's Vietnam." Spontaneously over the next several years, anti-IMF and anti–World Bank street marches spread to the other Latin American slums whose inhabitants had never heard of Lima's protests.

A fifth feature of the new politics was a *new labor militancy*. Wage workers in the factories, mines, and farms began asserting their rights not just to better work conditions but to a democratic say-so within their own labor unions or peasant organizations. In significant part, their militancy was a reaction against bossism, bureaucratism, corporativism, and often "class collaborationism" (union leaders siding with the bosses). The new labor militancy grew particularly threatening to old ways in Brazil, Colombia, Mexico, and Peru (see chapter 1, 12, 14, and 20). Similarly, the CIA and AFL-CIO funded AIFLD, once trusted by workers in countries like the Dominican Republic and Ecuador, was shunted aside and no longer, despite its millions of dollars, could easily divide labor unions in the name of free-trade unionism. Its role in the antidemocratic military coups of the 1960s and early 1970s left its reputation soiled.

A sixth feature of the new politics was the new assertiveness of women as political actors, including women workers in, or close to, the trade unions. An example was the Housewives Committee in the mining communities of Bolivia, one of whose leaders, Domitila Barrios de Chungara, brought working-class women to the center of the world's feminist stage at an international conference in the late 1970s by denouncing the middle-class biases and individualism of mainstream feminism. Throughout Latin America women were at the forefront of every slum-neighborhood mobilization, every human rights and peace march. As in Guatemala and Argentina (see chapters 2 and 18), examples of women human rights leaders abounded. Increasingly, women demanded a voice in running national political affairs as well. Two-time Nobel Peace Prize nominee Rosario Ibarra de Piedra, a human rights leader, twice ran for Mexico's presidency. Twenty-six women were elected to the Brazilian Congress in 1986.

As a result of the increased feminism sweeping the world, both Brazil and Argentina legalized divorce. Women in several countries marshalled campaigns to legalize abortion and outlaw and punish sexual violence. Sharing of housework began to occur as more women entered the labor force, although most still worked a "double day." According to social scientists Helen I. Safa and Cornelia Butler Flora, resistance to gender equality still persisted in Latin America's political and labor spheres even more than it did in the home (see Stepan entry in Selected Bibliography).

Gay liberation movements emerged throughout Latin America, occasionally encountering little backlash but more often evoking resistance. In 1990, the Second Lesbian Feminist Conference for Latin American and Caribbean women in Costa Rica met with so much rancor that it eventually had to go underground to conduct its meetings (see also Nacla entry in Selected Bibliography).

A seventh feature of the new politics was the "rediscovery" of Indians whose new militancy went beyond traditional land claims. Indians launched international campaigns to protect the environment and deter the pace of ethnocide decimating their ranks (see chapters 2, 16, and 20). In Ecuador, Indians mobilized for equal rights on an unprecedented scale. In Peru, the Indian half of the population finally won recognition of its majority language, Quechua, as the co-official language with Spanish—and hence the right to have public school instruction in Quechua.

In Mexico, Purépecha women led Indians in Michoacán to prevent the construction of a nuclear energy plant in the late 1970s and early 1980s—and won! As in so many recent instances of Indian militancy, they linked up with Indians elsewhere on the continent—especially those in Arizona and New Mexico. Then, in 1981 some eight hundred Indian delegates from as far north as Alaska and as far south as Patagonia held the Second Meeting of Independent Indian Organizations in Mexico, Central America, and the Caribbean in Michoacán. Despite language barriers, delegates were able to hammer out a common human rights platform against U.S. interventionism and in favor of revolutions like the one being fought in El Salvador. Other international meetings were also held. By the year of the Columbus Quincentennial (1992), Latin America's Indians (representing 6 percent of the population) and North America's Indians had launched major international campaigns against what they called "the great five hundred-year ethnocidal saga." In late 1993, an armed uprising by long oppressed Indians in southern Mexico gained world attention (see chapter 1).

An eighth feature of the new politics was the upsurge in peasant movements. As more and more rural inhabitants became pauperized and forced to migrate, they increasingly demanded not just land but jobs, a minimum wage, social benefits, cheaper food, or higher prices for farm products. Broad-based peasant movements showed particular strength in Brazil's impoverished Northeast and parts of the Andes, Central America, and Mexico.

A ninth feature of the new politics was the awakening of young people. There were three generations of youth in Latin America—the 1960s, older now, many demoralized and disillusioned; the 1970s, the middle-aged now, many traumatized but still anxious to see the new politics succeed; and the 1980s, many of whose youngsters grew up never knowing anything other than the long, dark night. This newer generation was still a question mark for observers of Latin America. With the spreading of drugs across much of the landscape, it was not certain to what extent they would become politically active. But their music and song festivals in South America's southern cone were often a way for them to sing their protest against tyranny. In Uruguay voices rose deliberately for the words "tyrants tremble" during singing of the national anthem. The military regime changed the anthem's melody. Very young people—children often—were at the forefront of many of the urban mobilizations among Latin America's poor. Still, the resurgent radical right attracted numerous young people.

A tenth striking feature of the new politics was the emergence of populist, reformist, and nationalist segments of the military (see chapters 2, 7, 13, 14, 15, and 20). Their populist efforts at reform, however, were usually checkmated by the forces of reaction. Nonetheless, with an occasional exception like Mexico's Lázaro Cárdenas or Argentina's Juan Perón (see chapters 1 and 18), the phenomenon of military reformism was relatively new in Latin America.

An eleventh feature of the new politics was experimentation with fresh approaches. These approaches included the introduction of new forms and hybrids of socialism and revolution/reform, from the "poder popular" movement of grassroots democracy in Cuba to the mixed economy attempts of the Sandinistas in Nicaragua or the National Assembly of Community Representatives that replaced the legislature under General Torrijos in Panama.

It was precisely the innovativeness of the new politics that made putting new politics into neat little sociological boxes impossible. One thing was certain, however. Its impact was widespread and would not disappear overnight.

Four obvious factors, nonetheless, threatened a rapid decline in the new politics. First, other than the theology of liberation, which itself had caused divisions in the Catholic Church, there was no cohesive organizational network to bring together even within a single country's borders the many groups being mobilized by the new politics. Latin America's Left had been largely smashed or dispersed, although its martyrs and its ideas still commanded considerable public sympathy. It had suffered the brunt of the long, dark night's traumatizing tortures and disappearances. An entire younger generation of idealistic activists, many of them bright and creative, had been wiped out or reduced to silence.

Second, this in turn had contributed to a demoralization of large numbers of people. Hopes were further dashed by the economic hard times weighing down on the shoulders of almost all Latin Americans by the early 1990s. In a region of the world long recognized for its traditions of extended family solidarity, human warmth, and generosity, symbolized by the everyday phrases *"Mi casa es su casa"* or *"Está en su casa"* (My house is your house), millions of families faced terrible strains because of deepening poverty. People migrated hundreds, even thousands, of miles in quest of decently paid work. Street crime and drug addiction, long associated with the United States, made their appearance south of the border. Observers of Latin America noted a dialectic of strengthened generosity in the face of hardship yet greater alienation and bitterness.

Third, as more and more new politics leaders entered mainstream politics there occurred a return of clientele "old politics" and a splintering of the new politics in old-style factionalism. New politics/populist broad fronts turned out to be very fragile processes, complicated by strong personalities and class divisions. Businessmen and presidents might welcome wage freezes to meet IMF conditionality clauses, but labor clearly did not. Result? More alienation, declining workplace productivity, new strikes or riots—and political instability.

Fourth, the very high-tech military muscle that helped provoke the birth of the new politics was still in place. Highly modernized military, police, and intelligence apparatuses operated at full capacity—with the names of new politics activists on the national security threat lists. According to Americas Watch and other human rights organizations, the militaries of the 1980s and 1990s were more brutal than even the ones that oversaw Latin America's "long dark night." Many high-ranking officers received their on-the-job training during earlier "dirty wars." In addition, those U.S. policymakers who for decades had helped build up Latin America's military establishments were still powerful voices inside the U.S. foreign policy community.

Learning from the Past: A Challenge for U.S. Policymakers

One such policymaker was Henry Kissinger (see chapters 17 and 18), the principal author of the newest major political analysis of Latin America coming out of Washington, the 1984 Kissinger Commission report. Both President George Bush's Enterprise for the Americas Initiative, backing privatization, free trade, and an eventual hemispheric common market, and President Bill Clinton's modified NAFTA approach, expanded upon doctrines already formulated by the Kissinger Commission and other earlier policy bodies.

Commission head Henry Kissinger was a longtime friend of the Rockefeller family, whose economic interests were extensive in Latin America. Financier David Rockefeller presided over the Council of the Americas (later called the Americas Society), the main corporate body advising U.S. policymakers on Latin America. Kissinger, as President Richard Nixon's secretary of state and NSC (National Security Council) chief, had reacted to Allende's 1970 election in Chile by describing it as a "contagious" example that might "infect" other pro-U.S. regimes in Latin America and Western Europe. Prior to Allende's election, he had stated: "I don't see why we need to stand by and watch a country go Communist due to the irresponsibility of its own people." He had then supervised the destabilization of Chile that led to the 1973 military coup and its killing of several thousand Chileans (see chapter 17).

In offering the carrot to Latin America, the 1984 Kissinger Commission Report went no further than the old Alliance for Progress. But on military aid and preventing leftist participation in reform or revolution, it took a hard line. It defended the Reagan administration's bellicose policies in Nicaragua, even though it recognized the Sandinista government had "made significant gains against illiteracy and disease." The report recommended renewal of arms shipments to Guatemala, even though it acknowledged the "morally unacceptable" and "brutal behavior of the security forces" that resorted to "the use of murder to repress dissent."

Perhaps the Kissinger Commission report's most innovative contribution was to acknowledge the past U.S. record of interventionism and to provide examples often omitted from U.S. textbooks. On the other hand, it chose to ignore the consequences of U.S. behavior: "What confronts us now is a question of what might become."

The "what might become" could not be removed from what had already happened. Because of the past, U.S. credibility was at a new low. During the previous twenty-five years' attempts at revolution in several countries the U.S. government had not only intervened and abetted the formation of national security states sponsoring torture and disappearances, it had *denied* doing so. These lies made Latin Americans skeptical of *any* preferred changes in U.S. policy toward genuine assistance for social reform or revolution.

Four lies undermining U.S. credibility stood out: the 1961 denial of planning an invasion of Cuba on the eve of the Bay of Pigs landing (see chapter 8); the 1970s' denial of intervening to destabilize the Allende government in Chile (see chapter 17); and in the 1980s the denial of planning to invade

Grenada on the eve of the sneak invasion and the denials of directing the contras' invasion of Nicaragua (see introductions to Part One and Part Two).

Earlier in history government officials openly stated the military and economic character of U.S. interventions. During the early 1900s they called it "gunboat diplomacy" and "dollar diplomacy." That aggressive honesty, however, had left a legacy of hatred and distrust in Latin America for the colossus of the North.

While the official explanations for U.S. interventions then and now were U.S. commitment to "freedom and democracy" and "defense of national security," the underlying motivation was invariably economic. As the *U.S. News and World Report* observed in its cover story of October 17, 1983, "Over a period of nearly 150 years, U.S. armed forces swept into Central America and the Caribbean more than 60 times to topple governments, install friendly regimes, and support American business interests."

Every intervention provoked disagreements among U.S. politicians and citizens. Significant U.S. "anti-imperialist" movements opposed U.S. expansionism in Latin America in the 1840s and 1850s and again in the 1890s and early 1900s. They recurred during the 1930s and after World War II, usually under the rubric of *"anti-interventionism"* instead of anti-imperialism. "Hands off (Cuba or some other country)!" became a rallying cry for anti-interventionist forces in the nineteenth century and continued to the present.

During much of the nineteenth century U.S. policy was guided by the notion of *Manifest Destiny*. Manifest Destiny proclaimed that it was the God-given destiny of the United States to populate and occupy the entire North American continent. Thomas Jefferson bluntly stated in 1809 that "no constitution was ever before as well-calculated as ours for extensive empire and self-government."

By implying it was God's will, Manifest Destiny justified relentless wars against the Amerindians and the seizure of Texas and the richest half of Mexico's national territory in the 1830s and 1840s (see chapter 1). It became the banner for a series of U.S. filibuster-adventurers like William Walker, who pronounced himself president of Nicaragua in 1855–1856 after a U.S. warship bombed San Juan del Norte (see chapter 5 for a chronology of U.S. interventions in that country).

The 1823 Monroe Doctrine established a U.S. claim to "protecting" Latin America by asserting that the United States would not tolerate European interference in the affairs of Western Hemisphere countries. It usually served, however, to legitimize U.S. interference in Latin America (see Parts One and Two). In fact until the 1890s when the "Olney fiat" proclaimed U.S. sovereignty over all Latin America (see chapter 8), the United States was militarily unable to enforce the Monroe Doctrine against major European powers. Indeed, far from standing up to European aggression in Latin America, the U.S.

government approved Britain's seizure of the Malvinas/Falkland Islands in 1834 and British expansion of its Central American territory in 1835 (once called British Honduras, now Belize). Recognizing the fact that Latin Americans viewed the Monroe Doctrine as a tool of U.S. intervention, the U.S. government never invoked it after mentioning it briefly just after the 1954 intervention in Guatemala.

The U.S. "Open Door Policy" of the 1890s, which declared that no nation should create colonial interests in China, had repercussions in Latin America. In harmony with the "free-trade" doctrine so important for any major power's expansion abroad, the United States maintained there should be an "open door" for traders and investors of all nations. This doctrine was then backed up by gunboat and dollar democracy that produced the conquests of Cuba, Puerto Rico, Hawaii, the Philippines, and the Panama Canal. The Dominican Republic, Haiti, and Nicaragua soon joined Cuba and Puerto Rico as virtual U.S. militarily occupied protectorates until the early 1930s.

In 1904 the Roosevelt Corollary to the Monroe Doctrine proclaimed that the United States would intervene in Latin America to correct any "misbehavior . . . which results in a general loosening of the ties of civilized society." This echo of the British empire's "white man's burden" theme served to protect burgeoning U.S. investments and to collect Latin American debts (partly a reaction to the Latin Americans' 1902 "Drago Doctrine"—see chapters 11 and 18). As President Woodrow Wilson stated in 1916:

> The masters of the U.S. government are the combined capitalists and manufacturers. . . .Do you know the significance of this single fact that within the last year or two we have ceased to be a debtor nation and have become a creditor nation? . . .We have got to finance the world in some important degree, and those who finance the world must understand it and rule it with their spirits and with their minds. . . .I am going to teach the South American republics to elect good men.

Wilson displayed his missionary zeal for democracy by invading Mexico twice to oppose revolution and sending troops into the Soviet Union to fight Lenin's new Bolshevik government and Trotsky's Red Army. Wilson's Secretary of State William Jennings Bryan acknowledged that the goal of U.S. foreign policy was "to prevent revolution," but he added the humanitarian sentiment that it was also "to promote education."

President Franklin D. Roosevelt rejected gunboat diplomacy when he endorsed his predecessor Herbert Hoover's recommendations for a "Good Neighbor Policy." Roosevelt sharply reduced the number of direct U.S. military interventions in Latin America while building up loyal national guards and armies in the Caribbean Basin and sending out U.S. warships and security forces whenever revolution loomed (see Part One and Part Two). The U.S.-trained "security forces" secured undemocratic governments throughout the region.

In 1940 Roosevelt stated that the United States "should invest heavily in Latin America to develop sources of raw materials needed in the United States." During the next decade U.S. control of Latin America's natural resources rose to 70 percent, and the U.S. share of Latin America's GNP (Gross National Product) increased to 50 percent. The Kissinger Commission Report acknowledged that the Good Neighbor Policy, designed "to signal the end of the era of intervention, had the paradoxical effect of continuing to identify the United States with established dictatorships . . . an identity between the United States and dictatorship in Central America that lingers."

Emerging victorious from World War II, the United States stood supreme in arms and wealth. By 1947 the CIA was in place and a new phase of U.S. interventionism was taking shape. In Greece the Truman Doctrine against "Communist aggression" was implemented to justify emergency economic and military aid to monarchist opponents of anti-Fascist resistance fighters. As the Cold War heated up, U.S. policymakers secretly called upon the advice of notorious war criminals—veteran anticommunist Nazis, many of whom found refuge in Latin America (often via Washington—see chapters 15, 16, and 18).

The Truman Doctrine for Europe had its Latin American variant, the "Rio Pact." In Rio de Janeiro, Brazil, a military pact was drawn up—the 1947 Inter-American Treaty of Reciprocal Assistance. It stated that "an armed attack by any state against an American state shall be considered as an attack against all American states" and would be countered by the assistance of the other American states. Also, mutually agreed upon measures—including if necessary "the use of armed force"—would be taken against "an aggression which is not an armed attack." A year later, in Bogotá, Colombia (see chapter 12), the old Pan American Union, founded in 1910 and derisively called by some Latin American leaders the "U.S. Ministry of Colonies," was renamed the OAS (Organization of American States).

The Rio Pact sidestepped the United Nations and provided a legally binding regional "self-defense" approach for future U.S. covert and overt interventions against reformist democracies in the name of combatting Communist aggression. The first full-scale test case was Guatemala, 1954 (see chapter 2). Once again, economic interests were involved in the making of U.S. foreign policy. The democratically elected government of Jácobo Arbenz was toppled on behalf of the United Fruit Company, whose properties the government had offered to purchase. In calling for the renewal of military aid to the sanguinary Guatemalan military dictatorships that had resulted from the 1954 intervention, the Kissinger Commission acknowledged that "the questionable practices followed by the fruit companies in those early years, together with the power they wielded over weak governments, did a lot to create the fear of "economic imperialism."' Vice-President Nixon's stoning in Caracas reflected Latin Americans' anger at the U.S. overthrow of Guatemalan democracy.

The United States was counting on favorable investment climates for its corporations, as businesspeople scoured the globe for more opportunities. As President Dwight Eisenhower noted upon taking office in 1953, "We need markets in the world for the surpluses of our farms and our factories; equally, we need for these same farms and factories vital materials and products of distant lands." Eisenhower asked Secretary of Treasury George Humphrey, former board chairman of the transnational mining firm M. A. Hanna Company with holdings in Latin America, if U.S. businesspeople would make sacrifices for world peace. Humphrey replied: "No, the American businessman believes in getting as much as he can while the getting is good."

The NSC issued a memorandum in 1950—"NSC-68." It defined Cold War containment policy against communism in terms of increased military spending, expanded covert operations, and a healthy U.S. economy fueled by defense production. There followed the 1950–53 Korean War, the 1953 return of the Shah to his "peacock throne" in oil-rich Iran, and the 1954 Guatemalan operation. These interventions in the internal affairs of other peoples were taught in U.S. schools and colleges as "victories" of U.S. foreign policy against communism. Their negative consequences were not examined by more than a few critics, who argued that in the long run they undermined U.S. credibility and security by placing the United States on the side of hated dictatorships.

In the name of what Eisenhower termed a "crusade against communism" but what in practice became a policy of guaranteeing and abetting U.S. corporate interests, 3 million U.S. soldiers fanned out to 3,000 bases around the globe and the United States became the world's biggest arms merchant. Ten percent of the U.S. employed labor force came to depend directly on defense production and another 25 percent on defense-related productive activities. A far-flung global military shield guaranteed stable conditions required for U.S. companies and banks to invest some $150 billion abroad between 1945 and 1978. These investments in turn created an overseas commercial empire that by 1980 was generating half a trillion dollars in sales and $20 billion in profits per year, or *one-fourth the world's GNP*. Military coups in Latin America and other Third World regions, often backed by the CIA and U.S. diplomacy, assured U.S. corporations that their profits would not be interrupted. Defenders of the coups asserted that they helped preserve U.S. national security.

President Eisenhower, a Republican, left a warning about the dangers of a "military-industrial complex" rising to dominance in the United States. During the next two Democratic party administrations the trend toward militarization of the Third World received major impetus. From 1962 to 1968 there occurred fourteen military coups in Latin America alone. The use of U.S. Special Forces (Green Berets), U.S. aircraft, and U.S.-supplied napalm reached into six Latin American countries, including Bolivia where U.S.-trained "Rangers" and the CIA captured and murdered Che Guevara in 1967 (see chapter 15).

U.S. military and police aid programs and counterinsurgency missions extended throughout the hemisphere, helping to train the forces that governed and controlled most of Latin America during the long, dark night. Local and foreign business firms prospered. CIA and AID monies and personnel became implicated in the formation of Fascist-style terrorist squads in several Latin American and other Third World countries. AID operative Dan Mitrione was later exposed as having helped teach Uruguayan security forces torture techniques (Mitrione was killed by leftist guerrillas— see chapters 19 and 20). The U.S. Congress voted to terminate the AID police program in 1974 because of evidence of its use in torture.

CIA-sponsored invasions and U.S. military intimidation or intervention continued apace—the Bay of Pigs invasion of Cuba, 1961; the Cuban Missile Crisis, 1962; the invasion of the Dominican Republic, 1965; and, of course, the Vietnam war. At one point in May 1965 U.S. troops in and around the Dominican Republic outnumbered those in Vietnam by two to one. President Lyndon B. Johnson justified this forceful prevention of the return to power of pro–Alliance for Progress reformer Juan Bosch (whom Dominicans had elected president in 1962 by a 60 percent majority before a military coup replaced him) by saying the United States would intervene in any country of the Americas where there existed a danger of Communists taking power (see chapters 8 and 10).

In effect, the Johnson Doctrine was applied worldwide—the Vietnam war being the most obvious case. Johnson shed further light on that war when he told Congress in January 1967 that "the Vietnam buildup virtually assured businessmen that no economic reverse would occur in the near future." U.S. Labor Department figures for 1965–67 attributed one-fourth of the overall job increase during those years to the Vietnam war. Also, in 1967 President Johnson told a group of U.S. soldiers stationed in South Korea that the Vietnam war had saved the country from a depression and that Third World people like the Vietnamese knew America was a rich country and so had to be defied— "they want what we got and we aren't going to let them have it," he said. A year earlier, General Westmoreland, commander of U.S. forces in Vietnam, pointed out that "We are fighting the war in Vietnam to show that guerrilla warfare does not pay." In other words, U.S. policy was still, as in the days of Wilson and Bryan, one of preventing revolutions from occurring.

In 1969 _The Rockefeller Report on the Americas_ was issued. It declared Latin America's military forces to be "the essential force of constructive social change." At the same time, it called for preparing Latin America for limited democracy, in effect the kind of Brazilian military introduced in 1983–84 through an electoral college and a political party it controlled (see chapter 20). It emphasized registering women to vote, since Latin American women tended to be more religious and conservative than men.

The Rockefeller Report pointed out that U.S. direct investment in manufacturing industry had increased in the 1960s from one-fifth to one-third of all U.S. investments in Latin America. The era of the TNC was in full swing. Based on GNP of nation-states and annual sales of corporations, half of the world's largest concerns were private companies, not nations, and two-thirds of the companies were headquartered in the United States. Moreover, the United States was moving into a computer-cybernetic stage of industrialization—high-tech. Traditional U.S. manufacturing concerns were suffering from outmoded machinery, steep labor costs, and the need to hide behind high tariff walls.

According to the Rockefeller Report, the future strategy should be:

> shifting workers and capital out of (tariff-)protected industries into industries where advanced technology and intensive capital investment permits the United States to pay high wages. . . .The goods the United States is now producing inefficiently would be imported, mainly from less developed countries. . . .Such nations would become better customers for the high-technology products.

Moreover, U.S. corporations could raise their capital abroad, as they had done in the past. Approving of "joint ventures with local private participation," the Rockefeller Report pointed out that "the United States is but one partner in a development effort which is about 90 percent financed by the other American republics."

The Rockefeller Report recommended on a regional scale what the Nixon Doctrine and the Trilateral Commission sought to implement globally. According to the Nixon Doctrine, the United States would share global police responsibilities with regional powers like the Shah's Iran and the generals' Brazil. The Trilateral Commission, inspired by Chase Manhattan Bank President David Rockefeller, incorporated political and business leaders from North America, Western Europe, and Japan to discuss and, where possible, coordinate long-range economic and governmental strategies.

The sophistication of the Rockefeller Report's economic recommendations was carried over into the ongoing modernization of Latin America's militaries being encouraged in Washington. The IADC (Inter-American Defense College) at Washington's Fort McNair expanded its curriculum for Latin American officers in the areas of industrial and financial management. As 1969–72 IADC director Admiral Gene LaRocque explained, "The college is training people to more efficiently manage a government." The admiral acknowledged that "it's unhealthy to build up a cadre of military governors all over the world and this is what we do to some extent."

A somewhat different view was stated in a special report known as the Linowitz Commission Report (after its chairperson, Sol Linowitz). Issued in 1976, it stated that Latin America posed no immediate strategic threat to U.S. national security but did "significantly influence how the international economic order evolves." Exposures of U.S. complicity in human rights violations by Latin America's military regimes in the mid-1970s were harming the United States. The Linowitz Commission, composed of luminaries in the foreign policy community, deplored human rights violations and recognized "the right and responsibility of the people of other countries to organize their own political systems."

President Jimmy Carter (1977–81) relied heavily on the Linowitz Commission's recommendations. His administration combined calls for "limited democracy" advocated by the Trilateralists with an emphasis on "human rights." Human rights proclamations appealed to the American public's belief in the humanitarian spirit that historically had been invoked to explain much of U.S. foreign policy. Upon taking office, Carter suggested that the United States should not be driven by its "inordinate fear of communism" and should recognize that it lived in a world of "interdependence." Carter's approach was a presidential response to U.S. citizens' post-Vietnam and post-Watergate sense of reality, of limits to power, of desire for peace. The Panama Canal treaties (see chapter 7) further reflected an effort in Washington to respond to Latin American nationalism and the world of interdependence.

But President Carter's credibility was undercut by some of his other actions, such as his toasting of the Shah of Iran "who shares my human rights standards." Although he implemented some prohuman rights measures such as cutoffs in military aid to Argentina, Guatemala, and Chile when their governments rebuffed his administration because of its human rights declarations, he did nothing to block Argentina's and Israel's provision of large-scale military aid for right-wing dictatorships fighting popular mobilizations in Central America (see Part One and chapter 18).

Carter wavered on the revolutionary turbulence shaking Nicaragua, attempting in July 1979 to have the OAS establish an alternative government to one run by revolutionists, as the OAS had agreed to do in 1965 in the Dominican Republic. Times had changed, however, and the OAS refused to go along with the U.S. president (see chapters 5 and 10). The 1960s' U.S. policy of isolating Cuba from its neighbors in Latin America had long since failed, and the OAS was in effect saying that any attempt to turn back Nicaragua's revolution would also fail.

At the same time, U.S. counterinsurgency and military programs were beefed up in El Salvador and several other Latin American countries. Former Salvadoran soldiers later testified that U.S. military advisers were present at "training sessions" where suspected guerrillas were tortured by army instructors. Among Salvadoran troops being trained by U.S. advisers were fourteen- and fifteen-year-old boys.

The Kissinger Commission Report maintained that the United States had to increase military aid to El Salvador's security forces and to eliminate the 1974 ban on aid to police organizations in order to help create "humane" counterinsurgency practices and "improve human rights performance." Past aid had not prevented the practices of torture and murder by security forces. Critics suggested that to speak of more military and police aid and yet "humanitarian relief" from its consequences (more than a million Central American refugees) was contradictory and hypocritical.

The Reagan administration pressured Congress to lift its 1974 ban on police aid by requesting a $54 million police-training aid package for Central America. Congress balked, as evidence of CIA complicity in murders of civilians by Honduran security forces came to light (see chapter 4).

As the Kissinger Commission Report was being prepared, the NSC was carrying out its war in Nicaragua through Lieutenant Colonel Oliver North's White House basement operation. Even the NED (National Endowment for Democracy), a supposedly bipartisan U.S. foreign policy body launched by the Reagan administration, became caught up in the Central American warfare through North, the contras, and a shady operation called "Project Democracy." Funded by the USIA (U.S. Information Agency), the NED also poured millions of dollars into the political campaigns of Conservative candidates in Costa Rica, Bolivia, and Colombia and into the coffers of the CIA-funded Nicaraguan newspaper *La Prensa*.

For their part, many Latin American nationalists found themselves left with only one viable alternative for establishing humane and independent societies: revolutionary nationalism. The only other political option offered them, despite U.S. talk of reforms, was usually pro-U.S. militarism. The U.S.-backed military overthrow of Chile's democratically elected President Allende in 1973 showed that the U.S. government and business interests would not tolerate a democratic, peaceful road to social change—and that only an armed people could prevent the imposition of dictatorship. This helped explain the virtual disappearance of the political "center" in many countries, as more and more people saw no option short of revolution left them in the struggle to have a voice in government—and to be fed.

According to its critics, the Kissinger Commission, in calling for an augmented economic and military aid program for Central America and the Caribbean Basin, offered no recognition of the past failures of precisely that approach. In the first half of the 1980s, Central America's elites stashed away

$15 billion in foreign real estate and banks, or twice what the Kissinger Commission proposed as "aid" for the next five years. Meanwhile, Central America became militarized at great cost to human life. Pro-democracy forces, accused of being "Communist," generally defeated or drove back the U.S.-commanded Nicaraguan contras and U.S.-backed El Salvador military forces.

It was the threat of communism on which the Kissinger Commission ultimately rested its case:

> The use of Nicaragua as a base for Soviet and Cuban efforts to penetrate the rest of the Central American isthmus, with El Salvador the target of first opportunity, gives the conflict there a major strategic dimension. . . .The Soviet-Cuban thrust to make Central America part of their geostrategic challenge is what has turned the struggle in Central America into a security and political problem for the United States and for the hemisphere.

This "Red menace" argument carried little weight in Latin America, where, as noted earlier, the perception was one of North-South economic inequalities, not East-West geopolitical conflict. The World Court, Europe, Japan, and many U.S. citizens did not see tiny impoverished Nicaragua (or even the robust island of Cuba) as a credible threat to U.S. national security. Elsewhere in its report, the Kissinger Commission acknowledged the indigenous roots of Central America's insurrections.

A closer look at each Latin American country revealed that the double-barrelled economic/military aid approach of the Kissinger Commission had been tried earlier with sad results. A pattern of "hard cop/soft cop" traditionally characterized U.S. policy toward Latin America. Each new civilian government attempting serious reforms was crushed by the "hard cop" approach of the U.S.-backed military dictatorship. Each successive "democratic transition" presented Latin America's popular forces the friendly "soft cop." Each new cycle of military coups introduced harsher "hard cops" brooking no dissent. Both "cops" held in check the advances of popular forces and guaranteed an hospitable atmosphere for foreign businesses.

The much ballyhooed "positive U.S. role" in the most recent "democratic transition" in Latin America represented a "soft cop" adjustment to the new politics rather than a basic change in course. Thus, over time, U.S. policies seemed to become part of the problem instead of the solution, laying the basis for the contemporary challenges of the new politics.

In the eyes of most Latin American scholars, the dilemma for U.S. policymakers was how to embrace, or at least integrate, the new politics—instead of remaining part of the problem the new politics confronted. Clearly, with the end of the Cold War, the credibility of "anticommunism" and ""Soviet influence" as a rationale for opposing democratic or social reforms was undermined. Yet withdrawal of Soviet aid and influence from Latin America was not reciprocated by the United States. Moreover, all Latin American reformers and revolutionaries—even Cuba's Fidel Castro—accepted some degree of privatization and expanded "free markets."

The threat to democracy in Latin America clearly came from within the continent, not outside it. Few U.S. policymakers or scholars on Latin America disagreed about that any more. The new politics' call for popular democracy recognized that the existing limited democracies would fall by the wayside without further democratization. Two interrelated economic obstacles to the survival of limited democracy were the region's paralyzing debt structure and widespread poverty. As Argentine President Raúl Alfonsín reportedly stated in 1987, the debt "conspires against the consolidation of democracy."

Alfonsín's assessment was confirmed by a nonpartisan panel of sixty prominent Western Hemisphere citizens, including former U.S. Secretary of State Cyrus Vance. In a 1989 report, the panel warned: "The Latin American debt crisis may soon touch off a political crisis. . . .As governments lose credibility and authority, the appeal of extremist solutions is rising. . . .Economic hardship and political turbulence . . . may force civilian authorities to yield to military rule." Kissinger Commission consultant Howard J. Wiarda, in a 1990 book, concurred, foreseeing the possible demise of "an entire framework, model, and system of more or less moderate, more or less centrist, and more or less democratic rule" and "a new wave of military coups." Wiarda, a political scientist, confirmed Latin America's "frustration and disappointment" with the new democratic governments, while also noting "Latin America shudders at the prospect of a new era of authoritarianism."

U.S. policymakers and advisers were well aware that debtor nations' inability to pay contributed to reduced U.S. exports to Latin America and a greater trade deficit, costing hundreds of thousands of U.S. jobs. Some policy advisers complained that when Latin America's debts were partially canceled, revenues in creditor nations went down—and the taxpayers again, as in the times of the banks' original excessive loans, picked up the tab. In this vein, economist Benjamin J. Cohen concluded that it was time for the banks "to pick up the tab," a not unrealistic proposal since the banks had "high levels of reserves already set aside to cover the costs of Latin debt reductions."[5] Some policy advisers recognized the hard truth expressed by economist Myron J. Frankman: "A major implication of the globalization of markets is the need for global income redistribution."[6]

Yet actual U.S. policy continued to be one of just muddling through on a case-by-case basis as poverty worsened under the impact of the decade-old neo-liberal approach to solving social problems. The usually reliable Latin American newsletters[7] issued a 1993 special report entitled "Is Neo-liberalism

Working?" that noted the pressure on Latin American governments to drop the neo-liberal approach as already a failure.

Every Latin American nation posed serious challenges to U.S. policy-makers that could be understood only after examination of each country's history and the U.S. role in it. In addition, placing U.S. policy in the larger global context of not just the worldwide spread of poverty and threats to the environment but also U.S. economic rivalries with the European Economic Community and Japan (both had stepped up trade and investment initiatives in Latin America) clearly was necessary. Only then could the challenge to U.S. policy-makers be finally addressed (see Conclusion).

Notes

1. TNCs are corporations that have their base in one country but draw much of their income, raw materials, and operating capital from several other countries, through ownership of foreign subsidiaries, joint ventures with foreign governments or investors, and a host of other means. The concept "transnational" is accepted UN usage. It combines the global aspects of "trans" with the control aspects of "national."

2. On the black legend, consult Lewis Hanke, *The Spanish Struggle for Justice in the Conquest of America* (Philadelphia: N.p., 1949); Lesley Byrd Simpson, *Many Mexicos* (Berkeley: University of California Press, 1960); and James D. Cockcroft, "Prescott and His Sources: A Critical Appraisal." *Hispanic American Historical Review*, Feb. 1967.

3. See John J. Johnson, *The Military and Society in Latin America* (Stanford, CA: Stanford University Press, 1964).

4. See James D. Cockcroft, André Gunder Frank, and Dale L. Johnson, *Dependence and Underdevelopment: Latin America's Political Economy* (Garden City, NY: Doubleday, 1972).

5. See Robert Bottome et al., *In the Shadow of the Debt: Emerging Issues in Latin America* (New York: Twentieth Century Fund Press, 1992).

6. See A. Ritter, M. Cameron, and D. Pollock, eds., *Latin America to the Year 2000: Reactivating Growth, Improving Equity, Sustaining Democracy* (New York: Praeger, 1992).

7. See Selected Bibliography.

Selected Bibliography

See also Selected Bibliography for the introduction to Part One, Part Two, and Part Three, and the Conclusion.

Alexander, Robert J. (ed.). *Biographical Dictionary of Latin American and Caribbean Political Leaders*. New York: Greenwood Press, 1988.

Baddeley, Oriana, and Valerie Fraser. *Drawing the Line: Art and Cultural Identity in Contemporary Latin America*. London: Latin America Bureau, 1989.

Banks, Arthur S. *Political Handbook of the World*. Binghamton, NY: CSA Publications. An annual reference book.

Bethell, Leslie (ed.). *The Cambridge History of Latin America*. New York: Cambridge University Press, 1989. Multiple volumes.

Black, Jan Knippers. *Sentinels of Empire. The United States and Latin America Militarism*. New York: Greenwood Press, 1986.

Boeker, Paul H. *Lost Illusions, Latin America's Struggle for Democracy, as Recounted by Its Leaders*. La Jolla, CA: Institute of the Americas, 1990. Interviews with twenty-five presidents, ex-presidents, and political heavyweights looking for more U.S. support for democracy.

Boff, Leonardo, and Clodovis Boff. *Liberation Theology: From Confrontation to Dialogue*. New York: Harper & Row, 1986.

Bottome, Robert, et al. *In the Shadow of the Debt: Emerging Issues in Latin America*. New York: Twentieth Century Fund Press, 1992. Mostly South America, also Mexico.

Burns, E. Bradford. *The Poverty of Progress: Latin America in the Nineteenth Century*. Berkeley: University of California Press, 1980.

Carothers, Thomas. *In the Name of Democracy: U.S. Policy toward Latin America in the Reagan Years*. Berkeley: University of California Press, 1991. By a former AID official in Reagan years.

Cavanagh, John, et al. (eds.). *Trading Freedom: How Free Trade Affects Our Lives, Work, and Environment*. San Francisco, CA: Food First Books, 1992.

Chalmers, Douglas A., et al. *The Right and Democracy in Latin America*. New York: Praeger, 1992. Examines a wide range of right-wing forces and their roles in the transition to limited democracy.

Chilcote, Ronald H., and Joel C. Edelstein. *Latin America: Capitalist and Socialist Perspectives of Development and Underdevelopment*. Boulder, CO: Westview, 1986.

Chomsky, Noam. *Year 501: The Conquest Continues*. Boston, MA: South End Press, 1993. Educational on U.S. role.

Cockcroft, James D. *Outlaws in the Promised Land*. New York: Grove Weidenfeld, 1986, revised ed., 1988. On U.S. immigration policy; complement to Mitchell book below.

Collier, Ruth Berins, and David Collier. *Shaping the Political Arena: Critical Junctures, the Labor Movement, and Regime Dynamics in Latin America*. Princeton, NJ: Princeton University Press, 1991.

Corradi, Juan, Patricia Weiss Fagen, and Manuel Antonio Garretón (eds.). *Fear at the Edge: State Terror and Resistance in Latin America*. Berkeley: University of California Press, 1992. Powerful social psychological insights into life under authoritarian regimes and their legacy.

Council on Hemispheric Affairs. *Washington Report on the Hemisphere*. Informed biweekly newsletter on Washington's role in Latin America.

Crosby, Alfred W., Jr. *The Columbian Exchange: Biological and Cultural Consequences of 1492*. Westport, CT: Greenwood Press, 1972. A classic.

Cultural Survival Quarterly. Cambridge, MA, 1982 to present. Reports on threatened indigenous peoples.

DataCenter. *Information Services Latin America* (ISLA). Provides ongoing clips of articles from nine U.S. newspapers and topic-specific clips on request (Oakland, CA).

Davis, Harold Eugene. *Latin American Thought: Historical Introduction*. New York: Free Press, 1974. Informed survey.

Deere, Carmen Diana, and Magdalena León (eds.). *Rural Women and State Policy: Feminist Perspectives on Latin American Agricultural Development*. Boulder, CO: Westview, 1987.

Dent, David W. (ed.). *Handbook of Political Science Research on Latin America*. Westport, CT: Greenwood Press, 1990.

Dunkerley, James, John King, and Jean Franco (eds.). *Critical Studies in Latin American Culture Series*. New York: Routledge, Chapman and Hall, 1992. Multiple volumes on twentieth-century literature and art.

Eckstein, Susan (ed.). *Power and Popular Protest: Latin American Social Movements*. Berkeley: University of California Press, 1989.

Epstein, Edward C. (ed.). *Labor Autonomy and the State in Latin America*. Boston, MA: Unwin Hyman, 1989. New labor militancy.

Fisher, Jo. *Out of the Shadows: Women, Resistance, and Politics in South America*. New York: Monthly Review Press, 1993.

Foster, David William. *From Mafalda to Los Supermachos: Latin American Graphic Humor as Popular Culture*. Boulder, CO: Lynne Rienner, 1989.

Frank, André Gunder, and Dale L. Johnson. *Dependence and Underdevelopment: Latin America's Political Economy*. Garden City: Doubleday, 1972.

Fusco, Coco (ed.). *Reviewing Histories: Selections from New Latin American Cinema*. Buffalo, NY: Hallwalls Contemporary Arts Center, 1987. Interviews with leading filmmakers.

Galeano, Eduardo. *Open Veins of Latin America*. New York: Monthly Review Press, 1973. Famous history of looting of a continent.

Gaspar, Edmund. *United States–Latin America: A Special Relationship?* Washington, DC: American Enterprise Institute, 1978. Conservative view.

Gerassi, John. *The Great Fear in Latin America*. New York: Collier Books, 1965. By former *Time* magazine correspondent, an on-the-scene, well-documented critique of U.S. policies.

Gilbert, Alan. *The Latin American City*. London: Latin America Bureau, 1994.

Green, Duncan. *Faces of Latin America*. London: Latin America Bureau, 1993. Human dimensions of current social ferment.

Greenfield, Gerald Michael (ed.). *Latin American Urbanization*. Westport, CT: Greenwood Press, 1994.

Gutiérrez, Gustavo. *A Theology of Liberation*. Maryknoll, NY: Orbis Books, 1973.

Hamill, Hugh (ed.). *Caudillos: Dictators in Spanish America*. Norman: University of Oklahoma Press, 1992.

Handbook of Latin American Studies. Austin: University of Texas Press. Alternating annual volumes on humanities and social sciences.

Handelman, Howard, and Warner Baer (eds.). *Paying the Costs of Austerity in Latin America*. Boulder, CO: Westview, 1989. Consequences of debt and IMF austerity programs.

Herman, Edward S., and Noam Chomsky. *Manufacturing Consent: The Political Economy of the Mass Media*. New York: Pantheon Books, 1992. Exposes media deceptions on U.S. policy.

Hispanic American Periodicals Index. Covers two hundred journals.

Huggins, Martha (ed.). *Vigilantism and the State in Modern Latin America: Essays on Extralegal Violence*. New York: Praeger, 1991. Complement to Corradi et al., *Fear at the Edge*, cited in this bibliography.

Information Services on Latin America (ISLA). See DataCenter.

Inter-American Development Bank (IDB). Washington, DC. Each year IDB issues an updated annual report.

Inter-Hemispheric Education Resource Center. *The NED Backgrounder*. Albuquerque, NM: Resource Center. A quarterly on bipartisan National Endowment for Democracy initiated during Reagan presidency.

James, Preston. *Latin America*. New York: Odyssey, 1969. Geography.

Jaquette, Jane S. (ed.). *The Women's Movement in Latin America: Feminism and the Transition to Democracy*. Boulder, CO: Westview, 1993.

Keen, Benjamin, and Mark Wasserman. *A Short History of Latin America*. Boston, MA: Houghton Mifflin, 1984.

Kicza, John E. *The Indian in Latin American History*. Wilmington, DE: Scholarly Resources, 1993.

Kissinger, Henry. *Kissinger Commission Report*. Washington, DC: U.S. Government Printing Office, 1984.

Klare, Michael, and Peter Kornbluh (eds.). *Low-Intensity Warfare: Counterinsurgency, Proinsurgency, and Antiterrorism in the Eighties.* New York: Pantheon, 1988.

Koning, Hans. *The Conquest of America: How the Indian Nations Lost Their Continent.* New York: Monthly Review Press, 1993.

Kuppers, Gaby (ed.). *Compañeras: Voices from the Latin American Women's Movement.* New York: Monthly Review Press, 1994.

Lappé, Frances Moore, and Joseph Collins. *World Hunger Twelve Myths.* New York: Grove Weidenfeld, 1986. Readable explanation of relationship between agribusiness, aid programs, and starvation.

Latin American Bureau (LAB). *The European Challenge: Europe's New Role in Latin America.* London: LAB, 1982.

Latin American Newsletters, Ltd. *Latin American Weekly Report.* Informed London-based newsletter.

Latin America News Update. Ohio-based monthly foreign press digest.

Latin American Perspectives. "Class Formation and Struggle." *Latin American Perspectives,* 10 (2,3) (Spring, Summer 1983).

_____. "Democratization and Class Struggle." *Latin American Perspectives,* 15 (3) (Summer 1988).

_____. "Voices of the Voiceless in Testimonial Literature." *Latin American Perspectives,* 18 (3,4) (Summer, Fall 1991).

Latinamerica Press. Timely background weekly report on the new politics (Apartado 5594, Lima 100, Peru).

Lernoux, Penny. *Cry of the People: The Struggle for Human Rights in Latin America—The Catholic Church in Conflict with U.S. Policy.* New York: Penguin Books, 1980.

Liss, Sheldon B. *Marxist Thought in Latin America.* Berkeley: University of California Press, 1984.

Loveman, Brian, and Thomas M. Davies, Jr. (eds.). *Politics of Anti-Politics: The Military in Latin America.* 2d ed. Lincoln: University of Nebraska Press, 1989. Includes documents from military brass rationalizing their nefarious human rights records.

Lustig, Nora, et al. *North American Free Trade: Assessing the Impact.* Washington, DC: Brookings Institution, 1992.

Malloy, James M., and Mitchell Seligson (eds.). *Authoritarianism and Democrats: Regime Transition in Latin America.* Pittsburgh, PA: University of Pittsburgh Press, 1987.

Martz, John D. (ed.). *United States Policy in Latin America: A Quarter Century of Crisis and Challenge, 1961–1986.* Lincoln: University of Nebraska Press, 1988.

Miller, Nathan. *The Hidden History of U.S. Intelligence.* New York: Paragon House, 1989. Secretive underpinnings of U.S. diplomacy.

Mitchell, Christopher (ed.). *Western Hemisphere Immigration and United States Foreign Policy.* University Park: Penn State Press, 1992.

Moody, Kim, and Mary McGinn. *Unions and Free Trade: Solidarity vs. Competition.* Detroit, MI: Labor Notes, 1992. Insightful critique of NAFTA.

Morner, Magnus. *Race Mixture in the History of Latin America.* Boston, MA: Little, Brown, 1967.

NACLA Report on the Americas. *"The Black Americas, 1491–1992." NACLA Report on the Americas, 15 (4)(Feb. 1992).*

_____. "A Market Solution for the Americas" The Rise of Wealth and Hunger." *NACLA Report on the Americas, 26 (4)(Feb. 1993).* Includes update on gay liberation struggles.

Nash, June, and Judith-Maria Buechler (eds.). "Household Production and Reproduction in the Latin American Economic Crisis." *Anthropology of World Review,* special issue, 1993. Women's struggles.

Parenti, Michael. *Inventing Reality: The Politics of the Mass Media.* New York: St. Martin, 1986. Helps students read the press critically.

Pearce, Jenny. *Under the Eagle: U.S. Intervention in Central America and the Caribbean.* Boston, MA: South End Press, 1981.

Petras, James, and Morris Morley. *Latin America in the Time of Cholera: Electoral Politics, Market Economics, and Permanent Crisis.* New York: Routledge, 1992.

Poitras, Guy. *The Ordeal of Hegemony: The United States and Latin America.* Boulder, CO: Westview, 1990. Major issues.

Rangel, Carlos. *The Latin Americans: Their Love-Hate Relationship with the United States.* New York: Harcourt Brace Jovanovich, 1977.

"Rethinking Columbus: Teaching about the 500th Anniversary of Columbus's Arrival in America," *Rethinking Schools*, Special Edition, 1991 (Rethinking Schools, 1001 E. Keefe Ave., Milwaukee, WI 53212).

Ritter, Archibald R. M., Maxwell A. Cameron, and David H. Pollock (eds.). *Latin America to the Year 2000: Reactivating Growth, Improving Equity, Sustaining Democracy.* New York: Praeger, 1992. Poverty as core problem; possible scenarios.

Rockefeller, Nelson A. *The Rockefeller Report on the Americas.* Chicago, IL: Quadrangle Books, 1969.

Rubenstein, Richard L., and John K. Roth (eds.). *The Politics of Latin American Liberation Theology.* Washington, DC: Washington Institute Press, 1988.

Silvert, Kalman H. (ed.). *The Americas in a Changing World.* Chicago, IL: Quadrangle Books, 1975. Includes Linowitz Report.

Spalding, Hobart A., Jr. *Organized Labor in Latin America.* New York: Harper & Row, 1977.

Stein, Stanley J., and Barbara H. Stein. *The Colonial Heritage of Latin America: Essays on Economic Dependence in Perspective.* New York: Oxford University Press, 1970.

Stepan, Alfred (ed.). *Americas: New Interpretive Essays.* New York: Oxford University Press, 1992. Covers state, women, religion, literature, race/color/class, and migration.

Stoll, David. *Is Latin America Turning Protestant? The Politics of Evangelical Growth.* Berkeley: University of California Press, 1990.

UN Economic Commission for Latin America (ECLA). *Economic Survey of Latin America.* Annual volumes.

UN/NGO Group on Women and Development. *Women and World Development Series.* London: Zed Books. Various titles, 1990s.

Weinberg, William J. *War on the Land: Ecology and Politics in Central America.* London: Zed Books, 1991.

Wiarda, Howard J. *The Democratic Revolution in Latin America: History, Politics, and U.S. Policy.* New York: Holmes and Meier, 1990. Somewhat pro-Reagan and Bush; criticizes U.S. ethnocentrism and advocates human rights policy.

Wilkie, James W. (ed.). *Statistical Abstract of Latin America.* Los Angeles: Latin American Center, University of California—Los Angeles. Many volumes over the years with detailed statistics and interpretive essays.

Wolf, Eric. *Sons of the Shaking Earth.* Chicago, IL: University of Chicago Press, 1959. Classic text on Indian cultures.

Films

For distributors of films and videos cited, as well as further information, consult the audio-visual media department of your institution or the public library.

53

The Amazon: A Vanishing Rainforest. 1988. 29 minutes. Color video.

Americas. 1993. Ten one-hour programs aired by PBS and distributed through CPB/Annenberg.

Americas in Transition. 1981. 29 minutes. Color film, primer on U.S.–Latin American relations.

Burn! 1970. 112 minutes. Color film and video about "Quemada," with Marlon Brando, capturing flavor of nineteenth-century Latin America.

Columbus Didn't Discover Us. 1992. 24 minutes. Color video documentary on 1990 Continental Conference of Indigenous Peoples in Ecuador.

Controlling Interests. 1978. 45 minutes. Color video (CBS News) with interviews of corporate executives of TNCs investing in Latin America.

The Double Day. 45 minutes. Film portraying working Latin American mothers' "double day."

The Global Assembly Line. 58 minutes. Award-winning color documentary on new international division of labor, women in the work force, and U.S. runaway plants.

Latin America: Intervention in Our Own Backyard. 1978. 30 minutes. Color film/video, giving eighty-year overview of U.S.–Latin American relations.

Proving Their Worth. 1990. 24 minutes. Color video on rain forest and local economy of Northeast Brazil's Indians (from Cultural Survival, Cambridge, MA).

The Secret Wars of the CIA. 1987. 94 minutes. Color video tour by former CIA officer and NSC adviser John Stockwell.

Professional Journals

Canadian Journal of Latin American and Caribbean Studies

Current History

Hispanic American Historical Review

Inter-American Economic Affairs

Journal of Afro-Latin American Studies and Literatures

Journal of Inter-American and World Affairs

Journal of Latin American Studies

Latin Anerican Perspectives

Latin Anerican Research Review

Nacla Report on the Americas

Resource Center Bulletin (Albuquerque, NM)

Studies in Satin American Popular Culture

Part One
Mexico and Central America

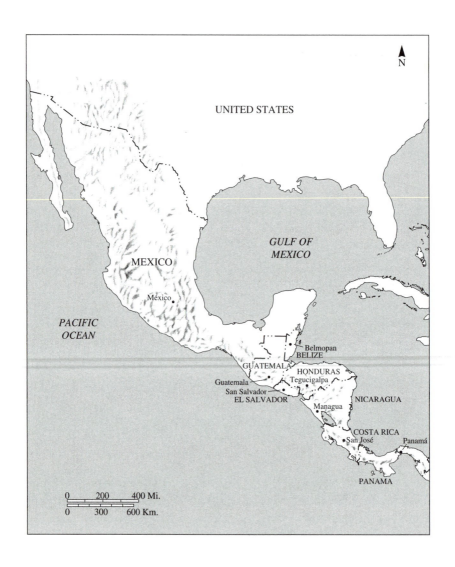

N

UNITED STATES

GULF OF
MEXICO

MEXICO

PACIFIC
OCEAN

México

Belmopan
BELIZE

GUATEMALA

HONDURAS

Guatemala
Tegucigalpa

San Salvador
EL SALVADOR

Managua

NICARAGUA

COSTA RICA
San José

Panamá

PANAMA

0   200   400 Mi.

0   300   600 Km.

56

Mexico and Central America

They [the contras] committed hundreds of civilian murders, mutilations, tortures and rapes . . .at the instigation of CIA training officers.—*Former contra public relations director Edgar Chamorro, 1985*

These freedom fighters [the contras] are our brothers . . . the moral equivalent of our Founding Fathers.—*President Ronald Reagan, 1985*

The inevitable result of the charges of illegal activities known as the Watergate affair has been to raise serious questions about the integrity of the White House itself. The public faith in the integrity of this office must take priority. Tonight I wish to address those questions.—*President Richard Nixon, in national TV address about Watergate*

My fellow Americans, your trust is what gives a president his powers of leadership and his personal strength, and it's what I want to talk to you about this evening. Well, the reason I have not spoken to you before now is this: you deserved the truth. I've paid the price for my silence in terms of your trust and confidence.—*President Ronald Reagan, in national TV address about Iran-contragate*

I have given him so many messages. He knows very well that the contras, from my point of view, are the problem and not the solution.—*Costa Rican President Oscar Arias, author of Arias Peace Plan and winner of Nobel Peace Prize, on President Reagan, 1987*

In October 1986, Nicaraguan teenagers changed the course of history by aiming their shoulder-braced rocket launchers at a low-flying U.S. cargo plane carrying weapons for a "drop" to some contras—U.S.-commanded Nicaraguan mercenaries fighting against the 1979 popular revolution that had overthrown the dictatorship of Anastasio "Tachito" Somoza. The plane crashed in the jungle, killing all of its U.S. crew members except one. The next day, newspapers all over the world showed a handcuffed U.S. cargo handler, Eugene Hasenfus, being taken prisoner with proud teenagers looking on. Nicaraguan President Daniel Ortega ordered Hasenfus released. Hasenfus acknowledged he was part of the CIA mission.

Iran-Contragate, Drugs, and Iraq-gate

The contras were a U.S. government creation. Their leaders were former members of Somoza's hated U.S.-trained National Guard who had fled to Florida and Honduras after losing a war, during which they slaughtered some 50,000 fellow Nicaraguans. The U.S.-contras' "dirty war" of the 1980s would claim as many lives again. Pentagon strategists called the war in Nicaragua and neighboring El Salvador "LIC"—low intensity conflict. But most observers accepted former CIA Director Stansfield Turner's assessment of U.S. policy in the region as "state-sponsored terrorism."

Prior to the Nicaraguan teenagers' 1986 action, evidence for Turner's analysis had surfaced here and there. For example, in 1984 the CIA acknowledged it had issued a contra training manual that called for assassinating civilians. In El Salvador there appeared on the CIA payroll the name of General Carranza, a known leader of ultrarightist death squads responsible for murdering priests, nuns, labor union leaders, and peasants. After the downing of Hasenfus's plane the evidence became more ample. It snowballed into a sequence of shocking revelations known as "Iran-Contragate," "the BCCI affair" (after the Bank of Credit and Commerce International), and "Iraq-gate."

It turned out that, in order to circumvent the 1982 Boland Amendment prohibiting aid to the contras (see Box I.1), the administration of President Ronald Reagan (1981–89) had sold weapons to the Iranian government of Ayatollah Khomeini (whom it accused of being a "terrorist") and then used the profits to arm, feed, and clothe the contras. The arms deals with Iran were also part of an unfulfilled "arms-for-hostages" exchange.

The entire Iran-contra operation was unlawful in a multitude of ways (see Documents). Violating the Arms Export Act, the Neutrality Act, and the Boland Amendment, it was coordinated by the government's National Security Council (NCSC), CIA Director William Casey (who died in 1987 after ordering the destruction of much damning evidence), and top Pentagon and State Department officials.

Besides the contras, U.S. soldiers fought and died in Nicaraguan combat. Throughout the 1980s, a U.S. "secret army" of the SOD (Special Operations Division of the U.S. Army) carried out several military actions. In 1983, the Associated Press wire service reported seventeen U.S. fatalities suffered in Nicaragua by the 160th Task Force of the army's 101st Airborne Division. U.S. troop maneuvers of up to 50,000 men regularly took place along Nicaragua's borders and offshore, as the Caribbean Basin became a virtual war zone. The U.S. invasion of Grenada in 1983 was a dress rehearsal for later military actions, such as the 1989 Panama invasion (see chapter 7 and Introduction to Part Two).

From the White House basement, NSC staffer Lieutenant Colonel Oliver North oversaw a wide network of arms dealers and secret bank ac-

---

Box I.1: Central America Crisis Chronology, 1950–1993

1950–1988 $18 billion foreign debt; 25,000 troops trained by the United States; $1 billion U.S. military assistance; cotton, sugar, and cattle agribusinesses boom as peasants are displaced and food imports rise; U.S. direct investment up fifteen-fold to $5.3 billion

1953 Democratic government in Guatemala offers to buy idle UFCO (United Fruit Company) lands for peasants

1954 CIA-directed coup overthrows Guatemalan democracy; 200,000 Guatemalans killed by military and death squads by 1993

1959–1961 Cuban Revolution and Alliance for Progress

1960 Panama Canal Zone used for U.S. counterinsurgency programs

1961 CACM (Central American Common Market) established

1964 "Flag riots" against U.S. dominance in Panama

1966 U.S. Special Forces participates in Guatemalan counterinsurgency campaign that kills 8,000

1968 General Torrijos, a populist, starts twelve-year rule in Panama; Noriega becomes his U.S.-trained intelligence chief

1969 Honduras–El Salvador war and collapse of CACM

1970s Low wages and U.S. aid bring assembly plants; Panama's International Finance Center attracts $2 billion

1974 U.S. Congress bans AID police program that taught torture; attempt to form Union of Banana Exporting Countries (later undermined by United Brands, ex-UFCO)

1975 $1.25 million United Brands bribe to Honduran government

1977 Guatemala and El Salvador reject U.S. aid because of human rights provisions; increase in Israeli and Argentine military aid

1977–1978 Bilateral Panama Canal treaties provide for Panamanian sovereignty by year 2000

1979 Nicaraguan Revolution; creation of U.S. Airborne Caribbean Task Force; military coup in El Salvador followed by short-lived juntas, erosion of political center, territorial gains for guerrillas

1980 In El Salvador escalation of death squad activities, murder of Archbishop Romero and four U.S. churchwomen; in Guatemala, start of five-year union struggle against Coca-Cola

1981 Military training camps allowed for Nicaraguan exiles in Florida; start of U.S. Army Special Operations Division secret operations and NSC/CIA-contra plan to overthrow Nicaraguan government: Senate and House Intelligence Committees informed of CIA arms program for contras; discredited "White Paper" on El Salvador, renewal of U.S. military aid, Honduras–El Salvador peace treaty and first twenty-one U.S. military advisers in Honduras, where military buildup starts; Belize independence

1982 President Reagan's CBI (Caribbean Basin Initiative calling for increased economic and military aid—see introduction to Part II); CIA use of Argentine

(Continued on next page)

Box I.1 *(Continued)*

officers to train contras in Honduras; "Project Democracy" set up within NSC under North as covert operation of bipartisan National Endowment for Democracy to help deliver arms to contras and to avoid congressional oversight; $20 million for contras from CIA contingency funds; year-end "Boland Amendment" to appropriations bill prohibits CIA and Defense Department from providing arms, training, or advice to any group "for the purpose of overthrowing the government of Nicaragua"

1983   U.S. blocks Contadora peace plan; U.S. invasion of Grenada; U.S. mining of Nicaraguan harbors; year-end Congress vote for $24 million in aid to contras, restricting CIA from using its contingency funds

1984   Kissinger Commission Report (see Overview and Documents); with CIA support, Duarte elected president in El Salvador; renewal of military aid to Guatemala; start of Saudi Arabia's $1 million a month contributions to contras; Boland Amendment bans all aid to contras; CIA assassination manual use in training contras acknowledged; Ortega elected president in Nicaragua's first democratic elections

1985   U.S. trade embargo on Nicaragua; Congress votes for $27 million in humanitarian aid for contras; start of arms-for-hostages deal with Iran; Congress votes for $1 billion a year through 1989 for Central America, per Kissinger Commission recommendations; 5,000 U.S. National Guardsmen dispatched by state governors to Honduras; General Noriega consolidates power in Panama; Cerezo elected president in Guatemala

1986   World Court decision against U.S. aggression in Nicaragua (see Overview and Documents); Congress votes for $100 million in aid for contras; U.S. arms plane shot down by Nicaraguans and Eugene Hasenfus captured; Esquipulas statement by Central American presidents against outside interference

1987   Congressional hearings on Iran-contragate; cutoff in U.S. aid to Panama; intensification of war in Nicaragua and collapse of its economy as contras are driven back; Arias Peace Plan signed and Nobel Peace Prize awarded Arias

1988   Congress votes against contra military aid; Miami federal grand jury indictment of Panama's General Noriega, U.S. suspension of Canal payments, U.S. steps to remove Noriega from power

1989   President Bush endorses Central America's peace efforts; El Salvador election of Cristiani, whose party included death-squad leaders; six Jesuit priests and two laywomen murdered by El Salvador's military; UN sends military peacekeeping mission to Central America; U.S. invades Panama and "captures" Noriega

1990   Electoral defeat of Sandinistas in Nicaragua's second democratic elections

1992   Peace accord signed between guerrillas and El Salvador government; Honduras–El Salvador border dispute resolved by World Court; Nobel Peace Prize awarded Guatemala's Rigoberta Menchú

1993   Nicaragua, Honduras, El Salvador, and Guatemala sign a common market agreement; Guatemalans turn back president's "self-coup" and the nation's human rights ombudsmen becomes president; peace accords in each nation strained by continued human rights abuses and political infighting

counts. Reporting to North on the contra gunrunning were retired air force Major General Richard V. Secord and former army Major General John Singlaub. Singlaub was the leader of the U.S. branch of the World Anti-Communist League. The league was known for its having recruited into its ranks former Nazi SS officers and many officials of dictator Stroessner's Paraguay (see chapter 16).

Further help for the contras was sought by the Reagan administration from the governments of Brunei, South Korea, Saudi Arabia, and Singapore. Some $10 million of contra funding from Brunei mysteriously disappeared. A 1984 plan to obtain money or arms for the contras from South Africa was reportedly scuttled because of the administration's fear of massive U.S. protests against apartheid (racial segregation).

From North in the White House basement the chain of the Iran-contragate command looped through other agencies on up to President Reagan, who, despite his official denials, told reporters in 1987 "It was my idea to begin with." In 1990 Reagan acknowledged the operation had been undertaken "at my behest."

Congressional hearings (see Documents) revealed some shocking developments, such as the fact that the Reagan-Bush administration had drawn up contingency plans to suspend the U.S. Constitution and to use already constructed "detention centers" as holding pens for up to 400,000 antiwar protesters in the event of a U.S. invasion of Nicaragua. The FEMA (Federal Emergency Management Agency) was staffed with right-wing ideologues charged with overseeing the mass arrests (a possible factor in FEMA's incompetence in handling subsequent natural disasters like Florida's 1991 hurricane). Congress's televised hearings converted North into an overnight television celebrity, while concealing more than they revealed. For example, a number of foreign links along the weapons and money trail, including those to Israel, Portugal, and Panama, were not investigated in depth, and plots to depose or assassinate foreign presidents went undiscussed (see chapter 4). Finally, an independent counsel was appointed to get to the bottom of the matter.

Seven years later, in September 1992, independent counsel Lawrence Walsh concluded a $40 million official investigation with little to show. Despite his impeccable Republican party credentials, Walsh had faced what he called a constant "cover-up" by the Republican presidencies of Reagan and George Bush under the guise of "national security." Thousands of computer tapes had been erased and documents shredded. After leaving office, President Reagan gave a videotaped deposition that the *New York Times* characterized as "friendly but forgetful." In 1993, Walsh told reporters that he was dealing with an administration "with no feeling for the rule of law." Walsh concluded in 1993 (when Bill Clinton was the new president) that both Bush and Reagan were implicated in constitutional crimes and Congress's only recourse would have been to impeach.

Among the criminal activities directed by the highest officials of the U.S. government were the following: murder; training of torturers; narcotics trafficking; a covert propaganda operation set up by military intelligence officers to "sell" President Reagan's Nicaragua policy to the U.S. public; and internal espionage and harassment of legal peace groups seeking to assist political refugees from Central America and otherwise end the warfare there. Perhaps most shocking was a CIA attempt to establish a permanent superagency immune from any checks or balances by other parts of the government—in other words, a secret government more powerful than the official one. In fact, congressional representatives learned in the early 1990s that an earlier secret intelligence agency, the National Reconnaissance Office, had existed since 1960 and been funded by a top-secret Defense Department "black budget" three times larger than that of the State Department.

According to Hedda Garza, award-winning compiler of the Watergate Index (see Selected Bibliography) who conducted a national speaking tour to point out the parallels to the obstruction of justice and other crimes of the Watergate era that led to impeachment hearings and President Nixon's resignation, the official government itself had become a "secret one." Garza pointed out that numerous Watergate veterans who had "slipped the net" back in the Watergate days served as top advisers to President Reagan (among them White House legal counsel Fred Fielding, Secretaries of State Alexander Haig and George P. Shultz, and UN Ambassador Vernon A. Walters). Other experts argued that however secretively or illegally the government acted at times, the cost was one citizens had to bear in order to enjoy security in their "democracy." Answered Garza: "How can a secret government be democratic?" On the incompatibility between secret policy making and democracy, the U.S. Congress agreed with Garza (see Documents).

Besides known crimes, alleged ones of an equally serious nature surfaced, such as the U.S. economic embargo of Nicaragua condemned by the World Court (see Overview and Documents). Perhaps even more serious was the "October surprise" case. Numerous witnesses claimed knowledge of a secret deal made in 1980 between Iranian officials and the Reagan-Bush campaign team that assured Iran would not spring an "October surprise" by releasing the fifty-two U.S. Embassy hostages *before* election day. Such a move might have led to President Carter's reelection and spared tens of thousands of Central American lives. The hostages were released *after* the election, the day Reagan took office.

No one served jail time for any of these actual or alleged crimes. A few individuals who went to jury trial were convicted but given probation. In 1990, an appellate court overturned convictions of North and NSC chief Rear

Admiral John M. Poindexter. North, who went on to launch a political career, asserted that he was acting on President Reagan's orders. For his part, Poindexter said he had acted loyally, "to give President Reagan plausible deniability." In 1991, Robert M. Gates, the CIA deputy director who actively participated in Iran-contragate, was promoted, becoming President Bush's CIA director. Donald P. Gregg, Vice President Bush's national security adviser, who also had participated, likewise was promoted to an important post.

Then, on Christmas Eve of 1992, outgoing President Bush issued a pardon letting everyone off the hook and momentarily nullifying the strong likelihood that his own claims of being "out of the Iran-contra loop" would be exposed as lies during the upcoming trial of Reagan's Secretary of Defense Caspar Weinberger. Bush pardoned Weinberger; Reagan's earlier NSC director, Robert McFarlane; Reagan's secretary of state for inter-American affairs, Elliott Abrams; Clair George (the convicted third- ranking officer of the CIA); and others.

Prosecutor Walsh opined that President Bush issued the pardon to save his own skin. Little noticed was a casual statement in October 1992 by Bush himself, not long after the end of Walsh's investigation, that as vice-president he had in fact known of the "arms for hostages" deal "and I've said so all along." After Bush's presidential pardon, former Secretary of State Shultz acknowledged that he had known that Bush was very much "in the loop" but had decided not to say anything so long as Weinberger might face trial.

How deeply into *both* political parties the cover-up went remained an unresolved question. On April 13, 1992, NBC television's "Now It Can Be Told" program aired the findings of a citizens' group called the Arkansas Committee that showed the state government under Governor Bill Clinton had failed to pursue investigations into an alleged guns-for-narcotics series of flights between Arkansas's Mena Airport and the contras in Central America. Among those in the know, besides Clinton, were North, Bush, Gregg, and the DEA (Drug Enforcement Administration), FBI, and CIA. Arkansas airport employees said they suspected a "bipartisan cover-up."

The 1988 and 1992 presidential campaigns, during which most Iran-contragate matters were swept under the rug even though the Republicans were obviously vulnerable, suggested to many that the airport workers were right in their suspicion of a bipartisan cover-up. The final report of the congressional hearings, in fact, partially exonerated (while also criticizing) President Reagan and completely exonerated Vice-President Bush: "There is no evidence that the vice-president was aware of the diversion" even though he "attended several meetings on the Iran initiative" (see Documents). There seemed to be concern in official circles about maintaining the stability of the U.S. government.

Ironically, only months before the Nicaraguan teenagers downed Hasenfus's plane, President Reagan went on national television with photographs purportedly showing Nicaraguan government officials loading narcotics onto airplanes at Managua's airport for eventual shipment to U.S. city streets. An embarrassed DEA had to announce the next day that the president's charge was false.

In fact, Iran-contragate revelations showed that the North White House basement operation was responsible for bringing back cocaine and marijuana in planes that dropped arms to the contras, using drug profits to help fund the war. Contra drug connections to Colombian drug lords Pablo Escobar and Jorge Ochoa (see chapter 12) became legend. A Texas investigation into the failure of twenty-two savings and loan institutions revealed that the CIA had used them to launder money for its illegal operations. Two of the airfields used by the CIA's drug runners were Florida's Homestead Air Force Base and the 1,750-acre Costa Rican ranch of CIA agent John Hull (who sometimes conferred with future Vice-President Dan Quayle and Quayle's secretary, Robert Owen, North's courier). In 1989, Costa Rica indicted Hull for murder, linking him to a CIA-contra narcotics and arms smuggling network that bombed a press conference of dissident contra leader Edén Pastora (see chapter 6).

Even worse, evidence showed that North, the FBI, the Department of Justice, the DEA, and President Reagan himself blocked further investigation into the drug-running. Vice-President Bush, heading up the "war on drugs" at the time, looked the other way. President Reagan ordered executive agencies not to deliver documents to a Senate committee investigating the impact of narcotics trafficking on U.S. policy. Reagan's concern at the time was to protect Panama's dictator Manuel Noriega, on whom the CIA was counting in its war against Nicaragua. Ex-CIA Director Turner said he had taken Noriega off the CIA payroll in 1976 but that Vice-President Bush had put him back on it in 1981. Noriega was used to infiltrate Cuba's and Nicaragua's intelligence networks.

A 1,116-page report by Senator John Kerry's Senate Subcommittee on Narcotics, Terrorism and International Operations shed further light on the Noriega connection. It stated: "We were told by a former U.S. ambassador to Costa Rica that a decision was made to "put Noriega on the shelf" and take no action against his drug trafficking until the Sandinista government [of Nicaragua] had been overthrown." Ironically, Noriega's public relations agent for the U.S. Congress in the mid-1980s became Vice President Quayle's manager for the 1992 election campaign—three years *after* the U.S. invasion of Panama and capture of Noriega as an officially recognized "prisoner of war" (Noriega was later convicted by a U.S. jury of drug-running and given a long prison sentence).

The Kerry committee found "that the State Department chose four companies controlled by drug traffickers to provide [humanitarian] assistance to the contras." A subsequent internal audit by the State Department released in early 1990 showed "a poor job of managing an expensive [antinarcotics] program with little to show for it . . . primarily concerned with the public relations aspect." The Kerry committee also stated: "We learned how high U.S. officials, including Lieutenant Colonel Oliver North, went to the Justice Department to intercede on behalf of a man convicted of a narco-terrorist assassination plot against a Honduran President— because the man had been the administration's liaison to the contras."

U.S. government involvement in drug trafficking and terrorism extended around the world. Gulbuddin Hekmatyar, the United States' well-armed ally in Afghanistan against the Soviet military incursion of the 1980s, ran a heroin factory and later became president. Several foreigners accused of bombing the World Trade Center and plotting other terrorist acts in New York City in 1993 were admitted into the country at CIA request. They had worked with Hekmatyar's group.

Similar CIA intervention on behalf of its friends occurred in the case of Mexico's notorious secret police chief Miguel Nazar Haro. The CIA asked the Justice Department not to prosecute him in 1982 in California for involvement in a $30 million car theft ring because he was "its most important source of information in Mexico and Central America." A known protector of druglords and torturer of Mexican political prisoners, he later became President Carlos Salinas's director of intelligence of the Mexico City Police before public protests caused his dismissal (see chapter 1).

A number of the names of U.S. military and CIA personnel allegedly involved in the Latin American drug and arms smuggling, such as Secord, Thomas Clines, and Theodore Shackley, had been involved in similar economic or political activities in Chile, Laos, Vietnam, and Iran under the Shah. And the suspected criminal trail led even further back in history. Félix Rodríguez (a.k.a. Max Gómez, known for his role in the CIA–contra operation and his connections with Vice President Bush) had links to the Cuban gangster network run by "Don" Santo Trafficante, some of whose members were Watergate burglars. (Trafficante had been chased out of Havana by the 1959 Cuban Revolution.) As far back as World War II, the U.S. government, through its Office of Naval Intelligence, had worked out arrangements with southern Italy's mafia for mutual protection prior to the U.S. invasion of Mussolini's Italy. Later, the U.S. government and gangster elements gave protection to Fascist and Nazi war criminals associated with mass murder and helped smuggle them to South America (see chapters 15, 16, and 18).

Numerous individuals blowing the whistle on governmental wrongdoing in the 1980s and 1990s mysteriously died. One was forty-four-year-old freelance writer Joseph Daniel Casolaro, who was found dead with his

65

wrists slashed in a West Virginia hotel room in 1991. Elliot Richardson, a former attorney general under President Richard Nixon, called for a federal investigation. Richardson explained: "It's hard to come up with any reason for his death other than that he was deliberately murdered because he was so close to uncovering sinister elements in what he called "the Octopus."" Those elements included Iran-contragate figures, the "October Surprise," and the international banking house BCCI, which collapsed in the early 1990s before a barrage of law suits. The BCCI reportedly laundered money for CIA terrorists and drug traffickers around the world and helped fund the contras and Afghan rebels.

Clark M. Clifford, an eminent figure in U.S. foreign policy circles throughout the Cold War and a former secretary of defense, was among several important persons implicated in the BCCI scandal that dwarfed the savings and loans scandals of the 1980s. The BCCI affair implicated other prominent government officials and businessmen in criminal activity, influence peddling, bribes for dictators like Haiti's Duvalier, the Phillipines' Marcos, Panama's Noriega, and siphoning off of U.S. aid monies in Asia and Africa. Among the BCCI's many unsavory clients was the renowned terrorist Abu Nidal. The CIA maintained secret accounts at the BCCI for years.

A related bank scandal in the early 1990s led to unsuccessful calls for the naming of a special prosecutor to look into "Iraq-gate." An Atlanta branch of an Italian bank and the CIA were implicated in Iraq's purchases of high-technology weaponry during its 1980s war with Iran. The Reagan and Bush administrations "tilted" toward Iraq at a time when the illegal U.S. arms sales to Iran were helping Iran militarily advance in southern Iraq. On the eve of Saddam Hussein's 1990 invasion of Kuwait and the Gulf war, President Bush's ambassador in Baghdad told Saddam Hussein in effect that the United States would not interfere if he invaded Kuwait. In those same months, billions of dollars of ostensibly agricultural loans guaranteed by the U.S. government went to buy weapons that would soon be turned against U.S. soldiers. Hussein felt betrayed by his U.S. sponsors.

U.S. pre–Gulf war support for Hussein was strikingly similar to its earlier support of Noriega before going to war against him in 1989. Some observers suspected that both the Panama invasion and the Gulf war were attempts by Bush to make up for "the wimp factor" and earlier setbacks for U.S. interests in Central America and the Middle East such as the Nicaraguan and Iranian revolutions. Both wars were sophisticated "hi-tech, quick war" operations carefully prepared in advance against former allies who claimed considerable knowledge of illegal behavior by U.S. officials. Both wars rallied U.S. public opinion during economic hard times, although strong dissent movements protested in the streets (300,000 attended one anti–Gulf war rally in Washington, D.C., the biggest turnout since the days of the anti–Vietnam war protests; the bloody Panama invasion and its aftermath of mass graves and poverty are discussed in chapter 7).

Several covert CIA operations throughout the Middle East and beyond were connected to "Iraq-gate." Like the BCCI affair, Iraq-gate seemed to dwarf Iran- contragate, which in turn had dwarfed Watergate! The post-Watergate record of literally getting away with secret, criminal politics, so roundly condemned by the Congress during Watergate (and even to some extent during Iran-contragate—see Documents), apparently encouraged high officials to continue business as usual and discouraged Congress from attempting any new investigations.

Protests, Arias Peace Plan, and Bush: War by Other Means

In the 1980s, the State Department called the entire area from northwestern Mexico through Central America and across the eastern Caribbean and northern South America "a circle of crisis vital to U.S. national security" (see map). Officials in both the Carter and Reagan administrations emphasized how close El Salvador was to the oil fields of the world's third largest oil exporter to the non-Communist world—Mexico. On the recommendation of the Kissinger Commission, Congress lifted the 1974 ban on U.S. aid to El Salvador's police (see Overview).

In 1982 Mexico's oil-inflated economy collapsed (see chapter 1) and by 1989 the value of the Mexican peso had plummeted more than a thousandfold from its value at the start of the decade. Former CIA Director William Colby stated that in future years Mexican immigrants would represent a greater threat to the United States than the Soviet Union. The CIA put the odds at one in five that the hemisphere's longest governing party would soon fall from power in Mexico. Political instability and hopes for democratic reform or revolutionary change spread throughout Mexico and Central America, rocked by Latin America's _new politics,_ including the embrace between the theology of liberation and the new Marxism (see Overview).

Even the English-speaking, largely Creole population (170,000) of the tiny new nation of Belize, after gaining independence from Great Britain in 1981, became caught up in the turmoil. Strategically located between Guatemala—which still harbored territorial claims on Belize (formerly British Honduras)—and Mexico's southern oil fields, Belize was viewed in Washington as an important part of the Central American chessboard. In 1986 British and Belize armed forces occupied the Zapotillos Keys, critical for the control of the Gulf of Honduras, said to be rich in oil. Honduras claimed the islands as its own. The Monroe Doctrine, originally aimed at the British, seemed to welcome the British in this instance (see Overview). In 1989, Belize's pro-U.S. governing Unified Democratic party (UDP) lost the general elections to the less conservative but still anti-Communist People's United party (PUP). The PUP had opposed the U.S. military intervention in Central America. Once a semblance of peace returned to Central America, Belize settled its dispute with Guatemala, gaining that country's diplomatic recognition in 1991 (see chapter 2). In 1993, Britain announced it was closing its 1,400-troop garrison and leaving only 150 soldiers in Belize. The projected loss in revenues for the local economy amounted to one-fifth of GDP, but the government hoped that ecological and archaeological tourism (rain forests and Mayan ruins) would make up the difference. Meanwhile, the United States maintained its small military assistance and training programs for the Belize Defense Force (BDF), made up of the Police Special Forces and the Volunteer Guard, while foreign interests and expatriate elites expanded tourism at the expense of the environment. In 1993, the UDP won the general elections and returned to power.

Frequently warning that "millions of feet people" might sweep across the United States' southern borders, President Reagan praised the new Immigration Reform and Control Act of 1986 (see chapter 1). Because of the stream of Central American refugees already fleeing the region's warfare, the 2,000-mile-long U.S.-Mexico border became a kind of political war zone. Unlike the generally well-off Nicaraguans who fled to Miami after the 1979 Nicaraguan Revolution, hundreds of thousands of poorer refugees fleeing Central America's U.S.-backed dictatorships were denied political refuge. This violated the 1980 Refugee Act that accepted UN criteria for defining "political refugees." The Act had been passed by Congress to help justify the admission of the "Marielito" boat-lift refugees from Cuba (see chapter 8).

Many refugees were herded into detention camps as bad as those housing Haitian refugees, which reporters described as "concentration camps" (see Introduction to Part Two). Detention camps in Arizona, California, Colorado, Florida, Louisiana, New York, and Texas housed "illegal" Central American and Haitian refugees, sometimes with Mexican "undocumented" migrant workers, including children. Human rights groups like Americas Watch and Amnesty International protested their mistreatment.

U.S. citizens, from the "Latino" and "Anglo" Roman Catholics of the Southwest to the southern Baptists and northern Presbyterians, built up a 100,000-strong "sanctuary movement," the nation's newest self-proclaimed "underground railroad." This movement spirited refugees fleeing the Central American warfare into safe houses away from the vans and helicopters of the INS (Immigration and Naturalization Service, known among Latinos as "la migra"). The FBI sent agents to infiltrate and harass sanctuary churches and some of the one thousand other organizations that sprang up to protest U.S. policies in Central America. Several sanctuary activists were tried and convicted for violating U.S. immigration law, in spite of the 1980 Refugee Act.

Salvadoran right-wing death squads began sending out threats against clergy-men in Los Angeles, California.

In 1984 Latinos in Los Angeles marched outside the summer Olympics shouting "Hell No, We Won't Go!" (to Central America to fight on the U.S. side) and "Hands Off Nicaragua!" In 1985, 1986, and 1987 marches of more than 100,000 people in Washington, D.C., and in San Francisco protested U.S. policies in Central America and South Africa. The organizers claimed that these mass mobilizations prevented a direct U.S. invasion of Nicaragua, El Salvador, or Guatemala more effectively than other modes of protest, such as isolated acts of civil disobedience or lobbying, which also occurred (see Conclusion and Documents).

Much of organized labor supported the protest marches, although AFL-CIO president Lane Kirkland hesitated to take a public position. Kirkland was serving as president of the controversial CIA-backed AIFLD (American Institute for Free Labor Development—see Overview). Decades of AIFLD support for Latin American dictatorships and trade unions without fighting spirit had undermined its credibility, causing AIFLD to redouble its efforts to bust fighting unions and create obedient ones (see chapters 2, 3, 4, and 7). In 1983 the AIFLD got behind Guatemala's CUSG (Confederation of Trade Union Unity), founded with the approval of the "born-again Christian" dictator, General Ríos Montt. But CUSG lacked credibility among most workers, since it opposed the Coca Cola bottling workers' strikes that cost at least eight workers' lives at the hands of death squads but won wages of as much as $7.50 a day (see chapter 2).

In El Salvador the AIFLD mounted its best-financed program in the late 1970s and early 1980s. Its efforts—intentionally or unintentionally abetted by El Salvador's military and death squads—succeeded in destroying all independent or left-leaning labor unions. Their leaders were imprisoned, eliminated, or driven underground. By 1983 the only significant trade unions allowed to function were AIFLD-assisted ones associated with the UPD (Popular Democratic Unity). But because of the intense repression brought down by the Salvadoran government, even these unions broke with the AIFLD, becoming in turn the targets of AIFLD union-breaking efforts. International labor solidarity and human rights campaigns helped gain the release of some jailed union leaders. As antigovernment guerrillas gained more territory and clandestinely moved into the major cities and towns, trade unionists recovered their ability to fight back. By 1987 the 300,000-strong UNTS (National Unity of Salvadoran Workers) was mounting huge demonstrations in San Salvador that called for trade-union rights, AIFLD's expulsion, and peace with the guerrillas—a major reason why the government decided to sign the Arias Peace Plan.

Growing numbers of AFL-CIO leaders criticized the blood-stained record of the AIFLD and played a vocal role in the anti-interventionist movement. The 1983 convention of the auto workers' UAW resolved: "We strongly oppose covert or overt U.S. aid to overthrow the government of Nicaragua, and urge a withdrawal of CIA and military involvement in Honduras aimed at harassment of Nicaragua." In October 1985 the AFL-CIO national convention resolved that "a negotiated settlement, rather than a military victory, holds the best hope" for establishing the "justice that the people of Nicaragua and El Salvador deserve." The National Labor Committee in Support of Democracy and Human Rights in El Salvador, composed of twenty-four top AFL-CIO union leaders, lobbied against contra aid and helped organize the nation's largest mass marches against U.S. intervention in Central America and apartheid in South Africa. At its seventeenth National Convention in 1987, the AFL-CIO passed a resolution on Central America condemning the unlawful contra war and urging acceptance of the Arias Peace Plan.

Vietnam War veterans also joined the protest marches. They pointed out that Oliver North had gone on television during the Vietnam War to defend the massacres of entire village populations like the highly publicized one at My Lai, which they compared to the massacres occurring in Central America. In 1988 a "Vietnam veterans' convoy" of thirty-seven trucks surmounted U.S. government harassment to deliver food, medicine, and clothing to the Nicaraguan people.

"Internationalists" from around the world rushed to support Nicaraguan democracy against the contras. Ageing U.S. veterans of the famed "Abraham Lincoln Brigade," whose courageous defense of the Spanish Republic's democracy in the 1930s against Hitler, Mussolini, and the invading fascist ("contra") general Francisco Franco had earned them places on Washington's "Communist blacklist," delivered medical supplies to Nicaragua. One internationalist, twenty-seven-year-old engineer Benjamin Linder, was gunned down in 1987 by a contra raid on a cooperative farm where he had been helping to build a hydroelectric project. His brother went on American television to state that Ben had been killed by the U.S. government, citing President Reagan's 1985 boast "I am a contra." Public opinion turned against the war.

Meanwhile, back at the U.S.-Mexico border, tensions escalated. In early 1988 the INS conducted a thorough investigation into border patrol agents' shooting of a Mexican national inside Mexican territory. The INS concluded that its agents had every right to shoot into Mexico in defense against acts such as people throwing rocks. Advocates of peace, human rights, and international law expressed shock.

A newly created Alien Border Control Commission brought together the INS, FBI, CIA, and Justice Department to coordinate mass internments. The INS Alien Terrorists Contingency Plan of May 1986 allowed the government "to isolate those members of nationality groups whose presence is inimical to national Security interests." National Security Directive 138 granted the U.S.

Armed Forces the right to use force against persons or groups "thought to be planning operations" inimical to national security. These unconstitutional draconian measures were aimed at discouraging popular protest about U.S. foreign policy and the treatment of both refugees and immigrant workers.

The Arias Peace Plan (see Documents) grew out of a long process involving larger issues of dictatorship and democracy. Starting in the 1960s, Costa Rica's presidents allowed U.S. administrations to begin militarizing their traditionally army-free democracy (see chapter 6). Arias and others worried that warfare in neighboring countries was contributing to stepped-up militarization of Costa Rica and the danger of regional war.

At the same time, popular mobilization in Central America against military dictatorships, combined with the economic crisis of the late 1970s and early 1980s, had led the militaries in several countries to permit a kind of limited "democratic opening." Into that opening walked a wide range of human rights activists demanding "accountability" from military and police officers for alleged crimes against humanity. Americas Watch, Amnesty International, and a newly organized international Coalition of Nongovernmental Organizations Concerned with Impunity for Violators of Human Rights launched campaigns against "amnesty" for those accused of torture and other crimes during the long, dark night of military repression in both Central America and South America (see Overview).

As these events were unfolding, other nations stepped in to offer their services in arranging peaceful solutions to the region's raging civil wars. In 1983–1984 Colombia, Mexico, Panama, and Venezuela worked out what was known as the Contadora twenty-one-point peace plan. Backed by several other Latin American nations emerging from their own long, dark night of state terror (see Introduction to Part Three), Contadora's twenty-one points provided for demilitarization of Central America and guarantees of "democratic pluralism." All foreign military personnel, whether Cuban or U.S., would have to leave.

In 1984, Nicaragua, most other Latin American countries, the EEC (European Economic Community), and Japan endorsed the Contadora peace plan, but the Reagan administration blocked it. As early as April 1983 the NSC issued a directive stating the U.S. intention "to coopt the [Contadora] negotiations to avoid congressionally mandated [peace] negotiations." On November 6, 1984, the *Washington Post* published parts of a leaked NSC background paper that boasted "We have effectively blocked Contadora Group efforts."

The Arias Peace Plan picked up the pieces of the shattered Contadora process. It became realizeable when Central American leaders met at Esquipulas, Guatemala, in 1986 and stated their opposition to "external interference of any kind." Costa Rica shut down the CIA's "secret" Murciélago airfield. The diplomatic momentum swung to the Organization of American States

(OAS) and the UN. The Arias Peace Plan, signed in 1987, called for cease-fires, peace negotiations, amnesties for armed opposition groups and political prisoners, formation of national reconciliation committees, and a cutoff in outside aid to rebels (Arias insisted on a prompt ending of U.S. aid to the contras). Signed by five Central American presidents including Nicaragua's, the Arias Peace Plan provided for regional demilitarization, democratic elections, political pluralism, and guarantees of civil rights and freedom of the press. It also provided for a UN presence to monitor the treaty's implementation and future elections. It commanded a wide international backing and earned its author the 1987 Nobel Peace Prize. Central America's acceptance of the Arias Peace Plan reflected a nascent regional trend among even pro-U.S. governments like Guatemala's and El Salvador's of defying U.S. policies in the region on certain international issues.

Mexico had traditionally preached a noninterventionist policy in foreign affairs ever since two U.S. invasions during its own revolution of 1910–20 (see chapter 1). Most Central Americans and Mexicans viewed the international axis of their problems as North-South, not East-West.

President Arias's strongest ally in pushing for the prompt implementation of his peace plan was Nicaraguan President Daniel Ortega (the nation's first democratically elected president—see chapter 5). The contras, badly beaten on the battlefield by Nicaraguan patriots and facing diplomatic isolation in Central America, announced in 1987 they could not win the war.

The diplomatic initiative passed to the Latin Americans. In March 1989, the new U.S. president, George Bush, asked Congress to support the Central American peace efforts but also to aid the contras. In August, Central America's presidents set a December 8 deadline for disbanding of contra bases in Honduras under international supervision—a decisive diplomatic blow against U.S. policy.

In October 1989, the OAS held a meeting of heads of state in Costa Rica to celebrate the peace process. A reluctant President Bush attended. While there he called Nicaragua's President Ortega "this little man" and confused him with Panama's General Manuel Noriega. Bush reportedly described Ortega as "an unwanted animal at a garden party." The Latin Americans were shocked but maintained their dignity. In November 1989, the UN Security Council voted unanimously to send a team of unarmed military observers to Central America to monitor the shaky peace process— the first such UN military peacekeeping mission ever undertaken in the Western Hemisphere.

When the United States invaded Panama in December 1989 and literally kidnapped its leader, Noriega, there was little the Latin Americans or the OAS (or the UN, for that matter) could do. Peace was a relative matter having to do with power.

Bush's actions changed the basic U.S. policy of pursuing war against revolution not in its ultimate goal but in its techniques and rationales. The winding down of the Cold War contributed to the change. Anticommunism and anti-Sovietism were no longer credible pretexts. Antiterrorism and controlling drug trafficking became the new banner for U.S. interventionism. The Panama operation was the first successful test of swift victory through decisive, direct force.

"Gunboat diplomacy" was dusted off and modernized, becoming "missile diplomacy." Future wars would be high-tech, short-term, winnable wars, with clearly stated moral goals. The press would be kept under far tighter wraps than had been the case in Vietnam. Little time would be permitted for public opinion to change. The Panama incursion, however much in violation of the UN Charter, OAS Charter, Canal Treaties, and U.S. Constitution, demonstrated the new approach. Called "Operation Just Cause" because of its nailing a presumed narcotics "biggie," its critics called it "Operation Just Business." The results in Panama included the return to full power of the financial and commercial oligarchy and the assurance that Panama's eventual ownership of the Canal would not lead to loss of U.S. control (see chapter 7).

But in military stalemates like those in Nicaragua and El Salvador, less invasive means could be used to better advantage—tied aid programs, "democratic" elections where money made a big difference, manipulation of burdensome state debt structures, propaganda about human rights. The Panama invasion was timed to occur at the height of the Nicaraguan presidential election campaign on which the Bush administration spent far more per voter than on its own campaign the previous year (see chapter 5). Noriega's removal served the U.S. policy goal of removing the Sandinistas from power through intimidation. The implicit message was: if the contras cannot do it and the voters do not elect our candidate, then missiles will do the job.

The lesson of the 1980s was that U.S. economic interests could better be served through less spending on unreliable generals like Noriega and more on building strong local economies tied through free trade and common markets to the United States. In addition, there were more important markets to consider than those of "economically backward" Central American—China, the former Soviet bloc, South America, Mexico.

Japanese and Korean investors had moved into parts of Mexico and Central America (see chapters 1 and 2), but a NAFTA-style free trade agreement requiring local inputs could assure U.S. advantages. The Bush administration (1989–1993) made NAFTA (North American Free Trade Agreement linking Mexico, Canada, and the United States) and an eventual hemispheric common market the cornerstone of not just its Latin America policy but its global strategy to out-compete Europe and Japan as well. The Clinton administration that followed added nonbinding environmental and worker protection

73

"side agreements" to NAFTA but did not fundamentally alter the underlying strategy.

To deflect organized labor's protests against low wages and poor work conditions, a new type of worker-management harmony would be championed. Called "solidarismo," or solidarity, it would pool matching worker and employer contributions to fund benefits that worker-funded unions could not afford. This approach was already working in Costa Rica, where there were more *solidarista* association members than labor unionists.

Finally, U.S. policy in Central America became one of steering all post-war reconstruction aid to governments it supported, as in the case of El Salvador's right-wing Cristiani regime elected in 1989 in elections that, unlike Nicaragua's, hardly could be called democratic (see chapter 3). The 1990 election victory of the U.S.-backed candidate in Nicaragua and Ortega's gracious acceptance of the results there re-energized the Arias Peace Plan. It facilitated the return and disarming of most of the contras. But other contras continued to fight. The United States provided less economic aid to rebuild the country than anticipated, and by 1993 Nicaragua was again one of the region's most unstable nations (see chapter 5).

In 1992, the World Court resolved the Honduras–El Salvador border dispute by assigning joint control of the Gulf of Fonseca to them and Nicaragua. Honduras kept Tigre Island. That same year, El Salvador's government signed a peace treaty with representatives of the guerrillas, and one thousand UN observers took up their posts. But UN "truth commission" findings of government and army responsibility for mass graves and horrifying massacres hardened the right wing's attitude and the peace remained a tenuous one (see chapter 3). The situation was somewhat similar in Guatemala, where peace talks sputtered (see chapter 2).

The Economic Legacy of the 1980s

The 1980s' warfare left an economic legacy of bloated debts, increased poverty, and entrenched civilian and military elites dividing up the wealth harvested from mostly U.S. loans. War combined with the prior decades' agricultural development for export (cattle and bananas) left two-thirds of Central America's tropical rain forests destroyed and basic water and food supplies contaminated or inadequate.

Central America's presidents announced that the decade's civil strife had killed 120,000 people and that billions had been wasted in military expenditures leaving 60 percent of the region's 30 million people "in extreme poverty." Despite billions of dollars in U.S. aid to wage the war, Central American per capita income had dropped 20 percent. Illiteracy still plagued half the citizens of Guatemala and Honduras. Land tenure remained skewed, with farms bigger than 75 acres accounting for 7 percent of all farms and 73 percent of the land. On the other hand, farms of less than 5 acres represented 78 percent of all farms and held only 11 percent of the land. The figures were similar in Mexico.

Only revolutionary Nicaragua and the guerrilla-controlled zones of El Salvador had significantly improved literacy rates and land distribution (see chapters 3 and 5). After the Sandinistas lost Nicaragua's 1990 elections, U.S. aid to Central America was slashed by 40 percent. In the eyes of the U.S. government, the tiger of revolution seemed adequately tamed for the moment.

Central American nations rushed to embrace the previously short-lived regional common market approach (see Overview). Combined with tax breaks, it had earlier helped attract more than $5 billion in U.S. investments. Panama, because of its International Finance Center introduced in the 1970s, had led the way (see chapter 7). The rapid economic growth rates of the late 1960s and early 1970s had helped expand middle classes and popular expectations, but the subsequent worsening of economic conditions had contributed to the mass mobilizations of the "new politics" that shook the region (see Overview).

Following Mexico's embrace of "free trade," Central American countries streamed into GATT (the global General Agreement on Tariffs and Trade). The presidents of Mexico, Venezuela, and Colombia agreed in February 1993 to establish a free trade area and left open the possibility of Central America joining it later. In April 1993, Nicaragua, Honduras, El Salvador, and Guatemala signed a preliminary common market agreement to permit the gradual phasing in of free movement of their products, primary resources, and work forces. Regional trade inside Central America had fallen in the 1980s to half the 1980 amount.

In the face of NAFTA, Central America's already small amount of trade might be diverted toward Mexico. Central America's economy was midget-sized compared to Mexico's, which in turn was dwarfed by that of the real economic powerhouse of the region: the United States. Unlike trade with Mexico (the third largest U.S. trading partner after Canada and Japan), Central American trade accounted for less than 1 percent of U.S. trade each year. The United States and Mexico remained Central America's major trading partners, but the dream of economic success through a common market remained a distant reality.

NAFTA triggered significant popular opposition among its member populations. The already accomplished pre-NAFTA "silent integration" of Mexico's economy with its northern neighbor's had not yet pulled Mexico's 90 million people out of their political and economic crisis (see chapter 1 and Conclusion).

Meanwhile, Central America's banana plantations were hard hit by the

European Economic Community's decision to restrict imports of Latin American bananas as part of the heating-up trade wars between the EEC, Japan, and the United States (see Conclusion). As prices on traditional exports stayed soft and newly developed exports like cut flowers and vegetables failed to make up the difference, trade deficits climbed. Unemployment worsened.

The only dynamic economic increase in Central America occurred in *maquiladora* (assembly plant) production, which received millions of dollars from the U.S. Agency for International Development (AID) to help develop it. It employed 735,000 workers and generated $1.5 billion in exports by 1992 (almost half from Costa Rica, followed by Guatemala, Honduras, and El Salvador). But workers earned as little as $2 a day, and U.S. textile jobs dropped by 40 percent. Much of the U.S. public's anti-NAFTA sentiment came from this phenomenon of "runaway plants."

Economic neo-liberalism and IMF-style austerity programs (see Overview) reigned supreme in both Central America and Mexico, but only Mexico showed any signs of economic hope—faint ones at that! The "lost decade" of the war-torn, depression-plagued 1980s seemed to be giving way everywhere to worse poverty in the 1990s.

U.S. Policy Debates Then and Now

In the 1980s, the debate focused on how to handle the inevitable revolutions generated by mass poverty. The Reagan White House boasted it had blocked the spread of the Cuban and Nicaraguan revolutions through its actions in Central America and Grenada. its critics countered that it had only increased anti-U.S. feelings and the likelihood of further revolutions in the region by placing the United States once again on the side of dictators and death squads instead of the forces for human rights and democratic change. After all, they suggested, Cuba's and Nicaragua's revolutions could not be such a terrible thing if they handed out weapons to the citizenry and the citizens did not turn them against their leaders. In any case, they said, no matter what U.S. policies were adopted, revolutions could not be "spread" or "exported" since they were generated by specific harsh conditions *within* each country.

Broadly speaking, U.S. policymakers were divided into two schools of thought—stabilization versus reform. The first school echoed the Kissinger Commission recommendations (see Overview). It advocated more U.S. military aid, privatization of state enterprises, an export-led economy, and IMF-style economic austerity measures to stabilize the region. The second school advocated structural changes to redistribute income, increase production for the internal market, diversify foreign dependence, and bring all social classes into the political process. Ironically, the stabilization advocates said they ap-

crs edu

proved of reforms, while the reform advocates claimed that only their policies would provide stabilization.

In the case of Mexico, few figures in either the Republican or Democratic parties protested the mid-1980s' "Mexico-bashing" in media and government circles, especially the use of Mexico as the scapegoat for drug problems in the United States. Mexico's 1988 "stolen election" and mass popular street demonstrations shocked policymakers into renewed awareness that Mexico represented potential trouble at the U.S. doorstep. The long ruling PRI (Institutional Revolutionary party) claimed barely 51 percent of the 1988 vote but in reality obtained less. Most policymakers agreed Mexico needed some modest relief for its whopping $110 billion foreign debt if political stability were to be maintained. The longstanding scheme for a North American common market originally championed by the Rockefeller interests suddenly loomed as an ideal solution (see chapter 1).

In the 1990s, policy debates continued along similar lines but with greater shared emphasis on improving the human rights situation in both Central America and Mexico. The stabilization versus reform debates shifted into arguments over NAFTA, the environment, labor's rights, and the social failures of recent neo-liberal economic orthodoxy and earlier populist-statist approaches. For Mexico, more conservative stabilization advocates hoped for the creation of a two-party system that would give the conservative PAN (National Action party) a chance to end more than sixty years of PRI rule. Some even welcomed a military coup.

More radical voices in the reform camp thought that U.S.-Mexico relations had to be approached less from the viewpoint of big business and more from the viewpoint of working people on both sides of the border. Improved Mexican wages would reduce the frequency of U.S. "runaway shops," save U.S. jobs, and provide for a larger Mexican market for U.S. goods, they argued. Some of these voices, like some of their Mexican counterparts in the new politics of labor reform and bottom-up organizing, believed Mexico might have to engineer another revolution to redistribute income and free itself from an unhealthy economic dependence on the United States,

No one believed that the problems in Mexico and Central America would go away overnight. As both NAFTA and neo-liberalism became the focus of raging policy debates, the U.S. economy continued to stagnate and Europe and Japan joined the worldwide economic slowdown. The mid-1990s witnessed renewed calls for more imaginative approaches by U.S. policymakers (see Conclusion).

Selected Bibliography

See also Bibliographies for Overview, Introductions to Parts Two and Three, and Conclusion.

Bagley, Bruce M., (ed.). *Contadora and the Diplomacy of Peace in Central America.* Boulder: Westview Press, 1990. Diverse views.

Barry, Tom, and Deb Preusch. *The Central American Fact Book.* New York: Grove Press, 1986. Country profiles; U.S. policy.

Barzetti, Valerie, and Yanina Rovinski (eds.). *Toward a Green Central America: Integrating Conservation and Development.* Austin: Documentation Exchange, 1992. Central American views on ecotourism in Costa Rica and Belize; war's impact in region.

Beverly, John, and Marc Zimmerman. *Literature and Politics in the Central American Revolutions.* Austin: University of Texas Press, 1990s. Introduces us to the new poetry and testimonial literature of both genders.

Blachman, Morris L., William M. LeoGrande, and Kenneth Sharpe (eds.). *Confronting Revolution: Security Through Diplomacy in Central America.* New York: Pantheon, 1987. Editors critical of Reagan policy.

Bolland, O. Nigel. *Belize: A New Nation in Central America.* Boulder, CO: Westview Press, 1986.

Bonpane, Blase. *Guerrillas of Peace: Liberation Theology and the Central American Revolution.* 2d ed. Boston, MA: South End Press, 1987. Inside account.

Booth, John, and Thomas Walker. *Understanding Central America.* Boulder, CO: Westview Press, 1993. Insightful.

Central America Newspak. Biweekly news and resources from Documentation Exchange, Austin, TX.

Central America and Panama Highlights, A Confidential Report. Conservative news source, Miami, FL.

Central Intelligence Agency. *The Freedom Fighter's Manual.* New York: Grove Press, 1985. How to assassinate civilians.

Christic Institute. *Contras, Drugs and the U.S.* Washington, DC: 1986. Affidavit submitted by attorney for two journalists accusing U.S. officials of violating U.S. racketeering laws.

Cockburn, Leslie. *Out of Control.* Boston, MA: Atlantic Monthly Press, 1987. NSC/CIA/contra drug network, Iran-contragate, by former CBS news producer.

Cockcroft, James D. *Outlaws in the Promised Land.* New York: Grove Press, 1988. On 1986 Immigration Act, immigrant workers, and political refugees.

Draper, Theodore. *A Very Thin Line.* New York: Touchstone, 1992. On Iran-contragate, well researched.

Dunkerly, James. *Power in the Isthmus: A Political History of Modern Central America.* London: Verso, 1988.

Emerson, Steven. *Secret Warriors: Inside the Covert Military Operations of the Reagan Era.* New York: Putnam, 1988. Information on several secret Pentagon units in early 1980s.

Faber, Daniel. *Environment under Fire: Imperialism and the Ecological Crisis in Central America.* New York: Monthly Review Press, 1992.

Garst, Rachel, and Tom Barry. *Feeding the Crisis: U.S. Food Aid and Farm Policy in Central America.* Lincoln: University of Nebraska Press, 1990. Eye-opening.

Garza, Hedda (compiler). *The Watergate Investigation Index.* 2 vols. Wilmington, DE: Scholarly Resources, 1982, 1984. Award-winning index, with in-depth entries on nearly one hundred volumes of hearings, memoranda, executive sessions of Senate Select Committee hearings and House Judiciary Committee hearings and Report on Impeachment.

Golden, Renny, and Michael McConnell. *Sanctuary: The New Underground Railroad.* Maryknoll, NY: Orbis Books, 1986. On Central American refugees and sanctuary movement.

Gonzalez, Nancie L. Solien. *Sojourners of the Caribbean.* Chicago: University of Illinois Press, 1988. On Central America's 30,000 to 50,000 Garifuna peoples (Afro-Indian).

Goodman, Louis, William LeoGrande, and Johanna Forman (eds.). *Political Parties and Democracy in Central America.* Boulder, CO: Westview, 1992.

Hunter, Jane. *Israeli Foreign Policy: South Africa and Central America*. Boston, MA: South End Press, 1987. On military aid (see chapter 2).

Inforpress Centroamericana. *Central America Report*. Weekly news report (Guatemala City).

Institute for Central American Studies. *Mesoamérica*. Informed monthly newsletter in English (San José, Costa Rica).

Inter-Hemispheric Education Resource Center. *Central America Inside Out*. Separate informed overviews of each nation, Albuquerque, NM.

Krauss, Clifford. *Inside Central America: Its Peoples, Politics, and History*. New York: Touchstone, 1992.

Kwitny, Jonathan. *The Crimes of Patriots: A True Tale of Dope, Dirty Money and the CIA*. New York: Norton, 1987.

LaFeber, Walter. *Inevitable Revolutions: The United States in Central America*. New York: Norton, 1993.

Landau, Saul. *The Guerrilla Wars of Central America*. New York: St. Martin, 1994.

Leiken, Robert S., and Barry Rubin (eds.). *The Central American Crisis Reader*. New York: Summit, 1987. Anti-Sandinista editors join the debate.

Liss, Sheldon. *Radical Thought in Central America*. Boulder, CO: Westview, 1993.

Nacla. "El Pueblo Unido . . . A Central America Retrospective." *Report on the Americas*, 36(3) (Dec. 1992).

National Security Archives. *The Iran-Contra Affair: The Making of a Scandal, 1983–1988*. Washington, DC: 1992. Includes documents obtained under Freedom of Information Act.

Nuccio, Richard A. *What's Wrong, Who's Right in Central America? A Citizen's Guide*. New York: Facts on File, 1986. Presents two sides on contra aid issue in Congress.

PACCA (Policy Alternatives for the Caribbean and Central America). *The Difficult Triangle: Mexico, Central America, and the United States*. Washington, DC, 1992.

Scott, Peter Dale, and Jonathan Marshall. *Cocaine Politics: Drugs, Armies, and the CIA in Central America*. Berkeley: University of California Press, 1991. Revealing.

Torres Rivas, Edelberto. *History and Society in Central America*. Austin: University of Texas Press, 1993. Overdue translation of 1969 social science classic.

Truell, Peter, and Larry Gurwin. *False Profits: The Inside Story of BCCI, the World's Most Corrupt Financial Empire*. Boston, MA: Houghton Mifflin, 1992.

Weinrub, Al, and William Bollinger. *The AFL-CIO in Central America*. Oakland, CA: Labor Network on Central America, 1987. On AIFLD.

Williams, Robert G. *Export Agriculture and the Crisis in Central America*. Chapel Hill: University of North Carolina Press, 1986. Cotton and beef export booms set stage for revolution.

Films

Coverup: Behind the Iran-Contra Affair. 1990. 76 minutes. Award-winning color video produced by Santa Monica's Empowerment Project, narrated by Elizabeth Montgomery, music by Ruben Blades, Pink Floyd, Lou Reed. Excellent for classroom use.

El Norte. 1983. 139 minutes. Feature color film and video about Guatemalans fleeing army destruction of village and living in United States.

Faces of War. 1987. 27 minutes. Color video produced for U.S. commercial television by San Francisco-based Neighbor to Neighbor Action Fund.

If the Mango Tree Could Speak. 1993. 58 minutes. Award-winning color video about children and war in Central America.

Is This Democracy? 1990. 25 minutes. Color video by Witness for Peace (Washington, D.C.). Answers "no" to U.S. claims to support democracy.

Latino. 1985. 105 minutes. Feature color film directed by Haskell Wexler about a Chicano training the contras.

Mexico   1

As for the nationalism of Mexico, that nation opens its doors to foreigners, as it always has done in the past. So nationalism is no problem in Mexico.—*Henry Ford II, 1970*

They like the Mexican a lot because he's the hardest-working person the United States has . . . No people work as hard.—*Immigrant worker from Michoacán, Mexico*

The [Salinas] administration offers the U.S. an implicit deal, of which free-trade is the latest step. Mexico will indiscriminately put in place the type of economic reforms [privatization] that the U.S. always wanted for Mexico, but the U.S. will accept and protect the existing political system. The Mexican people want a friendly and balanced relationship with the U.S., but not at the cost of bailing out Mexico's authoritarian government.—*Cuauhtémoc Cárdenas, 1990*

Poor Mexico—so far from God, so close to the United States.—*Mexican saying*

That night in 1985, while Mexico City's streets still trembled with the earthquake's aftershocks, more relatives from miles around rushed to the smoldering ruins of the garment district. Many were already dressed in black. They, like the others who had arrived earlier, soon heard the occasional moans of their loved ones from beneath the rubble of shattered sweatshop-factories.

Soldiers prevented relatives and youthful volunteers from advancing, explaining that their "relief efforts" were not necessary yet. But lorry trucks were allowed through.

Workers wearing bandanas over their mouths jumped down from the trucks. Nattily dressed "gentlemen" directed them into the ruins. Relatives sighed with relief. Help had finally arrived.

As the night wore on, the relatives' sighs turned into horrified shouts of rage. Workers emerged from the ruins hauling not stretchers bearing loved ones but sewing machines. The well-dressed men checked off on their clipboards each machine "saved" from the ruins as the workers loaded them on the trucks.

Meanwhile, the moans of the crushed seamstresses ebbed and then stopped. Except for the scraping feet of the workmen bringing out the machines, a stunned silence descended over the watching crowd like a veil floating down over a graveyard.

As a pair of workmen carried out the last machine, a young seamstress, luckily excavated along with it, crawled after them into the street. Her face was streaked with purple bruises and dried blood. Her dark eyes were glazed with terror. She pointed a bleeding finger at the "gentlemen":

"Scum!" she cried out. "Scum bosses! You care more about your machines than human life!"

The accused men turned away from her pointing finger. They climbed aboard the trucks, which sped away.

The woman collapsed onto the pavement. Two young soldiers rushed over and knelt beside her. Then they spun around.

"She's still alive!" they shouted to stunned onlookers.

In a matter of days the capital's streets trembled from a different cause—marching feet. The accusing seamstress, walking on crutches and supported by other seamstresses who did not work that doomed early morning shift, led a protest march of thousands. The demonstrators railed against the inhumanity of the government, its soldiers, and the "bosses."

No political party, no guerrilla band organized these people. The seamstresses and their families called for the march. They led all those willing to follow.

Every Mexican sensed it: The country would never be the same. It was as if the 1985 earthquake and its aftermath had brought down the curtain on an entire epoch and set the stage for a qualitatively new drama.

In the eyes of many Americans Mexico is Latin America's most important country. Second to Brazil in population (90 million), it is—with Argentina, Brazil, Chile, and Venezuela—the most industrialized. It is the best endowed with natural resources. It has oil, natural gas, gold, silver, copper, coal, iron, sulphur, manganese, and uranium. It also has an abundant, hardworking, inexpensive labor force. It is the United States' third largest trading partner, after Canada and Japan. The labor of its workers directly boosts the U.S. economy.

Foreign investors have billions invested in Mexico, where their profit rates surpass the world average because of abundant cheap labor. Two-thirds of foreign investment is in the hands of U.S.-based TNCs (transnational corporations). For decades these investors took out of Mexico twice the money they put in, leading some analysts to refer to the "suction-pump effect" of foreign investment.

With Mexico's decision to join Canada and the United States in NAFTA (North American Free Trade Agreement), foreign investment rose to $8 billion a year. Some of it went into manufacturing, but most new capital inflows increasingly fueled Mexico's world-scale stock market. A third of the stock market's transactions went through U.S. markets, where Mexican firms accounted for 11 percent of foreign stocks traded. The upper ten percent of Mexicans grew richer—the number of Mexican billionaires rose from two to twenty-four—while the rest of the population received a dwindling share of national income. Annual economic growth rates remained sluggish.

By the mid-1990s, many Americans associated Mexico with drugs, immigrants, NAFTA, or the place where U.S. "runaway shops" relocated. From two thousand increasingly hi-tech assembly plants (*maquiladoras*) U.S. companies were drawing profit rates nearly double those in the rest of Latin America. A strike at one of the *maquiladoras* could trigger layoffs of thousands of American workers who were dependent on parts assembled there, whereas a strike at an America plant could lead to a shutdown and a move to Mexico.

Economists called it the "silent integration" of the two nations' economies. U.S. labor-union activists excoriated it as shameless exploitation of labor. Corporate executives lauded it as "good sensible business." State Department analysts called it "mutual dependence." But because so much more wealth flowed out of Mexico than into it, a lot of Mexicans and even some U.S. scholars called it "imperialism."

Prior to the 1980s a few analysts called Mexico an "economic miracle," a classic case of successful "modernization" (see Overview). The country had introduced an agrarian reform, pulled in the reigns of the Church and military, and opened its doors to foreign capital, often in "joint enterprises" with the state. It had experienced rapid economic growth, a strong peso, and incorporation of the middle classes and organized labor into a stable political system of so-called one-party democracy. New oil discoveries in the 1970s augured more miracles, and U.S. banks stepped up their loans to Mexico.

But in 1982 the "miracle" dissolved into reality: Mexico suspended payments on its foreign debt and declared bankruptcy. Wondering where all the oil money had gone, people suspected corruption in high places. Mexico joined the rest of Latin America in the "lost decade" of the 1980s economic depression. Economic growth rates dropped to around 0 percent a year, the peso plummeted from 12.50 to the dollar to more than 3,000, and annual inflation zipped past 100 percent. The purchasing power of an average worker's wage fell by more than 150 percent. Mexico's total net payments to foreign countries from 1982 to 1989 exceeded $70 billion. Malnutrition came to affect the *majority* of Mexicans.

Some 40 million rag-clad Mexicans wandered across the volcanic landscape of mountainous escarpments, eroded hillsides, drought-plagued valleys, and arid deserts, following the harvest trail or searching for a day's work. They were the landless peasants, migrant workers, urban jobless, sierra Indians, homeless beggars, and occasional bandits. Three million of them were street vendors in the teeming capital of Mexico City—the world's most populous urban center (21 million), veiled in smog generated by industrial smokestacks and snarled automobile traffic. Less than half of the work force was regularly employed, and only one-third of those with jobs earned the minimum wage. According to the Mexican government itself, the legal minimum wage could not buy half of what a family of five needed to maintain itself.

Nearly one-fifth of all Mexicans received incomes lower than those in Haiti, Latin America's poorest nation. The top 5 percent of income recipients had nearly 50 times the income of the bottom 10 percent. They lived in luxurious homes protected by two-story-high walls topped with jagged glass. The bottom half of the population, including 90 percent of all preschool children, suffered from malnutrition and went barefoot. They had no plumbing, no potable drinking water, and no electricity. Their income was seldom more than 25 cents (U.S.) per person per day. "Today is like yesterday," wails the popular song. "in a world without tomorrow. How sad the rain beats on the tin roofs of the cardboard houses."

Although the U.S. government preferred friendly relations with the big neighbor on its southern flank, "Mexico-bashing," as the press called it, became accepted practice. Former CIA Director William Colby stated in 1978 that Mexican immigration would pose in future years a bigger threat to the United States than the Soviet Union. General Paul F. Gorman, commander of the U.S. Armed Forces Southern Command, described Mexico as the nation's biggest security threat for the next ten years. A 1982 NSC policy planning session concluded that "Mexico continues public and covert support for the extreme Left [in Central America] with propaganda, funds and political support." It called for the adoption of a "more active diplomatic campaign to turn around Mexico." President Reagan spoke of "millions of feet people" sweeping across the southern border.

In the 1988 presidential election half the registered voters abstained and a majority of the other half voted against the PRI (Institutional Revolutionary party, Latin America's longest ruling party). Computers conveniently "failed" on election night, and the director of the agency in charge of organizing 1994's national elections admitted that his predecessors had "opted for the system to fail" in 1988. Results from half the voting booths were never made public, many having been burned. The PRI "won" with 50.4 percent of the vote. Mexico went into political shock.

Then another miracle appeared on the horizon: NAFTA. Losing 1988 presidential candidate Cuauhtémoc Cárdenas, still claiming he was the legitimate winner, characterized it as a political bailout of the PRI's undemocratic system.

One thing is clear. Mexico is widely viewed as critical to U.S. interests. It has two attractive commodities in abundance: oil and cheap labor.

Mexico ranks a close second or third (with the former Soviet Union and Venezuela) to the middle East nations and Iran as a source of crude oil reserves (56.4 billion barrels in 1990). The state oil firm Pemex produces 2.7 million barrels a day, of which 1.4 million is exported. The United States accounts for over half, or 7 percent of all U.S. oil imports. Mexico is the only nation with a special oil deal with the United States: it guarantees the U.S. Strategic Oil Reserve at low cost.

Because of this deal and huge U.S. loans and technology sales to develop the petroleum industry, as well as concessions to U.S. corporations in the petrochemical sector, Mexico no longer securely controls the fate of its own oil resources. In 1993, Pemex arranged loans with Citibank that came close to pledging its oil as collateral. While President Carlos Salinas de Gortari insisted "the ownership and control of oil remains inalterably in the hands of the Mexicans," civil engineer Heberto Castillo, an authority on the oil question, charged "the government is handing over control of the oil to foreigners and private initiative through a series of subterfuges." *Fortune, El Financiero*, and other business media concluded that market forces would lead to the complete denationalization of Mexican oil, perhaps by modifying the Mexican Constitution as was done in 1992 in order to privatize *ejidos* (semi-collective landholdings—see below).

As important as Mexican oil is, Mexican immigrant labor is just as vital to the U.S. economy. Immigrant workers from many nations account for nearly 10 percent of the U.S. labor force. The biggest group comes from Mexico. The Mexicans are the pivot of the economy of the Southwest, the region experiencing the most economic vigor since the 1970s. As the *Wall Street Journal* headlined on May 7, 1985: "Illegal Immigrants are Backbone of Economy in States of Southwest—They Make Computer Parts, Package Arthritis Pills, Cook, Clean, and Babysit—Prisoners in the Bunkhouse."

That is why many employers supported the Immigration Reform and Control Act of 1986 (Simpson–Mazzoli–Rodino bill) with its provision for 350,000 or more "guest workers" from Mexico. They realized the new law would help them stabilize and guarantee the flow of Mexican labor much in the way the old *bracero* program of 1942–1964 had done. Low-cost immigrant labor could, as it had done before, help depress the average wages of Americans, provide "scabs" against strikes, and generate higher profits. Employer sanction laws were not seen as a big threat—they had never been enforced in the past.

NAFTA augured an even more abundant supply of cheap Mexican labor, whether exploited in Mexican *maquiladoras* or as immigrants to the United States. As projected U.S. grain and corn exports to Mexico (already large) increased under NAFTA and the Mexican government's few remaining price supports for small farmers disappeared (as an "unfair subsidy" under

NAFTA's terms), many more Mexican peasants would be driven out of business. In 1991, econometric researchers Raul Hinojosa-Ojeda and Sherman Robinson projected a resultant increase in Mexican immigrants of 610,000 household heads per year. NAFTA was already adding fuel to the U.S. fires of Mexican immigrant-bashing, despite the fact that some of the loudest bashers, such as California's Governor Pete Wilson, had often urged guaranteeing a permanent supply of immigrant laborers to keep industries like textiles, agriculture, and janitorial services going.

How did Mexico's labor become so cheap? Why did Mexico become the central pivot of U.S. relations with Latin America? What is the debt crisis all about? How do Mexicans perceive us? Will there by a military coup in "stable" Mexico? To answer these questions we need to review Mexico's amazing history.

The Colonial Heritage: Labor Oppression and State Corruption

The road to crisis in Mexico, as in most of Latin America, is marked by a long history of foreign intervention and competition among elites for control over a hard-working but rebellious labor force. Since colonial times production priorities were set with an eye upon foreign economic interests and quick profits based on cheap labor. Little attention was paid to complete industrial transformation and adequate wages for generating a steadily growing internal market.

Arriving in 1519, the *conquistador* Hernán Cortés was far more bedazzled by the gold jewelry of the Indian civilizations of Mexico than by marketplaces, sculptures, and engineering feats. He informed the Aztecs: "We Spaniards are troubled by a disease of the heart for which the specific remedy is gold."

Apparently suffering a similar "disease," Europe's enterprising elites entered a three-century period of colonizing Latin America for their own enrichment, leaving a yawning gap between the rich and the poor. In so doing, they reduced once proud Indian civilizations to historical relics. Mayan city-states, based on communally owned lands and governed by priests and nobles, had once dominated the southern lowlands of Mexico and the highlands of Guatemala and El Salvador. The Mayans invented an accurate calendar and introduced sophisticated mathematical and astronomical concepts long before the Europeans did. Mayan power ended by the tenth century A.D. The Olmecs of the Veracruz region of eastern Mexico also had an advanced civilization (800–400 B.C.).

All of these early civilizations declined, apparently because of severe droughts, internal worker and slave rebellions, or perhaps inadequate defense against outside attackers. The Aztecs (A.D. 1327–1519) of northern and central Mexico knew that without maize (corn), military strength, and strong state organization, they could not survive. They were fierce warriors and great builders. Aztec pyramids still dot the landscape of much of central Mexico.

But the Aztecs and other Indians of Mexico could not win against the superior weaponry of the Europeans. Moreover, such contagious diseases as smallpox brought over on European ships decimated the Indian population, which by 1650 was nine-tenths wiped out. Hard labor forced on them by the colonists also weakened the Indians' capacity to resist.

Europe's draining of wealth from Mexico, Peru, and other parts of the New World led to an outward-oriented, dependent economic development that some scholars later denounced as "the development of underdevelopment." European bankers and industrialists grew strong from the funneling of Mexican and Peruvian gold, silver, and other products through the markets and coffers of Spanish mercantilism and early European capitalism.

Behind the conquerors and European tradesmen came the bishops and friars. They tied their concern for saving souls to the colonists' grab for new riches and Indian labor. As Bishop Mota y Escobar remarked: "Where there are no Indians, there is no silver, and where there is no silver, the gospel does not enter." Under the sixteenth-century *encomienda* labor system the Spanish Crown owned the land and provided the colonists with Indian labor in exchange for their christening the Indians. By 1600 this slavery gave way in most of Mexico to "free" labor markets involving wages so abysmal that they amounted to a system of debt peonage.

By 1700 income from Catholic Church wealth in the New World was maintaining the Catholic establishment in Spain, Portugal, and Italy. A notable exception to this tale of empowerment was Bishop Bartolomé de Las Casas (1474–1567), a precursor of modern theologians of liberation (see Overview). Las Casas' angry denunciations of cruel acts by the Spaniards earned him the informal title of "Protector General of the Indians."

The Indians transferred their own religious customs to the new Catholic Church rituals imposed by their conquerors. In 1531, for example, a humble Indian named Juan Diego claimed to have seen an image of the "Virgin of Guadalupe" ("Earth Mother") miraculously coming to bless and heal her suffering people. The Church officially incorporated this myth in 1648, and the Virgin became a symbol of salvation for the oppressed. Her image today is borne by protesting farm workers from southern Mexico to northern California and central Ohio.

Many Indian social practices were also carried over into the new "mestizo" (mixed Indian-Spanish blood) culture. The Mayan system of *compadrazgo,* literally cofatherhood, was amalgamated with the European "godfather" system. Aztec *machismo*—the ideology of male supremacy and bravery—was reinforced by similar Spanish traditions. *Compadrazgo* and *machismo* fortified Spanish and mestizo control over Indian labor through a "patron-client" system of subservience. A better-off *compadre* was expected to assist his "godchild" with gifts on birthdays—keeping his eye on the activities of the peasant or worker family at the same time.

A class-stratified society, a strong state, and new forms of oppression and corruption developed alongside a colonial economy founded on a semienslaved, low-wage labor force. The Crown took its "royal fifth" of New World wealth, the Church its 10 percent "tithe," called a *diezmo*. The *diezmo* is still collected in parts of rural Latin America. There was an extreme concentration of power in the hands of *hacendados* (owners of plantationlike estates called *haciendas*), mine owners, traders, *obraje* (textile sweatshop) owners, bishops, and bureaucrats.

Many modern customs, however much altered in form by changes in technology and social organization, can be traced back to colonial times. Colonial social relations were often defined as "personal," giving rise to the tradition of *personalismo*. Colonial state regulations guaranteeing royal monopolies led to personal favors and graft in order to cut through red tape. The minuscule but growing middle classes of military officers, clergy, professionals, and intellectuals often depended on bribes for their advancement. This set an early precedent for Mexico's subsequently famous custom of "the mordida" (literally, "little bite," or bribe) and often proved both efficient and corrupt.

Caudillismo and *caciquismo* too had colonial roots. The *caudillo* was a strong regional leader "on horseback," often from the military, able to crush a revolt or, after independence from Spain, run a government. Below him was the *cacique,* the local boss or foreman—usually an Indian, sometimes a village headman—who was overseer of workers at a mine, *hacienda,* or labor gang. Mexicans still refer to some labor leaders, usually rural ones, or local officials as *caciques.*

The importation of African slaves and the mixing of different races created what became known as the *castas:* mestizos, mulattoes, zambos (Afro-Indians), Afro-mestizos. After Indians and blacks, the *castas* suffered from European racism the most. All the nonwhite groups periodically revolted. Their uprisings and food riots, known as "tumultos," caused grave concern among the elites. Two centuries prior to independence from Spain, "Death to the *gachupines!*"—(Spaniards)—was already a rallying cry of the oppressed.

The Spanish army crushed these revolts and then pinned the blame for the social unrest on the Jesuits, expelling them from Mexico (1766–1767). Many of the Jesuit properties were taken over by *criollos,* descendants of Spaniards born in Mexico. In this way, resentment among *criollos* at being lower in the social hierarchy than the Spanish-born bureaucrats (*peninsulares*) was momentarily tempered.

When Spain fell to Napoleon's armies in 1808, the New World's *criollo* elites realized they would have to control the tumulto-prone, dark-skinned "rabble" alone, or at least pick a new "mother country." Great Britain and the United States seemed the most interested. By 1762 the British had seized Havana and Manila and had threatened to occupy Veracruz. By 1786 Thomas Jefferson had cast his eyes toward Latin America: "Our confederacy must be viewed as the nest, from which all America, North and South, is to be peopled." By 1799 the majority of the foreign ships landing at Veracruz were of U.S. registry.

Spain had sought to meet these challenges with the so-called Bourbon reforms (1765–1788) that had allowed _criollo_ merchants to trade with the rest of Latin America. But the easing of trade restrictions only added to the wealth of Spain's European rivals and to the ambitions of _criollo_ elites. Mexican production of goods increased manyfold, exports doubled, and regional markets flourished, but the general populace did not benefit. Periodic droughts and famines stalked the New World landscape like a specter amidst wealth and plenty.

Foreign agents rushed to free Mexico from Spanish domination. The U.S. government backed Wilkinson's "Mexican Association" in 1805; the British sent their agent Williams in 1808; Bonapartist agents arrived from France in 1809; and slaveholding Americans carried out armed expeditions into northern Mexico, today's Texas.

Meanwhile, late at night, idealistic individuals from the middle classes met to conspire against colonial rule. Outside looking in were the dark faces of the huddled hungry. How long before they would launch a bigger "tumulto" that would lead to social upheaval and devastation of the economy? Independence from Spain or even increased autonomy could give the middle classes political control of the situation.

Independence, Foreign Invasions, and a New State

On September 16, 1810, Mexican Independence Day, a parish priest, Miguel Hidalgo y Costilla, _criollo_ son of a hacienda manager incensed by the embargoing of one of his three farms to force payment of his debts, called the people to mass in Dolores, Guanajuato. "Long live our most Holy Mother of Guadalupe!" Hidalgo intoned. "Long live [Latin] America!" he shouted. "Death to bad government! Death to the _gachupines_!"

Taking Hidalgo's words literally, the parishioners grabbed their machetes and stormed the Guanajuato granary where Spanish troops and wealthy _criollos_ had taken refuge. They set fire to Spanish forts and homes. Soon they were an 80,000-strong army, stampeding through towns and pushing fleeing Spanish and _criollo_ soldiers southward.

The sight of armed peasants dashing toward Mexico City terrified the *criollo* elites. Father Hidalgo ordered a pullback but it was too late. Spanish re-inforcements arrived, crushed the rebels and captured Hidalgo. he was tried and executed by the Catholic Inquisition.

Other groups of peasants rose up. To the south, the dark-skinned mestizo priest Father José María Morelos organized a guerrilla band by promising land, higher wages, and an end to slavery. A passionate antiracist, he forbade the use of the term "mestizo." When Spanish bishops excommunicated him as an "atheist and materialist," Morelos excommunicated the bishops as traitors to Christ. He was captured, defrocked, and executed in 1815, calmly puffing on a cigar as he faced a firing squad. The Indian leader Vicente Guerrero and Afro-Indian guerrilla warrior Juan Alvarez picked up where Morelos left off.

All Spanish American became engulfed in the flames of popular rebel-lion. Afraid of losing everything, elite landowners and merchants looked for a way to crush the rampaging rabble. As the *criollo* Liberator of South America Simón Bolívar explained in his famous "Letter from Jamaica" of 1815, the *criollos'* main grievance was Spain's not giving them sufficient authority to maintain "respect" among the aroused Indians and *castas* (see chapter 11).

Frightened *criollos* in Mexico turned to an *hacendado* named Agustín de Iturbide in 1820 to lead a movement for autonomy from Spain. Iturbide's "Army of the Three Guarantees" promised unity among *criollos* and Spaniards, protection of the Church, and independence. Indian leader Guer-rero, thinking independence would end injustice, joined his guerrilla army with that of Iturbide. Many Spanish soldiers and bureaucrats also joined Itur-bide.

Iturbide established himself as Emperor of Mexico and today's Central America, but his empire disintegrated in 1823. Mexican liberals in the army of Antonio López de Santa Anna toppled him and consummated Mexican inde-pendence.

A year later British Foreign Minister George Canning observed: "The nail is driven. Spanish America is free, and if we do not mismanage our affairs sadly, she is English." The Americans thought otherwise, and a European and U.S. scramble for Latin America's wealth entered high gear. Then, as today, foreign loans and investments indebted the Mexican government to outsiders. The war-torn mines were reopened. Moneylenders known as *agiotistas,* many serving foreigners, kept the Mexican government afloat in return for mort-gages on state property or custom duties.

Whenever popular rebellions interrupted the flow of dividends, foreign military intervention occurred. In 1829 the Spanish briefly invaded Tampico. In 1835 Americans in Texas undertook a decade-long bloody secession from Mexico. In 1838 the French invaded Veracruz to collect some debts. And in 1845 the United States annexed the rebellious province of "Texas."

Then, from 1846 to 1848, U.S. troops marched through Mexico, seizing almost half its territory. The U.S. government justified the war against Mexico under the ideological rubric of Manifest Destiny. Informed U.S. citizens protested. Ulysses S. Grant wrote in a letter home: "I am bitterly opposed to this war, one of the most unjust ever waged by a stronger against a weaker nation." Congressman Abraham Lincoln and Senator John C. Calhoun made speeches denouncing President James K. Polk's invasion. Writer Henry David Thoreau launched a movement to refuse to pay taxes for the war. Clapped in jail, Thoreau was visited by his philosopher friend Ralph Waldo Emerson.

"Henry David," asked Ralph, "what are you doing in there?"

Thoreau replied: "Ralph Waldo, what are you doing out there?"

The U.S. Army experienced its highest rates of desertion in any war before or since. A group of recent Irish immigrants deserted to form the "Saint Patrick's Battalion" and fought on the side of their Mexican "brothers."

Mexico City fell in 1847. General Santa Anna fled, but young military cadets, *los niños héroes,* stayed at Chapultepec Castle to defend national honor. Some of the youth reportedly wrapped themselves in Mexican flags and leaped from the cliffs shouting *"Viva México!"* Schoolchildren still recite their names. With fierce nationalist rancor, Mexicans remember a war about which most Americans know little.

All Mexico got out of the 1848 Treaty of Guadalupe Hidalgo was $15 million and some guarantees of Mexicans' property and language rights in the lost lands (a legal basis for U.S. bilingual education today). The treaty gave the United States some of Mexico's finest territory, today's Southwest. Mining and land tycoons took even more of the Mexicans' properties by systematically violating the 1848 treaty provisions protecting Mexicans. Historian Rodolfo Acuña, among others, has documented a large number of lynchings of Mexicans in the Southwest, pejoratively called "greasers."

Mexico's postindependence period was marked by continued armed rivalry between elite families and their military cliques. For their civil wars they recruited troops from seasonal farm workers and an immense urban mass of street vendors, beggars, semiemployed and unemployed. As government succeeded government (average life span: seven months), the ideological banners of liberalism and conservatism were unfurled to disguise what in fact was an interelite struggle for hegemony, wealth, and power.

Throughout Latin America the Liberals, often in alliance with foreign investors, advocated free trade and a secular state with limits on the Church and government. The Conservatives championed religion and a strong centralized state. Both camps, however, placed their highest value on owning land, mines, and factories and controlling labor. Neither hesitated to seek outside support.

Putting the lid back on the 1810–1820 rebellion of peasants and workers was no easy matter for Mexico's squabbling elites. Some 300,000 Mayans rose up in Yucatán in the mid-1840s in what became known as "the war of the *castas*." When the Bishop of Yucatán wrote Indian leaders imploring them to lay down their weapons, they replied, "Why didn't you take notice when the Governor began killing us? Why didn't you take interest when Father Herrera tossed his saddle on a poor Indian, mounted him, and began to whip him, lacerating his belly with lashes?"

The Liberals regained government power in the late 1850s and introduced a new constitution. To help finance their government, they confiscated Church wealth. The Conservatives eventually called for French assistance. Liberal leadership increasingly passed to a full-blooded Zapotec Indian named Benito Juárez who had left home to gain an education in law and to become a law clerk. Juárez had married into a family of wealth, served as governor of Oaxaca, and was to be remembered in history books as the "Abraham Lincoln" of Mexico.

In 1861 a joint intervention agreement was signed by England, France, and Spain. Spanish troops briefly occupied Veracruz. Then, in 1862 French troops invaded Mexico and set up Archduke Maximilian of Austria as emperor (1862–1867). Patriot guerrilla armies loyal to Juárez took on the French in a protracted war.

Juárez's guerrilla fighters repeatedly cut down the French Foreign Legion when it sent "search and destroy" missions to the interior. Some 50,000 men, women, and children perished before the firing squads and attacks of the frustrated Frenchmen, but Juárez's forces finally won.

In 1867 European leaders implored Juárez not to have Maximilian executed. Juárez replied that it was the "emperor" who had decreed the death penalty for prisoners, so justice must be done. Today's murals show a stern dark Indian (Juárez) facing a tall blond Nordic (Maximilian), the tips of guerrillas' rifles spitting fire at the emperor's head: a rare symbol of Indoamerica's revenge on imperialist Europe.

The Liberals' 1857 Constitution, once more the law of the land, laid the basis for a strong state and enshrined capitalist principles of "free wage labor," private property, and economic development. It forbade slavery and guaranteed workers' rights to "associate." It also prohibited any "corporation" from owning property, thereby legalizing attacks on Catholic Church properties, workers' guilds, and peasant *ejidos* (traditional Indian village lands and rural communes).

As a result, by 1911, 96.6 percent of rural households held no land whatsoever. High government officials described Mexican farming as "capitalist agriculture based on labor's cheapness . . . worked by a rural proletariat." Of Mexico's land surface, foreigners owned between 14 and 20 percent. U.S. investors owned more industries than Mexicans, dominated rails and mining, and, with the British, controlled Mexican oil (almost one-fourth of world production by 1921). Illiteracy plagued 84 percent of the populace. The gap between the rich and the poor grew wider than ever, although a handful of industrial workers fared better than their rural brethren and more middle-class people competed for jobs with the state bureaucracy.

White-haired Porfirio Díaz, a part-Indian Liberal general who had gained fame defeating the French at Puebla on May 5, 1862 (a national holiday), ran the country like a feifdom for his Mexican and foreign friends. His thirty-five year dictatorship (1876–1911) developed communications, energy, and transportation through concessions to foreign business interests and forced recruitment of labor and violent repression of strikes. A special rural police force, the *"Rurales,"* patrolled the countryside, while a strong army crushed strikes. Censorship and prison dungeons enforced Díaz's firm rule.

The Díaz regime's rapid modernization of Mexico contributed to an expansion of the middle classes. A "braintrust" of advisers known as "Científicos" advised Díaz and guided his economic policies. Firm believers in the European philosophy of "positivism" then fashionable in much of Latin America, they believed in "order and progress." Many lawyers, clerks, and intellectuals avidly discussed the pros and cons of this approach. Critics were often "coopted" by being offered government jobs. While radical dissent was not tolerated, there did develop in the inner circles of Díaz's government a certain degree of give-and-take.

A dissent movement launched by liberals in 1900, however, was driven underground and eventually took up guerrilla warfare—the PLM (Liberal Mexican party). Calling for "land and liberty," it sparked unsuccessful armed revolts throughout Mexico in 1906 and 1908. It was led by exiled anarchist Ricardo Flores Magón, whose frequent imprisonments by U.S. officials provoked large protest demonstrations by American radicals and by the rapidly growing Mexican communities of Los Angeles and the U.S. Southwest. Practicing the internationalism it preached, the PLM unionized workers and led or participated in strikes on both sides of the border.

Meanwhile, in Morelos, a dark-eyed small landholder named Emiliano Zapata, whose lands had been taken by the rich, echoed the PLM war cry: *"Tierra y Libertad!"* Historians variously described him as a mestizo, an Indian, or a mixed-blood of white, African, and Indian extraction. Those who heard his cry rallied to it. In just a few years he would be sitting beside a large mestizo cowboy named Francisco "Pancho" Villa in Mexico City's presidential palace. Mexico would never be the same again.

Today, old peasants say they can still see Zapata riding a white horse across the escarpments overlooking their *ejidos*. At official celebrations or after raucous drinking bouts, the visitor to Morelos can still hear the emotional shout of "Viva Zapata!"

A thousand miles north, a distant counterpoint: "Viva Villa!"

From generation to generation the word is passed along, in song, verse, and storytelling. Mexicans recall their revolution even more passionately than they do the U.S. invasion of 1846–1848.

Revolution, Oil, and the Modern State:
Populism and Corporativism

The Mexican Revolution erupted in earnest in 1910 when Berkeley-trained millionaire businessman Francisco I. Madero issued his "Plan de San Luis Potosí." Backed by many middle-class people, wealthy industrial and banking interests of Mexico's north, and U.S. oil firms, Madero had campaigned for the presidency in 1910 and been jailed. PLM soldiers and newly formed popular armies led by regional figures like Zapata defeated Díaz's *federales* and sent the dictator packing in May 1911. Later that year Madero was elected president in the nation's first "free election."

In 1913 a plot by former generals of Díaz's army was hatched in the American Embassy (the "Pact of the Embassy") and produced a military coup

---

Box 1.1: U.S. Intervention in Mexico before World War II

1906	Some 275 armed U.S. volunteers led by Arizona Rangers occupied Cananea, Sonora, to help put down a PLM-led strike against a U.S. copper company (100 workers killed).
1914–1915	U.S. troops seized Veracruz (hundreds killed during the invasion) in an attempt to isolate Huerta, who had sided with British oil interests; U.S. blocked arms shipments to Villa and Zapata and extended diplomatic recognition, loans, and arms to *hacendado* Venustiano Carranza, "First Chief" of the anti-Villa, anti-Zapata moderate wing of the revolution.
1916–1917	General John J. Pershing led a 6,000-man invasion of Mexico's north but failed to capture Pancho Villa or to defeat his army.
1919–1941	U.S. military planners drew up a secret 8-inch-thick "Special Plan Green" for an invasion of Mexico "and replacement of U.S. troops by a native Mexican constabulary" in the event of problems in oil fields or along the border.
1920–1923	After Carranza was assassinated, U.S. refused to recognize the elected government of Alvaro Obregón until it signed "Bucareli Agreements" protecting U.S. oil interests.
1924	During a revolt the U.S. supplied war material for Obregón and sent a cruiser to protect the oil port of Tampico.
1932–1933	U.S. blamed Mexican immigrants for high unemployment and deported more than 300,000 of them, aggravating unemployment in Mexico.
1938–1941	After Mexico nationalized oil, the U.S. terminated its silver-purchase program and withheld loans.

---

and the assassination of President Madero and his vice-president on the order of coup leader General Victoriano Huerta. Countless civilians were killed in the next ten days' fighting.

It was not the first or last time that the United States intervened in Mexico. Among Mexicans' most recounted tales of U.S. aggression prior to World War II, those presented in Box 1.1 are the best remembered.

Mexico's foreign-policy doctrine of "nonintervention" in other nations' internal affairs was a result of public reaction to these experiences. U.S. meddling also set a popular mood for the nationalization of oil in 1938.

The driving social forces behind the revolutionary upheavals of 1911–1916 and the mid-1930s were aroused peasants and workers. To the dispossessed peasant, small farmer (ranchero), Indian comunero, rural day worker (jornalero), or worker in a factory, oil field, or mine, the enemy was obvious: the landlord-capitalist-boss. The solution was equally evident: take back the land; seize the mine, mill, or factory; run things collectively. This is what thousands of peasants and workers did. Their actions sparked a prairie fire of revolt.

In 1913–1915 popular regional armies fought federal troops across the breadth of Mexico in a veritable dance of bullets. The revolutionaries split into two broad warring camps, a "radical" one led by Zapata and Villa and a "moderate" one led by Carranza (an ex-governor under Díaz) and Carranza's crafty military field marshall, Obregón (a sixth-grade graduate, ex-mechanic, and successful chickpea farmer from Mexico's north). Carranza decreed the death penalty for prisoners, adding to the carnage.

Obregón offered the leaders of Mexico's many, newly formed Socialist-oriented labor unions material aid in exchange for organizing union members into "Red Battalions" to help defeat Villa's and Zapata's armies. The deal split the ranks of workers and peasants and gave Carranza a military victory. A year later he showed his gratitude to the union leaders by invoking the death penalty for strikers.

By the time the Carrancistas voted on the 1917 Constitution, nearly 2 million Mexicans had perished (12 percent of the population). Zapata refused to surrender but was tricked into attending a "peace conference" in 1919 and was assassinated.

The results of the bloodshed were a defeated peasantry; a crippled labor movement dependent on state favors; a wounded but victorious set of elites led by industrialists, *hacendados,* and enterprising entrepreneurs like Obregón; and a paper triumph, the 1917 Constitution. A radical document for its time, the constitution guaranteed private property, effective suffrage, separation of Church and state, rights to "legal" strikes and land reforms, and national ownership of natural resources.

Mexico stumbled into the 1930s with no single group or class clearly in control. The Mexican economy was still very dependent on U.S. trade, loans, and investments. Competing elites and emergent powerful middle-class and military elements struggled bitterly for control of the government. A long and savage civil war raged from 1926 to 1929, the "Cristero revolt." It was sparked by the Catholic Church's resentment at the government's enforcement of anticlerical provisions of the 1917 Constitution. The bishops finally conceded defeat and accepted the constitution.

The hard times brought by the 1930s' Great Depression led to renewed social unrest and a wave of strikes and land seizures. General Lázaro Cárdenas, a young revolutionary soldier in the days of Carranza, was elected president. Cárdenas was a popular man genuinely interested in good government. His regime (1934–1940) distributed more lands than all its predecessors combined, although the most fertile lands remained in the hands of big landowners.

The Cárdenas administration also reached out to labor, supporting some major strikes. It armed and organized popular militias to defend the revolution against military coups and attacks from a resurgent extreme right led by Fascistic Catholic "Gold Shirts" known as Sinarquistas. When U.S. and British oil companies refused striking workers' reasonable demands, Cárdenas nationalized the oil. On this issue, even the Catholic Church rallied to his side.

Cárdenas's brilliant political entrepreneurship forced each special-interest group to organize itself—business, labor, peasantry, teachers, and so on. The state worked with these groups, ultimately regulating them in the interest of a more stable capitalist development. By granting concessions to peasants and workers, Cárdenas laid the basis for a more productive agriculture and industry worked by people who felt they finally had a voice in the government. His maximizing the power of the presidency for guiding the nation's affairs continued a long tradition of a strong state and "presidentialism."

Cárdenas was a true populist, offering something for everyone. He played one group against the other, backing strikers against unyielding bosses, but sending the army to break strikes in vital industries. He favored industrialists over lazy *hacendados,* state-controlled unions over independent ones. By reassuring Conservatives that the Mexican Revolution would always be "capitalist," he controlled the fires of renewed civil war. He prevented workers and peasants from uniting for social improvements by keeping them in separate organizations—the CTM (Confederation of Mexican Workers) and CNC (National Peasant Confederation).

Cárdenas's presidential populism, made possible by each competing group's inability to assert hegemony, consolidated a corporativist form of state tutelage. The official political party, founded in 1929 and known today as the PRI, assumed its present structure of three sectors: peasant, labor, and "popular," the latter sector composed of bureaucrats, professionals, small business-people, and so on. A fourth sector, the military, merged into the popular one in 1940. The corporativist state amounted to a centralized one-party system, run from the top down by a small executive committee. Competition among sector leaders for candidates chosen from "their" sector provided just enough democratic spice. The Cárdenas regime consolidated the methods of political control that marked the next half century of "political stability"—populism, corporativism, and presidentialism.

The State and Industrialization, 1940 to the Present

Unable to assert hegemony alone, Mexico's elites, old and new, called upon the assistance of a corporativist and increasingly authoritarian-technocratic state to mediate conflicts between themselves and labor. Peasants had their landholdings reduced. Workers' strikes were crushed. Not until 1968 did a person's wage recover to buy as much as it had done in the Depression year of 1939.

The corrupt right-wing regime of President Miguel Alemán (1946–1952) did not tolerate dissent. Alemán gutted agrarian reform, replaced honest or leftist labor leaders with thieving party hacks known as _"charros,"_ and opened the doors wide to foreign capital.

After World War II the elites used the state to subsidize their investments and negotiate old debts, new loans, and "joint enterprises" with foreign firms. The state "pump-primed" the economy by contributing more than 40 percent of total investment in every decade except the 1950s and by providing low-cost energy, transport, irrigation, and communication services. It financed free education that reduced the illiteracy rate 50 percent between 1940 and 1970. Price controls and subsidies kept food prices down.

From 1940 to 1960 Mexico's state-supported capitalism achieved what became widely reported as an "economic miracle." Agricultural production increased 100 percent, industrial production 120 percent. Government policies of import substitution (see Overview) helped mechanize agriculture and replace imported manufactures with domestically produced ones. But the cost was high in loans and imports of machinery and raw materials—82 percent of all imports today. By 1980 profits from new direct foreign investments and interest payments on the debt were removing from Mexico nearly five times the amount of incoming new direct foreign investment, which zipped past the billion-dollar mark. Despite losing some ground to the Japanese in electronics and _maquiladoras,_ U.S.-based TNCs, often through joint ventures with the state, dominated many of the commanding heights of the economy—capital goods and basic intermediate goods, automotive and petrochemicals, machinery imports, agricultural exports.

During the economic miracle period the "Monterrey Group" of investors in northeastern Mexico, whose steel, glass, and bottling factories still ban unions or operate with "white" company unions, tempered their opposition to "big government." The director of the private Banco Nacional de México summed things up: "In this country, the state and private enterprise are, at bottom, the same thing."

The "Green Revolution," a program of technification of agriculture through massive provision of credits, machines, fertilizers, pesticides, and hybrid seeds, was introduced to the world by the Rockefeller Foundation and Mexico's Ministry of Agriculture in 1943. It dispossessed the peasantry and concentrated lands in the hands of big agribusiness and modernized *hacendados*. Big growers paid a fee to indebted *ejidatarios* for the use of their parcels. As one U.S. agronomist noted, a fortunate *ejidatario* was "permitted to participate as a *peón* on his own land." The *ejido* and the *minifundium* (subsistence parcel), by providing a peasant with a little land, served as "shock absorbers" for the rapid expansion of agribusiness interests.

The state ejidal bank facilitated this trend. As one group of Michoacán *ejidatarios* growing sorghum for the booming cattle-export industry explained in 1980: "Banco Rural is our *patrón* [boss]. We're the workers and we don't even get a wage or have a labor union."

The Green Revolution made Mexico the world's ninth largest producer of food, but it failed to feed the hungry. Mexico ranked sixtieth in life expectancy and food consumption per person. Animals and foreign consumers ate more basic foodstuffs produced in Mexico than Mexicans did.

The Green Revolution benefited the owners of agribusiness, banks, and industry. Displaced peasants migrated to the cities, where they formed a cheap labor pool for industrialization. Increased food production helped provide sufficient low-cost foodstuffs for the work force and so reduced the need for wage hikes. Mechanization supplied inexpensive raw materials for industry (cotton, tobacco, hemp, etc.). Augmented agricultural exports provided foreign exchange for the importation of capital goods needed for industrial production.

Throughout the 1950s and early 1960s workers and peasants launched protest actions, but to little avail. The state either repressed or coopted dissident groups—buying off their leaders with government favors or positions. The carrot and the stick were alternated as needed. After sending the army to crush a militant strike wave in the late 1950s, the state introduced a profit-sharing law in 1962. Union *charros* took their "cut," leaving rank-and-file workers with little of the "shared" profits.

Laws were weighted against the right to strike. Official conciliation and arbitration boards could make one of three rulings on strikes: "legal," "illegal," or "nonexistent." The last two included no restitution of pay for days lost in a strike action. Dissatisfied workers learned to gain government approval *before* calling a strike. This kind of official labor unionism left Mexico with the world's third highest rate of industrial accidents.

In schools and workplaces the government trumpeted a revolutionary heritage, providing Mexicans with an imagery of their own victories against oppression. *Indigenismo*—official acts of celebration of the Indian heritage—served to mask the exploitation of the nation's Indians (today 30 percent of population is still predominantly Indian, although many share the culture of the 60 percent who are mestizo). The government quickly recognized the Bolivian, Cuban, and Nicaraguan revolutions, claiming that Mexico had been the first Latin American country to have a revolution and so did not need another one.

In these ways, the state not only controlled popular unrest but also acted as an agent of class formation, helping to "proletarianize" the peasantry and to impoverish a large segment of the urban masses. By the 1980s more than half of an estimated 7 million rural adult workers were landless. Another fourth held minuscule parcels of land incapable of feeding the family (*minifundistas*). Most of the 2 million *ejidatorios* were impoverished and gained most of their income from working on other people's farms. Whether or not holding land, nine-tenths of the rural population counted on abysmally low wages to survive. They were "proletarians" with a mixed peasant-worker political consciousness.

Meanwhile, the urban slums, swollen by outmigration from the countryside, became filled with families without regular jobs, decent housing, or adequate nutrition. Half of greater Mexico City's 21 million inhabitants resided in these "colonias proletarias" or "lost cities." Many families searched for rags, bottles, or paper to turn in for a few centavos. Those with irregular employment in garment sweatshops, furniture workshops, and even streetvending were integrated with larger business interests whose commodities they produced or sold. If they could not survive in the cities, the urban poor often drifted back to the countryside to take up *minifundista* farming—a little noticed "repeasantization" trend. Many went back and forth between the countryside and city.

State policies not only helped dispossess people from their land and expand a low-wage work force, but they also contributed to the creation of a bloated sector of middle classes in small businesses and the professions and in the ranks of an overstaffed government bureaucracy. The production or importation of many luxury consumer goods at the expense of basic necessities was encouraged by the government to satisfy the upwardly mobile yearnings of these expanding middle classes. This was part of what some observers called the "Americanization" of Mexico.

As the economic miracle revealed itself in the 1970s to be an economic debacle for the majority of Mexicans, frustrated middle-class youth turned to political agitation, even guerrilla warfare, and disgruntled workers introduced a new labor militancy to the nation's politics. The urban and rural poor began organizing themselves independently of the PRI.

But this was not the agitation of Zapatistas or Villistas. Nor was it the kind of protest that marked the 1930s, when Mexico was still a largely agrarian nation. Mexico was now an urban, semi-industrialized country, integrated with an international economy. It had three decades of institutionalized revolution under its belt. As might be expected, qualitatively new forms of political mobilization emerged.

The New Politics and Labor Militancy

As in the rest of Latin America, starting in the 1960s and early 1970s, the hopes for revolutionary change or at least democratic reform raised by the Cuban Revolution and the Alliance for Progress stimulated in Mexico a new politics of social agitation and consequent military repression (see Overview). Middle-class youth became fired up by the revolutionary ideals of Che Guevara and Colombia's guerrilla priest Camilo Torres (see chapters 8, 12, and 15). The PRI government talked up agrarian reform and "profit-sharing," but did little. Mass marches occurred. Catholics became revolutionaries. Violence erupted during the student revolt of 1968. But there were earlier historical precedents for the new politics.

In 1943 and again in 1953 veteran Zapatista Rubén Jaramillo, an ordained Methodist minister and member of the Communist party, rose in guerrilla war in the south. With the open Bible in his palm and a rifle on his shoulder, he preached revolution to the peasants. In 1962 army soldiers kidnapped him, his pregnant wife, and three sons and murdered them, but his movement continued. Eventually, the merging of the Bible with Marxism penetrated the nation's slums and campuses.

In 1958–1959 a national railway strike spread to schools, farms, and factories. The government broke the strike with troops and jailed its leaders. Mexico had its first modern generation of "political prisoners." Railway union leader Demetrio Vallejo was not released until 1971, when he helped found the Left-opposition party PMT (Mexican Workers' party).

Demanding democratic rights and the release of political prisoners, the student movement of 1968 began forming alliances with peasants and workers. Demonstrations of half a million flowed down the capital's Paseo de la Reforma. The government wanted tranquility for the Olympic Games. It called out the army. By September Mexico City glittered with burning jeeps, overturned buses, and barricades.

On October 2, 1968, as unarmed demonstrators streamed into downtown

Mexico City's housing project area of the Plaza Tlatelolco, troops opened fire. Many people ran to a nearby cathedral for shelter from the bullets, but the doors were locked against them. By the time the smoke lifted an estimated five hundred were dead, twenty-five hundred wounded, and fifteen hundred on their way to jail. Mexico had a "second generation" of political prisoners.

Mexico's boasted political "stability" had come to a bloody and tragic end; a new era of crisis had begun. In the early 1970s frustrated student militants took up guerrilla warfare. Most of it was quickly snuffed out by the military.

Other students and teachers, including former guerrillas, marshaled wider popular alliances. The government and right wing unleashed armed goons called "hawks" (*halcones*), who shot down peaceful demonstrators. Armed thugs known as *porros* roamed the hallways of high schools and colleges, beating up political dissidents. Hundreds of people were kidnapped and disappeared.

The most serious challenge to government authority came from the ranks of organized labor, where a movement for union democracy gained a powerful base in the automotive and aviation sectors before it was repressed. A more numerous though less radical wing of the new labor militancy, the "democratic tendency," gained leverage in other industrial sectors. It preferred to "work within the system." Sympathizers in the PRI eventually emerged, calling themselves by the same name—*tendencia democrática* (later, *corriente democrática*).

The new labor militancy generated waves of strikes in the mid-1970s. President Luis Echeverría (1970–1976) announced a "democratic opening." Speaking a populist language, he attempted to woo dissidents back into the official "revolutionary family." With other Third World presidents, he lambasted the TNCs and called for a "New International Economic Order."

Big businessmen of the "Monterrey Group" became alarmed, as did some of the U.S.-based TNCs. The FBI and CIA were ordered to destabilize the Echeverría government. Operating through the office of the legal attaché in the American Embassy, the FBI infiltrated the ministries of the interior, foreign affairs, national defense, public education, and the attorney general's office. FBI agents sponsored acts of terrorism in order to blame them on the left and to divide the opposition. FBI Director J. Edgar Hoover wrote the legal attaché of his "pleasure at the wave of night machine gunnings" and congratulated him for the "detonation of strategic and effective bombs."

Without sufficient resources to buy off the dissidents, Echeverría caved in and crushed labor and student strikes in 1976 by sending in the army. Jail doors clanged shut on his democratic opening and he bowed to the old economic order of the IMF—wage freezes and more profitable conditions for private investment.

But social protest would not go away. In desperation, the PRI played its oil card. President José López Portillo (1976–1982) announced what the PRI's top bureaucrats had known for three years: Mexico sat on a sea of oil. All was well, the economy would boom.

Good, said Mexico's poorly paid schoolteachers. Pay us a living wage. With its strikes of the 1980s, the hemisphere's largest teachers' union, with more than a half million members, moved to the front ranks of the new labor militancy. Blocked by corrupted leaders, members made their main demand internal trade-union democracy. They build alliances with other groups in labor and reached out to slumdwellers and peasants. A few teacher militants were mysteriously killed; many were hauled off to jail. CTM *charro* control of labor was ridiculed in the press. In one cartoon, one laborer asked another, "Trade-union democracy? Here?"—to which the other, clad in prisoner's garb, replied "Well, in Mexico, in Poland . . . " By 1989, the teachers' rank- and-file movement was sufficiently strong to have the union's *charro* leader replaced.

In order to bring protest back into official political channels, López Portillo announced a political reform, increasing the portion of minority seats in the Chamber of Deputies to one hundred, while still reserving three hundred for the PRI. Opposition parties would be part of "the national electoral system." Even the outlawed PCM (Mexican Communist party) was legalized. During election campaigns the state would pay for television time for all registered political parties. Constitutional amendments sanctioned the permanence of PRI control by speaking of "minority parties" as opposed to "the majority party."

The political reform was initially successful. Political unrest momentarily calmed down. But the government's increased borrowing to develop the petroleum industry caused "petrolization" of the economy in the 1980s. The result was runaway inflation, widespread corruption, and eventual state insolvency. The IMF imposed more wage ceilings and public grumbling grew louder.

In August 1982 the government announced its bankruptcy—it could not meet its debt payments. The "debt crisis" moved into high gear. López Portillo's administration started falling apart.

Before leaving office López Portillo rallied an angry nation back to the PRI's side by announcing the "nationalization" of the private banking sector (excluding foreign banks). Huge rallies cheered this blow against big bankers. Then López Portillo's PRI successors began selling state bank shares to the former owners and finally declared the banks' privatization.

The New Politics and Elections

The political reform brought members of left-wing opposition parties into the Chamber of Deputies. The two largest were the PCM and the PMT, symbols of the "old Left' and "new Left," respectively (see Box 1.2). Each in its own way embraced Latin America's new politics of popular grass-roots organizing, theology of liberation, new Marxism, and broad alliances (see Overview).

In an effort to change its image in the face of the anti-Communist atmosphere sponsored by the government and the Right, the PCM, the oldest Communist party of Latin America (founded in 1919), admitted priests into its ranks, replaced the goal of "dictatorship of the proletariat" with "workers' democratic power," and rebaptized its Marxist-Leninist ideology as "scientific socialism." Most of its members and sympathizers were journalists, scholars, and university students. In the 1979 congressional elections the PCM became the nation's third largest electoral force, garnering 5.4 percent of the vote.

The PMT, a loosely organized group of Marxists and Catholic activist supporters of the theology of liberation, claimed to have put down roots among workers, peasants, clergy, unemployed, and students in a dozen states. Emerging out of the student movement of 1968, it wrapped itself in the populist, nationalist *serape* of the 1917 Constitution. The PMT's strength was the Mexican spice of its call to revolutionary change.

The PRT (Revolutionary Workers party, a section of the Trotskyist Fourth International) advocated a worker-peasant alliance to bring down the regime. Its presidential candidate in 1982 and 1988 was a human rights activist, Rosario Ibarra de Piedra, affectionately called "la señora." The mother of one of Mexico's disappeared political dissidents, la señora reflected the growing importance of women in politics.

PRI dissidents formed several small parties over the years. All of them viewed the PRI as having surrendered its revolutionary traditions, although many ended up functioning as bought-off arms of the PRI (See Box 1.2).

In 1981 the PCM dissolved itself, joining with the PMT and four tiny leftist and liberal parties to form the PSUM (Unified Socialist party of Mexico). Riddled with factionalism, the alliance regrouped in 1986–1987 to become the PMS (Mexican socialist party). In the 1988 presidential race, it backed PRI dissident Cuauhtémoc Cárdenas, son of the president who nationalized oil in 1938.

Until the elections of the 1980s Mexicans rarely had any chance to vote for Left-opposition candidates. Even then there was justified fear that to vote for the Left was dangerous, since so many leftists had disappeared or been treated with violence. A case in point was the history of the COCEI (Coalition of Workers, Peasants and Students of the Isthmus). Despite killings and jailings of its members, the COCEI, practicing "broad-front" electoral politics, won such a huge following that in 1981 the PRI had to concede that it had won a majority of the seats on the city council in Juchitán, Oaxaca. Two years later the PRI suspended the city council, called in the army and police, arrested the COCEI leadership, and imposed a PRI-dominated council. After Cárdenas's stunning "victory" in 1988, the COCEI was again winning elections and holding office, but the fear remained.

Box 1.2: Mexico's Political Parties

PAN   National Action party, founded in 1939 as "sole independent opposition party" by Catholic conservatives; Right-populist

PARM   Authentic party of the Mexican Revolution, founded in 1954 in name of ideals of 1917 Revolution; viewed as PRI's right wing but embraced 1988 presidential candidacy of Cuauhtémoc Cárdenas of PRI Left splitoff "democratic current" and ran own candidate for president in 1994.

PCM   Mexican Communist party, founded in 1919, banned in 1929, legalized in 1935, banned again, relegalized in 1978; with PMT it created PMS in 1980s (the backbone of PRD with Cárdenas's ex-PRI followers)

PDM   Mexican Democratic party, founded in 1971 by ultrarightist Catholics and PAN dissidents

PEM*   Mexican Ecologist party, new name of mid-1980s Green party; weak and divided

PMS   Mexican Socialist party (ex-PSUM)—electoral alliance of PCM, PMT, PST, PPS, and other leftist parties initiated in 1981, renamed in 1986, backed Cárdenas candidacy in 1988, backbone of PRD with Cárdenas's ex-PRI followers

PMT   Mexican Workers' party, founded in 1974 by engineer Heberto Castillo and "new leftists" of 1968, including Catholic radicals; Left-populist, created with PCM and PMS in 1980s (the backbone of PRD with Cárdenas's ex-PRI followers)

PPS   Popular Socialist party, founded in 1948; has reputation of being PRI's left wing and ran own candidates in 1994 elections.

PRD   Party of the Democratic Revolution, founded after Cárdenas's 1988 "victory" by his ex-PRI followers and PMS

PRI   Institutional Revolutionary party, founded in 1929, reorganized in 1938, renamed in 1946; multifactioned ruling party; excluded "democratic current" from central committee in 1986 (see PARM and PRD)

PRT*   Revolutionary Workers party, Trotskyist

PSD   Pro-democracy Social Democratic party, founded by state technocrats to contest 1982 elections; unregistered

PST   Socialist Workers party, social-democratic, founded in 1973 by "new leftists" of 1968 and disciples of ex-president Echeverría, ally of PRI; renamed FCRN (Cardenist Front of National Reconstruction) in 1988 to draw off votes from PRD and became PFCRN for 1994 elections.

PT*   Labor party based on grassroots defense committees in north, close to PRI like PST, and ran woman presidential candidate Cecilia Soto González in 1994.

PVEM   Ecological Green Party of Mexico, first entered elections in 1994.

*Lost electoral registration because did not obtain 1.5 percent of vote in 1991 elections

---

Until Cárdenas's strong showing, most "protest votes" went to the candidates of the right-wing PAN (National Action party). It was founded in 1939 by Catholic Conservatives who advocated free enterprise. During the "economic miracle" years the PAN lost its base among big industrialists and bankers when they began to reap the benefits of state-supported capitalism. The PAN shifted to a more populist line in the 1960s, denouncing government repression and corruption, and reaching out to new constituencies from the economically squeezed middle classes and religious-oriented peasants. Traditionally, PAN was the nation's second largest electoral force.

An addition conservative party was the PARM (Authentic party of the Mexican Revolution), led by retired generals and viewed as the PRI's right wing, much in the way the PPS had gained a reputation as the PRI's left wing. PARM gained new life in 1988 when it offered its banner for Cárdenas's left-center coalition to run under.

The central trend of the post-1968 period was voter apathy, as shown by turnouts of less than half the eligible voters on election day. A 1985 newspaper headline trumpeted "Abstention Wins Again!"

The PRI attempted to reverse this trend and to expand its appeal by bringing more women into a newly created (1984) party national council and by loudly announcing new "internal party reforms." But the traditional hierarchical method of running party affairs from the small national executive committee down—a system known as *dedazo* ("fingering")—continued. So did presidentialism. When President Salinas's third "reformer" appointee to head the PRI publicly acknowledged in 1993 "we are neither a virtual single party nor the party of government" he was promptly removed.

None of the PRI's internal machinations mattered much to the general populace. The struggle to survive had intensified in the face of deteriorating living conditions. From the Indian backlands facing starvation to the sprawling shantytowns where squatters organized "proletarian colonies," Mexico's new politics saw the springing up of networks of protesting organizations—the peasants' CNPA (National Plan of Ayala Network), the CONAMUP (National Council of Popular Urban movements), the teachers' CNTE (National Network of Education Workers), and the slum-based Assembly of Neighborhoods, created in 1987 to combat poor housing and high rents.

In 1983–1984 Mexican workers launched two symbolic general strikes and one mass public protest march that brought production and distribution of goods to a partial halt. The government's response was stepped-up repression. Still seeking an accounting of five hundred disappeared people, la señora pointed out that in the early 1970s "they captured and 'disappeared' guerrillas. . . . Now they are repressing whole movements—peasants, students, unionists. They don't want centers of agitation anywhere."

On May Day of 1985 workers set off on their traditional march to the

Zócalo, many of them in contingents independent of the official CTM. When they got there, they found the immense plaza ringed by troops. Not even the CTM "official" march was allowed to enter. It marked a low point in the PRI's ability to control labor through cooptive and corporativist practices. In 1985's midterm congressional elections all eight opposition parties together polled more votes than the PRI in Mexico City. The electoral law, of course, gave the PRI all forty congressional seats.

The September 1985 earthquake destroyed a higher percentage of government-built structures than other buildings. The word spread that public housing complexes, hospitals, schools, and clinics had been built with inferior materials or designs. The money saved had gone into the pockets of officials. Mismanaged relief efforts and delays in providing new housing deepened public distrust of the government. In the effort to rebuild, people began turning to their own collective resources rather than to traditional leaders of either the PRI or the opposition parties. From the bottom up a protest leadership emerged from the ranks of self-organized quake victims, seamstresses, and slumdwellers, and demanded answers to the most pressing question: What was the future direction of the nation, now tottering on the twofold ruins of failed economic policies and quake-gutted downtowns and villages?

In 1986 the largest peaceful street demonstrations since 1968 took place. One was a combined effort of the CUD (Unified Quake Victims' Committee) and the powerful electrical workers' union SME that turned out 70,000 demonstrators during one of the coldest winters ever in Mexico City. The demonstrators called for "Jobs, Housing, Decent Wages!" instead of echoing the Left's decade-old shouts of "Cancel the Debt!" Tired of the debt being blamed for their worsening living conditions, they called for its cancellation *only if the government used it as an excuse for not finding the money to meet the immediate demands.*

The PRI response was an additional "political reform" in 1986. The number of opposition seats in Congress was expanded to 150 out of 500, an attempt to defuse the independent protest movement by channeling it into the electoral arena.

Nevertheless, in early 1987 students at UNAM (National Autonomous University of Mexico) launched demonstrations of 150,000 and more (the university's enrollment stood at 340,000, the hemisphere's largest). They were protesting tuition hikes and demanding a student voice in establishing stricter educational standards. Unlike 1968 the government did not send troops. It incorporated students into policy negotiations, and within a year the main student organizations had gained a significant voice in UNAM's policy-making.

Although there were many signs of demoralization in the populace, labor protest continued. In 1987 some 10,500 workers at the Volkswagen plant in Puebla won a fifty-seven-day strike that reversed company plans for massive layoffs and obtained a 72 percent wage hike. The extent of popular discontent with the government's acceptance of IMF-imposed austerity programs in exchange for stretching out debt-payment schedules was suggested by Congress's unprecedented rejection of the president's budgetary proposals in early 1987. For the first time the PRI-dominated body did not serve as a rubber stamp for executive policies.

Then Cárdenas, a former governor of Michoacán, stepped forward and announced his candidacy. He brought with him the "democratic current" of PRI leaders expelled by the party's "reformed" (expanded) executive committee in 1986. Because of their experience, the "new politics" appeal of the PMS, and above all the popularity of his father's name, Cárdenas drew immense crowds to his rallies that dwarfed those mobilized by PRI monies for their candidate, Salinas.

Once the vote-counting computers "failed" and an official result was finally announced several days later, president-elect Salinas announced that the era of the one-party state "is ending." Less than a quarter of the populace believed Salinas was a fairly elected president. Most thought Cárdenas received far more votes than the official 31 percent granted him and that the PAN's candidate received less than the standard 17 percent awarded the PRI's "loyal opposition." Huge rallies protested the "stolen election." With the PRI losing public credibility, the IMF monitoring a staggering economy, and protestors taking to the streets, talk of a military coup became more common.

Security Forces, Drugs, and Human Rights

After the 1940 election of the first civilian president since the writing of the 1917 Constitution, Mexico's military was widely viewed as having "returned to the barracks." Reduced percentages of the federal budget going to the army had many believing that attempted military coups were no longer possible.

Yet, greased by the oil "boom," actual military spending increased sharply in the late 1970s and the defense budget was doubled in 1981. A well-armed, modernized military establishment was created. Generals began running for office—particularly at the gubernatorial and congressional levels. Officers sat in the president's cabinet. Talk of a military presidential candidate became acceptable. Rumors of an impending military coup were taken seriously.

Mexico's 150,000-strong armed forces retain an exceptional degree of autonomy and are a powerful force in the nation's politics. Mexico is divided into thirty-five military zones that receive their orders from the minister of defense (himself a military officer). No state governor can give orders to the *jefe* of a military zone, who, as many a protesting peasant, worker, or student can testify, exercises well-known clout in putting down "social unrest."

More than 1,000 Mexican army officers have been trained at U.S. schools, including West Point. U.S. military assistance to Mexico shot up 60 percent from 1981 to 1991 to $256 million, ostensibly as part of the "war on drugs." Like the police, army personnel have been widely accused of complicity in narcotics trafficking.

The army defines its role as "maintaining national security." Everyone knows this means breaking up strikes and controlling mass protests. Some of the U.S.-trained officers of the elite counterinsurgency "White Brigade" at Mexico City's Military Camp 1 are believed to be responsible for torturing and killing some of the nation's five hundred disappeared persons. An army deserter told Canadian immigration officials in 1988 that his unit had gunned down between 60 and 140 political dissidents at Camp 1 in the late 1970s and early 1980s. Death squads, suspected of having links to the military or the police, assassinated thirty-six journalists in the 1980s. The murderer of one turned out to be the person covering it up, the director of the National Security Police.

President Salinas appointed a former White Brigade member to be chief of Mexico City's Federal District judiciary police. The new chief bluntly declared his mission: "to persuade the *cardenista* [PRD] majority in this city not to insist on its rights."

Various elite military units (Grenaderos, "antiterrorist" squads, etc.). intelligence-gathering agencies, and local and federal police forces enjoy a large degree of autonomy. As the United States' leading supplier of heroin and marijuana (and second to Colombia of cocaine), Mexico offers fertile terrain for corruption to flourish. For decades, police chiefs and their subordinates have made fortunes from drug trafficking, bribery, and other forms of crime.

The new director of intelligence of the Mexico City police under Salinas was none other than Miguel Nassar Haro, saved by the CIA from U.S. Justice Department prosecution for protecting drug traffickers and a known torturer of political prisoners (see Introduction to Part One). Later, when it was discovered that Nassar Haro had set up a new torture chamber, public outrage forced him to resign.

Not surprisingly, the Mexican government began receiving bad human rights report cards. In June 1990 the widely respected U.S.-based Americas Watch condemned Mexico's "policy of impunity for human rights abuses." A year later Amnesty International reported: "Torture remains endemic in Mexico." Salinas set up a National Commission on Human Rights, but it could not cope with the nearly five thousand complaints that poured in.

A number of high-ranking police officers were accused of involvement in the 1985 assassination of an American official of the DEA (Drug Enforcement Administration). Not all DEA officials focused on drug investigations. During the mid-1970s some 226 DEA advisers assisted seven thousand Mexican soldiers in fighting a "special war" against Indian land occupiers in the Sierra Madre of the northern states of Sinaloa and Durango under the pretext of searching for marijuana fields. Herbicides of a type used in the Vietnam War were sprayed on food plants, causing starvation among the Indians.

The 1993 killing of Cardinal Juan Jesús Posadas Ocampo in Guadalajara was attributed to crossfire between narcotics thugs. A 1993 U.S. State Department report sharply criticized Mexican government corruption in permitting Mexico to become a top money laundering and drug trafficking center. Mexican officials countered that the problem was centered in the United States, where the market for drug consumption was located. Some believed the U.S. "antidrug war" was a hype aimed at preventing profits from the U.S. drug trade, valued at $200 billion a year, from leaving the United States. The U.S. government attacked foreign narcotraffickers but did not touch the big U.S. drug lords or Oliver North's White House basement "contra" operation (see Introduction to Part One).

Also rankling Mexicans was the DEA's 1990 payment of a bounty for the abduction in Mexico of a doctor allegedly involved in the death of its agent in 1985. In 1992 the U.S. Supreme Court ruled that it was legal to seize people outside the country and bring them back for trial, thereby serving both the doctor's case and the conviction of captured Panamanian leader Manuel Noriega (see chapter 7). The Court's decision drew Mexican censure. The doctor was later acquitted and freed.

Among high government officials accused of having been involved in the 1985 murder of the DEA official were the defense minister and interior minister. Another suspected official, Enrique Alvarez del Castillo, was removed as head of Banobras, a government development bank, in 1993. But President Salinas steadfastly denied the charges against government officials. It was expected that NAFTA would increase narcotics trafficking because of drug traffickers' use of *maquiladora* warehouses and the favored treatment given by customs officials to *maquiladora*-related transportation.

The Salinas government appointed a new attorney general in 1993 to step up its less than model antidrug campaign. He was the former head of the National Commission on Human Rights who had long denounced corruption at the top.

Whether to "fight drugs" or deal with political dissidents, top Mexican security officials often coordinate their efforts with U.S. counterparts, further integrating the two nations. A February 1977 story in the *New York Times* reported that ex-president Echeverría had accepted CIA monies when serving as minister of interior (Mexico's top internal security body) under his predecessor, President Gustavo Díaz Ordaz (1964–1970). Promises of Mexican-U.S. cooperation in policing the two thousand-mile-long common border have been frequently implemented, including the 1986 "Operation Alliance" coordinating Mexican and U.S. military, federal, state, and local police agencies. But, as officials in the new administration of President Bill Clinton declared, the decade-long "war on drugs" remained a failure (see Conclusion).

Foreign Relations, Immigration, 1990s Politics, and NAFTA

Mexico's traditional nonintervention doctrine and the PRI's need to answer leftist critics led the government to become a moving power behind the peace-negotiating process in Central America (see Introduction to Part One). Its 1982 recognition of the political arm of the guerrilla army in El Salvador as a "legit · imate political force," like its earlier recognition of the Sandinista guerrillas of Nicaragua, won it support among left-leaning popular organizations protesting domestic policies. So did the government's condemnation of the 1989 U.S. invasion of Panama.

The Reagan and Bush administrations were miffed, but they still wrung concessions from the Mexican government during debt, trade, and oil negotiations in the 1980s, further integrating the two nations' economies. A debt agreement in 1986 tied future Mexican payments to the price of oil. A 1989 arrangement reduced the debt by $12 billion.

In exchange, Salinas, first as the minister of budget and planning for the administration of Harvard-educated President Miguel De la Madrid (1982–1988) and then as president, privatized a thousand state enterprises. In early 1992, some 285 remaining state companies employed only 7 percent of the work force. Pemex remained the largest state firm. It was blamed for the 1992 Guadalajara explosion that killed more than 180 people, leading momentum to calls for its privatization.

In 1992, an amendment to the Constitution uncapped restrictions on farm size and effectively privatized *ejidos*. It allowed the nation's *ejidatarios* to vote for conversion to private property or use of their land as collateral for loans. Affected would be a reported 28,000 *ejidos* occupying almost half the agricultural land, producing 56 percent of the food supply, and supporting 3.5 million families. This put the nail in the coffin of the agrarian component of the Mexican Revolution.

In brief, Salinas embraced the IMF and neo-liberal economic doctrines of the times. Above all, Salinas pushed hard for NAFTA, an old idea of David Rockefeller, former president of Chase Manhattan Bank. The goal was to make Mexico an "export platform" like Taiwan or South Korea. Mexican critics feared it would revert Mexico to an "enclave economy" of the United States. But Salinas insisted it was the only way to extricate the nation from its economic crisis.

A leaked memo from U.S. Ambassador John Negroponte in 1991 encouraged support for Salinas because his government was changing the attitude toward Washington "dramatically" and NAFTA offered a unique opportunity for expanding U.S. influence. (Negroponte had served as ambassador to Honduras during the military buildup of the contras in the 1980s—see Introduction to Part One and chapter 4.)

Investors watched Mexico cautiously. The nation still had a mega-debt problem—over $110 billion in 1993. Annual inflation rates of over 100 percent in the late 1980s dropped to under 10 percent by 1994. But the trade imbalance—worsened by the lowering of most remaining trade barriers in anticipation of NAFTA—ballooned. This left Mexico with a very perilous current account deficit of about $25 billion by the end of 1993. Talk of a peso devaluation, a possible stock market panic, and 1980s-style "flight of capital" became as common as the government's expectations of a NAFTA "miracle."

Starting in the late 1970s, Mexican and U.S. labor unions began to discuss more unified approaches to the issues of immigrant labor and "runaway shops." Conferences on "immigrant rights" and "international labor solidarity" were held. While the unionized portion of the U.S. work force had dropped from about 21 to 16 percent by 1986, Mexican immigrant workers in the United States had, despite overwhelming obstacles, been organizing themselves into independent unions numbering more than 25,000 members. This was a little noted reason behind U.S. employers' helping to whip up anti-immigrant sentiment in order to secure passage of the 1986 Immigration Act. The new law's guest-worker program, reinstituting a system of contract labor outlawed in 1886 and again in 1964, discouraged the feisty labor unionism of the immigrants. During the guest-worker program of 1942–1964, Americans' wages in agriculture had dropped steadily and five times as many illegals as legal *braceros* had entered the United States, assuring a large pool of willing, desperate workers and potential strikebreakers. With more than half the Mexican immigrant labor now employed in services and industrial workshops, U.S. employers obtained the same profit-boosting and union-busting results from the new guest-worker program. The original *bracero* program had been bilateral; the new one was unilateral. The Mexican government now had no say in the recruitment of "contract labor" from its citizenry. But it was in too weak a position to issue a serious complaint.

Mexico's economy needed the "escape valve" of emigration and the dollar its migrant workers sent home. U.S. preparations for the possible internment of thousands of immigrants in the case of a "domestic crisis" upset

Mexican officials, as well as members of the Mexican, Central American, and Arab communities of the United States. The Mexican government had protested violations of its citizens' rights inside the United States many times before, most notably in the cases of border area attacks on immigrant workers by terrorist organizations like the Ku Klux Klan. A U.S. border Patrol official's shooting into Mexican territory caused further border conflict. Televised reports of San Diego County teenagers shooting Mexican immigrants "for sport" added to the tensions in the 1990s.

Politically, the PRI's widening rifts continued. The last three Mexican presidents had come from outside the PRI's inner circle of politicians and had helped create a clique of "technocrats" inside the party. The two Harvard men, De la Madrid and Salinas, typified the new technocratic mind-set, as did Salinas's U.S.-educated successor, Luis Donaldo Colosio, former secretary of social development. When Colosio was assassinated while campaigning for the presidency in March of 1994, his successor was Yale-educated Ernesto Zedillo Ponce de León, Salinas's former budget and planning minister.

President Salinas introduced electoral reforms that rearranged voting districts favorably for the PRI and guaranteed the president an automatic majority of support in Congress. New grass-roots alliances for democracy took shape and eventually forced additional electoral reforms, allowing transparent voter boxes and domestic and foreign observer teams in parts of Mexico for the 1994 elections.

The PRI's old guard of so-called "dinosaurs" looked warily at Salinas who had never before run for political office. The old guard proved influential in the expulsion of more than one PRI "democratic current" and the removal of Salinas's "reformist" appointees to head the party. The "dinosaurs" were also widely suspected of having engineered the assassination of presidential candidate Colosio, a former head of the PRI. Official investigations of the assassination bogged down in frequent alleged cover-ups and the resignations of those appointed to investigate.

In the 1991 congressional elections, the PRI won 62 percent of the vote. A similar percentage of the electorate abstained from voting. Opposition parties charged widespread fraud and complained about the television coverage by the private monopoly Televisa, owned by a millionaire PRI member.

Confronted with mass protests against electoral fraud like the 1991 "March for Dignity" from San Luis Potosí to Mexico City and the following year's 680-mile march from Tobasco, President Salinas pursued his image of being a reformer committed to democracy. He nullified several disputed local election results by appointing interim officials or granting the opposition its victories. As a result, by 1993 the conservative PAN held three state governorships.

To further assuage right-wing opposition, Salinas defanged the Constitution of its anticlericalism. In 1992 new laws gave clergy the right to vote and churches the right to own property and run their own schools without state interference. Mexico restored full diplomatic relations with the Vatican.

Salinas was less generous with his left-center opposition. When peasants, workers, and students occupied municipal offices in the states of Michoacán and Guerrero in 1989 to protest the government's denial of PRD electoral victories there, the president sent in the army. Several people were killed or wounded. A near-repeat occurred in Michoacán in 1992, resulting in six deaths.

In an attempt to "depoliticize" the "new politics" mass movements of poor people and coopt their leadership, Salinas introduced a policy of _"concertación"_ (coming together). In the first half of the Salinas _sexenio_ (six-year administration), at least forty-four PRD activists and dozens more peasant and worker leaders fell before a hail of _"concertación"_ bullets.

To offset some of the harm done by the "stick" of repression, the Salinas government offered the "carrot" of some $3.4 billion of privatization proceeds to a new "Solidarity" program, mainly public-works projects in states where the PRI was weak. The program was meant to project Salinas's philosophy of "social liberalism," which in 1993 became part of the PRI's official ideology along with "nationalism" and "revolution."

Some of the urban poor movements were coopted in this way. But most were not. CONAMUP claimed democratic grass-roots organizations in a majority of states. Women activists organized community kitchens, laundries, and child-care centers, and campaigned against rape and battering.

Salinas had some success in coopting the new labor militancy. In 1989, he replaced the _charro_ leaders of the teachers and oil workers unions. (The Pemex _charro_ had brought corruption charges against a close friend of his.) The new Pemex union leader went along with the ongoing reduction of the oil firm's labor force—by another 50 percent to 124,000 workers. Salinas undermined the huge teachers' union by making education a responsibility of the thirty-one states, forcing the union to negotiate separate state-level contracts instead of a national one. As importantly, Salinas won over to his neo-liberal economic program the formerly militant telephone workers and electricians unions. They formed the backbone of a new 200,000-strong Federation of Goods and Services Union.

Rank-and-file movements against the corrupt _charrismo_ of ninety-three-year-old CTM boss Fidel Velázquez nontheless continued. More than one hundred unions, many sympathetic to the PRD, formed a new labor federation, the United Union Front in Defense of Workers and the Constitution.

In 1992 the Citizens Movement for Democracy brought together dozens of civic groups demanding an end to excessive presidential control, one-party rule, poverty, state manipulation of the media, and foreign dependence. It too included many PRD sympathizers.

Mexico's politics related to the NAFTA debates (see Conclusion). NAFTA was sponsored by the most powerful business organizations of each country, including Mexico's CCE (Management Coordinating Council), whose thirty-seven members reportedly held one quarter of the nation's GDP (gross domestic product). The secretly negotiated 2,000-page NAFTA, approved by the U.S. Congress in November 1993, was to go into effect in 1994 and phase out trade barriers over the next fifteen years. It augured a $6 trillion market for 363 million consumers, or one-fifth of world trade. NAFTA advocates called it a "win-win-win" situation for all three countries. Mexico was reaching out to other Latin American countries to form subsets of NAFTA (see Introductions to Part One and Part Three), and the Bush and Clinton administrations spoke of an eventual hemispheric common market.

Mexican critics saw NAFTA as an attempted political bailout for the PRI. Some said that Mexico's "brain drain" would increase as university graduates in computers and scientific research flocked northward for better paying jobs. Many worried that NAFTA would be dominated by the United States, where the GDP was eleven times bigger than Canada's and twenty times larger than Mexico's. In 1992, 7 percent of all U.S. exports went to Mexico, adding to Mexico's trade imbalance.

Critics charged "free trade" was a cloak word for "trade war" (between the EEC, the United States, and Japan) and a "free labor" pool of cheap Mexican labor for U.S. and Canada-based TNCs. A few asked: could this be another "big business scam"?

Of great concern was the need to develop Mexico in a way which would not keep its wages low and force more and more people to accept poor, unsafe work conditions or migrate northward just to survive. A "new politics" coalition called the Mexican Action Network on Free Trade forged links with its principal anti-NAFTA counterparts to the north: the Action Canada Network and the U.S.-based Mobilization on Development, Trade, Labor and the Environment. The three together proposed a Continental Development Pact modelled after Europe 1992's Social Charter (which spent $70 billion to upgrade wage levels in poor EEC nations like Spain and Portugal). Mexican Action Network's demands included equal pay for equal work, demilitarization of the U.S.-Mexico border, modification of Mexico's unfair electoral laws to permit fair elections, and the inclusion of nongovernmental organizations in all NAFTA negotiations.

Environment was also a concern. Mexico was one of the world's most "biodiverse" nations, but 98 percent of its tropical forests had been destroyed and one-third of its land desertified. A National Toxics Campaign Fund study concluded in 1991 that *maquiladoras* were "turning the [U.S.-Mexico] border into a 2,000- mile-long Love Canal," while an American Medical Association report called the region "a virtual cesspool and breeding ground for infectious disease." Among documented pollution-related diseases on both sides of the border were hepatitis, cholera, and a rare encephalitic brain disease (babies born without brains). A 1991 U.S.-Mexico Border Plan, geared toward doing something about the deteriorating environment, was underfinanced and under-staffed.

As the basis for the free-trade pact with Mexico, U.S. Trade Representative Carla Hills used the permissive Codex standards being pushed upon GATT (General Agreement on Tariffs and Trade). On one key issue—the use of the pesticide DDT, banned in the United States—Codex declared that there was nothing wrong with a little DDT on food. Mexico might argue that any prohibition of DDT-tainted food is a trade obstacle. Mexico's fruits and vegetables for export and agricultural workers were still routinely sprayed with insecticides banned in the United States.

Mexico's first serious environmental protection code was legislated in 1988, but it lacked enforcement. Mexico's SEDUE (the equivalent of the U.S. Environmental Protection Agency) employed only 1,600 people in 1993 with a budget of $65 million— nothing compared to EPA's $6.1 billion budget. And EPA itself was understaffed and underfinanced. President Salinas placed economic growth before environment, claiming that adequate funding for enforcement of environmental regulations could be budgeted only *after* the national debt problem was overcome, the economy was in a sustained growth phase, and the budget deficit and trade imbalance were corrected.

NAFTA's preamble included pro-environment goals like "sustainable development" (see Overview). Chapters 7 and 9 included vague language that implied upward harmonization of environmental standards. But environmental protection would hinge on how dispute resolution cases were handled. Only governments, not environmental or other citizen groups, would be allowed to initiate a dispute.

Both environmental and labor protection, as well as the immigration issue, were excluded from the secretive NAFTA negotiations. Because of the public outcry, the Clinton administration added nonbinding side agreements on environment and labor. But there was no White House suggestion of moving toward an EEC-style social charter.

International solidarity groups like the North American Worker-to-Worker Network, the AFL-CIO backed Coalition for Justice in the Maquiladoras, and the Mexican Action Network on Free Trade increasingly cooperated to apply pro-labor, pro-environment pressures against NAFTA. Some scholars called these grass-roots coalitions "citizen diplomats."

Those seeking a compromise solution *within* NAFTA also linked up across borders. For example, the well-financed, U.S.-based Environmental

Defense Fund built bridges to Mexico's "Group of 100" (prominent Mexican intellectuals who advocated NAFTA "with a human face"—see Conclusion). The "Group of 100" wanted Mexican labor's northward migration on the agenda to prevent low Mexican wages from becoming a permanent feature of the North American economic landscape.'

Acts of international labor solidarity, though still few, related to NAFTA. When one of the pro-democratization CTM workers in a Ford plant in Cuautitlán was killed by CTM hired thugs in 1990s, a trinational solidarity task force (MEXUSCAN) organized a Ford Workers Justice Day for the first anniversary of the murder, January 8, 1991. Speakers called for building international labor unity to assure upward harmonization of wages in all three countries, with or without NAFTA. Similarly, the Midwest's FLOC (Farm Labor Organizing Committee) cooperated with Sinaloa's SNTOAC (Mexican Farm Workers Union) in contract negotiations with Campbell Soup. Their earlier cooperation had prevented Campbell from moving its Michigan operations to Sinaloa.

The AFL-CIO critiqued NAFTA in a 1991 publication entitled "Exploiting Both Sides." But by limiting its cooperation to the CTM, whose ageing leader backed NAFTA and the PRI, and by shunning the leaders of Mexico's new labor militancy, the AFL-CIO was unlikely to see Mexican workers unionizing to harmonize wages upward.

In early 1994, the "Zapatista National Liberation Army," a pro-Indian guerrilla force in Chiapas State near the Guatemalan border, seized major towns to draw attention to the poverty and mistreatment of the region's predominantly Indian population. Government troops drove the guerrillas back into the hills, amid widespread accusations of indiscriminate bombing of civilians. Hundreds were killed. The unrest spread to the rest of the nation, and tens of thousands marched in Mexico City to support Chiapas's Indians. One of the main "Zapatista" complaints was that NAFTA would further impoverish Mexico's masses. The "Zapatistas" won concessions from the government but refused to sign a peace treaty until they were certain that the August 1994 elections were conducted fairly (an unlikely event in Mexico).

The August 1994 presidential race was won by the PRI's Zedillo with barely 50 percent of the votes. The conservative PAN candidate finished second, and the PRD's Cárdenas, charging widespread "fraud," came in third. No one denied there were shortages of ballots and other "irregularities." Turnout was higher than usual. One thing appeared certain: the political crisis was not over and the integrated economies of Mexico and the United States would grow noisier in the years ahead, as suggested by the collapse of the peso in late 1994.

Selected Bibliography

See also Bibliography for Conclusion.

Acuña, Rodolfo. *Occupied America: A History of Chicanos.* 3d ed. New York: Harper & Row, 1987. Definitive.

Barkin, David. *Distorted Development: Mexico in the World Economy.* Boulder, CO: Westview Press, 1990.

Barry, Tom (ed.). *Mexico: A Country Guide.* Albuquerque, NM: Inter-Hemispheric Education Resource Center, 1992.

Cockcroft, James D. *Mexico.* New York: Monthly Review press, 1990. Political analysis and "popular history . . . without doubt the best"—*Choice*

—— *Diego Rivera.* New York: Chelsea House, 1991. Short biography of famed muralist, with color plates.

—— *Outlaws in the Promised Land: Mexican Immigrant Workers and America's Future* New York: Grove Press, 1988.

Cypher, James M. *The Unmaking of the Mexican State: From State- Led Development to Neoliberalism.* Boulder, CO: Westview Press, 1990. Pioneering effort by economist.

Documentation Exchange (Austin). *Mexico NewsPak.* Biweekly newsclips.

Equipo Pueblo. *The Other Side of Mexico.* Bimonthly on grassroots movements (Aptdo. Postal 27–467, México 06760).

Foweraker, Joe, and Ann L. Craig (eds.). *Popular Movements and Political Change in Mexico.* Boulder, CO: Lynne Rienner, 1990.

Garza, Hedda. *Frida Kahlo.* New York: Chelsea House, 1994. Informed short biography of acclaimed artist.

Hart, John M. *Revolutionary Mexico: The Coming and Process of the Mexican Revolution.* Berkeley: University of California Press, 1987. Includes previously unexplored archival materials on U.S. role.

Harvey, Neil. *Mexico: Dilemmas of Transition.* New York: St. Martins Press, 1993.

Inter-Hemispheric Education Resource Center (Albuquerque). *BorderLines.* Quarterly on U.S.-Mexico border issues.

Knight, Alan. *The Mexican Revolution.* 2 vols. Lincoln: University of Nebraska Press, 1990.

La Botz, Dan. *Mask of Democracy: Labor Suppression in Mexico Today.* Boston, MA: South End Press, 1992.

Levy, Daniel C., and Gabriel Szekely. *Mexico Paradoxes of Stability and Change.* Boulder, CO: Westview press, 1987. "Stimulating, fresh, provocative"—*Choice*

Nacla. "Mexico Out of Balance." *Report on the Americas,* 38(1) (July/Aug. 1994).

Shaiken, Harley. *Mexico in the Global Economy: High Technology and Work Organization in Export Industries.* San Diego, CA: Center for U.S.- Mexican Studies, 1990.

Teichman, Judith. *Policymaking in Mexico: From Boom to Crisis.* Winchester: Allen & Unwin, 1988.

Wright, Angus. *The Death of Ramón González: The Modern Agricultural Dilemma.* Austin: University of Texas Press, 1990. Results of Green Revolution and ongoing pesticide use.

Films

Ballad of an Unsung Hero. 1988. Eloquent and dramatic feature color film produced by Jude Eberhard, directed by Isaac Artestein, on injustice done to a Mexican immigrant in 1920s and 1930s.

Memorias de un Mexicano. 45-minutes. Video in English of Salvador Toscano's classic documentary of the Mexican Revolution, all original footage, with instructional guide by University of California-Berkeley Prof. Alex M. Zaragosa.

Mexico: The Frozen Revolution. 1970. 60 minutes. Color film by Raimundo Gleyzer introducing Mexico then and now.

The Ragged Revolution. 55 minutes. Black-and-white film with excellent narrative and archival footage from early 1900s to 1920s.

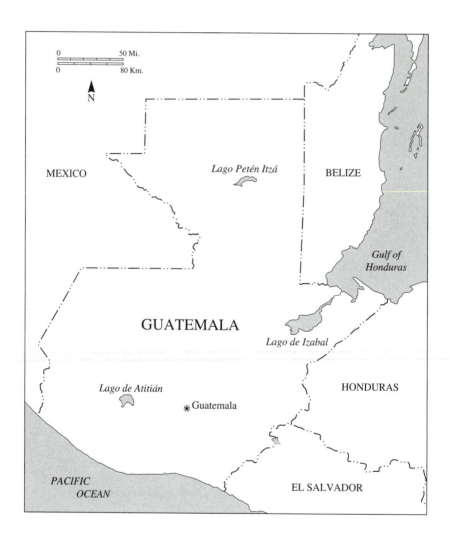

Guatemala   2

You needn't kill everyone to complete the job. . . . We instituted Civil Affairs [in 1982] which provides development for 70 percent of the population, while we kill 30 percent.
—*Former Defense Minister Gen. Héctor Alejandro Gramajo*

Why should we be worried about the death squads? They're bumping off commies, our enemies. I'd give them more power.—*Fred Sherwood, former president of American Chamber of Commerce in Guatemala, 1980*

We all know the history of the use of torture, the massacres of entire families and groups, above all Indians and peasants, including children, pregnant women, and old people . . . of how trade unions' numbers have been decimated, their main leaders murdered, disappeared, or forced to seek refuge in neighboring countries.—*Guatemalan Bishops Pastoral Letter, June 10, 1984*

The army hardliners are not willing to discuss land or social injustice, which are the real roots of the war.—*Ramiro de León Carpio, parliament-appointed human rights adviser and president after failed May 1993 coup*

It is night and we are encamped in a remote area. A ragtag group rests around a fire. They are rebels, trading war stories. They laugh at what they plan to do to the sons of bitches after they take over. They are driven by the prospect of power and wealth, not ideology. They haven't heard the president of the United States describe their mission as "preventing the establishment of a Communist beachhead in the Western Hemisphere." They intend to overthrow the government, period.

The scene is Honduras. But the year is 1954. The rebels are Guatemalan, not Nicaraguan. A tragic error is being played out—an error being repeated today.

As a CIA case officer, I trained Guatemalan exiles in Honduras to invade their country and oust their democratically elected president, Jacobo Arbenz. Our liaison officer with the Honduran military was Nestor Sanchez, now an assistant secretary of defense and a key policymaker in the current war against Nicaragua.

CIA Director Allen Dulles told us exactly the same thing that Reagan tells the American people now: that U.S. support for the rebels will foil the spread of communism.

Later I learned that Dulles had lied to us. Communism was not the threat we were fighting at all: Land reform was.

When I authorized Castillo Armas, then in a Tegucigalpa (Honduras) safe-house, to return to Guatemala and assume the presidency, I had no idea what the consequences of our meddling would be. "Operation Success" was a failure. The new regime burned books. It disenfranchised three-fourths of Guatemala's people. It dismantled social and economic reforms such as land redistribution, social security, and trade-union rights.

The coup I helped engineer in 1954 inaugurated an unprecedented era of intransigent military rule in Central America. Generals and colonels acted with impunity to wipe out dissent and amass wealth for themselves and their cronies. I now consider my involvement in the overthrow of Arbenz a terrible mistake, one that this administration seems bent on reenacting in Nicaragua.

I have grown up. I only wish my government would.

So wrote Philip C. Roettinger, a former CIA officer and retired U.S. Marine Corps colonel, in an "opinion column" published in several newspapers in July 1986. Most Americans still know little about what every Latin American students knows—how the U.S. government overthrew a popular elected government in Guatemala in 1954. The events of that year set the stage for everything that followed, including Guatemala's current crisis,

Without knowing about 1954, the student of Guatemala—indeed, of Latin America—learns in a vacuum. It was a textbook case of U.S. military interventionism recalled by Latin American nationalists ever since. It incorporated mass-media disinformation campaigns, talk of freedom fighters, and anti-Communist diplomatic moves.

Early in 1954 Secretary of State John Foster Dulles went to Caracas to persuade the Organization of American States (OAS) to pass a resolution censuring Communist threats to hemispheric security. Everyone knew the target was Guatemala. The OAS delegates voting for the resolution represented some of history's most notorious dictators. Yet even these representatives could not help applauding the Guatemalan delegate's eloquent speech denouncing the planned U.S. intervention. Guatemala's was the only "no" vote. Mexico and Argentina abstained.

The United States chose Colonel Carlos Castillo Armas, a graduate of the U.S. Command and General Staff School at Fort Leavenworth, Kansas, to head the coup. It fed him arms and set up training camps in Honduras and Nicaragua for a rebel force of two hundred men. These men fired scarcely a shot. U.S. aerial bombings did the job. CIA B-26 bombers, supplemented by U.S. Air Force planes, including six F-47s flown by U.S. "volunteers," bombed Guatemala City and other government strongholds. Several villages were leveled. The Guatemalan army stayed in its barracks, and President Arbenz resigned.

Arbenz's successor, Colonel Castillo Armas, was flown in from neighboring Honduras in U.S. Ambassador John Peurifoy's Embassy plane. Peurifoy was known as an anti-Communist troubleshooter who had helped demolish the pro-democracy, anti-Fascist resistance in Greece after World War II.

There were not many Communists in Guatemala, and most informed people knew that the Arbenz government had pledged to build a strong nationalistic capitalism. The coup enraged many, including a youthful Argentine physician who was in Guatemala helping with the agrarian reform when U.S. bombs rained down. He decided to dedicate his life to fighting for revolutions in Latin America. His name became legend: Ernesto "Che" Guevara (see chapters 8 and 15).

Known in CIA circles as Operation Success, the 1954 overthrow of Arbenz distracted the U.S. public's attention from the post–Korean War recession of 1953–1954 and a terrifying two-year assault by lawmen on Mexican American *barrios* (neighborhoods) known as "Operation Wetback." Scapegoated for economic hard times, 1.5 million Mexican workers were rounded up and placed in jails or deported across the border. House-to-house raids in the *barrios* scooped up numerous U.S. citizens who the next day found themselves across the border, disoriented, and "without a country."

The 1954 U.S. intervention in Guatemala also set the basis for later U.S. interventions against revolutions in Cuba, the Dominican Republic, Chile, Grenada, and Nicaragua (see chapters 5, 8, 10, 17, and Introduction to Part Two). Guatemala itself was used as a training base for Cuban exiles involved in the 1961 "Bay of Pigs" invasion. A top CIA official for the 1954 intervention, Richard Bissell, directed that venture. Veterans of both 1954 and 1961 played active roles in the 1965 invasion of the Dominican Republic, the 1973 overthrow of Allende in Chile, the 1983 takeover of Grenada, and the 1980s' attack on Nicaragua.

Despite the release of damning evidence about the earlier U.S. interventions, made possible by the post-Watergate Freedom of Information Act, there still remain records housed in the National Archives, Washington, D.C., ruled "off limits" to researchers of 1954's events for reasons of national security. Scholars may never get to see the forbidden files—as continues to be the case for the archival records of the sinking of the *Maine* in 1898 that led to the first landing of U.S. troops in Cuba (see chapter 8).

Nonetheless, there is no doubt that a Communist threat to Guatemala was not the real reason for the 1954 Operation Success. The U.S. intervention was in direct response to an attempt by a constitutionally elected government to carry out its campaign promise to deliver uncultivated lands to impoverished peasants. The 1952 land reform program, enshrined in Decree 900, was not a radical one. U.S. agronomists described it as "a remarkably mild and fairly sound piece of legislation." It distributed 400,000 acres of idle land to more than 100,000 peasants. The problem was that most of the unused land belonged to the powerful Boston-based United Fruit Company (UFCO), today's corporate conglomerate, United Brands. The government offered UFCO compensation based on the land values stated in the company's own tax records.

UFCO officers picked up the phones and called their friends in Washington, D.C. UFCO had no problem finding people with enough influence to encourage and coordinate the intervention. UFCO's law staff and shareholders included many top U.S. government officials. The law office of Secretary of State Dulles had drafted UFCO's 1930 and 1936 agreements with the Guatemalan government. The secretary's brother, CIA Director Allen Dulles, had been a member of UFCO's board of directors. The assistant secretary of state for Inter-American Affairs, John Moors Cabot, and Cabot's relatives, were UFCO shareholders. Cabot's brother was UFCO president in 1948. UN Ambassador Henry Cabot Lodge was also a UFCO stockholder. UFCO Public Relations director Spruille Braden was the former U.S. Ambassador to Argentina who had blatantly meddled in Argentina's 1946 elections (see chapter 18).

So it was that Guatemala's only full experience in democracy—the 1944–1954 period of ideological and party pluralism that resulted in two elected governments—was surgically terminated, to be followed by more than three decades of state terrorism. The thirty-eight-year horror: 160,000 dead, 40,000 disappeared, six hundred Indian villages destroyed, and more than a million refugees.

Known as the "land of eternal spring" because of the temperate climate of its highlands, Guatemala became after the 1954 coup the land of eternal military dictatorships and human rights abuses. The *New York Times* reported in September 1982 that the army and its civil defense patrols are "responsible for the torturing, burning, stabbing and shooting of entire families." The 1984 Kissinger Commission Report, even though recommending renewed military aid to Guatemala, acknowledged that the Guatemalan government was resorting to "the use of murder to repress dissent."

The transition from land reform to terror began immediately after the coup. Upon taking power in 1954, Castillo Armas returned lands to UFCO, let plantation owners slash wages 30 percent, closed down opposition newspapers, crushed free- trade unionism, and tortured and murdered critics. He himself was assassinated in 1957 by one of his bodyguards, a half-Indian named Romero Vásquez Sánchez who gained instant homage from Latin American democrats. The stoning and heckling of Vice-President Richard Nixon during his spring 1958 visit to Caracas, Venezuela, reflected Latin Americans' disgust not only with U.S. support of dictators but also specifically with the U.S. intervention in Guatemala that followed the 1954 OAS meeting in Caracas.

In a country where half the children of rural families die of hunger-related diseases before age five, where more than half the labor force is unemployed, and where 2 percent of the population controls 72 percent of the land, agrarian reform is taboo. Today, as yesterday, freedom of speech and a peasant's right to a piece of land or a decent job are intertwined issues.

Now there is much more than a highly profitable coffee and banana "enclave" at stake. As Secretary of State Alexander Haig said in 1981, Guatemala is "strategically the most important Central American republic." The region's most populous, industrialized, and Indian nation, it sits on oil deposits discovered by Texaco, extending southward from the recent Mexican discoveries (see chapter 1).

After the 1954 coup U.S. investors moved into Guatemala en masse. By the late 1980s, over three hundred U.S.-based corporations had $177 million invested in Guatemala. Four-fifths of the largest forty Guatemalan companies were U.S.-controlled. The visitor saw modern buildings with office names like Bank of America, Beatrice Foods, Coca Cola, Colgate Palmolive, Del Monte, Goodyear, Monsanto, Standard Oil, and Texaco.

For years these firms enjoyed extremely high rates of profit. Labor unions were practically nonexistent and wages were low. If trouble occurred, it was snuffed out by the military, the police, or death squads under their command. U.S. bankers acknowledged they made loans to businesses led by death-squad supporters. A U.S. Embassy report in 1981 encouraged new investors by announcing that the Guatemalan government permitted "full repatriation of earnings and payment for all imports without exception."

From Conquest to United Fruit: Indians, Ladinos, and Oligarchy

As already observed in chapter 1, Guatemala's original peoples helped construct one of the world's greatest civilizations, the Maya. After the Spanish Conquest of 1524, Guatemala's "Indians" (as Columbus called them because he thought he had discovered India) were subjugated and, in great part because of smallpox and other diseases previously unknown to them, reduced in number by nine-tenths within a century. The "conqueror" Pedro de Alvarado, whose pastimes included rape, child labor as tribute, and burning Indians alive, was so bloodthirsty that his own government undertook criminal proceedings against him in 1529.

Some scholars believe that the severity of the early Spanish colonists helps explain why Guatemala's Indians retain more tradition of revolt and cultural purity than many of their counterparts in the rest of Latin America. Even

125

those Indians who initially welcomed the Spaniards resisted assimilation. For example, the Cakchiquel of central Guatemala's Lake Atitlán area originally sided with the Spaniards because of their rivalry with the more powerful Quiche of the western highlands. But the destruction of their communities and enslavement of their people caused them to rise up against the Spaniards in a rebellion that was not subdued until 1530. Indian rebellions continued long after that.

Another reason for the small number of mestizos, however, may be Spain's relative neglect of Guatemala in colonial times, since the country lacked large quantities of gold and silver. Of today's inhabitants, 40 percent still speak as their primary language one of the twenty-two dialects associated with the Cakchiquel, the Pokoman, the Ixil, the Mam, the Tzutujil, the Quiche, the Pipil, and the Kekchi. They often practice their own religions and wear with pride one of 280 types of clothing marking them as Indian.

There were Indians who interbred with the Spaniards. Usually they were the relatives of the nobility or had serious economic or other pressures behind their interbreeding. Some mixed-race offspring resulted from rape. Mestizos were called *ladinos*. The ruling elites set up an acutely racist pecking order. Even a down-and-out *ladino* peasant was assigned higher status than his or her Indian equivalent. Today's middle classes, whether white, mestizo, or Indian, are often called *ladino*.

Most *ladinos,* however, are economically little better off than the Indians. They work as *colonos* (recipients of small land parcels as part payment for laboring on coffee, sugar, and cotton *haciendas,* or large estates), sharecroppers, tenant farmers, subsistence farmers, wage workers, and artisans. Those still suffering the abuses of debt peonage (outlawed in 1945 but never entirely abolished) are called Indian.

From the outset of its incorporation into the world economy, Guatemala was a typical Latin America monoculture—an economy based on virtually enslaved laborers producing a single agricultural commodity for export in exchange for imported manufactured and luxury goods. The first main crop was cacao, until the Spaniards shifted its production to Venezuela and Ecuador. Then indigo (*añil,* the base of blue dye) became the big export. By the nineteenth century the red dye cochineal had replaced indigo. Other exports included sugar (worked by black slaves imported from Africa and the Caribbean), cotton, tobacco, and hides. A sudden fall in export prices could propel thousands of bare-subsistence workers into the ranks of the starving unemployed.

In a pattern not untypical of all Latin America those Guatemalans who prospered most from the agroexport monoculture were the merchants of the capital, Guatemala City. They had good connections to the monopolistic merchant houses of Cádiz and Seville in Spain, through which the bulk of trade and profits flowed.

Prior to Guatemala's gaining independence from Spain, most small landowners lost their lands to the *hacendados* and the Roman Catholic Church. Five of the eight largest sugar mills and the leading banking institution were Church-owned. The landless peasants were then forced to work for next to nothing for the very people who had taken their land. Labor was also obtained forcibly through tribute, the seizing of Indian communal village lands, and disguised forms of slavery such as debt peonage.

By the eighteenth century Spain's wealthy monopolies were coming under the domination of the stronger, ascendant merchants, bankers, and industrialists of Genoa, Paris, Amsterdam, and London. A proxy war in the 1780s pitted Spanish-backed Guatemalan Indian forces against British-armed Jamaican "Zambos" (Afro-Indians), who were defeated in 1787. Last minute efforts by the Spanish Crown to save its empire through free-trade and other reforms in the late eighteenth century were not enough to stave off the North European challenge.

Guatemala's white merchant and landed elites feared the chaos augured by Spain's decline and the always present rumble of protest from the Indian masses. In July 1820 the Quiches of Totonicapán seized power from local officials administering the forced labor system and set up a new government that eliminated tribute. Shocked and bewildered, the elites opted for independence "to prevent the consequences to be feared in case the people themselves might proclaim it" (1821 Guatemalan Declaration of Independence). They did so, the Declaration read, in the name of "the preservation of order and tranquility."

The Mexican "empire" set up by Iturbide after independence from Spain soon unraveled, and Guatemala separated from Mexico in 1824. The Federation of Central American States depended on British loans, source of the famous *deuda inglesa,* or "English debt." British investors used it as a powerful bargaining tool to dominate much of the region until the end of World War I. When the Central American Federation dissolved in 1838, Guatemala was left with nearly half the debt (not fully resolved until 1966–1967). After 1838 the nation was ruled by dictators who were reinforced by the economic domination of outside powers—first Britain (less so, Germany), then the United States.

From 1838 to 1865 a powerful regional leader (*caudillo*) from eastern Guatemala named Rafael Carrera tyrannized the nation in the name of conservatism and the Catholic faith. He was a pig farmer described by some historians as an "illiterate Indian" but in actuality 70 percent Spanish by origin.

Carrera rode into power on the back of a massive Indian uprising shaking Guatemala and El Salvador that ended the seven-year reign of a Liberal (federationist), Mariano Gálvez. Much of northeastern Guatemala had been ceded by Gálvez to the British. The British exploited the nation's lavish mahogany resources, controlled Central America's only deep-water port in what is today's Belize, and imported so many textiles that Guatemala's textile industry could not compete.

The Carrera regime, backed by the British, conducted three wars with neighboring El Salvador, backed by American interests. The 1850 Clayton–Bulwer Treaty was one of many unofficial truces worked out between the British and the Americans in Central America. So was the eventual agreement to join forces against the American adventurer William Walker who almost ruled the entire region at one point during the 1850s (see chapter 5).

Guatemala's Liberals passed private property laws against corporate properties of the Church and Indian villages, deepening a long process of despoiling the Indians of their lands, their only source of survival. Aggressive and often desperate *ladinos* grabbed up some of the Indian lands, and from their ranks emerged many of the first *cafetaleros* (coffee farmers), who with other large landholders, sought to share power with the urban-based merchant elites that ran the country. By 1880 coffee accounted for 92 percent of foreign exchange earnings. Whenever the price of coffee on international markets dropped more than a fraction, Guatemala's economy collapsed.

Bananas also became a principal export. (The story of the rapacious behavior of U.S. banana interests, led by the UFCO, is told in chapter 4.) The combined aggressiveness of UFCO and the coffee market *hacendados* and merchants, many of them German, left only 7.3 percent of all Guatemalans owning land by 1926. Gifted with fertile soils, Guatemala was converted into an importer of food staples.

U.S. warships were sent to "protect American citizens and property" in 1885 and again in 1906. The 1923 "Washington Conference," called to settle Central American affairs, relegated Guatemala and the other republics to the status of "secondary partners." American ambassadors became virtual proconsuls.

During most of that time, from 1898 to 1920, one of the most tyrannical of the many Liberal governments, that of Manuel Estrada Cabrera, ran Guatemala. He created a secret police and granted big concessions to UFCO, even allowing it to use private armies to "pacify" labor protests on its properties. Popular protests forced him to resign.

There followed a brief democratic interlude in 1921, and then several undemocratic governments before the fourteen-year-long dictatorship of military strongman Jorge Ubico (1931–1944). When Ubico took over, foreigners, with UFCO in the lead, owned about one-third of all land under cultivation.

The U.S. State Department had been interested in Ubico since 1919. He had worked closely with the Rockefeller Foundation and seemed reliable. In

1930 the United States accounted for two-thirds of Guatemala's trade and the majority of its foreign debt, which stood at a whopping $16 million. Then the Great Depression caused an economic collapse and students and laborers began agitating for social change. A hastily called election, in which the United States refused to recognize candidates not to its liking, brought Ubico to power. His reelection in 1936 was also U.S.-supported and earned UFCO and its railroad subsidiary IRCA (International Railways of Central America) new contract concessions and privileges. The forces of repression were modernized—the Civil Guard and the army. A New York expert helped upgrade the police.

Posing as a friend of the Indians, Ubico decreed an end to peonage. In actual practice, however, he permitted UFCO and other big landowners to continue "business as usual." Even as earlier governments had used contract Indian labor to build telegraph, highway, and port facilities that were then turned over to private foreign interests, so Ubico issued a vagrancy law in 1934 that required all Indians to work 150 days a year and to carry a card ("libreta") showing the number of days they had worked. A 1944 law allowed landowners to shoot trespassers seeking food.

By the end of Ubico's regime, counting each foreign corporation as a person, 98 percent of all cultivated land was owned by 142 people. Thousands of U.S. troops were stationed in Guatemala during World War II to defend the distant Panama Canal. Their presence helped keep the proto-Fascist Ubico in line with the Allies against Germany and to guarantee dominant U.S. economic interests. Three U.S.-based monopolies prevailed: UFCO, IRCA, and EBS (Electric Bond and Share, controlling all electrical power).

In 1944, for the first time since an uprising in 1933 when the Ubico government had executed 100 protesting students and workers, a new opposition coalition launched a popular revolt. Indians were marginal to it, although they rose up in Patzicia in October and had to be subdued by troops.

The anti-Ubico protest movement started with a student strike that spread into a general strike. This forced Ubico's resignation in June 1944. When it became clear that the next government was "Ubiquista," students and workers armed themselves and joined dissident military officers to set up a revolutionary junta. Led by army officers Arbenz and Francisco Arana and civilian Jorge Toriello, the junta government was known as "the October Revolution," since it took power that month. It set up national elections, won easily by Juan José Arévalo, who became president on March 15, 1945.

Arévalo was no radical. He represented the middle-class democratic thrust of the revolution. A self-styled "spiritual Socialist," he opposed communism which he saw as "contrary to human nature." He believed in free elections up to a point—without the Communist party. After the 1954 U.S. coup against the revolution, Arévalo went through an "anti-Yankee" phase in exile.

His book *The Shark and the Sardines* became an international bestseller. In the 1960s he returned home to fail in a presidential bid and then to serve as an ambassador for reactionary administrations.

Arévalo's government spent an unprecedented third of the budget on schools, hospitals, and housing. The 1947 Labor Code provided workers their first legalized rights to unionize, strike, engage in collective bargaining, and have social security. The government retained the power not to recognize certain unions (and applied it to any found to be "Communist-dominated").

More than 90 percent of the work force was rural and remained untouched by these reforms. The only unions with any semblance of strength were those working for UFCO and IRCA. Arévalo's government respected but sought to regulate foreign capital. It engaged in no agrarian reform, other than to parcel out a few German coffee plantations expropriated during World War II (most of the other German estates had been taken over by Americans). Arévalo claimed that "In Guatemala there is no agrarian problem."

Arévalo's unique accomplishment was to preside over the nation's only free democratic election in history (although the Communist left was banned). Illiterate males were allowed to vote. In a three-cornered race Arbenz won 63 percent of the vote. Arbenz was backed by a coalition of workers and students that had helped fend off repeated attempts at a military coup in the late 1940s, including one during which Arbenz's more moderate junta partner Arana was mysteriously assassinated.

Although he legalized the Communist party (PGT—Guatemalan Workers party), Arbenz did not advocate communism. Adopting many of the 1950 World Bank Mission's recommendations, he announced his program to convert the nation into "a modern capitalist country." His agrarian reform law of 1952 vowed "to develop capitalist methods of production." But as the U.S. plans for overthrowing him became obvious, Arbenz reluctantly accepted the support of Communists in organized labor. He was influenced by his wife, María Vilanova, who had been born into a wealthy coffee baron's family and had later become active in left-wing politics.

The 1954 collapse of Arbenz's democratic-capitalist revolution made several things clear. First, the military could not be relied on to defend the country against aggression. Second, the middle-class and *ladino* revolutionaries never fully trusted the urban and rural masses—either with arms or power. Those who were able, with the help of the Arbenz reforms, to join the ranks of the "new bourgeoisie" (cotton growers, bankers, new industrialists) were even more distrustful of the masses and their few "radical" middle-class leaders. Thus the traditional coffee and merchant oligarchy and its foreign allies (the U.S. monopolies) found it easy to topple the Arbenz government and absorb much of its bureaucracy—after wiping out the radical opposition to the 1954 coup and any possible Arbenz or Arévalo "sympathizers." The oligarchy had a ready ally in the new bourgeoisie. Finally, the Indian majority and women were generally left out of the political process.

The main U.S. concern in 1954 was the preservation of traditional economic enclaves. In later years UFCO diversified into food processing and became a conglomerate. IRCA and EBS worked out deals with the government to be nationalized and handsomely paid off. The underlying economic rationale for U.S. interventions in Latin America remained after 1959, but the style became refined after Cuba's revolutionaries, perhaps learning from the Guatemalan experience, armed the Cuban people *before* they nationalized foreign firms.

Defeated in Cuba, U.S. strategy became one of avoiding "another Cuba." The Alliance for Progress was still guided by the need to assure "safe" environments for private investors. In Guatemala, as elsewhere, U.S. emphasis was placed on expanding and diversifying the private investment portfolio and upgrading the national security state—military and intelligence operations. Not too ambitious agrarian reforms were sometimes introduced to throw a bone to hungry and angry peasants. In Guatemala about 20,000 peasants were given lands in unsettled frontier colonies.

The style of U.S. policy had changed in Guatemala, but the U.S. enemy remained a nationalist-capitalist revolution of any kind, with or without the accompanying threat of socialism or communism. Military interventionism was now supplemented by local military dictatorship, counterinsurgency, and death squads.

From Ballots to Beans and Bullets: Liberation or Genocide?

In a mid-1954 television and radio address Secretary of State Dulles informed Americans that Guatemala had just experienced "liberation from the yoke of communism." The newly installed Castillo Armas government, assisted by lists of names provided by the U.S. Embassy and $80 million in U.S. grants (not loans, and not counting military assistance), unleashed a witch hunt against all possible dissenters. A bleak "normalcy" returned to the country. Ubico's secret police chief resumed his office, and the Catholic Church regained its pre-1871 privileges, including the right to teach religion in public schools.

A new Petroleum Code (1955), drawn up in English and translated only later, provided for the cession of subsoil rights to foreign companies. In the early 1970s lavish nickel resources were ceded to INCO (International Nickel Co., 20 percent owned by the U.S. firm Hanna Mining Co.); later, oil concessions were handed out. The main nickel mine stopped production in 1980 after making a fortune for its owners. Two members of a Guatemalan inquiry commission investigating the original contract had been killed after criticizing the giveaway terms. The government's refusal to institute more than a token tax on private property meant that it had to borrow heavily abroad to fund its road building, electrification, administration, and militarization. The foreign borrowing started a runaway debt cycle—$2.5 billion by 1987.

Guaranteeing this anti-Communist "liberation" was a vastly strengthened military, 30,000-strong, which ruled for more than three decades, attacking both its opponents and nonpolitical civilians. In addition, the United States funded, armed, and trained specialized military and police forces and intelligence-gathering agencies that became the backbone of a modernized national security state.

From 1954 to 1972 some 2,000 Guatemalan military officers were trained by the United States in counterinsurgency warfare. AID's Public Safety Program (1957–1974) helped create a police academy and train more than 32,000 Guatemalan police. In 1971 a U.S. Senate report noted that the police "are commonly held to be brutal" and that "the United States is politically identified with police terrorism." But Congress did not discontinue the program until 1974 when its torture-tarnished record became public knowledge.

Guatemala's first post-1954 civilian president, Julio César Méndez Montenegro (1966–1970), could take office only after signing an agreement with the military giving it full authority over internal security. It was during his regime that the most notorious right-wing death squads, the *"Mano Blanca"* (White Hand) and *"Ojo por Ojo"* (An Eye for an Eye), under the command of military and police officers and funded by the now merged oligarchy and new bourgeoisie, grew very powerful. These death squads, supplemented by others a decade later, kidnapped and murdered or disappeared people. By 1987 the number of disappeared from all walks of life, including children, approximated 40,000, the highest figure in the world.

The majority of Guatemalans entered the late twentieth century in worse conditions than during their short-lived democratic dawn of midcentury. Alliance for Progress programs had helped restructure much of the economy, particularly when Guatemala gained a dominant position inside the CACM (Central American Common market). By 1970 Guatemala was the area's only nation with a positive trade balance in the CACM and accounted for a third of the region's foreign investment. But as investors got rich, many Guatemalans got poorer. Agricultural and industrial production expanded for the export market, leading the country to import wheat and corn food staples. Land absorption for the development of beef and other agrarian exports drove small landholders and landless workers into the cities as a cheap labor force for industry.

As urban slums swelled with the arrival of thousands of hungry peasants every month, the country became more than 40 percent urban. Illiteracy continued to affect more than two-thirds of the populace. Guatemala's Archbishop told Guatemala City's poor in 1970: "You, the humble ones, are the most cherished by me . . . where there is poverty, there is happiness."

Peaceful forms of protest were repeatedly outlawed. Villages and rural families were decimated by army patrols. "Democratic" elections were fraudulent. Even foreign embassies became fair game for the forces of repression. In 1980 Spain shut down its embassy after thirty-nine persons were incinerated inside it. most of them were peasants who had occupied the embassy in an attempt to call the world's attention to what was happening to their communities. The Spanish ambassador blamed the police for excessive violence. Spain did not renew diplomatic relations with Guatemala until 1984, when Guatemala formally apologized.

Only a minority of political activists continued the many years of armed resistance launched in the late 1950s and early 1960s. The main roots of the guerrilla movement were in the November 1960 revolt of army officers against President Ydígoras Fuentes that brought students out into the streets, clamoring for democracy. Via UFCO-owned Tropical Radio, the Ydígoras government wired Washington seeking "naval and air support." U.S. warships arrived along the Guatemalan coast. The uprising was crushed by Cuban exiles being trained by the CIA at the not so secret Retalhuleu base in Guatemala in preparation for the 1961 Bay of Pigs invasion. Cuban mercenary pilots and CIA pilots from Retalhuleu bombed the rebels' strongholds and retook the Zacapa garrison. Three years later the United States instigated an army coup against the man they had saved, Ydígoras Fuentes, to avert an anticipated electoral victory by ex-president Arévalo.

Many of the frustrated junior officers leading the November 1960 revolt escaped to take up guerrilla warfare. Some joined small units launched in the late 1950s in response to the post-1954 wave of repression. Most of them went down in a hail of government bullets and bombs, but the survivors fought on.

In the mid-1960s the United States introduced in Guatemala's northern mountains what later became known as the technology of the Vietnam War. With the southern zone of Mexico, northern Guatemala became a free-fire military theater of operations for the armed forces of Guatemala and Mexico and the U.S. Rangers (Green Berets, up to one thousand). An estimated twenty-eight U.S. soldiers died in combat. This was the start of a prolonged "dirty war," Vietnam-style. In 1968 *Time* magazine quoted the U.S. military attaché's approval of the use of terror against noncombatants.

One of the guerrillas' first leaders was an army officer named Marco Antonio Yon Sosa, nicknamed "el chino" because some of his forebears were Chinese. Yon Sosa had been trained by U.S. soldiers, but he turned against the United States when he realized they were not going to carry through on the Alliance for Progress promises of agrarian reform. He was killed by Mexican soldiers.

Some of the guerrillas who outlived Yon Sosa were influenced by liberation theology's call for a "preferential option for the poor" (see Overview) and established in 1972 the Guerrilla Army of the Poor (EGP). They gradually built up a base among the highland Indians. For the first time in modern Latin American history guerrilla units commanded by Indian villagers became the spearhead of a national revolutionary movement. By 1980 Guatemala's various guerrilla armies had more than 6,000 members.

Long before that, however, Guatemala's national security state had started to earn its reputation as one of the world's worst violators of human rights. Among the first victims, particularly in the 1963–1973 period, were political centrists, moderates, and reformers—professors, lawyers, students, and politicians who opposed communism but because of their democratic convictions were viewed as "soft on communism." In just one year (1980) 86 professors and 389 students were killed. But most of the deaths occurred in the countryside and mountains, where the army sought to drain the Indian "sea" in which the guerrilla "fish" swam (the metaphor is from Pentagon counterinsurgency manuals, drawing upon a concept developed by the father of the Chinese Revolution, Mao Tse-tung).

In 1977 Guatemala's government reacted to a critical human rights report circulating inside the Carter administration by refusing further U.S. military aid. The U.S. Congress responded with a de facto arms ban. By then, Israel was becoming the Guatemalan military's main foreign supplier of counterinsurgency aircraft and light automatic weapons (at least 15,000 Galil submachine guns between 1975 and 1982). The Argentine dictatorship's military also stepped in to help out. The war against the Indians of Guatemala continued unabated as the government found new "shopping malls" for guns. Time was running out for Guatemala's Indians. In 1982 Guatemala's Conservative Catholic council of bishops condemned the dirty war as "genocide."

During General Romero Lucas García's reign (1978–1982) there were several massacres. The first wave was undertaken by the PMA (Mobile Military Police), an outfit organized and equipped by the United States. The military evacuated Indians from the northern highland guerrilla strongholds in Quiche and Huehuetenango departments and penned them into "model villages" (a U.S. policy perfected during the Vietnam War).

One of the military's first targets was the Santa Cruz del Quiche area, which since the early 1970s practitioners of the theology of liberation had begun to set up literacy classes and farming cooperatives among the Mayans. By 1980 people were fleeing for their lives and the bishop had to close the diocese because the army had killed so many priests.

New death squads also emerged to assist in Lucas García's "pacification program." These included the Anti-Communist Secret Army, the Anti-Communist front of the Northeast, the Band of Vultures, the Band of Hawks, the King's Band, the Centurions, the Death Squad, the Order of Death, the Southern Anti-Communist Commando, and Zero Organization.

The multimillion dollar programs funded by the U.S. AID, including shipments of food, focused on the northern Indian highlands where the pacification program was in full swing. The U.S. government called the program "Food for Peace," but with unusual candor the Guatemalan army called it "Beans and Bullets." Explained an army officer to villagers in Quiche department: "If you are with us, we'll feed you, if not, we'll kill you."

When Lucas García tried to impose his successor in a fraudulent election in 1982, other officers loyal to the ultrarightist pro-Catholic MLN (National Liberation movement), founded in 1960 by the clique behind the 1954 coup, ousted Lucas García and replaced him with General Efraín Ríos Montt.

Declaring himself "God's Choice," Ríos Montt was a non-Catholic, "born-again" Christian. He was a preacher for the Church of the Complete Word (a branch of California's Gospel Outreach). His government sponsored huge Christian revival meetings.

The Catholic-Protestant issue soon divided the MLN. Two of its many factions, the PDCN (National Democratic Co-operation party) and the PSC (Social Christian party), remained loyal to Ríos Montt's Protestant fundamentalism. The MLN itself, and a sister organization named the CAN (Authentic Nationalist Confederation), turned against Ríos Montt. Most of these powerful ultrarightist political parties, including the FUN (National Unity front, also close to the MLN and seen as representing big business), united behind common candidates for the elections of late 1985 and were dealt a stunning defeat.

The Reagan administration hailed Ríos Montt's "improvement" on the human rights scene. For his part, Ríos Montt explained on national television that he had "declared a state of siege so we could kill legally." Villagers who supported the government would be safe; those who did not would die.

On July 16, 1982, more than three hundred Indian residents of Finca San Francisco in Nenton, Huehuetenango, were driven out of their local church by marauding soldiers, gunned down, and then decapitated. Survivors were burned to a crisp in their homes. Two days later, villagers in Baja Verapaz witnessed an army unit rape young women and set fire to the homes of 250 peaceful residents. The 1981–1983 period alone claimed 440 Indian villages and nearly 100,000 lives. Human rights abuses included burning people alive, rape, electric shock, smashing children against rocks, and cutting off limbs. In August 1983, Ríos Montt was overthrown by another clique of military officers, who escalated the violence against the rural population and set up elections for the fall of 1985.

In response to the government's devastating attacks on villages, more guerrilla units sprang up. In 1981–1982 the four main guerrilla groups—EGP, ORPA, FAR, PGT—merged into the URNG (Guatemalan National Revolutionary Union; see Box 2.1).

Box 2.1: Guatemala's Political Parties and Guerrilla Organizations

ASC	Civil Sector Assembly, group of grassroots organizations gaining role in peace negotiations in 1994
CGUP	Guatemalan Committee of Patriotic Unity, coalition of exiled politicians, PSD, and FP-31, created in 1981–1982; sympathetic to URNG
EGP	Guerrilla Army of the Poor, founded in 1972, close to Indians, influenced by theology of liberation
FAR	Rebel Armed Forces, guerrilla organization rooted in 1960 junior officers' revolt and later led by PGT dissidents
FP-31	Popular front of January 31, named after date of attack on Spanish Embassy; coalition of labor, peasant, and student groups dominated by Christian radicals
MAS	Movement for Action and Solidarity, ultrarightist pro-Evangelical, won presidency in 1991
MLN	National Liberation movement, ultrarightist pro-Catholic, founded in 1960, often in power since; for 1990 elections ran as MLN/Frente de Avance Nacional
ORPA	Revolutionary Organization of the People at Arms, an FAR split-off of 1979
PAN	Plan for National Advance, a rightist electoral coalition for 1990 elections
PDCG	Guatemalan Christian Democratic party, founded in 1968, member of Christian Democratic International
PGT	Guatemalan Workers party, outlawed Communist party founded in 1949; all central committee members assassinated in early 1970s; has guerrilla army
PID/FRG/FUN	Ultrarightist electoral coalition for 1990 elections that superceded MLN in strength
PNR	Nationalist Renewal party, center-right, founded in 1979, close to PDCG
PR	Revolutionary party, center-right, founded in 1957, in power 1966–1970, close to PNR
PRTC	Central American Revolutionary Workers' party, Trotskyist, linked with similarly named parties in El Salvador and Honduras
PSD	Democratic Socialist party, member of Europe-dominated Socialist International, ran as Alianza Popular 5/PSD in 1990 elections
UCN	National Union of the Center, strong center-right party founded in 1983
URNG	(Guatemalan National Revolutionary Union), 1981–1982 guerrilla merger of EGP, FAR, ORPA, and PGT

Simultaneously, exiled politicians, the moderate PSD (Democratic Socialist party) and the FP-31 (Popular front of January 31, a coalition of labor, peasant, and student groups dominated by Christian radicals) formed the CGUP (Guatemalan Committee of Patriotic Unity). The CGUP had no direct links with the guerrillas but endorsed their program of equal rights for Indians, an end of repression, a pluralistic democracy, agrarian reform, and nonalignment in foreign affairs.

In response to the growth of the opposition, starting in 1982, the army organized compulsory "volunteer service" units called "Self-Defense Civil Patrols." By Decree-law No. 44-82 every villager had to participate. Those who refused were threatened with reprisals. Numbering 900,000 people, these patrols were made up mainly of Indians appointed by the military. Human rights groups called them instruments of oppression, but in 1986 the U.S. State Department claimed villages were better protected and "the pro's out-weigh the con's." The 1986 Constitution made the patrols "voluntary," and about 300,000 men quit them despite army threats of reprisal.

From the outset U.S. human rights legislation and congressional bans on military aid to Guatemala were circumvented with impunity. Using a license issued during the final year of the Carter administration, twenty-three helicopters worth $25 million fitted with .30-caliber machine guns were sent to Guatemala. They were used in village massacres along with CIA shipments of rifles and other equipment. At least two U.S. military officers trained Guatemalan officers at the time. Three U.S. clergymen were murdered in Guatemala during 1980–1981.

In April 1982 the U.S. NSC Planning Group in a closed meeting decided to continue circumventing Congress's ban on military aid in order "to assist Guatemala in dealing with its insurgency." Acting under the authority of a March 1981 presidential finding on Central America, the NSC Planning Group called for an increase in military aid from $19.5 to $22 million, using the CIA's reserve for contingencies. As a summary report leaked to the press noted, foreign military cash sales were "authorized immediately" and "up to $10 million in F.M.S. credits [were] reprogrammed to Guatemala."

In early 1983 Assistant Secretary of State for Human Rights Elliott Abrams acknowledged that the 1978–1982 counterinsurgency had been a "war against the populace." During that four-year period, however, the U.S. government had indignantly denied such charges. A month before Abrams's statement President Reagan, fresh from a meeting with Ríos Montt, said the Guatemalan government had been given "a bum rap" on human rights and had earned the right to military aid.

The increased influx of U.S. military equipment helped roll back the guerrilla movement, which announced a strategic retreat. By 1984 the general heading Guatemala's government announced (falsely) that the guerrilla movement had been "wiped out," conceding that "many innocent people who had nothing to do with it" had been killed. Guatemalan troops and airplanes had used napalm and white phosphorous bombs and massacred groups of unarmed civilians. According to the Guatemalan Church in exile, there occurred at least two hundred fifty government massacres of unarmed civilians alongside open-pit mass graves between 1980 and 1986. By all estimates, some five hundred Indian villages were razed to the ground and a million people were displaced from their homes—one-eighth of the 8.6 million population.

Many Guatemalans fled to southern Mexico, to face the threat of starvation rather than immediate death; others fled to the United States and Canada. Described as "economic migrants," Guatemala's refugees were deported by U.S. officials to almost certain death back home. In Mexico they were moved to remote parts of the interior.

Oliver North, subsequently famous in the 1980s as the White House basement operative in charge of circumventing Congress's ban on military aid to Nicaragua's contras, was also involved in circumventing the 1977 congressional ban on military aid to Guatemala. Those records not shredded in late November 1986 revealed that North had worked closely with Guatemala's generals since the start of the Reagan presidency in 1981 (see the introduction to Part One and Documents).

The Iran-contragate scandal of 1986 led to confirmation of earlier reports linking the American Embassy in Guatemala City to private mercenary groups of American "soldiers of fortune," including the National Defense Council and the Air Commando Association. These organizations claimed they were "helping Guatemala's Indians." They relied on the Michigan Air Guard and the U.S. Air Force to help them transport their "humanitarian" supplies.

Declaring it saw a hint of progress in Guatemala's human rights record and a good sign in promised elections, the U.S. Congress in 1984 acted on a Kissinger Commission recommendation and ended its ban on military aid. By 1986 it was approving $104 million in economic and military aid. Guatemalan refugees in early 1986 announced their villages recently had been bombed by U.S. planes and warships.

When another civilian, Christian Democrat Mario Vinicio Cerezo Arévalo, became president in 1986 with two-thirds of the popular vote, he wore a pistol to his inauguration. Thrice a victim of attempted assassinations by death squads, he openly acknowledged he could not control the military.

Cerezo's cautious political platform, even though offering voters more hope than that of his opponent from the UCN (National Union of the Center), promised *not* to cut the swollen military budget and *not* to prosecute those involved in the killings and murders. Cerezo's party, the PDCG (Christian Democratic party of Guatemala), had participated in many earlier fraudulent elections and for a number of months had supported the savage regime of the "born-again" Christian fanatic, Ríos Montt (1982–1983).

Cerezo's election was made possible in part by broad labor support. After the 1954 coup labor-union membership initially had dropped by 80 percent, as hundreds of unions were outlawed. By the 1970s a new leadership trained by the U.S.-dominated forerunners of the AIFLD (American Institute for Free Labor Development) had taken over the remnants of the union movement. Toward the end of the decade a fresh movement for the right to unionize led by elements less dependent on U.S. support started up—part of the new labor militancy observable throughout Latin America (see Overview and Introduction to Part One).

At a Coca Cola plant in Guatemala City a strike led to arrests and killings of workers. The plant manager had connections with right-wing death squads. Strikers occupied the plant and a worldwide campaign in their defense emerged. Troops seized the plant. In 1980 workers and management signed an agreement for troop withdrawal, union recognition, and relief for the families of assassinated strikers. But it was only a temporary victory. The Coca Cola workers next had to fight against firings and a plant closure.

They won again in 1985, with the backing of the newly formed 35,000-strong UNSITRAGUA (Union of Guatemalan Workers Unions). The new labor militancy, a growing human rights movement, and bold demonstrations by citizens from many walks of life forced the Guatemalan military to allow elections that year. The pattern was typical of the new politics shaking the continent (see Overview). The UNSITRAGUA joined two Christian Democratic labor federations in backing Cerezo's presidential candidacy, assuring that the right wing would not retain presidential power.

After taking office in 1986, President Cerezo undertook a foreign policy of "active neutrality," seeking peaceful resolutions of the larger regional conflicts shaking Central America. Later that year British and Belizian armed forces occupied the Zapotillos Keys, critical for the control of the Gulf of Honduras, believed to be rich in oil, Guatemala still did not recognize Belize's independence. The issue was important also because of increased U.S. military involvement in Central America.

In May 1987, U.S. pilots ferried Guatemalan troops into combat against the URNG guerrillas. The incident marked the first time the United States acknowledged its direct intervention in Guatemala's counterinsurgency war. President Cerezo reportedly requested the assistance.

Advocates of U.S. economic and military aid argued it might help move Guatemala closer to the U.S. position on the Contadora and Arias peace initiatives in the region (see Introduction to Part One). Aid supporters also said that the dirty war had subsided. More assistance would allow the military to "mop up" and Guatemala to "rebuild."

Opponents of U.S. aid, some of whom urged a total cutoff, maintained it would only send a signal to Guatemala's generals that a civilian presidency, or "façade," was all that was necessary for U.S. support. They said the war materials sent would help the military maintain its control over the country without making any real political, social, or economic reforms. People would see in the guerrillas their only hope, and so the dirty war would continue to be "war without end." U.S. troop involvement in 1987 augured a possible new Vietnam or Cambodia-type incursion, some claimed.

Meanwhile, America's newest "underground railroad," a church-based support network numbering some 100,000 U.S. citizens known as the "sanctuary movement," sought to hide and protect newly arriving Guatemalan (and Salvadoran) refugees. Some of its ministers and religious workers were tried, convicted, and jailed for their "illegal" activities. Its ranks, like those of other large movements protesting U.S. militarism and interventionism, were infiltrated by FBI agents, some of whom were ordered to plant guns or other weapons in order to prove the group was terrorist.

Because the roots of the current crisis go back to the U.S.-engineered coup of 1954, hatred among Guatemalans for the U.S. government runs deep. In the spring of 1986 distraught widows and mothers of Guatemala's disappeared occupied the cathedral. They belonged to the GAM (Group of Mutual Support, founded in 1984 by relatives of the disappeared), two of whose leaders had just been murdered by right-wing death squads. President Cerezo labeled the GAM "too radical." Thousands of peasants started marching on the capital demanding land.

In 1987, organized labor's UNSITRAGUA and the AIFLD-backed, 100,000-strong Confederation of Labor Unity (CUSG) formed a coalition with GAM and the Peasant Unity Committee (CUC) to demand improved wages, an accounting for the disappeared, and land distribution. As the "new politics" of broad popular coalitions gained momentum, the Cerezo government faced rejections of its tax package by the business community and two coup attempts by military hardliners and younger officers.

Human rights violations by the military escalated. In 1990, the Washington, D.C.–based Council on Hemispheric Affairs named Guatemala the "worst violator of human rights in the Americas." Typical violations included massacring dozens of unarmed townspeople carrying white flags and assassinating human rights activists. In December 1990, the Office of Human Rights for the Archdiocese of Guatemala reported a total of 50,000 widows and 250,000 orphans as a result of political violence.

The economy continued to decline in the 1990s, as unemployment surpassed half the work force. A strike by 40,000 underpaid teachers and public employees failed, as did one by sugar workers earning less than $2 a day. A burgeoning *maquiladora* (assembly plant) industry, benefitting from earlier

U.S. aid programs, paid a pittance to its nonunion workers—70 percent female. It was dominated by Korean investors. Textile exports rose to over $100 million a year, second only to coffee, but textile workers for J. C. Penney and K Mart earned only $2 for a sixteen-hour day in stifling, unsafe warehouses.

Malnutrition rose, as food production continued to be displaced in favor of growing opium poppies for heroin production. Dangerous pesticides increased short-term production for the exports of fruits, flowers, and vegetables. Half or more of the populace remained illiterate. Army officers, active and retired, consolidated large economic holdings in banking (the army has its own bank), hotels, television, cement, construction, and especially real estate. According to the government, remittances from the United States of more than $400 million by hundreds of thousands of Guatemalans who had fled the military's dance of bullets in the 1980s helped the rest of the people survive.

In January 1991, Stanford-educated Jorge Antonio Serrano Elías, an Evangelical Christian of the far-right Movement for Action and Solidarity (MAS), won a presidential runoff election. Twelve candidates ranging from the center-Right to the extreme Right contested the first round the previous November. The National Union of the Center (UCN), backed by the business association CACIF's secretive Pyramid Club, ran second.

The Christian Democrats polled only 6 percent of the vote. They were opposed by the Bush administration that had censored the Cerezo government for human rights violations, including the murder of an American innkeeper. U.S. officials alleged the PDC candidate was linked to Guatemala's growing narcotics trade. U.S. military aid was again suspended. Serrano's candidacy benefitted from a Supreme Court decision that ruled out a bid to run by another Evangelical, ex-dictator Ríos Montt. Serrano had served as president of the Council of State during Ríos Montt's savage sixteen-month dictatorship. By 1991, some three hundred Christian fundamentalist sects claimed to have won over a third of the population.

The Serrano administration extended diplomatic recognition to Belize (see Introduction to Part One). Serrano's neo-liberal economic austerity policies added to the nation's economic woes. A 1991 government report showed more than 80 percent of the population living in poverty and real wages having dropped 30 percent since 1980. Two percent of the population still owned 72 percent of arable land, and 80 percent of farms were small parcels of under 3.5 hectares.

"Ethnic cleansing" continued, as bombs rained down on the thousands of Indians who, rather than leave the country, had set up remote refugee camps known as CPRs—Communities of Resistant Populations. They demanded noncombatant status.

In 1992, UN-brokered peace negotiations started between the guerrillas' URNG (Guatemalan National Revolutionary Unity) and the government and military. The United Representation of the Guatemala Opposition (RUOG) attributed this U.S.- approved change in government policy to the Bush administration's preference for spending less on bloated military aid programs and more on converting Central America into an economic trade bloc. The Guatemalan military was split between hardliners and softliners. For their part, the guerrillas, now numbering only 3,000 realized that military victory was distant and unlikely to be tolerated by the United States, especially since the collapse of the Soviet Union and the electoral defeat of the Sandinistas in Nicaragua.

In 1992, mass demonstrations of 15,000 people and more, at continued risk of life, demanded an end to impunity for human rights violators. The strongest human rights group, the National Coordinating Committee of Guatemalan Widows (CONAVIGUA), obtained thousands of signatures on an anti-impunity petition presented to the peace negotiators. Human rights activist Rigoberta Menchú, an Indian peasant woman who had lost half of her family to right-wing violence, won the Nobel Peace Prize. The army called it a victory for the guerrillas.

In early May of 1993, shortly after the military rejected longstanding guerrilla demands for downsizing the 43,000-strong army by half, disbanding the Civil Defense Patrols, and purging human rights violators, the peace talks broke down. An increase in electricity rates sparked weeks of student protests and public marches. In Guatemala City, Nobel laureate Menchú convoked the first Summit of Indigenous Peoples.

Then, on May 25, 1993, Serrano dissolved parliament and the Supreme Court and reintroduced military rule. The president's *auto-golpe* (self-inflicted coup, a new phenomenon modeled after Peruvian President Fujimori's turning over of power to the military in Peru a year earlier—see chapter 14) was soon defeated, however, by a combination of mass street demonstrations, international protest, a cutoff in U.S. aid, splits in the military, and behind-the-scenes negotiations with the Clinton administration.

In the discredited Serrano's place, a "constitutionalist" president took office: Ramiro De León Carpio. At the time, De León Carpio was the parliament-appointed human rights adviser. Because of his human rights work, he had suffered various assassination attempts by ultra-rightist forces. His administration failed to deliver on the promise of social and economic reforms. In 1994, it momentarily steered the peace process back on track. The guerrillas' URNG and the government agreed to the creation of a human rights "truth commission" with no legal authority to punish abuses, and a Civil Sector Assembly (ASC) was granted input into the peace negotiations.

As Guatemala entered its fifth decade since the U.S.-crushed democratic revolution with its democratic hopes faint but alive, all eyes remained focused on the well-armed (though divided) military and the ongoing system of gross racial and economic inequality. The often silenced voices demanding agrarian reform and justice for the Indian majority were still making themselves heard in "the land of eternal spring"—a land long drenched in sorrow and blood.

Selected Bibliography

Anderson, Marilyn, and Jonathan Garlock. _Granddaughters of Corn: Portraits of Guatemalan Women._ Willimantic, CT: Curbstone Press, 1988. Compared to Anne Frank's diary, photos with words.

Carmack, Robert M. (ed.). _Harvest of Violence. The Mayan Indians and the Guatemalan Crisis._ Norman: University of Oklahoma Press, 1988.

Frank, Luisa, and Philip Wheaton. _Indian Guatemala._ Washington, DC: EPICA Task Force, 1984. A good history, including post–1954 events, with photographs.

Fried, Jonathan L., et al., eds. _Guatemala in Rebellion._ New York: Grove Press, 1983. Presents both sides on controversial issues.

Frundt, Henry J. _Refreshing Pauses: Coca Cola and Human Rights in Guatemala._ New York: Praeger, 1987.

Gleijeses, Piero. _Shattered Hope: The Guatemalan Revolution and the United States, 1944–1954._ Princeton, NJ: Princeton University Press, 1991.

Jonas, Susanne. _The Battle for Guatemala: Rebels, Death Squads, and U.S. Power._ Boulder, CO: Westview Press, 1991.

McClintock, Michael. _The American Connection_, vol. 2, _State Terror and Popular Resistance in Guatemala._ London: Zed Books, 1986. Detailed evidence on U.S. interventionism.

Manz, Beatriz. _Refugees of a Hidden War: The Aftermath of Counterinsurgency in Guatemala._ Albany: SUNY Press, 1987. Documents refugee situation.

Melville, Thomas, and Marjorie Melville. _Guatemala: The Politics of Land Ownership._ New York: Free Press, 1971. By two Maryknoll missionaries expelled by the government for their "liberation theology" practices.

Menchú, Rigoberta. _I . . . Rigoberta Menchú: An Indian Woman in Guatemala._ London: Verso, 1984. Gripping testimonial by Nobel Prize laureate.

Montejo, Víctor. _Testimony: Death of a Guatemalan Village._ Willimantic, CT: Curbstone Press, 1987.

Painter, James. _Guatemala: False Hope, False Freedom: The Rich, the Poor and the Christian Democrats._ London: Latin America Bureau, 1989.

Peterson, Kurt. _The Maquiladora Revolution in Guatemala._ New Haven, CT: Yale Law School Center for International Human Rights, 1992.

Report on Guatemala. Publication of the U.S.-based Network in Solidarity with the People of Guatemala, (P.O. Box 28594, Oakland, CA 94604).

Simon, Jean-Marie. _Guatemala: Eternal Spring, Eternal Tyranny._ New York: Norton, 1987. One hundred thirty color photos speak volumes.

Trudeau, Robert H. _Guatemalan Politics: The Popular Struggle for Democracy._ Boulder, CO: Lynn Rienner, 1993.

Films

The Dark Light of Dawn. 1987. 28 minutes. Color video on 1980s; Best Video, Global Village Documentary Festival.

Guatemala: A Journey to the End of Memories. 1986. 55 minutes. Documentary on contemporary refugee camps, "model villages," and a counterinsurgency state.

Under the Gun: Democracy in Guatemala. 1988. 40 minutes. Award-winning, highly informative color video.

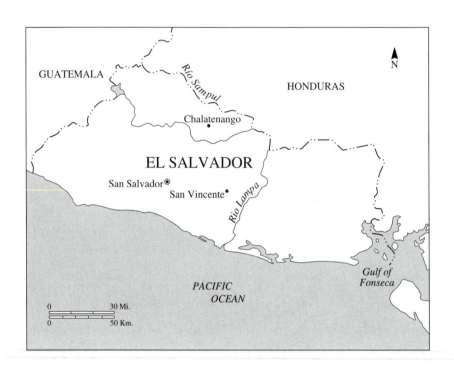

GUATEMALA

HONDURAS

Río Sampul

Chalatenango

EL SALVADOR

San Salvador⊛

San Vincente•

Río Lampa

PACIFIC
OCEAN

Gulf of
Fonseca

N

| 0 | 30 Mi. |
| 0 | 50 Km. |

El Salvador ___ 3

Be a Patriot. Kill a Priest!—*Slogan of White Warriors Union death squad*

30,000 Salvadorans have been murdered, not killed in battle, murdered.—*American Ambassador Deane Hinton, 1982*

The killings by the army have traumatized the Salvadoran people. . . . [I saw] the bodies of people sawed in half, bodies placed alive in battery acid or bodies with every bone broken. . . . That is why the army must eventually lose.—*Leonel Gómez, former Salvadoran land reform official, 1981*

The heterogeneous left must make up 80 percent of the Salvadoran population—*Murat W. Williams, former American Ambassador to El Salvador, 1980*

The cause of our plight is the oligarchy. . . . Another cause is industry, foreign and domestic, which keeps salaries at the hunger level to compete on the international market, thus explaining their blind opposition to any type of reform which tries to improve the living standards of the people.—*Archbishop Oscar Arnulfo Romero, 1980*

In the early morning chill, high above the village square, the volcano spewed out orange flames. Torrents of hot lava rumbled down the mountainside, clouding the sky with purple dust. A rivulet of red ran out from behind the back wall of the Church of Asunción and down into the ravine below; wisps of steam rose from it.

In the plaza, from the wooden table in front of the military command post, a line of people dressed in white and indigo colors stretched as far as the eye could see. Each peasant stepped up to the table to receive "clearance" papers, thereby proving noninvolvement in the previous day's uprising against the landlords. If the peasant looked like an Indian or carried a machete, as was typically the case, then his thumbs were tied to those of his neighbor. In groups of fifty, they were led to the massive stone wall behind the church. Every few minutes a volley of gunfire marked their final "clearance." The river of red was soon a bubbling cauldron of human blood.

Now the lines of thumb-tied victims backed and filled the plaza. The commanding officer, one of the region's *ladinos*, instructed the next group at the table to dig a giant pit in the plaza. Then the peasants were lined up in front of the pit, three and four deep. Trucks rolled in from behind the command post. Women and children ran to join their menfolk, screaming. Machine-guns mounted on top of the trucks opened fire. The pattering thuds of bodies falling the pit counterpointed the screams that bounced off the canyon walls of the surrounding mountains.

A week or so later a Salvadoran newspaper headlined: "The Indian has been, is, and will be the enemy of the Ladino." Inside, an article by a landholder stated: "There was not an Indian who was not afflicted with devastating communism. . . . We committed a grave error in making them citizens."

. . .

Guatemala, 1980s? No, El Salvador, 1932—the year of the *matanza,* or "slaughter." For a week soldiers of the Chilean-trained army and National Guard, together with "White Guards" (private armies of the landlords) "shot down anyone they came across," as one survivor put it. U.S. warships stood offshore. The *matanza* claimed up to 30,000 lives—4 percent of the population, mostly murdered peasants.

In the 1980s soldiers of the U.S.-trained army, national police, and other security forces, together with the "White Warriors Union" and similar death squads backed by the big landholders and the military brass, also offered people their clearance papers—the *"cédula"* that obligated one to vote in "democratic" elections. Now, however, the *matanza* was not a week's savage interlude. It was more or less ongoing, deepened under the "civilian" presidency of José Napoleón Duarte by aerial bombardments of guerrilla-controlled territories.

In the 1980s, outside the capital city of San Salvador, a bed of black lava was dotted with sun-bleached white human skulls that stretched all the way to the green hills in the distance. Each week a fresh load of bodies was dumped in this supposedly clandestine cemetery called "El Playón."

By 1988 the modernized *matanza* had claimed more than 70,000 lives. It had converted one-third of the population into homeless refugees. More than half a million had fled to the United States, even though their presence there was "illegal" and their deportation back home often meant death.

In 1932 the popular resistance lacked leadership or a program and was limited to a single area—the coffee-growing zone of the western highlands. Fifty-five years later the resistance had a leadership and a program uniting people from all areas of the country. A guerrilla army occupied nearly half the national territory and was able to launch surprise attacks upon the country's strongest military bases. Army officers said the guerrillas had infiltrated the conscript army.

In 1932 a handful of Communists led by Agustín Farabundo Martí participated in municipal elections. The government refused to certify their victories. Martí and his followers called for a popular uprising, but someone betrayed them and their plot was exposed. Martí tried to call off the revolt, but the village headmen of the Indian *cofradías* or Roman Catholic brotherhoods, who had decided to join in the rebellion, answered to their own gods. Were not the erupting volcanoes a sign that the end had come for the cruel landlords? In Sonsonate peasants armed with machetes stormed a fort but were driven back. Regrouping under the leadership of a woman called "Red Julia," they kept fighting until army reinforcements mowed them down.

With the electoral rolls carrying the names of the people who had voted Communist, it was an easy matter for the military to round up the "subversives" and execute them. A similar fate awaited many of the tens of thousands of rural workers who had joined the Regional Federation of Salvadoran Workers (FRTS), the key labor organization inspired by Martí and other labor militants at the height of the Great Depression. In 1932 there was no guerrilla army to protect the people from the *matanza*.

But the Salvadoran revolution was not permanently crushed by the 1932 *matanza*. The U.S. military attaché for Central American Affairs, Major A. R. Harris, warned in 1932: "A socialistic or communistic revolution in El Salvador may be delayed for several years, ten or even twenty, but when it comes it will be a bloody one."

In the 1970s hundreds of thousands of Salvadorans participated in fraudulent elections followed by peaceful protest marches. They were dispersed by army machine-gun fire. Many were killed or disappeared. The prisons filled to overflowing.

In the 1980s new so-called Communists, banned by law and bullet, many of them Catholics inspired by the examples of the Cuban and Nicaraguan revolutions, did not place their names on what they feared were death lists posing as electoral rolls. Now almost all the prodemocracy groups, including the ex-majority of the Christian Democratic party (PDC), were united into the FDR (Revolutionary Democratic front), the political arm of the guerrilla army FMLN (Farabundo Martí National Liberation front), led by Marxists and Catholic radicals.

From Mexico to France the FDR had obtained the political recognition of most of the world's governments as a legitimate representative organization of the Salvadoran people. But the military brass and the Duarte government labeled them Communist. The Reagan administration viewed El Salvador as the locale for the "decisive battle for the Western Hemisphere." Claiming that the guerrillas were directed and supplied by the Soviet Union through its surrogates Cuba and Nicaragua, the White House was not able to substantiate its charges in a hastily drafted 1981 "White Paper on El Salvador."

Military-Oligarchic Alliance

In the twentieth century El Salvador experienced the longest uninterrupted rule by the military of all of Latin America—over fifty-five years. Allied with rich landholders and traders known as "the oligarchy," the military became a kind of ruling caste. High military positions, when not reserved for the oligarchs' sons, served as stepping stones into the oligarchy.

The agricultural-export oligarchy was distinguished by its reactionary belief system, its disdain for workers and middle-class professionals, and its unwillingness to share power with anyone other than the military. Over the years, particularly after the influx of Alliance for Progress monies to make El Salvador a "showcase for democracy" in the 1960s, the oligarchy of fifty families (traditionally called "the fourteen families") diversified its economic holdings into industry, banking, and commerce. This added to its wealth and power.

Because of the oligarchs' ostentatious display of their wealth, nowhere in Latin America did there emerge such a stark contrast between the wealth of a few and the misery of many. Some rural people hacked out a substandard diet from maize grown on land rented from the landlords high up on the steep slopes above the lush coffee acreage. Others crowded into the shantytowns (*tugurios*) of the cities. Because of malnutrition and widespread gastrointestinal diseases, 47 percent of El Salvador's "natural" deaths today are of children under five years of age.

Most of the military's officers in recent decades have been graduates of the Salvadoran military academy, where U.S. officers began offering classes during World War II. By 1980 U.S. instructors had trained more than two thousand officers.

Each graduating class of the military academy formed a group known as a "tanda." Tandas made alliances with other tandas to share spoils and power. Cliquish loyalties within the military were cemented by these shared experiences. They were reinforced by bloated military budgets, anti-Communist indoctrination by U.S. military advisers, secrecy oaths, plush retirement and reservist benefits, and growing links to organized crime and the international arms and drug trade.

The military's power was further assured by the leadership role of its retired officers in death squads manned by thousands of former soldiers. For example, Roberto D'Aubuissón, the main candidate of the extreme Right in the limited 1984 elections, was a former military intelligence officer with close ties to the government-sponsored paramilitary organization ORDEN (Spanish for "order"). Documents seized when he was briefly detained for leading an attempted coup in the spring of 1981 indicated that he had ordered the 1980 assassination of the nation's popular archbishop, Oscar Arnulfo Romero. In

148

addition to D'Aubuissón's involvement in Romero's death, U.S.-backed contras invading Nicaragua were implicated by a Salvadoran colonel.

But even wealthy families and well-armed officers and death-squad commanders have their disputes, especially on tactics. The Cuban Revolution frightened El Salvador's elites. In the 1970s a few landholders and colonels thought it best to stem the tide of social protest with token reforms rather than with executions. They were a tiny minority of the oligarchy and were quickly eliminated or isolated. Some even joined the popular forces. They were called class traitors and Communists by the oligarchs and generals and were more despised than the guerrillas themselves.

Marxist-Christian Unity

The inflexible attitude of the ruling elites toward even minimal reforms partially explains a striking feature of modern El Salvador—the emergent alliance between Christian Democrats and diverse Marxists to bring about genuine democracy and social reform. As noted in the Overview, the United States had backed Christian Democracy throughout the hemisphere as an alternative to nationalist or Socialist revolutions like Cuba's.

But in El Salvador only a handful of Christian Democratic leaders remained loyal to the U.S. scenario. Many Christian Democrats were kidnapped or assassinated by government security forces and death squads. Liberation theology swept the field.

The breadth of government-sponsored terrorism galvanized world attention in 1980 when it touched the lives of prominent social figures and U.S. citizens. First, on March 22, Archbishop Romero was gunned down while saying mass. He had beseeched President Carter to end military aid because it contributed to injustice and repression. In his final sermon he instructed soldiers not to kill their fellow peasants and workers.

Then, on November 27, 1980, six civilian leaders of the FDR, the country's largest political coalition, including FDR president Enrique Alvarez Córdoba, a millionaire dairy farmer, and BPR's Juan Chacón, leader of the largest mass organization (see Box 3.3), held a press conference to explain why elections in El Salvador were not a viable alternative. What happened proved their point. They were seized at the press conference and their mutilated bodies were found the next day on a country road. The Maximiliano Hernández Martínez death squad (named after the general responsible for the 1932 *matanza*) claimed responsibility, but the FDR blamed the government.

Finally, in early December 1980, the bodies of three missing American nuns and an American lay worker were found. They had been shot in the back of the head, executioner style, and thrown in a ditch. The people who ordered their deaths—and the subsequent deaths of other Americans, including journalists and labor and agrarian reform advisers—were never brought to justice.

Nonetheless, by 1983, El Salvador was the world's third largest recipient of U.S. aid—over $2 billion a year—and U.S. military involvement was on the increase. In 1987 U.S. aid totalled more than El Salvador's own budget. What was the setting and historical background for the drama sweeping this tiny Central American nation—and why was the outcome so important?

Colonization and Anti-Indian Racism

Tiny, densely populated El Salvador—with 5.6 million people, more per square mile than any other Central American country—is a lush, earthquake-prone land, dominated by 8,000-foot high volcanoes that dot the sloping highlands reaching down from Guatemala. Its lava-rich soils are quickly eroded when the tropical rainforests are cut back. Its people are mainly mestizo (*ladino*) and poor. European-descended whites control the upper class. Indians are virtual outcasts in their own land.

People's struggles for a piece of land etch El Salvador's history in blood. Spaniards conquered the country by much the same means they took over Mexico and Guatemala (see chapters 1 and 2). Pedro de Alvarado invaded in 1524. He and subsequent conquistadores killed or enslaved any Indians who resisted. They branded some, like cattle, to use as slaves to work the silver and gold mines, first in El Salvador and later in Peru and Honduras. By the end of 1578 murder, harsh labor conditions, smallpox and other epidemics of imported diseases, and a terrible plague had reduced El Salvador's population from about half a million when the Spaniards arrived to less than 80,000.

Almost all the Indian groups, most of them descendants of the Aztecs and Mayas, had resisted the conquest. The most numerous, the Pipils, were expert maize growers. Their survivors and mestizo descendants at first produced sugar cane, indigo, and balsam for export to Europe. Much later, after the introduction of coffee plants from Brazil in 1840, they became the low-wage producers of "king coffee." That was shortly after El Salvador and the other republics of the United Provinces of Central America had become separate nations, having gained their initial independence from Spain along with Mexico in 1821.

The Pipils did not peacefully accept subjugation. One of their most famous uprisings was led in 1833 by Anastasio Aquino, who marshalled a self-proclaimed liberating army of four thousand. Shouting "Land to the tiller!" Aquino's forces took over the San Vicente area twenty-five miles south of San Salvador, heartland of the production of indigo (source of a blue dye). Soldiers of the creole elites captured and executed Aquino in June 1833, and placed his head in a cage in the main plaza as a warning to other Indians. His name reap-peared one hundred fifty years later when the guerrillas' FMLN established the Anastasio Aquino Paracentral front in his local homeland of San Vicente.

Unlike Aquino, Guatemalan pig farmer Rafael Carrera extended his rebellion far-and-wide four years later, leading to the dissolution of the Central American federation (see chapter 2) and El Salvador's going it alone. With separate nations came border wars—and competing foreign nations egging on the Indian cannon fodder. El Salvador conducted wars with Guatemala in 1844, 1851, and 1863, as well as one with Honduras in 1845.

The new republic's ruling elites initially conceded Indian rights to communal lands (*ejidos*) because they depended on Indian labor and needed Indian warriors to fight the border wars. Popular resistance movements kept cropping up. In the last third of the nineteenth century the elites, using British assistance and rural mounted police, were able to crush dissent. The effort required a terror campaign of armed force, rape, the stockade, torture, and defamation of all things "Indian" or "peasant." The Catholic Church looked the other way.

In 1900 the government founded a military academy, and in 1912 it created the National Guard. The Guard's mission was to control El Salvador's land-hungry peasantry, as well as student rebels.

Racism against the Indians, common to all of Latin America, became particularly endemic to El Salvador. The Pipil language survived, but by 1987 less than 1 percent of the population dared wear Indian clothing or conduct Indian festivals. The ruling families always sanctioned the killing of Indians. The 1932 *matanza* equation of "Indian equals Communist" was nothing new.

King Coffee and the Faces of Hunger

By 1875 coffee supplanted traditional export crops. European and North American demand produced a "boom" of coffee profits. Setting aside their ideological hairsplitting over liberal and conservative doctrines, the oligarchs had laws passed that did away with Indian rights to communal lands. The elites stripped the Indians and mestizos of their *ejidos* and converted them into debt-peon laborers for the coffee plantations. The value of the coffee crop increased tenfold in thirty-five years.

Among the competing foreign powers, Britain led the way with loans for railroad construction and agricultural machinery. By 1914 Britain was receiving from El Salvador $15 million a year in capital based on loan payments, investments, and gold mining concessions.

In 1906, however, the United States challenged British influence. As a result of Guatemalan exiles using El Salvadoran territory as a base for an attempted overthrow of Guatemalan dictator Manuel Estrada Cabrera (see chapter 2), El Salvador and Guatemala went to war. Acting as a "peacekeeper," the United States overcame a Nicaraguan effort to unify all Central America (see chapter 5) and arranged "peace and friendship" treaties that obligated the region's states not to recognize governments arising from revolutions or coups.

El Salvador's coffee exports skyrocketed from a value of $7 million in 1915 to $23 million in 1928, as lands planted with coffee increased 50 percent. Rural inhabitants had been driven off the best lands and forced to labor at abysmal wages. Now most of them no longer had even a small patch where they could grow food for their families. Worse yet, as coffee displaced corn and *frijoles* (beans), people had to rely on expensive imported foods. By the 1970s the majority of rural people had no land and no regular employment. Recently created capital-intensive industrialization programs in the cities offered few jobs. Out of shantytown shacks stared gaunt faces of hunger ready to welcome any force that promised liberation. Malnutrition had become the nation's major cause of "natural" death.

First U.S. Investments

Starting in 1913, the elites began shifting their alliances with foreign investors to the United States. A 1923 agreement between U.S. banks and El Salvador provided for major loans with a U.S.-controlled customs receivership in case of loan default. The money helped railroad magnate Minor Keith, a founder of the United Fruit Company, complete the rail line connecting El Salvador to Guatemala (1929), thereby speeding the delivery of coffee to the U.S. east coast. The United States went on to gain "most favored nation" status, prohibiting El Salvador from giving other nations better tariff terms. By 1930 U.S. investments of $34 million, mostly in railroads, were triple those of Britain. These were the investments being protected by U.S. warships at the time of the 1932 *matanza*.

From 1917 to 1927 the Meléndez-Quiñónez family network ran the presidency under a state of siege. Yet dissent would not go away. In 1922 the army machine-gunned several thousand women in San Salvador marching on behalf of an opposition presidential candidate. Workers and intellectuals organized labor unions (the FRTS) which were outlawed. In 1930 some FRTS members and a few intellectuals founded the PCES (Communist party of El Salvador). Other than the ideologically diverse FRTS and the tiny PCES, both violently suppressed, the only organization with any say-so in guiding the democratic opposition was the Salvadoran Red Cross. The government needed the Red Cross to clean up after army massacres. Later, because the word "Red" was viewed as subversive, it became the Green Cross.

From 1929 to 1930 the worldwide economic depression slashed coffee prices by half. Unemployment soared. The 1930 census showed society skewed between haves and have-nots—with 1 percent classified as upper class, 4.4 percent as middle class, and the rest as lower class. Over 90 percent of agricultural workers were landless—a huge rural work force that had to take whatever the wealthy landholders offered at harvest time. Hunger stalked the land, appeals for reforms were ignored, and—in 1932—protest shook the earth.

From *La Matanza to* the Alliance for Progress

Among the leaders of the protest movement was a founder of El Salvador's Communist party, a landowner's son named Agustín Farabundo Martí. After entering law school at the National University in 1914, Martí soon became embroiled in the politics of the democratic opposition. His efforts earned him repeated arrests and deportations to neighboring countries. In the early 1920s he worked picking crops and as a mason in Guatemala. In 1928 he joined Sandino, the Nicaraguan rebel fighting the U.S. Marines (see chapter 5), writing: "In Nicaragua the liberating struggle of the Americas has begun and it is to be hoped that the joint action of all the oppressed lands of the continent will sweep away the last vestiges of Yankee imperialism."

To calm things down, elections were called in 1931 and won by a populist candidate, an engineer named Arturo Araujo. Hoping to build a labor party similar to England's, Araujo owed his victory to the organizing efforts of the FRTS and PCES. When he failed to deliver on his campaign promises, those who had supported him took to the streets. The oligarchs called in the military. Araujo was overthrown in December 1931 by the vice-president and minister of war, General Maximiliano Hernández Martínez, the man responsible for the 1932 *matanza*.

A theosophist, General Hernández Martínez said he was protected by "invisible legions" who had telepathic communication with the U.S. president. When asked in 1944 by the archbishop of San Salvador to halt the executions of his opponents "in the name of God," he replied: "In El Salvador, I am God."

Hernández's dictatorship lasted from 1932 to 1944. His administration discouraged industrial diversification and catered to the interests of the large landholders. It was based on a mutual understanding: The military would control key political posts, leaving economic management to the wealthy elites.

In the spring of 1944 student protests and social unrest led to more executions. The response was a general strike on April 19 that paralyzed the economy. A few weeks later General Hernández fled the country and his defense minister took over, inviting into his administration members of a "developmentalist" faction of the army that advocated democracy, foreign investment, and industrialization.

These events opened a little space for labor union organizers and democratic reformers seeking fair elections. But old-line officers, frightened by the specter of Guatemalan democratic elections next door (see chapter 2), dared not risk genuine reforms. They carried out a coup. Then they staged a national election to bring one of their own to the presidency, General Salvador Castañeda. He dissolved political parties, student organizations, and labor unions, killing or exiling their leaders. Business resumed as usual.

Salvadorian politics continued for several decades in this seesaw fashion of protest, repression, more protest, promises of reform, and so on. Colonel Oscar Osorio oversaw the introduction of the 1950 Constitution, one that allowed labor unions for urban workers but barred unions from the countryside. The PCES heralded the new age as "the beginning of the bourgeois-democratic era." In 1956 Osorio's handpicked successor, Colonel José María Lemus, was "'elected" president. Lemus brooked no dissent. Soon the prisons were again filled.

The Cuban Revolution of 1959 frightened the ruling powers even more than the Guatemalan one had done, and by 1960 army troops were stationed everywhere—in the universities, on the streets, and in rural villages, maintaining order. On October 26, 1960, junior officers overthrew Lemus and established a military-civilian junta that promised free elections. People took to the streets demanding elections. Junta member Dr. Fabio Castillo later stated: "The American Embassy informed me that it did not agree with the holding of free elections."

On January 25, 1961, three months after Lemus's overthrow, there was another military coup, led by Colonel Julio Adalberto Rivera. A new junta of colonels and three civilians embraced the U.S.-sponsored Alliance for Progress, while gunning down street demonstrators protesting the coup, leaving ninety-six dead in a hail of bullets. Rivera created the PCN (Party of National Counciliation), which adopted the clasped-hands logo of the Alliance for Progress for its banners. Making room for an occasional voice of reform, the PCN ruled by force until 1979, after which it allied itself with the more rightist Arena (National Republican Alliance), headed by suspected death-squad leader d'Aubuissón.

1960s' Seeds of Revolution: "Development" Without Democracy

President John F. Kennedy praised the Rivera administration: "Governments of the civil-military type of El Salvador," he observed, "'are the most effective in containing communist penetration in Latin America." The Alliance for Progress funneled millions of dollars to its Central American "showcase." For a while these policies postponed revolution while sowing more of its seeds.

Economically, El Salvador's GNP growth rates fluctuated between 9 percent (1964) and 3.5 percent (1970). U.S.-based firms doubled their investments to $45 million by 1967. ESSO, Kimberly Clark, Procter & Gamble,

Westinghouse, and others joined El Salvador's "fifty families" to set up joint business ventures. Stimulated by the 1961 formation of the Central American Common Market (CACM), El Salvador's free- trade zone kept wages low and allowed the manufacturing sector to grow by 24 percent. Through CACM, El Salvador sold its textiles, chemicals, petroleum derivatives, paper, and processed foods to less-developed Honduras and Nicaragua. Jobs in manufacturing increased by a few thousand and an urban-based industrial working class took shape, fighting for—and sometimes getting—wage increases.

Meanwhile, coffee, cotton, and sugar production further mechanized. Together with the development of a cattle-export industry, this drove more peasants off their lands and into the cities, where they served as a surplus labor pool. The population of San Salvador, the capital, rose to a third of a million.

Politically, the Left was repressed. A few anti-Communist political parties and labor unions were allowed to organize. In 1964 the Christian Democrats' Duarte won the election for mayor of San Salvador. Efforts to extend democracy to those other than Christian Democrats and moderate politicians were crushed by the military.

For example, in 1968 the National Guard arrested, disappeared, tortured, and killed two independent labor leaders. This mode of operation was refined by National Guard General José Alberto Medrano's creation of the 80,000-strong organization of paramilitary patrols ORDEN (order). ORDEN was composed of desperately poor peasants commanded by 10,000 superiorly equipped military personnel. Its standard practice was to execute any suspicious person on the spot. U.S. intelligence officers assisted ORDEN's Medrano.

A 1967 report by the U.S. AID concluded that U.S. advisers had "efficiently trained the National Guard and National Police in basic tactics so that authorities have been successful in handling any politically motivated demonstrations in recent years." The police-training program of AID's Office of Public Safety (OPS) was terminated by Congress in 1974 when it learned of U.S. involvement in the training of torturers in Latin America. (A 1985 waiver allowed El Salvador to obtain more police aid.)

For decades, no elected official could act independently of the military. For instance, after an earthquake shook San Salvador in 1965, little aid reached the people because, according to Mayor Duarte, his hands were tied by the generals.

On balance, El Salvador's economic growth and limited democratic opening of the 1960s consisted of development for the haves without democracy for the have-nots. Expectations were lifted, there was a growth in the urban working and middle classes, but the underlying power structure was left untouched. As U.S. Ambassador Murat Williams later recalled, even moderate reforms were not implemented because of Washington's conviction that "'we must stay close to the oligarchy and the army because they have the power." In retrospect, the 1960s in El Salvador showed the futility of limited democratic elections in a country run by a military-oligarchic alliance. Twenty-one years later, after 1986's destructive earthquake, President Duarte's hands were still tied.

Escape Valve: The 1969 War with Honduras

There was an economic downturn in 1968. The moderate Christian Democrats and the more militant Left continued winning recruits. In spite of the grisly activities of the state security forces and ORDEN, people still protested. The oligarchs needed an escape valve if the seeds of popular revolt were not to sprout.

They found it a year later in a full-scale war with neighboring Honduras, during which the armed forces of both countries tested their new American weapons. The "hundred-hour war" of mid-1969, ridiculed by the foreign press as the "futbol war" because of a rivalry between the two nations' soccer teams, was based on the desire of both governments to distract their citizens from economic hard times and political repression.

The war was based on economics, not sports. One-third of a million landless Salvadoran peasants had migrated to sparsely populated Honduras for jobs. Of Honduras's banana workers, 30 percent were Salvadorans. Needing a scapegoat for its own economic problems, Honduras announced it was deporting all Salvadorans. The Salvadoran Air Force responded by bombing the Honduras capital on July 14, 1969. Then El Salvador invaded, taking huge chunks of Honduras territory and threatening a swift victory.

An OAS peace-keeping force rushed to the scene to end the war and oversee a truce, but not before three thousand lives had been lost. The war put an end to the CACM and sealed the Honduran border to landless and jobless Salvadorans. It made villainous generals into popular heroes in both countries and postponed any social uprising for at least two years.

1970s' Stolen Elections, Massacres, and Guerrilla Warfare

In the 1970s the outside world heard talk of "development," "agrarian reform," and "democratization" in El Salvador. But by the end of the decade the regime was more steeped in blood than before. El Salvador's popular forces took the talk of democratization seriously and mobilized on an ever larger scale, first for fair elections and finally for armed struggle.

After the 1968–1971 recession El Salvador's revolutionary process began in earnest. Real wages (what the wage can purchase) dropped. Labor unions no longer could deliver economic gains. The return of hundreds of thousands Salvadorans from Honduras fueled rural unrest.

Eventually, increased government expenditures based on an eightfold increase in the foreign debt revived the economy. Lured by a tax-free, duty-free trade zone outside San Salvador where strikes were outlawed, foreign investments revived. The zone became a haven for U.S. runaway shops that used Salvadoran laborers earning $4 a day to assemble products for reexport to the U.S. market. Companies like Texas Instruments and Maidenform made fat profits.

Land remained the perennial problem. Land concentration and an annual population growth of 3.1 percent were squeezing land resources to the limit. As early as 1971, six families alone possessed as much land as 80 percent of the rural population combined. In the mid-1970s agriculture still provided four-fifths of export revenues, and 60 percent of the population remained classified as agricultural. Three-fourths of rural families depended on wages for at least one-third of their income.

In response to increased peasant organizing led by priests and others, the government of Colonel Arturo Molina undertook a timid agrarian reform in 1975, setting aside 150,000 acres of public land and creating the ISTA (Salvadoran Institute of Agrarian Transformation). It was the first time since the 1932 _matanza_ that talk about changing the land structure did not trigger a massacre. Instead, it divided the ruling groups, pitting a reformist faction of the military and a minority of industrialists against the traditional oligarchy as represented by the ANEP (National Association of Private Enterprise) and FARO (Eastern Region Farmers' front). U.S. AID agreed to provide compensation for any affected oligarchs.

The carrot of reform and the stick of repression made it difficult for revolutionaries to organize the rural population. The number of small farmers (mostly in sugar) expanded with the doling out of some government land, and their economic interests did not mesh with those of a large number of permanent plantation workers. It was difficult to unite rural people around a common set of demands. Nonetheless, subsequent economic hard times and intensified repression drove most groups into the revolutionaries' broadening alliances.

The growth of these alliances only made the oligarchs more unyielding in their control over agriculture, industry, banking, and trade. Unlike the urban capitalists of Nicaragua, who felt shut out by the Somoza dynasty and therefore sympathetic to revolutionary demands, most of El Salvador's industrialists and bankers were not about to form alliances with labor unions or popular organizations organized by priests, Christian Democrats, and leftists. Only an occasional family, like the De Sola family, considered political liberation as an alternative by 1979.

Government repression undermined the historical unity between oligarchy and Church. ORDEN's founding in 1968 had coincided with the impact of the theology of liberation documents issued by Latin America's bishops at their 1968 conference in Medellín (see Overview). Priests and nuns in El Salvador's understaffed Catholic Church took seriously Medellín's definition of inequality and oppression as sin. They and many Christian Democrats soon became the victims of military and death-squad violence. The ruling military-oligarchic alliance made little distinction among Christians, reformers, Democrats, or Communists.

The death squads (see Box 3.1) consisted of groups of heavily armed men, often dressed in civilian clothes, who traveled in vans, kidnapped individuals before disappearing them, or killed people on spot. Like ORDEN, they were usually headed by military veterans and had the government's cooperation. As human rights protests mounted domestically and internationally in the late 1970s and early 1980s, El Salvador's military government blamed the civilian death squads for activities it ordered, encouraged, or tolerated.

The U.S. State Department's annual Human Rights reports in the 1980s blamed El Salvador's tens of thousands of deaths equally on forces of "the extreme Right and extreme Left." This implied that neither the Salvadoran nor the U.S. government was involved. But according to testimony by a former

---

Box 3.1: Military, Paramilitary, and Death-Squad Groups

Army, Navy, and Air Force—50,500+
National Guard—4,500
National Police-4,500
Treasury Police—2,500
(all under jurisdiction of Minister of Defense and Public Security)

ORDEN (Nationalist Democratic Organization)—80,000 people under direction of the president, founded in 1968, outlawed by Decree Law 12 of first (two-and-a-half month long) civilian-military junta that overthrew General Romero in 1979, but resurrected under other names by military sympathizers

Patrullas cantonales (rural patrols)—former servicemen authorized to carry weapons, a kind of army reserve

Death squads (right wing terror units emerging in mid-1970s with collaboration or acquiescence of government military forces)—Anti-Communist Political front (FPA); Anti-Communist Armed Force of Liberation-War of Extermination (FALANGE); Escuadrón de Muerte (EM); Maximiliano Hernández Martínez Brigades; White Warrior's Union (UGB), believed to be linked with eastern region's landowner organization FARO; and, created after 1979 overthrow of General Romero, the Eastern Antiguerrilla bloc (BAGO), the Commando Domingo Monterrosa, the National Liberation party–Anti-Communist Secret Army (PLN-ESA), the New Death Squad (EMN), and the Organization for Liberation from Communism (OLC)

---

captain in the Salvadoran army before the U.S. Congress in 1981, death squad acts "are, in fact, planned by high-ranking military officers and carried out by members of the security forces." The Salvadoran commander of the Treasury Police—a virtual death squad—was on the CIA's payroll.

Independent, nongovernmental investigations into kidnappings, assassinations, and torture concurred that most of the thousands of deaths in the 1970s and the 70,000 deaths after 1979 were caused by government security forces, many from aerial bombardments of villages in guerrilla-controlled territory. They attributed less than 1 percent of civilian fatalities to leftist or guerrilla violence.

Electoral frauds deprived the Christian Democrats and other opposition forces from gaining office peaceably in 1972, 1974, and 1977, thereby raising guerrilla warfare to the status of "only viable alternative." Later, President Reagan would accuse the guerrillas of trying "to shoot their way into power."

In 1972 the first vote count showed that the candidates of the Christian Democrat–Communist–Social Democrat alliance UNO (National Union of Opposition) had won. UNO's presidential candidate was Duarte and its vice-presidential candidate was Guillermo Manuel Ungo. Colonel Arturo Molina, the military's candidate, seized power. Troops occupied the National University and arrested eight hundred protesters. Duarte later said that had the 1972 election results been allowed to stand, none of the subsequent bloodletting and political crisis would have occurred.

After the 1972 election Duarte was imprisoned, tortured, and exiled, returning by grace of the military in 1980 to become president of a military–civilian junta in December. Ungo left a similar junta eleven months earlier (January 1980) because of its failure to change anything. He then became head of the Democratic Revolutionary front (FDR—allied with the guerrilla armies' FMLN), the nation's largest political formation. Duarte and Ungo, once allies, became enemies. After interviewing CIA director William Casey shortly before Casey's death in 1987, Journalist Bob Woodward reported that Duarte had been a CIA "asset" since 1980.

The stealing of the UNO's 1972 electoral victory had stimulated a resurgence in popular resistance. In March 1972 the minuscule guerrilla army FPL-FM (see Box 3.2) publicly announced its existence. An equally small guerrilla unit, the ERP, had been founded by disenchanted Christian Democrats and Marxists a year earlier. Now both groups began winning new recruits.

Guerrilla popularity increased after fraudulent 1974 legislative elections. This time the government posted no results for the full slate of UNO candidates and simply declared PCN the winner. In towns with strong UNO turnouts, ORDEN units accompanied the police and National Guard to point out the houses of those who had voted for UNO. Many disappeared in the following weeks.

Box 3.2: Guerrillas*

FMLN	Farabundo Marti National Liberation front, coalition of all guerrilla groups formed in October 1980; armed wing of broad front FDR
Clara Elizabeth Ramírez front	urban-based group founded in 1983, loyal to FDR-FMLN
ERP	Revolutionary Army of the People, founded in 1971 by both Marxist and Christian proponents of the foco theory (guerrilla warfare insurrectionist strategy)
FAL	Armed Forces of Liberation, military wing of the outlawed Communist party (PCES) founded in late 1970s
FARN	Armed Forces of National Resistance, a 1975 splitoff from ERP; strategy of popular insurrection; gained support of some labor groups
FPL-FM	Farabundo Marti Popular Forces of Liberation, founded in 1972 but initiated in 1969 by dissident Communist Salvador Cayetano Carpio, a baker and labor militant who objected to PCES support for war against Honduras and later, involved in fratricidal splits in the guerrilla movement, committed suicide; strategy of prolonged people's war, allied with PCES and BPR
Pedro Pablo Castillo front	founded in 1985 and responsible for kidnapping President Duarte's daughter (released in return for freeing of several political prisoners); disowned by FDR-FMLN
PRTC	Revolutionary party of Central American Workers, founded in 1979 and associated with similarly named parties in Guatemala and Honduras

*See also Boxes 3.3 and 3.5.

ORDEN, death squads, and the national security forces unleashed a wave of terrorism, assassinating trade unionists, peasant leaders, clergymen, and intellectuals. Every sector of the population began organizing to defend itself (see Box 3.3). Unlike the professionals and members of the middle classes who had the resources to flee and survive during the repression of the 1970s, members of the popular classes had no such advantage. When employed, 90 percent of the work force received less than the minimum wage. Group solidarity through mass organizations became their only protection.

The first mass-based coalition of popular organizations, the FAPU (United Popular Action front), was founded in 1974 to lead strikes, sit-ins, and land seizures. The largest popular organization, the BPR (People's Revolutionary Bloc), was founded after an army massacre of peaceful student demonstrators on July 30, 1975.

The activism of priests and others in organizing peasants in the mid-1970s posed an additional threat to the old order. New rightist terrorist groups were organized to concentrate on rural areas: in 1975 the FALANGE (Anti-

---

Box 3.3: Popular Organizations*

Mass organizations based on unifying people around demands for end to state terror and
introduction of social reforms (initially active in peaceful protest, later supplying guerrillas)

FDR   Democratic Revolutionary front, umbrella alliance founded in 1980.
Encompasses all major popular organizations and rural and urban labor
organizations; political arm of guerrilla groups' FMLN; since 1982, recognized
by most governments as a legitimate representative political force.

BPR   People's Revolutionary bloc, known as "el Bloque," largest of popular
organizations inside FDR; connections with PCES and Christian Democratic-
oriented organizations like the peasants' UTC and FECCAS; formed of diverse
organizations of shantytown dwellers, workers, students, and teachers during
1975 occupation of Metropolitan Cathedral to protest army massacre of students
July 30, 1975; links with largest guerrilla army FPL-FM

COPPES   El Salvador Political Prisoners' Committee, a human rights group founded by
political prisoners

FAPU   United People's Action front founded in 1974, included most powerful labor
federation, FENASTRAS; links with FARN

LP-28   Popular Leagues–28th of February, created by ERP in 1977 after massacre of
demonstrators protesting General Romero's fraudulent election; student-
dominated

MLP   Popular Liberation movement, created in 1979; links with PRTC guerrilla army

UPT   Union of urban dwellers; part of BPR

*See also Boxes 3.2 and 3.5.

Communist Armed Force of Liberation War of Extermination), in 1977 the
UGB (White Warrior's Union). After killing a priest, UGB vowed to kill all
Jesuits.

Also in 1977 a more conservative archbishop, Oscar Arnulfo Romero,
was named for San Salvador. He was highly critical of activist priests. The
more he learned about the interrelatedness of U.S. aid programs and repression, however, the more he altered his thinking in the direction of liberation
theology, particularly when he saw his own priests being gunned down.

Repression intensified, making almost any public meeting impossible.
In 1975, for example, troops killed several students protesting the government's use of $3.1 million to stage the Miss Universe contest in San Salvador;
twenty-four disappeared. The air force was beefed up in 1975 to combat the
guerrillas. Israel supplied eighteen refurbished French fighter bombers and
trainers for the first jet aircraft operation by Salvadorans (see Introduction to
Part One).

Despite the government's best efforts, by the late 1970s the BPR,
FAPU, and other popular organizations had established a kind of alternative,

neighborhood-level government. The military government responded with a series of armed attacks that broke up all public demonstrations.

In February 1977, after another fraudulent presidential election during which UNO supporters were assaulted at polling booths, General Carlos Humberto Romero seized power. The people exploded with anger. Security forces opened fire on a march of 50,000 to 70,000 people in San Salvador's Plaza Libertad, leaving one hundred dead. Two hundred UNO officials were detained. The military and police occupied BPR-controlled neighborhoods. Following the Carter administration's criticism of these and related human rights abuses, El Salvador's military rulers joined those of Guatemala, Argentina, and Brazil in rejecting U.S. military aid.

Actually, President Force had suspended such aid after learning of the conviction in New York of the Salvadoran Army Chief of Staff for trying to sell machine guns to the U.S. mafia. The military's growing integration with organized crime and the international drug trade probably dates from the 1970s.

In November 1977, General Romero issued the draconian Law for the Defense and Guarantee of Public order, banning public assemblies and authorizing security forces to break up strikes, jail critics, and kill as required. The International Commission of Jurists announced that the jailings and killings were "'not isolated incidents . . . but part of a deliberate campaign to preserve the privileged position of the ruling minority."

Political murders increased tenfold in the three years after the law was announced. The popular organizations resorted to street demonstrations, civil disobedience, and takeovers of government buildings or foreign embassies— but these too were repressed, often with gunfire. First the voting booth, now the last avenues of nonviolent protest, had been cut off.

The intense repression drove many people into the mountains to join the guerrillas. Most stayed in the political underground of the cities. More slaughters followed, leading up to the police opening fire on unarmed demonstrators on the steps of the cathedral in May of 1979, killing 23 and wounding 70. In the month of May alone, 188 people perished in such clashes.

Throughout the spring of 1979 factory workers launched illegal strikes, often winning their economic demands. The momentum of the popular forces seemed irresistible.

On July 19, 1979, the Sandinistas marched into Managua, ending Nicaragua's forty-five-year dictatorship. Two months later, as popular mobilizations spread throughout the rural and urban landscape, BPR and FAPU workers occupied four factories in San Salvador and declared 1980 the "year of liberation." From Washington it looked as though the Salvadoran dictatorship might fall as quickly as the Nicaraguan one had done.

162

1979 Coup, Elections, and U.S. Military Involvement

On October 15, 1979, a military coup sent General Romero and his cabinet packing to Guatemala. It came none too soon. As Assistant Secretary of State for Inter-American Affairs Viron Vaky later observed, only "a military-civilian junta" could prevent "'another Nicaragua.'"

At first the new junta's composition looked like a radical change. It included prominent civilians of the moderate opposition like UNO's Ungo and a representative of the De Sola family. A member of the tiny Communist party (PCES) became minister of labor. Roughly 10 percent of the officer corps was expelled for corruption and violence.

Duarte returned from exile to be met by an airport throng of 100,000. While moderates rushed to support the junta, the left opposition criticized it as an old fox in new lamb's clothes. The junta promised to disband ORDEN and to introduce an agrarian reform, freedom for labor unions, and respect for human rights.

Within a week its security forces broke up strikes, occupied rebellious towns, and killed more than one hundred people. On October 29, the police and National Guard mowed down eighty-six people marching in a demonstration. In December troops massacred forty peasants who had occupied a farm called "El Refugio." Nearly three hundred more protesters were gunned down in the next few days.

By early January 1980, Ungo and the entire cabinet, as well as thirty-seven other high-ranking officials, resigned, noting that the army high command still viewed the popular organizations as the enemy. Three weeks later security forces in the capital opened fire on a "March of Unity" estimated to number between 80,000 and 200,000. Most undecided moderates now rushed to join the forces of the revolutionary Left. One of the few who remained in government, Attorney General of Welfare Mario Zamora of the PDC, was assassinated on February 23. His brother, Rubén Zamora, left the PDC to become a major FDR leader and head of today's Democratic Convergence.

The 1979 junta's failure further militarized the social struggle for land, free-trade unionism, and democracy. It was clear to everyone from peasants to men of the cloth that there could not be peaceful change in El Salvador. Shortly before his March 24 assassination, Archbishop Romero proclaimed: "Christians do not fear combat; they know how to fight . . . the Church speaks of the legitimate right of insurrectional violence."

Some 80,000 people gathered for the Archbishop's funeral on March 30. In full view of television, another *matanza* occurred, leaving thirty-nine dead and two hundred wounded. Forty-eight hours later the U.S. Congress approved an additional $5.7 million in military aid, "nonlethal" equipment that included night-vision devices.

On April 18, 1980, the popular organizations and labor groups united to form the FDR, a coalition of moderate and leftist forces that left the junta isolated. The FDR's program called for an agrarian reform, low-cost housing, improved health care, and a literacy campaign. Banking, foreign trade, and utilities would be nationalized to provide the funding for those social necessities, but small and medium-sized private businesses and landholdings would not be touched. It called for a "popular, democratic and antioligarchic" revolution, the only way to achieve "'true and effective national independence." The Reagan administration later claimed that the FDR was committed "to the establishment of a Marxist, totalitarian government."

The military's cynical ruling inner circle, already an established bastion of wealth, grew wealthier after the 1979 coup. Called the Armed Forces Security Council and composed of seven to ten members of the most powerful tandas, it quickly purged the younger reform-minded officers and used their reforms—nationalization of the banks and export trade in March 1980—to enrich its own bank accounts. The stepped-up international arms and drug traffic and billions of dollars in U.S. aid over the next six years provided even easier fast bucks.

The Armed Forces Security Council made a pact with President Duarte similar to the one the oligarchs had made with General Hernández half a century earlier: You can hold political office but hands off our economic activities. Former U.S. Ambassador to El Salvador Robert White told Congress in February 1982 that the military elite profited from the war by "selling arms to the revolutionaries."

Duarte remained the civilian figurehead of the military coup but the real power changed hands during a series of military-civilian juntas. The original 1979 junta lasted less than three months. The second junta, nominally headed by Duarte, lasted from January 1980 to April 1982. A third junta governed from May 1982 until June 1984, when newly elected President Duarte started what was supposed to be a five-year presidential term. Many generals, businesspeople, and oligarchs distrusted Duarte but accepted him because the U.S. Congress approved larger sums of aid with Duarte in office.

Two Christian Democrat leaders joined the second junta in January 1980: Héctor Dada and José Antonio Morales Ehrlich. When they learned of an impending coup by an ultrarightist group, Dada and Morales Ehrlich announced that the Christian Democrats would leave the government if the plotters were not removed from the military. There was no response. Dada and most other Christian Democrats resigned in March, but Morales Ehrlich remained with Duarte beside him.

The reduced PDC, a shadow of its former self, stood isolated as the only remaining moderate force in an alliance with the military. In effect, the so-called "Center" that Washington claimed to champion against the forces of the Left and Right existed no more. Two sons of Morales Ehrlich joined the guerrillas, one of them writing his father: "It is really dishonorable to be in your situation, and still try to hide from the world the reality of violence and repression that our people suffer daily."

The next several years marked a period of increased U.S. aid and militarization of the conflict, more death-squad assassinations, troops mowing down protesters, electoral fanfare covered by the world press, and another tokenistic agrarian reform. The FMLN guerrillas extended their attacks to all but two of the nation's fourteen provinces.

U.S. policymakers during both the Carter and Reagan administrations viewed the events in Nicaragua and El Salvador as threats to U.S. national security. In April 1980, the Carter administration initiated a strategy of using Honduras military to crush El Salvador's guerrillas. It sold $3.5 million worth of arms to Honduras' military and leased ten Huey helicopters to the Honduran Air Force. It also dispatched Green Berets to train Honduran troops in border security operations.

On May 14, 1980, Honduran troops turned back six hundred Salvadoran men, women, and children crossing the Sampul River to escape from Salvadoran army gunfire. The desperate families recrossed the river and were slaughtered. Ten months later, in March 1981, a similar massacre of Salvadoran peasants occurred as they fled across the Lempa River border with Honduras.

Now that they were cooperating against the guerrillas, it was clearly time for El Salvador and Honduras to end the haggling over border issues resulting from the 1969 futbol war. The two old enemies, with U.S. advisers beaming approval, signed a partial agreement on October 30, 1980. The treaty permitted Salvadoran troops to make sweeps into demilitarized pocket areas of the border zone where refugee camps had been set up by forces believed friendly to the Salvadoran guerrillas.

Prior to 1980 El Salvador and Honduras had experienced many decades free of direct U.S. military intervention. But the Nicaraguan Revolution changed all that. U.S. military advisers soon accompanied Salvadoran troops on patrol. In the spring of 1983 San Salvador's Ilopango airport became a launching pad for the U.S. war against Nicaragua and a buildup of El Salvador's air force (by 1986: sixty helicopters, twelve helicopter gunships, five AC-47 gunships, ten combat jets).

On September 12, 1983, Undersecretary of Defense Fred Ikle rejected negotiations to end the Salvadoran war: "We do not seek a military stalemate," he said, "we seek victory." Universally condemned weapons like antipersonnel fragmentation bombs, white phosphorous, and napalm rained down on El Salvador's peasantry. As the Pentagon acknowledged on March 11, 1984, U.S. reconnaissance planes flown by U.S. pilots helped spot guerrillas and select targets for the Salvadoran military. The 10,000 peasants residing on the slopes of the Guazapa volcano outside San Salvador suffered more tonnage of nonatomic bombs per square inch of territory than any other people in history.

Despite the U.S. military presence and the modern armaments it contributed, popular support for the FDR-FMLN increased. They now added the popular theme of national independence to their program. The number of guerrillas rose from under 2,000 to over 10,000, and it was clear that they enjoyed the support of workers and students as well as peasants.

The guerrillas continued building up their support in the cities. Most leaders of urban labor organizations (see Box 3.4) had been jailed, tortured, killed, or forced into exile. But other workers kept organizing. On June 24, 1980, more than 125,000 workers launched a general strike. Business activity in the capital ground to a halt for two days. Support demonstrations took place at the campus of the National University. Troops occupied the campus, killed fifty students, closed the university, and the strike ended.

Public outrage over the November 1980 kidnap-murder of six FDR leaders from a press conference at a Jesuit high school surrounded by federal troops and the December killing of four American churchwomen, two of whom were raped, forced the U.S. government to set up a special U.S. investigatory commission headed by former Secretary of State William Rogers. The commission absolved the military high command of responsibility for the women's deaths and asked the junta to bring the women's killers to justice. Finally, the Rogers Commission successfully pressured the junta once again to accept Duarte as its president.

At the end of 1980 and start of 1981 the FMLN announced an offensive to try to defeat the junta before the Reagan administration took power. Ambassador White cited "circumstantial but compelling and convincing evidence" of Nicaraguan material aid to the FMLN, including a Nicaraguan invasion. Junta leaders, including President Duarte, acknowledged at the time that the FMLN's weapons came mainly from the black market and were U.S.-made. Nevertheless, on January 14, 1981, White stated: "We can't stand idly by and watch the guerrilla movement receive outside assistance." Three months later White retracted his charges, citing faulty military intelligence "intended to serve a particular kind of solution," but the concocted story provided the rationale the U.S. government needed for its "particular kind of solution"—a stepped-up U.S. military rescue of the Salvadoran regime.

Three days after White's allegation of "circumstantial but compelling evidence," President Carter initiated the U.S. policy of military intervention based on combatting "left-wing terrorism supported covertly by Cuba and other Communist nations." On January 17, 1981, Carter sent an emergency $5 million shipment of lethal weapons and six leased Bell UH-IH helicopters. He authorized twenty additional U.S. military trainers.

Box 3.4: Labor and Private Sector Organizations*

ANEP	National Association of Private Enterprise, founded in late 1960s to represent agroexport, commercial, and industrial interests, including Salvadoran Chamber of Commerce and Salvadoran Association of Industry (ASI)
ANDES	National teachers' union; part of BPR
AP	Production Alliance, founded in 1980 and dominated by industrial and commercial interests
CCS	Union Coordinating Committee, part of BPR
CGSS	General Confederation of El Salvadoran Labor Unions, founded in 1958 with assistance of government and ORIT as an alternative to CGTS; close ties to regime
CGTS	General Workers Confederation, formed in 1957 by militant trade unionists, repressed, and dissolved into FUSS in 1965
CNTS	National Coalition of Salvadoran Workers, founded in February 1986 and representing 300,000 workers and forty-six unions, most of them not recognized by Duarte government
FARO	Eastern Region Farmers' front, founded in 1975 by landowners to block Molina government's attempt at agrarian reform.
FECCAS	Christian Federation of Salvadoran Peasants, a merger of isolated peasant leagues launched in 1965 with Church support; part of BPR
FENASTRAS	National Labor Union Federation of Salvadoran Workers, the most powerful labor organization, part of FAPU and FDR and part of CNTS
FESINCONSTRANS	Federation of Unions of Construction and Transportation—most successful in gaining concessions since 1968; some links with government unions like UCS, more independent in 1980s
FTR	Revolutionary Workers' Federation, founded in 1980 to spread support for general strikes called by FDR
FUSS	formed by independent unions and remaining ones of CGTS in 1965
UCS	Salvadoran Communal Union, founded in 1968 with AIFLD support and alleged CIA influence
UNTS	National Union of Salvadoran Workers, a strong coalition of professional, labor, and peasant unions, founded in 1984
UPD	Popular Democratic Union, founded in 1980 with AIFLD support; a coalition of peasant and trade unions; supported Duarte in 1984 election but broke away in February 1986 to join the antigovernment CNTS
UTC	Union of Fieldworkers, founded by left-wing Christians and part of BPR

*See also Box 3.3.

The Reagan administration followed up with $25 million in military aid (doubled a year later) and fifty-six military advisers—ironically, the same number as those in Vietnam on the eve of the first big U.S. escalation of that war. Secretary of State Alexander Haig spoke of ending Communist subversion in the region, even if it meant "going to the source" (Cuba). From 50,000 to 75,000 demonstrators gathered in Washington, D.C., to shout a resounding "no" to the Reagan-Haig approach. Shortly thereafter, Washington's bellicose rhetoric eased but not its war efforts. In addition, the new Reagan team drew up and implemented war plans against the government of Nicaragua (see Overview, Introduction to Part One, and chapter 5).

Thanks to the emergency infusion of U.S. military aid and trainers, the FMLN's attacks of late 1980 and early 1981, which some had called the "final offensive," were eventually checked. Before it was, guerrilla forces had taken ninety-six cities and towns and proven their ability to occupy the suburbs of the nation's capital. The guerrillas' policy of not killing captured soldiers but turning them over to the Green Cross also bore fruit. Several military officers and troops in Santa Ana defected to the FMLN.

The next few years witnessed a further deterioration in the juntas' abilities to eliminate either the guerrillas or the nation's economic problems. Once again, it was time for a change.

Responding to U.S. pressures, the third junta sponsored limited democratic presidential elections in the spring of 1984. The stated purpose was to establish a civilian government that might quiet the international clamor about human rights violations and win over some of the populace.

Only right-wing and Conservative candidates ran (see Box 3.5). The government refused to guarantee the safety of the candidates of Left parties or even those of coalitions slightly to the left of Duarte's conservative remnants of the PDC. Most PDC members had long since turned to the FDR as the country's best hope. The FDR and other left-of-Duarte groups were either outlawed or chose not to participate, claiming the elections were a "public relations act" put on for the benefit of American television viewers to assure continuation of U.S. aid. Citizens had to show authorities their stamped *"cédulas,"* proving they had gone to the polls; more than a million did.

It was widely acknowledged that the U.S. government poured at least $1.4 million dollars into the final campaign against Roberto D'Aubuissón of the extreme-Right Arena (National Republican Alliance) to assure a victory for the PDC's Duarte. Because of D'Aubuissón's associations with death squads, the Reagan administration feared an Arena victory would repel U.S. public opinion and undercut congressional support for additional aid. Three days after Duarte's victory by seven percentage points, Congress approved an increase in military aid and for the first time did not attach conditions necessitating presidential confirmation of "improvements" in human rights conditions. Duarte had campaigned on a pledge to "dialogue" with the guerrillas, whereas D'Aubuissón had pledged "'war unto death against communism" and had called Duarte a "watermelon" (green on the outside, red on the inside).

The Reagan administration called the 1984 elections "an exercise in democracy" in contrast to the "totalitarian mockery of elections" held by the Sandinistas in Nicaragua later that year (for contrasting views, see chapter 5). But a Salvadoran churchman asked U.S. reporters: "They don't kill priests in Nicaragua, do they?" Detractors considered El Salvador's elections "an exercise in intimidation" that had left the majority of the electorate unrepresented yet forced to mark translucent ballots under implied threats of assassination if they could not produce their stamped cédulas.

Box 3.5: Political Parties*

AD	Democratic Action, political arm of Maximiliano Hernández Martínez death squad
Arena	National Republican Alliance, ultra-rightist party founded in 1981 by Roberto D'Aubuissón
CD	Democratic Convergence, electoral coalition of MNR, MPSC, and PSD, founded in 1988
FDR	Revolutionary Democratic front, political arm of guerrilla groups' FMLN
PAISA	Authentic Institutional party of El Salvador, 1982 right-wing splitoff from PCN
PAR	Renewal Action party, founded in 1944, suspended in 1968, failed in 1985 elections
Patria Libre	Free Homeland, 1985 rightist splitoff from Arena
PCES	Communist part of El Salvador, founded in 1930, outlawed ever since (see UDN, below)
PCN	National Conciliation party, founded in 1961, in power until 1979; often allied with Arena
PDC	Christian Democratic party, formed in 1960; most members joined FDR, leaving Duarte with party remnants in 1980s; in power with military since 1980; split in 1988
PSD	Social Democratic party, member of CD
PPS	Salvadoran People's party, founded in 1966, close to PCN and commercial-industrial sector
MNR	National Revolutionary movement founded in 1965, member of Socialist International; led by Guillermo Manuel Ungo, a law professor and businessman, who incorporated it into FDR and CD
MPSC	Social Christian People's movement, founded in 1980 by Rubén Zamora and PDC members opposed to Duarte; member of FDR and CD
UCA	Central American University (Jesuits), active in late 1980s as "third force" between government and guerrillas
UDN	National Democratic Union, founded in 1969 as legal expression of PCES
UNO	National Opposition Union, coalition of PDC, MNR, and UDN in 1972 and 1977 elections

*See also Box 3.3

In spite of Washington's support for Duarte, Arena and the PCN used their votes in the constituent assembly (elected in 1982) to cut off further applications for land under the agrarian reform program. The reform, decreed in 1980, had targeted 376 properties in excess of 1,224 acres. Some of the reform's top administrators had been assassinated by right-wing death squads—and in most rural areas the security forces made sure distributed lands ended up in friendly hands or those of the big landlords.

In the face of the early 1980s' recession and the costs of increased warfare, the Duarte government in 1986 announced an IMF-style economic recovery plan to diversify exports and beef up internal production. In spite of U.S. aid dollars in the 1980s totalling fifty times the amount pumped in during the Alliance for Progress "showcase" days, El Salvador's economy was on the ropes. Duarte's plan failed to address the most pressing problem—the concentration of economic power in a few hands.

The government's efforts to initiate "Phase II" of the agrarian reform ran into stiff right-wing opposition. Hardest hit by the economic program were the middle and lower classes. On February 21, 1986, the powerful independent National Union of Salvadoran Workers (UNTS), a coalition of professional, labor, and peasant unions, marched in San Salvador to protest the new austerity program. A few months later, on May 1, some 80,000 Salvadorans marched through the capital's streets demanding an end to human rights violations and emphasizing negotiations with the FMLN.

In late 1986, Duarte reiterated his desire to establish a dialogue with the FDR–FMLN. (The two sides had previously held unsuccessful talks.) Duarte's condition was that the guerrillas lay down their arms—"a dialogue of surrender" according to FDR leader Ungo. The FDR stated it would accept "power-sharing" with noncriminal elements of the military-oligarchic alliance waging the war. Halting steps continued toward a negotiated settlement, abetted by the pressures of the Arias Peace Plan (see Introduction to Part One). But the war continued and death squad killings increased in 1988. Duarte's ability to negotiate a middle ground with the revolutionary coalition was limited by threats from his Right flank. Private-enterprise forces led by ANEP and FARO, together with ultrarightist elements inside the government, wished to eliminate what they called the "watermelon" tendencies of post-1979 El Salvador. The U.S. Congress continued to fund the regime, based on the rationale that it was a "freely elected" one. But public opinion and continued mass demonstrations in Washington and other cities placed limits on U.S. war efforts.

Then, in April of 1987, the FMLN attacked the government's second strongest military base, El Paraíso, just north of San Salvador. It gutted the base and killed scores of people, including two Americans. One was a CIA agent. The other was a military adviser. Critics of U.S. policy were quick to point out that the killing of U.S. advisers in Vietnam had led to the Vietnam war. Four months later, northeast of the capital, a U.S. helicopter crashed, killing six U.S. servicemen. They were reportedly on a mission to assist a wounded U.S. military adviser. In September 1988 U.S. military trainers fired on guerrillas. Although Congress had long since outlawed U.S. military personnel from participating in combat, a 1985 report by a 130-member bipartisan congressional caucus had documented that "U.S. personnel are selecting targeting sites for bombing and maintaining equipment." Salvadoran right-wing death squads began threatening political refugees and peace activists in the United States.

The extreme Right swept the 1988 legislature elections (voter turnout was low). With President Duarte dying of cancer and the remainder of his PDC split, it was clear D'Aubuissón's Arena would win the 1989 presidential contest. To have the death squad leader whom Ambassador White had repeatedly described as "a pathological killer" elected president would be hardly becoming to the U.S. sponsors of the entrenched military-oligarchy alliance. So Alfredo Cristiani, a U.S.-educated forty-one-year-old businessman and a disciple of D'Aubuissón, was selected as the Arena candidate instead.

Cristiani promised a more moderate Arena and won the 1989 election with 53 percent of the vote. Arena had the backing of not just the landed oligarchy but most of the business community. Duarte's PDC was charged with corruption, failure to end the war, and ruining the economy. Its electoral defeat concluded another chapter in Latin America's typical "falling away of the political center" (see Overview) that the PDC itself had initiated years earlier.

The U.S. government hailed the El Salvador election as a democratic example that Nicaragua's Sandinista revolutionaries should be sure to follow in 1990. But unlike Nicaragua in 1990, El Salvador prohibited the opposition from participating effectively in its election in 1989. Many now feared a return to the death squad rampages of earlier years. Others expected Arena to consolidate a "legal" police state that could be marketed abroad as an improvement in "human rights"—a "jackboot democracy."

For its part, the FMLN stepped up its peace efforts and armed vigilance. It acknowledged it had committed some political killings but assured everyone they had been mistakes and would not occur in future.

In late October 1989, only hours after a bombing of the offices of the human rights group Co-madres, a bomb exploded in the headquarters of the National Federation of Salvadoran Workers (FENASTRAS), killing ten. Among dozens of wounded was a Connecticut man doing translation work for the unions.

The FMLN responded by launching a mid-November offensive that claimed hundreds of lives and once again penetrated San Salvador. President Cristiani declared a state of siege. Half the nation's mayors resigned because of death threats. Upon unanimous vote by the UN Security Council, the first

UN military observers headed for El Salvador and other Central American hotspots (see Introduction to Part One).

Also in November, uniformed assassins murdered six Jesuit priests, their housekeeper, and her daughter in a barbarous fashion that evoked world outrage. The priests were prominent university professors. Subsequent investigations placed the blame for the murders on the army's high command.

These tragic events in late 1989 redounded to the FMLN's favor. It set up governments in several newly liberated territories. On February 8, 1990, General Maxwell Thurman of the U.S. Southern Command in Panama told Congress that the FMLN could not be beaten militarily by El Salvador's army and that it was time for a negotiated solution to the war.

Nonetheless, the war dragged on for the next few years, despite pressures from Mexico, Venezuela, Colombia, Spain, and the United Nations to bring the combatants to the peace table. In 1990 ex-President Duarte died of liver cancer. U.S. military aid underwent reduction because of the government's ongoing human rights abuses, including the murder of trade union leaders and expulsion of peasants from their lands. The strong U.S. protest movement against aid to El Salvador was winning.

Yet more than one hundred fifty U.S. military "advisers" continued to appear in combat zones. One of their helicopters crashed in 1991 some seventy-five miles east of San Salvador. Two servicemen surviving the crash were killed by two FMLN soldiers (two years later, the soldiers were freed under an amnesty law). One U.S. military adviser reportedly told FBI investigators he would have agreed with the murder of the six priests in 1989.

The FMLN, no longer able to expect any help from Cuba or Nicaragua whose peoples were suffering their own aid reductions because of the demise of the Soviet bloc, made several concessions toward peace that were for the most part unreciprocated. In the March 1991 elections for a new National Assembly, the FMLN and its sympathizers fielded candidates. Many of their supporters found it either impossible or too risky to register to vote. Yet Arena won only thirty-nine of eighty-four seats. The Christian Democrats' PDC won twenty-six seats, the right-wing National Conciliation party nine seats, and guerrilla representatives eight. Rubén Zamora, head of the Democratic Convergence, a left-center coalition of parties, produced a long list of government violations of voting rights.

In November 1991, the FMLN announced its last unilateral cease-fire, saying it would stick until a peace treaty was signed. The army viewed this as a ruse and immediately invaded FMLN bases and shut down the National University.

The U.S. citizens' movement against the U.S. government's expulsion of Salvadoran refugees gained momentum. In early 1992, the Bush administration decided to allow 200,000 refugees to remain because of war conditions in El Salvador. But there were still many more unprotected.

In January 1992, under mounting international pressure, the Arena government finally signed a peace accord with the FMLN. The agreement called for: the removal of more than one hundred high ranking officers implicated in human rights violations and a 50 percent army troop reduction to 31,000 men; depoliticalization of the military academy; dismantling of the military's National Intelligence Directorate; a new police force to replace paramilitary police like the Treasury Police and National Guard with civilians, including former FMLN soldiers; completion of the 1980 agrarian reform; human rights guarantees; democratic elections; and disarming of the FMLN in exchange for land and resettlement compensation for its troops and the right to become a political party.

UN Secretary General Boutros-Ghali called the peace accord "a negotiated revolution." The United Nations sent one thousand observers to El Salvador. In February 1992, tens of thousands of people turned out in downtown San Salvador to greet the FMLN General Command and hundreds of FMLN troops.

The remaining issues in the Honduras border conflict were now resolved by the World Court (see Introduction to Part One). In October, the bodies of 38 children were discovered in a shallow grave in El Mozote, believed to be the victims of a 1981 army massacre of 794 local villagers.

The major obstacle in the implementation of the 1992 peace accord was the Cristiani government's reluctance to purge high ranking military officers and disband the hated U.S.-trained Atlacatl battalion, National Guard, and Treasury Police (the government sought to fake its compliance by assigning such groups new names). The Arena government hoped to use promised international aid of $1 billion on projects in the disputed areas controlled by the FMLN in order to win over FMLN loyalists to its side.

The government's foot dragging on the peace agreement led to its being censured by every interested party in 1993. Most of the FMLN's eight thousand guerrillas disarmed, but they suspended destruction of their last fifty surface-to-air missiles pending government compliance.

Then, in March 1993 a UN-appointed Truth Commission of three international jurists, including a George Washington University law professor, named sixty-two Salvadoran officers responsible for the worst massacres, tortures, and murders of the twelve-year war. It called for the immediate dismissal of forty of them. The Panama-based U.S. Army School of the Americas (now in Fort Benning, Georgia—see chapter 7) had trained forty-seven of them. The pride of the U.S. military training missions, the army's Atlacatl Battalion, was accused of several major massacres, including those in Morazán province in 1981.

The report also noted FMLN human rights abuses, naming commander Joaquín Villalobos as the one responsible for the killings of some mayors and recommending that he be barred from public office for ten years. But it found the U.S.-trained Salvadoran military responsible for 85 percent of the war's dead. The late D'Aubuissón, who had died in 1991 of lung cancer, was confirmed as the man who ordered the assassination of Archbishop Romero and the mastermind of the death squads. The UN Truth Commission also concluded that the current defense minister, General René Emilio Ponce, had ordered the grisly murders of the six Jesuit priests and two laywomen in 1989 (a finding first put forth in 1991 by a U.S. congressional panel). An earlier trial of nine military men had resulted in irregularities, including disappearing witnesses, but for the first time in history two Salvadoran officers in that trial were convicted of human rights violations.

Despite their denials of knowing about any of these matters, the Reagan and Bush administrations knew all along. The *New York Times* reported on March 21, 1993, that it had obtained formerly classified government documents proving "that American officials knew far more about the workings of the military and right-wing death squads than they told Congress or the American people." The UN Truth Commission said that U.S. intelligence agencies withheld requested information. There were calls for a congressional investigation and the naming of a special prosecutor.

But for 80,000 Salvadoran dead and well over a million refugees, it was too late. Billions of dollars in U.S. aid, most of it military, had contributed—in the words of a September 26, 1991, *New York Times* editorial—"to the destruction of this tiny country."

In El Salvador, the army charged that Communists were behind the UN Truth Commission report. President Cristiani rushed through an amnesty bill to spare the accused, including those convicted of the murder of the six Jesuit priests. Only the PDC and the Democratic Convergence voted against the special amnesty bill. The head of the manufacturing Asociación Salvadoreña de Industriales called for the appointment of a civilian to head the defense ministry. U.S. congressmen, including Robert Torricelli (after whom the anti-Castro Torricelli Amendment was named—see chapter 8), announced a review of Reagan administration statements to Congress that now looked like total fabrications.

The administration of President Bill Clinton (1993–) suspended military aid because of the government's failure to implement the peace accord. It called for completion of a purge of military officers implicated in human rights violations.

In May 1993, police opened fire on a protest march by disabled army and guerrilla combat veterans demanding medical care, killing two. Another mass grave was uncovered, this one having six hundred bodies presumed to be the civilian victims of the joint Salvadoran-Honduran military massacre thirteen years earlier. A Catholic bishop was assassinated in June. Three high-level FMLN leaders and several political activists were murdered in the months leading up to the March 1994 elections.

The peace process sputtered because of army resistance. According to the Christian Democrats and the ex-guerrillas and their Social Democratic allies, the Cristiani government used its control of the Supreme Electoral Tribunal to prevent opposition voters from registering for the elections. One-third of the potential electorate remained unregistered. Some 600,000 refugees had returned home after the signing of the 1992 peace accord.

The FMLN split on electoral strategy, with Villalobos of the ERP faction warning that to win the election would risk alienating U.S. and other investment needed for postwar reconstruction. The numerically stronger FPL faction backed the candidacy of dissident Christian Democrat legislator Rubén Zamora, who, in a runoff election, lost out to Arena candidate Armando Calderón Sol by a margin of two-to-one. The FMLN and many centrists denounced the election for numerous technical frauds and "irregularities" committed by the well-financed Arena and its government. Foreign observers gave mixed reports, none denying that several irregularities had occurred and that there remained an atmosphere of fear in El Salvador. The Left emerged as the second electoral force after Arena, winning twenty-one seats in the Legislative Assembly, compared with Arena's thirty-nine seats and the PDC's eighteen.

Economically, El Salvador was still suffering, and cholera struck seven hundred in the last week of 1993. The Arena government privatized banks, other financial institutions, and the state monopoly on sugar and coffee sales. A preliminary common market agreement was signed with Nicaragua, Honduras, and Guatemala (see Introduction to Part One). Drug smugglers increased their use of El Salvador as a way station. Most Salvadoran families barely survived economically by means of cash remittances of some $350 million sent them by the one-fifth of the population that had fled to Canada or the United States.

Some former FMLN guerrillas started attending U.S.-financed courses on capitalism and democracy. Others began receiving FBI training to become part of the new police force required by the peace agreements. But, as an eighty-one year-old peasant woman told reporters, "Many of those in the death squads are still around, in the towns. Everything's calm now, but who knows what might happen later? I don't want to die yet. I want to live to see the liberation."

Selected Bibliography

Anderson, Thomas P. *Matanza, El Salvador's Communist Revolt of 1932*. Lincoln: University of Nebraska Press, 1971.

Bonner, Raymond. *Weakness and Deceit: U.S. Policy and El Salvador*. New York: Times Books, 1984. By former *New York Times* correspondent.

Cagan, Beth, and Steve Cagan. *This Promised Land, El Salvador*. New Brunswick, NJ: Rutgers University Press, 1991. Photographs and story of refugee camp in Honduras.

Clements, Charles. *Witness to War*. New York: Bantam, 1984. Informative account by Vietnam War veteran who became a doctor and went to FMLN-controlled zones to tend the ill and wounded.

A Dream Compels Us:Voices of Salvadoran Women. Boston, MA: South End Press, 1991.

Gettleman, Marvin E., et al. (eds.). *El Salvador: Central America In the Cold War*. New York: Grove Press, 1987. Documents and opposing views on controversial issues.

Montgomery, Tommie Sue. *Revolution in El Salvador: Origins and Evolution*. Updated ed. Boulder, CO: Westview, 1990.

National Security Archive. *El Salvador: The Making of U.S. Policy, 1977–1984*. Alexandria, VA: Chadwyck-Healey, 1987. Revealing government documents.

North, Lissa. *Bitter Grounds: Roots of Revolt in El Salvador*. Toronto: Between the Lines, 1982. Good brief backgrounder.

Romero, Oscar A. *Voice of the Voiceless*. Maryknoll, NY: Orbis Books, 1987. Martyred archbishop's letters and statements.

Russell, Philip L. *El Salvador in Crisis*. Austin, TX: Colorado River Press, 1984. Good short history.

Stephen, Lynn M. *Testimonial: The Story of María Teresa Tula and the Co-Madres of El Salvador*. Boston, MA: South End Press, 1994.

Sundaram, Anjali, and George Gelber (eds.). *A Decade of War: El Salvador Confronts the Future*. New York: Monthly Review Press, 1989. Includes analyses by participants.

Tula, María Teresa. *Hear My Testimony*. Boston, MA: South End Press, 1994. How the civil war destroyed families and led to author's activism in CO-MADRES (Committee of Mothers and Relatives of Political Prisoners, Assassinated, and Disappeared of El Salvador).

Films

El Salvador: Another Vietnam. 1981. Gold Hugo Award documentary, Chicago International Film Festival, an informed documentary.

In the Name of the People. 1984. 45 minutes. Award-winning color documentary, narrated by Martin Sheen; only film shot by Americans behind guerrilla lines and showing Guazapa and Dr. Charles Clements.

A Question of Conscience: The Murder of the Jesuit Priests in El Salvador. 1990. 43 minutes. Color video by Ilan Ziv, Icarus/Tazmouz Media, on the 1989 slaughter.

Romero. 1989. 105 minutes. Color film; Raul Julia as the archbishop.

The Situation. 1986. 90 minutes. Color video acclaimed for its musical score and coverage of recent events.

A Time of Daring. 1983. 40 minutes. Prize-winning color film and video by FMLN media collective.

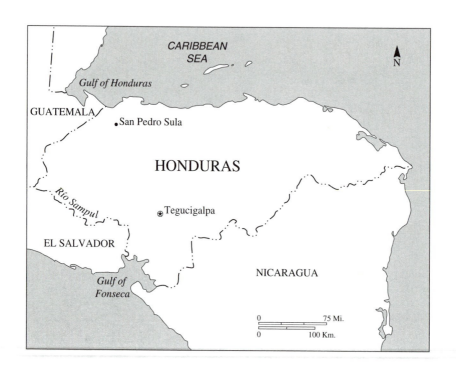

Honduras   4

Honduras is a pawn of the United States.—*Vice-President Jaime Rosenthal, 1986*

Honduras must be independent and must not be manipulated by any power.—*Archbishop Hector Enrique Santos, 1985*

This dump is the center of the world now.—*U.S. Army Captain Michael Sheehan, 1985*

It was the middle of March 1986, a sunny springlike day with temperatures rising above 70°F. The only sounds were an occasional vendor's shout of *"Montuca! Tortillas!"* or an army truck's backfiring. Then, a thin line of dust rose past the thousands of hovels covering the hills around the capital city of Tegucigalpa as thousands of people silently streamed past the fortresslike colonial presidential palace. They headed down the narrow road past the far end of the palace's courtyard, past its 25-foot-high wall of immense stones once fulcrumed by Indian hands. To one side of the wall, soldiers stood thirty-deep. Smaller army groups in jeeps and trucks waited at the intersection below.

At the foot of the hill some marchers turned left, some right. They followed the winding downtown streets and poured out into the central plaza. At a rear corner of the park stood a cluster of shy-looking U.S. servicemen, talking with Honduran soldiers and a bevy of heavily made-up women.

An orator stood up to address the crowd, raising his fist and shaking it. At first his words were the usual denunciations of taxes, high prices, inadequate land reform, government indifference to the poor. But as he saw more and more placards with a single slogan, his focus shifted. He spoke of the need for neutrality in the Nicaraguan conflict. People shouted their approval and waved their signs high.

The orator called on the government to account for the many union leaders, students, teachers, priests, and leftists who had disappeared. People became agitated. They began shaking and banging their signs one against another in a rising crescendo of wood and cardboard colliding. The orator paused to sip from a glass of guayaba juice. With a slight tremor in his voice, he continued, now urging the government to cancel military treaties with the United States.

The people began shouting *"Dále más duro!"*—"Give it to 'em harder"—over and over, and turned their placards toward the American servicemen. They stopped talking.

The orator hesitated. Then, inhaling deeply, he lifted his voice to call for the expulsion of all contras and U.S. troops. The crowd responded instantaneously with shouts and yells. Some of the placards raised the highest were in English. Their crude black lettering translated the chants of the crowd: "If the Yankees don't go, they will die in Honduras!"

The servicemen scrambled aboard the soldiers' jeeps and drove off. The voices, now in unison, shouted after them: "You will die in Honduras!"

.   .   .

Of all Latin America's countries that day, Honduras had the most U.S. troops permanently stationed in its territory (eleven thousand) and the most U.S. military bases (thirteen); eight airfields were capable of handling C-130 transport planes. Yet unlike its neighbors—Guatemala, El Salvador, Nicaragua—Honduras had no big guerrilla forces, no frequent mass street demonstrations against oligarchs or generals. In spite of the outpouring of fifteen thousand people that day and the recent unification of minuscule guerrilla units vowing to "throw out the Yankee occupiers," Honduras did not have a well-mobilized nationalist movement against Yankee intervention.

Why had Honduras become—in the words of Latin American nationalists—"a Pentagon Republic, the United States' newest land-based aircraft carrier"? One answer offered by cynics and apologists alike was that Honduras, as the original "banana republic," had never overcome its "Americanization" and alleged "fondness for Americans."

Most analysts dismissed this answer as a joke in poor taste. They attributed the U.S. military presence to the success of the Sandinista guerrilla war against the Somoza dictatorship in neighboring Nicaragua. U.S. military officials acknowledged that their purpose was to intimidate Nicaragua, coordinate the antiguerrilla war in El Salvador, and prepare for an invasion of either one. The U.S. General Accounting Office (GAO) concluded that many of the U.S.

military installations in Honduras were illegal, since they were permanent and therefore should have been approved by Congress before being built. President Reagan declared in 1988 the bases *would* be permanent.

When public protest against the U.S. Armed Forces' role became vocal, the U.S. government tried to put a "good face" on its intervention. In 1985 and 1986 it sent to Honduras five thousand National Guardsmen on a "goodwill mission" to build roads. The state guardsmen came from Alabama, Arizona, California, Missouri, and North Dakota. The roads connected the military bases in northern Honduras. In Minnesota the governor refused to order the guard to Central America. Then, in May of 1987 the biggest exercise yet, involving fifty thousand U.S. troops, was carried out. In March 1988, some thirty-two hundred U.S. troops were airlifted to Honduras to assist in the repulsion of an alleged Nicaraguan incursion. They left after a spate of militant protests by anti-interventionist groups in major U.S. cities, reportedly leaving behind an arsenal of weaponry for Nicaragua's contras.

How could the Honduras government tolerate what appeared to be an obvious compromise of national sovereignty? The answer was lodged in a series of debilitating conditions that distinguished Honduras from its neighbors.

First, even though it ranked among the hemisphere's poorest nations, Honduras had a history of fewer social protest movements than its neighbors. Whenever popular movements occurred they were not just crushed—often they were coopted through partial concessions, including an agrarian reform. Second, the Roman Catholic Church in Honduras was weaker than elsewhere and more reluctant to take political action. Third, Honduran elites were weak and fractionalized—so they were easily dominated by either the United States or the strong Honduran military created after World War II by U.S. aid programs. Fourth, Honduras's military in turn was too weak to defend the nation's sovereignty—as shown by the Salvadoran army's overrunning of the country in less than five days of 1969 during the misnamed futbol war (see chapter 3).

Of overriding importance was the way U.S. influence started. The arrival of U.S. banana companies in the early 1900s ended four centuries of lethargic economic activity and commenced an era of blatant U.S. manipulation of Honduran politics.

A Legacy of Poverty: From Colonial Backwater to Banana Republic

Honduras's original peoples included the Maya in the north and the Lenca in the center and west. The magnificent Maya ruins of Copán near the Guatemalan border testify to their scientific accomplishments (see chapter 1). Today, most of the population of 5 million is mestizo. The country is 55 percent rural and has a literacy rate of only 27 percent. Some 40,000 Miskitus,

15,000 Caribs, and 25,000 Garifuna (Afro-Indian) peoples live along the Atlantic coast.

During the 1980s the Miskitus became embroiled in the CIA-contra maneuverings along the border with Nicaragua. Contra troops invaded their lands and tried to recruit them into the war, often brutalizing those who refused to cooperate. Contra atrocities included kidnappings, rapes, and acts of torture (see chapter 5).

The Spaniards, who arrived in Honduras in 1524, were almost driven out by Indian revolts like that of 1537, led by the Lenca chieftain Lempira, whose name graces Honduras's currency. Although not pouring as much effort into developing Honduras as other parts of their colonial empire, the Spaniards did mine Honduras's gold and silver deposits. This laid the basis for the development of mule, cattle, hide, and dairy production—the backbone of Honduran agriculture over the next four centuries.

After the sixteenth-century reduction of available Indian labor by conquest and disease, slaves were imported. Later, English-speaking blacks were brought in to harvest the northern banana plantations. Two percent of today's population is black.

From 1600 to 1900, the majority of Hondurans scratched out their survival through subsistence agriculture. British, U.S. and German capital redeveloped silver mining at the end of the nineteenth century, when silver accounted for half of the exports.

Unlike its neighbors, Honduras did not develop a multimillion-dollar coffee economy. The cattle barons stuck to their sprawling ranches worked by peon labor. Because land was abundant, land sharks never had to pass liberal, private property laws confiscating communal or unsettled territories for themselves, the way elites did in most of Latin America.

Even if they had wanted to, Honduran landowners were not well equipped to jump on the coffee bandwagon. Except in the extreme north, the soils of Honduras were poor and most of the terrain mountainous and poorly watered. With a sparse population scattered over an immense territory, recruitment of an adequate labor supply was difficult. Big landholders lacked a transportation network, surplus capital, and commercial know-how.

After Central America's nations gained independence from Spain in 1821 and their federation collapsed in 1838, the shaky Republic of Honduras had undergone decades of devastating civil war and plunder by outside powers. Some eighty-five presidents "governed" between 1821 and 1876, many of them appointed by stronger regimes among Honduras's neighbors. The "Liberal-Conservative" conflict between Honduran landlords took the form of favoring or opposing Central American federation. The federationists (Liberals) carried the banner of Tegucigalpa's martyred Francisco Morazán, who had died fighting for Central American reunification in 1842. The frequent wars left the landowners with their economic reserves exhausted and dependent on foreign loans. Honduras became hopelessly in debt, weak, and unstable.

The 1876–1891 Liberal reform confiscated lands of the Catholic Church and secularized primary education and marriage. But since the Church did not own wealthy properties, the seizures did not provide enough to cover the Liberal governments' debts. It left the Catholic Church economically and politically even weaker.

By the mid-1980s the Roman Catholic Church faced a further threat to its already fragile power base from Protestant Evangelicals (see Introduction to Part One). The "Delegates of the Word" theology of liberation movement that generated some of the Central America's first "Christian base communities" started in Honduras in 1966 as a Catholic Church effort to compensate for Honduras's low number of ordained priests. These conscientious lay delegates, men and women alike, were often arrested, tortured, or murdered by the government for being subversive or Communist.

As elsewhere in Latin America, the nineteenth-century elites welcomed outside help. Britain had loaned various Honduran governments 6 million pounds in the late 1860s, presumably to build a coast-to-coast railway. But the rails were never laid, and the debt rose sixfold over the next fifty years, not being fully paid off until 1953. After the arrival of U.S. banana companies Honduras mortgaged itself yet further to outsiders. It did not develop its own currency or central bank until 1950.

Honduran elites were no match for the British navy or American mercenaries who declared themselves presidents of Central American nations—like William Walker (see chapter 5). Britain occupied the Bay Islands from 1850 to 1859, returning them in exchange for railway and other concessions. The Methodist Church is still the main religious institution there. Walker declared himself president of Honduras, Nicaragua, and El Salvador in 1860. He relegalized slavery and made English the official language. British forces put an end to his escapades, handing him over to Honduran authorities for execution by a firing squad.

Because a superrich oligarchy of coffee barons never developed, Honduras entered the twentieth century with one of Latin America's weakest elites. They and their political representatives became easy "marks" for banana company agents on the prowl for quick profits. As the future president of United Fruit Company (UFCO) Samuel ("Sam the banana man") Zemurray put it: "In Honduras a mule costs more than a deputy." In 1920 UFCO's H. V. Ralston wrote his lawyer that "none of them has any convictions of character, far less patriotism; they seek only position and rank, and on being granted them, we will make them hungry for more."

The elite families and politicians lavished generous concessions on three banana companies: Standard Fruit, Zemurray's Cuyamel Fruit Company, and

UFCO, which finished absorbing Zemurray's outfit in 1929. Backed up by the landing of the U.S. Marines to crush periodic revolts, these firms converted the lush lands of northern Honduras into their own private feifdoms, paying workers an average wage of less than $25 a month. The wage was often paid in tokens redeemable only at the company store.

Few laborers lasted more than a dozen years at the back-breaking work, putting in twelve-hour days at harvest time. In 1930 UFCO estimated that nearly one-third of the work force suffered malarial infection. They lived in wretched unscreened camps. Paramilitary "white guards" and well-armed overseers enforced their obedience. In his 1950 book *Green Prison* Ramón Amaya Amador wrote: "Amidst the confusion of toilers and banana plants, sun and pestilence, sweat and machines, creeks and malaria, there rang out the cocky shouts of the foremen, the whistling of the overseers, and the arrogant, all-powerful gringo slang."

Between 1910 and 1930 banana exports multiplied fivefold; but Hondurans saw little of the profits. The government's emphasis on developing remote banana enclaves meant that the rest of the nation went ignored. By 1979 Hondurans had a per-capita income half that of Nicaraguans. The infant mortality rate in Honduras, like Nicaragua's, was twice that of El Salvador's. The Kissinger Commission Report pointed out: "half the population is unemployed or underemployed . . . 57 percent lack sufficient income to cover the cost of the basic basket of food . . . 54 percent of rural Hondurans don't have access to safe water."

U.S. Occupation and the Power of Traditional Parties, 1910–1957

With the help of U.S. Marines, the banana companies converted Honduras into an occupied country. The much decorated marine commandant Major General Smedley D. Butler later recalled: "I helped make Honduras 'right' for American fruit companies."

The banana firms bankrolled Honduras's two traditional political parties and governed through them. Zemurray's Cuyamel got behind the Liberal party while UFCO supported the National party. In 1924, out-of-power National party forces led by General Tiburcio Carías Andino bombed the capital. U.S. Marines marched in "to protect American interests." They tipped the balance of power to the Nationals, although a Liberal president ruled from 1929 to 1933. Later, when the Great Depression led to social unrest and all Central America fell to strong-armed dictators, the Nationals' General Carías set up his sixteen-year-long rule by martial law (1933–1949), guaranteeing the properties and profits of UFCO and Standard Fruit.

After World War II the democratic "revolution" shaking Guatemala (see chapter 2) reverberated in Honduras. Banana executives and the elites recognized that General Carías's continued rule risked upsetting the Liberals and the moderate Nationals. They eased out Carías and replaced him with a new president, Juan Manuel Gálvez (1949–1954), a National party moderate.

A 1950 World Bank mission laid out a typical Third World game plan for modernizing Honduras. The government central bank would finance the "infrastructure" (roads, bridges, etc.), and additional foreign investment would be welcomed. Foreign bank loans proceeded to finance the development of cotton, sugar, coffee, and select industries.

"Modernization" money increased the National party–Liberal competition for power. The Nationals denied the Liberals an electoral victory in 1954. Strikes by banana workers and students shook the nation. Liberal leaders were banished, and a Liberal revolt erupted in 1956. The military stepped in to break the stalemate and preside over new elections. In 1957 the winning Liberal candidate, Ramón Villeda Morales, was allowed to assume the presidency (1957–1963).

The traditional rotation of power between the two parties regained a semblance of its historic rhythm. Government patronage in the form of jobs and favors flowed more evenhandedly. An individual's membership or support for either party had deep roots in personal loyalties on a local level. Godfather (*compadrazgo*) kinship systems of support and subservient patron-client relations had been passed down for generations (see chapter 1). Systematic repression of ideologies or groups outside the two parties further assured "party loyalty."

Political differences got worked out by means of competition between factions inside each party. This style was often repeated in the labor movement and even inside the one institution that had any real power in "modern" Honduras—the military.

Labor Unions and a Weak Military-Dominated State, 1957–1980

It is not surprising that direct and indirect military rule characterized "modern" Honduras. Weak elites, a cautious Church, recurrent labor unrest, and two traditional parties filled with factionalism left only the military to guarantee the political stability required for gradual modernization.

In 1954 some 50,000 laborers led by the banana workers launched a nationwide strike that paralyzed economic life for sixty-nine days and threatened a popular upheaval. Almost every working Honduran got involved in the unprecedented action. The strike won workers their major demand—the right to have trade unions—plus some modest wage hikes.

Labor strikes had occurred as early as 1916–1918, when banana strikers were beaten back by company goons and Caribbean workers were imported to weaken the unions. By 1928 a majority of banana workers had joined the

Communist-dominated FSH (Honduran Union Federation). After FSH walkouts were repressed in the early 1930s the companies enforced labor obedience through a system of military control, corrupt patronage, and internal union spies. The semiclandestine character of trade-union work meant that the most disciplined and tightly organized group—the Honduran Communist party—survived best.

Communists took charge of the big 1954 strike action, provoked by UFCO's refusal to pay dockworkers overtime. Employers and the government offered to negotiate and stalled for time to whip up an anti-Communist publicity campaign. Then they arrested radicals on the strike committee. Moderates trained or influenced by the U.S.-sponsored ORIT (Inter-American Regional Organization of Labor—see Overview and Introduction to Part One) stepped in and signed the final strike settlement. The agreement allowed the banana firms to mechanize and lay off thousands of workers with impunity.

The strike frightened the government sufficiently to agree to the signing of a military treaty with the United States. The 1954 treaty gave the Americans the right to conduct military maneuvers on Honduran soil and provided them access to Honduran raw and semiprocessed materials in cases of deficiencies in U.S. sources. The treaty became the "legal" grounds for the stationing of U.S. troops in Honduras in the 1980s.

In spite of these unforeseen consequences, the strikers succeeded in winning legal recognition of their unions. Next to revolutionary Nicaragua, Honduras had the highest percentage of organized rural and urban workers in Central America in the late 1980s.

The strongest labor organization—the CTH (Honduran Confederation of Workers, founded in 1964)—had its roots in the conservative union leadership that emerged during and after the 1954 strike. The powerful CTH included the ANACH (National Association of Honduran Peasants, founded in 1962). Its leaders, many U.S.-trained by ORIT and after 1962 by the AIFLD (American Institute for Free Labor Development), served employers by moderating members' demands. They were coopted by the infusion of U.S. aid, as well as by political patronage payoffs. As a UFCO employee noted in 1957, "After the strike, the AFL–CIO, the U.S. Embassy, and ORIT offered us scholarships to 'study in Puerto Rico' . . . upon their return, these scholarship students were placed very 'democratically' as union leaders."

The government responded to labor unrest with both military repression and agrarian reforms (1962, 1972, 1975). Since half of the nation's land was state-owned or village communal property, these reforms barely touched big landowners.

Most peasants who benefited were organized in 1970 into production and service cooperatives—the FECORAH (Federation of Agrarian Reform Cooperatives). Producing for the export market, they became dependent on state or private loans and marketing facilities controlled by big growers. They took the risks of bad weather and did all the work while agribusiness scooped up more profits from increased exports (mainly bananas, coffee, and beef, but also cotton, sugar, tobacco, and vegetables for the U.S. winter market). In order to pay the interest on foreign loans originally taken out to modernize export agriculture, the government encouraged farmers to produce more for the foreign market instead of food for Hondurans.

While tempering peasant unrest, the agrarian reform did not benefit more than one-tenth of rural Hondurans. Four-fifths of them still suffered malnutrition and lived without electricity in thatched huts with dirt floors. Some 60 percent remained landless or land poor. Children with bloated bellies stumbled across parched hillsides scratching for edible berries or cactuses. Big farms dominated, and a few giants among them still owned half of the land. In the west, cattle grazing for the export market took the place of the cultivation of basic grains.

The humiliating defeat suffered by Honduras during the brief futbol war with El Salvador in 1969 (see chapter 3) destabilized its politics. The Central American Common Market collapsed, leaving Honduras with a $20 million trade deficit. A 1971–1972 national unity government supported by Liberals and Nationals tried to reclaim national honor. The patchwork "unity" ended with the killing of seven peasants at La Talanquera in 1972.

General Oswaldo López Arellano, who had ruled from 1965 to 1971, seized power in November. He nationalized the timber industry and announced more land handouts. But the 1975 "Bananagate" scandal undid his administration. United Brands (formerly UFCO) was caught giving a $1.25 million bribe to the finance minister. A year later a U.S. SEC investigation revealed that Castle & Cooke (Standard Fruit) had paid $1.2 million to foreign government officials "for security purposes" such as "during an unruly labor strike."

Matters deteriorated further under the notoriously corrupt reign of a military clique headed by Colonel Juan Alberto Melgar Castro (1975–1978). Soon after taking power, the colonel's soldiers and local landowners killed fifteen peasant demonstrators and two priests at Los Horcones.

Then, in 1977 Lt. Col. Gustavo Alvarez, who was on the payroll of Castle & Cooke, used his troops to smash the Isletas cooperative, founded two years earlier by laid-off Standard Fruit workers. One coop member had boasted: "We wanted to show that we didn't need the companies to cultivate bananas—and that's what we did." By the end of the 1970s most of the military high command, including Castle & Cooke's Alvarez, were millionaires.

Meanwhile, U.S.-based corporations like Alcoa, AMAX, Colgate Palmolive, Del Monte (R. J. Reynolds), ITT, Phelps Dodge, Sterling Drugs, and Texaco moved in and enjoyed profit rates on a par with those of the recently diversified banana giants United Brands and Castle & Cooke. By the early 1980s U.S.-based TNCs controlled 88 percent of the nation's twenty largest firms.

In the free-trade zone outside the industrial center of San Pedro Sula a typical low-wage assembly plant owned by the Worth Sports Company was set up. Rows of women sat deftly sewing softballs—a fifth of the world's supply.

After enjoying an agreed-upon five years of tax exemption, Texaco refused to pay taxes. The government could not enforce even its lenient regulations. When it protested in 1981, Texaco closed the nation's only oil refinery.

A small Honduran bourgeoisie became junior partners of foreign investors. There also grew up a powerful mercantile group of traders and financiers, known as "turcos" because of their Middle East lineage. But Honduras still remained Central America's least industrialized nation, and neither the nascent bourgeoisie nor the landed oligarchs could hold a candle to the military's club of millionaires or their U.S. partners.

By the early 1980s a worker earning the legal minimum wage still received less than $15 a week, the second lowest in the Caribbean Basin (after Haiti). The U.S.-trained leadership of organized labor's CTH welcomed U.S. troops. These circumstances contributed to a nationalist backlash and the renewal of Communist influence among railway and other workers in the banana enclave.

In the 1970s and 1980s disgruntled workers had already begun to rebel against their "sellout" leaders. They joined organizations like the CGT (General Congress of Workers, founded by Christian Democrats in 1970), the UNC (National Union of Peasants, formed by Christian Democrats in 1970), and the FUTH (United Federation of Workers of Honduras, formed in 1981 by Communists). Even the progovernment ANACH and the smaller FECORAH joined a national unity organization of peasants organized by Christian Democrats and leftists. Hondurans were testing the waters of the *new politics* of broad alliances uniting Christians and Marxists (see Overview).

This gave strength to a sharp escalation in peasant land grabs in the 1980s. The ANACH and FECORAH bowed out of the peasant alliance in 1985, charging leftist "manipulation." The alliance was renamed the CNTC (National Congress of Rural Workers), but its original membership had been halved. Similarly, the Christian Democrats' UNC split between a rightist group and a leftist group. A partial unity was reestablished when the UNC, CGT, and FUTH later issued a joint call for the expulsion of U.S. troops.

Organized labor's factional difficulties spilled over into the two-party system, making it easier for the military to control the situation. Majorities in both parties, but especially the Nationals, curried favor with the military to assure stability in the work force and to have better access to state resources, including the frequent payoffs from corrupt officials and foreign investors. This proved an easier avenue of wealth for politicians and the elite families they represented than the risk of introducing new crops or industries.

Thus neither modernization nor democratization noticeably improved the lives of the general populace. But the U.S.-trained and "professionalized" military became powerful and prosperous beyond its wildest dreams. In 1952 the Francisco Morazán Military Academy, an officer-training school under the direction of U.S. officers, was inaugurated. The 1957 Constitution made the military independent of any elected government and gave the head of the armed forces the right to disobey presidential orders he considered unconstitutional. More than two thousand military personnel received U.S. training during the 1970s. Honduran army officers consolidated their power by forming alliances with other groups besides the landed elites, such as peasant and labor confederations or budding industrialists. The officers grew astute at striking a deal with a powerful foreign government or a big foreign investor. The elites followed suit. It was only a matter of time before Honduras would be, in the words of indignant nationalists, "a nation for sale," or, by the mid-1980s, a "captive nation."

U.S. Reoccupation and Nationalism: The 1980s and 1990s

Once again, the United States was the "captor" and anticommunism the ideological rationale. The Nicaraguan Revolution of 1979 alerted Washington to the consequences of social unrest and agitation for democracy shaking Central America, a trend increasingly evident in Honduras. U.S. aid to the military junta governing the country after the 1978 overthrow of the corrupt Melgar Castro regime was quickly tied to elections, a façade of civilian democracy.

The elections-aid trade-off started during the Carter administration, which in April of 1980 sold $3.5 million worth of arms and leased ten Huey helicopters to the Honduran military. It also dispatched Green Berets to train Honduran troops in border security operations. The Carter government also got Honduras and El Salvador to sign a peace treaty resolving the border dispute left over from the 1969 war. Salvadoran soldiers were given the right to make sweeps into Honduran camps where Salvadoran refugees had fled. The Honduran military joined forces with the Salvadoran army to carry out numerous massacres of fleeing refugees, including the Sumpul River massacre of 1980 and the Lempa River one of 1981 (see chapter 3).

So it was that in 1981 there occurred the first direct elections for president and congress since 1957. The two major contending parties were the same reactionary ones that had dominated the scene for most of the century. Five years later, after another round of elections, one civilian president passed the sash to another for the first time in five decades. Both were Liberals, a fact attributed by some to public dissatisfaction with military rule—because traditionally the Nationals had been popularly identified with the generals.

Actually, the Nationals campaigned on an antimilitary platform in 1985 and claimed they had won the close election. Outgoing President Roberto Suazo Córdova (1982–1986) had provoked a constitutional crisis earlier that year when he arbitrarily arrested the head of the Supreme Court and four other justices appointed by the national assembly. This crisis had been overcome by the military's intervention, but it led to the formation of an unprecedented parliamentary alliance named CODECO (Democratic and Constitutional Coordinator) that linked the unions, the Christian Democrats, and factions of the National party. The broad alliances of the new politics were getting even wider. By then, however, everyone knew that the actual power in Honduras was the military, with the Pentagon firmly behind it.

Soon after taking office in 1982, President Suazo Córdova approved an augmented U.S. aid program and the consolidation of a centralized military command structure reaching from the COSUFA (Armed Forces' Superior Council) to the American Embassy. A group of seven COSUFA officers known as "the iron circle" chose Suazo's (and Castle & Cooke's) close friend, Colonel Gustavo Alvarez, as commander-in-chief. Alvarez had the strong endorsement of the CIA and the new Reagan administration in Washington. He had been trained in counterinsurgency at Fort Benning, Georgia, and the School of the Americas in Panama and had learned police operations in Washington under the later discredited AID-sponsored OPS (Office of Public Safety) program (see Overview). It was Alvarez who had been paid by Castle & Cook to use his troops to dismantle the Isletas banana cooperative in 1977; he also had ordered a police attack on striking workers at the Bemis Handal textile factory in San Pedro Sula in 1979.

As head of Public Security forces in 1980, Colonel Alvarez controlled the secret police (DNI). With CIA support, he organized a new army intelligence unit known as Battalion 316. An inveterate anti-Communist, he worked closely with Argentine military advisers brought into Honduras to help train Nicaragua's contras. He was a personal friend of General Videla (who oversaw the 1976–1979 dirty war against civilians in Argentina) and an admirer of Chile's dictator General Pinochet (see chapters 17 and 18). In February 1982, at a time when the Reagan administration was pledging a 50 percent increase in military aid to Honduras, four clandestine cemeteries were discovered— confirming widespread charges of death-squad or military operations against leftists. One such death squad was MACHO (Honduran Anti-Communist movement). Alvarez was known to be close to such groups. In January 1983, Alvarez became president of a right-wing pressure group, APROH (Association for the Progress of Honduras), which included conservative representatives of big business, the landed elites, and organized labor's CTH and

ANACH. Alvarez signed a secret agreement setting up the CREM regional military training center at Puerto Castilla, a base for U.S. training of Salvadoran and Honduran troops to combat unrest. Encouraged by his Argentine advisers and his friends in the Unification Church (the "Moonies"), Alvarez prepared to invade Nicaragua but was prevented from doing so by U.S. pressure. In September 1983, he established the CIE (Center for Emergency Information), ordering the Honduran people to inform the organization "about any attitude which they consider suspicious and that concerns security."

On March 31, 1984, Alvarez's attempts to impose his control totally on the military command triggered his removal by a coup d'état by disgruntled officers. U.S. Ambassador John D. Negroponte characterized his deposed clique, which had embezzled over $30 million of public funds, as an "open book of corruption." APROH was disbanded, and the new head of the armed forces, General Walter López Reyes, closed down the CREM in June 1985. According to reports by the U.S. GAO, both Alvarez and López Reyes received substantial CIA funds. Alvarez owned a half million dollar home.

The Reagan administration's investments in military and economic aid to Honduras dwarfed those of the Carter team. By 1982 the U.S. diplomatic mission in Tegucigalpa was one of the largest in Latin America. AID and AIFLD also had established big offices and staffs there. The U.S.-sponsored contra war against Nicaragua swung into high gear, with Honduras as the major command post. A protocol to the 1954 treaty, in effect long before it was approved by the Honduran legislature in 1986, provided for Honduran jurisdiction over U.S. troops, thereby tacitly accepting a permanent U.S. military presence. In exchange, U.S. aid dollars flowed in, totaling $230 million in 1984 alone. At least one-third of it was military aid. In 1985, a special waiver allowed Honduras to receive U.S. aid for its police.

During the alleged Nicaraguan invasion of Honduras on the eve of the U.S. House of Representatives vote on contra aid in the spring of 1986, the Honduran president chatted with Nicaragua's President Ortega by phone and then went to the beach. The Nicaraguan incursions during the mid-1980s were in fact frequent. Hondurans and most of the world understood them to be defensive in nature. Nicaraguan soldiers were chasing contras back into Honduran camps. Honduran officials later stated that they were pressured by the Reagan administration to go along with the invasion story so that the U.S. Congress might be persuaded to pass the $100 million contra aid package. A larger Nicaraguan military sweep into Honduras early the following fall evoked no U.S. protest and little media coverage. Then, when the "Iran-contragate" scandal broke (see Introduction to Part One), the "Nicaraguan invasion" scenario was replayed and U.S. helicopters ferried Honduran troops into action. Honduran planes bombed two Nicaraguan towns.

U.S. policy in Honduras evoked sharp debate. The debate in the United

States pitted national security hardliners and the radical Right against human rights advocates, legal-minded moderates, and the anti-interventionist movement. Hardliners said that the U.S. troop presence in Honduras kept pressure on the Sandinistas to negotiate with the contras and showed allies in the region that they would not be "abandoned to Marxists." A diminished U.S. presence, they asserted, would allow the Sandinistas to consolidate their power and act with a free hand in the region. Critics of this position pointed to the illegality and questionable morality of U.S. intervention in Honduras and Nicaragua and to the stepped-up human rights violations and growing anti-Americanism in the region, suggesting that U.S. policy might produce more enemies than friends and thereby undermine national security. This was partially evidenced in April 1988 when anti-U.S. demonstrations shook Tegucigalpa. A better alternative, critics suggested, might be to stop supporting dictatorships and outdated oligarchies and start working with moderate and even revolutionary forces gaining ascendancy in Central America.

The presence of U.S. military units and 15,000 contras on Honduran soil created a crisis of conscience for Honduran intellectuals. A few began to speak out. Very few worried about "Communist aggression from Nicaragua." If the Contadora peace treaty took effect, Honduras's 21,000-man army, whose commanding officers had long been helping deliver supplies to the well-armed contras, would have to expel or disarm the contras—hardly an easy task. This concern reached into the halls of congress in late 1986, where National party congressman Nicolás Cruz Torres, although opposed by the party leadership, drafted a motion to expel the contras within ten days.

There were additional reasons for alarm. The contras, with the Honduran military's cooperation, had chased thousands of Hondurans from their homes along the border. The forced recruitment of Miskito Indians was provoking a nationalist response among that long-oppressed minority. To make matters even worse, in 1985 the AMAX subsidiary Rosario Resources laid off 120 union employees involved in silver, lead, and zinc mining, and replaced many of them with Nicaraguan contras. That same year the military was forced to exonerate itself by announcing that the contras were involved in the disappearance of at least eighteen Hondurans.

There was also fear that the Honduran military, under U.S. tutelage, was becoming more savage. In 1985, for instance, Honduran soldiers swept through refugee camps looking for Salvadoran guerrillas, killing and brutalizing as they went. Then, more disappeared people began turning up as mutilated corpses, including a former officer and critic of close U.S.-Honduran ties.

In February 1986, this concern deepened when two U.S. government officials and a Honduran military officer acknowledged that the CIA had "aided Honduran security forces that it knew were responsible for having killed a number of people they detained for political reasons between 1981 and 1984." These officials also noted that the CIA knew about many of the two hundred disappearances of politically suspect people (many of them labor unionists) but "looked the other way." In October 1986, the United States sold eight F-5-3 offensive fighter jets to Honduras This added to the superiority of the region's most powerful air force and laid a basis for Nicaragua to seek Soviet MIGs to defend itself.

A June 5, 1988, story in the *New York Times Magazine* reported CIA connections to the torture and murder of Hondurans and other Latin Americans through its cooperation with a Honduran Army death squad. A mid-1986 public opinion poll showed 83 percent of Hondurans opposed U.S. troop presence. The government joined other Central American nations in refusing permission for U.S. advisers to accompany the $100 million aid package approved by Congress for the contras. The United States began training some of the contras on nearby offshore locations.

Honduras also faced World Court proceedings brought against it by Nicaragua for its role in the contra invasion. Although respecting the Court's jurisdiction with regard to its border dispute with El Salvador and a 1960 Court decision in its favor concerning the Nicaraguan-Honduran border, Honduras, like the United States, refused to recognize the Court's jurisdiction in the case of the new dispute with Nicaragua.

Further embarrassing Honduran officials were revelations around the Iran-contragate scandal. Lieutenant Colonel Oliver L. North and his operatives, for instance, were reportedly linked to a 1984 assassination plot on President Suazo, funded by the selling of more than $10 million worth of cocaine in the United States.

The 1980s' first deployments of U.S. troops in Honduras had provoked the formation of guerrilla units pledged to throw them out. Most guerrillas united in 1983 to form the DNU (United National directorate), ceasing military action in order to build a larger social base among the people.

One of the guerrilla martyrs was a fifty-eight-year-old Jesuit priest from St. Louis, Missouri, Father James Carney, who died in August or September 1983. Father Carney's death was cloaked in mystery, but *The Nation* published an article in August 1984, stating that "there are strong suggestions that U.S. intelligence and military personnel took part in the Honduran combat operations and may have been present when Father Carney died." A U.S.-trained Honduran interrogator in an army death squad later said he had interrogated Carney.

The four main guerrilla organizations were the Marxist-Leninist FMLH (Morazanist front for the Liberation of Honduras); the Maoist-oriented FRP Lorenzo Zelaya (Lorenzo Zelaya Popular Revolutionary forces); the MPLC (Cinchonero People's Liberation movement, a breakaway group of the Honduran Communist party); and the PRTCH (Revolutionary Workers party of Central America, led by dissident Christian Democrats of the Socialist party of Honduras and linked with similar groups in El Salvador and Guatemala). In 1985 the MPLC called for the creation of a united guerrilla front to confront the U.S. military presence.

In the late 1980s the political situation in Honduras was as tense as ever. The government of President Azcona was reluctant to carry out the "reconciliation with amnesty" process called for by the Arias Peace Plan (see Introduction to Part One). In spite of more than $600 million in U.S. economic assistance since 1980 and Pentagon plans to spend another $45 million on new bases by 1990, Honduras's economy was growing at only 3 percent a year, not enough to make up for a per-capita GNP drop of 12 percent from 1980 to 1983. Unable to meet its debt payments, the government had agreed to IMF guidelines for economic austerity in 1981, but renewed strikes and the threat of a general strike had caused it to hold back implementation. The relative strength of labor unions still kept private investment sluggish, despite Central America's lowest inflation rates.

In an unusual move, the Catholic Church lent its support to the two main human rights groups, CODEH (Committee for the Defense of Human Rights in Honduras) and COFADEH (Honduran Committee of the Families of Disappeared Persons). Chief of the Honduran armed forces General Humberto Regalado Hernández vowed to hunt down every Honduran involved in "a Communist plot against Honduras," based on three things: "Discrediting the contras; forcing the withdrawal of North American troops; and denunciations about disappearances." In January 1988, several political assassinations occurred, taking the lives of one CODEH leader and one junior officer about to testify against his commanders at a human rights hearing.

President Reagan once described Honduras as "'an oasis of peace." But in the late 1980s the nation was on the brink of war. Those Hondurans who could afford it fled. They sometimes found themselves as unsafe in the United States as at home. Typical disasters included being stopped in Texas and thrown into detention camps and the famous New York City social club fire that killed more than a hundred people, many of them Hondurans.

In the early 1990s, Honduras withdrew from the brink of war because of the success of the Arias peace plan, the Sandinista 1990 electoral defeat, and the amnestied contras' return to Nicaragua (see chapter 5 and Documents). Resolution of the border conflict with El Salvador soon followed (see Introduction to Part One). The National party was allowed back into power when, bolstered by its flirtation with the "new politics," its candidate Rafael Leonardo Callejas won the 1989 elections with 50.97 percent of the vote. Outgoing President José Azcona Hoyo (1986–1990) acknowledged unsolved human rights cases that included the assassination of popular leaders.

Incoming President Callejas refused to carry out any reform of the military, however. According to a 1993 U.S. State Department report, the military's human rights abuses continued as the military acted with impunity. Among more recent victims of disappearances and assassinations were journalists and businessmen. Implicated in some of the killings were former members of the intelligence Battalion 316, set up during the contra war, supposedly disbanded because of its poor human rights record, but presumed to be active still as part of army "counterintelligence." When in early 1993 the public demanded disbanding the DNI (secret police), troops briefly occupied the streets of Tegucigalpa and San Pedro Sula.

President Callejas carried out a tough neo-liberal style economic program that reduced inflation, brought some economic growth (2.2 percent in 1992), but worsened social conditions. One cost of poverty involved an open black market in babies for adoption in the United States that included numerous _casas de engorde_ ("fattening houses"—private homes where children sold by impoverished mothers were taken until adoptive parents were found). Evidence of trafficking in human organs for medical transplant also surfaced.

In 1992, Congress approved the Agricultural Modernization Act. It modified Honduras's agrarian reform to allow United Brand (Chiquita Bananas) and Castle & Cooke to buy out the cooperatives. Workers of the United Brands subsidiary Tela Railroad Company staged eight strikes in the early 1990s. A 1993 strike delayed the closing of four banana plantations hard hit by the EEC's decision to restrict imports of Latin American bananas (see Introduction to Part One and Conclusion).

With the population (5.5 million) growing restless, Callejas introduced a social spending program in 1993 geared to win support for the Nationals in the November 1993 presidential elections. The Inter-American Development Bank approved a $500 million loan aimed mainly at social projects. But it was too late, and the Nationals' Oswaldo Ramos Soto, an active "Moonie" close to more conservative elements of the military, lost by eleven percentage points to the Liberals' Carlos Roberto Reina, a human rights lawyer.

One of President Reina's first acts was to declare that the land claims of five thousand Indians who marched two hundred miles from western Honduras to Tegucigalpa were "just." The military, preoccupied with its new economic role in several privatized companies and not yet reunified, watched carefully to see if the "new politics" would need more of its "discipline" beyond the crimes it already had committed.

Selected Bibliography

Acker, Alison. *Honduras: The Making of a Banana Republic*. Boston, MA: South End Press, 1992.

Carney, Father J. Guadalupe. *To Be a Revolutionary*. New York: Harper & Row, 1984. By martyred guerrilla priest from St. Louis, MO.

Latin America Bureau. *Honduras State for Sale*. London: Latin America Bureau, 1985. Well-researched short history.

Morris, James A. *Honduras: Caudillo Politics and Military Rulers*. Boulder, CO: Westview, 1984.

Peckenham, Nancy, and Annie Street (eds.). *Honduras: Portrait of a Captive Nation*. New York: Praeger, 1985. Presents opposing views on controversial issues and many primary documents.

Shepherd, Philip L. *The Honduran Crisis and U.S. Economic Assistance*. Boulder, CO: Westview, 1988. Sees U.S. AID as a "shadow government."

Wheaton, Philip E. *Inside Honduras: Regional Counterinsurgency Base*. Washington, DC: EPICA, 1981.

Films

Elvia: The Fight for Land and Liberty. 1989. 27 minutes. Color video documentary from Food First Books about landless poor in midst of U.S. military intervention.

Honduras: America's New Policeman. 1982. 28 minutes. Color film and video by Yvan Patry with interviews of Gen. Alvarez and a guerrilla spokesperson.

HONDURAS

Rio Coco

Puerto
Cabezas
•

NICARAGUA

*Gulf of
Fonseca*

•Léon

*Lago de
Managua*

Managua
⊛

Granada•

Bluefields
•

*Lago
de
Nicaragua*

*PACIFIC
OCEAN*

*CARIBBEAN
SEA*

COSTA RICA

0   75 Mi.

0   100 Km.

N

Nicaragua 5

Our cause will triumph because it is justice and love.—*Sandino*

Those three days were like three years to me—three years of being raped by those animals. . . . Somoza's National Guard thought that by torturing people they would force us to abandon the struggle. It wasn't true. When they burned houses—often with children inside—we fought all the harder.—*Amanda Piñeda, peasant mother of nine (four still alive)*

Marx helps us understand the connection between liberal philosophy, capitalism, and imperialism, and the connection between liberal thought, capitalism, and racism. . . . No one has influenced my own life more than Martin Luther King.—*Father Miguel d'Escoto, Sandinista Minister of Foreign Affairs*

No one is going to make war on us from Central America. There is something genuinely zany in thinking about the area in those terms.—*McGeorge Bundy (President Kennedy's former National Security Advisor)*

I am a contra.—*President Ronald Reagan, 1985*

On July 19, 1979, the first rays of sun touched the tips of high weeds that covered the vacant lots of downtown Managua, the nation's capital, destroyed by the 1972 earthquake. Of all the elegant government and private buildings that had once graced the now deserted area, only the Bank of America building remained. Scrub grass marked the crevices of the cracked pavement of the empty streets. Vultures cruised overhead, their black wings mottled by remnants of smoke curling from the northern industrial zone bombed by planes of the dictator Anastasio ("Tachito") Somoza Debayle before his flight to Miami three days earlier. An occasional crackle of gunfire could be heard from behind the hill above the Hotel Intercontinental, where the dictator's notorious underground armed garrison, "the bunker," ruled the landscape.

That day would be long remembered. People poured out of their homes and ran through the streets, dancing and shouting *"Llegan los muchachos!"* ("The kids are coming!") Men, women, and youngsters of the guerrilla army of the Sandinista Front of National Liberation (FSLN) entered the capital. Some sat atop tanks they had captured from the National Guard; others rode double on horses and mules, or crammed into backfiring pickup trucks; most walked, trailed by barefoot street urchins and smiling toddlers high-stepping in mock military formation.

It was the day a popular revolution took power in Nicaragua, ending nearly half a century of dictatorship by the Somoza family, a dynasty installed after a twenty-one year military occupation by U.S. Marines. Catholic priests, anti-Communist moderates, and atheistic Marxists headed the new revolutionary government.

In the months that followed the government appealed for U.S. aid to help rebuild bombed-out factories, warehouses, and bridges. But the country was soon invaded by former "Somocista" Guardsmen known as "contras," armed and trained by the CIA and Pentagon.

The Sandinista anthem excoriated "the Yankees" as the enemy. Yet the government, proclaiming a foreign policy of nonalignment, acknowledged it would forever remain in "the U.S. sphere of influence." It was prompt in its payments of the large debt it had inherited from the Somoza regime (except the portion owed Israel and Argentina, which had supplied arms to the National Guard). In the next several years, Nicaragua received more than 150,000 visitors from the United States. Some were known as "internationalists" because they helped with the coffee harvests and other tasks.

What did all the controversies swirling around their country mean concretely for Nicaraguans? Were the contras freedom fighters or murderers—or a mix of the two? What was the impact of what the World Court defined as the U.S. illegal and unjust war against Nicaragua (see Overview and Documents)? Was the new political system introduced by the Sandinistas, in President Reagan's words, a "totalitarian dungeon," fundamentally "Marxist" and antithetical to "Christianity"? Or was it, in the words of the 1987 Nicaraguan Constitution (passed in the name of all Nicaraguans, including "Christians who out of their faith in God are committed to the struggle for the liberation of the oppressed") a democracy characterized by "political pluralism" and a "mixed economy"?

Social Classes and Nationalism: Blaming Uncle Sam

Nicaragua's 4 million citizens populate a lush landscape rich in timber and minerals. Roughly the size of Florida, Nicaragua has potential hydroelectric power from its many northern rivers and geothermal energy from its southern volcanoes. It has a potential interoceanic canal route—cause of frequent foreign interventions—following the San Juan River along the southern border with Costa Rica and passing through two large lakes. The smaller of the two lakes, Lake Managua, is dead, killed by 40 tons of mercury dumped into it between 1968 and 1981 by the caustic soda chemical plant of a U.S. corporation, Pennwalt.

Nicaraguans share with Haitians, Bolivians, and Hondurans the dubious distinction of being the Western Hemisphere's poorest people. In 1992 the average Nicaraguan's life expectancy at birth was under fifty years, 80 percent of children suffered malnutrition, and cholera cases were reported.

For most Nicaraguans national independence and economic oppression are vital political issues. After one hundred fifty years of formal political independence, during which they experienced repeated U.S. military interventions (see Box 5.1), Nicaraguans were left with dead rivers and lakes, stripped forests, and the stark contrasts of extreme wealth and poverty. Most blamed the country's ills on the United States—and the forty-six-year reign of the Somoza family's clique, "the Somocistas."

Box 5.1: Nicaragua, a Century and a Half of U.S. Domination

1837　Vanderbilt issues plan for Accessory Transit Company (ATC) to build a canal.

1850　Clayton-Bulwer Treaty obligates Britain and United States not to hold exclusive control over a canal route.

1854　To avenge attacks by angry protestors on a U.S. diplomatic official in Greytown (as the British had renamed San Juan del Norte), U.S. warship _Cayne_ shells and destroys the Atlantic coast port city.

1855　Vanderbilt's ATC obtains concession to build a canal. William Walker, a 100-pound proslavery Tennessee filibuster, fresh from his 1853 invasion of Mexico's Baja California, invades Nicaragua with fifty-six men and proposes an empire to include Central America, Mexico, and Cuba. A celebrated hero in the United States, he is a despised villain in Nicaragua.

1856　Walker has himself "elected" president of Nicaragua, makes English the official language, reinstitutes slavery (outlawed since 1823), and cancels Vanderbilt's canal concession. Vanderbilt, together with the British, finances invasion by Central American troops opposed to Walker. Defeated, Walker escapes in an American ship.

1857　Walker returns to seize the port of San Juan del Norte, only to be driven out by the British.

1860　Walker invades Bay Islands (Honduras) and declares himself president of El Salvador, Honduras, and Nicaragua. He is captured by the British and executed.

1867　Violating the 1850 treaty with Britain, United States accepts exclusive rights of transit across Nicaragua.

1907　Responding to Liberal president Zelaya's threats to create a united Central American federation, United States imposes on Central American nations "peace and friendship" treaties providing for nonrecognition of governments established by revolution or coup d'état.

1909–1910　Sending its warships, troops, and arms to the Atlantic coast city of Bluefields, United States backs a successful insurrection against the Zelaya government, which had started negotiating with Germany and Japan for a canal and had taken out a big loan from a London syndicate. Zelaya is overthrown, and U.S. bankers Brown Brothers and Seligman replace the British as Nicaragua's creditors.

(_Continued on next page_)

Box 5.1 *(Continued)*

1912   U.S. Marines crush rebel forces trying to overthrow a corrupt Conservative government and remain until 1925.

1912–1933   Nicaragua is a virtual U.S. protectorate. A U.S. representative, Irving A. Lindberg, collects its customs revenues and serves as "American High Commissioner." Marines guarantee "law and order."

1916   Bryan-Chamorro Treaty cedes United States "in perpetuity and for all time" ownership rights to a proposed canal.

1925   U.S. Marines withdraw after thirteen-year occupation.

1926   Several thousand U.S. Marines return to protect dictatorship of Conservative president Díaz and oversee creation of a military police force, the National Guard, commanded by U.S. officers until 1933 when it is turned over to General Anastasio Somoza García. Marines unable to defeat guerrilla army of Sandino.

1933   U.S. Marines withdraw, leaving Somoza in power. Somoza has Sandino assassinated.

1953   Bilateral treaty for U.S. Army Mission in Managua to renew U.S. command and training of National Guard (except for Nicaraguan commander, a Somoza).

1956   U.S.-Nicaragua Treaty of Friendship is signed.

1961   Puerto Cabezas used as launching pad by CIA for the "Bay of Pigs" invasion of Cuba.

1976   In operation "Aguila Z" some three thousand Salvadoran and Guatemalan soldiers join U.S. Rangers and Nicaraguan National Guard in Jalapa mountains searching for Sandinista guerrillas.

1980s   United States backs the contra war and involves U.S. helicopter, warship, and special forces in combat.

1990   U.S.-funded Violeta Chamorro wins presidential election.

1992   Bush administration withholds aid in attempt to eliminate Sandinistas from alleged power-sharing with Chamorro.

What distinguishes Nicaragua from the rest of Latin America (even Cuba or Mexico) is the length and intensity of U.S. domination. Since the 1840s' California Gold Rush and Commodore Cornelius Vanderbilt's efforts to secure an interoceanic passage, Nicaraguans rarely have experienced a long period without the presence of U.S. troops and mercenaries—or gunboats offshore (see Box 5.1).

Nicaragua's "army," the National Guard, differed from those of the rest of Latin America. It was not a force composed of recruits. Rather, it was a praetorian guard, subject to foreign orders, made up of specially trained men with loyalty only to Somoza and his foreign sponsors—a loyalty many of its members were to prove after 1979 by joining the contras.

Nicaragua's long history of foreign subjugation and of frustrated negotiated truces eventually generated a fervent nationalism that spread across social classes. By the late 1970s it affected even wealthy elites who joined the revolutionary camp.

Nicaragua's social classes never achieved the cohesiveness or strength observable in other Latin American countries. Most people were family and subsistence farmers or landless peasants, who, besides farming, labored in whatever new areas of mineral, timber, or agricultural production were developed for export. A seemingly endless agricultural frontier made for residential impermanence. Neither a full-fledged peasantry nor an urban or rural working class ever fully took shape.

People were divided between rich and poor, light skinned and dark skinned. Weak, regionally based elites competed for control of the central government and the country's labor supply and natural resources. They raised Latin America's usual banners of liberalism and conservatism, pitting anticlericals against the Church and those advocating local rule against those seeking a stronger central government. The wealthy León-based Liberals (Zelaya and other families) and Granada-based Conservatives (Chamorro and other families) pressed "their" peasants into service to fight their civil wars. Both sides often sought outside support.

The majority of Nicaraguans reacted to the armed repression of social protest by the elites and their foreign sponsors with growing resentment. Economic hardship and outside interference thus fueled a popular social rebelliousness robed in the banner of nationalism.

Historical Background

The pattern of foreign domination started with the arrival of the Spaniards during the 1520s, when the conquistadores Gil González de Avila and Francisco Hernández de Córdoba (for whom the Nicaraguan monetary unit is named) marched up from Panama in quest of gold. The main Indian chieftain, Nicarao, after whom the country received its name, agreed to negotiate with the invaders. This was a costly mistake Nicaraguans were to make more than once in their history. The Spaniards promptly laid claim to all their land and labor.

The poorly armed followers of less cooperative Indian leaders, national heros like Diriangen, were quickly put to the sword. In 1542 Bishop Bartolomé de las Casas characterized the Spaniards' depopulation of Nicaragua as "so much evil, butchery, cruelty, and injustice that no human tongue would be able to describe it."

In 1625 the British conquered the isolated Atlantic coast of Nicaragua and Honduras and colonized it as a British protectorate. To secure their control, the British armed the Miskitu Indians as a kind of constabulary, sending some off to Jamaica to subdue slave revolts there.

These developments, along with the intervening mountains and rain forests, assured the linguistic separation of the peoples of Nicaragua's Atlantic coast, where English, Creole, and Caribbean-style Indian and African dialects still prevail. In the more populous Pacific, central, and western sections, Spanish and remnants of Nahua, Aztec, and Maya Indian dialects are spoken. The arrival of North American timber, mining, and fruit companies consolidated the separation of the Atlantic region from the Pacific. Even the dominant churches are different—the Moravian Church establishing its influence over the Atlantic coast's Creoles and Miskitus late in the nineteenth century.

From conquest, colonization, and intermarriage came both the cultural gaps separating the Pacific and Atlantic regions and the ethnic composition of today's Nicaragua. Nationally, mestizos compose an overwhelming majority (80 percent). Less than 5 percent of the population is ethnic minorities, all on the Atlantic coast.

Some 67,000 Miskitu Amerindians are the largest minority. Along with 5,000 Sumu Amerindians, the Miskitus are concentrated in the northeast of Nicaragua. Creoles, an English-speaking Afro-Caribbean people, are the second largest minority group, numbering 26,000 and concentrated in the southern coastal port of Bluefields. Farther to the south there reside about six hundred Rama Amerindians and fifteen hundred Garifuna, a people of Afro-Amerindian descent.

In their efforts to control Nicaragua foreign powers often focused on the less populated and easily accessible Atlantic coast. Foreign invasions contributed to the collapse of the Central American confederation in 1838 when Nicaragua decided to go it alone as an independent republic.

After the invasions of U.S. adventurer William Walker were put down at a great cost of Nicaraguan lives (1855–1860), Nicaragua's leading Conservative families established a dictatorship that governed for thirty years. Their 1858 Constitution freed the peasants from forced labor. Many Nicaraguans became small family farmers.

Then, in 1877, the Pedro Chamorro government promulgated a law that aimed to take all Indian communal lands and recruit peasant labor to harvest the coffee and cut the mahogany trees to sell in the growing European and U.S. markets. This provoked an uprising by Indian and peasant communities that was crushed in 1881, leaving seven thousand dead.

The dictatorship of Liberal President José Santos Zelaya (1893–1909) differed from the previous Conservative dictatorship by limiting the wealth of the Roman Catholic Church and attempting to modernize the economy and lessen its dependence on the United States. It allowed the Church to continue religious instruction in the public schools, a practice that continues today, but made both Church and Indian lands subject to seizure. It sought to make small farmers dependent on bonuses and loans. Those who defaulted on their loans would lose their land and be forced to join the larger wage work force the elites wanted to create to harvest the coffee. Until the "cotton boom" of the 1950s, coffee accounted for more than half of the nation's exports.

When Zelaya showed signs of allying Nicaragua with Britain, Japan, or Germany, the United States financed and armed his overthrow. From 1909 to 1912 U.S. gunboats and troops became the guarantor of a Conservative, pro-U.S. government that ceded the customs revenues, railroads, and banks to U.S. interests. As Major General Smedley D. Butler of the U.S. Marine Corps later recalled, "I helped purify Nicaragua for the international banking house of Brown Brothers in 1909–1912."

U.S. Marine Occupation and Sandino, 1912–1933

In 1912, a nationalist doctor and teacher named Benjamín Zeledón led a revolt against U.S. control. Again, the Marines invaded. U.S. artillery bombed Zeledón's forces in Masaya, and Zeledón and his three hundred followers were captured. Some had their throats cut, and the rest were shot.

A short, skinny seventeen-year-old watched Zeledón's casket being taken to the cemetery. His name was Augusto César Sandino, and he would grow up to be the leader of an armed struggle to free Nicaragua from U.S. "protection." The son of a wealthy Liberal landowner and an Indian peasant woman who had been the family servant, he was to become the Nicaraguans' "George Washington." He would later fight a prolonged guerrilla war against the Marines in a "lost cause"—and win. His name would join those of Bolívar, Hidalgo, and Martí in the pantheon of Latin American "Liberators."

Sandino, like Cuba's José Martí and Fidel Castro (see chapter 8), started out by working "within the system." His ideology eventually blended currents of liberalism, free masonry, and theosophy with anarchism and communism. On two issues he brooked no compromise—national independence and improving the lot of Nicaragua's peasants. Recent scholarship has shown that Sandino's thinking was far to the left of the "pluralistic, mixed economy" notions espoused by the Sandinistas of the 1980s.

In 1921 Sandino wounded a politician during a dispute. He fled from the police and worked in Honduras and Guatemala for the United Fruit Company as a mechanic's assistant. Later he worked in Mexico for the South Penn Oil Company and as a gasoline sales director for the Huasteca Petroleum Company in Tampico.

From the struggles of the labor unions and the sight of U.S. gunships sent to Tampico in 1924 to guarantee Standard Oil interests, Sandino learned more about "imperialism." He wrote,

> About 1925 I decided everything in Nicaragua had gone sour and that honor had disappeared before the advance, by treachery or force, of Yankee imperialism. . . . if there were one hundred honorable men who loved their country as I did, the absolute sovereignty of our country would be restored.

Sandino went home and found his first "honorable men" among exploited miners in northern Nicaragua. Buying guns with his savings, he armed twenty-nine of them. Then, in 1926, the United States imposed a Conservative president in Nicaragua. A number of Liberals organized an army and allied themselves with Sandino's troops. They obtained arms from the Mexicans.

The Marines, withdrawn from Nicaragua in 1925, returned in 1926 to crush the uprising, pounding the rebels' northwestern stronghold of Chinandega to rubble. U.S. Undersecretary of State Robert Olds proclaimed, "Until now Central America has always understood that governments which we recognise and support stay in power, while those which we do not recognise and support fall—-Nicaragua has become a test case."

The chief of staff of the Liberals' army, José María Moncada, caved in to U.S. pressure to negotiate a compromise. Sandino called him a traitor, proclaiming that "The sovereignty and liberty of a people are not to be discussed but rather to be defended with weapons in hand." In 1927 the American diplomat Henry L. Stimson arranged a political truce that gave Liberals the presidency. The truce called for dismemberment of the Liberal and Conservative armies and the creation of a national guard to be trained, led, and armed by the United States. This is what the Marines had done earlier in the Dominican Republic and Haiti.

Stimson's translator during the 1927 negotiations was a general in Moncada's army, Anastasio Somoza García. The son of a coffee planter, Somoza had graduated from Philadelphia's Pierce School of Business Administration and had worked as a used car dealer in the United States. He had married into the Liberal elite family of Juan Batista Sacasa. Six years later General Somoza, the ex-translator, would become head of the National Guard and Sacasa would become president.

In May 1927 Sandino married a telegraph operator named Blanca Arauz. Refusing countless bribe offers, he kept the armed struggle for national sovereignty alive. Receiving an ultimatum from U.S. Marine Captain G. D. Hatfield to "surrender or else," Sandino replied, "I will not surrender; *patria libre o morir* (a free fatherland or death)." With eight hundred recruits, he attacked the town of Ocotal, where Captain Hatfield's Marines were stationed. U.S. airplanes flew low over the town, bombing and machine-gunning the populace, leaving three hundred dead. Overwhelmed by four thousand Marines, Sandino's forces retreated.

Sandino wrote:

From now on, our enemy won't be the forces of the tyrant Díaz, but the marines of the most powerful empire in history. We will fight against them. We will be ruthlessly killed by bombs dropped from the air, stabbed by foreign bayonets, and shot by modern machine-guns. Nicaragua vencerá [Nicaragua will triumph].

His prophecy came true. In seeking to kill or capture Sandino, known through-out Latin America as "The General of Free Men," U.S. military occupation forces bombed towns, shot and abused prisoners, used "water torture," muti-lated victims' bodies, and created a "concentration program" of civilian "relo-cation camps."

Appalled by what they had been called upon to do, some Marines went over to Sandino's Defensive Army of National Sovereignty. There, they dis-covered a band of youthful guerrillas called the "Choir of Angels," who be-tween battles taught the peasants of the mountainous provinces of Matagalpa, Jinotega, and Nueva Segovia how to read. These provinces later became the main base for the Sandinista Revolution of 1979.

Sandino remained a thorn in the side of U.S. bankers, investors, and troops. He kept attacking their installations in guerrilla-style warfare, winning more and more recruits as he "hit and ran."

Back in the United States the war against Sandino's Nicaragua was un-popular. In response to mass protests in the streets, Congress had to cut off funds. On January 1, 1933, the Americans gave up the fight. By then a huge portion of Nicaraguan territory had come under the control of Sandino's three thousand guerrillas—six times the number of Sandinista guerrillas that later took power in 1979! In the words of American Ambassador Matthew Hanna, Sandino was "as strong as, if not stronger than at any time."

The National Guard was turned over to General Somoza, said to be a lover of Ambassador Hanna's wife. Within twenty-four hours all the Marines were scrambling aboard ships to head for home. Left in the presidency was Sacasa, who promptly signed a peace pact with Sandino that promised land for peasant guerrillas and guaranteed the safety of Sandino and his troops. Sandino left the security of the hills for the insecurity of Managua.

American Ambassador Arthur Bliss Lane held a series of conversations with Somoza and Sandino and assured Sandino that Somoza would not do anything rash. Then, on February 21, 1934, the end came. Shortly after conferring with Ambassador Lane, Somoza ordered Guard troops to detain Sandino's party as it left a dinner at the presidential palace. Sandino and his brother were taken to a nearby airfield. There, a little after 11:00 P.M., machine-gun fire cut down Sandino, his brother, and his two leading generals. First thing next morning, Guard troops seized the Sandinista cooper-ative farm at Guiguili and massacred three hundred unarmed men, women, and children. In a matter of weeks scores of prominent Sandinistas were executed and the movement was crushed. Somoza told his officers, "American Ambassador Arturo Bliss Lane has assured me that the govern-ment in Washington supports and recommends the elimination of Augusto César Sandino."

In 1936 Somoza assumed direct power in a coup against President

Sacasa. The following year he was himself "elected" president. The very name "Sandino" was forever purged from the pages of Nicaraguan school books—but his story has passed down through the generations.

The U.S. government said nothing about the 1936 coup. President Franklin D. Roosevelt said of Somoza in 1936, "He is an S.O.B., but he is our S.O.B."

The Somoza Kleptocracy, 1933–1979

The dynasty of Somoza and his sons was an unusually grisly one. The Somozas' elite army, the EEBI, was made up of young boys trained to torture and dismember. Prominent poet Ernesto Cardenal, a priest who in the 1980s became Minister of Culture, told UNESCO in Paris in April 1982 of how these boys were instructed:

> The trainer would shout:
> "What are you?"
> And they'd shout back in chorus, "Tigers."
> And, "What do tigers eat?"
> "Blood."
> "Whose blood?"
> "The people's."

Like El Salvador's generals of the time (see chapter 3), General Somoza consolidated his power in the 1930s through terror. Twenty thousand peasants, workers, and students perished. Not anxious to kill off the entire work force, Somoza offered the carrot instead of the stick in 1944 by decreeing a progressive labor code in response to labor unrest. That gesture won him the backing of the newly founded Communist party (PSN—Nicaraguan Socialist party). The labor code was never enforced, though, and the word "strike" became as forbidden as the word "Sandino."

On September 21, 1956, worker-poet Rigoberto López pumped four bullets into Somoza, receiving sixty bullets in exchange from the tyrant's bodyguards. A U.S. medical team rushed the bleeding dictator to a hospital in the Panama Canal Zone, where he died on September 29. His eldest son, Luis Somoza Debayle, became president and another son, West Point graduate Anastasio Somoza Debayle (Tachito), took over command of the National Guard. When Luis Somoza died suddenly in 1967, Tachito assumed control of both the presidency and the Guard.

Tachito Somoza knew where his ultimate power lay. As he told the Mexican newspaper *Excelsior* in 1974, "Nicaragua is not a Third World country but a country economically, politically, and militarily dependent on the

United States." By 1979 the United States had trained more Nicaraguan soldiers per capita than any other nation's in the world.

In the 1950s the Somozas made a tenuous peace with Nicaragua's elite families by dividing the ownership of the nation's wealth three ways: the Somoza group, the Bank of Nicaragua group (mostly Liberals in cotton and commerce), and the Bank of America group (mostly Conservatives, cattlemen, merchants, and the traditional oligarchy). Lacking arms or the will to revolt, the out-of-power elites settled for a cut of the economic action and the right to publish a mildly critical "opposition" newspaper, the Conservatives' *La Prensa.*

A journalist writing for the French newspaper *Le Monde* gave the Somozas' "economic development" model a name—"kleptocracy." It rested on thievery not only from working people but also from elites and foreign investors. The Somozas regularly took "their cut" from any private investment or public aid package. The Somoza brothers reportedly raked off one-quarter of Alliance for Progress aid, and Tachito pocketed much of the aid sent for victims of the 1972 earthquake (20,000 dead, 200,000 homeless).

Foreign investment in Nicaragua totaling $180 million, while not large, was strategically placed. U.S. firms were prominent in agriculture, chemicals, and forest and mineral products—all major exports. They also invested in banking, transportation, energy, and packaging sectors closely related to these activities. By 1971 foreign credit accounted for 90 percent of Nicaragua's agricultural production.

By the end of the "long, dark night" (see Overview) of Somocismo, the Somozas' wealth was estimated at just under a billion dollars. It included one-tenth of the nation's cultivable land. Prior to his death in 1967, President Luis Somoza, Tachito's brother, owned the largest slaughterhouse in Central America and six Miami meat-packing plants. In the 1960s his fortune-making from the "cattle boom" made Nicaragua unusual in its having more head of cattle than people.

The Somozas' and foreign capital's hurry to loot Nicaragua produced human displacement and ecological havoc. The 1950s' cotton boom drove food-producing farmers off the fertile Pacific plains into the hills. The subsequent cattle boom stripped 30 percent of the nation's extensive tropical rain forests. More than 60 percent of rural people were left without land. Half the children were undernourished. Nearly one-fifth of "natural" deaths came from polluted water.

Tachito Somoza left the Sandinistas a national foreign debt of $1.5 billion, roughly equal to the annual gross national product (GNP). Half came from loans granted during his regime's final two years, when the dictator needed money to finance his war against an aroused populace. It included a $22.3 million IMF (International Monetary Fund) standby credit granted over the protest of the Sandinistas and most of the elite families two months prior to the government's fall. The Sandinistas found only $3.5 million left in the national treasury. The rest had disappeared. From Miami, Tachito found a plush refuge in fellow dictator Stroessner's Paraguay. There, however, he was assassinated (see chapter 16), causing jubilation in Nicaragua.

From Sandino to the FSLN

Not all of Sandino's soldiers were killed back in 1933. One veteran, Ramón Raudales, his spirits lifted by the news of guerrillas under Fidel Castro gaining ground against Batista in eastern Cuba, led a guerrilla action in October 1958 in the mountains of Jalapa. He was killed, but dozens of uncoordinated guerrilla actions spread across the nation in subsequent years. Many were led by semiliterate peasants and well-educated but disillusioned youth, fired up by the Cuban Revolution.

Using the old black and red flag of Sandino, the FSLN came into being to unite the diverse strands of guerrilla resistance in 1961–1963. Among those arrested after the 1956 assassination of Anastasio Somoza had been two of the ten FSLN founders, Carlos Fonseca Amador (1935–1976) and Tomás Borge. By 1979 Borge was the only FSLN founder still alive. The son of a humble cook, Fonseca was an internationalist who frequently invoked the examples of Sandino, Ché Guevara (see chapters 8 and 15), and the Vietnamese people, swearing "to fight for the redemption of the oppressed and exploited in Nicaragua and the world." He was killed in action in 1976, the same year U.S. Rangers launched operation Aguila Z (see box 5.1). In 1979 an "eternal flame" memorial was set up opposite the main cathedral in Managua to commemorate his life.

During its years of armed struggle the FSLN built ties to people in the mountains, towns, and cities. On December 27, 1974, an FSLN guerrilla unit burst in on a party honoring the American ambassador and grabbed several high-ranking hostages. They obtained the release of fourteen political prisoners and a big ransom, as well as wage hikes for workers and circulation of their statements in the media.

One of the freed prisoners was Daniel José Ortega Saavedra, a Jesuit-educated, Catholic law student and Nicaragua's first democratically elected president (1985-1990). Son of a poor accountant and trader (father) and baker (mother), Ortega had spent most of his teenage and adult life in a tiny jail cell, where torturers had hooded him, broken his ribs, burned him with cigarettes, and almost starved him to death. He had joined the guerrillas at age fourteen and entered his first jail a year later.

In January 1978, *La Prensa* editor Pedro Joaquín Chamorro, husband of Nicaragua's second democratically elected president, Violeta Barrios de

Chamorro, was assassinated, allegedly on the orders of Tachito's son and heir apparent, Anastasio Somoza, Jr. This caused an immediate split between the Somozas and the rest of Nicaragua's elites. A group of prominent business-people, intellectuals, and priests known as "los doce" ("the twelve") de-manded Somoza's resignation. Even the dictator's American wife left him, since he had long ignored her and showered his favors upon a prostitute.

During the last week of February 1978 Indians in Monimbo, Masaya, rose up in arms against the National Guard but were bombed into submission. Spontaneous uprisings spread across the nation. On August 22, 1978, an FSLN unit seized the National Palace when congress was in session and forced the release of Borge and other political prisoners and publication of its program.

This fueled the popular insurrection during which the FSLN frequently found itself outpaced by the spontaneous actions of the people in the towns. In December 1978 the three competing tendencies of the FSLN ("proletarian," "protracted people's war," and "tercerista insurrectionist") set up a unified command structure—to coordinate the steamrolling insurrection.

In June 1979, as Somoza's planes roared overhead dropping their bombs, civil defense committees (CDCs) in neighborhoods and factories called a general strike. The days of the tyrant were numbered. The United States pressured for an interim government without Somoza—"Somocismo without Somoza"—but it was too late. Except for a few of the wealthier elites, the broad alliance of forces behind the mass insurrection wanted Somoza _and_ Somocismo out.

Finally, Secretary of State Cyrus Vance proposed to the OAS (Organiza-tion of American States) that a "peacekeeping force" be sent to Nicaragua. Only Argentina's military dictatorship backed the idea. Latin America's new politics of broad alliances against bloody dictatorships was getting its first test in tiny Nicaragua. The "rubber-stamp" character of OAS votes to bless U.S. interventions like the one in 1954 in Guatemala and the one in 1965 in the Do-minican Republic (see chapters 2 and 10) was a thing of the past.

The Revolution in Power: Reconstruction and Capitalist Economy

Somoza's indiscriminate bombing left Nicaragua's economy in a shambles. An estimated 50,000 persons perished in the insurrection and 100,000 were wounded—all told, nearly 5 percent of the population. One-third were left homeless and without food. In 1979 major export crops went unplanted, un-employment approached 50 percent, and the GNP plummeted 25 percent.

The new government called itself the Provisional Junta of National Re-construction. It included multimillionaire Alfonso Robelo, a subsequent leader of the contras. Defining the revolution as "popular, democratic, and anti-impe-rialist," it pledged itself to "go slow" in making radical changes. The junta nationalized without compensation the properties of Somoza and his friends, a popular move. It also took over, usually with compensation, banking, insurance, transportation, mining and forestry, most of construction, and foreign trade. It did not nationalize the private agroindustrial businesses of the anti-Somoza elite families, but it did initiate an agrarian reform.

These measures shifted only one-quarter of industrial and agricultural production to the state sector. In industry, half of production remained in the hands of private owners employing five or more workers. During the mid-1980s large-scale capitalist enterprises produced one-third of agricultural exports; state farms and co-ops produced one-quarter; and private peasant farmers grew the rest. This was the "mixed economy" that stirred so much interest among those who believed a capitalist system with a social conscience could "develop" Latin America (see Overview).

The government encouraged small private industry and artisan production. Together with new agricultural and service co-ops incorporating the landless, these smaller producers soon accounted for 40 percent of the GNP and two-thirds of productive employment.

Additional steps taken by the government to generate economic recovery were a cut in luxury imports, diversification of trade and credit relations, and enactment of carefully phased income-redistribution policies. By the mid-1980s one-quarter of Nicaragua's exports still went to the United States, but the rest went to Western Europe, the Socialist bloc, and the Third World.

Surprisingly, in the early 1980s when most nations were experiencing economic downturns Nicaragua's economy grew at a 6 percent annual clip. This happened even though U.S. aid was cut off, the nation's harbors were mined by the CIA, and the U.S.-backed contras were invading. Nicaragua turned to other countries for aid. Its foreign debt rose to a staggering $4 billion (two-fifths of it Somoza's). The country's recovery occurred despite 1982's flood and big cotton farmers' reduction of production by 7 percent. A "decapitalization" law allowed the government to confiscate any firm that suddenly disinvested. This happened to Sears, Roebuck & Company. Contra attacks, "flight capital" sent abroad by big businesspeople, and a U.S. economic embargo declared on May 1, 1985, ended the period of economic recovery and introduced a period of severe economic crisis. President Ortega's IMF-style austerity program of the late 1980s added to an economic decline from which Nicaragua has yet to recover.

Streams of refugees from the war zones flooded into Managua, where the population mushroomed to 800,000 by 1987. Many of these people accounted for a doubling of the number of street vendors and market-stall operators in the Mercado Oriental (Eastern Market). In addition to Managua's old slums, new ones called "barrios salvajes" (literally, savage neighborhoods) sprang up to house recent rural migrants. The government installed sewage and electrical and water systems for all of Managua and other cities.

By 1990, Nicaragua was in deep economic trouble. Right-wing critics attributed the economic slowdown to investors' loss of confidence caused by Sandinista mismanagement and lack of state support for private capital. The government responded by pointing to investment incentives it had provided the private sector through subsidized loans and access to scarce foreign exchange and voluntary labor. The 1987 Constitution declared the nation's commitment to building a "mixed" economy that allowed for capitalist enterprises. The government said that many big capitalists were shifting investments to the contras, whose U.S.-backed invasion was destroying major facilities. The U.S. embargo was also blamed.

Leftist critics said the government left capitalists with so much economic clout that they found it easy to destabilize the economy and dilute the revolution's social reforms. These critics asserted that whatever the government did, including the holding of elections in 1984, the United States called it "Marxist-Leninist" and mounted an attack against it. Using scarce resources in a vain effort to outspend Uncle Sam on elections like those scheduled for 1990 was an immoral waste. A more direct democracy was necessary, one based on workers' control from the workplace to the National Assembly. This would instantly rally all working people to the defense of the nation. The ultimate guarantee, a few of these critics suggested, was a unified socialist Central America.

Government supporters answered that the Sandinistas' moderate approach helped win European support, diversify the nation's sources of trade and credit, and maintain the pluralistic democracy the revolution had promised. Holding elections helped the FSLN to raise the consciousness of the masses who were being swamped with Church and "pro-imperialist" propaganda. A humane and democratic socialism had to be created in stages, not overnight. Saving the nation from the talons of the American eagle could occur only by making the political costs of U.S. military intervention prohibitively high, which the Nicaraguan government and the American people's protest movement abroad were doing, they claimed.

Social Reforms

The revolution's social reforms drew high praise from international organizations. UNESCO (United Nations Educational Scientific, and Cultural Organization) issued an outstanding achievement award to Nicaragua for its 1980–1981 education campaign that reduced illiteracy from 52 to 12 percent. In 1982 the WHO (World Health Organization) declared Nicaragua a model for primary health care. Women's organizations applauded Nicaragua's new law providing equal pay for equal work. Nicaragua's land reform was similarly lauded for distributing 2 million acres to 60,000 landless rural families and granting land titles for 4.6 million acres to another 60,000 families already working the land.

The rural majority benefited most from the revolution's social reforms. In spite of shortages and rationing, nutrition initially improved, as the government carried through on its promise to deliver the "canasta" (basket) of nine basic food items to outlying areas. To many families the government brought electricity, potable drinking water, and adequate food for the first time. These gains were undermined by acts of sabotage, by contras, however.

The reforms got rolling in 1980–1981 when more than 100,000 people, mostly youngsters and their teachers from the cities and towns, packed their knapsacks and went to the countryside to teach the poor how to read and write. In the process they learned about rural people's hard lives and generous hearts. Half a million peasants became literate. Even ex-National Guardsmen serving jail sentences, half of whom were illiterate, received instruction during the campaign. Minister of Culture Cardenal observed, "The revolution taught to read and write those whom the dictatorship had taught how to kill."

Literacy campaign workers suffered casualties: fifty brigadistas died, six of them murdered by the contras. But the campaign continued. A follow-up program dispersed 24,000 educators to teach 185,000 adults in a two-year program designed "to create a nation of not only literate, but critical revolutionaries." Between 1979 and 1984 the number of students from preschool through university and adult education doubled, and the number of schoolteachers quadrupled. The casualty rate also increased. According to Minister of Culture Cardenal, in 1984 the contras destroyed fourteen schools, killed 113 teachers, and kidnapped 187 others.

Reforms in health care were no less dramatic. Under Somoza, few had access to medical care of any kind. Health campaigns modeled after the literacy campaign swept the nation, and by 1985 an estimated 80 percent of the population had some regular access to medical care. The number of medical students increased tenfold. Infant mortality decreased by nearly half, life expectancy momentarily rose, immunization programs wiped out polio and measles. The number of citizens covered by social security doubled, increasing to one-third of the working population. Again, because of the contras' war the toll was high: sixty-three health workers were killed, including two European doctors, twenty-seven wounded, thirty kidnapped and tortured, and two hospitals and nineteen health centers destroyed.

Nicaragua's agrarian reform altered the shape of the nation's total farm area, reducing the portion belonging to farmers holding more than 850 acres from 36 percent to 11 percent. State farms accounted for 19 percent of the farming land, and the new production co-ops comprised another 9 percent.

Because they represented three-fifths of the poorest segment of the population, women benefited from the revolution's social programs. Women had been very active in the insurrection. Some had risen to the position of commander in the FSLN guerrilla army. A quarter of the FSLN fighters were women. In 1985 women occupied 37 percent of the leadership positions in the FSLN—more than in any other political party in Latin America. They also made up half of the membership of the citizens' militias and the CDSs (Sandinista Defense Committees).

One-third of all Nicaraguan households were headed by a woman. The agrarian reform mandated by law a separate paycheck for each working family member, something new for rural women in Latin America (except Cuba). Family laws obligated men to help in the housework. Debate was initiated on highly controversial issues like abortion and woman-beating, but it remained to be seen how much women's liberation ideology would penetrate the popular culture. Before the contra war diverted funding into defense, the government built forty-three day-care centers accommodating four thousand children.

Labor unions also received a boost from the revolution. Union militants began organizing publicly for the first time since the repression of 1944–1945. Most Nicaraguan workers joined pro-Sandinista labor organizations like the CST (Sandinista Workers Confederation) and the ATC (Association of Farm Workers).

According to the Ministry of Labor, by 1984 there existed eleven hundred unions representing 260,000 workers or 55 percent of the work force—a tenfold increase since Somoza's time when several trade unionists had been jailed, beaten, or killed. During forty-three years of Somocismo, only 160 collective bargaining agreements were signed. A U.S. West Coast trade-union delegation said these new agreements were "ahead of contracts in the United States" and included "full health and maternity coverage" and "access to the company's books." The same delegation noted that in spite of periodic government emergency bans on strikes, they did occur.

The Reagan administration, on the other hand, accused the government of a terroristic campaign against democratic trade unionism—specifically, the AFL-CIO–backed CUS (Confederation for Labor Unification) and the CTN (Nicaraguan Workers Central, Huembes faction), representing less than 2 percent of organized workers. It quoted former Vice-Minister of Labor Edgard Macías, "On one side the workers who are protected and privileged by the FSLN, and on the other side those who . . . belong to the 'second class' labor unions and for whom life is much harsher."

Whatever the difficulties, Nicaraguan workers organized feverishly in the 1980s. Besides the labor confederations already mentioned, they built the 45,000-strong National Union of Public Employees, the 17,000-strong CGT (General Confederation of Labor-Independent), and the 19,000-strong FET-SALUD (Nicaraguan Health Workers Federation).

The New Politics

The new politics of the 1980s in Nicaragua echoed trends in the rest of Latin America, particularly in the unity forged between the forces of the theology of liberation and those of the new Marxism (see Overview). Unlike the new politics elsewhere, however, Nicaragua's was based on an armed revolution that had destroyed the military machine of the ancien regime. Of course, Cuba's revolution two decades earlier had done that. But Nicaragua remained unique because it held a nationwide election (conducted in the midst of war) in which several widely divergent political parties participated with equal access to the mass media—something unheard of in the rest of Latin America.

As a result of those elections, on January 10, 1985, Daniel Ortega was sworn in as president, and a Western-style, multiparty, elected National Assembly was seated. The Assembly drafted the 1987 Constitution. The parliament's Constitutional Commission was made up of twenty-two members, of whom only eight were FSLN members (ten were from six other parties, three were independent liberationist Christians, and one was an independent journalist).

The Assembly itself consisted of members of seven parties, including some representing as few as 1 percent of the voters. Opposition parties held over one-third of the seats. One-fifth of the FSLN electoral slate sitting in the Assembly was nonparty members. They included Ray Hooker, a black educator from Bluefields, and Sixto Ulloa Dona, a Baptist evangelical leader. Nicaragua's was probably the only parliament in history that allowed supporters of an outside invasion force (the contras) to hold seats and speak freely— as some PCD (Democratic Conservative party) members did.

In the 1984 elections, in which 84 percent of registered voters cast their ballots, more than 30 percent voted for parties to the right of the Sandinista slate of candidates. The FSLN obtained only 67 percent of the vote. A team sent by the largest organization of experts on Latin America in the United States, LASA (Latin American Studies Association), declared the 1984 elections "a model of probity and fairness." U.S. State Department critics said the elections were a sham because the participating parties agreed with the dominant FSLN on major points. LASA responded that a broad range of disagreements existed among and within the seven parties and that the election results were the proof of their fairness. "There is *nothing* that the Sandinistas could have done to make the 1984 elections acceptable to the U.S. government," LASA observed.

The Democratic Coordinating Board (Coordinadora), whose candidate was banker Arturo Cruz (a founder of "los Doce" and one-time ambassador to Washington), boycotted the elections at the last moment. Cruz's main backers were the COSEP (Superior Council of Private Enterprise, a group of the country's largest capitalists) and the Reagan administration. Next time around, in 1990, these forces would take advantage of Nicaragua's young democracy and unite behind the victorious candidacy of Violeta Barrios de Chamorro.

The centerpiece of Nicaragua's new politics was a network of mass organizations, many of which had sprung up during the insurrection. The FSLN did not lead these groups, but it was often the dominant voice (see Box 5.2).

New Controversies: Human Rights, the Church, the Press, and Soviet Aid

After the overthrow of Somoza the Sandinista government was accused of several human rights violations (although nothing as extreme as the political assassinations and disappearances that were occurring in several other Latin American counties—see Overview). Although the Sandinista regime and the 1987 Constitution outlawed the death penalty, by January 1988 there were reportedly more than one thousand political prisoners. President Ortega, as part of Nicaragua's commitment to the Arias Peace Plan (see Introduction to Part One), released all but a few of the prisoners by January 1990, even though the contras did not meet the preceding month's deadline for disbanding and killed two hundred more Nicaraguans during the 1990 election campaign. Among the contra and National Guard prisoners released by Ortega were the ones who had killed his brother Camilo and FSLN founder Fonseca.

Box 5.2: Mass Organizations of the "New Politics," 1980s*

AMNLAE   Association of Nicaraguan Women Luisa Amanda Espinoza (60,000 members). Over FSLN objections, it won the right for women to volunteer for the Patriotic Military Service.

ATC   Association of Farm Workers (125,000 members, mostly state-farm workers). It sought and won wage increases and represented the most impoverished rural people.

CDS   Sandinista Defense Committees (600,000 members, one-fifth of the population, all volunteers, organized in 15,000 block organizations). Each block committee elected its own leadership. The CDSs provided vigilance against contra sabotage, helped with vaccination campaigns, distributed rationed foodstuffs, and reduced crime rates.

CST   Sandinista Trade Union Federation (112,000 workers, most of them in industry). Merger of all trade unions with FSLN ties.

UNAG   National Union of Farmers and Cattlemen (over 100,000 members, including large landowners). In 1986 it won increases in distribution of land to individuals.

"19th of July"
Youth Organization   30,000 members organized in 880 base assemblies, or 16 percent of students between the ages fourteen and twenty-eight.Active in literacy campaign and reserve battalions of Popular Sandinista Army.

* In addition, there were smaller organizations like ANDEN (National Association of Teachers), CEPAD (Evangelical Development Support Committee), and UNEN (University Students Union).

In the early years of the Sandinista regime the government was accused of abusing the human rights of the Miskitu Indians. But the prestigious Amnesty International concluded that "reports of [Sandinista] shootings and other deliberate brutality" during the transfer of Miskitus out of contra war zones "were later shown to be false." Abuses of the Miskitu people's rights by the CIA-sponsored contras, on the other hand, were found to be systematic. The Sandinista government eventually acknowledged its occasional abuses of the Miskitus' human rights and began to enforce laws it passed on behalf of the nation's ethnic groups. The 1987 Constitution granted autonomy to the Miskitus and other minorities. It provided for local community elections of local councils and local administration. Many Miskitus moved back to their original lands, and large numbers began returning to Nicaragua from Honduras and Costa Rica.

By then all Miskitus except for a tiny minority expressed reservations about fighting for the contras. Residents in the Honduran refugee camps accused a CIA-financed and trained Miskitus guerrilla band, known as Kisán, of dragooning young men into its ranks and brutalizing women (see chapter 4).

Another controversy raged around the role of the Roman Catholic Church in the revolution. At first, the Catholic Church issued a "Carta Pastoral" that advocated "true socialism," as contrasted to the image of "repression and tyranny" sometimes associated with socialism. But this "honeymoon" period soon ended. The Church split between those upholding traditional hierarchical norms and those advocating and implementing what was known as the popular church.

The traditional Church opposed the revolution and claimed the folloing of the very rich and a growing percentage of the small middle class. The popular Church championed the revolution and claimed the adherence of a majority of the poor. The pope rushed to Nicaragua to tend to his flock. Sandinistas heckled him, and the conflict intensified. Many felt that the pope failed to condemn the crimes of the Somoza regime and of the contras.

The roots of the popular Church included more than the general "preferential option for the poor" theology sweeping the continent (see Overview). Somoza's dictatorship had allowed no outlet for protest or independent labor organizing except the Church. Consequently, in 1976, "delegates of the Word" had formed committees of agricultural workers on Nicaragua's coffee estates and organized protests over work conditions. When these efforts were repressed by kidnappings, assassinations, and torture, many Christian militants joined the guerrilla struggle. As a joint statement of Nicaraguan Roman Catholic and Protestant organizations explained, "It was very difficult for many Christians to choose armed struggle, but it was the last and only alternative which was left to them in order to stop the terror and genocide." The popular war against Somoza's dictatorship solidified the new politics of Marxist-Christian unity.

Three priests became high government officials: Miguel d'Escoto, minister of foreign affairs; Fernando Cardenal, director of youth organizations; and his brother Ernesto, minister of culture. The papacy in Rome instructed them to resign from the government, since religion should be personal and not political. They responded that the personal *was* political—and why had the pope not issued instructions forbidding Archbishop Obando y Bravo from being political? Obando y Bravo had told U.S. businesspeople in August of 1984 that he and his diocese were actively involved in efforts to remove the FSLN government. Subsequent investigations into Iran-contragate revealed that the CIA funded Catholic Church elements opposed the government.

In July 1986, President Ortega told a gathering at New York City's Riverside Church that none of the 138 deaths or 264 disappearances of clergy and religious workers in Central America since 1980 had occurred in Nicaragua. The only places where the lives of priests and nuns were in danger were "in those countries that have the U.S. government's official blessing and approval"—places like El Salvador (see chapter 3).

The Nicaraguan government expelled ten foreign priests for their subversive activities, including defense of a priest caught on videotape drinking with CIA agents and exclaiming "What's needed is four bullets in one of those [government] *jodidos* (literally, 'fucked-up ones']." Archbishop Obando y Bravo expelled far more priests for their support of the revolution. Despite all of this, in 1987 President Ortega invited Archbishop Obando y Bravo to mediate the conflict with the contras, and Obando y Bravo accepted.

Controversies about press censorship focused on the newspaper *La Prensa*. After the 1978 killing of *La Prensa* editor Pedro Joaquín Chamorro, the slain editor's youngest son, Carlos Fernando Chamorro, had joined the Sandinistas. Somoza's National Guard responded by destroying the newspaper plant.

After the triumph of the insurrection the Chamorro family still ran the nation's press. The slain editor's oldest son Pedro Joaquín Chamorro Barrios and brother Jaime Chamorro Cardenal turned *La Prensa* into an antigovernment advocate of sedition. Another brother, Xavier Chamorro, took his quarter of the paper's assets to found a competing daily, *El Nuevo Diario*. Meanwhile youngest son, Carlos Chamorro, became editor of the official FSLN daily *Barricada*.

Few outside the middle and upper classes read any of the competing papers. For most Nicaraguans radio remained the main medium of communication. More than half of the nation's fifty radio stations were privately owned, and none of them was subjected to prior censorship, although the Catholic Church's radio station was periodically censored. Television sets were not common in Nicaraguans' homes, and only two television channels existed, both operated by the FSLN. Merely 10 percent of TV programming was locally produced, most of the rest coming from Mexico and the United States.

The main case of press censorship in the 1980s was the government's periodic closing of *La Prensa* and frequent prior censorship of its contents. The government justified its actions by noting the newspaper editor's own acknowledged support for the contras and receipt of CIA funds. Nicaragua was unique in allowing such a seditious newspaper to print during wartime.

On the controversy about Soviet and Cuban aid the Nicaraguan government did not deny that it was receiving substantial amounts of such aid and indeed welcomed Cuban, East European, and other "foreign" personnel, or "internationalists," interested in assisting it to defend or build the revolution. Periodically, the government announced the departure of several of the largest group of foreign advisers, the Cubans (most of whom were involved in medicine and education). This was part of Nicaragua's effort to show its willingness to achieve a peaceful settlement with the United States.

The U.S. government, on the other hand, aware that the Soviet aid was defensive in nature, continued arming the contras and blocking the implementation of the Arias Peace Plan, even after the Iran-contragate revelations about Lieutenant Colonel Oliver North's White House basement arms and drug trafficking operations. By May 1987, annual U.S. troop "exercises" in Honduras and off Nicaragua's coasts involved 50,000 U.S. military personnel and 20,000 contras. U.S. helicopters, C-123 cargo planes, and airmen continued to be shot down over Nicaraguan territory. After 1990 the issue of Soviet aid became mute because of the stunning military and diplomatic victories of the Sandinistas in 1987–1988, their electoral defeat in 1990, the collapse of the Soviet bloc, and Cuba's growing economic crisis (see below and Overview, Introduction to Part One, and chapter 8).

CIA-Contra Activities and War's Impact

Practically all of the contra aid went to the Somocista FDN (Nicaraguan Democratic Force). According to the bipartisan U.S. Congress Arms Control and Foreign Policy Caucus, "While the 'foot soldiers' of the FDN army are largely peasants, forty-six of the forty-eight positions in the FDN's command structure are held by former National Guardsmen." The FDN's commander was Enrique Bermúdez, a former colonel in the National Guard who had led the Nicaraguan contingent in the OAS occupation of the Dominican Republic in 1965. In 1991, he was assassinated. The head of FDN counterintelligence was Ricardo Lau—an ex-Guard officer known to have committed systematic atrocities in both the Guard and the FDN. Lau's presence in the FDN was cited by the Costa Rica–based Democratic Revolutionary Alliance (ARDE), a tiny band of contras headed by ex-FSLN commander Edén Pastora, as a reason for its refusal to be part of an FDN coalition. Unsuccessful militarily, Pastora withdrew from battle in 1985, after which only remnants of ARDE remained active.

Human rights organizations generally condemned the FDN for systematic atrocities. According to Americas Watch, the FDN forces routinely "kidnap, torture, and murder health workers, teachers, and other government employees." A CIA manual instructing the contras and their sympathizers on how to sabotage the Nicaraguan economy and kill teachers, nurses, and other noncombatants had long since been made public. Former contra leader Harvard-educated Edgar Chamorro, who for four years was FDN public relations director, stated, "Unfortunately, the contras burn down schools, homes and health centers as fast as the Sandinistas build them."

Chamorro called the contras "a CIA puppet." For the World Court he provided a notarized affidavit stating that the contras' "hundreds of civilian murders, mutilations, tortures and rapes" were committed "at the instigation of CIA-training officers." He said:

> The Sandinistas, for all their faults, have made enormous advances in education, housing and health care . . . and must be credited with generating an atmosphere of genuine equality for the first time in Nicaragua's history. By contrast, the "contras" who were my colleagues talked mostly of recovering their lost wealth and privileged status.

A U.S. House of Representatives Select Committee on Intelligence report concluded that the contras' "indiscriminate attacks on civilian and economic targets" had led to "an exponential growth in the loss of innocent life." One such loss was the already-mentioned death of twenty-seven-year-old engineer Ben Linder (see the Introduction to Part One).

The Iran-contragate revelations confirmed these assessments, but the Reagan administration did not alter its policies. Frequent mass demonstrations of 100,000 or more people in Washington, D.C., kept public pressure on the U.S. government to desist from intervening in Nicaragua. Public opinion polls showed most Americans opposed aiding the contras.

The effects of the contra war inside Nicaragua were complex. Politically, it polarized the nation into rival camps about how to construct the new democracy. For many Nicaraguans the concern was not some East-West or superpower conflict, but rather, one of defending their country against the traditional military incursions of the United States and its proxies. Thus, the word most often heard in Nicaragua was "imperialism."

Economically, shortages of milk and other items became a serious problem. As inflation passed 1,000 percent a year in early 1988, the government followed the examples of Argentina and Brazil (see chapters 18 and 20) by issuing a new currency and slashing the federal budget by 10 percent. Socially, reform programs were cut to the bone. These and related economic austerity measures made many question the ability of the Sandinistas to meet the people's basic needs. The military draft also became unpopular.

In sum, the war devastated tiny Nicaragua without defeating it. Some 50,000 Nicaraguans perished in the war. Countless more were left wounded or maimed for life. The revolution's social gains were undermined, and the economy was left in a shambles. The war's ultimate and most ironic political impact was to make it possible for the anti-Sandinistas to achieve at the ballot box what they had been unable to accomplish on the battlefield: removal of the Sandinistas from state power.

The U.S. policy of slow strangulation of the Nicaraguan Revolution worked, but at what price? Internationally, the U.S. performance earned its government the worst public image it had experienced since the Vietnam war. Domestically, it gave rise to a large array of anti-interventionist groups that stayed the hand of U.S. interventionism and helped forge the tenuous peace that Central America enjoys today.

1990 Elections and the Chamorro Government

On February 25, 1990, as two thousand official foreign observers looked on, Violeta Barrios de Chamorro of the multi-party UNO coalition (National Opposition Union) scored an upset victory over President Ortega with 55 percent of the vote. Like Ortega, Chamorro campaigned for peace. From the upper crust of Nicaraguan society, she openly welcomed President Bush's support, leaving the impression that obviously a friend of the U.S. president could end the war more quickly than the man Bush had called an "animal" (see the Introduction to Part One). Some voters said they feared an Ortega victory would produce an "overkill" U.S. military invasion like the one in Panama two months earlier (see chapter 7). Official U.S. support for Chamorro ran as high as $10 per Nicaraguan voter, roughly thirty times what Bush had spent per voter in his presidential campaign. The universal tradition of buying poor people's votes helped tilt the balance in Chamorro's favor.

The first day after the election resembled a day of national mourning. There were no wild celebrations in the streets. That evening Ortega visited Chamorro to assure her of a smooth transition to power. Each expressed love for the other, with Chamorro calling Ortega "my beautiful little father." Next day, Chamorro gave her acceptance speech: "This election will produce no exiles, no political prisoners, no confiscations."

Two days after the election nearly 200,000 people overflowed Managua's Omar Torrijos and Non-Aligned plazas to cheer Ortega. Encouraging saddened militants of the "new politics" mass organizations, Ortega said "We were born at the bottom and we are used to fighting from below. . . . We will continue governing from below." Back in Washington, President Bush signed a formal determination that Nicaragua was not "a Marxist-Leninist country" and promised hundreds of millions in U.S. aid.

Chamorro's governing coalition soon fell apart. Its extreme right wing resented the new president's agreeing to allow Humberto Ortega (Daniel's brother) to stay on as defense minister. Chamorro's vice president led an open campaign to turn her out of power, and because of UNO defections she lost her majority in the National Assembly. Chamorro promised to replace Humberto Ortega later in her administration.

Most of the contras were resettled with government assistance. Some, known as *"recontras,"* kept fighting, forcing President Chamorro to declare a state of emergency in northern Nicaragua in 1993.

The Sandinista army budget was slashed by 80 percent and its troop force reduced from 90,000 to 15,000 by mid-1993. Some demobilized soldiers and members of cooperatives known as *"recompas"* (for "comrades again") formed self-defense groups against *recontra* attacks. Veterans and relatives of both enemy camps sometimes joined together to demand war injury compensation and widow benefits.

In July 1990, when Chamorro began selling off state properties and returning confiscated lands, Sandinistas conducted a ten-day general strike. Chamorro stopped returning the lands and Daniel Ortega helped negotiate an end to the strike. Some said this illustrated the Sandinistas' "governing from below." But as the economy failed to recover over the next few years, the Sandinistas became as badly divided as the government on what to do.

The Chamorro government reversed social programs, causing health conditions to deteriorate. Unemployment jumped to 60 percent. Illiteracy rates shot back up to more than 30 percent. Runaway inflation eventually eased. European and U.S. creditors forgave 75 percent of their share of the still rising foreign debt in 1992. Exports to the United States remained at less than 10 percent of their 1980 level. Strikes, armed skirmishes, and political turbulence became more frequent than at any time since the end of the contra war. A 1993 UN study stated that poverty and malnutrition in Nicaragua and Somalia were at similar levels.

A partial form of very tenuous power-sharing between the Sandinistas and the Chamorro administration called by some rightists "co-gobierno" failed to deter the growing autonomy of the "new politics" mass organizations. For example, in May 1992 armed women from all sides of the political spectrum blocked roads in Ocotal and seized the city hall to demand a maternity ward and day-care center.

The Bush administration tied much of its promised aid to the return of properties and the removal of Sandinistas from the security forces. The Clinton administration released $50 million in aid to bolster the unpopular Chamorro government. In September 1992 President Chamorro agreed to allow beneficiaries of the Sandinista agrarian reform to keep their lands and to compensate former property owners with shares in state companies undergoing privatization. Some former landowners accepted the deal.

Many scholars believed this compromise to be an important step in the consolidation of Nicaragua's "bourgeois democratic revolution." Private property rights were more respected than ever; the state sector was being privatized; and free market competition would likely impoverish most of the small farmers who had benefited from the Sandinista agrarian reform. In 1993 Nicaragua's revolution thus resembled Mexico's or Bolivia's more than it did Cuba's (see chapters 1, 8, and 15), except for the fact that it occurred at a later time in a poorer country in a world transformed by the rise of transnational corporations and hi-tech military weaponry.

Selected Bibliography

Cockcroft, James D. *Daniel Ortega*. New York: Chelsea House, 1991. Award-winning biography.

Diskin, M. et al. *Peace and Autonomy on the Atlantic Coast of Nicaragua. A Report of the LASA Task Force on Human Rights and Academic Freedom*. Washington, DC: Latin American Studies Association, 1986. Available from Central America Resource Center, P.O. Box 2327, Austin, TX 78768. Short, informed account on indigenous peoples.

Ezcurra, Ana Maria. *Ideological Aggression against the Sandinista Revolution: The Political Opposition Church in Nicaragua*. New York: Circus Publications, 1984.

Foroohar, Manzar. *The Catholic Church and Social Change in Nicaragua*. Albany: SUNY Press, 1989.

Hodges, Donald C. *Intellectual Foundations of the Nicaraguan Revolution*. Austin: University of Texas Press, 1986. Includes new scholarship on Sandino.

———. *Sandino's Communism*. Austin: University of Texas Press, 1992.

Lancaster, Roger. *Life Is Hard: Machismo, Danger, and the Intimacy of Power*. Berkeley: University of California Press, 1993. Ethnography of working-class Managua *barrio*.

Latin American Studies Association. *Electoral Democracy Under International Pressure: The Report of the LASA Commission to Observe the 1990 Nicaraguan Election*. Washington, DC: LASA, 1990.

Macauleay, Neill. *The Sandino Affair*. New York: Quadrangle Books, 1967. By U.S. military officer, fair account.

National Security Archive. *Nicaragua: The U.S. and the Nicaraguan Revolution, 1979–1989*. Alexandria, VA: Chadwyck-Healey, 1991. Revealing government documents.

Nicaragua Network Education Fund. *Nicaragua Monitor*. Bimonthly update on Nicaragua (1247 "E" St. SE, Washington, DC 20003).

Robinson, William I. *A Faustian Bargain: U.S. Intervention in the Nicaraguan Elections and American Foreign Policy in the Post-Cold War Era*. Boulder, CO: Westview, 1992.

Rosset, Peter, and John Vandermeer (eds.). *Nicaragua: Unfinished Revolution*. New York: Grove Press, 1986. Compendium of opposing views, including many primary sources; includes article by Robert Leiken often used by President Reagan in denouncing Sandinistas.

Rius (Eduardo del Rio). *Nicaragua for Beginners*. New York: Writers and Readers Publishing, 1982. Illustrated introductory history.

Vanden, Harry E., and Gary Prevost. *Democracy and Socialism in Sandinista Nicaragua*. Boulder, CO: Lynne Rienner, 1993.

Walker, Thomas W. (ed.). *Reagan Versus the Sandinistas. The Undeclared War on Nicaragua*. Boulder, CO: Westview, 1987. Well-researched policy critique.

Films

Destination Nicaragua. 1986. 58 or 28 minutes. Color video covering U.S. visitors to Nicaragua and the U.S. policy debate. Best Documentary, Philadelphia International Film Festival.

Fire from the Mountain. 1987. Color documentary film on Omar Cabezas' widely acclaimed book on "coming of age" under Somoza and joining the Sandinista guerrillas, directed by Academy Award winning director Deborah Shaffer *(Witness to War: Dr. Charlie Clements*, 1985) and produced by Shaffer and Adam Friedson in association with Common Sense Foundation.

From the Ashes. 1982. 60 minutes. Color film showing Nicaragua through the eyes of a typical family during the rebellion against Somoza and the contra war and revealing Nicaragua's past, present, and future "from the bottom up."

Neighbors Working with Neighbors. 1986. 60 minutes. Color video by U.S.-based Prismatic Productions on foreign delegations and work brigades revealing grassroots life in 1980s' Nicaragua.

Nicaragua: The Dirty War. 1987. 68 minutes. Color film of National Film Board of Canada.

Queremos La Paz (We Want Peace). 1986. 33 minutes. Color video; Nicaraguans speak to North Americans.

Ten Days/Ten Years: The Nicaraguan Elections of 1990. 54 minutes. "On the scene" video by Mickey Friedman and John MacGruer (22 Railroad St., Great Barrington, MA 01230.)

Who's Running This War? 1986. 60 minutes. Color video, PBS.

Women in Arms. 1980. 59 minutes. Color documentary film written and directed by Victoria Schultz (Hudson River Productions).

Costa Rica ___ 6

It would be wise if the United States withdrew economic occupation.—*José Pepe Figueres, three-time president, 1953*

Jeane Kirkpatrick [U.S. Ambassador to United Nations] told Costa Rican officials in 1981 they shouldn't expect to receive any U.S. assistance until they agreed to build an army.—*Former Vice-President José Miguel Alfaro*

President Oscar Arias Sánchez had just learned the exciting news. He had been awarded the Nobel Peace Prize for 1987 for his Central American peace plan, signed the previous August by five Central American presidents in Guatemala.

Since he had become president in 1986 Arias had made many attempts to demilitarize Central America. His government had closed contra bases and shut down a secret airstrip near the Nicaraguan border used by Lieutenant Colonel Oliver North's associates to supply the contras invading Nicaragua. In response the U.S. government had temporarily frozen economic aid to Costa Rica in 1987. Despite the pressure from Washington and the economic hardships it caused Costa Rica, the majority of the Costa Rican people were supporting the Arias Peace Plan.

In June 1987, President Arias had gone to Washington to meet with President Reagan and Vice-President Bush. He had not gotten very far—the U.S. leaders were still taking a negative approach to his peace plan. Now perhaps the prestige of the coveted Nobel prize would change all of that. It might be the last chance for peace in Central America. After all, the Contadora peace process had bogged down for six years while the war raged on and Costa Rica itself became less and less the peaceful country Arias had known as a boy.

After receiving the news of his prize, the young Costa Rican president flew off to Stockholm to receive it. Upon his homecoming, he was received with cheers and accolades. Not satisfied merely to have come up with the plan, he began to push for its implementation in meetings with the region's presidents. He also again urged U.S. cooperation.

But by early 1988 President Arias had not yet succeeded. "Peace in 1988 depends on the prevalence of reason over madness," he wrote in a special article for U.S. newspapers. "Those fueling this war are neither the ones dying in the battlefields nor the mothers who, with heavy hearts, see their sons go off to fight."

It should surprise no one that the impetus for the Central American peace plan came from Costa Rica, a nation known for its peaceful and democratic traditions. Costa Rica is so unlike the rest of Central America that it is often compared with Argentina and Uruguay. It is likened to those two countries because of its high literacy rate (90 percent) and predominantly Euro-Caucasian population (85 percent, mostly of Spanish descent but also of German, Dutch, and Swiss origin). To Uruguay it is compared for its pro-middle-class social welfare system and history of "Swiss-style" democracy. These traditions help explain the low degree of organized popular opposition to Costa Rica's political and economic system in the 1970s and 1980s, in contrast to the massive upheavals rocking its neighbors.

There was no denying Costa Rica's distinctness for most of the second half of the twentieth century—a land of democracy in a region of dictatorship. In Costa Rica no superwealthy oligarchy enslaved a huge mass of landless peasants. A sizable set of middle classes, including semiprosperous family farmers, existed. There were no major Indian problems, no guerrilla movements or significant number of rebel-priests, no military coups, and no people "disappeared." While as in most countries few citizens had a voice in the candidate selection process, ever since 1948 there had occurred regular multiparty elections with everyone over eighteen years of age obligated to vote.

Costa Rica was often called "an oasis of peace in a region of war and revolution." It was known as a country almost unique in human history for its constitutional prohibition of a standing army (Article 12 of the 1949 Constitution). A common saying was that in Costa Rica there were more teachers than soldiers.

Yet Costa Rica did once experience an actual violent armed uprising, however abbreviated—in 1948. Moreover, under the impact of subsequent U.S.-aid programs Costa Rica's claims to complete demilitarization were invalidated. Its longstanding Civil Guard and Rural Guard were supplemented by the creation of a volunteer Organization for National Emergencies in 1982. Together with paramilitary organizations, all these armed forces incorporated a total of over 20,000 armed men.

By the mid-1980s Costa Rica was still an oasis of peace but it was being lapped by a "ripple of war" along the shores of its San Juan River border with Nicaragua, where Lieutenant Colonel North's operatives were active (see Introduction to Part One). Costa Rica's much-vaunted social welfare system was reduced and endangered by Latin America's largest per-capita debt and by IMF-imposed austerity programs. In spite of $600 million of U.S. economic aid from 1982 through 1985 (more per capita than any country other than Israel), Costa Rica was on the verge of bankruptcy and social unrest.

Observers recalled that economic hard times and signs of radical discontent a decade earlier had led to the collapse of the hemisphere's other "Swiss democracy," Uruguay (see chapter 19). Eyeing the clouds of war and chaos billowing to their north, Costa Rican politicians proudly but nervously spoke of the virtues of their social democracy, foreign investment with regulations and neutrality.

What then was to be the future for this unusual experiment in democracy once without an army? What was the role of the United States in its incipient militarization? And how did Costa Rica gain its reputation for uniqueness in the first place?

A Different History

The roots of Costa Rica's differences may be found in its relative isolation from the conquering European powers during the colonial period. Even though in 1502 Columbus called it the "rich coast," because of the sparkling gold ornaments the Indians wore, Costa Rica lacked rich mineral deposits. From 1511 to 1517 the conquering Spaniards seized Costa Rica's Indians and shipped them off to work in Cuba. The country remained an economic backwater for almost four centuries.

Costa Rica's Indian settlements were in all of its main geographical areas: the dry tropical forests of the northern Pacific coast and hills of the northwest; the humid tropical forests of the south on both coasts near the Panama border; and the long cordillera of mountains rising from the northwest to the southeast, in the midst of which sits the green temperate intermont basin where today's capital city of San José is located. Four major active volcanoes ranging from 9,000 to 11,000 feet rise northeast of San José to dominate this central plateau of exceptionally fertile lands, where three-fourths of today's 3 million Costa Ricans reside. The concentration of people in fertile plateaus and valleys resulted in Costa Rica's having one of the highest _rural_ population densities of all Latin America.

In the northwest, Indians established a maize-based and stone-carving civilization during the eighth century. Fishing, hunting, and food-gathering Indians from South America's Amazon region inhabited the Atlantic coast and much of the central plateau. The Chiriquí Indians, some of whom survive today, populated the Panamanian border area of the southern Pacific coast.

Epidemics of smallpox and other imported diseases decimated Costa Rica's Indian population of 100,000. Conquest, subjugation, and virtual enslavement also took a toll. Only an estimated one thousand Indian descendants survive today, mostly Chiriquís. Costa Rica has a larger racial minority—some 20,000 blacks, whose ancestors were imported from the British West Indies in the 1880s to build the railroad and again in the 1900s to work on the banana plantations. Most of them still speak a Jamaican-style English.

The scarcity of Indian labor meant that few Europeans were interested in colonizing Costa Rica. The first sustained settlement did not begin until the 1560s, and then only fifty families arrived. The next settlers—a few hundred families—did not arrive until 1736, when San José was founded. Costa Rica was colonized by independent-minded people from the Basque, Cartago, Galicia, and Aragón regions of Spain (and other parts of Europe) seeking a peaceful life as farmers, artisans, or businessmen.

By the time of independence from Spain, 1821, there were fewer than 60,000 people in Costa Rica, mostly self-sufficient farmers, traders, and artisans who valued equality and enterprising hard work. The more successful of them became the nation's "first families." They introduced coffee cultivation to Central America, shipping the product to foreign lands in the 1830s. By 1850 coffee was the nation's main export.

Costa Rica's first families never became deeply involved in either the Mexican Empire of Iturbide (1822–1823) or the Central American Federation (1823–1838) to which they technically belonged. In 1842 Francisco Morazán seized power in order to bring Costa Rica back into the recently dissolved federation. But most of the first families did not welcome this. Their troops captured Morazán and executed him.

In 1848 Costa Ricans, numbering only 85,000, formally established the Republic of Costa Rica. Disdaining the swashbuckling antics of the American mercenary William Walker, they organized a small but professional army and a popular militia to repel his repeated invasions of the 1850s (see chapter 5). The anti-Walker agitation in turn led to Costa Ricans' developing a genuine sense of national solidarity based on a profound mistrust of foreigners and of puppet military dictators tied to outside economic interests.

As in so much of Latin America, Liberal reforms limiting the power of the Roman Catholic Church and introducing free secular education came to Costa Rica after the establishment of a coffee export monoculture. A kind of Liberal dictatorship emerged when Tomás Guardia seized power from the loosely knit group of first families in 1870, crushed dissent, and served as president or guiding influence behind other presidents until 1882.

Guardia's strong government sponsored changes in Costa Rican transportation and trade that dynamized the economy. It enlarged trade, built public schools, and granted lucrative railroad concessions to the American adventurer Minor Cooper Keith, nephew of Henry Meiggs, the famous railway magnate of Chile and Peru. By 1884 Keith had a contract with the Costa Rican government granting him a tax-exempt area the size of Rhode Island and earning him the popular reputation of "uncrowned king of Central America." It was Keith who introduced banana production into Costa Rica and, later, into Honduras; the many small companies consolidated in 1899 as the United Fruit Company (UFCO).

During the second half of the nineteenth century several ambitious and successful Costa Rican first families consolidated into a small oligarchy of coffee plantation owners and import-export merchants tied to foreign interests. Costa Rica's new economic dynamism stimulated demands in its population of family farmers for equal rewards for hard work and a voice in the nation's politics. Consequently, in 1889 the nation held one of Latin America's freest elections involving opposing parties and a relatively honest ballot count. With the exception of 1917–1919 (dictatorship of Federico A. Tinoco), 1932 (aborted revolution), and 1948 (another revolt), Costa Rica entered into a hundred years of democracy, tempered by—in the words of a former member of the U.S. Foreign Service—"various techniques of manipulation and outright chicanery" that formed "in effect, a part of the electoral process."

The twentieth century opened with a delicate balance between democratic freedoms and a skewed division of wealth. In the country of "family farmers" seven out of ten rural families no longer had land, as 5 percent of the growers produced more than half of the nation's coffee exports on large estates. Most other landholders were *minifundistas*—holders of tiny parcels. UFCO was fattening from a banana boom that saw Costa Rican exports peak in 1913 at 11 million bunches. Funguses and diseases led to a decline, and UFCO began shifting production to the Pacific coast in the late 1920s. Labor unrest speeded UFCO's move. Because of Communist influence in organizing them, banana workers proudly called their union "the red union." It later integrated with the Communist party, known as the Vanguardia Popular.

In 1932 falling coffee prices and the Great Depression plunged the nation into crisis. A revolt sparked by the Communists' Workers and Peasants bloc was put down without much bloodshed because the government passed laws permitting the occupation of public lands—an escape valve for social pressures among landless peasants and farmers displaced by the big coffee and banana growers. By 1936 nearly one-quarter of Costa Ricans resided in newly colonized parts of the lowlands, compared to little more than one-tenth fifty years earlier.

"Don Pepe" and a Different Revolution

Despite the reforms, social protest continued. In the 1942 congressional elections disaffection with the established traditional political parties was widespread. The Communists garnered 16 percent of the vote, and independents and smaller parties polled another 20 percent.

President Rafael Angel Calderón García, a physician, formed a controversial alliance with the Communists' Vanguardia. This momentarily helped to keep labor peace and to broaden the appeal of his National Republican party. Prosperous landowner José ("Pepe") Figueres Ferrer, an anti-Communist Social Democrat enchanted with the capitalist democracies of Europe and the United States, gave a radio speech in mid-1942 claiming President Calderón had turned the nation over to the "Reds." An indignant Dr. Calderón responded by exiling Figueres. The head of Costa Rica's Communist party helped smooth Figueres' way in Mexico with a letter of introduction to friends there. Figueres' martyrdom earned him the nickname "Don Pepe" among some middle-class Costa Ricans.

In 1944 the National Republican–Vanguardia alliance candidate for president, Teodoro Picado, narrowly won a fiercely contested election. The conservative camp, led by the right-wing National Republican defector ex-President León Cortés Castro (whose 1930s government had routinely rigged electoral results) cried "fraud!" A year later Figueres and his followers founded the small Social Democratic party. In the name of popular suffrage and "honest elections," they joined a right-wing electoral alliance led by Cortés, who died in 1946. Funded by the oligarchy, the new alliance, known as "the Opposition," vowed to win the 1948 elections.

In actuality, Figueres's Social Democrats believed the only way they could take power was through armed revolt. They recognized that the Communist-influenced government had popular appeal because of its reformist promises and legislation. Accordingly, they formed secret cells that sabotaged public facilities in preparation for implementation of "Plan Sunday," an armed insurrection. They portrayed the government as alternatively a lackey of the Soviet Union and a puppet of Nicaraguan dictator Anastasio Somoza.

Figueres gained support from Guatemala's anti-Communist reformist leader Juan José Arévalo (see chapter 2) and other democrats fighting right-wing dictatorships in the Caribbean Basin. In this way he was able to downplay the right-wing character of his allies in the Opposition and appeal to democratic-minded youth from the middle classes.

By 1948 antirightist democratic revolutions were sweeping Central America. The Cold War was heating up and the United States, in the name of anticommunism, was moving to crush or control revolutionary processes underway throughout the region, most notably in Guatemala. In Costa Rica U.S.

choices were limited. A social reform process guided by the government was in full swing. If the Opposition failed to win the 1948 presidential elections, Figueres seemed—in Washington circles—the next best alternative.

The populist "Calderonista" government was a coalition of Calderón's moderate conservatives, Catholic Church progressives (including San José's Archbishop), and the Communists' Vanguardia. Its social base included the banana workers' unions. It had passed social security legislation, a big income tax, the eight-hour workday, and a very progressive social welfare program. It had only a small standing defense force.

Alleged irregularities in the 1948 elections were all it took for Figueres' insurrectionary Army of National Liberation to swing into action. It received economic and military assistance from the U.S. government. When federal troops loyal to Calderón proved unable to repel Figueres' better equipped forces in outlying and coastal areas, the government asked for help from the Vanguardia. The Communists and their working-class supporters rushed to defend government offices in San José.

For a week heavy fighting flared throughout the nation. Figueres' troops, advancing on San José, overcame poorly armed government supporters in many cities and towns. Well-armed Nicaraguan troops of dictator Somoza's U.S.-created National Guard (see chapter 5) helped the anti-Communists. The American ambassador conferred several times with Figueres.

On April 17, 1948, the U.S. government let it be known that its military forces were on standby alert in the Panama Canal Zone, ready to rid San José of "Communist control." Figueres followed this up with a threat to march on San José and a statement that no negotiated settlement would conflict with the anti-Communist policies of the United States. Outgunned, the government called off the Vanguardia forces and negotiated its own surrender.

President Picado wrote a letter to his supporters explaining that he was capitulating because he feared that "unbeatable forces [presumably the U.S. military] were on the point of taking control of the fatherland." Hundreds of lives (some estimates ran as high as two thousand) had already been lost in heavy fighting, most of them defenders of the government. The Communists' Vanguardia managed to obtain as part of the negotiated settlement a general amnesty and a guarantee that "the social rights and guarantees of all employees and workers be respected and extended."

As de facto leader of the eighteen-month Founding Junta of the Second Republic in 1948–1949, Figueres carried out amazingly progressive reforms. He disbanded the government army, taxed the very wealthy, nationalized the banking system, and extended full political rights to women and blacks. He and his successor, Otilio Ulate (a man accused of anti-Semitism) also abolished many labor unions, however. They outlawed the Communist party and jailed and exiled opponents. Figueres then devoted his energies to building his own political machine, the PLN (National Liberation party). As PLN candidate in 1953, he won the presidency. The PLN joined the Social Democrats' International, dominated by Europe's Social Democrat parties.

From his exile in Nicaragua, Calderón and some of his followers mounted two unsuccessful invasions (1949, 1955), each swiftly condemned by the OAS (Organization of American States), the same body that gave advance approval for a CIA-sponsored right-wing invasion of democratic Guatemala in 1954. In 1958 Calderón returned to Costa Rica to run in the elections and lost.

The PLN government of 1953–1958 adopted much of the earlier Calderonista government's programs. It introduced government regulation of the economy. The state ran banking, insurance, transportation, and utilities and entered into jointly financed enterprises with private capital. It provided social welfare programs of medical care, social security, and housing subsidies that favored the middle class.

As president, Figueres initially condemned foreign capital's role as "economic occupation." Through "import-substitution" policies common to much of Latin America at the time (see Overview), he sought Costa Rica's industrialization. As time went on, however, he emphasized more partnership with foreign capital. His government renewed contracts with UFCO, which provided the state with 30 percent of profits. It extended concessions to Standard Fruit Company to develop plantations on the Atlantic coast. It consolidated a conservative leadership in the remaining unions (14 percent of the work force) and became a major voice inside the U.S.-sponsored ORIT (Inter-American Regional Organization of Labor—see Overview).

"Don Pepe," patriarch of the revolution's PLN who served as president three times, was a curious blend of pro-Americanism, anticommunism, and lofty idealism. He embraced President John F. Kennedy's Alliance for Progress. A former MIT student, speaking fluent English and twice married to American women, he was later to joke that he was "first Catalán, second gringo, and third Costa Rican." A friend of Richard Nixon and the 1950s' CIA director Allen Dulles, he admitted to CIA connections. He also reportedly had close ties with Robert L. Vesco, an American who fled to Costa Rica when he was criminally charged with business theft and illegal campaign contributions to Nixon.

With the assistance of the CIA-tainted Kaplan Fund and his Social Democrat friends in Peru's APRA and Venezuela's AD (Democratic Action party), Figueres devoted much of his energy to the creation and expansion of the International Institute for Political Education on the hills overlooking San José. A center for the training of anti-Communist political and labor leaders from other Latin American republics, it was characterized by former *Time* correspondent John Gerassi as a "capitalist comintern."

During his third presidency (1970–1974) Figueres sent police officers to

Panama for U.S. training and had the U.S. military mission in San José set up a police academy. Yet during the 1980s Figueres was closer to the Sandinistas of the Nicaraguan Revolution than he was to much of the PLN leadership. "At least the Sandinistas have a core of idealism," he said. "The Somozas and the rest of the dictatorships of the right that I've dealt with are all alike. The only thing they're interested in is power and money."

The PLN government's alliance with foreign investors strengthened the power of foreign banks and industries over Costa Rica's destiny. The electorate turned the PLN out of office in the 1958 elections and gave the victory to defeated 1953 candidate Mario Echandi. The Echandi administration carried out policies even more favorable to foreign investors than those of Figueres. In 1962, it, too, was voted out and replaced by the PLN's Francisco Orlich. By then the nation was caught up in the dramatic changes taking place in Cuba.

Anti-Castroism, Industrialization, and the Debt

Costa Ricans welcomed the Venezuelans' overthrow of General Pérez Jiménez and the Cubans' military victory over Batista's army in 1959. But the PLN, which dominated the political scene for most of the post-1948 period, turned against the Cuban Revolution when Fidel Castro introduced far-reaching agrarian and housing reforms, nationalized the properties of foreign corporations (1960), and established what the PLN called a Communist dictatorship. From that point forward the PLN strengthened its powerful regional alliance with Venezuela's governing AD party and other social democratic movements to back the kind of "democratic reformism" advocated by President Kennedy when he announced the Alliance for Progress. The government of Costa Rica supported the Bay of Pigs invasion of 1961 and became a leading voice in the U.S.-sponsored campaign to isolate Cuba politically and economically.

This anti-Communist antirevolutionary fervor reached an extreme in 1965 when the PLN turned against its former ally Juan Bosch, whose democratic election as president was denied him in the Dominican Republic by a U.S. invasion (see chapter 10). Costa Rica joined the military dictatorships of Brazil, Honduras, and Nicaragua in sending troops to Santo Domingo to "keep the peace."

The anti-Bosch action was an early sign of the increased voice being asserted by the nation's military forces, despite the nation's antimilitary political culture. Some military officers had been infused with a virulent anticommunism by U.S. instructors. The PLN shared the radical Right's anticommunism. In such a climate Costa Rica's tiny oligarchy and its ultrarightest shock troops were able to reassert their power. A number of paramilitary groups took shape, including the Free Costa Rica movement, which developed close ties with

Guatemala's death squads. In 1965, Cuban exiles established a military base in Costa Rica only to have it closed down when protesting citizens gained support from the international community. But soldiers of fortune, drug-runners, smugglers, and criminal elements managed to develop a nascent base of operations in Costa Rica—one that expanded in the 1980s when the contras invaded Nicaragua from Costa Rican soil.

Newly created rightist political parties formed a coalition with older conservative parties in 1966 and defeated the PLN presidential candidate backed by Figueres. In the next election Figueres was reelected president. He promptly called for an inter-American invasion of Cuba, even while he protested CIA meddling in the internal affairs of his own country.

Costa Rica's PLN-dominated governments built up a huge foreign debt by taking out loans to help create conditions favorable to foreign investment and to defer the costs of chronic trade and budget deficits. The state paid for roads, dams, and other "economic infrastructure." It also kept up the earlier social welfare programs that provided it a social base among the middle classes.

In agriculture the U.S. firms United Brands (formerly UFCO), Castle & Cooke (formerly Standard Fruit) and R. J. Reynolds's Del Monte controlled banana production. The export-oriented cattle industry opened up new lands for grazing, reducing the nation's forest reserves from 71 percent of the total area in 1955 to 15 percent in 1981. Local beef prices rose and big ranchers drove small farmers from their lands, much as the earlier coffee and banana developers had done.

In the past displaced peasants had been able to move to new frontiers. But as those frontiers were stripped by lumber and cattle interests, a vast migration to teeming urban slums *(tugurios)* began. The new urban immigrants joined the cheap labor pool required for ongoing industrialization efforts.

Investors in Costa Rican industry took advantage of the CACM (Central American Common Market) to export their manufactured goods, three-fourths of which were produced by companies owned or controlled by U.S. firms. During the heyday of the CACM, the second half of the 1960s, foreign investments in Costa Rica increased by more than 3,000 percent.

The 1980s: Economic Crisis

The impact of these policies was very clear by the 1980s. Wages were driven down. In 1982 Costa Rican clothing workers were receiving wages half those of their counterparts in Taiwan. The daily minimum wage in 1984 was $3.48, lower than many other Central American countries. Two new free-trade zones were created to compete with Hong Kong and neighboring Panama. Foreign firms enjoyed duty-free imports of capital goods and a five-year exemption from income taxes. U.S. industries included American Cyanamid, Coca Cola,

Consolidated Foods, Crescent Corset, Firestone, Hirsch Fabrics, Kaiser, IBM, ITT, Lee Jeans, Loveable Brassiere Co., Quaker Oats, and United Brands. Americans bought up chunks of Costa Rican real estate at bargain prices and set up vacation and retirement communities, home to 20,000 U.S. citizens.

Two former presidents who actively stimulated these developments later summed up Costa Rica's situation as one of loss of independence. "Costa Rica is not a country," said "Pepe" Figueres. "It is a pilot project. It is an experiment." Francisco Orlich observed, "Decisions are made in accord with the expansion of foreign enterprise and not the needs of Costa Rica."

Costa Rica entered the 1980s with a population that remained about half rural despite the growth of San José to nearly 600,000, one-fourth of the total. Internal migration into the deteriorated neighborhoods of the cities' *tugurios* was accelerating. The government still talked about colonizing new lands and developing the agricultural heart of its economy, where more than one-quarter of the labor force was employed.

But industrialization since the Alliance for Progress days had brought industry's share of the GNP (gross national product) to a level equal to that of agriculture (21 percent each). The expanded public sector accounted for 15 percent of the employed labor force and almost one-fifth of GNP. The nation's per-capita GNP remained lower than the Latin American average but higher than that of other Central American countries (except Panama). Nine-tenths of the populace remained eligible for government-sponsored health care, the reason for Costa Rica's low rate of infant mortality and high life expectancy (seventy-two years).

But the economic crisis of the 1980s, brought on by falling coffee prices and higher oil prices and interest rates, threatened to tumble the social gains of half a century. The decline in the purchasing power of an average worker's wage that began in 1973 accelerated. Combined unemployment/underemployment surpassed 25 percent.

Declining living standards reawakened labor unions, sparked by the 1980 founding of the independent and left-oriented CUT (Unitary Confederation of Workers), with more than fifty affiliates. During 1980 there occurred some sixty-three labor strikes, as many as had taken place during the previous five years. The Civil Guard fired upon striking banana workers. Because of government cutbacks on consumer subsidies and reductions of guaranteed prices on farmers' produce, the economic crisis also fueled discontent among the urban and rural middle classes.

Costa Rica's income distribution, once considered one of the hemisphere's fairest, became as skewed as that of most other Latin American countries. Of national income, a meager 3.3 percent went to the bottom one-fifth of the populace, whereas a whopping 40 percent went to the top one-twentieth.

The government continued to welcome foreign investment, which poured into agribusiness, tourism, and light industry (food processing, textiles and clothing, construction materials, and fertilizer). Although increasingly dependent on U.S. aid, Costa Rica carried on considerable business with Japan, West Germany, and the rest of Central America. Nevertheless, it faced a growing trade deficit because it depended on lower-priced agricultural exports (coffee, bananas, beef, sugar, and cocoa) and had to import expensive oil, manufactures, and capital goods.

Worse yet, because of the IMF's and World Bank's insistence on increased exports to finance the debt, Costa Rica was turning more farmland over to export crops and less food was being grown for domestic consumption. Major new exports included fruits, vegetables, and cut flowers. Like Mexico, an agriculturally rich nation was importing more and more of its basic foodstuffs, and food prices rose.

The year 1981 was a turning point. By September the government could no longer meet interest payments on the debt. The IMF and a group of more than one hundred fifty foreign banks imposed a conditionality agreement that froze wages, ended price supports for basic items, increased utility rates, and reduced public sector welfare programs. For its part the United States conditioned its aid on Costa Rican cooperation with its military and diplomatic plans for the region, including a stronger Costa Rican military.

U.S. military aid tripled in the next two years. In the last year of the conservative presidency of Rodrigo Carazo (1978–1982) Costa Rica joined the U.S.-sponsored organization aimed at isolating the Nicaraguan Revolution, the Central American Democratic Community (CDC, composed of the dictatorships of El Salvador, Guatemala, and Honduras). Pleased by Costa Rica's move away from neutrality, the United States lifted a two-year ban on Costa Rican tuna. Popular discontent with the Carazo government's policies and deteriorating economic conditions contributed to a decisive victory of the PLN in the 1982 presidential election.

The economic crisis deepened in 1982. The IMF, foreign bankers, and the U.S. government pressured the government into privatizing more of the state sector. AID (Agency for International Development) programs soon surpassed $100 million a year. By 1986 Costa Rica's debt rose above the $4.5 billion mark, the highest in Central America. A common saying on the streets of San José was "Here Mr. Fondo [IMF] rules."

Economic hard times hurt the PLN at the polls in the 1986 presidential elections. Its candidate, Oscar Arias Sánchez, barely defeated Rafael Angel Calderón Fournier, candidate of the Christian Democrat–dominated opposition coalition PSUC (Social Christian Unity party) and the son of the mid-1940s populist political leader. Enough voters considered Calderón's call for the breaking of relations with Nicaragua a dangerous escalation of the simmering war along the border to prevent his victory. Calderón also championed harsher actions against strikers. Thus Arias won as a "peace" candidate who was less inimical to labor.

Two small right-wing armed movements emerged in the mid-1980s, the EPC (Costa Rican People's Army) and Homeland and Truth. The Left fared poorly in the election process, although the PU (People United), founded in 1978, had elected a number of its candidates to the unicameral Legislative Assembly. Costa Rica's Communist party showed strength in organized labor, dominating the CUT. But in August 1987 the party lost its stronghold in the banana industry when some three thousand workers signed nonunion agreements with Standard Fruit (subsidiary of U.S.-based Castle & Cooke). The agreements, backed by the Catholic Church and the labor ministry, were hailed by moderates as the "Costa Rican road to labor peace." The agreements combined dimensions of private company unionism with a workers' cooperative movement launched in 1978. The Left continued to decline in the 1990s.

Militarization of Costa Rica and Foreign Relations

U.S. military aid programs ($18 million in 1984–1985) had partially militarized a country once known for its absence of armed forces. Anti-Nicaraguan military operations by U.S.-backed contras were being launched from Costa Rican territory.

Public resentment began growing when President Luis Alberto Monge Alvarez of the PLN accepted U.S. Special Forces advisers to train Costa Rica's National Guard in counterinsurgency in 1982. The Guardsmen and Green Berets operated in close proximity to the contra bases. Some citizens protested that their government was directly collaborating with the invasion of Nicaragua (charges later borne out, in part, by the Iran-contragate revelations). Disagreeing with the conservative PLN majority on the issue of U.S. military advisers, PLN founder Don Pepe Figueres launched on May 26, 1982, the Patriotic Forum for Peace and Sovereignty. Minister of Public Safety Benjamín Piza Escalante, founder of the fascistic Free Costa Rica Movement, stated, "I cannot guarantee that a couple of our men might not have been involved with the contras."

Two longtime U.S. residents in Costa Rica, journalists Martha Honey and Tony Avirgan, lodged a controversial lawsuit against twenty-nine U.S. and Costa Rican officials, including leading figures in the Iran-contragate affair such as Richard Secord, John Singlaub, and Robert Owen. They charged these men with violation of U.S. antiracketeering laws—that is, illegal drug trafficking. The Costa Rican ranch of American John Hull was a key "drop" point in the operation. According to witnesses' statements, U.S. pilots flew weapons to the contras in Nicaragua and returned with planeloads of drugs that received clearance to land at U.S. Air Force bases in Florida. The two journalists suffered numerous death threats but pursued their suit. During their investigations they also uncovered evidence of the CIA's and Hull's involvement in the 1984 bombing of a press conference held by Edén Pastora (whose contra army refused to unite with the mainstream contras and later disbanded) at La Penca, Nicaragua. Later evidence suggested a faction of the Sandinistas may have been responsible for the incident.

A few miles from a Civil Guard training camp at Murciélago, near the northwestern border with Nicaragua, an airfield large enough to handle transport planes was built by a shadowy company based in Panama with links to Oliver North and contragate (see Introduction to Part One and chapter 7). U.S. troops and military engineers were very active in the area. President-elect Arias announced in early 1986 an agreement with Nicaragua to set up a bilateral border vigilance commission. The United States responded by sending 186 more Army engineers to renovate border airstrips.

Nicaragua filed charges against Costa Rica before the World Court for allowing its territory to be used by the contras to mount an invasion. In September 1986 Minister of Public Safety Hernán Garrón Salazar said the Murciélago airfield was being closed because "we feared it was being used by the counterrevolutionaries or by drug traffickers."

That fall the government deported Armando López Estrada, a Cuban-American who claimed past CIA connections and to have been a liaison with the Costa Rica–based contra supply network. López gave officials details of his past that went back to espionage activities at the time of the 1961 Bay of Pigs invasion and included narcotics trafficking as well.

The Costa Rican government also jailed some U.S. mercenaries. One of them later gave a televised interview stating that he had been instructed by the CIA to participate in a plot to blow up the U.S. Embassy in San José. The aim was to create an incident that could be blamed on Nicaragua's Sandinista government and used to justify a U.S. military response. The young man expressed his disillusionment and returned to his home in Florida, where his mother told him to flee for his life. A week later he turned up dead in California, allegedly of a drug overdose. Other individuals involved in the same alleged plot reported "suspicious" deaths and, on U.S. television, told interviewers they expected to testify before congressional hearings on Iran-contragate in 1987. They were never called, however (see Introduction to Part One).

The role of the U.S. Embassy in San José in the creation of a contra military network operating out of Costa Rica was not well known until 1987. In December 1986 American Ambassador Lewis Tambs resigned. He later testified before the U.S. Congress that during his ambassadorship he had acted on orders from the State Department, the CIA, and Oliver North "to open a southern front" for the contra invasion against Nicaragua. National Security Council head Rear Admiral John Poindexter testified that he had briefed President Reagan on the Costa Rican airstrip built as part of the U.S.-created "southern front" operation. Costa Rica was, more than ever, being sucked into the international maelstrom. For Costa Ricans the burning issue was national sovereignty.

President Arias's peace efforts finally succeeded. In July 1987, Nicaragua dropped its World Court charges against Costa Rica. The following month Nicaragua's President Daniel Ortega joined four other Central American presidents in signing the Arias Peace Plan in Guatemala (see Introduction to Part One and Documents). But Costa Rica was still left with the legacy of the 1980s.

Crisis Prolonged

The year 1990 marked a symbolic watershed in Costa Rican history. Pepe Figueres, the leader of the 1948 "revolution," died, and the PLN's presidential candidate lost the election to the PUSC's forty-one-year-old Calderón Fournier. An era was ending. The revolution's social programs had been slashed to the bone. The 1990s started with real wages still below their 1980 level.

Incoming president Calderón Fournier had served in the 1980s as executive director of the Costa Rican Association for the Defense of Democracy and Liberty, a right-wing group critical of the Arias peace plan and largely funded with monies from the National Endowment for Democracy and U.S. Information Agency. Calderón Fournier had run a populist campaign. Ironically, his 51 percent tally was a protest vote against Nobel laureate Arias's presidency, which had been rocked by drug scandals and a sputtering economy.

Under Calderón Fournier, Costa Rica's economy still sputtered. The population living in poverty rose from 18.6 percent in 1987 to 24.4 percent in 1991. A 1991 earthquake devastated the country's main port of Limón on the Atlantic coast. Economic growth approached 3 percent in 1992, but the annual inflation rate was 17 percent, considered high. More of the state sector was privatized. The government opened financial markets, with the state monopoly on insurance being the last one under review.

Delighted U.S. creditors renegotiated Costa Rica's debt and extended new loans that further swelled the debt. But U.S. courts balked at accepting cases launched by banana workers against Shell Oil, Dow Chemical, and Occidental Petroleum for selling the pesticide DBCP (dibromochloropropane) in Costa Rica after the U.S. Environmental Protection Agency banned its use in 1979.

Costa Rica's trade deficit and foreign debt doubled in 1991–1992. Banana plantations were hard hit by EEC's decision to restrict imports of Latin

American bananas (see introductions to Part One and Part Two and Conclusion). Rising *maquiladora* production contributed $689 million worth of exports in 1992.

Eco-tourism brought in even more foreign currency. It flourished with the world's growing concern for the protection of rainforests (see Overview and chapter 20). Costa Rica boasted of 3.7 million acres placed under protection since the early 1970s. After that, almost as much land was deforested by expanding banana and cattle concerns. The government worked with Merck and Company to explore the forests for medicinal plants. Poor people found themselves forced to collect firewood or burn forested areas to grow food for survival. Some 30,000 Costa Rican women organized to help the poor construct new housing.

Corruption, street crime, robberies, kidnappings, and drug addition rose at an alarming rate. Charges of embezzlement of $2 million from a government emergency fund implicated ex-President (1982–1986) Monge and eighteen others. In April 1993, five gunmen, on orders from a former narcotics detective in need of money for a liver transplant, took eighteen Supreme Court justices hostage for three days and demanded a $20 million ransom. They released the hostages when promised safe exit from the country; then they were arrested. Complained one store owner: "This is no Swiss democracy—we're looking more like the rest of Central America every day."

The electoral campaign of 1994 was one of the dirtiest in history. The PLN's thirty-nine-year-old José María Figueres Olsen, son of "Don Pepe" and a West Point graduate, won handily by campaigning against the economic neo-liberalism of the administration's PSUC. The new president promised to beef up the nation's dwindling social welfare programs to help the needy.

Selected Bibliography

American Friends Service Committee. *Report on Costa Rica 1985.* Philadelphia, PA: AFSC, 1985. Surveys the controversies.

Bell, John P. *Crisis in Costa Rica: The 1948 Revolution.* Austin: University of Texas Press, 1971. By a former member of U.S. Foreign Service.

Bird, Leonard. *Costa Rica: The Unarmed Democracy.* London: Sheppard Press, 1984. Dedicated to "Don Pepe" Figueres; argues against a permanent army.

Edelman, Marc, and Joanne Kenen (eds.). *The Costa Rica Reader.* New York: Grove Press, 1989.

Edelman, Marc, and Rodolfo Monge Oviedo. "Costa Rica: The Non-Market Roots of Market Success," *Nacla Report on the Americas,* 26(4) (Feb. 1993).

Hall, Carolyn. *Costa Rica: A Geographical Interpretation in Historical Perspective.* Boulder, CO: Westview, 1985. "Excellent synthesis" (*Hispanic American Historical Review.*)

Honey, Martha. *Hostile Acts: U.S. Policy in Costa Rica in the 1980s.* Gainesville: University of Florida Press, 1993.

Saxe-Fernández, John. "The Militarization of Costa Rica," *Monthly Review,* 24(1) (May 1972). Pioneering study.

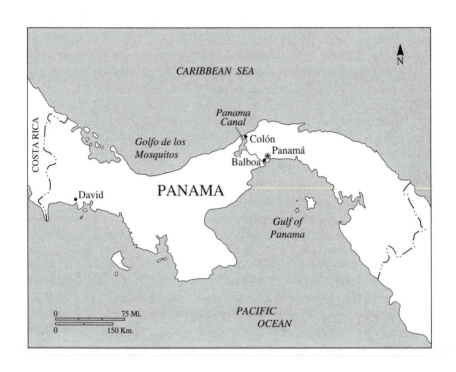

244

Panama 7

I took the Canal.—*Teddy Roosevelt, 1911*

We bought it, we paid for it, we built it, and we intend to keep it.—*Ronald Reagan, 1980*

If the students break into the Zone again I have only the alternative of crushing them or leading them. I will not crush them.—*General Omar Torrijos Herrera, "Chief of the Revolution," 1976*

In early January 1964 a visitor to Panama could sense the tension. Radios were blaring out news of the controversy over the recent implementation of a 1959 order by President Eisenhower to fly the Panamanian flag alongside the U.S. flag in sixteen designated Canal Zone locations in recognition of Panama's "titular sovereignty." Street agitators were working the sweltering crowds of "Hollywood" and other slum communities traditionally known as *barriadas brujas* ("witch quarters") that festered only minutes away from the luxurious U.S.-controlled Zone. People were "taking the air" on the balconies of Hollywood's tottering wooden houses. Brown-tinted rainwater and mud were the "streets"; without sewers, the whole place reeked from the stench of communal lavatories. A woman hanging her laundry on a Hollywood balcony could see a half-mile away the manicured golf courses, grass tennis courts, and racially segregated schools, housing, and public facilities of "Little America," as the Zone colony was called by its U.S. residents.

On January 7, U.S. students hoisted an American flag on the flagpole in front of the Balboa High School on the Pacific Ocean side of the Canal Zone. Two days later about 150 Panamanian high-school students entered the Zone and marched to the Balboa High School, bearing their seventeen-year-old Panamanian flag that had been used in similar student demonstrations in 1947. Zone police nervously accompanied the Panamanians.

U.S. students clustered around "their" flagpole and shouted racial epithets at the Panamanians. The police captain ordered the Panamanians to cross the street. A scuffle ensued, and the Panamanian flag was torn. The Panamanian students fought briefly with the police, then made a dash back through the two miles of the U.S.-controlled Zone for safety in Panama. En route they tried to haul down a U.S. flag in front of the Zone Administration Building, smashed car windows, and overturned trash cans.

Within hours all hell broke loose. Incensed at the desecration of their flag, some three thousand Panamanians stormed the Canal Zone and started to burn and sack the Ancon freight house and a nearby railroad station. U.S. troops were called into action. War tanks rumbled into Panama City. Helicopters and fighter planes swooped over Hollywood. Demonstrators torched U.S. cars and businesses. On the roads entering towns, students toppled the Walt Disney figures that bore the towns' names. The protests leapfrogged across the nation's jungles, reaching as far as the farming-commercial center of David 314 miles to the west, near the Costa Rican border and the 11,000-foot-high volcanic cone of Mt. Chiriquí.

By the time the dust settled twenty-four Panamanians and four U.S. soldiers were dead; hundreds were wounded. Before the OAS (Organization of American States) Panama charged the United States with armed aggression. It broke diplomatic relations for four months. President Lyndon B. Johnson agreed in December to open negotiations on new canal treaties, recognizing that Panamanian feelings were "based on a profound sense of the necessary honor and justice of Panama."

. . .

Panama's politics, like its economy, has been shaped by the history of the forty-mile canal connecting the Atlantic and Pacific oceans. U.S. control of the canal has long been an affront to Panamanians' sense of national independence, while for many Americans it has symbolized world power status and a cause for pride. The so-called "flag riots" of 1964 epitomized this clash.

Prior to the U.S. invasion of Panama in 1989, the 1977–1978 Canal Treaties sought to prevent any future clashes on the canal issue. They provided for Panamanian assumption of the chairmanship of the Panama Canal Commission in 1990 and Panamanian control of the Canal Zone in the year 2000. The Zone is a 550-square-mile strip of land extending for 5 miles on either side of the canal that separates the northwestern half of Panama from its southeastern half, making Panama the only nation to be divided by an area owned by a foreign power. A citizen of Panama did become commission chair during the U.S. military occupation in January 1990. However, by the time of the 1994 elections, the government of Guillermo Endara Galimany, installed at the height of the invasion, lacked strong public support. Panama was still rocked by political instability.

The main causes of the Canal Treaties and Panama's subsequent political instability were complex. Responding to nationalist sentiment, Panama's popular leader General Omar Torrijos Herrera (1968-1980) declared that if the United States did not agree to a new treaty by the end of 1977 it was possible the Canal Zone would be without "water, light, or gringos." The Pentagon informed President Carter that it would take 100,000 U.S. soldiers to defend the canal. Carter and Torrijos initialed the canal treaties in September 1977.

The following month, Panamanians voted their approval of the treaties by a two-thirds majority. In March 1978, the U.S. Senate ratified them, first adding amendments stating that the United States had the right to defend "forever" the canal or a future sea-level canal, but intervention would not be "against the territorial integrity or political independence of Panama." The amendments called for future bilateral "agreements or arrangements for the stationing of any U.S. military forces" in Panama after the year 2000. The treaty also provided for unilateral "use of military force in the Republic of Panama to reopen the Canal or restore the operations of the Canal." Yet President George Bush did not invoke the treaties when listing the reasons for the 1989 U.S. invasion. Bush preferred to emphasize the illegitimacy of the Noriega government and the "pro-democracy" mission of installing in the presidency the presumed winner of the nullified May elections.

While being negotiated, the canal treaties of 1977–1978 aroused strong conflicting views. Opponents of the United States claimed that Panama was bound forever by the original 1903 treaty that gave the United States control over any future canal "in perpetuity" and the right to act "as though it were sovereign" in the land surrounding the canal. Treaty supporters answered that the 1903 canal agreement did not conform with the UN Charter and would never survive a challenge before the World Court. The new treaties provided for neutrality of the canal, guaranteed access to passage for U.S. and other shipping, and laid a basis for improved relations with all Latin America and greater credibility in the Third World. Disagreeing with fellow conservatives, William Buckley returned from a visit to Panama to state that he trusted Torrijos and believed the United States should "get out—while the initiative is still clearly our own. That is the way great nations should act." Influential TNCs (transnational corporations), with a lot to lose in Latin America, also rallied behind the treaties.

Panamanian supporters viewed the treaties as a long overdue concession of real sovereignty by the United States. Detractors, however, pointed out that the treaties could legitimize future U.S. military interventions in Panama and increase Panama's dependence on the United States by means of the treaties' economic aid and joint defense clauses.

Calmer voices on both sides noted that the Panama Canal was becoming an obsolete relic, unable to handle the huge, deep-draught ships of the late twentieth century. Canal use was tapering off in the face of air transport, the U.S. creation of a three-ocean fleet, and a defense system based on thermonuclear weapons, electronic warfare, and outer-space vehicles.

The presidency of Ronald Reagan (1981–1989), however, viewed U.S. military installations in Panama as an essential component of its war-by-proxy being conducted against the Nicaraguan Revolution of 1979 and popular insurgencies in El Salvador and Guatemala (see Introduction to Part One). As pro-Reagan right-wing ideologue Roger Fontaine explained to a conference on international security in 1987: "Howard Air Force Base is well sited for logistical operations and force projection throughout the region." Moreover, Fontaine pointed out, a refuelling station on Panama's Atlantic Coast could support "the by now small but permanent U.S. naval presence off the coast of El Salvador."

Although a media blitz persuaded the U.S. public that the 1989 "Operation Just Cause" invasion of Panama was a good thing, Latin American nationalists thought otherwise. One more unsavory dictator's removal from power paled before the hi-tech overkill of the invasion and the symbolic import of the canal. The one issue that first came to Latin Americans' minds when complaining about domination by "the colossus of the north" remained the Panama Canal. Some suspected the hidden long-range purpose of the 1989 invasion was to make the Canal Treaties either irrelevant or a cosmetic cover for continued denial of genuine Panamanian national sovereignty. The invasion violated both the UN Charter and the treaties' specific prohibition of intervention "against the territorial integrity or political independence of Panama."

Nationalism: Lower-Class Revolt versus Concessions to Foreigners

Panamanian nationalism always related to the country's unique linkages to world trade through its optimal geographical location. The lower classes often resisted subjugation in the name of defending the nation. Although the elite families made concessions to stronger outside powers in order to maintain their privileges, they often catered to the nationalism of the masses by posing as "defenders of national honor."

The Spaniards made Panama one of their earliest settlements, using it as a springboard for the conquest of North and South America and as a storage and shipping depot for the wealth of all the American colonies. An estimated half million Indians of sixty tribes (related to the Nahuatl and Maya of Guatemala and Mexico and the Chibcha of Colombia) strongly resisted the conquest but could not withstand the contagious diseases that accompanied it. Most perished, while survivors persisted in their independent ways. About 7 percent of today's 2.4 million Panamanians are Indian. They include the Kuna who live on the 365 Mulatas (San Blas) Islands off the Caribbean coast. The Kuna enjoy local autonomy, pay no taxes, and have their own treaty with Colombia.

Many African slaves imported by Spain to carry booty across the isthmus escaped to set up independent "kingdoms." They were known as *cimarrones*. Today, blacks compose 14 percent of the population, speak mainly English, and are the backbone of the Canal Zone work force. Most of them descend from West Indians brought from the Caribbean to build the Canal.

Throughout history, Panama's white elites enforced racial segregation codes. The otherwise progressive constitution of 1941, approved during the short-lived presidency of Nazi sympathizer Arnulfo Arias, called for the exclusion or deportation of Caribbean blacks, Chinese, and other "undesirable colored aliens." About a tenth of the present population is caucasian. The majority of Panamanians are mestizo or mulatto, who, except for those few assimilated into the upper class, also suffer racial discrimination at the hands of the whites.

Buccaneers unsuccessfully sought to seize Panamanian wealth throughout the colonial period. Panamanians put up strong defenses. In 1572 Sir Francis Drake destroyed the city of Nombre de Dios; in 1671 Sir Henry Morgan burned and looted Panama City.

All the major powers thought about building a canal across Panama. When Spain's decline became obvious in the early 1800s two independence leaders, Simón Bolívar and Francisco de Miranda (see chapter 11), made offers of canal rights to the British in return for weapons and support against the Spanish. When the Spanish colonies declared independence in 1821, Panama proclaimed its own separate freedom before voluntarily federating with Gran Colombia (now Venezuela, Colombia, Ecuador, and Peru).

As early as 1815 Bolívar envisioned a confederation of Central American states centered at a canal in Panama that would "bring that happy region tribute from the four quarters of the globe. Perhaps some day the capital of the world may be located there." By 1826 the great Latin American Liberator was calling a Pan American Conference in Panama to unite all the Americas. But the United States, having already warned Bolívar not to liberate Cuba or Puerto Rico, failed to attend. Three years later a disillusioned Bolívar warned, "The United States appears to be destined by Providence to plague America with misery in the name of liberty."

U.S. meddling in Panama started early. In 1840–1841, after unsuccessful revolts in 1830 and 1831, Panama attempted once more to break away from Colombia. But Colombia, gaining U.S. support in exchange for future trade and navigation privileges on the isthmus, crushed the revolt.

The California "gold rush" brought U.S. investors to Panama. They imported Caribbean blacks to build the private transisthmus Panama Railroad, which opened in 1855. U.S. troops appeared almost yearly in the 1850s to crush popular rebellions and guarantee Colombian sovereignty.

During the 1880s a private French company headed by engineer Ferdinand de Lesseps attempted to build a canal. Malaria and yellow fever killed off 20,000 imported black West Indian workers, and Panamanians rose up again for independence in 1885, burning the Caribbean port city of Colón. U.S. troops occupied the land adjacent to the railway for fifty-six days, once more assuring Colombian sovereignty.

Eighteen years later, in 1903, Colombia rejected the terms of a U.S. offer for construction of a canal. The United States promptly dropped its pretended concern for Colombian sovereignty and became a supporter of Panamanian independence.

Military needs generated by the U.S.-Spain-Cuba War of 1898 had heightened U.S. interest in building a canal. So had lucrative investments by U.S. corporations. The United Fruit Company (UFCO), for instance, owned one-quarter of the value of all private property in Panama. William Nelson Cromwell, of UFCO's hired law firm Sullivan & Cromwell, was virtual head of the Panama Railroad and part owner of the bankrupt French Canal Company. He and the company's chief engineer, Phillipe Bunau-Varilla, bribed U.S. congressmen to choose Panama over Nicaragua as a route for a future canal.

Realizing the historic yearning of Panamanians for independence, the administration of President Theodore Roosevelt plotted Panama's independence from Colombia that would guarantee a U.S. canal in perpetuity. In August 1903, Colombia rejected the proposed treaty terms for a U.S. canal. The United States made contact with Panamanian separatist leaders. A tiny group of well-to-do Panamanians, some of them patriots and all of them fearing renewed labor unrest or popular revolution, welcomed the support of U.S. Marines to secure their own political interests and future wealth.

On November 3, 1903, Panama became an independent nation. U.S. warships stood by offshore, and personnel operating the U.S.-built railway denied passage for Colombian troops in direct violation of the railroad's original concession terms. The 1903 canal treaty signed two weeks later granted U.S. eminent domain throughout Panama and perpetual control over the future Canal Zone.

The Panama Canal took a decade to build. It was completed in 1914 and cost the lives of more than five thousand workers, mostly West Indians. The canal was touted as a marvel of modern engineering. It was also a model of racial segregation. Panamanian and black workers were paid in silver and white workers were paid in gold, a distinction passed on for generations in job appointments distinguishing high-paid security positions for U.S. citizens from low-paid nonsecurity positions for Panamanians.

The new Panamanian government reluctantly accepted the 1903 treaty because it feared loss of its independence if U.S. backing against Colombia was withdrawn. The treaty, not made available in Spanish until 1926, became the target of repeated nationalist uprisings over the next three-quarters of a century. Panama's elites were able to maintain what little real political power they had only by launching demagogic tirades against "Yankee imperialist" control of national territory.

Presumably to "defend the canal," thousands of U.S. troops took up positions in the Canal Zone. They repeatedly invaded Panama to assure the interests of U.S. banana companies, banks, and corporations and to protect Panama's elite families—known as "the twenty families," or the *rabiblancos* ("white tails" or "white fury," after a game bird hunted out of season).

The U.S. military interventions of 1908, 1910, 1918–1919, and 1921 were all initiated by the United States because it refused to tolerate a presidential candidacy of someone not to its liking. Popular mobilizations for improved economic or social conditions also brought U.S. troops. In 1925, for instance, U.S. Marines entered Panama City to put down a strike by workers demanding lower rents. The Marines killed many of the strikers with their bayonets and were thanked personally by Panama's foreign minister. Subsequent street protests against attempts to lock Panama into a military alliance were also crushed by U.S. troops, but twice—in 1926 and 1947—the elite-dominated National Assembly felt the pressure and voted against a military alliance.

Panama's elites were not the "landed aristocracy" typical of so much of Latin America. They based their wealth on international commerce, urban rents, and circulation of goods rather than on rural land ownership and the production of goods.

In the 1930s Panama's dependent economy was pummeled by the Great Depression. A new middle class led the struggles of labor and minorities for survival wages. Two mestizo brothers, Harmodio and Arnulfo Arias, who had made their fortunes in the provinces, gained a large popular following. Running on the Liberal party ticket, Harmodio Arias became president in 1932.

Behind the scenes he and the oligarchy agreed to negotiate. A 1936 revised canal treaty made some moderate concessions to Panama in the spirit of President Franklin D. Roosevelt's "Good Neighbor" policy (see Overview). The Panamanian oligarchy benefited from increased access to lucrative Canal Zone markets. Panama's annual lease fee for the canal was also increased.

Those middle-class families who gained some political power during the

1930s rapidly adapted to the old elites' ways. One political scientist later observed, "The state came to be controlled by a small group of families who treated the national treasury as their personal preserve."

In the next two decades powerful political machines based on state patronage were developed, and some public services were finally offered to the urban masses. The "personalismo" of patron-client relations so typical of Latin America flourished in Panama, where single individuals often developed large political followings on the basis of populist-style appeals to the masses.

One such individual was Arnulfo Arias. He dominated Panamanian politics for five decades. In a way similar to Velasco Ibarra in Ecuador or Perón in Argentina (see chapters 13 and 18)), he trumpeted an anti-Communist nationalism that also tugged at Uncle Sam's beard. Arias became president three times, but each time he was thrown out of office (1941, 1951, 1968) by U.S.-backed Panamanian police and National Guard forces. In 1984 he claimed that he was cheated again of an electoral victory and blamed the Guard and the United States.

The United States had created Panama's national police in 1936, much in the way it had created the other military forces of the Caribbean Basin (see chapters 5, 8 and 10) Police chief José Antonio Remón, who over the years unseated five presidents, helped transform the police into the National Guard and ruled Panama with ruthless venality from 1952 until his assassination in 1955. He gained some new concessions on the canal treaty right before his death, notably an increase in the lease fee to $1,930,000.

Remón's regime modernized the National Guard and involved it in drug-running and organized crime activities that grew enormously in the 1980s. Remón also legitimized Guard intervention to mediate conflicts among political elites and to preserve oligarchical privileges.

The New Politics and a Crisis of Hegemony

One of the anti-Arias Guard coups occurred in 1968 at a time when the continent was shaking with the new politics (see Overview). Women agitators and priests led slumdwellers in street demonstrations. An Alliance for Progress report of 1973 revealed why. It stated that by 1966 unemployment stood at 25 percent. The largest employers were the government (30,000 employees), the Canal Zone (13,000), and UFCO (now United Brands, 11,000). One-third of national income went to 5 percent of the population, and "the great majority of farmers earned less than $100 a year." This was in Central America's most urbanized country with the highest per-capita income and second highest literacy and life expectancy rates.

The "flag riots" of 1964 started a crisis of political hegemony. Middle-class elements, workers, and peasants were pitted against divided ruling elites.

The powerful CONEP (National Confederation of Private Enterprise) split between those commercial and high-finance elements seeking to convert Panama into a free-trade zone, Hong Kong-style, and those industrial interests seeking more import substitution, protective tariffs, and integration into the CACM (Central American Common Market).

General Torrijos, Populist Military Reformism, and Corporativism

Such was the unstable situation faced by the National Guard, eight thousand-strong and well-equipped, when it took power in 1968. This time, a strong populist leader emerged within the Guard to assert control within two years. The son of a poor rural schoolteacher, he was Omar Torrijos Herrera. Trained by the United States, General Torrijos had killed student and peasant guerrilla fighters in Panama's remote Cerro Tute in 1959 and had watched from the Guard's barracks as students invaded the Canal Zone in 1964. His heart was with the students—the canal was rightfully Panama's. Torrijos was an admirer of Yugoslavia's Tito and eventually got on good terms with Cuba's Castro. According to personal confidants, Torrijos dreamed of an independent social democratic Central America that would be no menace to the United States.

Now as "Maximum Leader of the Revolution," Torrijos used the canal issue as a nationalist rallying cry to unite all social classes in a state-organized corporativist manner similar to what General Velasco was doing in Peru and Mexico's PRI (Institutional Revolutionary party) had done for decades (see chapters 1 and 14). Six months after Ronald Reagan became president, Torrijos died in a suspicious plane crash. Years later, Colonel Roberto Díaz charged that U.S. General Wallace Nutting, head of the Southern Command based in Panama, conspired with Torrijos' chief of intelligence, future dictator Manuel Noriega, and the CIA to plant a bomb on the plane. Whatever the truth, for Panamanian nationalists it was bad enough that in 1973 Watergate luminary John Dean had revealed an earlier plot on Torrijos' life by two leaders of the Bay of Pigs invasion of Cuba (see chapter 8), Watergate defendant E. Howard Hunt and his CIA cohort Cuban exile Manuel Artime.

Torrijos' thirteen-year reign epitomized the new politics trend of populist-reformist segments of Latin America's military emerging in the name of revolution. At first Torrijos and the guard looked like "hard-cop" types. They jailed Communists, occupied the national university, launched search-and-destroy missions against guerrillas near the Costa Rican border, and established "order." Then, playing "soft cop," Torrijos awarded ministerial posts to members of the Communist-dominated FEP (Federation of Panamanian Students) in exchange for their support for his policies. Panama recognized Cuba in 1974, joined the nonaligned movement in 1975, and offered political refuge for those fleeing ultrarightist military dictatorships in the rest of Latin America. Torrijos supported Nicaragua's Sandinista guerrillas—quite a reversal for a U.S.-trained expert in counterinsurgency warfare!

General Torrijos also sought the support of the lower classes and the advocates of the new theology of liberation (see Overview). An American priest, Father Leo T. Mahon, impressed him. From 1963 to 1970 Father Mahon, who had developed consciousness-building programs in Chicago's Puerto Rican and Mexican neighborhoods, had successfully implemented his "conscientización" programs among the shantytown dwellers of San Miguelito, northeast of Panama city. Torrijos authorized autonomy for San Miguelito and adopted its model of local participation. In place of the elite-dominated legislature, he established the NACR (National Assembly of Community Representatives), composed of 505 *juntas comunales* or local participatory bodies similar to San Miguelito's.

In the countryside Torrijos handed out 4.4 percent of agricultural lands to the peasants, creating *asentamientos,* or peasant settlements, in the least fertile regions. Large cattle estates went practically untouched. The nation's best land remained owned by the twenty-two large plantations.

A new labor code granting urban labor many benefits was approved in 1972. Using the flexibility made possible by corporativist organizations that helped bring previously unrepresented slumdwellers, peasants, and workers into the political mainstream, Torrijos was able to juggle the demands of conflicting groups while centralizing power in himself and his trusted advisers. A new constitution in 1972 granted extraordinary powers to the general for a period of six years.

The elites fought Torrijos' populist policies with considerable skill, managing to preserve their privileged positions. The 1972 labor code, for instance, gradually ceased to be enforced. General Torrijos eventually gave in to the antilabor demands of big business' CONEP and medium-sized and small rural producers, particularly after the economy suffered a downturn in 1974.

The Torrijos regime's corporativist populism stabilized the nation's politics for a decade and strengthened the economic power of wealthy domestic and foreign investors. According to political scientist George Priestley, Torrijos' "military dictatorship of the bourgeoisie" had two goals. First, it sought to modernize production based on industry and agribusiness and to improve the commercial-financial economy based on the 1977–1978 Canal Treaties, the Colón Free Trade Zone, and a liberal banking and tax code. Second, it sought to "coopt" (buy off) organized labor and incorporate it into a democratic framework to support the industrial wing of the bourgeoisie. Until the economic downturn of the mid-1970s, the two-goal project proceeded smoothly. Panama became momentarily self-sufficient in the production of basic foods and increased its exports of bananas, shrimp, sugar, tobacco, rice, cattle, and the petroleum products of refineries processing Venezuelan oil. New hydroelectric plants fueled 90 percent of the country's energy needs. Contracts for extraction of the world's largest copper deposits were handed out to foreign firms like Texasgulf Corporation and the Canadian firm Pavonia, S.A.

Liberalized banking and tax laws attracted more than 134 international banks from all over the world to Panama's newly created International Finance Center (IFC)—the world's sixth largest. Bank secrecy laws more stringent than Switzerland's made Panama a haven for "narco-dollars," "capital-flight" deposits, and the millions stolen by military dictators such as Haiti's Duvalier and the Philippines' Marcos.

Transnational Service and Counterinsurgency Platforms

By the early 1980s services accounted for 72 percent of Panama's gross domestic product. Panama accounted for 85 percent of all U.S. direct investments in Central America, including $2 billion socked into the IFC. Panama also offered shipping firms its flag to avoid shipping and cargo taxes. Most U.S. oil tankers flew the Panamanian or Liberian flags.

An additional 150,000 nonfunctioning "paper companies" (fronts for TNCs whose facilities are located in other nations) were registered in Panama to take advantage of the many tax and accounting benefits. Three such companies—Udall Resources, Stanford Technology Corporation, and Lake Resources—served as conduits for "illegal" dollars being transferred from Iran to support Nicaragua's contras (see Introduction to Part One).

The Colón Free Zone on the Atlantic coast became one of the world's most important trading areas. More than eight hundred companies conducted $1 billion of business a year—double the total of CACM's internal trade. There were no export duties and often no corporate taxes. U.S.- and other foreign-based TNCs set up assembly plants in the Free Zone in electronics, book binding, garments, and pharmaceuticals.

Panamanian economists characterized the financial and services sectors as a "transnational service platform," since most of the profits went overseas to foreign interests. But Panama's "twenty families" also benefited. They modernized themselves into a junior-partner financial bourgeoisie by means of deals made with the TNCs. Many National Guard officers also prospered, often by means of bribes paid them by big-time investors, bankers, or drug traffickers. Panamanians recognized the corruption spreading throughout their country. "To get anything done," they said, "you have to put a colonel on your payroll."

Panama also continued to serve as a counterinsurgency platform. For more than three decades the Canal Zone had been the headquarters of the U.S. Southern Command and its "School of the Americas" (temporarily moved in 1985 to Fort Benning, Georgia, leaving a navy school and an air force school behind). The school trained 45,000 Latin American military officers (earning it the nickname "School of military coups"). A model Vietnamese village was created to train Green Berets before their departure for Vietnam. U.S. military trainers taught Bolivian Rangers who in 1967 participated in the capture and murder of Ché Guevara (see chapter 15). A major cause of the new canal treaties was Panamanians' indignation at the use of their territory for the launching of military missions against other Latin Americans, including the Dominican Republic invasion of 1965.

After the signing of the treaties the United States continued to run its Army Jungle Operating Training Center for U.S. soldiers in Panama. The Pentagon's Mobile Training Teams for Central American troops consisted mainly of members of the Army Special Forces attached to the 193rd Infantry Brigade stationed in Panama.

In spite of its role in the Contadora peace-making process (see Introduction to Part One), Panama was still a major communications base for U.S. military operations being conducted against Nicaragua and guerrillas in El Salvador and Guatemala. The canal treaties allowed the continued presence in Panama of COPECOM (Permanent Commission for Interamerican Military Communications). Together with Honduras, Panama was host to the Pentagon's "Exercise Blazing" in 1986, a construction project involving 10,000 U.S. active-duty soldiers and Army reservists.

The Crisis of the 1980s and U.S. Invasion

Following Torrijos' death, Panama underwent increasing crisis. Advocates of the new politics, including some industrialists, fought to retain the momentum of the "revolution." They were opposed by high-finance and commercial families who longed for the pre-1968 "good old days" when they enjoyed complete oligarchic power. A third key actor was the military.

In 1984 General Manuel Antonio Noriega consolidated his power in the National Guard and renamed it the PDF (Panama Defense Forces). When still a youth from a poor background, Noriega had been trained by the U.S. military. In the 1980s, Noriega played all sides in the counter-intelligence game: Cuba, Nicaragua, and the United States. He did the same in the drug business. DEA officials described his cooperation as "superb." After 1984, Panama's role in narcotics trafficking was cut back.

Reforms in 1983 provided for a president, two vice-presidents, and a sixty-seven member National Assembly to be elected for five-year terms in 1984. Noriega tampered with the election results, allowing the U.S.-backed candidate Nicolás Ardito Barletta to win by 1,173 votes over the octogenarian Nazi sympathizer Arnulfo Arias. A former minister of planning under Torrijos (1973–1978), Barletta had received a doctorate in economics at the University of Chicago and shared the laissez faire free-market doctrines of Milton Fried-man and the "Chicago Boys" (see chapter 17). U.S. embassy officials, aware of the vote tampering, later acknowledged that the Reagan administration had approved Barletta as the best possible candidate. His campaign was partly funded by the AIFLD (see Overview and Introduction to Part One) through its affiliate, the Confederation of Panamanian Workers.

Not long after the inauguration of Barletta as president, the political tide seemed to turn against General Noriega, particularly in Washington. It was not the first time Noriega had experienced U.S. ill will. In 1972 the Nixon admin-istration had considered the idea of assassinating him, presumably to reduce drug trafficking in Panama. Now, in the summer of 1985, the CIA leaked re-ports indicating the general had been involved in drug trafficking and had given away CIA secrets to Cuba's intelligence agencies. The U.S. Embassy found the time ripe to acknowledge it had known all along that Noriega had "rigged" the 1984 elections.

Further pressure was put on Noriega by President Barletta's decision to launch an official investigation into the torture-murder of a former deputy minister of health who allegedly had been killed by a PDF-linked death squad known as "F-8 Terrorista." The general had the president out-gunned, however. Behind the scenes Noriega arranged for President Barletta's resignation. First Vice-President Eric Arturo del Valle, a powerful industrialist from the small conservative PR (Republic party), who was widely viewed as a Noriega figurehead, became president in the fall of 1985. Gone were the days of Torrijos-style populist-corporativist stability in Pana-manian politics.

Economic problems did not help. The 1981–1983 international reces-sion left the economy on the ropes. Banks closed down in the IFC and invest-ments plummeted by one-third. By 1986 unemployment/underemployment rates surpassed 45 percent. Panama's foreign debt reached $3.7 billion, one of Latin America's highest per capita. Hundreds of thousands of street demon-strators protested the imposition of IMF and World Bank anti-labor reforms and economic austerity measures.

Noriega ruled with an iron hand. Colonel Díaz's charge that he had "murdered" Torrijos added fuel to the political fires. In 1987, a political al-liance of mostly conservative opposition parties, businesspeople and profes-sionals known as the Civil Crusade demanded that Noriega and del Valle step down. The crusade was backed by the Roman Catholic Church and found a sympathetic ear in Washington, D.C. Its main sponsors, the financial oli-garchy, wished to substitute privatization of the canal for the national recuper-ation project of Torrijos and Noriega.

Noriega arrested Díaz, declared a state of emergency, suspended opposi-tion newspapers, and sent troops into the streets to "maintain order." The

United States closed its embassy and suspended economic and military aid to Panama.

Initially, Noriega survived by building his bridges with labor and the Left, currying favor with Castro's Cuba and the Non-Aligned movement, and pinning the blame for his troubles squarely on the tip of Uncle Sam's beard. The local press printed a document allegedly drafted by a U.S. State Department official that called for Noriega's ouster and a revision of the canal treaties.

In February 1988, del Valle dismissed Noriega as PDF commander. Noriega refused to leave his post, and the National Assembly voted to dismiss del Valle instead. The Reagan administration called this "undemocratic," imposed economic sanctions, and proclaimed its intent to remove Noriega from Panama and try him for drug trafficking.

In the May 1989 presidential election, Guillermo Endara Galimany was winning a majority of votes when Noriega nullified the results and installed a figurehead president. Prior to the election, the CIA, despite protests by some congressmen, poured in millions of dollars to defeat Noriega and warned him not "to rig" the election. This time, unlike 1984, the U.S. government did not approve of Noriega's tampering with elections. It tightened the economic embargo, suspended Canal payments in violation of the Canal Treaties, and beefed up U.S. troop strength to 12,000 troops.

Noriega attributed the stepped-up U.S. pressure against him to his having refused National Security Adviser John Poindexter permission in December 1985 to use Panama "as the spearhead for an invasion against Nicaragua." The U.S. economic embargo's questionable legality and the rest of Latin America's view of U.S. policy as interventionist contributed to the initial failure of the U.S. attempt to overthrow Noriega. But because of the importance of the IFC, the economic embargo quickly brought business to a grinding halt. Banks closed down and much of industry went bankrupt.

In early October of 1989 U.S.-backed middle-ranking officers attempted a coup against Noriega and failed. A series of provocative acts by U.S. soldiers led to counteractions by members of Noriega's PDF and newly created "Dignity Battalions." The shooting of an American soldier served as the ideal pretext for an invasion, but the plan was well in place before that.

At midnight on December 20, 1989, some 25,000 U.S. troops backed by helicopter gunships, F117 Stealth bombers, a naval armada, tanks, and artillery, invaded and occupied Panama. Eyewitness reports over the next few days told of U.S. soldiers incinerating corpses with flamethrowers and entering homes not destroyed by bombs to torch them. Troops invaded foreign embassies and human rights offices.

U.S. officials oversaw the "swearing in" of President Endara and vice-presidents Ricardo Arias Calderón and Billy Ford. Noriega sought refuge in the Vatican Embassy but was eventually delivered over by Church officials to U.S. custody. The U.S.-Endara government began building a new military apparatus called the "Panama Public Force."

Flown to Miami, Noriega was officially declared a "prisoner of war." Despite this status, granted him in part to meet international law requirements, he was eventually tried and convicted for narcotics trafficking and sentenced to forty years in jail. Among many resultant issues in national and international law were the precedent established for kidnapping a country's leader and judging him under another nation's laws.

While the U.S. mass media focused on Noriega and the hi-tech proficiency of the invasion, international commissions of inquiry, Catholic bishops, and human rights activists discovered bodies bulldozed into graves. They put death tolls at from three to four thousand mostly unarmed civilians. Thousands more were wounded, and Panama's homeless population increased up to 30,000. A ten square block section of the predominantly black, working-class "new politics" district in El Chorillo was levelled. Similarly, inhabitants of San Miguelito (population 224,000) suffered heavy casualties. Yet U.S. military press releases described "collateral damage" to noncombatant civilians as minimal. (Only later did the United States bring murder charges against three of its soldiers.)

Anti-interventionists held rallies in major cities. New York City's Town Hall rally drew an overflow crowd; those not admitted heard eye-witness accounts of grisly U.S. "war crimes" by sidewalk loudspeaker. A university dean told of a fresh U.S. military assault on the slum of Curundu in March that amounted to "a second invasion."

The dean was subsequently threatened by roaming vigilante squads reminiscent of the death squads of El Salvador. Ten thousand government employees were dismissed as "politically suspect." Labor unions were smashed, dissident journalists detained, and an atmosphere of terror and repression spread across Panama. The film *The Panama Deception* documented the "war crimes" and subsequent repression and won the 1992 Academy Award for the Best Documentary. The woman accepting the Oscar complained that even PBS was still refusing to air the film.

For the moment, white racism and the financial oligarchy once more prevailed. Concluded political scientist Priestley: "Under the guise of constructing a democracy in Panama, the United States and its white business class allies are attempting to roll back all of the cultural, economic, and political gains of Panama's majority [non-white] population."

The invasion's destruction caused more than $2 billion in industrial losses. Investments nose dived, and half of Panama's remaining private businesses went bankrupt. The United States delivered $1 billion in aid, but most of it went to pay the debt and to private banks. It did not suffice to rebuild the industrial and IFC economy to its pre-invasion levels. In 1993, unemployment remained at 20 percent.

U.S. companies that left Panama during the Noriega regime did not return in large number. Asian and European companies arrived in the early 1990s to take advantage of what Colón Free Zone administrator Jaime Ford Lara called "the Hong Kong of the Americas."

Drug trafficking and money laundering continued. President Endara initially refused to tighten up the lax regulations on Panamanian banking. He was a longtime director of Banco Interoceánico de Panamá, reputedly a main source of drug money laundering. Endara was also a business associate of Carlos Eleta, arrested by U.S. officials on cocaine smuggling charges. Second Vice-President Ford was part owner of the Dadeland Bank of Florida, reportedly linked to Colombia's Medellín drug cartel. First Vice-President Arias Calderón, Attorney General Rogelio Cruz, and other officials in the new U.S.-imposed government were said to have similar narcotics money-laundering links. A new jingle was soon heard in the streets of Panama City: "We got rid of one drug thief, now we have three/Long live democracy!"

Political instability characterized the 1990s, evident in several coup attempts and bitter disputes between the government and opposition parties. In 1991, President Endara kicked the Christian Democrats out of his cabinet when they pushed for more social programs. He allowed some of the banks to open their records to investigators pursuing money-laundering trails.

A constitutional referendum in November 1992 showed how dissatisfied Panamanians were with Endara and his neo-liberal laissez-faire economic policies. By a two-to-one margin voters rejected fifty-eight reforms of the constitution, including one that would have permanently eliminated any defense forces.

The May 1994 elections were won by Ernesto Pérez Baladares, the candidate of the party of Noriega and Torrijos, the Revolutionary Democratic party. A U.S.-educated former City Bank executive, Pérez Baladares distanced himself from Noriega and claimed the populist heritage of Torrijos. He won only a third of the vote. Pro-government candidate Mireya Moscoso, widow of former president Arnulfo Arias, finished a close second. Left-of-center salsa singer Rubén Blades came in third, slightly ahead of another pro-government candidate.

The legacy of the 1989 invasion was a virulent undercurrent of anti-Americanism. Demonstrators threw stones at a welcoming ceremony for President Bush's 1992 visit. Victims of the invasion were still demanding compensation for their destroyed homes and properties. Every anniversary of the invasion became the occasion for a protest rally honoring the nation's "martyrs." President Pérez Balladares declared the invasion's fifth anniversary a "day of national mourning" and ordered Panamanian flags lowered to half-mast. In the Canal Zone, U.S. authorities did not comply. Given the history of Panamanian nationalism, it was obvious that the canal, due to come under Panamanian sovereignty in the year 2000, might again be the lightning rod for turmoil.

Selected Bibliography

Conniff, Michael L. *Black Labor on a White Canal.* Pittsburgh: University of Pittsburgh Press, 1985.

Dinges, John. *Our Man in Panama: How General Noriega Used the United States—and Made Millions in Drugs and Arms.* New York: Random House, 1990.

Independent Commission of Inquiry on the U.S. Invasion of Panama. *The U.S. Invasion of Panama: Operation Just Cause.* Boston, MA: South End Press, 1991. Revealing.

LaFeber, Walter. *The Panama Canal.* New York: Oxford University Press, 1978.

Moffett, George D., III. *The Limits of Victory.* Ithaca, NY: Cornell University Press, 1985. Insider's view of ratification of canal treaties by former Carter White House staff member

Nacla. "Panama: Reagan's Last Stand." *Report on the Americas,* 22(4) (July/Aug. 1988). Pre-invasion backgrounder.

Pippin, Larry L. *The Remón Era.* Stanford, CA: Institute of Hispanic and Luso-Brazilian Studies, 1964.

Priestley, George. *Military Government and Popular Participation in Panama: The Torrijos Regime, 1968-1975.* Boulder, CO: Westview, 1986.

Ropp, Steve C. *Panamanian Politics.* New York: Praeger, 1982.

Weeks, John, and Phil Gunson. *Panama: Made in the USA.* London: Latin American Bureau, 1992. The 1989 invasion and its aftermath.

Zimbalist, Andrew, and John Weeks. *Panama at the Crossroads: Economic Development and Political Change in the Twentieth Century.* Berkeley: University of California Press, 1991.

Films

The Panama Deception. 1992. Oscar-winning best documentary film by Empowerment Project (Santa Monica, California) on what U.S. media left out of its coverage of 1989 invasion.

Part Two

The Caribbean

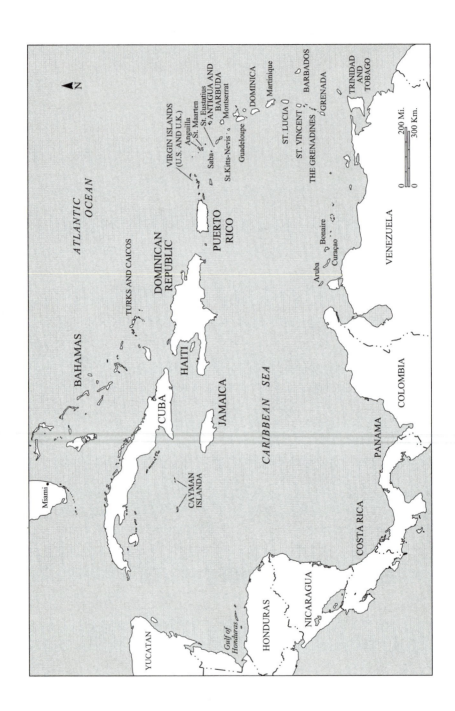

The Caribbean

The Caribbean is not the calm sun-soaked paradise of the tourist books. Despite the culturally distinct easygoing and friendly behavior of its people, in the 1980s and 1990s it was racked by political turmoil. A decade of falling world prices on sugar, mineral, and hydrocarbon exports had taken the wind out of the sails of economic expansion stimulated by the Alliance for Progress and the arrival of foreign-based transnational corporations and banks. Revolutionary uprisings surged here and there, rekindling the previous ninety years of U.S. interventionism. (Three of the recent "hot spots"—Grenada, Haiti, and Suriname—are discussed in this introduction.)

As throughout much of the Caribbean Basin (see Introduction to Part One and chapters 5, 7, and 12), race relations were ostensibly cordial yet actually not so tranquil. Racial differentiation was defined more by class than actual racial derivation. Jean-Jacques Acaau, a Haitian peasant leader of the 1840s, used to say: *"Nèg rich se milat pòv se nèg"* ("A rich black was a mulatto, a poor mulatto was a black"). Not much occurred after 1840 to change the Caribbean's class-based racism (the historic legacy of colonial plunder and slaverunning carried out by foreign white interests). What made the class/race ranking system more subtle and insidious in the multiracial Caribbean than elsewhere, however, was the fact that nonwhites usually composed the majority, yet social status and economic opportunity corresponded closely with whiteness. People were ranked on a sliding scale of extremely subtle shades of negritude, with the darkest usually at the bottom.

Seeking to correct this class/race inequality, a "black power" movement swept the area in the 1960s and 1970s. As in the case of radical reform attempts elsewhere in Latin America, it usually met with severe military repression. Nonetheless, its impact lingered, and a few dark-skinned individuals broke out of the pack to achieve success. Several contemporary prime ministers are black.

While U.S. warships and tourist-packed ocean liners cruised the Caribbean's deceptively still waters, many groups contested the region's future. They included Communists, socialists, political centrists, pro-free enterprise conservatives, Rastafarians, Baptists, Evangelicals, fundamentalist Muslims, clergy for and against the theology of liberation, young people for and against the new Marxism (see Overview), politicized calypso and reggae singers, guerrillas, urban youth gangs, angry slum dwellers, hungry peasants, overworked miners, black power and women's liberation groups, students, job-hungry workers, political refugees migrating by boat, political exiles, tourists and hotel magnates, foreign investors seeking tax havens, low-wage labor for assembly plants, international gangsters setting up drug-running networks, soldiers of fortune, U.S. troops and, in Cuba until 1991, Soviet advisers.

Much of the Caribbean's politicking took place outside each home country. One-fifth of the population lived off-and-on in the United States, while many others lived in Europe or Canada. Either Manhattan or the South Bronx in New York City, or Miami in Florida, qualified as one of the most populous cities of Spanish-speaking Caribbean peoples. Large black and East Indian Caribbean communities could be found in Brooklyn (New York), London, Liverpool, Paris, Amsterdam, Montreal, and Toronto.

Economically, the Caribbean was never a U.S. lake. Canada had a big stake there. So did Great Britain, France, and the Netherlands. For three decades, the Soviet Union had significant trade with Cuba, as well as a big political investment there. According to the U.S. Chamber of Commerce, U.S. direct investments, most of them in banking and finance, totaled $30 billion in 1982 (excluding Puerto Rico and the U.S. Virgin Islands). That was sixteen times more than the 1970 figure. Adding to the traditional activities of tourism, tropical agriculture, oil refining, and transshipment terminals, offshore banking and drug trafficking had become the principal Caribbean money-making ventures.

Militarily, the United States had naval and air force bases in several places, including Cuba (Guantánamo), Puerto Rico, and, off the coast of Honduras, Swan Island (for training Nicaragua's contras in the 1980s). The British, Dutch, and French also had a Caribbean military presence, however small.

With a population of more than 33 million, the Caribbean's scattered island nations and colonies had more people than Central America. Most islands had populations of about 60,000 (Aruba), and only six had as many as a million or more. Cuba, the region's most economically developed nation, was home for one-third of the Caribbean's people.

Cuba's highly educated 11 million citizens enjoyed Latin America's best housing and health care—most of it free. Its Marxist leader Fidel Castro, a Jesuit-educated son of the landholding aristocracy, was still popular (and controversial) after thirty-five years in power. Had his alliance with the Soviet Union been avoidable? Was Castro's regime "the source" of terrorism and revolution in the rest of Latin America, as alleged in 1981 by U.S. Secretary of State Alexander Haig? And what was likely to happen after Castro left the scene (see chapter 8)?

The Caribbean's second most populous country was its most debt-ridden: the Dominican Republic. In the spring of 1965, there were more U.S. troops mobilized to crush a popular movement for the restoration of democracy there than in all Vietnam. After that, Dominican democracy was partially restored. The CIA-funded AIFLD (American Institute for Free Labor Development—see Overview and Introduction to Part One) sought to expand its influence after earning worker animosity for its support of U.S. intervention. U.S. corporate investments and profits skyrocketed. In the 1980s rising unemployment, food riots, and protests against the IMF (International Monetary Fund—see Overview) kept soldiers of a beefed-up Dominican army at every street corner. Seeking economic survival, young and old Dominicans jumped on rickety boats to go to Puerto Rico; sometimes the boats sank, drowning all aboard. From San Juan, some of the Dominicans flew to the United States, posing as Puerto Ricans (i.e., U.S. citizens). Dominican Spanish was increasingly heard in New York and New Jersey. If the Dominican Republic had another revolutionary upsurge, its shockwaves would likely be felt in the United States even more than those of 1965 had been (see chapter 10).

Puerto Rico was the Caribbean's fourth most populous nation (after third-place Haiti), as well as its most polluted island. It was described as "a colony" by the United Nations and "a geopolitical bastion of the United States" by former UN Ambassador Jeanne Kirkpatrick. "Dress rehearsals" for the 1983 invasion of Grenada were staged in Vieques, Puerto Rico, where the U.S. Navy conducted regular bombing practice. What were the views on Puerto Rico's future political status? Did most politicians support the island's "commonwealth" status? What about "terrorist" groups and the FBI's role in

Puerto Rico's "Watergate"? And what was the situation among the half of the Puerto Rican population residing in the United States (see chapter 9)?

Foreign Domination, Economic Dependence, and Revolution

Historically, as the chapters in Part Two reveal, the Caribbean was so highly valued by Europe's colonizing powers they fought several wars to retain or expand their political control in the region. The lucrative traffic in slaves from Africa and indentured agricultural workers from India, Java, and China generated a rich blend of races and cultures that distinguished the Caribbean from the rest of the world. The terrible living conditions faced by these workers in turn produced a tradition of rebellion along race/class lines for emancipation, political independence, and social justice.

The growing influence of U.S. economic and military interests from the mid-nineteenth century forward added to Caribbean traditions of foreign domination, economic dependence, and local revolt. Nearly half a millennium of such patterns created a Caribbean political culture that extended its influence worldwide. For generations the Caribbean peoples established their poets, writers, and political exiles on the world stage of literature, art, and politics. That such tiny island-states could have such apparently exaggerated importance remained a marvel during the post-1959 era of Cuba's Socialist revolution, a period that brought all the Caribbean to the center of world attention.

Foreign domination of the Caribbean only made its revolutionary upheavals more frequent, explosive, and difficult to carry through to complete social justice. Haiti's remarkable slave revolts generated early independence (1804) despite the proslavery efforts of French, English, and Spanish troops. At the time Haiti was one of the Caribbean's most prosperous and profitable colonies. But Toussaint L'Ouverture's faith in French republicanism spelled his defeat. He was taken prisoner, his land reduced to ashes. Foreign economic groups gave very little attention to war-destroyed Haiti after that. Later, they were able to reassert their hegemony over an impoverished people. The rended fabric of Haiti's economic dependence was gradually restitched. But the people's tradition of revolt never died.

Other revolts for independence evoked prompt interventions by outside powers (Dominican Republic 1865, Puerto Rico and Cuba 1868–1898). In the twentieth century Haiti, the Dominican Republic, and Nicaragua joined Cuba and Puerto Rico as virtual U.S.-occupied protectorates until the early 1930s. Afterward the United States left behind local national guards, police forces, or armies that spawned some of history's most notorious dictators: Haiti's Duvaliers, the Dominican Republic's Trujillo, Nicaragua's Somozas, and Cuba's Batista.

This legacy in turn led to new revolutionary upsurges and U.S. interventions. U.S. troops crushed the Dominican revolutionary upheaval of 1965, bled Nicaragua's Sandinistas in the 1980s, and eliminated the remnants of Grenada's attempted revolution of 1979–1983. Only Cuba's Revolution of 1959 succeeded in avoiding foreign overthrow, and to do so it had to turn to the Soviet Union for military and economic assistance. For better or worse, the Cuban Revolution's arming of the masses, building of a socialist economy, and "sticking its chest out at the rich uncle" instead of "saying uncle" appealed to countless Latin Americans. The Alliance for Progress and U.S. counterinsurgency programs were in large part a response to the Cuban challenge (see Overview).

Grenada and British Caribbean

The Caribbean's vulnerability to outside intervention and its political volatility were dramatically illustrated by events that shook the tiny island of Grenada (population 100,000) from 1979 to 1983. Prime Minister Maurice Bishop's New Jewel movement was embarked on a revolution in education, employment, housing, and health care when divisions in its leadership led to his assassination and the U.S. "rescue mission" of October 1983 (opposed by the Conservative party Prime Minister Margaret Thatcher of the former "mother country"). Being "rescued" by thousands of U.S. troops (while the U.S. press was kept from observing) were medical students attending a private U.S. medical school. Declassified Defense Department documents later showed that the students were not in danger. Grenada would-be doctors could not afford an education at home and so had journeyed to Socialist Cuba to receive their education free. They were allowed to return to post-Bishop Grenada only if they agreed to "stay out of politics." Later, one of them, Dr. Terry Marryshow, helped create the Maurice Bishop Patriotic Movement to enter elections in the 1990s and keep alive the idea of reform.

Another reason given for the U.S. invasion of Grenada was the construction of a large airport with Cuban assistance to further tourism. The British government looked favorably on the project, but the U.S. government, which completed construction of the airport after the invasion, alleged it had military purposes. After U.S. "mopping up" operations against suspected rebels, a small number of U.S. troops remained. A "moderate" from the newly formed NNP (New National party) was elected prime minister in elections that banned the Left. Reforms of the Bishop administration were shelved, day-care centers shut down, and unemployment rose from 14 percent to 40 percent.

The U.S. invasion of Grenada was condemned around the world as a blatant violation of another nation's sovereignty. Cartoonists caricatured it as an elephant stepping upon an ant. Observers of the Caribbean Basin recognized the message it sent to the Sandinista government of Nicaragua: "You could be next."

A number of British Caribbean prime ministers tied to Conservative elite interests welcomed the U.S. crushing of Grenada's socialist-oriented attempt at political and economic reforms. The lightning military takeover of Grenada was also well received in the United States, where people were told that their government had "saved" freedom from a small group of murderous Marxists. The New Jewel movement had indeed split into warring factions, but most Grenadans were not so sure how much freedom the United States brought them. Prior to Bishop the country had been ruled by a fanatical U.S.-backed dictator who claimed he had psychic powers and had seen flying saucers, Sir Eric Gairy (1967–1979). Gairy's Mongoose Gang had beat up opponents, as his army, known as the Green Beasts, maintained "order."

Most Caribbean nations and colonies, like Grenada, belonged to what was commonly referred to as the British Caribbean. A visit to any of the British colonies and ex-colonies showed how distinct their politics and culture were from Latin America. For instance, despite the sweltering tropical climate, court justices usually wore British-style thick white wigs and heavy black robes. Parliamentary debates resembled those of London's House of Commons in their acerbic verbal innuendos and back-bench grumbling of "Hear! Hear!" or "Shame!" rather than the personal direct threats to life or honor (even occasional gunplay) observed in Latin American congresses.

An early drama of independence in the greater British Caribbean that involved the United States took place in Guyana on the mainland of South America during the 1950s and 1960s. The racial factor there divided people who otherwise shared common class-based, proindependence goals. In the final years of British colonialism two parties fought for control: Cheddi Jagan's PPP (People's Progressive party) and Forbes Burnham's PNC (People's National Congress). Indo-Guyanese (East Indians) composed a majority of the population and for the most part backed Burnham, a black. Fearing Jagan might pull off a social revolution or move Guyana into the Soviet camp, the CIA incited race riots to help topple his government in 1961. Independence was delayed until 1966, by which time Burnham was entrenched in power.

Burnham formed a "Cooperative Republic." It was more republic than cooperative. It evoked frequent charges of electoral fraud and violent treatment of Indo-Guyanese and leftist opponents. Seeking to correct the situation, a new multiracial left-wing party, the WPA (Working People's Alliance), denounced Burnham's proclamations of socialism and use of the word comrades as phony. It gained support among strategically placed bauxite workers (black) and sugar-cane cutters (East Indian) but was weakened by government repression and political murders. World famous historian and political scientist

270

Walter Rodney, a WPA leader, was gunned down by hired killers. Border quarrels with Venezuela added to Guyana's political instability—and vulnerability (see chapter 11). Burnham died in 1985, and his party was voted out of power in 1992 in the nation's first democratic election in twenty-eight years. The winner with 54 percent of the vote was Jagan, still a parliamentary Marxist at age seventy-four. He pledged continued free-market reforms short of completing the privatization of Guyana's mineral resources.

As throughout Latin America, political conflict in the British Caribbean intensified after the 1959 Cuban Revolution and during the economic crisis of the late 1970s and early 1980s. The Caribbean's fifth and sixth most populous nations, Jamaica and Trinidad and Tobago, became centers of unrest and regional influence (the seventh most populous Caribbean nation was Guyana with a population of almost a million, after which came Suriname on the South American mainland with 400,000 people).

Unemployment affected one-quarter of Jamaica's work force. Nearly half the population resided in other countries. Two parties, the moderately social democratic PNP (People's National party) and the profree enterprise conservative JLP (Jamaica Labor party) contested Jamaica's future. The CIA helped "destabilize" the PNP government of the 1970s to pave the way for the 1980 election of its favored candidate, the JLP's Harvard-educated Edward Seaga (eight hundred died from political violence during the electoral campaign). In 1989, PNP leader Michael Manley was reelected, but for health reasons he resigned three years later. In 1993, PNP Prime Minister Percival Patterson was reelected by a landslide. He promised continued privatization of the economy and more jobs. Angry reggae lyrics still blasted from store-front speaker systems in Kingston's sweltering slums, where no one was ever sure when a fresh crisis might explode.

The economic giant of the British Caribbean was Trinidad and Tobago. Fueled by oil-refining revenues (90 percent of export earnings), it faced the consequences of a thirty-year economic "modernization" (see Overview). Any visitor could see the stark contrasts between the plush estates of the *nouveau riche* and the rundown hovels of the poor. Once a net exporter of food (mostly sugar), Trinidad and Tobago had to import three-fourths of its food needs. It had more U.S. direct investments than any other Caribbean nation. With over a million people and a fairly strong trade-union movement led by the OWTU (Oilfield Workers Trade Union), Trinidad and Tobago remained a regional economic pivot. A fundamentalist Muslim uprising there almost succeeded in 1990 against an unpopular government that had been elected after many years of rule by the People's National Movement (PNM), founded in colonial times by famed historian and independence leader Dr. Eric Williams. In 1992, the PNM, despite its reputation for corruption, was reelected to power.

Britain's other ex-colonies were Antigua and Barbuda, the Bahamas,

Barbados, Dominica, Grenada, St. Kitts-Nevis, St. Lucia, and St. Vincent and the Grenadines.

Antigua and Barbuda gained independence in 1981 (Barbuda soon petitioned to secede, hoping to gain economic benefits by becoming a dependency of the United Kingdom). The United States had two military bases in this nation of 77,000, which received more tourists each year than it had residents. Prime Minister Vere Bird's Antigua Labour party government joined in the U.S. military occupation of Grenada in 1983 on the basis of an agreement of the OECS (Organization of Eastern Caribbean States). Bird announced he would retire in 1994.

Newly Independent (1983) St. Kitts-Nevis was hard hit by low sugar prices, firebombings, and political feuding. Its sugar cane cutters could no longer find work in nearby Trinidad, and it was hanging out the welcome sign for foreign electronics firms. Disputed election counts in late 1993 led to brief rioting and a short state of siege, as the British governor-general asked Dr. Kennedy Simmonds of the People's Action Movement to remain as prime minister. The losing St. Kitts-Nevis Labour party called for new elections.

Dominica remained one of the British Caribbean's least economically developed countries. After gaining independence in 1978, it became the object of plots by U.S. soldiers of fortune, evangelical campaigns by the American Bible Society and the Southern Baptist Convention, and union-control attempts by the CIA-backed AIFLD. Its political life was as tempestuous as the hurricanes that annually wreaked havoc on its mostly impoverished 75,000 citizens. The Caribbean's first woman prime minister, Dominica's Eugenia Charles, rushed to endorse President Reagan's 1983 decision to send troops to Grenada. Meanwhile, at home, her government's soldiers had killed more people than the few victims of the previous (equally tempestuous) twenty years. New assembly plants and tourist facilities were established in the 1980s.

After gaining independence in 1979, St. Lucia offered generous terms to foreign investors, seeking to diversify its economy from reliance on tourism and banana and sugar exports. But militant labor unionists and a weak economic infrastructure discouraged foreign capital, and the contest for power between the pro-U.S. United Workers party (UWP) and the more independent-minded St. Lucia Labor party heated up after that, with the UWP winning the 1992 election.

The eruption of St. Vincent's volcano La Soufriere in 1979, the year of independence for St. Vincent and the Grenadines, was followed by severe political tremors in a populace numbering 135,000. Poverty was widespread, intestinal diseases were rampant, and there was a shortage of potable drinking water, some of which had to be imported. Energetic Rastafarians, restive labor unions, and a leftist coalition contesting power in the 1984 elections gave the two major parties a scare. In 1989, the New Democratic party swept the legislative elections against the St. Vincent Labour party.

Densely populated (275,000) Barbados had more tourists in a year than it had residents. But tourism was in decline, as was the sugar industry. The late Prime Minister Tom Adams (d. 1985), butt of a critical calypso song "Mr. T.," supported the 1983 U.S. rescue mission in Grenada and implemented economic austerity measures recommended by the IMF. His Barbados Labour party administration, like its opponents who later ousted it, began opening the island to foreign assembly plants. In 1991, the Democratic Labour party was reelected to govern the island.

Were things, in the words of the government-sponsored advertising campaign, "Better in the Bahamas"? This deteriorating tourist attraction found itself in the midst of a political crisis involving government corruption linked to narcotics trafficking. Also causing alarm were the expulsion of Haitian immigrants and a burgeoning women's movement against recent increases in rape incidents. Rastafarians and Baptists once again joined the political fray. A reform candidate opposed the six-term prime minister, Sir Lynden Pindling, in 1992 and won on an anticorruption, antinarcotics platform.

Remaining as British colonies were Anguilla, Bermuda, British Virgin Islands, Cayman Islands, Montserrat, and Turks and Caicos. Because of aid received from the United Kingdom, these colonial dependencies were somewhat better-off economically. They were also less populated than the independent mininations. The largest colony, Bermuda, a group of islands 580 miles east of Cape Hatteras, North Carolina, had 75,000 people. Tension between black militants and white merchants sent ripples of unrest through Bermuda in the 1980s, during which strikes, murders, and vandalism spread. Blacks rallied to the PLP (Progressive Labor party), whereas whites backed the United Bermuda party. Besides tourism, Bermuda attracted many banks and insurance companies to its tax haven.

Haiti and French Caribbean

The former French colony of Haiti was the Caribbean's third most populous nation, as well as the first land in the Caribbean or Latin America to gain political independence (1804—see chapter 10). Haiti was the Western Hemisphere's poorest and most illiterate nation. It was also the one most affected by politician's appeals to traditional folk religion (voodoo). Because of undernourishment and food scarcities, it also had a long tradition of food riots. More than 1.5 million Haitians, one-fourth of the populace, lived abroad, about half of them in the United States and Canada.

In 1985–1986 a mass uprising of protesters in the streets toppled the family dynasty of Francois "Papa Doc" Duvalier (d. 1971) and his playboy son

President-for-Life Jean-Claude "Baby Doc" Duvalier—or so it seemed. A U.S. Air Force plane flew Baby Doc and his trunks of furs, jewels, and stolen millions to a comfortable exile in France, where, like the late Shah of Iran in the United States, he was greeted by irate demonstrators.

Bolstered by fresh infusions of U.S. aid (more than $100 million in 1987) and apparently guaranteed by U.S. warships offshore, Haiti's interim military government fired some Duvalier supporters while retaining others. The infamous Duvalierist death squads, the "Tonton Macoutes," still murdered citizens, some of whom formed self-defense squads armed only with knives, sticks, and stones.

In late 1987 Haitian troops killed more than thirty citizens as they attempted to vote in the first post-uprising elections. The United States responded by suspending $60 million in aid. Then, in early 1988, new elections were held at bayonet-point. The 1988 elections were widely viewed as a cosmetic cover-up for continued military rule. The victor was overthrown by the military, and yet another military coup occurred in September 1988, as the generals had a falling out among themselves. A continuing revolution from below against the nation's continued direct and indirect military rule-by-terror gained momentum. The only political voices permitted to speak out were from the clergy, and often they, too, were beaten up or killed.

Finally, in December 1990, international human rights pressures and the strength of the popular movement for carrying through "the revolution against the Duvaliers" led to genuinely democratic elections. The winner with two-thirds of the vote was the Reverend Jean-Bertrand Aristide. A thirty-seven-year-old priest advocating the theology of liberation (see Overview), he was affectionately called "Titid" by the masses. He was overthrown by the generals after only eight months in office and went into exile. A fresh, even more savage reign of terror was unleashed against the populace, which vainly sought to bring back Aristide. A 1,150-member national police force increased its power. Some 5,000 Haitians were killed and a half million were driven into hiding. Huge protest rallies for Aristide were held in Miami and New York.

The international community, including the United Nations and the United States, censured the coup makers and set up a negotiating process between military and police commanders and civilian politicians. Eventually, in 1993, a UN-brokered agreement with the officers allowed for Aristide's resumption of the presidency, albeit without substantive power. But the military backed out of even that agreement and refused to allow Aristide's return from U.S. exile. The Clinton administration then attempted to provide a military escort for Aristide's return. Right-wing armed groups vowed to attack U.S. soldiers, as the ruling officers refused to cooperate. The example of Somalians killing U.S. troops in Africa further helped deter the U.S. forces from landing in Haiti.

Meanwhile, Haiti's reign of terror continued, overseen by police and military officers linked to drug trafficking and past CIA payrolls. A new Tonton Macoute–style group called the Haitian Front for Advancement and Progress employed face slashings, murder, and rape as political weapons against several independent peasant, labor, neighborhood, student, Christian-based-community, and women's organizations. The Clinton administration further reduced its support for Aristide, leading the moderate human rights group Americas Watch to conclude in April 1994: "The U.S. government has embraced a murderous armed force to act as a counterweight to a populist president it distrusts." A month later, the U.N. Security Council voted to impose an economic embargo on Haiti to force the military rulers to permit Aristide's return.

On July 31, 1994, the Security Council authorized a U.S.-led invasion to restore Haitian democracy. Except for Argentina, Latin American nations refused to endorse the idea of another U.S. military intervention—and Argentina later refused to offer troops. It looked like U.S. intentions in Haiti might be linked to an attempt to overthrow Cuba's revolutionary government, as a subsequent crisis involving U.S. detention of would-be Cuban refugees clearly suggested (see chapter 8). Numerous observers pointed out that the guiding thread of U.S. policy was to find a way to maintain Haiti as a source of cheap labor for U.S.-owned assembly plants.

Although many of Haiti's mulatto elite (3 percent of the population) held overlapping interests in land, commerce, and business, landed oligarchs close to the Duvalier camp had political disagreements with professional technocrats and modernizing segments of the export-import bourgeoisie close to foreign investors. Other export-import merchants felt threatened by increased direct foreign investment. The administrations of both Bush and Clinton tilted toward the modernizers, but almost all the elites, domestic and foreign, were uneasy at the prospect of Aristide's return. He had promised agrarian reform and an increase in the minimum wage, when foreign-owned assembly plants were paying as little as fourteen cents an hour. The legacy of shifting military/business/oligarchy alliances that previous U.S. administrations had helped forge or protect was proving difficult to break.

More than 90 percent of Haitians spoke Creole, while the small mulatto and black upper and middle classes conducted the nation's affairs in French. Most Haitian professionals, often educated abroad, lacked the independent economic means to become a "political class" (see Overview). Trade unionists and leftists were practically unknown after decades of Duvalier banishment and the opening up of Haiti to foreign-owned assembly plants (by the mid-1980s, light manufactures accounted for 65 percent of exports from the predominantly agricultural nation). Analysts agreed that any moderate or political "center" in Haiti was at the mercy of military, economic elite, and foreign influences, leaving a yawning gap between the few rich and the numerous incensed masses.

Aristide was the logical bridge across that gap, but the U.S. government continued to waffle in its support for either him or democracy in Haiti. Several factors explained why. First, there was the heritage of proreform voices in Washington being overridden by promilitary solutions in the name of antirevolutionism ("anticommunism") and "economic stability." Second, there was a traditional reluctance to commit U.S. troops to defend genuine democracy. Third, U.S. business interests benefitted from Haiti's low wage structure. Even in the next-door Dominican Republic, where Haitian sugar cane workers were treated as virtual slaves on government-owned lands, U.S. companies benefitted from the resultant sugar trade they dominated. Finally, most Haitians were black, unemployed, and suffered from ongoing racism.

Until August 1994, the biased treatment of Haitian refugees showed up in U.S. immigration policy. A U.S. "double standard" existed, granting political asylum to (mostly white) Cubans but denying it to Haitians fleeing the infamous Tonton Macoute and military killers (see chapter 8). For years the U.S. explanation had been that the Duvalier dictatorship was a "friendly government" and that the refugees were "economic," not political. But the U.S. Air Force's role in arranging the removal of the "friendly" government of Baby Doc had undercut the credibility of that rationale. Some Haitian refugees had been housed so long in Miami's Krome detention center that it could be argued they qualified for amnesty under the 1986 Immigration Reform and Control Act since they could prove continuous U.S. residence since 1982—behind bars! Reporters described the camps as concentration camps.

As more Haitian refugees fled the terror in the 1990s, tens of thousands in rickety boats were turned back by U.S. Navy ships and housed temporarily at the U.S.-owned Guantánamo Naval Base in Cuba. The refusal to admit Haitians into the United States on grounds that they were either economic refugees or had HIV (the AIDS virus) caused a loud international outcry against blatant discrimination in violation of standard UN and U.S. political refugee criteria.

The rest of the French Caribbean consisted of colonies known as *départements:* Martinique, Guadeloupe, and, on the South American mainland, Guyane. Independence movements existed, speeding the integration of the *départements* with France. In the 1980s, the social democratic Mitterand government authorized regional councils to increase popular participation among the 700,000 residents, most of whom lived in Guadeloupe or Martinique. Left-leaning parties fared well in subsequent elections. Major social and political tensions followed a clear race/class line: the "béké" merchants (under 1 percent of the population), descendants of white slaveholders resisting the increased integration with France; their political rivals among the mulatto (*mulâtre*) and black middle classes (10 percent); and the black masses, employed and unemployed. An influx of white French immigrants further complicated the picture. In general, though, conditions in the *départements* were more prosperous than in most of the neighboring islands.

Suriname and Dutch Caribbean

Located on the South American mainland, Suriname, which became independent in 1975, was the most troubled part of the Dutch Caribbean. Like its western neighbor, Guyana, it was economically important for its abundant bauxite mines on which it depended for the bulk of its export revenues. Unemployment was rife among its 400,000 inhabitants (37 percent Hindustani, 31 percent Creole, 15 percent Javanese, 10 percent black, 2 percent Chinese).

A 1980 "sergeants' coup" in Suriname established the MNR (Nationale Militair Raad, or military council). Leftists obtained ministerial posts in the MNR government of Sergeant Major Dési Bouterse. Its populist-style rule was marked by a campaign against corruption, the murder of political opponents, general strikes, cutoffs in Dutch aid, guerrilla warfare backed by conservative domestic and foreign interests (including U.S. mercenaries), and the imposition of martial law. In the fall of 1987, the electorate opted for a return to democracy in a constitutional referendum. The opposition won the November elections, but Bouterse remained the real power, as evidenced by a bloodless Christmas Eve military coup in 1990. New elections in 1991 returned the country to a shaky civilian government that sought closer ties with the Netherlands.

The remaining Dutch colonies in the Caribbean were known as the Netherlands Antilles: Aruba, Bonaire, Curaçao, Saba, St. Eustatius, and St. Maarten. They had one-quarter of a million people, 170,000 of them on the island of Curacao. Oil refining, offshore financing and banking, transshipment terminals, and tourism constituted the economic lifeline of these generally prosperous but unemployment-plagued islands. The safety valve of jobs in Holland, unemployment insurance, free medical care, and other social benefits provided by the Dutch social democracy, combined with an expansion of the tourist industry, alleviated the impact of the closing of Aruba's oil refinery, which had brought the island considerable prosperity in the 1960s and 1970s. As tourism expanded and the refinery reopened in the 1990s, cheap labor from the Dominican Republic, Venezuela, and Colombia was imported. Because of the general prosperity, Arubans debated whether to opt for independence tentatively set for 1996 or remain a Dutch colony. Curaçao voted against independence in 1993 and to remain in the Netherlands Antilles federation.

Caribbean Basin Initiative and Policy Debates

The economy of the Caribbean, like that of the rest of Latin America, remained hurt by falling export prices, a bloated foreign debt, and the worldwide recession of the early 1990s. Devastating hurricanes added to the economic problems. The region had followed a continent-wide pattern of welcoming or submitting to IMF dictates, privatization of state enterprises, attempted union busting, rampant narcotics trafficking, corruption, ongoing militarization, and aborted revolution or limited democracy. In addition, it had developed one of the highest rates of AIDS in the world—nearly a million reported cases among 33 million people.

Caribbean politicians increasingly turned to the United States, Great Britain, France, and the Netherlands for help. The region's pleasant beaches and casinos could not remain attractive as economic beggary and social unrest closed in from the urban slums and impoverished countryside. Something had to be done. Recognizing that economic hardship might fuel the flames of popular discontent, the Reagan administration introduced the CBI (Caribbean Basin Initiative). The CBI aimed to generate economic recovery through private investment and the lowering of trade barriers. But the CBI budget only gradually reached $400 million a year (1987), and it encountered opposition from several quarters. For example, as the CBI was working its way through the U.S. Congress in 1983, organized labor's AFL-CIO expressed concern that yet more "American jobs" would be moved overseas to less expensive workplaces. It proposed reforms to safeguard the interests of its members while creating improved work conditions for Caribbean and Central American laborers. These included guarantees of human rights, freedom of speech, press, and assembly, workplace safety and health standards, and the right to organize and collective bargaining. A lobby more powerful than the AFL-CIO was behind the CBI bill, however. Headed by banker David Rockefeller and Eastern Airlines President Frank Borman, this corporate lobby won the day in Congress. When CBI passed, labor's interests had been virtually ignored. Neither human rights violations nor lack of trade union freedom was a mandatory ground for denying a country CBI privileges. On the other hand, expropriating a U.S. firm's property was a mandatory ground.

Because of CBI, more than twenty nations in the Caribbean Basin were allowed to ship a range of duty-free exports to the United States. In practice, under CBI the United States reduced its sugar imports from the area while increasing its trade surplus ($1.5 billion in 1989). It exported expensive capital goods and raw materials for the production by underpaid Caribbean workers of inexpensive products to be imported back into the United States—imports of manufactures from U.S.-owned subsidiaries. When workers attempted to unionize or improve their wages, they were usually met by armed soldiers or police. The cycle of poverty for many and enrichment for a few went unbroken. Puerto Rico's "twin plant" initiative (see chapter 9) received CBI endorsement as well, auguring a continuation of the pattern.

Caribbean state leaders worried that the introduction of NAFTA would drain investment and trade away from the Caribbean and toward low-wage Mexico (see Overview, chapter 1, and Conclusion). Members of CARICOM (the thirteen-country "Caribbean Community" of English-speaking nations, including Guyana and Central America's Belize) rushed to sign a framework trade agreement with the United States in 1992 that promised an eventual hemispheric free-trade area. CARICOM envisioned a Caribbean-wide common market with a regional currency by the year 2000. In the early 1990s, CARICOM approved trade pacts with Venezuela, Colombia, and Mexico. It also opened negotiations with Central America for trade agreements. Then, despite U.S. objections, CARICOM signed a trade pact with Cuba in December 1993. Jamaican and other investors began investing in Cuban hotels and tourism.

The consolidation of the European Economic Community trade bloc in 1992 affected non-Caribbean Latin America more severely than it did the Caribbean, where integration with Europe's economy was already strong. European restrictions on Latin American exports such as bananas (see introductions to Part One and Part Two and Conclusion) did not radically hurt the Caribbean. The British-based Geest retained its exclusive marketing arrangements with the Eastern Caribbean. But the yields in banana production there were only a third of those in Central and South America.

The CBI's unimpressive record and heightened political turmoil in the Caribbean heated up the foreign policy debate in Washington. Besides Haiti and the free-trade issues, two central questions remained: the pros and cons of the stiffened economic embargo against Cuba and of proposed statehood for Puerto Rico (examined in chapters 8, 9, the Conclusion, and the Documents section).

Caribbean intellectuals and politicians continued debating the issues of social reform and economic development. Every country, including Cuba, was experimenting with greater "free market" approaches to economic change. Some dreamers envisioned a Caribbean political or economic confederation pulling the diverse mini-nations together and even uniting them with the "mini-giants" of Cuba, the Dominican Republic, Jamaica, and Trinidad and Tobago. Others felt that "small" could be "beautiful," and that the major task was to bring into convergence the capital, labor, and natural resources of the island-states through increased state intervention in the economy—socialism if need be—and the conditioning of outside aid. Still others marched to the IMF–World Bank beat of "privatization" of the state sector and a more efficient "modernization."

In 1992, the Nobel Prize for literature went to St. Lucia-born Derek Walcott, a West Indian poet-playwright known for his celebration of Caribbean multiculturalism. The region sports an unusual record of producing famous internationally minded intellectuals like C. R. L. James, Eric Williams, Frantz Fanon, and other champions of anticolonialism; racial tolerance, peace, and freedom—a kind of multiculturalism from which many in the United States and elsewhere continue to learn much.

Selected Bibliography

See also the bibliographies to Overviews, introductions to Part One and Part Three, and Conclusion.

Aristide, Jean-Bertrand. *Aristide: An Autobiography.* Maryknoll, NY: Orbis Books, 1993.

Barry, Tom, Beth Wood, and Deb Preusch. *The Other Side of Paradise: Foreign Control in the Caribbean.* New York: Grove Press, 1984.

DeWind, Josh, and David H. Kinley III. *Aiding Migration: The Impact of International Development Assistance on Haiti.* Boulder, CO: Westview, 1987. Up-to-date analysis of migration, food, foreign aid, and politics.

Dupuy, Alex. *Haiti in the World Economy: Class, Race, and Underdevelopment Since 1700.* Boulder, CO: Westview, 1988. Historical analysis including post-Duvalier prospects.

Ecumenical Program for Interamerican Communication and Action (EPICA). *Grenada: The Peaceful Revolution.* Washington, DC: 1982. On Bishop's reforms and foreign policy.

Farmer, Paul. *The Uses of Haiti.* Monroe, ME: Common Courage Press, 1994. Includes critique of U.S. press coverage.

Ferguson, James. *Grenada: Revolution in Reverse.* London: Latin America Bureau, 1990.

Heine, Jorge (ed.). *A Revolution Aborted: The Lessons of Grenada.* Pittsburgh: Pittsburgh University Press, 1990.

James, C. L. R. *The Black Jacobins.* New York: Random House, 1963. Classic account of Toussaint L'Ouverture and Haitian independence by famed Caribbean intellectual.

Keith, Nelson W., and Novella Z. Keith. *The Social Origins of Democratic Socialism in Jamaica.* Philadelphia, PA: Temple University Press, 1992.

Knight, Franklin W. and Margaret E. Crahan (eds.). *Africa and the Caribbean: The Legacies of a Link.* Baltimore, MD: Johns Hopkins University Press, 1979.

Latin America Bureau (LAB). *Guyana: Fraudulent Revolution.* London: LAB, 1984.

————. *Haiti: Family Business.* London: LAB, 1985. Duvalier era.

Lewis, Gordon K. *Grenada: The Jewel Despoiled.* Baltimore, MD: Johns Hopkins University Press, 1986. By a leading Caribbeanist.

Maingot, Anthony P. (ed.). *Trends in U.S.-Caribbean Relations.* Special issue of *The Annals of the American Academy of Political and Social Science,* v. 533 (May 1994).

North American Congress on Latin America (NACLA). "Haiti: Dangerous Crossroads," *NACLA Report on the Americas,* 27(4) (Jan.-Feb. 1994).

PACCA (Policy Alternatives for the Caribbean and Central America). *An Alternative U.S. Policy toward Cuba.* Washington, DC: 1988. See Documents.

————. *In The Shadows of the Sun: Caribbean Development Alternatives and U.S. Policy.* Boulder: Westview Press, 1990.

Paus, Eva (ed.). *Struggle against Dependence: Nontraditional Export Growth in Central America and the Caribbean.* Boulder, CO: Westview, 1988. Original research on Caribbean Basin Initiative, Cuba, Dominican Republic, and Jamaica.

Richardson, Bonham C. *The Caribbean in the Wider World, 1492–1992.* New York: Cambridge University Press, 1993. Award winner.

Safa, Helen I. *The Myth of the Male Breadwinner: Women and Industrialization in the Caribbean.* Boulder, CO: Westview, 1994. Path breaking.

Stone, Carl. *Democracy and Clientelism in Jamaica.* New Brunswick, NJ: Transaction, 1980. Good case study.

Sunshine, Catherine A. *The Caribbean: Survival, Struggle, and Sovereignty.* Boston, MA: South End Press, 1986. Readable country accounts, updated in 1988.

——— and Philip Wheaton. *Death of a Revolution.* Washington, DC: EPICA, 1984. On U.S. invasion of Grenada.

Tardanico, Richard (ed.). *Crises in the Caribbean Basin.* Beverly Hills, CA: Sage, 1988.

Thomas, Clive Y. *The Poor and the Powerless: Economic Policy and Change in the Caribbean.* New York: Monthly Review Press, 1988. By one of Latin America's most original thinkers, a colleague of Guyana's late Walter Rodney.

Trouillot, Michel-Rolph. *Haiti: State against Nation.* New York: Monthly Review Press, 1988. Thematic analysis including post-Duvalier period.

Waters, Anita M. *Race, Class, and Political Symbols: Rastafari and Reggae in Jamaican Politics.* New Brunswick, NJ: Transaction, 1989.

Watson, Hilbourne A. (ed.). *The Caribbean in the Global Political Economy.* Boulder, CO: Lynne Rienner, 1993.

Watts, David. *The West Indies: Patterns of Development, Culture, and Environmental Change since 1492.* London: Cambridge University Press, 1987.

Films

Grenada: Portrait of a Revolution. 1982. 28 minutes. Color video by Cinewest with some of last interviews of Bishop.

Haiti Dreams of Democracy. 1987. 52 minutes. Color video on Haiti's revolution against Duvalierism, based on popular music.

The Man By the Shore. 1992. Remarkable dramatization of contemporary Haiti through the eyes of an eight-year-old girl.

Sugar Cane Alley. 1985. Award-winning feature film on sugar, politics, and Caribbean life.

Professional Journals

Caribbean Affairs

Caribbean Insight. London-based newsletter.

Caribbean Quarterly

Caribbean Review. Cultural monthly.

Caribbean Studies. Puerto Rico–based journal.

Caribbean Update. Monthly business-oriented newsletter.

Centro de Estudios Puertorriqueños Bulletin. City University of New York (Hunter College) research publication.

Cimarrón. City University of New York research publication.

Haiti Info. Bimonthly news from "the popular movement" published by Ft. Lauderdale-based Haitian Information Bureau.

Haiti Report. Exile left-wing political quarterly published by New York-based *Friends of Haiti.*

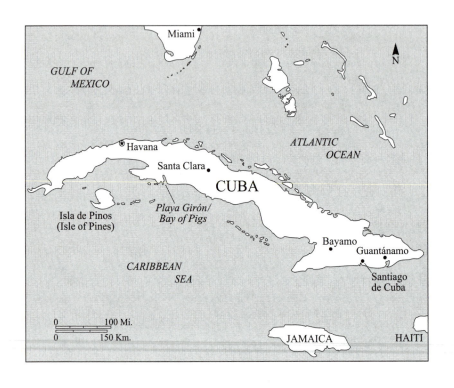

GULF OF
MEXICO

Miami

ATLANTIC
OCEAN

N

Havana

Santa Clara

CUBA

Isla de Pinos
(Isle of Pines)

Playa Girón/
Bay of Pigs

Bayamo

Guantánamo

Santiago
de Cuba

CARIBBEAN
SEA

0   100 Mi.
0   150 Km.

JAMAICA   HAITI

Cuba _____ 8

It is my duty . . . to prevent, by the independence of Cuba, the United States from spreading over the West Indies and falling with that added weight, upon other lands of our America. . . . I have lived inside the monster [United States] and known its entrails."—*Last letter written by José Martí, father of Cuban independence, killed in battle, 1895*

Let me say, with the risk of appearing ridiculous, that the true revolutionary is guided by strong feelings of love. It is impossible to think of an authentic revolutionary without this quality.—*Ernesto "Ché" Guevara, from somewhere in Africa, 1960s*

I believe that there are two different concepts of freedom. You [the United States] believe that freedom can exist with a class system, and we believe in a system where everyone is equal, where . . . there is no pyramid, no millionaires, no multimillionaires, no jobless. . . . We believe that without equality there is no freedom because you do have to speak about the freedom of the beggar, the prostitute, the exploited, the discriminated, the illiterate.—*Fidel Castro, 1975*

On October 16, 1953, soldiers escorted a tall, twenty-seven-year-old man nicknamed "El Caballo" ("the horse") into the nurses' lounge of the Civil Hospital. The Emergency Tribunal of Santiago de Cuba had moved there to avoid the crowds this young leader of the aborted July 26 uprisings had been drawing at the downtown courthouse as he defended himself and his companions. Armed attacks on July 26 against the Moncada military garrison in Santiago and other targets in Bayamo in the eastern province of Oriente had failed to topple the dictatorship of Fulgencio Batista, originally installed with U.S. backing in 1934.

The public was barred from attending the proceedings at the hospital. Only a few reporters were allowed to observe, but they took notes on the two-hour-long speech that was to become the clandestinely circulated program of the Cuban Revolution.

The young man started by chastising his accusers for not permitting him to have the books of José Martí, Cuba's liberator and national hero. "It seems the prison censors considered them too subversive," he mocked his jailers, "or is it because I named Martí as the instigator of the 26th of July events?" Next, he outlined the problems of Cuba and his proposed solutions, pitching his populist-style words to "the people":

The people we counted on in our struggle were these:

Seven hundred thousand Cubans without work. . . .

Five hundred thousand farm laborers inhabiting miserable shacks. . . .

Four hundred thousand industrial laborers and stevedores whose retirement funds have been embezzled. . . .

One hundred thousand small farmers who live and die working on land that is not theirs. . . .

Thirty thousand teachers and professors who are so badly paid. . . .

Two hundred thousand peasant families who do not have a single acre of land. . . .

Ninety percent of rural children consumed by parasites. . . .

When the head of a family works only four months a year (during the sugar planting and harvest), how can he purchase clothing and medicine for his children? . . .

A revolutionary government will settle the landless . . . solve the housing problem . . . improve public health . . . undertake integral reform of the educational system . . . solve the problem of unemployment. . . .

Then, he described the tortures of prisoners taken after the July 26 attacks:

The Army shattered their testicles and they tore out their eyes. . . . Photographs—which do not lie—show the bodies to have been dismembered.

Finally, he concluded, again with an accusatory tone:

Cuba is suffering under a cruel and base despotism. You are well aware that resistance to despots is legitimate. . . . I do not fear prison, just as I do not fear the fury of the miserable tyrant who snuffed life out of seventy brothers of mine. Sentence me. I don't mind. *History will absolve me.*

He remained standing, his head held defiantly high. No one spoke. The guards stared open-mouthed at the young man, waiting for more. Finally, he slapped his hand on the table in front of him and said, "Well, I'm finished, that's all."

Then the startled judge rang his bell and barked "Order! Order!"—in the midst of silence. Gradually, whispering began. The judge pronounced sentence: thirteen years in prison.

From his cell in the circular prison on the Isle of Pines, he used lime juice as invisible ink to record his speech between the penned lines of letters sent out to friends and family. They in turn printed 10,000 copies of "History Will Absolve Me," which circulated clandestinely throughout Cuba. The dictator Batista sent his minister of interior to offer him amnesty if he dropped out of politics. He issued a public statement refusing, "One thousand years of prison before I renounce any of my principles." Cubans loved it.

Soon afterward, Batista announced presidential elections. His one opponent, who withdrew on the grounds that the vote would be rigged, forced him to make a campaign promise of amnesty for the "Moncadistas"—as the young man and his comrades who had launched the July 26 attacks were known.

After his inauguration in early 1955 Batista was paid a friendly visit by U.S. Vice-President Richard Nixon on behalf of President Eisenhower. Batista also signed a sugar sales agreement with the Soviet Union. Feeling secure with such powerful friends abroad, he gave in to public pressure to keep his campaign promise and signed an amnesty law on May 7, 1955. It was a seemingly minor decision, but it altered the course of world history.

As the newly freed young man and his comrades crossed the waters on a ferry boat from the Isle of Pines to mainland Cuba, they pledged to mount an armed revolution against the dictatorship. Within weeks, numerous political dissidents had joined the "26th of July movement," as it became known. Next, the young man, imitating Martí, went into exile to build an invasion force.

A little over a year later, on November 24, 1956, he and eighty-one other armed men, denounced by the Cuban Communist party as "crazies," "putschists," and "adventurers," returned in a rickety old fifty-eight-foot yacht called the *Granma* (later the name of Cuba's official daily newspaper). The craft smashed up on rocks during their landing west of the Sierra Maestra mountains in Oriente and one thousand soldiers mowed half of them down. Another twenty-one fled.

One of the survivors, an Argentine doctor, bleeding from a flesh wound in the neck, became known within a year as the world's foremost new strategist of guerrilla warfare: Ernesto Ché Guevara. For years CIA and Pentagon counterinsurgency experts studied his manuals late into the night, before capturing and murdering him in Bolivia in 1968 (see chapter 15).

When fifteen survivors reassembled inland, El Caballo announced: "The days of the dictatorship are numbered." Batista declared that all of the invaders had been killed, but Cubans whispered behind closed doors, "He's alive, he and the boys are up there in the hills." Then the Cuban "underground" smuggled a *New York Times* reporter, Herbert Matthews, in and out of Cuba to photograph him and his bearded followers among the 7,000-foot-high peaks of the

Sierra Maestra. Mysterious notes began appearing in Cuba's plazas: "Beware, the bearded ones have shaved their beards and descended into the cities."

By the fall of 1958 the guerrillas' numbers had grown to hundreds, and they enjoyed the support of millions. They had set up other battle fronts, including one in central Cuba. They treated captured soldiers humanely and won over portions of Batista's 40,000-strong army. Heavy air force bombardments earned them the compassion of the surrounding peasantry; schools and clinics set up in the "liberated zones" drew widespread approval. The national police decapitated and dismembered their messenger boys and girls and threw their corpses into the streets, repelling all Cubans and bringing fresh support for the bearded ones.

On New Year's Eve, his army chewed up by casualties and desertions to the guerrilla cause, Batista and his henchmen fled Cuba. The ragtag guerrillas paraded from Santa Clara, site of the final military battle in the center of the island, to Havana, cheered along the way by huge throngs. A general strike lasted until they were firmly in power, January 7, 1959.

Cuba, indeed the world, would never be the same. Ever since, people wondered what would have happened if Batista had executed Fidel Castro.

.   .   .

The former center of the Western Hemisphere's "white slave trade" (trafficking in prostitutes) and an important drug-trade crossroads, Cuba eliminated these "traditions" during a revolution led by that same man, Fidel Castro, in 1959. At one time little more than a U.S. colony and later a playground for organized crime and America's wealthy, Cuba is the West Indies' most populous nation and the world's biggest producer of sugar. Once plagued by widespread poverty and racism, it became by the 1980s remarkable for its relative absence of both. Hunger and involuntary unemployment were rare until 1993. Income is still distributed relatively equally, leading some observers to call Cuba the most egalitarian nation in the world. Cuba's standards of nutrition and health are among the world's highest. No more does one see beggars in the streets, underfed children, homeless people sleeping on the sidewalks in front of shop windows filled with U.S. appliances.

Once in power, Castro tried to implement the promises of reform he had outlined in his 1953 speech. When landowners or employers balked, he expropriated their properties. He would not break his promises, he said. Economically well-off Cubans shuddered, while workers and peasants applauded. The U.S. government clamped an economic embargo on Cuba. By 1961 Castro had carried through many radical reforms and was riding a tidal wave of popularity. When Havana's suburbs were bombed by U.S. planes in April 1961 on the eve of the Bay of Pigs invasion by U.S.-trained Cuban counterrevolutionaries,

Castro declared to cheering throngs that Cuba was the Western Hemisphere's first Socialist revolution. At the end of that year, he declared himself a Marxist-Leninist.

The consensus among most biographers and political analysts is that Castro's conversion to Marxism-Leninism came after he took power and was consistent with his pragmatic political style. He had always tailored his uncompromising idealism to the circumstances of the moment, and events like the U.S. economic blockade and Bay of Pigs invasion intensified his leftist inclinations. To fulfill his promises of reform and to rescue the revolution, he turned to the Soviet Union for help.

He asked for—and got—Soviet missiles, leading to the October 1962 missile crisis and a U.S. promise never to invade Cuba (President Reagan disavowed this part of the settlement in the 1980s). Castro later made Cuba the only non-European country other than Mongolia to become, in 1972, a member of the Soviet-dominated common market COMECON (Council for Mutual Economic Assistance). While many people in the West viewed Castro as a Soviet puppet, the Non-Aligned Movement of Nations, viewing him as independent, elected him as their president.

Thirty-five years after Fidel Castro took power, Cuba's 11 million people have Latin America's best, although still inadequate, housing, with rent payments limited to 10 percent of the renter's income. Cubans have free health care in a system of preventive medicine where there are more doctors per capita than in France, half of them women. The WHO (World Health Organization) has lauded Cuba's public health programs as "on a par with Sweden." More than three thousand Cuban doctors and health technicians serve voluntarily in twenty-seven needy countries.

Although Cubans enjoy a wider range of economic and professional activities than ever before, they still depend economically on the bounty of their sugar harvests—seventy percent of the value of exports compared with prerevolutionary figures of 82 percent and higher. Nontraditional exports (everything but sugar, tobacco, and nickel) grew at an annual clip of 39.3 percent in the 1980s. A world-class biotechnology program developed by the revolution generated additional exports. Prior to the collapse of the Soviet block in 1989-1990, Cuba conducted up to 20 percent of its annual trade with nonsocialist countries, mainly Canada, France, Japan, and Spain. In the 1990s it increased trade with them and China.

The 1980s' precipitous fall in world sugar prices crippled most neighboring nations (see Introduction to Part Two), but Cuba's economy chugged along, until 1986 at least, with 6 percent annual growth rates in "real income" (what the peso buys). Bilateral agreements with the Soviet Union in Cuba's favor linked the price of Cuban sugar sales to Soviet oil prices, giving Cuba up to ten times the market price of sugar. One-third of the sugar crop was still sold on the open world market. Depressed sugar prices in the 1990s added to Cuba's economic woes that followed the end of Soviet aid, and the economy nosedived.

There were three important differences in Cuba's sugar monoculture as compared to the pre-1959 days. First, the sugar worker earned enough to pay for a year's expenses plus guaranteed vacations. Second, Cuba could choose its trading partners, sometimes obtaining higher sugar prices than what it had received under the monopolistic U.S. "quota." Third, the sugar was owned by the state instead of by foreign or private corporations. This made it possible to reinvest "profits" in new equipment, expand the use of sugar by-products, or invest in the development of other sectors of the economy, such as biotechnology, citrus fruits for export, fishing, and steel (all new industries). Because of this relative economic diversification, sugar's share in the total production of goods and services fell from 22 percent in 1959 to 6 percent in 1986.

Cubans also developed one of Latin America's strongest military arsenals, supplied no longer by the United States but instead by the Soviet Union. Cuba was capable of dispatching troops to points halfway around the globe, as happened in the late 1970s in Angola and Ethiopia. Some called these actions "aggressive"; others, like Andrew Young, President Carter's troubleshooter on African affairs, acknowledged them to be "stabilizing"; and still others applauded them as "internationalist" acts of solidarity in the battle against apartheid, colonialism, and counterrevolution.

Foes of the Cuban Revolution called the 745-mile-long island a bayonet-ruled house of fear and launching pad for overseas aggression. Friends described it as an egalitarian safe house for the development of what Cubans called "the new man and new woman," committed to the cause of human liberation everywhere and an end to "the exploitation of man by man." There were no disappeared or death squads in Cuba, they noted. But there were political prisoners, some of whom charged the regime with torture. The U.S. government and major human rights organizations called on Cuba to open its doors to international inspection of prison and human rights conditions, and Cuba agreed to do so in 1988. The State Department forbade Cuban inspection of U.S. prisons. Few denied that Castro's was the first honest government in Cuban history and the first to put a stop to institutional racism. But some said it practiced new forms of nepotism and corruption.

Was Castro's alliance with the Soviet Union avoidable? Could Cuba "return" to "the family of American nations"? Had it ever "left"? What was life like in Cuba? What about Cuba's economic slump of 1986–1987 and Castro's crackdown on internal free markets? And what would happen if Castro died?

Cuba as Colonial Pivot: Spanish-Cuban-American War

From the time Christopher Columbus claimed it for Spain in 1492, Cuba became the Caribbean's prize jewel, fought over by the world's great powers. Consequently, external forces of domination and internal ones of liberation developed a tradition of violent extremism in their contest for control over Cuba's destiny.

Located 90 miles south of Florida and 75 miles east of Yucatán, Mexico, the island is the largest in the West Indies, twelve times the size of nearby Puerto Rico. Cuba's excellent harbors made it an ideal jumping-off point for the conquest of North America, Central America, and South America. From early on the transshipment to Europe of gold and silver from Mexico and Peru and the African slave trade made Cuba a commercial crossroads. But for settlement and profitable agriculture, Cuba also had deep, fertile soils and a balmy semitropical climate, made comfortable by the prevalent trade winds.

The *conquistadores* and imported diseases wiped out Cuba's Arawak, Carib, and Taino Indians even more rapidly than they did Puerto Rico's (see chapter 9). The Indian chieftain Hatuey was burned alive. The British, Dutch, French, and North Americans—pirates and governments alike—repeatedly tried to grab Cuba away from Spain, which in turn built its best fortresses and most infamous dungeons for prisoners in Cuba.

As Europe's and North America's demand for sugar and tobacco rose during the eighteenth century, Cuba's dominant Spanish merchant families in the cities and landholding Creole elites (Spanish descendants born in Cuba) converted the island into a nascent agroindustrial plantation and factory. More than one-quarter of a million slaves worked in Cuba by the early 1820s. In the 1840s U.S. investors brought rails, telegraphs, gas lighting, and the first steam-operated sugar refineries.

For many decades U.S. presidents and diplomats viewed Cuba as de facto American. President Thomas Jefferson (1801–1809) stated in 1809 that "Cuba would be naturally taken by the United States, or the island would give itself to us." President James Monroe (1817–1825) wrote Ambassador Nelson in Spain, "Cuba and Puerto Rico are natural appendages of the United States."

When Latin America began winning its Wars of Independence against Spain, South America's self-proclaimed "Liberator" Símon Bolívar considered freeing Cuba and Puerto Rico, but U.S. Secretary of State John Quincy Adams told him to stay out. Adams's Monroe Doctrine became the diplomatic banner for U.S. interests in the Americas (see Overview). He viewed Cuba as "an apple that had to fall by gravity into the hands of the United States."

President James Polk (1845–1849) and his Secretary of State James Buchanan tried to buy Cuba from Spain but failed. From 1849 to 1851, in their efforts to extend slave territories, U.S. proslavery filibusters aided the prostatehood Cuban annexationist Narciso López in three aborted invasions of the island. Buchanan railed, "We must have Cuba. We can't do without Cuba, and above all we must not suffer its transfer to Great Britain. We shall acquire it by coup d'état at some propitious moment. . . . Cuba is already ours, I feel it in my finger ends."

In 1854 three proslavery U.S. ministers issued the Ostend Manifesto, recommending that in case Spain refused to sell Cuba, "Then by every law human and divine, we shall be justified in wresting it from Spain." Secretary of State Marcy publicly disavowed the Ostend Manifesto but privately endorsed its spirit in his instructions to the new American ambassador to Spain, "The president regards the incorporation of Cuba into the American Union essential."

After the Civil War in the 1860s the United States underwent rapid industrial expansion and stepped up its quest for control over natural resources, markets, and ports in the entire Caribbean Basin. Cuba fell under the increasing economic control of U.S. sugar, iron ore, manganese, tobacco, rail, and trading interests. Nearly half its sugar production was based on the *central* system—a big plantation around a mill, worked first by slaves and later by low-wage free laborers. So-called *colonos* (small farmers) cultivated smaller land parcels nearby. In 1890 the McKinley Tariff placed raw sugar on the free list of U.S. imports. This and subsequent U.S. tariff policies created a "quota" system of guaranteed Cuban sugar for the U.S. market—40 percent of the U.S. supply by 1958.

The wealth and influence of coffee growers and cattle ranchers in Cuba's largest province, mountainous Oriente, had already been reduced by Spanish customs duties and income taxes.Creole sugar estate owners could not compete with the modern technology and guaranteed quotas of bigger U.S. firms. Oriente was also a favorite hiding area for the *cimarrones* (runaway slaves). Consequently, it was not surprising that leaders in the fight for independence came from Oriente.

U.S. diplomacy backed up U.S. business interests in Cuba. In the early 1870s the United States blocked Colombia's "Pan-American" plan for nineteen American republics to recognize Cuba's right to independence. The Cubans' so-called Ten Years War (1868–1878—named by most Cubans the "Thirty Years War," 1868–1898), was in full swing. It started with the "Proclamation of Yara" by Carlos Manuel de Céspedes, an Oriente landowner who freed his slaves but later pulled out of the fight when he saw how radical it was becoming. More than 100,000 perished in the Ten Years War.

The main general leading the independence fighters was a sympathetic foreigner, Afro-Dominican exile Máximo Gómez—an early forerunner of Cuba's later internationalists fighting foreign control in Latin America. The main Cuban guerrilla commander was Afro-Cuban Antonio Maceo, known as "the bronze Titan." In the 1880s an exiled Maceo planned further invasions of Cuba. Also supporting the fight was a diminutive, poetry-writing seventeen-year-old youth named José Martí, who was arrested in 1870 and sentenced to six years in jail. He was deported to Spain. Like his yet-to-be-born disciple Fidel Castro, he eventually obtained a law degree.

The "father" of Cuban independence, José Martí, like Castro, the son of a Spanish immigrant army sergeant, condemned the U.S. for refusing arms to Cuban exiles and blocking the struggle: "We had but one neighbor who confessedly 'stretched the limits of his power and acted against the will of the people' to help the foes of those who were fighting for the same Chart of Liberties on which he built his independence." Martí spent fourteen years in exile (1881–1895), mostly in New York City where he served as a correspondent for Latin American newspapers.

While serving as Uruguay's Consul in the United States in 1890, Martí attended the First International American Conference held in Washington. He warned Cubans not to trust such U.S.-dominated Pan-American ventures. As for potential U.S. aid in Cuba's fight for independence, he said, "Once the United States is in Cuba, who will get her out?" During his guerrilla days in the Sierra Maestra, Castro read and marked many similar passages from Martí's collected works.

As Cuba's independence forces conducted their on-and-off war against Spain during three decades, the U.S. grew more committed to seizing the island. In 1891 U.S. Secretary of State James G. Blaine wrote President Benjamin Harrison that he considered "only three places that are of value to be taken: one is Hawaii and the others are Cuba and Puerto Rico." Four years later Secretary of State Olney issued his famous "fiat"—"Today the United States is practically sovereign on this continent, and its fiat is law upon the subjects to which it confines its interposition."

Some Cubans harbored other ideas, though. Their earlier attempts at winning independence had taught them that their task was not easy. Spanish troops had crushed them mercilessly, as in the case of the rebellion by tobacco growers (*vegueros*) in 1717 or slaves backed by University of Havana intellectuals in 1812. During the 1820s U.S. and British naval forces helped Spain secure its ports in Havana and Santiago to protect their trade in slaves, rum, tobacco, and sugar. Scattered bands of *cimarrones* kept up the independence fight, and in 1842–1844 slaves backed by educated Creoles launched a series of bloody uprisings, and again were crushed.

Three ideological camps took shape: annexationists, favoring U.S. statehood; autonomists, preferring self-government under Spanish sovereignty; and separatists, demanding independence. The first two were usually Creole big landowners, planters, merchants, and shipowners, reluctant to free the slaves. The separatists incorporated some Oriente landowners, many intellectuals, small traders, émigré tobacco workers in Florida, artisans, slaves, and *cimarrones,* anxious to free the slaves and "go it alone." The ruling Spanish elites, of course, opposed all three.

Antislavery exiles organized the Republican Society of Cuba and Puerto Rico in New York in 1865–1866, and the separatists gained ascendancy in the Cuban opposition over the next three decades. The separatists' armed resistance contributed to Spain's decision to free the slaves in 1880, a process they did not complete until the early 1890s, often with the guns of pro-independence guerrillas pointed at them. By the mid-1890s Spanish authorities had their hands full with the growing strength of the separatist guerrillas.

In 1892 the proindependence First National Workers' Congress convened in Havana. Led by radical artisans and tobacco workers, it opted for "revolutionary socialism." As head of the newly founded PRC (Cuban Revolutionary party), Martí rejected demands by moderates that Socialists and blacks be excluded. On the other hand, he excluded autonomists and annexationists. Article 9 of the PRC Program stated, "Anyone in Cuban ranks who presents ideas other than independence should be tried and shot."

On February 24, 1895, the final phase of the War of Independence began in Oriente with the "Grito de Baire." Martí, Gómez, and others left the neighboring island nation of the Dominican Republic and landed in Cuba on April 11. Martí wrote, "The Cuban war has broken out in America in time to prevent . . . the annexation of Cuba to the United States." On May 19, 1895, Martí was killed riding headlong into a Spanish force near Dos Rios, Oriente.

A new military governor of Cuba, the infamous "Butcher Weyler," ordered thousands of Cubans killed and thousands more herded into concentration camps. Some 200,000 Spanish soldiers squared off against 4,000 guerrilla fighters. The Spaniards retreated before Maceo's "invasion of the West" that advanced the guerrillas from Oriente to the other end of the island. Yellow fever, malaria, and dysentery cut down Spanish reinforcements as quickly as they arrived. Shortly before his death, Maceo wrote, "Nor do I expect anything from the Americans; we must confine all to our own efforts. It is better to rise up or fall without help than to contract debts of gratitude with so powerful a neighbor."

In 1896 President Grover Cleveland warned Spain that should she lose Cuba "higher obligations" would fall upon the United States, which, he pointed out, had $30 to $50 million of capital tied up in Cuba. In 1897 Spain tried to save Cuba by granting it autonomy—but it was too late. Realizing the Cuban guerrillas had won the war, as shown in the testimonies of General Blanco (Weyler's successor) and other Spanish officials, Spain sought a final settlement in Cuba.

Meanwhile President McKinley dispatched the battleship *Maine* to a tightly guarded Havana harbor. One night in February 1898, it blew up, killing

U.S. sailors aboard. The U.S. National Archives' files on the incident are still ruled "off limits" to historians. "Remember the *Maine!*" became the battle cry of Americans seeking to seize Cuba.

The day before President McKinley delivered a war message to Congress, he received a cable from the American Ministry in Madrid advising him that Spain was willing to grant Cuba's rebels autonomy or independence or to cede the island to the United States. McKinley knew that if the United States received Cuba from Spain, they would still have to face the victorious Cuban guerrillas. If he refused to negotiate with Spain, however, he could come in as an "ally" of Cuba against the Spanish. Congress was clamoring for war. After falling to his knees and praying to God, McKinley stood up and opted for war.

The Spanish-Cuban War became the Spanish-Cuban-American War. Initially, the U.S. Senate voted to recognize Cuban independence and the guerrilla leadership, but a Joint House-Senate Resolution deleted this. Instead, the "Teller Amendment" to the war declaration disclaimed any U.S. intention to annex Cuba.

Among the U.S. officers gaining fame in the short war were political and economic giants like Teddy Roosevelt, Cornelius Vanderbilt, and J. P. Morgan. Many Americans opposed the war, calling it "imperialist." Desertion and draft evasion were proportionately higher than in any other U.S. war since the Mexican War (see chapter 1) and until Vietnam. Cubans did the fighting against the Spaniards, and there was only one major U.S. battle—San Juan Hill. Roosevelt acknowledged, "It wasn't much of a war, but it was the best war we had."

On December 10, 1898, Spain and the United States inked the Treaty of Paris ending the war. Cuba was not represented, but the treaty granted "independence" to the U.S.-occupied island.

U.S.-Regulated Republic, Frustrated Cuban Nationalism

U.S. direct and indirect rule over Cuba combined the ideals of free enterprise capitalism and democracy with the firm, often violent hand of a stern "uncle." After disbanding the "Mambises," as the Cuban independence fighters were called, the United States repeatedly used military force to put down Cuban nationalist rebellions and to protect mushrooming U.S. investments. U.S. troops invaded and occupied Cuba in 1898–1902, 1906–1909, 1912, and 1917–1922, with Protestant missionaries not far behind. U.S. warships stood offshore during the unsuccessful Revolution of 1933 and the triumphant arrival of Fidel Castro in Havana in 1959.

When U.S. Marines squashed an Afro-Cuban uprising in 1912, Secretary of State Knox observed," "The United States does not undertake first to consult the Cuban Government if a crisis arises requiring a temporary landing somewhere." U.S. Marine Major-General Smedley D. Butler later recalled, "I helped make Haiti and Cuba a decent place for the National City Banks boys to collect revenues in." By 1914 Cuba's economy was almost entirely controlled by U.S. interests, and the island was the world's sixth largest customer of U.S. goods and services.

The U.S. government invoked various doctrines to justify its interventionism: the 1902 Platt Amendment to the Cuban Constitution, abrogated in 1934 after Batista's dictatorship was installed; the "international police power" of the 1904 Roosevelt Corollary to the Monroe Doctrine; and Dollar Diplomacy (see Overview). The Platt Amendment gave the United States the right to intervene to secure "the preservation of Cuban independence [and] the maintenance of a government adequate for the protection of life, property, and individual liberty." It also gave the United States the right to oversee Cuba's foreign policy, to limit Cuba's debts to what its "ordinary revenues would cover," and to purchase or lease "land necessary for coaling stations and naval bases."

The Cubans agreed to the Platt Amendment in exchange for withdrawal of U.S. forces and formal independence. A U.S. naval base was established at Guantánamo on the eastern end of Cuba, creating a bilateral bone of contention.

When necessary, the United States appointed its own citizens to govern Cuba. In 1906, for example, Secretary of War and future U.S. President (1909–1913) William Howard Taft served as provisional governor of Cuba, followed by Governor Magoon until 1909. Even when Cuba had its own president—an army general or a civilian backed by the army until the advent of Castro—the American ambassador apparently still had considerable power. One ambassador to Cuba in the 1950s, for instance, observed that he "sometimes" was "more important than the president of Cuba."

U.S. presence contributed to the eradication of diseases; the construction of highways, railroads, and hotels; the development of a modern army and national police force; and the growth of middle classes of tradesmen, lawyers, teachers, and other professionals. Cuban culture underwent a high degree of "Americanization," especially in the areas of consumerism, tourism, and gangsterism. Organized crimes' Meyer Lansky came to oversee gambling and other rackets.

Few other Latin American countries experienced as virulent a racism as Cuba did in the six decades prior to 1959. Beaches and other public facilities were segregated. Bars became private "clubs" to keep blacks out, and racial intermarriage was prohibited. Nearly one-quarter of all Cubans could "pass" as white, whereas the rest were unmistakably mulattoes, blacks, or Chinese. Afro-Cubans, composing one-third to half of the population, were the majority of the unemployed, had the worse jobs, and were kept from rising in the pro-

fessions. Dictator Batista, a man of mixed mulatto-Asian background, was unusually powerful in a nation ruled by whites.

The value of U.S. investments in Cuba passed a billion dollars by the
1920s. In 1959 they were among the highest in book value of all U.S. business
portfolios in Latin America. United Fruit Company and other U.S. firms dominated sugar, while U.S. companies also prevailed in oil refining, mining, rails,
tourism, communications, electricity, pharmaceuticals, rubber, chemicals, and
banking. Banks like Rockefeller's Chase Manhattan grew so powerful that
they could dictate the Cuban government's budget and tax policies and force
cabinet changes.

Students and workers led Cuba's attempted Revolution of 1933, gaining
a progressive reputation as "the generation of the thirties." Their roots, however, were in the 1920s. After another U.S. troop withdrawal, Julio Antonio
Mella and other students founded the FEU (University Student Federation) in
1923; Mella joined the Communists' PSP (Popular Socialist party) a year later.
The PSP led illegal general strikes in 1930 and 1932 that dictator Gerardo
Machado (1925–1933) drowned in blood. A *New York Times* reporter wrote
that under Machado assassination rose "to the dignity of a political art." On the
eve of his overthrow in1933, Machado told the American ambassador that his
use of widespread assassinations had been "a stupid mistake."

In April of 1933 the United States dispatched Special Ambassador Sumner Welles to Cuba to oversee Machado's removal, the exclusion of leftists
from the new government, and the negotiation of a Reciprocal Trade Treaty
that, in Welles' words, "will give us a practical monopoly" of the Cuban market. By August 7, however, Welles had to cable the State Department, "The
general strike has now extended to all of the Republic." Two days later he requested U.S. warships. On August 11, 1933, Machado fled Cuba. Thirty-six
sugar mills had been seized by their workers, and it seemed that the Revolution of 1933 had triumphed.

Not for long. On September 4, a "*sargents'* revolt," led by Batista in the
name of crushing pro-Machado counterrevolutionaries, led to the suppression
of the Left. Thirty more U.S. warships were sent to Cuban waters, and the
United States refused to recognize the interim government of Professor Grau
San Martín.

After meeting with Batista and representatives of the right-wing student
and professional society ABC, Welles wired the State Department: "I told him
that in my opinion he was the only individual who represented authority today
in Cuba. . . ." Welles asked Batista to take charge, and "Batista agreed to it in
the most emphatic manner."

On January 15, 1934, confronted with an ultimatum from Batista and
U.S. Ambassador Caffery, Grau resigned. Batista's troops occupied factories
and murdered striking workers, establishing a "reign of terror." Another gen-

eral strike was crushed in 1935, leaving more than one hundred strikers dead. In 1936 Batista dissolved the Senate, closed down the University of Havana, and muzzled what was left of the press.

Batista legalized the PSP in 1939 and took two Communists into his government in 1940 as "ministers without portfolio." They were no longer organizing against his government. The PSP, like Communist parties all over the world, had decided to make the defense of the Soviet Union against Nazi Germany's invasion the major item on their agenda. The United States and its "friends" like Batista had allied themselves with the Soviet Union in the fight against Hitler's aggression in Europe. Just like movie fans everywhere else in the free world, Cubans jammed the Saturday matinees to cheer the Soviet freedom fighters against German fascism and to hoot and howl at the Nazis.

When the Cold War reached Cuba's shores after World War II, anticommunism returned. But when the first Soviet ships arrived with supplies to break the U.S. economic blockade against the 1959 Cuban Revolution, Cubans again cheered Soviet freedom fighters. The only remnant of Cuba's Revolution of 1933 to survive was the 1940 Constitution, a document that called for electoral democracy and the type of labor and agrarian reforms Castro implemented in 1959–1960.

After World War II Batista retained military power while two civilian presidencies (1944–1952) of the "Auténtico" party governed, each more corrupt than any before. The Auténtico party, founded in 1936, claimed to represent the aspirations of the Revolution of 1933, but its governments assassinated leftist labor leaders and drove the PSP underground. Gangster elements took over organized labor's CTC (Cuban Workers' Confederation, founded in 1939).

The most popular voice of the opposition was Eduardo Chibás, founder of the "Ortodoxo" party, which claimed it truly represented the Revolution of 1933. In 1952, after delivering an impassioned speech on his popular weekly radio program, Chibás shot himself while the microphone was still on. Fidel Castro and other admirers of Chibás and the Ortodoxos rushed him to a hospital, but it was too late.

In 1952 Castro announced his candidacy for Congress in upcoming elections on the Ortodoxo ticket. Polls showed the Ortodoxos would likely win. On March 10, Batista carried out his military coup. He suspended the 1940 Constitution and closed down the University of Havana. Ever the lawyer, Castro first sent a brief to the Court of Constitutional Guarantees accusing Batista of treason—in vain, of course. Then, on July 26, 1953, Castro led the botched attack on the Moncada garrison in Santiago.

Batista reintroduced a reign of terror. Gangsterism and corruption reached new heights during the next five years. An estimated 2,000 to 20,000 Cubans were murdered, most of them city youths suspected of burning sugar cane fields and bombing electrical installations, or of running messages to Castro's guerrillas.

At first the opposition to Batista stumbled badly. On November 30, 1956, Frank País led an uprising in Santiago. It was intended to coincide with Castro's invasion, but a storm delayed the arrival of the *Granma* until December 2. On March 13, 1957, the Student Directorate in Havana attacked the presidential palace. Student leader José Antonio Echeverría seized Radio Reloj and exhorted Cubans to rise up. He and others fell in a hail of lead near the University of Havana, the walls of which are still pockmarked by the ricocheting bullets. Two weeks later, though, Castro's guerrillas captured the army barracks at El Uvero in Oriente, preserving some faint hope of victory.

In July 1957 mass support changed the nature of the resistance. Frank País was assassinated in Santiago. A massive march at his funeral was followed by a one-week strike. A general strike called by Castro failed in April 1958, because of poor coordination and PSP opposition to Castro's "adventurism." Three months later Communist leader Carlos Rafael Rodríguez treked to the Sierra Maestra to begin mending political fences with Castro.

In an action that Castro disapproved, Raúl Castro, his brother, led a band that captured seventy U.S. soldiers from the Guantánamo Naval Base. They were released in exchange for a promise that aerial bombardments of peasant-civilian zones would stop. But the bombing was renewed. Believing that the bombing depended on U.S. supplies and diplomatic support for Batista, Fidel Castro wrote Celia Sánchez, his long-standing companion, that after the guerrillas' triumph they would still face one more battle, "the battle against the United States."

After Batista's midnight escape New Year's Eve from Cuba with nearly all of the national treasury, U.S. officials maneuvered to establish a "provisional government," excluding the guerrillas. Castro responded with a successful call for a general strike. On January 8, 1959, Castro, Guevara, and other guerrillas entered Havana to joyous public acclamation. Chants of "Fidel! Fidel!" and *"Cuba sí, Yanqui no!"* filled the air. From the Columbia military barracks, renamed, *"Ciudad Libertad"* (Freedom City), Castro announced on radio and television, "We have won only the right to begin."

Changing the System

Most writers agree on the facts and historical context of the Cuban Revolution. None deny the pre-1959 pattern of U.S. economic and cultural domination. All concur there was some revolutionary input from the rural proletariat (sugar workers), the peasantry, urban workers, middle-class elements, and generations of students (1933, 1953). Major disagreements crop up over Castro's motivations and the events after the actual taking of power.

Some believe Castro misled the Cuban people and "betrayed" the revolution, particularly its promises of free elections and a free press. They argue that Castro was a shrewd and conscious Marxist-Leninist bent on one-man rule long before 1959. They say Castro made Cuba more dependent on the Soviet Union than it ever was on the United States.

Others believe that hostile U.S. actions rather than prior ideological commitments "pushed" Castro into the arms of the "Russian bear." They point out that Castro's pre-1959 ideology was a mix of many elements and that even his later Marxism was more populist and pragmatic than dogmatic. They maintain that Castro was a moralist and nationalist in the Martí tradition, intent on overcoming the evils of corruption, unemployment, and disease. To carry out pervasive reforms, he had no choice but to reduce the power of some U.S. companies, such as United Fruit. The revolution became Socialist because powerful interests fought against the agrarian, housing, and other reforms tooth-and-nail, leaving the revolution's leadership two alternatives: surrender or "go all the way" and nationalize their opponents' properties (usually with compensation). Since genuine reforms were proving to be impossible under the profit system, elementary logic pointed to replacing that system with a nonprofit one—socialism.

Still other authors emphasize the role of the individual in history, noting the exceptional or "charismatic" qualities of Castro's leadership and his great popularity among "average" Cubans. He moved freely around the country and delivered not only promised reforms, but also weapons with which to defend them—establishing the popular militia. He held regular rallies attended by a million or more to give blow-by-blow explanations of every revolutionary step the government took.

No act had as great an initial impact as the land and housing reforms. Castro started by expropriating his own father's estate. The land reform redistributed more than 10 million acres, ended rural unemployment, and raised rural workers' wages. It rapidly terminated decades of large private estates and minuscule land parcels by establishing a maximum size for private farms of first 994 acres and then 163 acres and a minimum size of 66 acres. The huge task was run by INRA (National Institute of Agrarian Reform). It administered state farms, payment of wages and vacations, distribution of land, fertilizers, and seeds. Private farmers received or owned some 30 percent of the land area. Later organized into the ANAP (National Association of Small Farmers), the farmers received government credits and technical assistance and generally cooperated with government marketing and production schedules. Starting in 1975, private farm cooperatives were encouraged by government incentives such as new housing. They soon outproduced the state farms.

Unlike any other revolution, Cuba's emphasized improving the countryside even, if need be, at the expense of the city. New housing construction focused on rural areas, where the traveler today sees prefab houses and recently built health centers in what are called "new towns." The *bohío,* or one-room, dirt-floor, windowless thatched hut that once housed most rural people, is seldom seen.

The slashing of urban rents and the application of rent payments to eventual purchases of dwellings turned Cuban real estate practices upside-down. While renters celebrated, big landlords headed for Miami and the homeless moved into their abandoned houses. Mansions in Havana's fashionable Miramar section became schools, day-care centers, youth hostels. Electricity and phone rates were slashed; public telephones and local buses were made free of charge. The Cuban Revolution closed down casinos, some of which had become gathering places for racketeers, drug-pushers, and pimps. Brothels were also shut, but instead of pouring out into the streets, prostitutes were offered rehabilitation and job training. Massive antidrug and antialcoholism campaigns were launched. There was much work to be done and jobs for all. After a few years poverty disappeared from Havana's streets. With the emphasis on rural housing, run-down buildings remained in the "Old Havana" section until a renovation program in the 1980s.

The "government," still an informal band of ex-guerrillas led by Castro and Guevara, announced that 1961 was "The Year of Education." Some 200,000 young people left their classrooms to go into the countryside and teach reading and writing to illiterates, 24 percent of the population in 1959. The successful campaign practically eliminated illiteracy and became a UN-recommended model for other nations, including Nicaragua in the 1980s (see chapter 5).

By the mid-1980s Cubans had the highest level of education in Latin America, all of it free, including school lunches. Every Cuban youth completed ninth grade. Many went on to finish high school. University enrollments increased eightfold. Since foreigners had usually held all the key technical jobs, the sciences and technical training were emphasized. Learning by doing through "work-study" became the norm from junior high school on up.

Competition for good grades was de-emphasized, and brighter students were obligated to help out slower ones. Ideological content was based on the tenets of "Marxist-Leninist internationalism," which claimed to help others instead of competing with them. Thousands of Cubans volunteered to work overseas as teachers, nurses, doctors, or technicians.

With increased education came expanded cultural programs and international recognition of new Cuban accomplishments in literature, art, music, dance, and cinema. While a minority of intellectuals grumbled about the loss of artistic freedom and even left the island, most stayed or returned from their places of exile under Batista. Some fought for changes and felt free to do so "within the revolution." But within the revolution had its limitations. One dissident, Ariel Hidalgo Guillén, a forty-one-year-old Marxist historian and textbook writer, wrote a book critical of "the new class," the PCC (Cuban Communist party), ruling Cuba. That was too much for some people, and in 1981 he was arrested by the DSE (Department of State Security) and charged with subversion "against the social order." Tried and convicted, he was sentenced to eight years in prison.

In the area of health half of Cuba's doctors suspected socialized medicine was around the corner and left. They were right. Free of charge health-for-care replaced expensive health-for-profit. New doctors were trained and clinics were established. The number of hospitals and hospital beds nearly quadrupled. Every medical student was required to practice for two years in the countryside. Preventive medicine eliminated malaria and polio and radically reduced tuberculosis, diphtheria, and gastroenteritis (a big killer in pre-1959 Cuba). Mortality rates plummeted, and life expectancy rose to seventy-five years for women and seventy-one for men.

Before the revolution newspapers were often pro-Batista, paid for by government subsidies and commercial advertising. Castro eliminated the big newspapers' subsidies and their circulation declined in favor of new prorevolution newspapers. Advertisers stopped paying for ads in unread papers. Protesting the loss of Cuba's freedom of the press, the old newspaper owners closed their presses and went to Miami. The end result was a quasi-official press with articles about cattle and egg production instead of debutantes' coming-out parties. Either way, it made for dull reading.

The Cuban Revolution won enthusiastic support from women with its land, housing, health, and educational reforms. Centuries of Cuban "machismo" and an inferior status assigned to women could not be overcome with laws alone or educational campaigns in the schools and on the mass media, but there were huge and rapid changes. The problem of getting Cuban women to give up their traditional roles and gain their economic independence through wage employment was tackled from a legal and cultural angle. The Family Code of 1972 provided generous maternity leaves and other benefits for mothers. It required that if both partners worked, the husband had to share the housework equally with the wife. Day-care centers were introduced. The FMC (Federation of Cuban Women) campaigned vigorously to persuade women to leave the home and take paying jobs. More and more women entered training programs and enrolled in colleges to become technicians and professionals. Many housewives who did not take full-time jobs were trained as lay lawyers/judges for evening duty in neighborhood "peoples' courts" created to adjudicate minor crimes.

Having a big influence on recalcitrant men was Fidel Castro. Known as a macho himself, he became one of the most outspoken advocates of the anti-machismo campaign. The concrete examples of women as members of the guerrilla force that won the revolution as well as women's participation in the militia went a long way toward abolishing the image of the "señorita," going on a date chaperoned by an older female. One high-school militia woman on late-night guard duty informed a foreign visitor, "This rifle is my chaperone." The award-winning film *Lucía* poked fun at incurable male chauvinists.

The Cuban Revolution's "Women's Liberation" movement succeeded on some levels, but it still had barriers to overcome, particularly in employment and political leadership. In 1985, 22 percent of the deputies in the National Assembly that elects the president and Council of State were women. By Latin American and U.S. standards this was high, but it was far lower than what the Cuban Revolution had promised. In 1986, since most of the top leadership of the revolution remained in the hands of older white and mulatto men, the PCC congress emphasized the promotion of women, blacks, and young people to leadership positions.

Most Cuban "minorities" fared well, especially blacks and young people. Racial segregation was outlawed. Afro-Cubans were given better job opportunities. Youth were made the main targets, agents, and "heros" of the reforms being implemented. Sports and cultural programs were given a big boost. When the Cuban team defeated the U.S. team in the amateur world series of baseball in 1969, there was an all-night celebration in Havana.

One minority that did not improve its social status was the homosexual community. Heterosexual prejudices against homosexuals were harder to overcome than other forms of sexism. Homosexuals were barred from teaching. Some homosexuals were imprisoned and abused by their guards, a policy Castro reversed when he heard about it.

Attacking the Revolution

The swiftness and depth of Cuba's reforms provoked instant reaction among the former power brokers. Batista loyalists schemed to get rid of Castro. Cuba's wealthy went to Miami or kept their bags packed.

In both Havana and Washington, the example of the 1954 U.S.-backed overthrow of the reformist Arbenz government in Guatemala was still fresh (see chapter 2). The Eisenhower administration refused a Cuban request for military aid and set in motion a plan to pull off "another Guatemala." It led to the aborted 1961 Bay of Pigs invasion.

Six months into the revolution, Cuban authorities intercepted shipments of U.S. arms destined to "counterrevolutionaries." Castro believed that it was only a matter of time before the United States would cut off Cuba's sugar quota and, using Batistiano exiles, invade Cuba.

Meanwhile an aroused Cuban public clamored for more executions of well-known "hired guns" of the Batista dictatorship and army and police "murderers." Headlines in Havana's conservative dailies and the U.S. press excoriated "summary executions," calling them a "bloodbath." Castro tried to provide trials for the accused and to calm down the tempers of irate Cuban parents who were grieving for their murdered children. In the end, only 550 Batistianos were "put to the wall," accused of responsibility for the killing of thousands of civilians. Most Cuban dissidents were permitted to go into exile. The Miami "escape valve" let off the pressures of counter-revolution. Many Americans were persuaded that Castro was a bloodthirsty fanatic.

Years of cold war indoctrination had also convinced most Cubans that communism was evil. Yet they liked all the reforms and realized that they were pointing the country toward socialism and communism. A typical cartoon showed Cuban musicians playing bongos and maracas and saying "If what Fidel does are Communist things, sign me up, brother, 'cause they're my thing."

The Roman Catholic Church was never very strong in Cuba. Only a little more than half of Cuba's population was Roman Catholic, and the rest practiced Yoruba religious rites and were spiritualists, masons, Protestants, agnostics, Jews, or atheists, more or less in that order. At first the Church supported the revolution, but soon many religious leaders followed their rich parishioners into exile. Others, usually from poorer areas, stayed in Cuba and kept their churches functioning.

The rhetoric against "*el imperialismo yanqui*" in Havana and U.S. support for "Cuban freedom fighters" in Washington heated up throughout 1959. Then, in February 1960 Cuba and the Soviet Union signed a trade agreement calling for the Soviet purchase of one million tons of sugar a year (not unlike Batista's earlier sugar deal with the Soviets).

In the summer of 1960 U.S.-owned oil refineries refused to refine Soviet crude oil sent to Cuba in partial payment for sugar. The Cuban government took over the refineries and announced that it would determine its own trade policies. The United States retaliated by revoking its sugar quota agreement and refusing to go through with a purchase of 700,000 tons of Cuban sugar. In effect, as the *Wall Street Journal* reported, Eisenhower "declared economic war on Fidel Castro's Cuba." Cuba responded by nationalizing more U.S.-owned properties.

In August 1960 the OAS (Organization of American States) passed a U.S.-sponsored resolution condemning Chinese and Soviet influence in Cuba. A U.S.-sponsored economic blockade of Cuba picked up steam after that, and the OAS expelled Cuba by a fourteen to six vote, January 25, 1962.

Aerial and terrorist bombings in Cuba escalated during 1960. When four bombs exploded at a huge rally in Havana's Plaza of the Revolution on September 28, 1960, Castro proposed that people elect block-by-block CDRs (Committees in Defense of the Revolution). The CDRs became a permanent grassroots mass organization to help maintain vigilance, as well as to implement programs such as vaccination campaigns and equitable distribution of scarce food supplies and medicines.

Before leaving office, President Eisenhower broke diplomatic relations with Cuba (January 3, 1961). For a year Castro had been telling the world Cuba was about to be invaded. The *Hispanic American Report,* a scholarly journal published at Stanford University, leaked the news about U.S. military preparations at bases in Guatemala many months prior to the actual invasion. The mass media, however, agreed to White House requests to keep the news from reaching the American public. Opponents of U.S. interventionism launched "Fair Play for Cuba" committees to educate the public to oppose a U.S. invasion of Cuba. They were labeled "Communists" and "unpatriotic."

A month before the invasion, Cuba's Minister of Industries Ché Guevara told a group of journalists his views on the impact of the U.S. economic embargo:

> We had to nationalize U.S. industry. And when we did, the United States cut us off. . . . It's too bad, though; it will mean many shortages for us. We will run out of food. Our buses will stop. Everything will go down until we can raise the food we need and manufacture our own buses. If we can last until then, the United States is lost, because as soon as Latin America sees our economy going up, more revolutions will explode. That's why the United States must destroy us— before we recover completely, before we have rebuilt our economy. (John Gerassi, *The Great Fear in Latin America.* New York: Collier, 1963, p. 258)

The invasions's opening act occurred on April 15, 1961. Cuban exiles used U.S. B-26 bombers to attack Castro's tiny air force. Many suburban homes near the Havana airport were hit. Ambassador Adlai Stevenson first told the United Nations the planes were not American but then had to correct himself, embarrassing Kennedy. Counter to CIA expectations, the attack rallied wavering middle-class Cubans to defend Cuba. The next day they joined more than a million other Cubans at the Plaza of the Revolution to cheer Castro's announcement that the revolution was "socialist."

Instead of canceling the plan, on April 17 the CIA gave the go-ahead to some sixteen hundred Cuban exiles who had been trained in Guatemala, Nicaragua, Honduras, and Florida. They landed at Playa Girón (Bay of Pigs) in southern Cuba, backed by U.S. naval and air support. The CIA had predicted the Cuban people would rise up to join the attackers, but instead, they rose up to repel them. Castro led the defense in the front lines of battle.

A few days later President Kennedy went before the television cameras to take full responsibility for the invasion's failure. He promised to defend the heroic freedom fighters captured at the Bay of Pigs, and later commented that their flag would some day fly over Havana.

Alarmed as these truculent boasts, Castro asked for and got what he called "defensive" missiles from the Soviet Union in the late summer of 1962. On October 22, 1962, the Kennedy administration called for removal of the missiles and declared a naval blockade of Cuba to prevent the arrival of Soviet ships already on the way. In the midst of the crisis Robert Kennedy, apparently looking for a way to justify U.S. intervention in Cuba, suggested that perhaps there was "something . . . you know, sink the *Maine* again or something." On October 26, 1962, President Kennedy received a letter from Khrushchev offering to withdraw the missiles in exchange for U.S. assurances of no future invasion of Cuba. A second letter arrived the next day proposing that the United States also dismantle missile bases in Turkey. Overruling his top advisers, who favored air strikes or an invasion, Kennedy publicly accepted the first letter's proposal and had his brother Robert assure Soviet Ambassador Anatoly Dobrynin that the Turkish missiles could be removed in the near future (as they were). Nikita Khrushchev ordered his ships to head for home.

Although Castro resented being left out of the missile crisis negotiations and refused to allow UN officials to enter Cuba for on-site inspections, the missiles were dismantled. "We disagreed that the missiles should be taken away," he said then and later. He had no faith in U.S. "no-invasion" pledges.

Indeed, Cuban exile organizations continued to harass Cuba with terrorist acts and attempted landings. The CIA, sometimes enlisting its Mafia friends, engaged in about thirty attempts on Castro's life. The exiles set up training camps in Florida, most recently in the early 1980s when President Reagan announced he would not be bound by the Kennedy-Khrushchev accords.

Foreign Affairs

Despite the intensity of the Cuba-U.S. conflict, some efforts at healing the rift were made by every American president and by Castro. On December 24, 1962, the U.S. and Cuban governments carried out an exchange of 1,113 Bay of Pigs captives for $53 million worth of food and medicine. The Johnson administration (1963–1969) signed a "Memorandum of Understanding" that provided a special airlift for Cubans wishing to leave the island. By 1970 more than half a million Cubans were residing in the United States, most of them from the upper and upper-middle classes.

Cuba's foreign policy went through a phase in the 1960s of encouraging revolutions abroad. For example, in Venezuela where ultrarightist Cuban exiles had organized terrorist units and Venezuelan students had organized guerrilla bands, Castro criticized the Communist party as antirevolutionary and backed the guerrillas (see chapter 11). OLAS (Organization of Latin American Solidarity) was established in Havana, and many leftists and political refugees from right-wing dictatorships in Latin America were given sanctuary in Cuba. Ché Guevara went to Bolivia to try to spread the Latin American revolution (see chapter 15).

As it became clear that quick victories for guerrilla "focos" were not in the cards, Castro shifted gears and befriended reformist regimes, such as the Velasco military government in Peru (see chapter 14). This helped break Cuba's diplomatic isolation in the Americas, and by 1975 the OAS economic embargo of Cuba was lifted, but the more damaging U.S. embargo held firm.

In October 1975 a South Africa–sponsored invasion of newly independent Angola from its southern neighbor of Namibia caused the Angolan government to request Cuban military aid. In November, as Castro later said, Cuba sent "a battalion of regular troops with antitank weapons to help the Angolan patriots resist the invasion of the South African racists." Outside Angola's capital city of Luanda, Cuban and Angolan troops repulsed the invaders, who included hundreds of white South Africans and had U.S. backing.

For a dozen years more, half a million Cubans served at one time or another in Angola, helping the Angolan government hold back the U.S. and South Africa backed "rebels." Most anti-apartheid forces supported the Cuban presence. Even Gulf Oil appreciated Cuban troops guarding its installations in northern Angola. After a major military victory in 1988, Cuba helped broker a peace accord that led to Namibia's independence and the withdrawal of all Cuban troops by early 1991. Two years later Angola's "rebels" refused to accept a defeat in UN-monitored national elections and seized the northern oil fields.

In famine-plagued Northeast Africa Cuban soldiers helped turn back a Somalian invasion of Ethiopia's Ogaden province in 1978. The Soviet Union had backed revolutions in both Ethiopia and Somalia but viewed the former as more important. So when a counterrevolution toppled Somalia's government, the Soviets chose to limit their support to the Ethiopian revolution. Somalia's new rulers could count on U.S. military aid. Soon Somalia became a veritable arms depot, ruled by thugs interested in food shipments only as a means to wealth. Death by starvation stalked both Ethiopia and Somalia. By late 1993, U.S. "aid" in Somalia included food shipments protected by UN troops and elite U.S. military units. Meanwhile, in Ethiopia, the rulers had been overthrown by the Eritrean and other movements for regional independence. People still went hungry in both countries.

The first real breakthrough in normalizing Cuba-U.S. relations occurred during the Carter administration (1977–1981). The United States granted Cubans who were U.S. citizens the right to obtain exit visas for travel to Cuba, while Cuba issued visas to many political prisoners wishing to go to the

United States. Diplomatic "interest sections" were set up by each government in the other's capital (they still exist).

Further rapprochement, however, was undercut by the "Mariel boatlift" of 1980. More than 100,000 Cubans went by ship to Florida in a poorly coordinated process that left bad feelings on both sides. Castro's willingness to let such a large number of Cubans go into exile in such a short time puzzled many observers. It turned out that more than a few of the émigrés were the dregs of Cuban society—shiftless workers, alcoholics, petty criminals, even mentally disturbed people. Some were housed for years in U.S. detention camps, joined by many more convicted in the United States of drug-related and other crimes, including murder. When the Reagan administration announced in late 1987 it had reached a new agreement with the Cuban government to renew the flow of immigration of Cubans wishing to leave Cuba and to send back to Cuba those in the camps, the detainees seized hostages and revolted at Oakdale, Louisiana, and Atlanta, Georgia.

Until mid-1994, the U.S. government provided the majority of newly arriving Cubans with favored treatment, including subsidies and job opportunities. Miami blacks and New York Puerto Ricans complained at being "passed over" on the job market by each new wave of Cuban arrivals. Black riots in Florida cities in the 1980s were fueled by unemployment and these resentments. Haitians, Salvadorans, Guatemalans, and civil libertarians complained that the U.S. government applied a "double standard" when it came to granting political refuge, one that welcomed anti-Communists but turned away anti-Fascists and preferred whites to blacks or Indians. Black Haitians fleeing the pro-U.S., right-wing dictatorships of Papa Doc and Baby Doc (Duvalier and son) ended up in detention camps, whereas anti-Communist Cubans, usually white or mulatto, received favored treatment. To facilitate the admission of the 1980 "Cuban boat people," or "Marielitos," and to answer the criticisms of a double standard, the U.S. Congress passed the Refugee Act in 1980, redefining "refugee" to conform with UN criteria. Yet refugees fleeing rightist, U.S.-backed regimes and death squads in Haiti and Central America continued to be deported or placed in detention centers in spite of the law. President Reagan's 1981 Task Force on Immigration and Refugee Policy warned that "detention could create an appearance of 'concentration camps' filled largely by blacks" (see introductions to Part One and Part Two).

Some of the early Cuban emigrants who fled to the U.S. later decided that maybe communism wasn't so bad and returned to their homeland. But most adapted to U.S. ways and stayed. A minority of their children—adults in the 1970s and 1980s—publicly complained about U.S. racism and the U.S. economic blockade of Cuba. They launched an effort to reestablish friendly relations between the two nations, and even met with Castro.

Some of these prorapprochement Cubans were terrorized, even killed, by right-wing Cuban exile organizations. But the terrorist groups were rapidly losing support in the Cuban communities of Florida, New York, and New Jersey. Their reputations had suffered from the exposure of their role in the Watergate burglary and the murder of Chile's ex-foreign minister Orlando Letelier and his American research assistant Ronni Moffitt in Washington, D.C. (see chapter 17). Then when these terrorists blew up a civilian airliner, killing all aboard (see chapter 11), they were looked at even more critically. One of the terrorists escaped from a Venezuelan prison with the help of "The Enterprise," a shadowy operation headed by Richard Secord and Albert Hakim, later indicted by the special prosecutor in the Iran-contragate affair.

In the early years of the Reagan administration U.S.-Cuban relations became worse. After remarks by Secretary of State Haig about "going to the source" or "terrorism," Cubans began digging trenches and building air-raid shelters in anticipation of a possible U.S. attack. In 1982 Reagan reimposed the U.S. ban on tourist travel to Cuba previously lifted under Carter. Cubans helping to build an airport in Grenada died in combat when they were attacked by U.S. troops invading and occupying that tiny island nation in October 1983 (see Introduction to Part Two). The U.S. government set up "Radio Martí" to beam broadcasts into Cuba.

Yet even under Reagan efforts at rapprochement were not abandoned. In the fall of 1987 Cuba released hundreds of political prisoners for transferral to the United States as a "goodwill" gesture, and the United States upgraded its "interest section" in Havana.

The Bush administration, however, did not take these steps further, despite signs of Cuban cooperation. It welcomed the pullout of the remaining 11,000 Soviet troops from Cuba and Cuba's UN Security Council votes condemning the Iraqi invasion of Kuwait and demanding Iraqi withdrawal. But it was miffed when Cuba's UN delegation voted against U.S.-sponsored resolutions authorizing an economic embargo and the use of military force against Iraq. Naturally, Cuba did not want to establish a precedent for acceptance of the U.S. embargo and any threatened invasion against its revolution.

In 1990 the U.S. government started beaming television propaganda into Cuba from its "TV Martí" station, an act ostensibly in violation of the 1982 International Telecommunication Convention. Cuba jammed first the tv signal and later the radio signal from "Radio Martí."

The United States tightened up its thirty-two-year-old embargo against Cuba. The "Cuban Democracy Act" passed by Congress in 1992 prohibited foreign subsidiaries of U.S. companies from doing business with Cuba and banned ships trading with Cuba from entering U.S. ports for six months. Britain, Argentina, and other nations protested this infringement on their sovereignty, and the UN General Assembly called for an end to the embargo. Several prominent dissidents inside Cuba and U.S.-based exiles also criticized the "hard-line" approach to the Cuban people. Even former top aides of President Reagan said the time had come to lift the embargo, yet President Bill Clinton championed the stiffened embargo in his speeches through mid-1994 (for pros and cons, see Documents).

In August 1994, a new crisis erupted in U.S.-Cuban relations. It started when protestors in Havana objected to the Castro government's detention of a ferryboat hijacked by would-be refugees heading for Florida. The Cuban government responded to the protest by allowing anyone who wanted to leave by boat or raft to do so. As the number of "boat people" increased to two thousand a week, the Clinton administration responded by proclaiming a new immigration policy ending the "double standard" of free admission for Cubans and detention for Haitians. It dispatched Coast Guard and warships to patrol Cuban shores and sent new refugees picked up at sea to Guantánamo Naval Base in eastern Cuba. It tightened the embargo by prohibiting remittances of dollars by Cubans in the United States to Cuba (depriving Cuba of $500 million a year) and outlawing charter flights to the island. It rattled its sabers and talked about a blockade of Cuba to force the country to become "a democracy."

Most scholars on Latin America supported an end to the Cold War against Castro and the start of a new approach respecting Cuban sovereignty (see Documents). Earlier in the Clinton administration, the House Appropriations Committee had ended funding for TV Martí, the first major crack in Washington's cozy relationship with the extreme-rightist exiles' Cuban-American National Foundation. But the 1994 crisis seemed to seal that crack, at least for the moment. Raymundo del Toro, president of the New Jersey–based Cuban American Committee for Peace, asked in a letter to the *New York Times*: "If the United States can maintain most-favored-nation trade status with China, end the embargo against Vietnam, and begin negotiations with North Korea, how can it not lift the embargo and normalize relations with Cuba?"

Economic Incentives and Political Institutionalization

Cuba's economic and political development since 1959 was accompanied by a pattern of extremes not unlike its foreign policy. During the 1960s the excitement of revolutionary change generated an emphasis on moral incentives to raise production levels—reliance on collective work spirit and voluntary labor brigades modeled after the literacy brigades. Numerous "mini-plans," often conceived by Castro, Guevara, or others high up in the government, were attempted. At one point, for instance, everyone pitched in to build a "green belt" around Havana—city people growing their own crops!

The emphasis on moral incentives peaked during the so-called Revolutionary Offensive of 1969–1970, when the entire island was mobilized to produce 10 million tons of sugar. Although a record high figure of 8.5 million tons was achieved, Castro declared the effort a failure and assumed personal blame for it. Scarce resources had been squandered in the big push for the sugar harvest, leaving the economy in a precarious state. In subsequent years nearly 60 percent of the cane-cutting was mechanized, a welcome relief for Cubans' backs. All the machinery was produced in Cuba. Irrigated lands increased tenfold in area. Two new refineries—the first in fifty years—were built, and forty old ones were modernized or expanded. Sugar production averaged nearly 7 million tons a year after that, reaching 8 million in 1979, 1989, and 1990.

The failure of the 10-million-ton harvest left deep scars on the face of moral incentives. The government decided to shift its emphasis to material incentives—the wage system, production norms, and the distribution of scarce consumer goods according to work performed. While technicians and workers producing more got higher wages, the general wage scale remained unusually egalitarian. The government also decided to shift from miniplans to more global, long-term economic planning, but not at the expense of decentralization or active input by local communities.

Shortly before 1969 and for a long time afterward Castro moved Cuba closer to the Soviet Union on both domestic and foreign policy. The old Communist Carlos Rafael Rodríguez, demoted in the 1990s, gained greater influence over economic planning, and Castro's pronouncements on revolutions elsewhere in Latin America lost their stridency. He even approved of the Soviet military intervention in Czechoslovakia in 1968, although tempering his "solidarity" with subtle, indirect criticism of bureaucratism.

The revolution's post-1969 institutionalization took place amidst island-wide discussion, revision, and promulgation of a Socialist constitution, also influenced by the Soviet Union and overwhelmingly approved by plebiscite in early 1976. The Cuban Constitution defined Cuba as "a socialist state of . . . manual and intellectual workers." Cuba's economy was the most socialized in the world—it had little private enterprise left. The constitution made the ballot secret and universal, but not obligatory, for all citizens sixteen years of age and older. It defined Cuban émigrés as Cuban citizens, if they had not already lost their citizenship or if they were not actively seeking the government's overthrow.

To govern Cuba, the constitution established a five-hundred-member National Assembly of People's Power to be elected for five-year terms by delegates to municipal assemblies, themselves elected every thirty months by popular vote at the local level and subject to popular recall. The National Assembly of People's Power elected the president, five vice-presidents, a secretary, and twenty-three other members of the Council of State, the nation's highest political organ. The National Assembly passed on the president's proposed Council of Ministers, a powerful group like the president's cabinet in the United States. Starting in 1976, Castro was elected and reelected president of the Council of State and reconfirmed as commander-in-chief of the Revolutionary Armed Forces.

To counter the dangers of top-down bureaucratism, a "people's power" movement was institutionalized, allowing some supervision over state agencies at the local level (schools, supermarkets, etc.). Directors of numerous enterprises were made answerable to local people's power assemblies. Despite opposition to the plan by some high-level bureaucrats, by 1981 there were 169 municipal assemblies with literally thousands of elected delegates, about two-thirds of them PCC members. While critics viewed the frequent elections as mere window-dressing for continued centralized or personal rule, Cubans participated in them in large numbers. Critics saw the rising percentages of PCC people's power delegates as counter to democracy, whereas enthusiasts of the elections said that people voted for those who worked hardest and did the most to serve the public.

The 1976 Constitution recognized the leading role of the PCC. The party was created in 1965 out of a combination of all previous prorevolution parties or groups, including the Communists' old PSP. It had started out relatively small but grew to be more than 600,000-strong by the mid-1990s. Its members worked hard recruiting in the numerous "mass organizations" that sprang up after the overthrow of Batista—organized labor's CTC, the CDRs, the women's FMC, and a medley of others among students, youth, intellectuals, and farmers. Party members won the reputation of being skilled and dedicated workers and organizers. Half of the PCC's members by 1980 were workers in industry, agriculture, construction, and services.

Even a scandal in 1967–1968 seemed to help the PCC achieve a reputation for open debate within the party. Frictions between the "old" Communists and the new "Fidelista" ones (26th of July) peaked in the trial and conviction of Anibal Escalante and other old Communists accused of forming a "microfaction" within the government in an attempt to make Cuba a Soviet puppet. They were sentenced to from two to fifteen years. Recruitment increased after the "housecleaning" campaign, and Cuba moved closer to the Soviet Union later.

With the revolution's institutionalization came a rapprochement with the Catholic Church. Castro began appearing in public parades side by side with the Archbishop of Havana. He pointed out that the revolution had always welcomed sincere Christians—people like student martyr Echeverría or the "Catholic Action" youth group that backed the 26th of July movement. Times had changed. Castro's Jesuit teachers had been very conservative, but by the late 1970s, many of Latin America's Jesuits had become militants of the new theology of liberation (see Overview). Cuba's Catholic church backed the

310

government's campaign to cancel the Latin American debt. As of 1991, religious believers could become PCC members.

There were notable gains in Cuba's economy in the late 1970s and early 1980s, especially in tourism. But world sugar prices falling to 1930s levels more than halved Cuba's foreign exchange earnings desperately needed for the importation of capital and consumer goods. Cuban reexport of excess Soviet crude oil also brought in less money because of a decline in world oil prices. Cuba still had one-tenth of the world's nickel reserves, but nickel prices were also down. Finally, a decline in the comparative value of the dollar in international trade hurt Cuba since it had to pay for most imported goods in currencies that appreciated in value via-à-vis the dollar—the yen, for instance.

All of these problems eventually caused a slump in Cuba's economy in 1986–1987. Annual growth rates in real income terms dropped from an average of 7 percent in 1980–1985 to 1.4 percent. To make matters worse, 1987 was the third consecutive year of extremely poor rainfall. For the first time international banks, which for years had gladly renegotiated Cuba's foreign debt without insisting on IMF-type conditionality clauses as they did in the rest of Latin America, began to hesitate. Cuba's debt to the West of about $5 billion was more than one-third what it owed the Soviet bloc. Cuba stepped up offshore oil exploration and planned to build nuclear energy plants to try to reduce its dependence on oil imports. It welcomed foreign private investment in joint ventures with the state.

On April 19, 1986, Castro dropped a bombshell that some interpreters believed marked a return to moral incentives. He announced that the free market established earlier for housing sales and farm products was to be modified or discontinued. Party-headed commissions were appointed to work centers to crack down on corruption. Castro denounced "the guilty ones, the administrative personnel." In 1987, Castro declared: "A Communist spirit and conscience . . . always will be a thousand times more powerful than money." At the same time, he insisted that "idealistic mistakes" of the past would not be repeated. In 1988, he criticized the Soviet Union for its possible economic compromise of "socialist principles." And in 1989, a Cuban military court gave four former officers the death penalty for trafficking in Colombian cocaine. Corruption at high levels was clearly a problem.

Cuba's renewed emphasis on egalitarianism was symbolized by a wage reform favorable to the lowest paid workers, the reintroduction of construction microbrigades, and the assignment of control over wage funds and the means of production to small groups of workers at the plant level in sugar and other industries. But actual power over economic planning was centralized more than ever in a small circle of officials loyal to Castro. It appeared that top leaders, most of them from non–working class backgrounds, continued to encourage workers to participate but not to control. The message to any worker was clear: "I trust you to put lots of suggestions in the suggestion box, but don't tell me which ones to use!" The future of Cuba still pivoted around issues of democracy, workers' control, and economic survival.

After the collapse of the Soviet bloc, on which 75 percent of Cuban trade depended, Cuba's political and economic administration underwent further changes. Castro characterized Cuba as more threatened by external forces than at any other moment in the revolution's past. He announced the country would go through an adjustment "period special in peacetime." The gross national product fell 24 percent in 1991 and the number of rationed or unavailable goods skyrocketed. Personal consumption plummeted, while wage and social security costs rose. Black market cash flows surpassed those of the retail market. New contingents of emigrants headed for Miami.

To conserve energy in the face of having to pay cash for reduced Russian oil shipments, Cuba slashed electrical output by half and shifted from buses to bicycles for much of its public transportation. It halted construction on two nuclear power plants. Castro's scientist son was removed from the energy program's directorship because of "inefficiency."

Constitutional amendments recommended by the PCC's Fourth Congress in 1991 included: direct, secret elections for the National Assembly, with the PCC removed from the nominating process and candidate slates reviewed for final selection by the government; the prohibition of religious discrimination; removal of the mention of the Soviet Union in the preamble; and attribution of educational policies to the thought of Martí instead of Marx and Lenin. The "independent Cuban socialist line" was reaffirmed. After the Fourth Congress, more than a few leaders under forty years of age (children at the time of the triumph of the revolution) assumed top government positions, including the all-important stewardship of the economy and the foreign ministry. Two-thirds of the 225-member PCC Central Committee (average age forty-seven) were either newly elected or promoted at the 1991 party congress.

In the final round of elections in February 1993 to renew 80 percent of the seats in the 589-member National Assembly, dissidents hoped for a vote of no confidence in Cuba's leadership. Instead, official figures showed support for the government and a 98.8 percent voter turnout (compared with 97.2 percent in the previous December's municipal elections). Castro chided the dissidents for not daring to put themselves forward as candidates, but the dissidents saw the deck as "stacked." Blank or incorrectly filled out ballots accounted for 7.2 percent of votes cast. About a third of those elected were from outside the PCC.

The average age of the new legislative deputies was forty-three. Sixty-seven-year-old Castro, himself reelected, announced he probably would not run next time around. Some saw this as a kind of negotiating offer to the

United States. Many believed Castro hoped to see a younger generation guide the revolution into the future.

As early as 1980 a group of well-educated "new professionals," most of them born into the working class, already outnumbered older, less professionally trained administrators as the majority of Cuba's intermediate-level personnel. Many were committed to market reforms introduced in the late 1970s to "rectify" overemphasis on moral incentives. They saw the 1986 "rectification" as a "correction," not a change in course. They favored opening Cuba to private foreign investment.

A leader of Mexico's powerful, conservative "Monterrey Group" (see chapter 1) announced his intention to invest in Cuba. He was impressed with the low cost of labor that resulted from state provision of social services such as health, education, and housing "which they do extraordinarily well." By 1994, Cuba had opened up more than one hundred kinds of jobs to individual private enterprise. It had undertaken two hundred joint ventures with foreign companies, mostly with European, Canadian, and Latin American firms. Officials assured investors that the government's 51 percent share was negotiable.

Earnings in the expanded tourism industry, dominated by joint ventures with Spain, rose. As world sugar and nickel prices showed signs of recovering, the widely respected _Latin American Weekly Report_ concluded: "Cuba's energetic efforts to break out of its isolation and reinsert itself into the world market are beginning to pay off." But that was before the 1994 crisis.

Some observers wondered if the 1993 outbreak of a mysterious disease in Cuba affecting vision and nerves might not be related to a sudden increase in people's consumption of casava to offset food shortages. Casava contains traces of poison that are harmless when the food is consumed in normal amounts. According to the _New York Times,_ visiting foreign medical experts were baffled by the epidemic. A few suspected one more CIA plot. Past alleged instances of U.S. bacteriological warfare against Cuba included the 1971 introduction of African swine flu and Sogata rice blight.

Most visiting health experts were impressed by Cuba's medical research and heart disease prevention efforts. Cuban-developed pharmaceutical goods unavailable in the United States included new meningitis and hepatitis vaccines and heart and livestock drugs.

Cuba in the mid-1990s faced serious problems, including health-care cutbacks and the tightened U.S. economic embargo. Right-wing Cuban and most U.S. critics claimed that only a return to capitalism could save Cuba. They also said centralized authority was bound to leave people demoralized and less productive. Left-wing critics agreed that power was too centralized but saw no solution in a return to capitalism. They emphasized more workers' say-so in decision making, through "workers' control" and "self-management by workers" of economic enterprises.

Few denied that Cuba's revolution had made several advances that would be difficult to turn back. The revolution's institutionalization had proceeded steadily, and the army remained strong. The big question marks remained what would transpire in U.S.-Cuba relations and whether the majority of Cubans, those born after the guerrillas entered Havana in 1959, would put up with the new constraints they faced in the "special period."

Selected Bibliography

Areito. A bilingual magazine by Cuban émigrés seeking end of U.S. economic blockade and restoration of diplomatic relations.

Bourne, Peter G. *Fidel.* New York: Dodd, Mead, 1986. Biography by psychiatrist who served as President Carter's Special Assistant for Health Affairs and participated in attempt at U.S.-Cuba rapprochement.

Castro, Fidel. *History Will Absolve Me!* New York: Lyle Stuart, 1961. Speech that became 26th of July movement's program.

Cuban Studies/Estudios Cubanos. An annual journal edited by Cuban émigré scholar and labor expert Carmelo Mesa-Lago, Center for Latin American Studies, University of Pittsburgh.

Cuba Update. Monthly publication of Center for Cuban Studies including eye-openers such as Gabriel García Márquez's "Operation Carolota: Cuba's role in Angolan Victory" (April 1977). The Center's library, 124 West 23rd Street, New York City, is excellent. Its *Newsletter* features valuable materials.

Erisman, H. Michael, and John M. Kirk (eds.). *Cuban Foreign Policy Confronts a New International Order.* Boulder, CO: Lynne Rienner, 1991. Chapters by Cuban and U.S. scholars.

Feinsilver, Julie M. *Healing the Masses: Cuban Health Politics at Home and Abroad.* Berkeley: University of California Press, 1994. Includes biotechnology industry.

Fitzgerald, Frank. *The Cuban Revolution in Crisis: From Managing Socialism to Managing Survival.* New York: Monthly Review Press, 1994. Well researched pioneering work on the "new professionals."

———. *The Cuban Revolution in Crisis: From Managing Socialism to Managing Survival.* New York: Monthly Review Press, 1994.

Fuller, Linda O. *Work and Democracy in Socialist Cuba.* Philadelphia, PA: Temple University Press, 1992. Examination of workplace democracy.

Gomez Treto, Raul. *The Church and Socialism in Cuba.* New York: Orbis Books, 1988.

Hinkle, Warren, and William Turner. *The Fish Is Red: The Story of The Secret War Against Castro.* New York: Harper & Row, 1981.

Kaplowitz, Donna Rich (ed.). *Cuba's New Ties to Changing World.* Boulder, CO: Lynne Rienner, 1993. On recent changes in foreign relations.

Latin American Perspectives. "Cuba: Labor, Politics, and Views." *Latin American Perspectives,* 20(1)(Winter 1993).

Liss, Sheldon B. *Roots of Revolution: Radical Thought in Cuba.* Lincoln: University of Nebraska Press, 1987.

———. *Fidel! Castro's Political and Social Thought.* Boulder, CO: Westview, 1994. Pioneering work.

Lockwood, Lee. *Castro's Cuba, Cuba's Fidel.* New York: Macmillan, 1967. Superb photographs and interviews.

Medin, Tzvi, *Cuba: The Shaping of Revolutionary Consciousness.* Boulder, CO: Lynne Rienner, 1990. Short and insightful.

Mills, C. Wright. *Listen Yankee: The Revolution in Cuba.* New York: Ballantine Books, 1960. By prominent sociologist, presents Cuban nationalist views.

Morley, Morris. *Imperial State and Revolution: The United States and Cuba, 1952–1986.* New York: Cambridge University Press, 1988.

Nacla. "Cuba: Facing Change." *Report on the Americas,* 24(2)(Aug. 1990).

Nathan, James A. (ed.). *The Cuban Missile Crisis Revisited.* New York: St. Martin, 1993.

New University Conference (NUC). *Cuba.* Chicago: NUC, 1969. On-the-scene impressions by first U.S. delegation of academicians to break U.S. ban on travel to Cuba.

Pérez-Stable, Marifeli. *The Cuban Revolution: Origins, Course, and Legacy.* New York: Oxford University Press, 1993.

Platt, Tony (ed.). *Tropical Gulag: The Construction of Cold War Images of Cuba in the United States.* San Francisco, CA: Global Options, 1987. Revealing study of anti-Cuba lobby, U.S. press.

Randall, Margaret, *Cuban Women Now.* Toronto: The Women's Press, 1974. Interviews; daily life.

Rius. *Cuba for Beginners.* New York: Pathfinder Press, 1970. "An illustrated guide for Americans (and their government)" by internationally renowned Mexican caricaturist Eduardo del Río; pro-Cuban Revolution.

Smith, Wayne S. *The Closest of Enemies: A Personal and Diplomatic Account of U.S.-Cuban Relations Since 1957.* New York: Norton, 1987. By former head of U.S. Interest Section in Havana.

Stubbs, Jean. *Cuba: The Test of Time.* London: Latin America Bureau, 1989. Good short-backgrounder on 1959–1988.

Tablada, Carlos. *Che Guevara: Economics and Politics in the Transition to Socialism.* New York: Pathfinder, 1987. By Cuban economist.

Zimbalist, Andrew (ed.). *Cuban Political Economy Controversies in Cubanology.* Boulder, CO: Westview, 1988. Good collection on key debates.

Films

The Battle for Cuito Cuanavale. 120 minutes. Color video made by Cubans documenting the 1988 turning point in thirteen-year war in Angola and Namibia.

Cuba Va: The Challenge of the Next Generation. 1993. Up-to-date documentary by San Francisco's Cuba Va Video Project.

Lucia. 1969. 160 minutes. A widely acclaimed three-part epic in black and white, revealing women's oppression and ways of fighting back in Cuban history, including postrevolutionary period.

Portrait of Castro's Cuba. 1991. 60 minutes. PBS film narrated by James Earl Jones.

The Uncompromising Revolution. 1988. 45 minutes. Directed by Saul Landau, maker of earlier 1969 film *Fidel.*

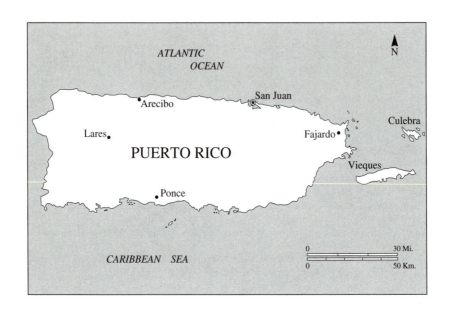

Puerto Rico   9

To take our country they must take our lives.—*Pedro Albizu Campos, Nationalist party martyr (d. 1965)*

The regime implanted by the United States in Puerto Rico is essentially colonial.— *Governor Luis Muñoz Marín, 1963*

On July 25, 1978, as they climbed the final 100 feet up the mountain in southern Puerto Rico, the three men were out of breath. Then, suddenly, Carlos Soto Arriví, eighteen, Arnaldo Darío Rosado, twenty-four, and Alejandro González Malave, twenty, found themselves surrounded by police.

"*Coño!*" the first two cursed.

It was a setup. The third man, González Malave, was a police agent who had lured them into an ambush. Outmanned and outgunned, Carlos and Arnaldo surrendered. The police began beating them. They fell to their knees. More clubbing. Then, the beating stopped, the policemen's voices hushed, and the high-pitched whistle of Puerto Rico's unusual tree lizard, the *coquí*, was heard.

Carlos and Arnaldo looked up from the ground.

A deafening noise. High-powered rifle fire cut them down.

. . .

The administration of Puerto Rico's Governor Carlos Romero Barcelo (1976–1984) claimed that the youths, one of them the son of a prominent novelist, had intended to blow up a communications tower on top of Cerro Maravilla, or Mountain of Wonder. The police had fired in self-defense. Four investigations by the Puerto Rican and U.S. Departments of Justice between 1978 and 1980 cleared the police.

But then a former president of the Puerto Rican Bar Association released 1979 FBI memoranda that the FBI had requested Puerto Rican officials *not* to investigate. Suspicions grew of an official "cover-up."

Finally, the Puerto Rican Senate conducted televised hearings into the matter in 1983. As Puerto Ricans sat glued to their television sets, they learned that the Cerro Maravilla killings were cold-blooded murder, planned at high levels of the Puerto Rican government as part of its strategy to repress and discredit the independence movement. Three policemen testified on the planning of the murder and their role in it.

The investigations went on to reveal a deliberate cover-up by various U.S. federal agencies and the Romero Barcelo administration. FBI agents had witnessed the police agent González Malave's conduct in an earlier bombing mission and done nothing. The FBI office in the capital city of San Juan was informed of the Cerro Maravilla operation before it happened. The hearings also showed widespread corruption in Puerto Rico's government, including involvement of top figures in Romero Barcelo's party, the prostatehood PNP (New Progressive party), in a Mafia-related drug, arms, and stolen goods racket.

"Puerto Rico's Watergate," as the "Cerro Maravilla affair" became known, contributed to the electorate's voting the PNP out of power in 1984. In 1985 ten policemen were convicted of perjury in the case and received long prison sentences. In 1990 the U.S. Justice Department refused court orders to turn over its Cerro Maravilla files to Puerto Rico. The president of the Puerto Rican Senate reportedly said this indicated high-level U.S. involvement in the cover-up.

Few Americans at the time knew much about Puerto Rico. Few realized that the FBI's apparent condoning of state terrorism in the affair was part of an historical pattern of extralegal acts the FBI, the CIA, the Navy, the Army, the State Department, the Secret Service, and other U.S. agencies had carried out against advocates of Puerto Rican independence in violation of their rights as U.S. citizens. Under the Freedom of Information Act passed by the U.S. Congress during the Watergate scandal of the Nixon presidency in the early 1970s, it was discovered that the FBI had a long history of interfering in Puerto Rico's elections and harassing advocates of Puerto Rican independence. FBI tactics included the opening of mail; use of agent-provocateurs; dividing nationalist elements against Socialist ones; anonymous mailings to create suspicion and distrust; and the planting of explosives. In 1967 the FBI director claimed the tactics had worked "to thwart any prospect of unity."

A particularly vicious FBI campaign had been launched in the early 1960s against Juan Marí Bras, secretary general of the MPI (Pro-Independence movement), the forerunner of the PSP (Puerto Rican Socialist party). Marí Bras was an early precursor of the theology of liberation (see Overview), in the sense that he was a devout Catholic who became convinced that socialism was the answer "here on earth."

In addition to FBI harassment, U.S. grand juries held hearings on proindependence groups in the 1970s and 1980s. When witnesses, including teachers, lawyers, and students, refused to cooperate because they viewed the grand juries as part of an antidemocratic witch-hunt, they were thrown into jail. Civil libertarians questioned the legality and propriety of the use of grand juries to suppress dissent. Also criticized was the FBI's use of hidden cameras to gather evidence against independence advocates.

Puerto Rico, then, was not only a central pivot for U.S. foreign policy, but it was also a testing ground for traditional American civil liberties. Yet few Americans knew a thing about the country. Most college textbooks on Latin America not only lacked a chapter on Puerto Rico but seldom even mentioned its 6.3 million people. Most Americans knew only that many Puerto Ricans lived in New York City and that the racist derogatory term "Spics" was often applied to denigrate them.

Yet Puerto Rico had always been the Latin American country with the closest ties to the U.S. Ceded by Spain to the United States in 1898, "Puerto Rico" had been misspelled by Americans as "Porto" Rico until 1932 when an Act of Congress corrected the error. It became the relatively self-governing Commonwealth of Puerto Rico in 1952, "a free state in association with the United States." But the United States retained full say-so on most important Puerto Rican matters, including foreign policy, immigration and tariff policy, defense, environment, labor law, and judicial review. According to the U.S. government, Puerto Rico was a U.S. dependency or territory. The United Nations called it a "colony."

About 100 miles long and 35 miles wide, Puerto Rico is situated just east of the Dominican Republic and Cuba. It is criss-crossed by mountain ranges up to 4,400 feet high. Nearly 3.7 million Spanish-speaking people, mostly of mixed African and Spanish ancestry, reside there, making it one of the world's most densely populated areas. Only one-fifth of them know English well.

Puerto Rico is almost as central to the workings of the U.S. economy as any bigger Latin American nation, such as Mexico (see chapter 1). In the mid-1970s it was generating one-quarter or more of U.S. corporations' profits in all of Latin America. It was the world's fifth largest market for U.S. exports, importing more U.S. products per capita than any other country. Since it was not represented in Congress, Puerto Rico paid no U.S. taxes. The island government granted manufacturing and hotel enterprises large exemptions from local taxes. Because of these favorable tax breaks and the low cost of labor, in 1978 U.S. corporations held a whopping $7.4 billion of retained earnings on their investments in Puerto Rico.

Yet even before the economic "hard times" of the 1980s and 1990s, unemployment in Puerto Rico averaged three times the U.S. rate. Foods as basic as eggs had to be imported, and the majority of the population depended on food stamps. Often imported necessities were products like razor blades, which Puerto Ricans produced for a low wage on the island for export to the U.S. market and then bought at their local supermarkets at a price 25 percent above what the Americans paid. A big producer of salt, fish, sugar, coffee, and tobacco, Puerto Rico imported its iodized salt, canned and frozen fish, refined sugar, ground coffee, and cigarettes.

About 40 percent of Puerto Ricans, close to 2.6 million, reside in the United States, half of them in New York and New Jersey, and most of the rest in Florida, Massachusetts, Pennsylvania, Connecticut, Illinois, California, Ohio, and Texas (in that order, numerically, 1990). They are economically more impoverished than African Americans. A Ford Foundation report notes that forty years of "devastating circular migration" back and forth between the island and the mainland has been "disastrous for Puerto Rican families, employment and income."

The large-scale "commuter migration" had started with an economic development program called "Operation Bootstrap," later trumpeted by President Kennedy's Alliance for Progress and President Reagan's Caribbean Basin Initiative as the "model" for the rest of Latin America. Puerto Rico is *critically* important for an understanding of Latin America and U.S. policies there.

In fact U.S. government officials routinely emphasize Puerto Rico's importance. Former UN Ambassador Jeanne Kirkpatrick called it a "geopolitical bastion of the United States." Twelve percent of Puerto Rico's arable land consists of U.S. military bases, including the world's largest naval base—Roosevelt Roads. "Dress rehearsals" for the 1983 U.S. invasion of Grenada were staged in Puerto Rico's east-coast island of Vieques, where the U.S. Navy regularly conducted bombing practice. In 1984, some 50,000 Puerto Ricans marched in protest against the use of bases and personnel on the island for "Operation Ocean Venture," a U.S.-sponsored Central American naval exercise the demonstrators believed was intended to intimidate the Nicaraguan government.

The Reagan administration's budgetary cutbacks on social welfare programs in the 1980s had a deleterious impact on the lives of Puerto Ricans. Some 24,000 employees under CETA (Comprehensive Employment and Training Act) were laid off, undermining many towns' basic municipal services that they had carried out (garbage collecting, road maintenance, etc.).

The towns could not pay people from local taxes since taxes could not be collected from unemployed people. Puerto Rico's commissioner in Washington soberly warned that more cutbacks might make Puerto Rico "the next Cuba in the Caribbean." The time had come for the American public to know more about Puerto Rico.

From Spanish Colony to U.S. Possession

Puerto Rico (Spanish for "rich port") was originally settled by Carib, Arawak, and Taino Indians. The Arawaks called the island Boriquen ("Land of the Great Lord"). Spain's Juan Ponce de León conquered the peaceful agricultural island from 1508 to 1511, enslaving its inhabitants. Early Indian rebellions were quelled by force, and in less than forty years the entire Indian population was eliminated by the combination of armed repression, overwork, and diseases brought by Europeans. The first African slaves arrived in 1513.

For nearly three centuries the island served as a way station for European slave traders, merchants, and pirates. It passed momentarily into the hands of the British (1598) and Dutch 1625). The Spanish settlers became *hacendados* (owners of large estates) or *colonos* (small farmers) in the countryside and merchants in port cities like San Juan. The majority of people, though, were slaves and laborers, completely under the thumb of the Creoles (descendants of Spaniards born in Puerto Rico) and Spain's colonial administration.

When most of the rest of Latin America was fighting its Wars of Independence (1810–1825), U.S. and British forces were securing for Spain its military bases in Puerto Rico, assuring for Americans and English increased trade in sugar, coffee, tobacco, rum, and slaves. U.S. politicians and diplomats spoke of eventually owning Puerto Rico and Cuba (see chapter 8). Puerto Rico's scattered anticolonialists could not mount a successful revolt against Spanish rule. Nonetheless, some of Puerto Rico's 30,000 slaves launched rebellions in 1796, 1821–1822, 1825, 1843, and 1848, and revolutionary plots against Spain were discovered in 1838 and 1867.

In early 1868 the Puerto Rican liberal Dr. Ramón Emeterio Betances learned of a U.S. offer to buy Cuba and Puerto Rico from Spain. He made up his mind to mount a revolution for independence before that could happen. On September 23, 1868, in the mountain town of Lares, the *"Grito de Lares"* (Yell of Lares) proclaimed the "First Republic of Puerto Rico." The first of Betances' "Ten Commands" was the abolition of slavery. Spanish troops put down the Lares insurrection, but soon granted some of its demands. These included the emancipation of the slaves in 1873 and the holding of limited, periodic elections pitting wealthy "assimilationists" (mostly Spaniards wanting to remain within the Spanish empire) against well-off "autonomists" (mostly

Creole advocates of local rule similar to what Canada enjoyed with Great Britain). These reforms took the steam out of the independence movement, whose exiled militants began linking up with Cuban patriots in New York City.

In 1897 Puerto Rico's autonomists won their demands. Spain, bogged down in the Cuban "Thirty Years' War of Independence" (see chapter 8), granted Puerto Rico its Charter of Autonomy, making the country a separate, self-governing legal entity. International recognition of Puerto Rico's nationhood came with its admission into the Universal Postal Union. Spain agreed in the Charter of Autonomy never to cede or sell Puerto Rico without the consent of its inhabitants, an agreement it would break a year later. Heading up the new autonomous government of Puerto Rico was Luis Muñoz Rivera, father of Luis Muñoz Marín (first elected governor under U.S. rule, serving four terms, 1948–1964).

In 1898 the United States launched its war against Spain. The day after Spain surrendered to U.S. forces in Cuba and offered to sign an armistice, U.S. troops invaded Puerto Rico, which Spain surrendered on October 18, 1898. The Treaty of Paris, December 10, 1898, granted independence to U.S.-occupied Cuba and ceded Puerto Rico and the Pacific Ocean island of Guam to the United States.

Not one of Puerto Rico's nearly one million citizens participated in the Treaty of Paris negotiations. Some assumed self-government would come as a matter of course and were looking forward to new economic opportunities promised by the Americans. Few noticed a U.S. government press release, dated July 21, 1898, "Puerto Rico will be kept. . . . That is settled, and has been the plan from the first. Once taken it will never be released. It will pass forever into the hands of the United States." Eugenio María de Hostos, a famous Puerto Rican patriot, declared the Treaty of Paris null and void. Since Puerto Rico had its own autonomous government, it was "a legal entity and could not be stripped of any of its prerogatives as a nation by a war which was not of its making."

U.S. military commanders governed the island until 1900, when the Foraker Act was passed by the U.S. Congress. It set up a political system of U.S. rule that lasted until 1948. School instruction was to be in English, and students daily had to pledge allegiance to the U.S. flag. Protestant missionaries arrived in droves. The dollar replaced the peso. Puerto Rico was permitted to have a governor appointed by the U.S. president; a relatively powerless two-house legislature; and a resident commissioner who had a voice but not a vote in the U.S. House of Representatives.

In 1917, a month before the United States entered World War I, the Jones Act made Puerto Ricans U.S. citizens. It subjected them to the wartime draft and granted them a bill of rights. Three years earlier Puerto Rico's only popularly elected body, the Chamber of Delegates, had unanimously voted to send the U.S. Congress a statement of "our opposition to being made, against our expressed consent, citizens of any country, other than the beloved land to which God gave us an inalienable right." Puerto Ricans suffered a dispropor-tionately large number of casualties in all of the United States' subsequent wars, even though they had no say in the decisions to enter the wars.

Meanwhile the arrival of the Americans transformed Puerto Rico econ-omy. Coffee declined, as "King Sugar" rose. By 1930 sugar accounted for 44 percent of the island's cultivated area and, during the sugar harvest, employed half the agricultural work force. Four U.S. corporations, including the Rocke-feller-dominated South Porto Rico Sugar Company, controlled one-third of the sugar cane crop. Thousands of *colonos* cultivated small cane parcels in areas outside the big plantations and sugar mills.

Future governor (1948–1964) Muñoz Marín called the Puerto Rican economy of the late 1920s "Uncle Sam's second largest sweatshop." He de-scribed the island as "a land of beggars and millionaires . . . a factory worked by peons, fought over by lawyers, bossed by absentee industrialists, and clerked by politicians."

Labor Unions and Political Parties, 1900–1940

During the early 1900s a vigorous labor movement emerged. Tobacco, sugar, and other workers influenced by the radical artisan and guild traditions of the late nineteenth century launched strikes, issued newspapers like *Yo Acuso* (I Accuse) and *Alba Roja* (Red Dawn), and even burned cane fields when their demands went unmet. Many trade-union leaders were anarchists or libertarian Socialists. Artisans, suddenly driven out of business by the "invasion" of mass-produced U.S. products, contributed to labor's radical leadership.

The labor movement's main leader was a Spaniard named Santiago Igle-sias. He helped found the FLT (Free Federation of Workers), affiliating it with Samuel Gompers' AFL (American Federation of Labor). In 1915 Iglesias and others launched the PS (Socialist party), a predominantly workers' party.

Other political parties also developed. Puerto Rico's Republican party (an ally of its U.S. namesake) was led by professionals, merchants, and mid-dlemen who were dependent on the U.S. trade and business network. They saw their futures in statehood, not independence. The old *hacendados,* on the other hand, no longer the main economic power, came out for independence in 1913. Not wanting to return to the old days of absolute *hacendado* power, FLT workers followed Iglesias and the PS's lead in supporting statehood as a more desirable alternative.

In 1928 a Ponce lawyer and Harvard graduate named Dr. Pedro Albizu Campos founded a proindependence Nationalist party. Disagreeing with the theories of conflicting class interests put forward by the Socialist PS and the island's Communists, Albizu Campos hoped to attract all Puerto Ricans under a patriotic banner of Puerto Rico for the Puerto Ricans. In the 1932 elections the Nationalists lost and boycotted future elections. They claimed that Puerto Ricans could not have fair elections so long as they had to vote at "the gunpoint" of thousands of U.S. troops occupying the island. They began organizing workers and *jíbaros* (landless peasants, four out of five rural Puerto Ricans). The Nationalists' popularity grew enormously—in part because of the Great Depression of the 1930s, which left 60 percent of the work force unemployed and desperate for a change.

When the FLT failed to organize the unemployed, the Nationalists and newly founded PCP (Puerto Rican Communist party, 1934) seized the unionizing banner and replaced the PS as the major political force among workers. In 1934 a strike sparked by workers at the Fajardo Sugar Company mill was opposed by the FLT. Backed by the Nationalists and the Communists (who otherwise were at each others' throats), it rapidly grew into a general strike. Newly appointed governor General Blanton Winship used U.S. troops to break the general strike, but not before some workers had forced wage concessions out of their employers. Their movement expanded during an islandwide port workers' strike in 1938. Most labor unions coalesced into the CGT (General Workers Confederation) that supplanted the FLT by 1940.

As the Nationalists gained a popular following, repression against them grew. In 1935, police under the command of U.S. Police Captain Francis Riggs killed the Nationalist party's labor secretary, Ramón S. Pagán, and three students at the University of Puerto Rico in Río Piedras. The following year Riggs himself was assassinated by two young Puerto Ricans. At that point the dynamic Nationalist leader Dr. Albizu Campos was arrested and charged with advocating the "overthrow of the government of the United States established in Puerto Rico." The rest of the Nationalist leadership was also jailed, and rallies were held to demand their release. Of Puerto Rico's seventy-seven municipalities, more than forty lowered the U.S. flag and replaced it with the Puerto Rican flag.

The first jury trial of Albizu Campos failed to convict him; its Puerto Rican members favored acquittal. The next jury, in which only two Puerto Ricans participated, did convict him. Albizu Campos was sentenced to ten years' imprisonment. He served his sentence in the penitentiary of Atlanta, Georgia. He suffered repeated jailings after that, spending all but four years of the remainder of his life as a prisoner.

The persecution of Albizu Campos and the Nationalists had the unintended effect of increasing sympathy for the Nationalist cause. Albizu Campos gained almost mythological status as a symbol of Puerto Ricans' desire for independence. Statues of him were erected in other parts of Latin America. The island's country people, most of them illiterate, knew all about Albizu Campos. His American defense attorney, black civil rights activist Conrad Lynn, called him "very religious . . . the most completely selfless and humble man I had ever met."

On March 21, 1937, in the island's second largest city of Ponce, Nationalists called for a peaceful demonstration demanding the release of Albizu Campos and other political prisoners. It was Palm Sunday. As men, women, and children dressed in their "Sunday best" paraded to the cathedral to celebrate a Te Deum mass in memory of independence martyrs, U.S. troops sealed the street behind them and opened fire, killing twenty and wounding more than a hundred. The U.S. government commissioned Professor Robert J. Hunter to investigate. "Most of the dead," he wrote, "were little more than children; none were armed; many were shot in the back while seeking refuge."

More than 2,000 sympathizers of the Nationalist movement were put in prison. Beheaded of its leadership, the independence movement appeared to be finished. Nonetheless, 25,000 people attended the funerals of those killed in what became known as "the Ponce Massacre."

A stroke in 1956 left Albizu Campos paralyzed on the right side and unable to speak more than two words at a time. His cellmate, Carlos Feliciano, who in the early 1970s was acquitted of trumped-up bombing charges in New York City, claimed Albizu Campos's failing health was brought on by deliberate prison mistreatment. Shortly before his death in April 1965, Albizu Campos was pardoned by outgoing Governor Muñoz Marín. His funeral elicited the largest public mourning in Puerto Rican history. Entire peasant families walked miles to attend.

A skilled politician emerged in the late 1930s to lead Puerto Ricans supporting independence and trade unions. Less insurrectionist and more reformist than Albizu Campos, Luis Muñoz Marín had participated in Iglesias's PS during his youth before emigrating to the United States where he lived among the intellectuals and artists of New York City's bohemian Greenwich Village of the 1920s. Returning to Puerto Rico, he commented in 1936, "Since statehood is impossible, the only alternative to colonialism is independence." This "young Turk" was too radical for Puerto Rico's old Liberal party, which expelled Muñoz Marín in 1937.

He and his followers founded the PPD (Popular Democratic party) in 1938, an Aprista-type reformist party (see Overview and chapters 11 and 14). The PPD brought together sons and daughters of the proindependence *hacendados* and scores of U.S.-educated new professionals. It also incorporated many of organized labor's CGT militants and the countryside's *colonos*.

The PPD quickly decided to let the independence issue rest in order to focus on their New Deal-type program of economic reforms. The New Deal was the name given to President Franklin D. Roosevelt's program of reforming capitalism in order to—as he promised the U.S. electorate—"save it" during the Great Depression. The PPD emblazoned the figure of a red *jíbaro* on its white banner and used the slogan of *"pan, tierra, y libertad"* (bread, land, and freedom).

Muñoz Marín cultivated close friendships with many of Roosevelt's advisers and Democratic party leaders. He made speeches all over the countryside, attacking the sugar interests. Seventy percent of Puerto Ricans were still peasants or rural workers. Muñoz Marín told them that he had friends in Washington and that if they voted for him, there would be an agrarian reform and eventual independence. The PPD won impressive victories at the polls in 1940 and 1942, becoming the dominant political party for the next twenty-six years.

"Operation Bootstrap"

The PPD used its majority in the insular legislature from 1942 to 1968 to undertake a series of economic and political reforms that radically altered the face of Puerto Rico. Economic reforms, known after 1948 as "Operation Bootstrap," industrialized and urbanized the island. PPD governments built hospitals, roads, electrical installations, and other so-called economic infrastructures. They raised the literacy rate to nearly 90 percent. A "new middle class" of professionals and white-collar employees emerged, many of its members aspiring to "the American way of life." A means of economic betterment through military service or employment with the CIA attracted thousands of Puerto Rican youth.

"Law 53" was issued in the late 1940s to harass independence advocates. Used to jail the leadership of the Nationalist party, it was dubbed "the Little Smith Act" because of its similarity to the U.S. Smith Act that called for the imprisonment of anyone "conspiring to teach" the overthrow of the government. (The Smith Act was widely applied during the anti-Communist "witch-hunt" days of the late 1940s and early 1950s in the U.S.) Later, Law 53 was replaced when similar local laws in the United States were found to be unconstitutional.

The PPD refused to recognize CGT Communist and radical leaders and sometimes sent goons to beat them up. Governor Muñoz Marín invoked the U.S. antilabor Taft-Hartley Act (1947) to break the power of the CGT's left wing. Strikes became less common. In this atmosphere, Operation Bootstrap got underway.

The preliminary steps for Operation Bootstrap were carried out during World War II under the governorship of Rexford G. Tugwell, a prominent figure in President Roosevelt's first New Deal administration. Back in 1934 Tugwell had recommended to Roosevelt that Puerto Rico "socialize the sugar industry along the lines of a Soviet collective farm."

Tugwell used the PPD's Land Law of 1941 to create state-owned "proportional-profit" farms and to resettle sharecroppers (*agregados*) on small land parcels near the sugar plantations. Overseeing the land redistribution program was an institution created by the 1941 Land Law, the Land Authority. The agrarian reform vastly increased the popularity of Muñoz Marín and the PPD. It gave the landless hope. It benefited many small *colonos,* while not affecting most of the old landed oligarchy or the large *colonos.* It confiscated, with compensation, the bulk of the U.S. sugar estates, although most of the Rockefellers' Eastern Sugar went untouched. Since three-fourths of the cost of sugar production was in cultivation, the sugar companies did not object to paying the lowest possible prices for the raw sugar and passing the costs and headaches of growing and cutting it on to the numerous small producers who benefited from the agrarian reform. Land planted with sugar expanded by 100,000 acres in the 1940s.

U.S. wartime needs energized Puerto Rico's economy. Unemployment dropped, as 60,000 Puerto Ricans went off to fight World War II and others worked, building U.S. military bases on 78,000 ares of arable land. Tugwell used the War Powers Act to create a public electricity corporation. The garment industry recovered, employing 80,000. Rum production skyrocketed. Tugwell left Puerto Rico after the war and wrote a book, *The Stricken Land* (1947), in which he praised the results of "our colonial policy."

Operation Bootstrap's leading advocates were Governor Muñoz Marín (1948–1964) and Teodoro Moscoso, who later headed up President Kennedy's Alliance for Progress (see chapter 11). Moscoso had directed the wartime PRIDCO (Puerto Rican Industrial Development Corporation) that had set up a few state-owned factories in bottling, cement, paper, ceramics, and shoes. Moscoso believed that private business could do the job better than the state since "government capital and government know-how were too scarce." But first, as Moscoso said in a speech in 1950, the labor movement had to create "the favorable conditions" necessary for attracting private investment. This meant acceptance of low wages and no strikes.

To a significant degree labor leaders cooperated. The days of collective solidarity among workers were over. Many Puerto Ricans, including World War II veterans, found it easier to advance individually by means of the Veterans Administration benefits they received or by migrating to New York City.

Moscoso believed Operation Bootstrap's success depended on controlling unemployment and social unrest through out-migration and population control. PPD governments organized both. Starting in the late 1940s, they organized the out-migration of more than a million Puerto Ricans to serve as migratory farm workers and low-wage industrial employees in the United States.

U.S. economic expansion after World War II generated a need for more laborers that Puerto Ricans (and Mexicans, see chapter 1) helped meet. Meanwhile, a new "birth control" policy took shape in the maternity wards of Puerto Rico's newly constructed hospitals, as PPD administrators encouraged postnatal sterilization. By 1965, more than one-quarter of Puerto Rican women of reproductive age had been sterilized.

During the 1950s U.S. investors took advantage of tax-free conditions and hourly industrial wages one-fourth what they paid Americans to set up more than five hundred manufacturing plants that provided 35,000 jobs—mostly to women in light industry. One-fourth of all manufacturing workers were employed by the garment industry. After 1955 additional opportunities were offered to U.S. private investors, including tax-free environments for supermarkets and other enterprises involved in the distribution of goods. By the early 1960s net income from manufacturing exceeded net income from agriculture by 50 percent. In 1960 about 135,000 persons worked in agriculture, 94,000 in manufacturing. The average Puerto Rican family was able to buy twice as many goods and services as in 1940.

In the 1960s workers won some wage hikes and transportation costs rose. Investments began shifting from light industry to more profitable capital-intensive heavy industry. U.S. investments tripled during the 1960s. Oil refineries, petrochemical and chemical industries, as well as high-tech industries in electronics, scientific equipment, and pharmaceuticals moved to Puerto Rico, but there were not enough new jobs to go around. The arrival of thousands of Cubans disgruntled with the Cuban Revolution added to the tensions, since they often got the best jobs. Big corporations monopolized larger percentages of Puerto Rico's economy than they did in the economies of the U.S. or Great Britain. By 1977, for example, a handful of U.S. pharmaceutical companies accounted for one-fourth of the island's gross domestic product.

The more the island industrialized, the more the sugar industry was allowed to decline. Small cane farms went bankrupt. Displaced farmers and farm workers flocked into the cities hoping to get the "new jobs" they had heard were opening up. In turn, at least half of the immigrants to New York City in the late 1940s and early 1950s was skilled or semiskilled workers from the manufacturing sector who also hoped to better their lot.

As the sugar industry declined, business in real estate, insurance, hotels, and banking flourished. The financial sector became dominated by a handful of "new rich" Puerto Rican families allied with U.S. bankers (the Ferré, Carrión, Bird, and García families, among others). The Ferré economic "empire" became an important power supporting statehood status. With economic change, then, came political change.

Commonwealth Status and Decline
of the Nationalist Party

In 1948 Muñoz Marín was elected governor, ending fifty years of Puerto Rican life under U.S.-appointed governors. During World War II, the PPD had recognized a big sugar strike and promised a postwar referendum on the ever controversial subject of independence. Because of these positions, most radicals and Liberals had joined the PPD in the early 1940s.

But in 1948, with Operation Bootstrap and the Cold War in full swing, the PPD openly distanced itself from the independence issue. A student organization at the University of Puerto Rico invited Dr. Albizu Campos to speak during one of his brief periods of liberty. University Rector Jaime Benítez, a PPD loyalist who later served as resident commissioner in Washington, D.C., refused to approve the invitation. Students launched a four-month protest strike. Police occupied the campus. The students' organization was dissolved. During that same year, unable to control its militants in organized labor's CGT or the independent Congress for Independence (founded in 1943), the PPD expelled them. They in turn founded the PIP (Puerto Rican Independence party).

In response to rising proindependence agitation by the old Nationalist party and the newer PIP, on July 30, 1950, the U.S. Congress passed Law 600, establishing Puerto Ricans' right to write their own constitution but within the framework of the "compact" between the two countries. The Nationalist party agitated that Law 600 was a club over the heads of Puerto Ricans to keep them under the thumb of the United States.

Rumors flew that there was a U.S. plan to jail the Nationalist party leaders and kill those who resisted. In late October policemen attacked a small farm in Peñuelas, killing three Nationalists. Deciding to resist with armed force, the Nationalists attacked a police station in the mountain village of Jayuya, on October 30, 1950. Other uprisings took place in Arecibo, Ponce, Mayaguéz, Utuado, and elsewhere. U.S. troops were ordered into the streets to help the police restore order, and a state of siege was declared. Under martial law the outgunned Nationalists were quickly subdued and jailed. Many Puerto Ricans who agreed with the Nationalists on the independence issue saw their actions as desperate, ill-timed, and unwise.

This defeat and loss of public support only heightened the Nationalists' sense of desperation. On November 1, 1950, in Washington, D.C., Nationalists Oscar Collazo and Griselio Torresola attempted to assassinate President Harry Truman at his temporary residence in Blair House. Torresola and one Secret Serviceman were killed. Collazo was wounded. At his subsequent trial, he was sentenced to death. Truman commuted his sentence to life imprisonment. Albizu Campos was languishing in jail again and it seemed that the Nationalists were finished. But the independence issue remained very much alive.

In the 1952 elections PIP became Puerto Rico's second largest party, outpolling the prostatehood party. There was no independence referendum on the ballot, but Puerto Ricans ratified their new constitution by better than a four to one margin. The U.S. Congress later added amendments to the document. Puerto Ricans never voted on the amendments, a practice the U.S. repeated with the 1977–1978 Panama Canal Treaties (see chapter 7).

As amended, the Constitution of the Commonwealth of Puerto Rico made the island "a free state in association with the United States . . . within the terms of the compact between the people of Puerto Rico and the United States of America." It retained the main points of the 1917 Jones Act. It left Puerto Rico subject to "the statutory laws of the United States . . . except for internal revenue laws."

To assure Puerto Ricans that they were not a colony but a self-governing people, President Eisenhower sent a message to the UN General Assembly in 1953 stating that "if at any time the Legislative Assembly of Puerto Rico adopts a resolution in favor of more complete or even absolute independence," he would "immediately thereafter recommend to Congress that such independence be granted." This pledge went unhonored even in the case of moderate reforms pointing toward independence. For example, in 1959, Puerto Rico's legislature and governor recommended extremely minor reforms that were incorporated into a bill before the U.S. Congress known as the Fernos-Murray bill. The Congress let the bill die.

On March 1, 1954, members of the Nationalist party grabbed the headlines again. The 1952 change in the political status of Puerto Rico had dimmed even further their hopes for independence. Three Nationalists entered the visitors' gallery in the U.S. Congress and shot and wounded five congressmen. This was followed by widespread arrests of suspected Nationalists. Both the 1950 and the 1954 events led to long prison terms for many Nationalists, who claimed to be "prisoners of war." An international campaign to release the four involved in the attacks on Truman and the congressmen led to President Jimmy Carter's granting them amnesty in 1979. Some admitted that their actions had been unwise acts of desperation, and all vowed to continue championing independence.

Meanwhile the independence torch was passing to a younger generation. In 1956 dissident university students, unable to organize since the police attacks of 1948, founded the FUPI (Federation for Puerto Rican Independence).

Rise of the New Left and New Right

In the continentwide atmosphere of radical nationalism created by the Cuban Revolution of 1959, the torch passed to a "new Left." Student militants of the FUPI helped found the MPI (Pro-Independence movement), the forerunner of the PSP (Puerto Rican Socialist party, 1971). In the 1960s and early 1970s revolutionary fervor swept not only young Puerto Ricans on the island, but also on the mainland. Initiated by students in the FUPI and MPI, large-scale street demonstrations by the new Left became a younger generation's way of expressing its frustration with both the corrupt PPD government and the apparent failures of the old Left and Nationalist party. The U.S. military draft, the U.S. invasion of the neighboring island of the Dominican Republic (1965, see chapter 10), the murder of Latin America's most famous guerrilla Ernesto "Ché" Guervara in Bolivia (see chapter 15), and the Vietnam war swelled the ranks of opposition movements.

Antidraft protest marches, firebombings of ROTC and other military installations, and talk of socialism and independence spread rapidly as the "body bags" came home from the Vietnam War. Popular movements were mounted against the "nuclearization" of Puerto Rico—the use of U.S. bases there for storing nuclear weapons. A long and bitter protest movement to defend Puerto Rican fishermen on the nearby eastern island of Culebra ended the U.S. Navy's bombing exercises there. Independent labor unions challenged the AFL's and Teamster's grip on organized labor. Strikes involving as many as 20,000 workers a year occurred.

In New York and Chicago street youth joined students in forming the Young Lords Organization, which proudly donned red and black berets to march in Puerto Rico Day parades. "Revolution" became a more favorable word than "independence." The Young Lords linked up with the Black Panthers and organizations of southern white migrants in Chicago's ghettos to launch what they called a "rainbow coalition."

FBI and police infiltration and repression, combined with the successes of the massive antiwar movement and the "winding down" of the Vietnam War, led to the breakup and decline of Puerto Rico's new Left in the 1970s. Yet most of the issues it raised did not disappear. Its sudden and massive appearance on the political scene caused Puerto Rican politics to change once more (see Box 9.1).

The U.S. government and the PPD quickly prepared a referendum to try to stop the new Left in its tracks. The largest crowd ever to attend a political rally demonstrated against the referendum on July 16, 1967. A week later Puerto Ricans voted on whether to become a state or remain a commonwealth. Only 38.9 percent opted for statehood, whereas 60.5 percent voted for retaining the commonwealth status. Some 30,000 Cuban "refugees" and 60,000 U.S. residents contributed to a big turnout among conservative, prostatehood voters. New Leftists called for a boycott of the referendum as just one more "colonialist" exercise. Their call was not unheeded: More than half the eligible voters and more than one-third of those registered did not cast ballots.

The threat of the new Left brought into the open long-simmering disputes

---

Box 9.1: People's Political Parties and Guerrilla Groups

EPB	Boricua People's Army, also known as Los Macheteros (The Canecutters), leftist, proindependence guerrilla group, active against U.S. military presence
FALN	Armed Forces for National Liberation, Socialist, proindependence guerrilla group, active in United States and Puerto Rico since 1972
MRA	Armed Revolutionary movement, leftist, proindependence guerrilla group, two of whose members were murdered by police in 1978 "Cerro Maravilla" incident
National Association for Statehood	Prostatehood group that testified at UN Committee on Decolonization in 1981
OVRP	Organization of Volunteers for the Puerto Rican Revolution, leftist, proindependence guerrilla group active since late 1970s
PCP	Puerto Rican Communist party, founded in 1934
PIP	Puerto Rican Independence party, founded in 1948, social democratic, proindependence, consultative member of Socialist International
PNP	New Progressive party, founded in 1967, prostatehood, one of two major parties
PPD	Popular Democratic party, founded in 1939, pro-Commonwealth, one of two major parties
PRP	Puerto Rican Renewal party, founded in 1983, led by San Juan mayor who broke with PNP while contesting its 1984 gubernatorial nomination
PSP	Puerto Rican Socialist party, founded in 1959 as MPI (Pro-Independence movement) and renamed in 1971, socialist, proindependence

---

inside the two dominant parties, the PPD and the Republicans. In 1964 the PPD split. A younger generation, led by Muñoz Marín's secretary of state, Roberto Sánchez Vilella, advocated limits on U.S. corporate power, an end to government corruption, and more political autonomy for Puerto Rico. The old guard, led by Senator Luis Negrón López and backed by Muñoz Marín, held the PPD fort and forced Sánchez Vilella to run on a separate ticket in the 1968 elections.

This opened the door to a victory for the pro-statehood Republicans, who had renamed themselves in 1966 the PNP (New Progressive party). Many workers voted in 1968 for Sánchez Vilella or the PNP as a protest vote against the failures of the PPD. The PNP's Luis A. Ferré won by three percentage points. Ferré represented a kind of "new Right," the newly dominant financiers, industrialists, and middlemen who had grown wealthy during Operation Bootstrap by making connections with big U.S. investors. They replaced Puerto Rico's old merchants and middlemen as the dominant power among the pro-statehood forces. Voted out of power in 1972, they regained the governor-ship in 1976 and held it for eight years.

The victorious PNP candidate in 1976, Carlos Romero Barcelo, con-ducted a populist-style campaign appealing to the poor to win in a close con-test. PPD Governor Rafael Hernández Colón (1972–1976) campaigned under the shadow of widespread charges of corruption and repression against his government and an unfavorable economic situation (30 percent unemploy-ment).

1980s and 1990s: Economic Stagnation, "Terrorism," and Political Disaffection

By the 1980s and 1990s there was widespread disaffection among Puerto Ri-cans with both their economic and political situation. Whenever workers won wage hikes or the local government attempted to tax U.S. corporations that controlled 85 percent of the insular economy, the firms "ran away" or threat-ened a plant shutdown. Labor unions went on the defensive. The militancy of the independent unions faded. Only about 15 percent of the labor force was or-ganized into unions, the strongest of which were in the public sector (around 180,000 unionized employees). The electrical workers' union UTIER had con-ducted long and bitter strikes in 1967, 1973, and 1978 that had exhausted their strike funds.

Half of the island's 150,000 workers in manufacturing were female. From one-third to a half of all families were headed by women. Research stud-ies showed that their "class consciousness," while rising, remained held back by patriarchical traditions and the double duty of child-rearing and earning a living.

Unemployment grew worse as more youngsters entered the labor force and foreign firms continued modernizing their technology. The local govern-ment debt grew as rapidly as the lines of people on the dole. From 1968 to 1980, federal assistance funds spent in Puerto Rico rose from $68 million to $2.3 billion. In the 1970s and 1980s the United States, acting unilaterally as they had done earlier in the case of Cuban refugees, decided to let thousands of Haitian refugees live on the overcrowded island, adding to the competition for scarce jobs. The contrast between San Juan's teeming slums of wood-crate shacks and the high-rise luxury tourist area of El Condado beach became a glaring symbol of the "two Puerto Ricos," poor and rich.

The PPD and PNP governments hoped an oil "bonanza" might bail out the economy. The island's northern coastal area was part of the same conti-nental shelf that provided Venezuela and Trinidad and Tobago with oil. In the 1970s the government signed oil exploration contracts with Mobil, Shell, Exxon, and Continental. Plans for construction of a deep-water oil tanker port, a "superport," were drawn up. With pollution already a major issue because of spilloffs from existing oil refineries and petrochemical and pharmaceutical plants, tens of thousands of Puerto Ricans mobilized in the streets to shout "No!" to the superport. People began hearing about something called the "2020 Plan"—a scheme of U.S. corporations and the U.S. government to strip mine Puerto Rico's interior of its rich copper reserves, iron, and other minerals and to convert the island's shoreline into eleven military-industrial parks.

Independence advocates usually were the ones who led the popular campaigns against pollution, the superport plans, nuclearization, corruption, and more concessions to U.S. corporations. But they fared poorly in elections. The PSP stopped running candidates after getting less than 1 percent of the vote in 1980. The PIP received less than 4 percent of votes cast in the 1984 gubernatorial election. Some thought economic hard times made people afraid of losing the right to go back and forth to the United States. Others thought the behavior of the Nationalists in the 1950s had left a long-term black mark on the independence movement.

Some youth believed that only an armed struggle would work to free Puerto Rico from its colonial status. A number of small guerrilla groups sprang up, attacking U.S. military installations and personnel and bombing corporate offices, stores, and hotels on the island and occasionally on the mainland. Although Cuba denied being involved in the guerrilla attacks, Governor Rafael Hernández Colón (1972–1976) said that "Cuba is training and aiding terrorists to overthrow the government of the island commonwealth." The *New York Times* quoted an unnamed high-ranking U.S. government official, who stated "We have no evidence of the Cubans" being involved except for "providing free vacations for the leaders."

The EPB (Boricua People's Army), momentarily crippled the island's U.S. Air National Guard in January 1981 by bombing nine jet fighters. Guerrilla bombings contributed to increased FBI and grand-jury roundups of independence advocates. The FBI ascribed half the "acts of terrorism" in the United States in 1982 to Puerto Rican independence groups. In the mid-1980s the FBI claimed that it had broken the back of the independence movement with its many arrests.

In the 1984 elections the PPD's Hernández Colón was voted back into office. The incumbent was defeated for much the same reasons that Hernández Colón had lost in 1976. The preceding pro-statehood PNP government was blamed for economic failure, repression, and corruption (revealed during the Cerro Maravilla televised hearings). After his election Governor Hernández Colón announced he would abandon his party's push for more political autonomy for Puerto Rico and would maintain tax exemptions for foreign corporations. Thousands of Puerto Ricans responded by holding a giant peaceful rally on July 4, 1985, in San Juan, calling for complete independence.

The new governor introduced a "twin-plant initiative" to attract more foreign investment. Under the scheme, a company set up one plant for the unskilled part of a job in a nearby Caribbean country paying 70 cents an hour and a "twin" plant for the skilled labor in Puerto Rico. Because of tax exemptions in Puerto Rico, the company kept all its profits after shipping the final products back to the United States or other markets.

Governor Hernández Colón said twin-planting made the Caribbean "the major alternative to Far Eastern production for U.S. corporations seeking lower production costs." Nine plants were opened in 1986, and more followed. Despite these steps, by 1987, a number of U.S. corporations, including Honeywell and Intel, had announced their intent to close plants on the island.

Other major controversies began to overshadow debate over political status. With more than 60,000 U.S. military personnel on the island, pollution and prostitution had grown alarmingly. High crime rates and an enormous drug addiction problem in the Puerto Rican neighborhood of New York City (El Barrio) had come back to roost in Puerto Rico itself. Guerrilla and state terrorism and nuclear/military issues had been added to the list. Health issues were also on the agenda when the U.S. environmental watchdog agency EPA (Environmental Protection Agency) reported on serious disease-endangering deficiencies in Puerto Rico's sewage systems. Another scandal erupted when it was revealed that standards for hormone injections in poultry were less strict in Puerto Rico than on the mainland. Estrogen-laden chickens had caused premature sexual development in Puerto Rican girls and breast development in boys who ate the chickens. Even more frightening was the appearance of AIDS (Acquired Immune Deficiency Syndrome) on the island. By 1990, San Juan rated second to San Francisco in new AIDS cases reported per year.

All political parties expressed dissatisfaction with the commonwealth status, sending representatives to appear before the UN Decolonization Committee in 1978 to denounce the colonial features of Puerto Rico's status. An economic obstacle faced both statehood and independence advocates, however. The burden of local taxation fell on the very group from which they drew most of their support—the middle classes—who would have to pay even more taxes if Puerto Rico became the fifty-first state or an independent nation.

With one-third of its work force unemployed and many more underemployed, Puerto Rico was more dependent on the U.S. economy than any other Latin American country. More than half its people received food stamps and depended on one or another program of the U.S. welfare system. Alcoholism was widespread. U.S. corporate investments surpassed $15 billion and drew off more than $1.5 billion a year in profits, dividends, and interests. Those championing independence spoke of economic relations with the rest of the Caribbean, Europe, and Japan, but they offered gloomy short-run prospects if the United States cut off Puerto Rico the way it boycotted the Cuban and Nicaraguan revolutions.

In 1991, when the U.S. Congress cancelled a scheduled status referendum, Governor Hernández Colón held a complex one of his own. It sought constitutional amendments to bar a simple yes-or-no vote on statehood and to provide guarantees for Puerto Rico's culture and Spanish language should the island ever become a state. Only 59 percent of the electorate turned out, voting 53-to-45 percent against amending the Constitution. The poor economy, AIDS crisis, and rising crime rate were hurting the PPD.

The next year, the PNP's Pedro Rosselló, a pediatric surgeon, defeated the PPD's Victoria Muñoz Mendoza, daughter of former Governor Muñoz Marín, by 75,000 votes. Rosselló took office in 1993. The new U.S. president, Bill Clinton, sought to bolster the federal budget by removing some of Puerto Rico's tax-free benefits, forcing companies to pay $3.75 billion in federal taxes over the next five years.

In November 1993, Puerto Ricans voted in a nonbinding referendum on the future status of the island. Only island residents were allowed to vote, causing some protest among mainland Puerto Ricans. By a narrow 48 to 46 percent margin, the electorate opted for a modified Commonwealth status over statehood, with only 4.5 percent voting for independence (some pro-independence voters chose Commonwealth in order to defeat statehood). Among modifications the PPD sought in early 1994 were complete and permanent restoration of tax exemptions for U.S. subsidiaries; expanded Supplemental Security Insurance benefits for island residents; more food assistance; and protection for Puerto Rican farm products. An oil spill near the main resort area of San Juan in January 1994 wreaked havoc with the tourist industry, leaving the island more economically vulnerable than ever.

Selected Bibliography

Acosta-Belén, Edna (ed.). *The Puerto Rican Woman*. New York: Praeger, 1986.

Dietz, James L. *Economic History of Puerto Rico*. Princeton, NJ: Princeton University Press, 1987.

Fernandez, Ronald. *The Disenchanted Island: Puerto Rico and the United States in the Twentieth Century*. New York: Praeger, 1992. Helpful overview.

Meléndez, Edwin, and Edgardo Meléndez (eds.). *Colonial Dilemma: Critical Perspectives on Contemporary Puerto Rico*. Boston, MA: South End Press, 1993. Fifteen essays on status issue.

Morales-Carrión, Arturo. *Puerto Rico: A Political and Cultural History*. New York: Norton, 1983. Comprehensive, informed.

Pantojas-García, Emilio. *Development Strategies as Ideology: Puerto Rico's Export-Led Industrialization Experience*. Boulder: Lynne Rienner, 1990. Insightful.

Peoples Press Puerto Rico Project. *Puerto Rico: The Flames of Resistance*. San Francisco, CA: Peoples Press, 1978. History from the bottom up.

Silén, Juan Angel. *We, the Puerto Rican People*. New York: Monthly Review Press, 1971.

Films

Los Sures. 1983. 58 minutes. Award-winning color film and video on Brooklyn (New York) *barrio*.

Manos a la obra. The Story of Operation Bootstrap. 1983. 59 minutes. Color film and video.

Puerto Rico: A Colony the American Way. 1982. 27 minutes. Color film and video directed by Diego Echeverria.

Siempre Estuvimos Aquí/We Were Always Here. 22 minutes. Video examining women's participation in Puerto Rican history; English soundtrack available.

A Show of Force. 1990. 93 minutes. Feature movie (and video) with Amy Irving and Lou Diamond based on Cerro Maravilla affair.

Dominican Republic _____ 10

Although the sun was bright and the sea breeze welcomed on that February afternoon in 1985, it was not a normal day in Santo Domingo's old city, oddly called "la ciudad nueva" despite its tottering colonial balconies and large shuttered windows. Uncollected garbage was piled high at curbs. The stores were closed, the streets silent. Troops were everywhere. The paper signs pasted to stucco walls denounced the government's jacking up of food and gasoline prices and blamed the IMF and American banks. Several protesters had been shot the previous week. The jails had run out of space. A general strike had paralyzed the capital.

Carlos was on his way back to snowbound New York City and the job of hauling racks filled with coats through the traffic-jammed streets of the West Thirties—the garment district. He had managed to scrape together enough money for his two-week home visit, but the strike had made if difficult to get around the city to meet his many relatives and old friends or to get prescription drugs for his ailing mother. He agreed with the strikers, of course, but he wondered how many of the younger ones would believe him if he told them that this was pretty tame stuff compared to what he had gone through twenty years earlier—in 1965—when he was a high-school kid.

Then, too, the uncollected garbage was piled high, but so were burning bodies. Under siege from the U.S. Marines, people had no time to conduct burials. Except for the San Isidro Air Force Base, a few luxurious suburbs and the polo field, the entire capital had been liberated by the constitutionalists, thanks to people's getting their hands on more than 20,000 guns from the armories and forts. Signs everywhere read "The 1963 Constitution is the only solution," "Yankees—murderers."

The U.S. jets, tanks, and troops had cut a swathe through the city. They called it a "Safety Zone," but it wasn't safe for Carlos. It had cut off communications between the industrial hub to the north and the downtown business district and slums, and he had been asked to run a message through it!

Carlos's home was a second-story flat only a block from Parque Independencia, where he and other youths had helped construct the barricades of orange crates and torn-up street pavement. They had been issued M-1 rifles, helmets two sizes too large, and instructions.

During one of his missions Carlos had been detoured by gunfire and found himself only a block away from a Marine checkpoint. He saw an old man and young boy riding on a bicycle. The boy, who couldn't have been more than eleven years old, was obviously a "*hijo de machepa*," one of the many street kids who had joined the revolution because his buddies had taken a vote and decided the constitutionalists were right. Under the youth's torn shirt Carlos could see the butt of a submachine gun.

Carlos raced to the side of a building as the Marines opened fire with their .50-caliber machine guns. The old man and the boy were ripped to shreds. Carlos ducked back around the side of the building. Bullets ricocheted all around him. He crossed himself, made a dash down an alley, and dove behind some scattered oil barrels, hoping no one had seen him.

Then he noticed he was not alone. A tall, lanky American dressed in a guayabera shirt was crouched only a few feet away.

"What the hell . . . " Carlos almost screamed.

"Peace Corps," the Yank whispered.

"Coño! Why are your Marines doing this? What have we ever done to you?"

"Nothing! But back in the States they think this is another Cuba, they think you're all communists."

"Communists? Are you crazy?"

"No, but my government is."

"Coño! You can say that again!"

Before any of the cease-fires really took hold, hundreds of Carlos's neighbors had been killed. It was a bloodbath, alright. The one chance for a democratic country went up in smoke. Later, in New York City, where he had gone to escape death threats from "La Banda," Carlos heard from some gringo professor giving a talk that the United States had sent twice as many troops as they had in Vietnam at the time. No wonder his country was in the mess it was in!

Oh well, he thought. People live to fight again another day.

. . .

Twenty years had changed very little. There had been several elections of dubious honesty. Everyone knew that real power still rested in circles outside the civilian government—the Dominican Armed Forces, the United States, the International Monetary Fund (IMF)—even though the 1966 Constitution called for a powerful civilian presidential system. Times were hard, and nearly one-seventh of the populace had migrated to New York and other American cities in quest of economic survival or political refuge. By 1995, more than a million Dominicans resided in the United States—as many or more than the number of Cubans.

Many blamed the new Dominican crisis on the earlier 1965 U.S. military incursion that put down a popular revolt for restoring democracy. But "blaming the Yanks" explained little without more knowledge about the nation's violent and personalist politics.

History of Foreign Control and Politics by Assassination

The roots of the Dominican Republic's political system go back to its colonial history and its nineteenth-century enmeshment in foreign intrigues in the Caribbean. National sovereignty was never securely obtained, and racial/personalist factors intersected economic ones to generate a country fired with antagonisms and instability. The Spanish-Latin American version of that universal phenomenon known as machismo affected Dominican politics in the form of *caudillismo*—strong male political leaders building political cliques of loyal followers.

Although "*Hispaniola*" ("Spanish island," the name given by Columbus in 1492 to the landmass occupied by today's Haiti and Dominican Republic) became the site of the first permanent European settlement in the New World, there existed insufficient wealth to attract Europeans in large numbers. There were inhospitable deserts in the west, 10,000-foot high peaks in the central cordillera, lush valleys to the north and south—but no gold, silver, or obedient Indian labor. The Arawaks fought and died. Many also perished from diseases imported by the Spaniards. As late as the mid-nineteenth century, fewer than

100,000 people, mostly former slaves, populated the Dominican Republic—a nation of 7.2 million today.

The country remained an economic backwater, periodically fought over by marauding pirates and filibusterers from England, France, Holland, Spain, and the United States. France eventually established juridical control, first over the Haitian west in 1697 under the Treaty of Ryswick and then over all Hispaniola in 1795 under the Treaty of Basel. The French developed the west, which they called Saint-Domingue, into a booming sugar/slave economy. In 1786–1787 nearly 70,000 slaves were imported as sugar workers. The terribly severe conditions they experienced provoked their rebellion a few years later, led by Toussaint L'Ouverture—and the establishment of Latin America's first independent nation, Haiti (1804).

Defeating Europe's most powerful army, Napoleon's, proved costly for Haiti's slave rebels. The burning of sugar plantations and the scorched-earth policies of successive European powers attempting to retake Haiti left a land in ashes, an economy in ruins. The new nation was further saddled by a gigantic cash indemnity conceded to France in exchange for diplomatic recognition in 1825.

The Haitian people never did recover from the abject poverty that they inherited during their first decades of independence. The stirring Hollywood movie *Burn* captured the character of the history of Hispaniola and the Caribbean from the early slave revolts to the mid-nineteenth century (see Overview Select Bibliography). It dramatized the meddling by foreign powers, the bribing of officials, the savagery of the wars, the popularity and certain death of that archetypical hero of Caribbean history: an ex-slave and honest leader.

When Spain was no longer able to control its colonies during the Napoleonic Wars, the Spanish settlers of the eastern region known as Santo Domingo, outnumbered by dark-skinned Haitians by more than five to one, sought incorporation into Simón Bolívar's "Gran Colombia." Bolívar could not help them, and by 1822 Haiti controlled all Hispaniola. The bankrupt Haitian government abolished slavery and introduced the present legal system of the Napoleonic Code. In 1844 a group of ambitious, well-off lighter-skinned and mulatto Dominicans rose up to declare independent nationhood.

The country's new rulers lacked a popular following among the dark-skinned masses and lacked economic leverage against stronger foreign interests. Two camps took shape, one favoring annexation to Spain and one annexation to France. A few leaders looked to Britain, one of the first powers to establish diplomatic representation in Santo Domingo, or to the United States, whose southern states could not find enough "white" Dominicans to merit recognition.

Meanwhile the Haitian government coveted control of Dominican customs revenues to help meet its debt payments to France. In 1861 Haiti almost took back control of the country, so the president had it annexed to Spain. In 1863 there was a revolution against this surrender of Dominican sovereignty. It was led by a black man named Gregorio Luperón, the hero of the Dominican Republic's "Second Independence," won in 1865.

Luperón and other victorious generals inherited a land almost as badly devastated as Haiti had been when it gained independence sixty years earlier. The generals divided into two rival camps, the Reds and the Blues. The Reds' General Buenaventura Báez negotiated the 1869 Hartmont loan with Britain that initiated a long chain of debts that led to the American customs receivership of 1905. His government, fearing another Haitian invasion since Luperón had retreated to Haiti, sought annexation by the United States. But the U.S. president, Ulysses S. Grant, was bogged down in a corruption scandal, and his opponents in the Senate defeated the annexation proposal. They feared another racial conflict as bloody as the recently concluded Civil War. Senator Charles Sumner denounced U.S. warships' maintaining Báez in power so that the tyrant might "betray his country . . . [in a] dance of blood."

The warring generals of the Dominican Republic continued leading the young nation down the path of economic indebtedness. The ruthless dictatorship of General Ulises Heureaux (1882–1899) based itself on anti-Haitian propaganda, internal espionage, rigged elections, a tenfold increase in the foreign debt that effectively handed over the customs houses to European and U.S. financiers, and political assassinations. Heureaux died the way he ruled—by gunfire. His eventual successor was his assassin, Ramón Cáceres, whose administration proved unable to quell a peasant insurgency in the east against encroaching U.S. sugar companies.

Weak elites and aspiring professionals competed for government power—the main avenue for advancement. Landed oligarchs, political _caudillos,_ merchants, and intellectuals, many calling themselves "generals," vied for a taste of power. Political infighting became personalist and violent, a tradition that underwent refinement in later decades.

The United States, already having seized nearby Cuba and Puerto Rico, took over the collection of Dominican customs duties in 1905, which it continued to manage until 1941. In this way Dominican government debts to private companies were regularly paid off. It was a more reliable method than the ones applied by today's IMF, but it generated a legacy of anti-Americanism. When Cáceres was assassinated in 1911 the country's less than 1 million mostly rural inhabitants once more vented their anger at foreign sugar companies and quarrelsome politicians. Revolutionaries from the lower classes threatened the previous half-century's arrangements of foreign domination. The U.S. Marines invaded Haiti in 1915 and occupied it until 1934; they did the same in the Dominican Republic from 1916 to 1924.

One of the first U.S. Marine units to land in 1916 rushed to protect a U.S.-owned sugar estate. Other units secured the banks and customs houses. The U.S. administration passed a land registration act that effectively broke up peasant communal landholdings and helped U.S. sugar companies consolidate control over the economy.

Marine officer Major General Smedley D. Butler later recalled,"I brought light to the Dominican Republic for American sugar interests in 1916." Sugar production peaked in 1920, and by 1926 almost as much land as today was under sugar cultivation—largely in the rich southern coastal plains.

For five years U.S. troops tried to enforce "law and order" against Dominican insurgents, mostly peasants. The popular resistance ended only when the United States submitted plans for withdrawal of the Marines. Under the banner of the newly created UND (National Dominican Union), Santo Domingo intellectuals and professionals led an international campaign against U.S. occupation. A strong movement of American citizens protesting "U.S.imperialism" emerged, causing the Republican party presidential candidate in 1920, Warren G. Harding, to advocate Marine withdrawal in his successful electoral campaign against Woodrow Wilson.

The delay in U.S. troop withdrawal until 1924 was partly due to fear in Washington that the UND would take power. U.S. generals and politicians felt that more time was needed to train and strengthen the U.S.-sponsored constabulary, the Dominican National Guard (later to be known as the Army). Under the leadership of former sugar-plantation guard and future dictator (1930–1961) Rafael Trujillo, this newly created force would become the surrogate of U.S. interests, a role similar to that of the National Guard under Somoza in Nicaragua (see chapter 5).

Economic hard times triggered by the Great Depression fueled social unrest. In 1930, when aging General Horacio Vásquez sought to extend his presidential term, an uprising aided by Trujillo, now commander of the army, toppled the government. Trujillo had himself elected president with more votes than there were eligible voters. For the duration of the Depression the United States maintained its customs receivership.

World War II and the Korean War stimulated U.S. demand for Dominican sugar and ferro-nickel exports that helped pay for expanded public construction projects. Trijillo lavished economic concessions upon U.S. investors and made generous campaign contributions to U.S. congressmen.

Political support in Washington helped Trujillo consolidate one of history's most ruthless dictatorships. It incorporated seven categories of intelligence agencies and obligated citizens to carry good-conduct passes from the secret police. Labor strikes or dissent of any kind met with rapid response from the army and police. Imprisonment, torture, and murder wiped out tens of thousands of political opponents. Discipline from the army meant massacres.

In 1937, for example, Trujillo ordered the army to slaughter more than 20,000 Haitians who had set up squatters' hovels in the western border provinces. Individual assassinations were also carried out, as in the 1956 New York kidnapping and subsequent murder of Jesús María de Galíndez, a professor critical of the tyrant.

The Dominican economy chugged along on the backs of contracted Haitian cane-cutters and underpaid Dominican workers and peasants. Starting in 1952, Haiti and the Dominican Republic signed bilateral agreements providing about 20,000 Haitian cane-cutters a year for state-owned sugar plantations. They worked in conditions bordering on slavery. The example of the 1937 massacre chilled labor unrest.

With his relatives and friends, Trujillo eventually came to own more than half the country's assets. The Trujillo clique employed nearly half the labor force, not counting another one-third employed by the government. Government employees were dunned for 10 percent of their salaries for Trijillo's political party, the PD (Dominican party).

Successful movements to topple dictatorships in Venezuela, Colombia, Cuba, and elsewhere made Trujillo's tyranny less tenable by 1960. The order of the day was democracy and reform, the Alliance for Progress. As part of its policy of isolating the Cuban Revolution, the United States had to make concessions to Latin America's democrats who wished to isolate Trujillo. Nicaragua's Somoza and Paraguay's Stroessner wisely distanced themselves from the sixty-nine-year-old Dominican strongman.

In February of 1960 President Dwight Eisenhower, whose administration was already preparing the 1961 Bay of Pigs invasion (see chapter 8), gave the go-ahead to the CIA to consider aiding Trujillo's opponents. Getting rid of Trujillo on the Right and Castro on the Left would make U.S. policy appear evenhanded. On May 3, 1961, Trujillo was in his car being driven to visit his mistress. Using weapons supplied by the CIA, a group backed by Dominican business and military leaders ambushed the car and gunned the old man down.

All but two of those carrying out the assassination were in turn executed by military troops loyal to Trujillo. Nonetheless, people danced in the streets and political exiles returned. Trujillo's eldest son, Ramfis, and his brothers ("the wicked uncles") reestablished control during the next few months. As a result, workers struck and people again took to the streets to demand the Trujillos' departure and confiscation of their properties. A U.S. naval flotilla stationed itself just off the coast (a scene to be replayed in Haiti in 1986 after the overthrow of the Duvalier dynasty—see Introduction to Part Two).

In November of 1961 Ramfis and the wicked uncles skipped town, taking with them much of the government treasury. People again rejoiced, toppling busts commemorating Trujillo and restoring to Ciudad Trujillo its original name of Santo Domingo.

An interim government took over and confiscated Trujillista properties. But under U.S. pressure, its titular president remained the man who had been serving in that capacity at the time of Trujillo's death—the dictator's presidential secretary, Joaquín Balaguer. Balaguer brought into the ruling interim "council of state" the two surviving members of the Trujillo ambush group, Generals Antonio Imbert Barrera and Luis Amiama Tío, both friends of the CIA.

Although he was not involved, Balaguer was implicated in an ultra-rightist Trujillista coup attempt checkmated by a general strike in early 1962. Army officers arrested coup leaders and exiled Balaguer to Puerto Rico, where he founded the PR (Reformist party) a year later. Popular street demonstrations continued to pressure the government to distribute Trujillista properties and tó conduct fair elections.

An interim ruling council set up national elections, which were held in December 1962. A huge turnout of nine-tenths of eligible voters cast 64 percent of their ballots for novelist and scholar Juan Bosch, candidate of the anti-Trujillo PRD (Dominican Revolutionary party). Bosch became the country's first democratically elected president on February 27, 1963.

Bosch, U.S. Occupation of 1965–1966, and Balaguer

The 1963 Constitution was an unusually democratic document that thrilled Dominicans. But their infant democracy lasted only seven months. A military coup ousted Bosch on September 25, 1963. It was headed by Air Force Colonel Elías Wessin y Wessin, the chief of the National Police, and Generals Imbert Barrera and Amiama Tío. Democrats ran for cover. At the time of the next coup, 1965, the military split, and people rallied to the prodemocracy wing of the military to resurrect the 1963 Constitution. In a popular insurrection they called for the return of Bosch. This provoked the largest U.S. invasion of a Latin American country in modern history.

It was an ironic twist, considering the fact that starting with CIA aid to Trujillo's opponents, the United States had been influential in bringing Bosch to power in the first place. U.S. taxpayers had invested heavily in the Alliance for Progress alternative to Castroism—"democratic reformism"—as epitomized by the Social Democrat oriented governments of Costa Rica's Figueres, Venezuela's Betancourt, Puerto Rico's Muñoz Marín, and Bosch. Personal friends, these four men had been the main leaders of the "Caribbean Legion," a broad alliance committed to the replacement of dictatorships with democracies.

One of their most active "braintrusters" was Sacha Volman, a close adviser of Bosch during his earlier seven-month presidency allegedly on the CIA payroll. Although the U.S. government backed the losing conservative candidate in the 1962 election won by Bosch, Volman's friendship with the Kennedy White House was said to have helped assure Bosch's being allowed to take office and to have influenced Kennedy to withhold diplomatic recognition of the so-called Triumvirate that replaced Bosch after the 1963 military coup. What, then, caused Bosch's fall from grace in Washington?

First, economies like the Dominican Republic's that depended on large estates geared for export production required fundamental land and labor reforms—something the prevailing sugar magnates and generals were not about to permit. Second, the situations inside several key countries changed.

Shortly before the 1963 anti-Bosch coup President Kennedy, already under attack for his botched Bay of Pigs invasion, received photographs of Soviet missile sites in Cuba. He was too preoccupied with Cuban and Soviet relations to pay much attention to Dominican matters. Nor did he have a unified administration (see chapter 8). U.S. military personnel in Santo Domingo were, according to a wide range of Dominican political leaders, active coconspirators with the Dominican officers behind Bosch's overthrow. Volman later claimed Kennedy offered Bosch U.S. troop support to resist the 1963 coup but that Bosch declined.

Reformist policies of the kind Bosch supported were challenged long before his election and overthrow in 1963. After Trujillo's death, only some of the ultrarightists of the Trujillista army and state bureaucracy were removed. Those who remained refashioned their political program to one of "Trujillismo without Trujillo"—a program implemented during the iron-fisted reign of President Balaguer (1966–1978) after the U.S. military invasion of 1965 had frustrated Bosch's attempted comeback. Earlier in the 1960s in the name of anticommunism and free enterprise, these Trujillo admirers marshaled anti-Bosch campaigns that included armed violence against Bosch sympathizers, including moderate Christian Democrats. The Trujillistas, then, were at the very core of the 1963 coup and the 1965–1966 U.S. intervention that rolled back the country's democratic-reformist forces.

Armed, trained, and enriched by U.S.-aid programs in the first years of the Kennedy administration, the Dominican military, although no longer unified, effectively replaced Trujillo as the nation's power center. The National Police, whose chief cosponsored the anti-Bosch coup, also gained strength. Never popular with the citizenry, it tripled its numbers to 10,000 men under the auspices of a U.S. training program. As president, Bosch discontinued the program, raising doubts in Washington about his reliability.

After Kennedy's assassination in November 1963, President Johnson recognized the post-Bosch governing Triumvirate. Later, one of the Triumvirate's members, right-wing oligarch Donald Reid Cabral, sought to bring the military more firmly under his personal command. This angered senior right-wing officers. Junior officers sympathetic to Bosch seized the opportunity to launch a countercoup in April 1965. They were joined by some of the disgruntled rightists.

The new military rulers soon split into armed camps, however. The pro-Bosch junior officers led by U.S.-trained Colonel Francisco Caamaño Deñó were called constitutionalists. The rightists led by General Wessin y Wessin were known as loyalists.

PRD supporters, in alliance with the Christian Democrats' PRSC (Social Christian Revolutionary party) and a handful of leftist organizations including the tiny outlawed PSP (Communist party), took to the streets to demand weapons to support the constitutionalists. General Wessin y Wessin sent air force planes to bomb and strafe constitutionalist neighborhoods. Tens of thousands of Dominicans rose up in cities and towns denouncing the loyalists as loyal only to Trujillismo, the oligarchy, and U.S. economic interests. Once the people had arms, the vastly more popular constitutionalists counterattacked, gained control of Santo Domingo, and threatened the nation's second major city, Santiago de los Caballeros. Everywhere there sprang up clinics for the wounded, food dispensaries, a communal system of organization involving priests, soldiers, street kids, and the entire citizenry. Some thirty Peace Corps volunteers lived and worked in the liberated areas. Their generous help was welcomed by the people.

At that point President Johnson ordered the Marines to invade the Dominican Republic "to save American lives" and "prevent a Communist takeover." Ironically, prior to the invasion, no American lives were lost. After it, however, several Americans were killed in the warfare. U.S. officials released a swiftly drafted list of fifty-eight "Communists," who allegedly were involved in the fighting. Most on the list were dead, in prison, or simply not Communists.

The powerful U.S. Marine force gradually rolled back the constitutionalists from the areas they controlled. Bloody battles in May and mid-June took thousands of Dominican lives. The marines were soon joined by troops from U.S. allies in the region. The OAS (Organization of American States), with five dissenting votes, approved the U.S. invasion by passing a resolution creating the Inter-American Peace Force (IAPF). The IAPF merged the U.S. forces with smaller units sent by the dictatorships of Brazil, Paraguay, Honduras, and Nicaragua—and the democracy of Costa Rica, a nation supposedly without an army (see chapter 6). The IAPF stayed in the Dominican Republic until September 1966.

President Johnson's diplomatic troubleshooter throughout the U.S. reoccupation of the Dominican Republic was special ambassador Ellsworth Bunker, Jr., a wealthy stockholder of the National Sugar Refining Company. He later served as U.S. ambassador to South Vietnam and negotiated the 1977–1978 Panama Canal treaties (see chapter 7).

348

Bosch was allowed to return to Santo Domingo in late September 1965, but his PRD forces were never able to recuperate from the defeats inflicted over the summer. His campaign for the presidential elections of June 1, 1966, was conducted from his home, where he remained under virtual house arrest. Hundreds of his active supporters were murdered and many more were deported or forced into exile. Bosch's son was shot; a bodyguard of Bosch was killed.

For the 1966 elections the United States supported the candidacy of ex-Trujillista Balaguer who won by a margin of 57 percent of the vote to Bosch's 39 percent. Oddly, with a lower voter turnout than in 1962, the total number of votes counted was 25 percent higher. Ex-CIA officer Ray Cline later recounted President Johnson's orders on Balaguer: "Get this guy in office down there!"

With the backing of the military, Balaguer served as president until 1978. His first administration revised the 1963 constitution to remove limits on foreign land ownership. Introducing tax abatements and other benefits, Balaguer welcomed foreign investment on a grand scale. U.S. aid flowed in— more per capita in 1966 than any nation except Vietnam. Labor unrest and political dissent were controlled by tried-and-true Trujillista methods. There were more than one thousand political murders between 1966 and 1971. The nation's soft-spoken and conservative Catholic Church condemned the government's human rights record as early as 1969.

As in Brazil and Guatemala during the 1960s, the term "death squad" became part of everyday parlance. The most notorious group was "La Banda" (The Band), directed by National Police commander General Enrique Pérez y Pérez. Responding to international protests as well as to an ultrarightist plot against his government allegedly led by General Wessin y Wessin, Balaguer dismissed Pérez y Pérez in October 1971. Little was heard of La Banda after that.

In 1973, Colonel Caamaño, whose whereabouts had been a mystery since the 1965 defeat of his constitutionalist forces, led a ten-man guerrilla landing and headed for the hills. Some two thousand troops chased him down. He was taken prisoner and, five hours later, summarily executed. Balaguer used the incident to justify the detention of fourteen hundred political opponents, mostly young leftists or PRD leaders. To appear evenhanded, he also deported General Wessin y Wessin.

Subsequent harassment of the democratic political opposition caused all the main parties to boycott the 1974 presidential elections, a macabre victory for Balaguer's PR (Reformist party, founded in 1963) during which soldiers stuck PR flags on the ends of their bayonets. More than half the electorate stayed home.

Not surprisingly, Bosch blamed the United States for democracy's failure. In 1967 he wrote a lengthy analysis that viewed Fidel Castro as a typical Latin American nationalist who "knew—and knows—that what has kept the democratic reformist parties in our countries from gaining the support of young people are the close relations between their governing officials and the United States."

In 1974 outvoted by his PRD colleagues, Bosch withdrew from the PRD to found the PLD (Dominican Liberation party). The Socialist International (SI), led by moderate European reformist parties, continued to recognize the PRD as its Dominican affiliate. PRD presidential candidates ever since came from the party's right or center wings. Much of the PRD party leadership passed to José Francisco Peña Gómez, an SI vice-president elected mayor of Santo Domingo in 1982. The son of Haitian victims of the 1937 massacre, Peña Gómez was said to be popular among the urban poor. Despite his frequent denunciations of Cuba and Nicaragua, military officers still referred to him as "that Haitian Communist."

The 1978 elections produced a new crisis. When it was clear that the PRD's Antonio Guzmán, a wealthy rancher, had taken a lead in the count, troops occupied the headquarters of the central election board. President Jimmy Carter, concerned that his human rights policy was about to be ignored, warned that future U.S. support depended on respect for the electoral process. It took seven weeks of secret backroom bargaining to prevent a military coup, but Guzmán was finally declared the winner by 150,000 votes. The process of recounting the vote shifted four Senate seats initially in the PRD column to Balaguer's PR, giving it a majority there and the ability to block future legislation.

In 1979 Guzmán claimed to have uncovered another coup plot and arrested several officers, replacing some top generals and promoting junior officers more sympathetic to the PRD. He also promoted into the top leadership of the Dominican military the two nephews of Major General Antonio Imbert Barrera, the CIA friend who had helped kill Trujillo and then had spearheaded the 1963 coup against Bosch. The Imberts became the military's most powerful faction.

Post-1965 Society and Economics

From 1965 to 1990 the Dominican population doubled to 7.2 million. Since most peasants were landless or owned *minifundios*—subsistence parcels that couldn't even feed a family—migration swelled the urban population from 30 percent of the total population to nearly 60 percent. With its overflowing slums, Santo Domingo held nearly one-fifth of the national population. Santiago de los Caballeros, in the fertile northern valley of Cibao, had 400,000 residents.

Rural poverty was extreme. The palm-thatched *bohíos* of the peasantry generally had dirt floors and no plumbing. Malnutrition was widespread. The minimum wage in 1985, a little under $3 a day in cities, was less than $2 a day in the countryside. Growing numbers of workers migrated to the United States—nearly a million by the mid-1980s, more than half of them to New York City. Meanwhile 200,000 impoverished Haitian laborers and political refugees had moved to the Dominican Republic, soon joined by hundreds of thousands more fleeing the reign of terror launched by the military and police against supporters of popular exiled President Aristide (see introduction to Part Two). For generations, Haitians had been used as sugar cane cutters in the Dominican Republic. In the 1990s, UN observers and U.S. reporters characterized the conditions of the Haitian sugar workers, many of them children, as "slavery."

As reflected by the abuse of the Haitians, racial prejudices followed a typical Caribbean color line of shades of darkness. About 16 percent of the Dominican population was white, 11 percent black, and the rest mulatto, plus a few Asians. There also remained a handful of descendants of Jewish immigrants from Hitler's Germany allowed in by Trujillo in his attempt to "whiten" the population in the late 1930s, and a very occasional Arawak survivor.

The dark-skinned majority were economically and socially worse off than the lighter-skinned mulattoes or whites. In the words of an old folk expression, "a rich Negro is a mulatto and a rich mulatto is a white man." Hostility toward whites was on the rise. With more than $500 million in U.S. investments, the Dominican Republic was "home" to 20,000 U.S. citizens in 1985. U.S. warships regularly made passes along Dominican shores. In 1981, and again in 1983, several thousand protestors turned out to denounce their arrival.

The Dominican Republic had a small traditional oligarchy whose economic roots went back to the landed wealth of the white Spanish settlers and the tobacco profits of the late nineteenth century in the fertile northern valley of Cibao. Refugees from Cuba's nineteenth-century Wars of Independence intermarried with Dominicans and helped create an aristocratic culture in Cibao's main city, Santiago de los Caballeros.

But by the 1980s traditional oligarchs were outnumbered by new elites spawned by the country's post-1965 semi-industrialization, state/military corruption, and the development of banking and tourism. The private sector's CNHE (National Businessmen's Council) incorporated the business representatives of all elites, including those of many foreign interests. Behind the scenes, the nation's elites, including senior military officers, ran politics from their men's clubs, country clubs, and private estates. Economic policies were coordinated through the CNHE and the government, in consultation with the U.S. government and foreign banking officials.

A sizable middle class grew up alongside the newer elites, much of which staffed the government and corporate bureaucracies. Under the PRD governments of Guzmán and lawyer Salvador Jorge-Blanco (1978–1986), the number of government employees doubled to 250,000. A constitutionally mandated strong presidency meant that the president ultimately controlled nearly half the nation's jobs. Meanwhile four-fifths of the population remained immersed in poverty, with Haitian immigrants at the bottom of the economic/race hierarchy.

After the U.S. military occupation of 1965–66 the Dominican Republic became a low-wage heaven for foreign companies. The two biggest were Gulf & Western and the Canada-based mining firm Falconbridge. With a majority of its capital U.S., Falconbridge owned the nickel mine at Boanao. Miners there complained that the company did nothing to control the silica dust that was destroying their lungs. Other powerful foreign companies included Nestle, Royal Bank of Canada, and Shell.

"Gulf & Western's newest acquisition" was what some called the Dominican Republic. Until January 1985, when it was purchased by a group of Florida investors headed by the fanatically anti-Castro Cuban brothers Alfonso and José ("Pepe") Fanjul, Gulf & Western held more than $200 million in some ninety businesses. It also owned about 8 percent of arable land, including the La Romana sugar plantation and refinery complex, and produced one-third of the nation's sugar. Near La Romana it set up a tax-free zone for companies, surrounded by a high fence topped with barbed wire, after police and troops broke up a labor-organizing effort in the mid-1970s with submachine guns. AFL-CIO officials visited the zone. They compared it to "a modern slave-labor camp."

Various firms, mostly in garment, footwear, and electronics manufactures, took advantage of handsome government subsidies and no taxes to set up shop in the country's twenty-six free-trade zones. Most of the workers there were women paid under a dollar an hour. Joint corporate-government security measures made labor organizing virtually impossible. A common Dominican saying was, "Civil liberties stop at the door of the factories."

Government connivance with foreign corporations produced widespread corruption. Investigations by the U.S. Securities and Exchange Commission (SEC) found that Gulf & Western speculated with Dominican officials in sugar deals and owed the Dominican government millions of dollars. It also found that Philip Morris made monthly payments of $1,000 to four-time President Balaguer.

Still the dominant economic power, the United States supplied half the nation's imports and purchased three-fourths of its exports. More than a hundred U.S.-based companies dominated banking and manufacturing, especially the textile and food processing industries. Among the largest were Citibank,

Colgate-Palmolive, Exxon, GTE, Philip Morris, Texaco, and Wometco. Tourism was built into a booming business, replacing sugar as the top earner of foreign exchange in 1983.

With food imports costing dearly, the Guzmán government (1978–1982) helped increase the production of rice and beans to levels approaching self-sufficiency. But as unemployment passed 30 percent in 1985, more than half the population still lacked sufficient food and almost half had no access to safe drinking water.

When sugar prices were up the economy chugged along. But the price of sugar plummeted from 76 cents a pound in 1975 to 6 cents a pound in 1984, less than half the cost of production. This skyrocketed the nation's trade deficit to an annual $100 million by the early 1980s. The foreign debt passed $3 billion. In 1987, to protect U.S. cane and beet sugar production, the United States halved the Dominican Republic's sugar quota to 160,200 short tons. The Soviet Union agreed to buy 50,000 short tons a year over the next three years at 8 cents a pound, slightly above the world price. In 1991 the United States slashed the country's duty-free sugar quota by a third. Twenty years earlier sugar had accounted for half the nation's export revenues, but now it brought in less than 8 percent, surpassed by ferronickel, gold, and light-industry exports (mainly apparel). The ongoing economic crisis of bloated foreign debts and huge trade imbalances threatened the nation's future.

In March of 1990, a group of UN economists from Harvard laid out a fresh plan for President Balaguer: increase import taxes; raise income taxes on individuals or groups earning more than a modest amount; regulate banking better. The IMF and World Bank, whose "experts" held key positions in the Central Bank and Ministry of Finance, called for further economic austerity measures. The U.S. government advocated more free trade agreements and complete privatization of the sugar sector, a step advocated by Balaguer's political rival Bosch. Additional pressures on the government came from the nation's trade unions and the AFL-CIO, which demanded a new labor code for the free trade zones employing 145,000 underpaid workers.

Questionably reelected in 1990 and 1994 (see below), President Balaguer proceeded to implement partly or fully _all_ the recommendations except for privatizing sugar. Attractive 20 percent interest rates in Dominican banks, tourism revenues, and nearly a billion dollars a year of dollar remittances from Dominicans working in the United States served to ease the trade deficit crisis. But President Balaguer also introduced pesos without Central Bank backing— and the annual inflation rate zipped past 100 percent in 1990–1991. Naturally, scarcity of basic goods for the masses grew more severe.

Worse yet, even though most working people did not have to pay direct income taxes unless very highly salaried, an indirect tax on gasoline drove them to the wall. Using the Persian Gulf War as a pretext, Balaguer hiked the gasoline price from 6 pesos to 20 pesos a gallon (12.50 pesos = 1 dollar). The IMF said this was a necessary measure for keeping up with foreign debt payments.

Recent Elections, the IMF, Social Unrest, and U.S. Troops in Haiti

The 1982 elections went more smoothly than those of 1978. PRD candidate Jorge-Blanco, with a strong following among government technocrats and bureaucrats, won 47 percent of the vote, followed by the PR's Balaguer with 39 percent and the PLD's Bosch with 10 percent. Two months later lame-duck President Guzmán committed suicide. Many speculated that he was depressed by the rapidly emerging evidence of widespread corruption in his regime in which his politically influential daughter Sonia was implicated.

President Jorge-Blanco dismissed the Imberts but otherwise kept the good favor of the Dominican military. He continued most of Guzmán's programs. In 1982 and again in 1984 he partially complied with IMF demands for wage freezes and tax and price hikes. Protesting the government's austerity program and failure to address the land problem, peasants temporarily occupied the Ministry of Agriculture in 1983. That same year the U.S. Agency for International Development (AID) conditioned its balance-of-payments support agreement on having access to government financial information and Dominican compliance with IMF loan terms.

In January 1984 President Jorge-Blanco sent a personal message to President Reagan explaining that IMF negotiating terms threatened Dominican democracy by placing too great a burden on the nation's working people. He received no help from the White House, however, and by mid-April he bowed to fresh IMF and AID demands.

IMF and U.S. power over Dominican affairs evoked a broad and hostile response from the populace in 1984. Just two weeks after President Reagan had praised the Dominican Republic as a beacon of freedom, a popular revolt erupted. Poor people, workers, and students took to the streets. They were no longer defending the program of the anti-Trujillo, reformist PRD, as they had done in 1965. Now, after seven years of PRD rule, they fought *against* the PRD government and its soldiers.

Troops attacked crowds of angry protesters, killing more than one hundred. Most of the shooting was done by the elite U.S.-trained Highland Rangers. Four thousand people were arrested. National police occupied labor union headquarters. The DNI, a powerful government intelligence agency reputedly linked to the CIA, filled its files with new names. A preventive detention law was passed.

Less than a year later an ultrarightist organization called MACI (International Anti-Communist movement) appeared on the scene. Staffed by military men, it reminded people of the notorious La Banda, although it did not carry out as many murders.

Then, in January 1985, the government signed a new IMF accord and hiked food and gasoline prices. A general strike in February forced several price reductions. There were more shootings and arrests, and ex-president Bosch was put under house arrest.

The May 1986 presidential elections produced yet another constitutional crisis. Disgusted by the government's failures to deliver on promises of reform, many voters turned against the PRD. Some who voted for Balaguer associated the economy's greater buoyancy of the early 1970s with his regime. PRD candidate Jacobo Majluta of the party's right wing denounced an early vote count, causing two of the three members of the election board to resign. The archbishop, senior military officers, and the American Embassy intervened to work out a solution. The final results of the interrupted vote count were announced in June. Balaguer, nearly blind and pushing eighty, was declared the winner. He took office for his fifth term as president in August. The man who President Johnson had ordered into power twenty years earlier was back in the saddle, now as head of the PRSC (Social Christian Reformist party, a 1985 merger of the PR and small Christian Democratic party). The PRSC is a member of the Europe-based Christian Democratic International. Outgoing President Jorge-Blanco was later accused of corruption, jailed, and faced criminal charges in Dominican courts.

Responding to militant pressures from below like fiercely repressed forty-eight-hour general strikes in June 1989 and August 1990 that left scores dead and wounded and hundreds arrested, Balaguer hiked the minimum wage and introduced lavish construction projects for the 1992 Columbus Quincentennial celebrations. Though items like the new lighthouse to honor Columbus and new modern race tracks were criticized as wasteful, the programs momentarily lowered the 25 percent unemployment rate.

The 1990 and 1994 elections repeated the 1978 and 1986 pattern of alleged fraud and prolonged delays in declaring the winner. Former U.S. President Jimmy Carter played a key role in mediating the 1990 dispute, when Balaguer was declared the winner by 24,000 votes over Bosch (35 percent to 34 percent, with the PRD's Peña Gómez finishing third and Majluta of the PRD splitoff Independent Revolutionary party a distant fourth).

In 1994, the electoral crisis was complicated first by the U.S. economic embargo of the neighboring Haitian dictatorship and then by the September U.S. military occupation of Haiti (negotiated by a U.S. team headed by Carter). Balaguer used the historic public (and often racist) feeling among Dominicans against Haitians to undermine the campaign of Peña Gómez, a black. The number of voter abstentions again outnumbered the votes of any single candidate. It appeared to most observers that Peña Gómez, whose party won a majority in Congress's lower house, handily defeated the eighty-seven-year-old Balaguer, a white. But the election commission awarded the victory to President Balaguer by a questionable two thousand votes. In the summer of 1994, Balaguer accepted a "Pact of Democracy" compromise of taking office for only two years before new elections to be held in 1996.

Dominicans wondered how long their limited "democracy" (and their aging *caudillo*-politicians) could last. A number of new political groups had emerged in the democratic space that had begun to open up after the end of Balaguer's first long reign. One of the most powerful was the FID (Democratic Left front), a coalition of about ten left-wing groups and forty-three other organizations, including the Communist party (legalized in 1978). The FID had the support of a majority inside organized labor's 40,000-strong CGT (General Confederation of Labor, where the Communists were strong) and the biggest university student organization. It was the main grouping behind the 1984–1985 popular protests, and suffered the most arrests. "Popular Struggle Committees" also sprang up during that period to guide the nascent mass movement.

The Left's strength in labor was owed in part to the demise of the nation's largest labor confederation in the 1960s, the CONATRAL (National Confederation of Free Workers). Backed by the CIA-funded AIFLD (American Institute for Free Labor Development—see Overview), the CONATRAL had earned workers' ill will by its failure to support the democratic pro-Bosch revolution of 1965. From 1962 to 1969 the AIFLD had poured $1.6 million into the Dominican Republic, more than in any country except Brazil. But workers did not trust AIFLD-trained leaders. The Christian Democrats, who supported the pro-Bosch 1965 revolution, developed muscle in organized labor. They were the dominant element among sugar workers, who composed much of the 70,000-strong CASC (Autonomous Confederation of Christian Unions).

Labor unions represented less than 12 percent of the work force. Strikes still were illegal or barely tolerated, and labor organizing remained a function of political parties. Besides the CGT and the CASC, the PRD had put together the UGTD (General Union of Dominican Workers), claiming 35,000 members, many at La Romana. The only politically independent worker group was the tenant farmers' and small peasants' MCI (Independent Peasant movement), which claimed 75,000 members.

The theology of liberation was making its weight felt. While the Church hierarchy still maintained its close ties to the ruling elites, local priests had started up Christian base communities in Santo Domingo's poorest slums as early as 1970. These had spread to the countryside. On the right were various small political parties, most of which cooperated with each other and, off-and-on, with Balaguer's PRSC.

Political sociologist Emelio Betances noted that Dominican politics was rhetorically populist but in reality highly personalist and elitist, since little was ever done for the masses. While each party drew support from different economic groups in the ruling class—for example Bosch's PLD was close with Cibao valley elites—no single party could consolidate clear-cut hegemonic support from all the elites combined. Moreover, the elites were influential in every party. Jan Knippers Black, among other political scientists, noted that Dominican politics remained a "family affair." In light of increased narcotics trafficking, the worst economic crisis in half a century, the swift and large-scale arrival of U.S. troops in neighboring Haiti, and the Dominican people's growing discontent with poverty, corruption, and fraudulent "democratic" elections, the nation's future remained grim.

Selected Bibliography

Betances, Emelio. *State and Society in the Dominican Republic*. Boulder, CO: Westview, 1994. Pathbreaking analysis.

Black, Jan Knippers. *The Dominican Republic: Politics and Development in an Unsovereign State*. Boston, MA: Allen & Unwin, 1986. Well-researched account, rich with interviews.

Bosch, Juan. *The Unfinished Experiment: Democracy in the Dominican Republic*. New York: Praeger, 1965. Former president's analysis of his own downfall.

Gleijeses, Piero. *The Dominican Crisis*. Baltimore, MD: Johns Hopkins University Press, 1978.

Grasmuck, Sherri, and Patricia R. Pessar. *Between Two Islands*. Berkeley: University of California Press, 1991. Covers the exodus to the United States.

Herman, Edward S., and Frank Brodhead. *Demonstration Elections: U.S.-Staged Elections in the Dominican Republic, Vietnam, and El Salvador*. Boston, MA: South End Press, 1984. Critical look at U.S. foreign policy.

Logan, Rayford W. *Haiti and the Dominican Republic*. New York: Oxford University Press, 1968. Well-researched history by scholar of black history.

Martin, John Bartlow. *Overtaken by Events: The Dominican Crisis from the Fall of Trujillo to the Civil War*. New York: Doubleday, 1966. Anti-Bosch account by President Johnson's special envoy.

Moreño, José A. *Barrio in Arms: Revolution in Santo Domingo*. Pittsburgh, PA: University of Pittsburgh Press, 1970. Well-researched firsthand account of 1965 revolution.

NACLA Report on the Americas. "Smoldering Conflict: Dominican Republic 1965–1975" (April 1975) and "The Dominican Republic, A Study of Constraints" (Nov.-Dec. 1982). Excellent examinations of economic constraints on a pseudo-democracy.

Vedovato, Claudio. *Politics, Foreign Trade and Economic Development: A Study of the Dominican Republic*. New York: St. Martin, 1986.

Wiarda, Howard J., and Michael J. Kryzanek. *The Dominican Republic: Caribbean Crucible*. Boulder, CO: Westview, 1982.

Deputy police lead Nationalist Party leader Pedro Albizu Campos (second from right) from his home in San Juan, Puerto Rico, in an island-wide roundup touched off by the Puerto Rican revolt and the attempt on the life of President Truman in 1950.

Armed troops attempt to keep back jeering mobs at Caracas Airport, Venezuela, upon Vice-President Richard Nixon's arrival in 1958.

Cuban Premier Fidel Castro (center left) listens to Major Ernesto "Che" Guevara (center right) while reviewing a peasant militia parade at San Julian Air Base, a former U.S. Air Force installation, in 1960.

Violeta Chamorro campaigning for the presidency of Nicaragua in 1989.

The wealthy elite in Chile includes new entrepreneurs. The man seated at the table built his explosives company into Chile's largest privately owned arms manufacturer, with exports in weapons worth more than $100 million.

American troops on patrol in Panama in 1989 the morning after the U.S. invasion.

Cuban refugees (raft people) departing from Cojimar Beach, east of Havana, in 1994.

A march of the Brazilian landless arrives
in the city of Porto Alegre in 1991.

Women Zapatistas
in the state of Chiapas,
Mexico, 1994, training
for military action.

Political campaign art
being painted on the
walls of Quito, Ecuador,
in 1984.

In 1987, El Salvador protestors confront government troops during a funeral march for slain human rights activist Herbert Anaya.

Mothers of missing children protest in Buenos Aires, Argentina. The "lost" ones are the victims of state-sponsored terror, as acknowledged by several military officers in 1995.

Military interrogation of a Mayan woman in the Quiche province of Guatemala.

Peruvian soldiers with displaced Indians in the war against leftist Shining Path guerrillas in the early 1990s.

Mexican workers in a U.S. owned maquiladora in Ciudad Juárez, across the border from El Paso, Texas.

The industrial complex of Cubatão City, the most polluted area of Brazil.

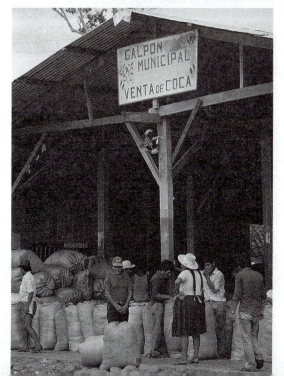

A coca market in the Chapare Valley, Bolivia.

Urbanization takes on a multi-national look in Asunción, Paraguay.

Slums on the outskirts of the city of Tegucigalpa, Honduras.

Public housing in Bogotá, Colombia.

Part Three
South America

Caracas

VENEZUELA

GUYANA

Georgetown
Paramaribo
Cayenne

Bogotá

GUYANE

COLOMBIA

SURINAME

Quito

ECUADOR

Amazon River

PERU

BRAZIL

Lima

Brasilia

La Paz

BOLIVIA

PARAGUAY

Asunción

CHILE

PACIFIC
OCEAN

ARGENTINA

Santiago

Buenos
Aires

URUGUAY

Montevideo

ATLANTIC
OCEAN

N

Falkland Islands/Islas Malvinas

0   800 Km
0   500 Mi.

South America

South America, the world's fourth largest continent, is marked by its immense diversities: earth's largest rain forest (Amazon Basin), colossal mountain ranges (Andes), vast deserts (Atacama), frigid fiords (Tierra del Fuego near the Antarctic Circle), remnants of great Indian civilizations (Inca), cosmopolitan cities (Buenos Aires, Rio de Janeiro), modern industrial hubs (Caracas, Santiago, São Paulo), and a multitude of peoples, languages, products, and cultures. Many of its nations are—although scarred by the malnutrition and health problems typical of "less developed countries"—veritable industrial giants if compared to the countries of Central America or the Caribbean.

Simón Bolívar, the self-proclaimed "liberator" of South America from Spanish rule, dreamed of a united Latin America (see chapters 7, 11, and 12). But geography and history made that impossible. South America's strong regional diversity, even *within* nations (see chapters 12 through 14, 18, and 20), was assured by extensive river systems, extremes of climate, and gigantic mountain ranges (three in Colombia alone)—as well as the desire of Great Britain and other world powers to "divide and rule" the continent.

Regionalism remains a hallmark of South America, accentuated by the rich mixture of peoples who settled there. Some nations are notable for their Euro-Caucasian populace (Argentina, Uruguay), while others are still heavily populated by Indians (Bolivia, Peru). Mixed-blood "mestizos" compose more than half of the populations of Venezuela and Colombia. The lush fertile plains of Argentina and Uruguay produced not only grain and cattle but also a unique rural *gaucho* (cowboy) culture—a kind of nationalist symbol in the face of waves of new European immigrants arriving in the late nineteenth and early twentieth centuries (see chapters 18 and 19).

Italian immigrants settled much of Argentina, Uruguay, and southern Brazil. English investors and settlers introduced soccer there and left their names and influence throughout the "southern cone" of South America. Brazil, noted for its alleged "genocide" against Indians of the Amazon Basin, incorporated all the races, including Asians; cultural and religious contributions of Brazil's black minority affected the entire society (see chapter 20).

Along the northern coast, including Venezuela and Colombia, South America's diversity is enriched by a significant Caribbean influence. Three of the nations on the northeastern coast—Guyana, Guyane, and Suriname—recently gained their independence from Britain, France, and the Netherlands (respectively) and are examined in the Introduction to Part Two as political extensions of the Caribbean.

Since differences are more marked than commonalities in South America's history and culture, generalizing can be a hazardous pastime. Yet some features do appear to be common to the area's history (see Overview), particularly the traditions of centralized colonial authority and postcolonial economic dependence, regional bossism (*caudillismo*), personal leadership with exaggerated influence (*personalismo*), patriarchical male chauvinism (*machismo*), urbanization, "new politics," and military rule or control over the affairs of state versus "civilismo"—civilian resistance to military rule.

The continent's military praetorianism goes back at least as far as its Wars of Independence against Spain and Portugal, after which military heroes and nationalist myths received lasting embellishment (Bolívar, Sucre, O'Higgins, San Martín, Artigas). As Part Three's chapters reveal, military careers offered aspiring individuals a chance to gain power, wealth, or influence. Some of the twentieth-century's populist leaders like Argentina's Perón, Bolivia's Torres, Brazil's Vargas, Ecuador's Rodríguez Lara, or Peru's Velasco emerged from the ranks of the military (see chapters 13 through 15, 18, and 20). Also coming from military backgrounds were several bloodthirsty tyrants, their names held in disrespect today.

Although most writings on South America emphasize the roles of powerful individuals and military-civilian conflicts, there exist also traditions of mass movements for social justice and commitment to lofty humanist and communitarian ideals. South America's world-renowned art, literature, and film usually deal in one way or another with social tensions generated by gross inequalities of wealth and opportunity. Writers, journalists, artists, and film-makers traditionally have been targets of state repression and yet agents of social change. In the words of Jeane Franco, an English authority on Latin American culture, to "declare oneself an artist in Latin America has frequently involved conflict . . . [but] has kept alive the vision of a more just and humane form of society."

State Terror, Democratic Dawn

For as long as two decades most of South America epitomized Latin America's "long, dark night of state terror" (see Overview). In the 1960s and 1970s the heads of the armed services and national police forces seized the reigns of government to silence what they viewed as dangerous revolutionary voices tolerated or spawned by democratic institutions. They feared the spreading influences of the 1959 Cuban Revolution and the internationalist example of Argentine-born guerrilla fighter Ernesto "Ché" Guevara (see chapters 8, 15, and 18). The Latin American public's clamor for reform or revolution penetrated the militaries themselves, leading to the sudden emergence of reformist and populist officers and junior officers who were killed or silenced during the long, dark night of right-wing military authoritarianism (see chapters 13 through 15, 17, 20).

South America's military dictatorships "disappeared," tortured, and waged "dirty war" against the local citizenry in the name of "saving Christian Civilization" from the evils of "communism" (and even "Zionism" in countries like Argentina where anti-Semitism was severe—see chapter 18). Implementing what they called the "doctrine of national security," South America's modernized military and police forces eliminated all democratic institutions, murdered tens of thousands of opponents, and forced into exile millions of their own compatriots. Many were tortured and killed under the doctrine of "preventive repression" (eliminating one's opponents before they have a chance to resist—see chapter 16). In the 1960s and early 1970s this doctrine was implemented throughout the southern cone and was publicly revealed at a meeting of U.S. and Latin American officers of the Inter-American Defense Board in 1972, a time when the last lights of South American democracy were being snuffed out. But preventive repression could not prevent new candles of freedom from being lit in the back rooms of urban apartments, slum shacks, and rural huts.

Brazil was the first country to experience the long, dark night. Masterminds of its 1964 coup and subsequent campaign of torture and intimidation spread their repressive know-how to fellow officers who launched coups in other South American lands. (Brazil also spread its economic muscle, taking over the economy of eastern Paraguay and becoming one of the world's fore-most producers and sellers of military armaments—see chapters 16 and 20.) Brazil's initial leadership of South America's militarization became a shared one, as each dictatorship assisted the other in rounding up political exiles and often killing them in their adopted countries. In the 1970s, first Chile under de-mocratically elected Socialist president Allende and then Argentina under re-turned populist hero Perón became havens for political refugees, who nonetheless suffered sudden disappearance or death when both countries expe-rienced coups more intolerant than Brazil's of 1964. Chile's state terror reached as far as Rome, Italy, and Washington, D.C. (see chapter 17).

Although the military dictatorships were substantially autonomous, members of U.S. military missions and police aid programs also participated in the international coordination of repression, particularly in high-tech intelli-gence work, as well as in the training of special counterinsurgency forces and even torturers (see chapters 14 through 20). In December 1992 raids on police offices in Paraguay uncovered what became known as the "Horror Files." Ac-cording to the *Miami Herald,* the files offered "the first substantial public doc-umentation of the systematic 'dirty war' against suspected leftists by South American police and military—and the U.S. role in that endeavor." The U.S. AID (Agency for International Development) immediately promised a grant to help process and index the files, leading one former torture victim to charge that the United States was "cleansing" the files. U.S. encouragement of tortur-ers and endorsement of the "preventive repression" doctrine was, however, by then well known, even if not completely documented. While the final respon-sibility for the crimes committed against people's human rights rested with South America's military and police forces (and those civilian doctors, judges, bishops, and others who cooperated—see chapters 18, 19, and 20), the U.S. role of complicity by commission and omission came in for worldwide cen-sure.

Several U.S. human rights activists and politicians condemned the use of the AID for training South American torturers. This led to Congress' ending AID's police training program in 1974, although President Reagan sought its renewal (see Overview and Introduction to Part One). The active role of U.S. government officials and military personnel in South America's rash of mili-tary coups from Brazil's of 1964 to Chile's of 1973 raised many eyebrows (see chapters 17 and 20). Apparently, even Argentina's dirty war was known about and approved by top authorities such as Henry Kissinger (see chapter 18).

President Jimmy Carter attempted to address the problem through public emphasis on "human rights." This produced little initial change in Latin Amer-ica, although it did cause some of the dictatorships to distance themselves from Washington and to give hope to prodemocracy civilian forces (see chap-ters 2, 17, and 18).

Economically, the military regimes welcomed foreign-based TNCs (transnational corporations) and made possible a relative "denationalizaiton" of home industry. Brazil's high command built what one scholar called a "tripod" of state, private, and foreign capital that accelerated industrialization at low-wage levels and expanded the industrial working class. Later illegal strikes by Brazilian workers in heavy industry sparked other strikes and demonstrations by millions of people that caused the military to hand the reigns of government back to civilians in 1985 (see chapter 20).

South America's national security states broke the momentum of common markets like the Andean Pact that would have limited foreign economic control (see Overview and chapters 13, 14, and 17). U.S. direct private investments in South America expanded greatly during the 1960s and first half of the 1970s. The military dictatorships crushed free-trade unionism and sometimes imposed economic austerity programs even more antilabor than those recommended by the IMF (International Monetary Fund—see Overview). The generals and admirals went on borrowing sprees that made them wealthy and left their nations hopelessly indebted to foreign bankers. Military rule seemed, for awhile at least, "good for business."

For nearly two decades the military regimes' maintenance of "law and order" guaranteed high returns on investments and contributed to spurts of economic growth. In the long run, however, declining living standards of South America's peasants, workers, and all but the top layers of the middle classes contributed to economic sluggishness followed by severe depression in the 1980s. Private investments in productive areas of the economy other than mining or agriculture increasingly went into offshore production platforms— low-wage, capital-intensive assembly plants for export—similar to the models of Taiwan, San Juan, Mexico's _maquiladoras,_ and San Salvador (see chapters 1, 3, and 9).

Growing amounts of both South American investment capital and foreign investments shifted from industrial to speculative activities, such as real estate, stock markets, and drug trafficking. Monies generated by the production, processing, and sale of cocaine created a new kind of "monoculture" (see Overview), matching or surpassing the traditional products of tin, copper, coffee, and sugar as the principal source of income for much of the region (Bolivia, Peru, Colombia). Billions of dollars "flew" to untraceable bank accounts in Switzerland, Panama, or the Caribbean.

In the early 1980s, facing economic hard times and foreign debt difficulties, most of South America experienced a near-halt to new direct foreign investments. By then the net result of long-term military dictatorship was the partial "deindustrialization" of several countries, rampant corruption, and public scorn for the officer corps and their wealthy friends.

Venezuela's entrenched but challenged two-party democracy was the only exception to this dark picture in South America (yet corruption, drug trafficking, economic slowdown, and attempted military coups eventually became problems there as well—see chapter 11). Colombia, because of its civilian government, was sometimes alleged to be an exception. However, Colombians lived under decades of an almost uninterrupted "state of siege" and then faced what became known as a dirty war by their own military against guerrilla and political opposition figures (see chapter 12).

In the midst of South America's authoritarian gloom there appeared the first rays of a possible democratic dawn lit not by outside agitators, Communists, or Zionists, but by housewives' committees, urban youth and slumdwellers, parish priests and nuns, shopfloor labor groups, "illegal" strikers, students, office workers, and former political prisoners and exiles. Leaders of previously conflicting political parties or ideologies organized "broad fronts" (*frentes amplias*) calling for a "democratic transition." In short, South America became a cauldron of Latin America's new politics (see Overview).

The long, dark night crushed South America's revolutionary Left, but apparently not for good. Theologians of liberation and Marxists made common cause, often supported by "moderates" who themselves had been politically silenced. The jackboots of military repression left deep footprints filled by intense citizen interest in "democratization." At the same time, poverty worsened and people became either accustomed to state-sponsored violence or exhausted from it. Most South Americans wanted peace, improved living standards, and a democratic voice in their governments.

Even conservative business leaders, no longer pleased by what the military had wrought, spoke of "the need for democracy." During the 1980s the generals, unable to handle either the rising political protest or the collapse of the national economies, launched a strategic retreat. They handed power back to the civilians, after first assuring their own "amnesties" (guarantees against prosecution for their infamous records of human rights violations discussed in Part Three's chapters).

South America's new democratic governments of the mid-1980s had to deal with herculean problems: ballooned foreign debts, high rates of inflation, stagnant economies, mass unemployment, aroused workers and peasants, disgruntled middle classes, irate relatives of the tortured and murdered crying out for justice—and well-armed militaries protective of their amnesties ready to resume power at a moment's notice. Argentina alone suffered two attempted military coups in less than a year during 1987–88 (see chapter 18).

One way the new civilian governments sought to assert both their limited power and their legitimacy was to express a more independent foreign policy. Argentina, Brazil, Peru, and Uruguay were the first to form a Latin American "support group" for the Central America peace-making efforts of "Contadora" and what became the Arias Peace Plan (see Introduction to Part

One). Brazil's President José Sarney asked fellow Latin American presidents in late 1987 to endorse Cuba's return to the OAS (Organization of American States). Argentina, Colombia, Mexico, Panama, Peru, Uruguay, and Venezuela agreed.

This same "Group of Eight" called for the world's "rich countries" to make concessions to the "poor countries" on the debt question. The main international problem was not East-West (or Communist-capitalist) in their eyes, but North-South. As Argentine President Raúl Alfonsín put it, "We cannot accept that the South pay for the disequilibrium of the North." Much of South America was expanding its relations with Western Europe, Japan, and in many instances the Soviet Union (e.g., Argentina, Brazil, and Peru—see chapters 14, 18, and 20). The general view was that this added to the region's ability to negotiate its dependence on the United States and to diversify its economic lifelines. The subsequent collapse of the Soviet Union dampened that possibility.

Brazil and Peru both experimented with sharp challenges to the IMF and World Bank on the debt question, but by 1988 they were, in the words of the London-based _Latin American Weekly Report,_ "returning to the fold" of IMF economic orthodoxy. In fact, by the early 1990s both countries were implementing economic shock treatments stronger than anything the military dictatorships had dared. For their part, foreign creditors wrote off small portions of South American's unpayable debts and used the rest to gain equity in industry, banking, and services (so-called "debt for equity swaps"). As the purchasing power of the minimum wage continued to decline in the 1990s, protest movements of "the new politics" again surfaced, this time against the fashionable economic doctrine of "neo-liberalism" (see Overview). Uruguay's electorate overwhelmingly threw out the neo-Liberals' "privatization" program in a 1992 referendum, and Venezuelans voted out their two-party system a year later.

South America's "democratic dawn" of the 1980s appeared to be fragile, complex, and tense. Conditions of political instability and sudden changes were widely forecast for the rest of the twentieth century and on into the next. People were wondering if the continent's early rays of democratic hope could break through and dissipate the storm clouds of persistent unemployment, a debt burden that could not be met, and the military's historically proven propensity to meddle.

Policy Debates

Policy debates on South America focused on subjects similar to those affecting most of the rest of Latin America. Some of the main topics were economic development, neo-liberalism, free trade pacts, democratization, human rights and amnesty, drug trafficking, corruption, and the role of the United States.

Most of the economic policy debates inside South America revolved around the pros and cons of neo-liberalism and privatization. The early 1990s' influx of foreign capital, much of it European and Japanese as well as U.S. (see Conclusion), and the collapse of the Soviet model of socialism (Stalinism) left the advocates of either a "mixed economy" or a democratic socialism in a weakened position (see Overview). The only countries where they were strong in an organized and only mildly repressed way were Brazil and Uruguay. On the other hand, any middle ground of modified privatization or use of the state to guide economic development in a way beneficial to the majority of citizens raised the specters of a tightened debt "noose," disinvestment by big bankers and industrialists, and a military coup. Public disgust in South America with the economic suffering caused by privatization was clearly evidenced by a sudden resurgence in mass protest movements and food riots; growing numbers of middle class people packing their bags to leave; or, various forms of military interventions, including the "self-coup" by a civilian president in Peru (see chapter 14).

Another economic debate revolved around future free trade. South America's economies were vulnerable to being left behind by the more industrialized countries who dominated world trade through the GATT (General Agreement on Tariffs and Trade). Weaker economies inside South America could not compete with more robust ones like Chile's or Argentina's. The creation of NAFTA (see chapter 1 and Conclusion) lent momentum to the idea of a hemispheric common market championed by U.S. business interests and their "junior partners" in South America. Chile, which led South America in knocking down its tariffs worldwide, signed a free-trade framework agreement with the United States. Chile and Mexico agreed to phase out bilateral tariffs by 1996, and both countries joined the Asia Pacific Economic Cooperation Forum (APEC). Chile went on to court economic integration with Argentina as an opening to benefits from the newly formed MERCOSUR (Southern Cone Common Market, founded in 1991 by Argentina, Brazil, Uruguay, and Paraguay). MERCOSUR members aimed to knock down tariff barriers by 1995 or 1996. The four MERCOSUR nations also planned to construct a billion-dollar seaway to make the Paraná-Paraná River system navigable and provide Bolivia with an Atlantic outlet (see chapters 15, 16, and 20).

The Andean countries liberalized trade among themselves through the resurrected Andean Pact. However, Peru withdrew temporarily in 1992 when its exports to Colombia fell by 30 percent. Pact members Venezuela and Colombia signed trade agreements with the English-speaking Caribbean countries and with Mexico (see chapters 11, 12, and Introduction to Part Two). Bolivia belonged to the Andean Pact but also sought participation in MERCOSUR.

All the free trade measures stimulated the return of domestic and foreign private capital investment and in some cases economic growth. But few of the benefits trickled down to the masses, and environmental protection codes, where present, were rarely enforced. Moreover, transnational corporations based abroad still held key competitive advantages through their domination of technological know-how, patents, and "intellectual property rights"—a bone of contention in both trade negotiations and discussions about the environment (see chapter 20 for Earth Summit 1992, Conclusion, and especially Documents).

Much of South America, like Mexico, offered economic bonanzas for investors in mining, agriculture, manufacturing "export platforms," and banking, insurance, and tourism services. But there remained the manifest need for South Americans to invest more in R&D (research and development) to create their own technological base for sustained economic development. Moreover, the celebration of "free trade" masked two darker realities: growing trade wars both globally and within regional common markets, and increased distribution of income upwards, leaving an expanded bottom tier of humanity in desperate straits. The real question was "free trade for whom?" (see Conclusion).

Lurking behind the economic debates were some hard political dilemmas, for if democratic reforms did not deepen and take hold—and there was scant evidence of any lasting success in the 1980s and early 1990s—then the old political choice of popular revolution versus military repression might reassert itself. The political "center" would move to the Right, as was already happening in several countries, or to the Left—or else disappear the way it did in the 1960s and 1970s. As in the rest of Latin America, South America's "democratic transition" might abort, be stamped out, or be pushed to a more truly democratic phase (see Overview and chapter 20). The underlying dynamic of "reform versus revolution versus state-terror national security regimes" still asserted itself.

Nowhere was this more clearly shown than in the ongoing use of military force by civilian governments to crush dissent. Human rights violations in some parts of South America were reaching new extremes, including ethnocide (see chapters 16 and 20). Central to even a limited democracy's chances for survival, then, was not only the state of the economy but the state of human rights.

Yet the civilians' return to power had been conditioned on their not prosecuting human rights cases from the past (or, alternatively, their allowing military courts to handle them). This was called "amnesty." The mass movements of the new politics that made necessary the return to democracy were not about to stop in their tracks and look the other way while some of their members recognized the faces or voices of their torturers on the streets or in the shops. The cry for justice could not be silenced by a mere shifting of personnel in a nation's presidential palace and congress.

Or major concern for human rights activists was the continuation of "Operation Condor," a state-terror plan developed jointly by the heads of military intelligence of Chile, Argentina, Paraguay, Uruguay, and Brazil in the mid-1970s to assist in the detention or assassination of dissidents wherever they went into exile. Condor's ongoing efficacy became clear when its operatives smuggled a fugitive Chilean chemist-terrorist first out of Chile to Uruguay (1991) and then to Brazil (1993). The chemist had been implicated in the development of a spray can method for torturing prisoners with the Nazi nerve gas "Sarin" and was also wanted for questioning about the 1976 Washington, D.C., car bombing assassination of former Chilean diplomat Orlando Letelier (see chapter 17). Uruguay's civilian president was unable to punish the head of military intelligence responsible for the fugitive's escape.

The amnesty issue went far beyond South America, since in Central America, Haiti, the Philippines, and other parts of the world similar demands were being heard from victims of torture and murder. The "Nuremberg principle" (of individual responsibility for crimes committed even at the order of others, originally applied to Nazi war criminals involved in the genocide against the Jews) had become an accepted and mandatory part of contemporary international law governing violators of human rights. If South America's human rights violators went unpunished, then what would this mean for other parts of the world and for international law? Not surprisingly, the best-selling nonfiction books in Argentina and Brazil in the 1980s were both (independently) titled, *Never Again.*

In a broad public mailing campaign, the newly formed international Coalition of Non-Governmental Organizations Concerned with Impunity for Violators of Human Rights issued an appeal in 1988 that highlighted the issue of the Nuremberg principle. It emphasized the official position of the respected international human rights organization Amnesty International that "essential guarantees for the future protection of human rights are that the truth about the occurrence of such events in the past be made public, that those responsible for such violations are brought to justice and that government undertakes all necessary measures so that it is firmly established . . . such abuses will not be tolerated in any circumstances."

Most observers concurred that the success of South America's democratic transition depended on a fair and lasting resolution of the amnesty issue. The concern of citizens was evidenced in Uruguay where more than 600,000 registered voters signed a petition calling for a democratic vote on the amnesty question. The resultant referendum that narrowly defeated the anti-amnesty forces reflected people's real fears that stripping away amnesty might bring back a "long dark night" of military terror (see chapter 19). Even in the one country where a few top state-terror generals were tried for torture and mass murder, convicted, and jailed—Argentina—a new civilian president pardoned them in 1990 (see chapter 18).

Other focuses of the democratization debate included how much tolerance should be extended to South America's tattered but surviving Left and how greatly the state should intervene to improve the living standards of the majority. In a sense, of course, these were economic debates that were transferred to the political arena. Often their results were being predetermined by the outcomes of other discussions concerning how the new democracies should be structured institutionally: constitutions, stronger or weaker executives and congresses, autonomy or civilian control for the military, maintenance or elimination of secret intelligence networks, and so on. Most guerrillas from the 1960s had returned to the electoral arena, where some were enjoying moderate success (see chapters 11 and 12). Chile's old Left and Center had largely regrouped to hold off the still strong Right and maintain a Christian Democrat in the presidency (see chapter 17). The burgeoning "new Left" of the new politics faced an uphill battle but was chalking up occasionally impressive electoral victories (see chapters 11, 19, and 20).

Drug trafficking was a critical issue throughout South America, especially in those countries where "drug czars" had established themselves as key political actors (see chapters 12, 14, and 15).Drug cartels often cultivated close relations with those military officers most responsible for Latin America's long, dark night. In one nation the phrase "cocaine coup" was introduced to describe the connection (see chapter 15). The power of drug traffickers, even when challenged by periodic arrests of "raids," showed no signs of real decline; quite the contrary. By the mid-1990s, drug-related corruption had penetrated every government of South America, adding to political discontent.

The role of the United States related to all of these policy debates. Indeed, the drug issue itself moved to the center of the stage of U.S.-Latin American relations in the late 1980s and early 1990s (see Overview, Introductions to Parts One and Two, and Conclusion).

Not only were politicians of both the Republican and Democratic parties clamoring for a crackdown on Latin America, the so-called source of the U.S. drug problem, but also U.S. troops were being sent into action, especially in Bolivia, Peru, and Colombia. Several observers noted that the U.S. troop presence was aimed against guerrilla movements like Peru's "Shining Path" or against the advance of the new politics mass movements. This was the conclusion of the U.S. House Government Operations Committee in December 1990. The Bush administration's mid-1991 whitewash of Peru's ongoing military and police violations of the human rights of noncombatant civilians lent credence to this perspective. U.S.military personnel again were helping their

South American counterparts conduct international operations, such as the joint Ecuadorian-Colombian army border patrols.

Like Mexicans (see chapter 1), many South Americans believed the real source of the drug problem was U.S. consumption of narcotics and U.S. sending abroad precursor chemicals and weapons. They feared the spread of drug consumption into the ranks of their youth. They also wondered about the growing evidence of CIA and U.S. government and banking officials' complicity in drug trafficking revealed during the "Iran-contragate," "Iraq-gate," and BCCI scandals (see Introduction to Part One and Conclusion). In late 1993 U.S. officials noted that three years earlier a CIA anti-drug program in Venezuela "accidentally"' allowed the shipping of a ton of cocaine to the United States.

Also in 1993 a report by the UN International Narcotics Control Board confirmed that Latin American drug addiction was on the rise and that the "war on drugs" was failing. Narco-traffickers had spread their activities to other countries, the report noted—a reality revealed in almost every chapter of this book. The governments of Peru and Bolivia, as well as top authorities in the new Clinton administration, admitted that the U.S. sponsored military strategy for combatting drug producers and traffickers was not working (see chapters 14 and 15 and Conclusion). In Colombia the Cali drug cartel had long since superceded the more publicized Medellín cartel (see chapter 12). Millions of peasants in the Andean countries, where cocaine was often a nation's leading export, depended on coca crops for their livelihood.

The movement to center stage of "corruption" as a political issue always involved charges of governmental complicity with the drug trade. Most of the corruption involved officials' embezzlement of state funds and/or collaboration with business groups through kickbacks, influence peddling, and the like. While the shocking corruption charges often had a basis in reality, they also represented a political acting out of the crisis of the state where no single social class or economic group could assert clear-cut hegemony (see especially chapter 20). The impeachments of Venezuela's and Brazil's presidents in 1992–93 reflected this state crisis, as well as the influence of popular mass mobilizations against neo-Liberal economic policies.

The role of all U.S. civilian and military programs was being reexamined in Washington. The CIA-backed AIFLD (American Institute for Free Labor Development—see Overview) was still very active in South America. But in some countries it had lost respect (such as Brazil after 1964 and Chile after 1973 where it had helped prepare the conditions for the coups that ended democracy). Moreover, many members of the AFL-CIO were questioning the AIFLD's earlier practices. Although U.S. trade unions were dwindling in strength in the 1980s, the U.S. public's anti-interventionist movement gained much of its momentum from organized labor's active role (see Overview, Introductions to Parts One and Two, and Documents). So did the political fight against NAFTA that almost succeeded in blocking its passage in Congress (see Conclusion).

This complicated the U.S. foreign policy debate. Presidents Reagan and Bush, most Republicans, and several Democrats, including President Clinton at times, backed a "quiet diplomacy" and a strong military presence not just in Haiti and off Cuba's coasts but in or near South America as well. On the other hand, several Democrats and Republicans advocated a more vocal and genuine human rights policy and greater aid for South American's nascent democracies. In the absence of radical changes in U.S. policy, critics argued, democracy might well suffer "crib death" or "infanticide." New policy alternatives were being debated by powerful coalitions inside both parties and the nonintervention movement (see Conclusion).

Selected Bibliography

See also Selected Bibliography for Overview, Introduction to Part One, and Conclusion.

Baily, Samuel L. *The United States and the Development of South America, 1945–1975*. New York: New Viewpoints, 1976.

Drake, Paul W. *The Money Doctor in the Andes: the Kemmerer Missions, 1923–1933*. Durham, NC: Duke University Press, 1989. U.S. economic advisory missions remarkably like later ones (e.g., Chile's "Chicago Boys"—see chapter 17).

Freemantle, Brian. *The Fix*. New York: Tom Doherty Associates, 1985. On region's drug czars.

Galeano, Eduardo. *Days and Nights of Love and War*. New York: Monthly Review Press, 1983. Short prize-winning memoir of exiled Uruguayan journalist on night of the generals—"not knowing when someone you love will be picked up or killed."

Kelly, Philip, and Jack Child (eds.). *Geopolitics of the Southern Cone and Antartica*. Boulder, CO: Lynne Rienner, 1988.

Herman, Edward S. *The Real Terror Network*. Boston, MA: South End Press, 1982. On U.S.-backed state terrorism, by professor at University of Pennsylvania Wharton School of Business.

Lindquist, Sven. *Land and Power in South America*. New York: Penguin, 1979. On land/power nexus, reform problems.

Linz, Juan J., and Alfred Stepan (eds.). *The Breakdown of Democratic Regimes: Latin America*. Baltimore, MD: Johns Hopkins University Press, 1978.

North Americans Congress on Latin America (Nacla). "Carter and the Generals: Human Rights in the Southern Cone," *Nacla Report on the Americas*, 13(2)(March/April 1979).

O'Brien, Philip, and Paul Cammack (eds.). *Generals in Retreat: The Crisis of Military Rule in Latin America*. Manchester, England: Manchester University Press, 1985.

O'Donnell, Guillermo, et al. *Transitions from Authoritarian Rule*. Baltimore, MD: Johns Hopkins University Press, 1986.

"State and Military in Latin America." *Latin American Perspectives*, 12(4)(Fall 1985). Focuses on South America.

Steward, Julian H., and Louis C. Faron. *Native Peoples of South America*. New York: McGraw-Hill, 1959. Based on data in *Handbook of South American Indians*.

Weschler, Lawrence. *A Miracle, a Universe: Settling Accounts with Torturers*. New York: Pantheon, 1990.

Films

Araucanians of Ruca Choroy. 1974. 50 minutes. Color film by Argentine Jorge Preloran introducing past 100 years of Indian life.

The Missions. Feature color film on eighteenth-century Indians, Jesuits, plantation owners, slaverunners, Spanish-Portuguese rivalry.

CARIBBEAN
SEA

Grenada

Trinidad and
Tobago

Maracaibo •

Valencia •

⊛ Caracas

Lake
Maracaibo

• Mérida

VENEZUELA

• Ciudad
Bolívar

Ciudad
Guyana

Rio Orinoco

GUYANA

COLOMBIA

BRAZIL

N

0   200 Mi.

0   300 Km.

Venezuela _____ **11**

In Venezuela there exists the tyranny of the landlord, industrial, merchant *class*—in one word, capitalism.—*Rómulo Betancourt, 1932*

If I weren't an official and if I were younger, I would be in the streets too, to tell [U.S. Vice President] Nixon what we all think of U.S. complicity with Pérez Jiménez [recently deposed Venezuelan dictator residing in Miami].—*President Wolfgang Larrazabal, 1958*

It was a pleasantly warm day that June 14 of 1961. Evening showers had cleared some of the smog generated by Avenida Sucre's clogged traffic. A limousine drove onto the campus of Caracas's Central University. Students chased it, chanting "Return Pérez Jiménez!" and "Cuba, Sí! Yanqui, No!" Out of the car stepped a balding dark-skinned man with a pockmarked face who was distinguished by a white moustache and a typical Caribbean guayabera shirt. He glanced up at the bright sun and removed his eyeglasses to wipe his forehead with a handkerchief. He didn't look North American, but he was in fact the newly appointed American Ambassador to Venezuela, a Puerto Rican named Teodoro Moscoso.

As he entered a nearby building the ambassador was grabbed and shoved. Detained for three hours, he later returned to his limousine to find it a smoking, ashened hulk. The students had burned it.

This time it was only an ambassador. Three years earlier it had been a vice-president—Richard Nixon—whose car demonstrators had pelted with stones to protest the 1954 U.S.-conducted coup in Guatemala (see chapter 2) and President Eisenhower's awarding Venezuelan dictator Marcos Pérez

Jiménez the Legion of Merit. Pérez Jiménez had fled to Miami after a popular revolution overthrew him in January 1958, and for three years Venezuelans had been demanding his return for public trial. In 1958 the students had been unable to do more than smash three of Nixon's car windows with rocks. Now, three years later, they broke into the ambassador's car and snatched a ticking political time bomb: a briefcase stashed with top-secret documents.

Some weeks later at the ceremonies inaugurating the Alliance for Progress in Punta del Este, Uruguay, stunned delegates from every Latin American nation listened as Cuban Minister of Industries Ernesto "Ché" Guevara read from the documents the Venezuelan students had found in the briefcase:

> So long as this [Venezuelan] administration is characterized by stupidity, indifference, inefficiency, formalism, party interests, corruption, duplicity and ill will, it will be practically impossible to make efficient and dynamic the development projects . . . not only is it unfair to ask the American middle class to pick up the tab while the Venezuelan oligarchy and the *nouveau riche* do not pay their share, but it is equally unrealistic to think that a modern industrial society could be built here on the basis of a medieval system of economic privileges.

The memo from which Guevara read was addressed to Ambassador Moscoso and had been prepared by two American Embassy staffers, Irving Tragen and Robert Cox. Its authenticity was never questioned. It stated that if the United States did not want to support a complete overhaul of Venezuela's "medieval system," then "it would be preferable to buy time, preserving as much as possible and as long as possible the actual status quo." Another embassy document from the briefcase asserted that "If the reformers do not hurry, they will soon see themselves deprived of popular support and cornered in an impossible situation between the extreme Right and Left." The implication was clear: short of overhauling Venezuela's existing system, or at least speeding the reform process, the best alternative was to back the status quo for as long as possible and, in effect, side with the Right.

In the aftermath of the defeated invasion of Cuba at the "Bay of Pigs," President John F. Kennedy had assigned Moscoso to Latin America's wealthiest nation to prove his "sensitivity" to Latino nationalism at home and abroad. Moscoso had been the director of Puerto Rico's "Operation Bootstrap" (see chapter 9), a program that became the model for the Alliance for Progress. In the eyes of many Venezuelan students, however, Puerto Rico was a colony, Moscoso a "turncoat," and the Alliance for Progress a figleaf for "Yankee imperialism." They viewed the material in the stolen documents as representative of typical U.S. double-dealing.

Some saw them as "proof" that Venezuela's reformer-president, Ró-mulo Betancourt, elected in the nation's second free election, would eventually be overthrown the way the nation's only other freely elected president, novelist Rómulo Gallegos, had been in 1948 or Arbenz of Guatemala had been in 1954. Others claimed that the documents proved the United States would back gradual tokenistic reform to block revolution. As one of the documents stated, "there will be a race between those who try to set those reforms by evolution and those who try to stir up the people in favor of a fundamental economic and social revolution."

Reform or revolution? That, as President Kennedy had said (see Overview), was the burning issue in all Latin America in 1961. In South America the country with the longest history of dictatorship—Venezuela—was to be a major testing ground for reform.

Spain's and Bolívar's Legacy: *Caudillos* and Dictators

Until the second half of the eighteenth century, when the "Bourbon reforms" liberalized trade (see chapters 1 and 14) and Venezuela's deep-water harbors attracted ships in record numbers, Venezuela was a colonial backwater. Discovered by Columbus in 1498, it had been named "Little Venice" by Alonso de Ojeda to describe the Indian huts built on stilts over the water of South America's largest lake, Lake Maracaibo.

Initially the colonial economy was founded on livestock and petty trade. Then, early in the seventeenth century, Spain transferred the cacao monopoly from Mexico to Venezuela and the era of "King Chocolate" began. Venezuela's Indians, who had lost many of their people in pitched battles against the conquering Spaniards, had been even more thoroughly reduced by smallpox and other diseases imported from Europe. Venezuela's landed oligarchy of cattle barons and cacao plantation owners, known locally as "Gran Cacao," brought in African slaves as their main labor supply.

The colony's land-based merchants, many of them dominating the thriving city of Caracas, sold cacao to Mexico's mining elites and to Spain. The oligarchy used harsh measures to assure labor discipline, sometimes burying disobedient workers to their waist. Many landlords, merchants, and labor foremen also used their positions of power to take advantage of the wives and daughters of the slaves, giving rise to the black-white racial mixture known as "pardo." Venezuela today is about two-thirds mestizo (counting the pardos), 20 percent white, 10 percent black, and 2 percent Indian. Some 200,000 Indians, speaking various dialects, inhabit the eastern Orinoco Basin and southern states of Amazonas and Bolívar; blacks are concentrated on the Caribbean coast.

The War for Independence against Spain in the 1810s was in large part a race war, reflecting long, simmering tensions between masters and slaves. Blacks rose up in the west as early as 1795, causing oligarchs there to side with the pro-Spain royalists. By 1810 pardo cacao producers and artisans, who also suffered racial discrimination, were challenging the colony's light-skinned landed and mercantile elites, known as "Creoles" because of their having been born in America and not Spain. Some of the upwardly mobile pardos had become professionals and traders.

The self-proclaimed liberator Simón Bolívar (1783–1830), a Creole, spoke with disdain of Venezuela's "pardocracy." In his famous 1815 "Letter from Jamaica" he displayed a typical Creole fear of rebellious pardos by asserting that "We [Creoles] have been deprived of an active tyranny, since we have not been permitted [by Spain] to exercise its functions."

Besides Bolívar and countless unsung lower-class heroes, Venezuela contributed more than its share of big names to Latin America's struggle for liberation from Spanish colonialism. They included the pamphleteer "Precursor" Francisco de Miranda, who scoured Europe for funds and arms; the brilliant military tactician José Antonio Páez, a former royalist from the *llanos* (central and eastern plains); Antonio José de Sucre, the liberator of Ecuador; and Andrés Bello, the great literary figure. But no one could hold a candle to Bolívar, whom Venezuelans then and later championed as a national hero without earthly parallel.

Under the strong leadership of Bolívar and Páez, Venezuela's Creole elites won the War of Independence in 1821 and set up the century-long dominance of landlords, merchants, and moneylenders that was not to be weakened until the advent of "oil prosperity." Bolívar's dream of a unified Latin America (see Introduction to Part Three) soon became a nightmare of civil war. When he died in 1830 his multination merger of Venezuela, Colombia, and Ecuador, created in 1822, fell apart. Venezuela, which the liberator had called "a barracks," became a republic.

Rule in Venezuela was by strength of arms. The capital of Caracas changed hands frequently, as warring regional caudillos—strong figures on horseback usually from the *llanos* or the Andes Mountains—fought mightily to become another Bolívar. These lesser imitations of the real thing rose and fell as swiftly as new constitutions could be drafted (more than in any other Latin American country). The "Age of Caudillos" institutionalized Venezuela's "Bolivarian culture," as it became known, of individualism, "macho" heroism, and strong government.

Meanwhile, as early as the 1850s, foreign powers, including the United States, sent their warships to the coast of Venezuela to support the financial claims of their citizens who were engaged in the cacao trade (and later, gold and coffee). Britain grabbed much of eastern Venezuela. In 1899 an international tribunal awarded Britain 90 percent of its claims. The land, still disputed, is over half of today's independent Guyana.

In Venezuela the squabbles of anticlerical Liberals and pro-church Conservatives were dwarfed by the battle among caudillos for control over first the cacao trade and then, after 1873, the lucrative coffee production of the fertile Andean foothills south of Lake Valencia. Some caudillos formed Liberal–Conservative "fronts" to consolidate their power—an early precedent for the many "pacts" between Venezuela's dominant political parties in recent decades.

The Roman Catholic Church became very weak after the dictator Antonio Guzmán Blanco (1870–1888) dissolved the preceding Liberal–Conservative front, expelled the bishops, and shut down seminaries. Today, despite the fact that 96 percent of the people call themselves Catholic, Venezuela is said to be Latin America's least Catholic country—less than 10 percent attend mass. Up to a quarter million of Venezuela's population of 20 million practice the María Lionza devotion, a mixture of African voodoo, Catholic ritual, and Indian nature worship.

In 1899, the frequent civil wars between caudillos became a thing of the past. The self-styled "Lion of the Andes," Cipriano Castro, recruited a private army in neighboring Colombia and seized Caracas. His victory initiated forty-five years of fairly stable rule by military figures from the Andean chain of mountains running from the central part of the western border to lower elevations around Caracas.

Castro soon faced economic and diplomatic troubles. A nosedive in international coffee prices caused Venezuela to default on its loans, many of which had been taken out by Guzmán Blanco in his efforts to modernize Venezuela the way Porfirio Díaz had done in Mexico (see chapter 1). In 1902–1903 German, Italian, and British naval units blockaded Venezuelan ports to demand settlement of debts. Amicable terms of payment were arranged, but not before Argentina's Foreign Minister Luis M. Drago issued his famous "Drago Doctrine" against foreign intervention for the collection of debts (see Overview and chapter 18).

Castro's stubborn nationalism irritated President Theodore Roosevelt, whose famous 1904 corollary to the Monroe Doctrine stated that the United States had the "duty" to intervene to safeguard the investments and standards of "civilized society." Castro viewed himself as not only "civilized," but also "the Moses of the Republic." He severed diplomatic relations with the "colossus of the north" twice. He also jailed, murdered, or deported his critics and stashed untold sums of money in his private accounts in New York and London banks.

By 1908, Castro's health was failing him. He handed the government over to an aide, Juan Vicente Gómez, and sailed for Europe for medical care.

Since many in Castro's clique did not trust Gómez, Venezuela swiftly collapsed into renewed civil war. Before his departure Castro had again broken relations with the United States. Gómez quietly asked for U.S. aid, which arrived in the form of two battleships and some diplomats. Relations were promptly restored, and Gómez paid out millions of dollars in compensation to foreigners. Many concluded Gómez was a "U.S. puppet."

Puppet or not, Gómez earned the nickname of "El Brujo," or wizard, by governing the country with an iron will as his private fiefdom. He used many techniques to terrify potential critics, including mass killings. He retained as his advisers three executives of foreign oil companies who had supported him in the showdown with Castro loyalists. On sales of Venezuela's newly discovered oil deposits, he settled for a one-eighth "*regalía*," or fraction of the well-head price of crude. That was enough to pay off the country's foreign debt. By 1940, the *regalía* was still under 20 percent.

King Oil: Bourgeoisie, Middle Classes, and Labor, 1922–1958

The twentieth-century rise of the Andean caudillos coincided with oil's supplanting of coffee as Venezuela's major export. Large-scale oil production started in 1922, and by the 1950s, when production doubled to over a billion barrels a year, Venezuela ranked third after the United States and the Soviet Union.

"King oil" converted Venezuela from a predominantly rural economic backwater where cattle outnumbered people to an urban semi-industrialized society. Eighty percent rural in 1920, Venezuela is 80 percent urban today. Creole (Standard Oil of New Jersey, a main source of Rockefeller wealth), Shell, and Gulf dominated the enclave economy. Texaco and Mobil also participated. The oil giants took billions of dollars out of the country, leaving much of a rapidly growing populace penniless. Rockefeller-funded anti-malaria campaigns and other health measures reduced the death rate, while one of Latin America's highest birthrates (over 3 percent) increased the number of Venezuelans from 2 million in 1920 to 20 million today.

Oil meant political changes. The nation's Andean-based mercantile capitalists generally cooperated with the foreign oil firms in order to increase their own wealth. They grew in strength not as an independent national bourgeoisie, but as a comprador bourgeoisie. Using their new-found riches, they were soon able to challenge the agricultural oligarchy for political power.

Oil also meant huge federal budgets, construction of new schools, office buildings, and roads, and a vastly expanded cash economy. This contributed to the development of the middle classes and organized labor as political forces. They first flexed their political muscles in 1928.

The oil workers rebelled against the abominable conditions of their labor camps around Lake Maracaibo. Their one-room shacks, stained black with oil, stood in stark contrast to the huge white houses of the foreign community in its fenced-off, heavily policed "safe area." A quarter of the petroleum work force was foreign-born: some were skilled U.S. workers but most were low-paid West Indians who spoke English. Language and other divisions among workers made them difficult to organize. Nonetheless, the first group of unions, the Syndicalist Labor Federation of Venezuela, emerged in oil in 1928. Repressed by dictator Gómez, it mushroomed after his death in 1935.

The year 1928 also marked the birth of the student movement. The government arrested students attempting to politicize a university festival. Spontaneous worker and student demonstrations and an aborted general strike resulted in the momentary release from jail of the students, most of whom then went into exile. The year 1928 was a political "baptism of fire" for later presidents like Rómulo Betancourt (1959–1963) and Raúl Leoni (1963–1968) and would-be presidents like Jóvito Villalba of the URD (Democratic Republican Union). Over the next sixty years the "spirit of '28" was invoked by radicals and moderates alike.

In 1931 a dozen of 1928's exiles, including Betancourt, issued the "Plan de Barranquilla," calling for a social revolution. Although as president Betancourt would disavow his Communist past, in his exile days he joined the Third International and was closely associated with Costa Rica's Communist party.

When Gómez, the "Tyrant of the Andes," died in 1935, Venezuelans broke the imposed silence and sought radical changes. All hell broke loose in the oil fields around Lake Maracaibo, where workers struck for wage hikes, improved work conditions, equal access to skilled positions, and more Venezuelan control of the industry. Nationalist slogans whipped them into a fury, and Shell Oil saw fit to evacuate the wives and children of its management personnel from its Lagunillas complex to a nearby tanker. Meanwhile 25,000 marched on the presidential palace in Caracas, and peasants in the interior rose up in revolt.

Military and political power was still concentrated among the Andean officers. Gómez's successors, General Eleazar López Contreras (1936–1941) and General Isaias Medina Angarita (1941–1945), were, like Gómez, from the western state of Táchira. They dealt with the eruption of public protests by means of concessions, yet using repression.

For the first time civic and political organizations were allowed to function publicly, although not on a regular basis. Betancourt's group formed the Marxist-oriented ORVE (Venezuelan Organization, 1941 renamed Democratic Action, AD). The Communists founded the PRP (Progressive Republican party). The popularity of these two groups frightened the López Contreras government, which packed some of the Communists off to concentration camps and forced both groups underground. The Communists and Betancourt's ORVE then combined to form a popular front known as the PDN (National Democratic party), or the "single party of the Left." But their unity was short-lived. In 1937 Betancourt's minority forces "expelled' the Communists, who renamed themselves the PCV (Venezuelan Communist party). In 1941 the Medina government and the Communists worked out a tacit agreement of mutual support, and the PCV and Betancourt's AD received legal status.

The emergent bourgeoisie and middle classes sought to use this unprecedented "democratic opening" to create a stronger, more centralized state and a more professional military by means of which they could transfer political power from the agricultural oligarchy to themselves. Workers and peasants sought to use it to demand long overdue economic and social revindications. Nationalism was the one banner around which most Venezuelans could rally. The post-Gómez governments talked about "sowing the oil" or diversifying and industrializing the economy.

In 1943, with popular sentiment rising against the oil companies, Medina's government issued a radical petroleum law that would remain unmatched for years to come. The law raised the *regalía* to a percent of the wellhead price that, from 1943 through 1945, averaged about half of the oil industry's actual declared profits. More significantly, the 1943 law allowed the government to tax the companies' profits directly. The companies could live with the new law because it helped stabilize the political situation without expropriating their wealth. Indeed, it renewed their lucrative concessions and excused them of past underpayments and frauds.

During the 1940s, AD contested the military for the backing of the bourgeoisie and fought the Communists' PCV for control of labor. AD had four distinct advantages: (1) it did not suffer extreme red-baiting; (2) it was considered less radical than the Communists by the country's "Fuerzas Vivas" (economic elites); (3) it made a big push to organize the peasants; and, most important, (4) it edged out the Communists in grappling for the banner of nationalism. The PCV, as part of its all-out effort to support the United States and the Soviet Union against the Nazi aggression of World War II, had restrained oil-workers' wage demands and discouraged strikes. AD, on the other hand, mobilized the oil workers behind the slogan of "Venezuela First."

The turning point came at the 1944 National Workers Congress. Although it had a majority of delegates, the PCV was accused of breaking an agreement with the Medina government to keep delegates' party affiliations secret. The government decreed the dissolution of PCV-controlled unions, and AD moved into the labor leadership vacuum.

Venezuelans were not tolerant of a return to government by decree and by force of arms. AD had a growing base in organized labor, a presence in the peasantry, a strong student branch, and a number of powerful friends among the Fuerzas Vivas. With this leverage, it was able to win over disgruntled young army officers fed up with the forty-five-year-long "Táchira dynasty." Together they organized a coup d'état that toppled the Medina government in 1945. One of the officers behind the coup was Captain Marcos Pérez Jiménez, who eventually emerged as the ruthless dictator of the 1950s.

AD's Betancourt headed up the new civilian-military junta until the nation's first free elections in 1947, when AD's Gallegos was elected president by a four to one margin. AD used the "trienio"—as the 1945–1948 period of AD rule became known—to some advantage. It set up political cells in cities and towns. It employed state patronage and police power to dislodge further the Communists from the labor movement. Later, in the 1960s and 1970s, AD labor leaders split with Betancourt and founded left-wing parties.

During the trienio AD introduced the controversial 50/50 petroleum law, a less radical measure than Medina's 1943 law. Under the AD law the government would tax the oil companies enough to guarantee Venezuela's receiving half of the industry's profits. Unlike the 1943 law, however, which set *no* limits, the AD law would *limit* Venezuela's share to 50 percent. As revealed by the 1958 interim government of Admiral Wolfgang Larrazabal, Betancourt reached a secret agreement with the oil companies *before* the 50/50 law was implemented. The companies trumpeted the new arrangement's virtues when dealing with some of the more nationalist regimes in the Middle East.

AD touted the 50/50 law as "nationalist." It pointed to the clause prohibiting *more* concessions for the oil companies. Actually, the clause helped the larger companies consolidate their monopolistic position since they *aleady* had huge concessions. It was during the trienio and the later Betancourt presidency of 1959–1963 that Betancourt and Nelson Rockefeller built their famous friendship. The biggest U.S. oil firm in Venezuela was the Rockefellers' Creole.

President Gallegos' world-acclaimed novel *Doña Bárbara* (1929) had portrayed a powerful female caudillo from the *llanos*—but Gallegos lacked her power during his ten months in office. The AD trienio had upset many powerful generals, landowners, and businesspeople who feared the party's populist rhetoric of nationalism and reform. A military coup in 1948 toppled Gallegos, banned the AD, and sent most democrats packing for exile. Prior to the coup, labor-union militants called for strikes and arms to defend the democratic government. Betancourt and other moderates restrained them. Gallegos claimed at first that the oil companies and American Embassy had orchestrated the coup. Later, he retracted the charge.

A three-man military junta governed until 1952. It eliminated civil liberties, crushed sporadic revolts, and incarcerated labor leaders. Because the Tenth Pan American Conference was scheduled for Caracas, the United States pressured the junta to hold elections in 1952. The outlawed AD instructed its cells to bring out the vote for the Christian Democrats' COPEI (Independent Electoral Political Organizing Committee) in conservative rural areas and for the URD (Democratic Republican Union) in the cities. The URD had been organized in 1946 as a moderate party of professionals and businesspeople, led by Villalba. When initial returns showed the URD and COPEI outvoting the government by two to one, Pérez Jiménez seized power and announced he had won the election hands-down.

Pérez Jiménez's "New National Ideal" was almost as savage in its dictatorial methods as Gómez's "Democratic Caesarism" had been. Opponents were sent to a jungle concentration camp, prison torture became widespread, and the Central University was closed. The head of the Gestapo-like national security forces, Pedro Estrada, was a notorious sadist. Pérez Jiménez and his coterie of friends established a private resort on a Caribbean island to which prostitutes from Havana, Cuba, were flown. Oil revenues built skyscrapers and superhighways for the wealthy and public housing projects for some of the urban poor.

The 1950–1957 period was known as the "oil boom." Oil production more than doubled, and foreign investments rolled. U.S. investors' capital returns amounted to at least 25 percent of book value, and profits were remitted tax-free. About one-third of all U.S. investments in Latin America and half the profits on them were in Venezuela. Creole's 1957 declared profits approached a 50 percent rate. The country attracted a million European immigrants, mostly from Spain and Italy, who added to one of Latin America's most racially mixed populations. Consumerism ran rampant. A popular saying based on seemingly endless oil reserves was "God is a Venezuelan."

People flocked to the cities. Urbanization during the next few decades undermined traditional rural values of family solidarity. More than half of new births were illegitimate, two-thirds of all children were raised without fathers, a million were abandoned. By 1990, half of the population was under eighteen years of age.

An economic recession shook Venezuela in 1957. The United States restricted oil imports, and "capital flight" worsened. After years of corrupt military rule the democratizing forces of the mid-1940s resurfaced. People clamored for jobs, free speech, and nationalization of oil. Youthful protesters took to the streets and clashed with army troops. Pérez Jiménez became the target of popular wrath, and nothing short of his removal from office and trial for criminal acts would satisfy the public outcry.

Popular movements against dictators and overbearing foreign interests were shaking Venezuela's regional neighbors as well—Colombia, Peru, Brazil, Guyana, Cuba, Panama, and so on. In 1957 President Eisenhower named Roy Rubottom to take over as Assistant Secretary of State for Inter-American Affairs. In his confirmation hearings Rubottom told the U.S. Congress, "A policy contrary to the interest of an oil company is automatically contrary to the interest of the U.S.government." He then issued an ultimatum to Venezuela's opposition to keep the Communists out of their movement.

The main opposition parties AD, URD, and COPEI (in order of size) proceeded to sign the so-called Punto Fijo unity pact. It ruled the Communists' PCV outside the system and laid the roots of a two-party system (AD and COPEI). In December 1957 the numbers of street protesters escalated, and officers in the navy and air force declared their opposition to the dictatorship. In January 1958, after some priests were arrested, the Church added its voice to the popular call for democracy.

Even big business' Fuerzas Vivas backed the movement. Venezuela's bourgeoisie was miffed at the dictatorship's "betrayal" of their support of an alliance with foreign corporations in opposition to new taxes. Pérez Jiménez had increased Venezuelans' taxes but worked out a separate and less burdensome arrangement with the foreign oil companies.

The opposition called a general strike in January 1958. Estrada's "Gestapo" responded by killing three hundred students. Pérez Jiménez stuffed his bags with funds from the treasury and, on January 23, took refuge in Miami, Florida. A military-civilian junta took power. Incensed by the Americans' giving Pérez Jiménez refuge, the opposition demanded his extradition and trial. Vice-President Nixon was stoned by angry mobs a few months later.

Interim President Admiral Wolfgang Larrazabal sympathized with the public's outrage. He hiked the government's share of oil profits to 60 percent (the "60/40 formula") and set up the nation's second free elections in December 1958. Backed up by the URD and the Left, Larrazabal won more than 80 percent of the vote in the capital city of Caracas. But AD's strong cell system elsewhere gave the nation's nod to Betancourt with 49 percent of the total vote.

Betancourt took office at a time when oil production was booming but an immense gap yawned between the upper classes and the rest of the working population. Oil workers, who accounted for less than 3 percent of the nation's work force, earned up to $3,000 per year. Peasant wage rates ranged from $10 to $100 a year. More than 80 percent of peasants with access to land hacked away on *conucos* (as "slash-and-burn" woodland patches were known). People's expectations ran high for radical changes to close the gap between the rich and the poor and to introduce basic social justice.

In early January of 1959 Fidel Castro's guerrillas marched into Havana (see chapter 8). Castro was immediately invited to Caracas where, according to government officials and press reports, he received "the greatest reception in the nation's history." His fiery oratory fueled Venezuelans' rising expectations.

Reform versus Revolution

During his January 1959 visit to Caracas, the tall, bearded, cigar-puffing Castro gave the short, chunky, pipe-smoking Betancourt a typical Latin "abrazo." Both men were popular heroes, and over the next few years all Latin America watched as they slipped into a kind of personal rivalry. "Pipa sí, chiva no" (Pipe yes, beard no) slogans began to appear on Caracas walls. So did pro-Castro slogans. Betancourt championed gradual reform, Castro immediate revolution. The United States rushed to support Betancourt and to isolate Castro.

A shrewd politician from a rural middle-class family, Betancourt had worked his way through the Central University, schooled himself in Marxism, and then turned to the Right. He believed in political democracy but felt that economic changes would have to come gradually. "We had always rejected the possibility of nationalizing oil," he stated in 1956.

President Betancourt announced there would be no new concessions to foreign oil companies. The United States responded in March 1959 with new ceilings on oil imports. Next month Venezuela organized a secret conference with Iran, the UAR (United Arab Republic), and Kuwait that set the groundwork for what in 1960 became the Organization of Petroleum Exporting Countries (OPEC). Venezuela and Ecuador became Latin America's only two OPEC members.

As Venezuela's anti–Pérez Jiménez coalition began to disintegrate, Betancourt backed the U.S. effort to isolate Castro from the inter-American system. He broke relations with Cuba in November 1961, charging Cuba with interference in Venezuela's internal affairs. A series of leftist-supported riots had threatened his government that month. Discoveries of Cuban arms shipments were reported. Betancourt was a major force behind the expulsion of Cuba from the OAS (Organization of American States) in 1962 and the OAS-declared economic blockade of the island in mid-1964 (by a fifteen to four vote).

In 1960–1961 the nation's economy suffered another recession, worse than the one of 1957. Popular unrest spread. Most of Venezuela's powerful student movement turned against Betancourt, as did the Left-oriented AD labor leaders from the trienio days and numerous slumdwellers. Demonstrations of the unemployed and street fighting became a monthly occurrence. A kind of "civil war" raged. In November 1960, students at Central University's Industrial Technical School set up barricades, renamed the school "Stalingrad," and returned the fire of federal troops. The violence spread to other college campuses and to high schools. Some 300 students were gunned down in frequent pitched battles. Casualties mounted.

Many of the Venezuelan dissidents admired Fidel Castro and called themselves "Fidelistas." They saw the go-fast approach of the Cuban Revolution as producing deeper, more genuine changes on behalf of the people than the go-slow approach of the Bolivian and Mexican revolutions. They viewed Betancourt as not moving even as fast as the Bolivians or Mexicans had done. They objected to his not cleansing the armed forces of collaborators from the dictatorship, the way Castro had done in Cuba. They viewed Betancourt as caving in to U.S. pressures and as a "traitor" to AD's original goals and to true Latin American nationalism.

The Betancourt government responded by jailing congressmen, suspending opposition newspapers, and unleashing armed AD "goon squads" against dissident student, labor, and peasant groups. It sent troops to quell disturbances in the nation's universities, high schools, and urban slums. During the November 1961 disturbances women in the high-rise "superblocks" of the "23 de Enero" and "El Silencio" neighborhoods of Caracas dumped buckets of boiling water on surprised soldiers. Shortly after that some firebrand leftist students from the upper classes treked to the mountains to launch a guerrilla war against Betancourt and AD.

The government stepped up its repression. It threw thousands into jail. It routinely violated "university autonomy," a much cherished Latin American tradition dating from the Argentines' 1918 University Reform of Córdoba (see chapter 18) and the Venezuelan student "generation of '28." Civil liberties guarantees of the 1961 Constitution were repeatedly "suspended." Troops and police were ordered "to shoot to kill."

In May and June 1962, two leftist-tinged military coup attempts failed in one of Latin America's first signs of the new politics developing *inside* the military (see chapters 7, and 13 through 15). Betancourt banned the two major leftist opposition parties, the PCV and the MIR (Movement of the Revolutionary Left, an AD splitoff). These parties and a few officers and soldiers from the aborted coup attempts openly added their muscle to the guerrilla struggle as the only option left them.

In June 1962 a saddened upper-class father wrote Betancourt's minister of justice, a personal friend, a letter reprinted by the conservative daily *La Esfera* complaining of the government's torture of his son, a leftist: "the goal of defeating Communism is not attained by applying to Communists, contrary to Christian ethics, inhuman methods of violence which make us equal to beasts. . . . With the fall of Pérez Jiménez, we came to think that the nightmare of prison tortures had ended once and for all. But our affliction has not ended."

Defenders of the government did not excuse such excesses. They portrayed the government's policies as a righteous struggle for democracy's survival against both the Left and Right. In this spirit the "Betancourt Doctrine," discarded by subsequent presidents, meant that Venezuela would not recognize Latin American dictatorships of any stripe, including governments established by military coup. Betancourt's own administration was plagued by five attempted right-wing coups in 1961 alone. In June 1960 Betancourt had narrowly escaped an assassination attempt widely attributed to Dominican dictator Trujillo. Venezuela's 1961 Constitution outlawed military coups or armed revolution.

In 1963 AD candidate Raúl Leoni was elected president, and the nation experienced its first "democratic succession." Venezuelans were still demanding the return of Pérez Jiménez for trial. Many Americans had learned about the case and also felt it only fair that he confront Venezuelan justice. On August 12, 1963, the United States extradited the ex-dictator. After a three-day delay caused by a paternity suit against him, Pérez Jiménez was flown to Venezuela where he underwent detention in a four-room apartment in a model prison and a lengthy trial. In 1967, he was found guilty of embezzling $13 million in public funds. Nonetheless, the ex-dictator still had followers among some of the urban poor who remembered his public housing projects and helped elect him to the Senate in 1968. He was barred from taking his Senate seat and gradually faded from the political scene, a "powerless" millionaire.

That same year a divided AD turned the government over to COPEI, whose candidate lawyer-sociologist Rafael Caldera garnered 29.9 percent of the presidential vote. AD candidate Gonzalo Barrios polled 28.2 percent, whereas former AD leader Luis Beltrán Pietro of the newly formed MEP (Popular Electoral movement) drew 19.2 percent.

The successful transition to democracy and punishment of Pérez Jiménez owed much to Venezuelans' dissatisfaction with more than a century of caudillo and military praetorianism. AD's reforms, however mild, were highly appreciated by key segments of the populace. Educational and health reforms initiated by Betancourt and extended by subsequent AD and COPEI administrations provided opportunities that many people had never dreamed possible. Today illiteracy is down to 14 percent and life expectancy is sixty-seven years, even though four-fifths of the population lives in poverty.

A controversial agrarian reform distributed land to 140,000 peasant families by 1968. Half the distributed land was public property. Big commercial farms went untouched, and expropriated *latifundistas* used the government's generous compensation to buy up better lands elsewhere. Most of the reform's land parcels were so small that only a few families could survive by farming. A longtime Betancourt friend and drafter of the reform law, Congressman Ramón Quijada, bitterly observed, "My law, our law, has become a farce." He bolted AD and founded an opposition party called AD-Ars.

During the 1973–1978 presidency of AD's Carlos Andrés Pérez (the architect of OPEC) the government admitted that the agrarian reform was a failure and undertook steps to strengthen large-scale commercial farming and to create some peasant cooperatives. About 5 percent of those benefiting from the original reform were regrouped into the co-ops.

Meanwhile up to a million poorly paid Colombian migrant workers became the shame of "modern" Venezuelan agriculture. Today 3 percent of the population owns 90 percent of the land. The landed oligarchs still emphasize cattle for export. Venezuela imports more than 60 percent of its basic foodstuffs, including the traditional black beans.

U.S. aid programs helped the AD and COPEI regimes in both their social reforms and their military defense against popular protest. The Kennedy and Johnson administrations made AD the "darling" of Alliance for Progress social programs in housing and agrarian reform. They also poured police and military aid into Venezuela. U.S. AID (Agency for International Development) established a police mission to train Venezuelan police in "riot control." In 1961 a million-dollar-a-year technical assistance program for Venezuela's military was launched. The U.S. military mission in Venezuela became the largest in Latin America. In February 1964 hundreds of U.S. military advisers teamed with the Venezuelan Army in "Operation Hammer and Anvil" to route out guerrillas of the Armed Forces of National Liberation (FALN). By the end of that year 1,195 Venezuelans had graduated from the U.S. Army School of the Americas in Panama. For the 1960s U.S. military aid to Venezuela was higher than anywhere else in Latin America if calculated on a "per-soldier" basis.

U.S.-guided "counterinsurgency warfare" succeeded. Because of the agrarian reform and traditional AD strengths among the peasantry, the guerrillas' FALN lacked a large rural base. According to German political scientist Wolfgang Hein, the guerrillas also underestimated the strategic importance of the nation's oil workers and the developing alliance between the Venezuelan bourgeoisie and powerful foreign-investor groups like the Rockefellers.

In 1966 the Communists' PCV renounced guerrilla warfare, leaving the FALN isolated except for occasional support from Cuba. In March 1967, Fidel Castro called the Venezuelan Communists traitors to the revolutionary cause. The PCV labeled Castro a "Revolutionary Pope." The MIR also abandoned guerrilla tactics, and in 1969 President Caldera's COPEI government relegalized both the PCV and the MIR. Rural and urban guerrilla actions occurred once in a great while over the next two decades, but by 1975 the FALN was defeated. Its leader, Douglas Bravo, accepted an amnesty in 1979.

With the help of oil dollars and U.S. aid programs, Venezuelan reform had momentarily beaten back the challenge of Venezuelan revolution. So long as oil prices stayed high the AD and COPEI governments were able to budget social security programs, school lunch programs, public housing projects, agrarian co-ops, and the construction of clinics, hospitals, and schools. For the time being no deeper structural changes seemed urgent.

"Pactocracy," Democracy, Corporativism, and Populism

The 1957 Punto Fijo unity pact excluding the Communists was reinforced by subsequent AD–COPEI pacts in 1958, 1964, 1970, and 1973 that excluded the PCV, the MIR, and other leftist formations that had split off from the AD. The 1970 and 1973 pacts provided for AD's and COPEI's dividing up appointments to the judiciary and leadership positions in Congress. Critics called the nation's young democracy the "pactocracy," that is, democracy by the consent of those who govern rather than of the governed. Nonetheless, Venezuela joined Colombia as South America's longest lasting exception to military rule in the 1960s and 1970s. Most observers attributed the success of civilian rule to the steady flow of oil-generated federal revenues for funding modest social reform programs.

There were political reasons as well. The government's frequent crackdowns on the Left and favoring of traditional privileges for the officer corps reassured the military, the business community, and the United States that Venezuela would never become "another Cuba." Therefore, no need existed to reintroduce rule by military dictatorship. At the same time the relative strength of leftist parties and Socialist sentiment in the younger generation, as contrasted to the weakness of extreme right-wing forces after the falling from favor of Pérez Jiménez, meant that the chances of an extreme right-wing takeover were reduced.

Both AD and the Christian Democrats' COPEI, initially at least, were oriented toward social democracy and had strong Left-oriented youth contingents. The parties' older leadership, on the other hand, was populist in rhetoric and centrist-to-conservative in practice. Proportional representation allowed for a medley of smaller, mostly Left-oriented parties (see Box 11.1), but their power was limited to the congress. Since 1968 all leftist candidates combined polled a steady 12 percent (or more) of the vote. Although public opinion polls suggested Venezuelans preferred socialism to capitalism by a two to one margin, the high costs of presidential campaigns during which AD and COPEI hired Madison Avenue ad agencies from New York City minimized the chances of a leftist becoming president.

Like Mexico's PRI, both AD and COPEI were organized along corporativist lines (see chapter 1). Every sector of society had a unit inside the party—labor, peasants, students, business. When governing the two parties also operated on a corporativist basis. A political patronage system served the different corporately organized groups. A swollen government bureaucracy regularly sapped the federal budget of half its funds.

Venezuela's ruling parties engaged in unusually high degrees of corruption. But for a while their periodic acts of reform, often under the rubric of "revolutionary" populism, helped them—and Venezuelan democracy—to survive the widespread negative image their corruption gave them.

The mid-1970s witnessed a populist high point in Venezuela, as elsewhere in South America. U.S. ability to intervene was at a low point because of the Vietnam War, the 1973 OPEC oil boycott (Venezuela and Ecuador did not honor it), and the Watergate scandal. On January 1, 1975, the government expropriated (with compensation to Bethlehem Steel and U. S. Steel) the nation's extensive

---

Box 11.1: Venezuela's Main Political Parties

AD	Acción Democrática, founded in 1936, legalized in 1941, outlawed in 1948, broad-based centrist party; alternated presidency with COPEI, 1969–1994
Bolivarian Liberation Forces	Armed underground group echoing rhetoric of February 1992 coup leaders
Causa R	La Causa Radical, a left-wing party founded in late 1980s by iron and steel workers opposed to labor's corrupt leadership; claimed to have been cheated of victory in 1993 presidential election
CN	National Convergence, a predominantly left-of-center, seventeen-party coalition led by a COPEI breakaway faction and MAS that ran Caldera for president in 1993 and won
COPEI	Independent Electoral Political Organizing Committee, a centrist Christian Democratic party that alternated presidency with AD, 1969–1994
MAS	Movement toward Socialism, founded in 1971 as a Euro-Communist splitoff from PCV; ran third in 1983 and 1988 presidential races and joined CN in 1993
MEP	People's Electoral movement, founded as an AD splitoff in 1967, left-wing Social Democratic; supported NA in 1983 presidential election
MIR	Movement of the Revolutionary Left, founded as an AD splitoff in 1960, Marxist-Leninist, banned in 1962, legalized in 1969 after opting for parliamentary strategy; in 1987 merged with MAS
NA	Nueva Alternativa, founded in 1982 as electoral coalition of twelve left-wing groups; mostly regrouped into CN in 1993
NGD	New Democratic Generation, right-wing electoral group founded in 1979, led by a retired general
PCV	Communist party of Venezuela, founded in 1931, often banned, legalized in 1969; backed NA in 1983, MEP candidate in 1988
PRV	Party of the Venezuelan Revolution, founded in early 1980s by ex-FALN guerrilla commander Douglas Bravo
URD	Democratic Republican Union, founded in 1946, centrist-personalist party of Jóvito Villalba
VU	Unity Vanguard, founded in 1974 as a PCV splitoff, Marxist, supported NA in 1983 presidential election

iron ore reserves. A year later it nationalized oil, again with compensation. President Pérez (1973–1978) used populism to centralize the state and make it more bureaucratic and authoritarian. He poured money into education. He granted wage hikes to labor, but also meted out more repression against labor dissent. His many "decree laws" earned his administration the nickname "decretocracia."

In 1975 Pérez renewed diplomatic relations with Cuba and, together with Mexican President Luis Echeverría, founded the SELA (Latin American Economic System). SELA was an attempt by twenty-two Latin American nations to assert stronger leverage in negotiating the terms of trade with the "developed" world. Pérez's move toward friendship with Cuba was undercut by an anti-Castro terrorist act that embarrassed his government. A Cubana airliner exploded off the coast of Barbados, killing all seventy-three aboard (see chapter 8). One of the plotters linked to the explosion was a CIA-trained Cuban exile who had recently served as an operations chief for Venezuela's DISIP (intelligence service).

Pérez tried to "sow the oil." He poured oil revenues into expensive industrialization projects like the iron-and-steel one initiated by Betancourt in Ciudad Guayana at the mouth of the Orinoco River. His administration took out additional billions of dollars in short-term, high-interest loans backed by expected oil income that suddenly, in the 1980s, did not materialize. "Kickback" scandals rocked the final days of the Pérez government, and COPEI's Luis Herrara Campins easily won the 1978 presidential race on a populist platform of "government for the poor."

Oil Nationalization: "Figleaf Imperialism" or "Venezuela First"?

President Pérez's January 1, 1976, nationalization of oil fulfilled longstanding popular demands. The foreign oil companies were compensated at roughly the book value of their properties—$1 billion. They complained, but nevertheless accepted the nationalization. The "reference price system," established by OPEC in the late 1960s, had made it more practical for some of them to make their profits from service contracts with the state rather than through direct ownership.

The reference price system allowed the host country to determine the wellhead price *without regard to the actual market price*. The Shah's Iran and the Arab countries used this system in 1973 when they hiked oil prices fourfold. The sudden influx of oil revenues after their action allowed Pérez to carry out his populist program of reforms. Nationalization of oil meant that the oil companies no longer bore the risks of sudden changes in the reference price. Nor did they bear the risk of the exploration and extractive phases of oil production. Instead, the state took the risks. The companies meanwhile could profit from service contracts for the production and marketing of the oil. Left-wing parties and COPEI criticized the loopholes of Article 5 of the nationalization law, which allowed the state oil firm Petróleos de Venezuela (PDVSA) to share its control over oil with foreign investors in "mixed enterprises" so long as technological needs made it advisable.

Critics of the way Venezuela nationalized its oil asserted that it was an artful piece of "figleaf imperialism" perpetuating the power of foreign oil firms and a situation of Venezuelan "dependence." Defenders asserted that it was a model of international cooperation that avoided the kinds of retribution that other countries had experienced from similar acts, notably Mexico in 1938, Iran in 1953, and Cuba in 1960. They said it carried out the original AD program of "Venezuela first," while making sure that the "sowing of the oil" should not be disturbed by a sudden pullout of foreign technology and know-how. While not noticeably reducing the country's dependence, they noted, the policy at least made possible greater *future* independence.

Crisis, Elections, New Labor Militancy, Military Praetorianism

But that future independence remained a dream. When oil prices took a nose-dive at the end of the 1970s and interest rates skyrocketed, Venezuela entered an economic contraction that threatened to alter the nation's new-found democratic stability. By 1984 one-third of export revenues had to be set aside to pay the interest and service payments on the public sector's $21.2 billion share of the $36 billion foreign debt (1984). More than $20 billion in Venezuelan private capital had fled overseas since 1978. Venezuelan businesspeople holding the flight capital said they would reinvest only if the government guaranteed them full control of firms in which they invested. Unemployment rose from under 5 percent in 1977 to almost 17 percent in 1983, according to official figures. To make matters worse, the nation's third largest and most popular bank, the BTV (Venezuelan Workers Bank), went bankrupt. Its main shareholder was organized labor's CTV (Confederation of Venezuelan Workers).

The electorate responded on December 4, 1983, by voting out COPEI. Its presidential candidate was highly respected ex-president (1968–1973) Caldera, who could muster only 34.6 percent of the vote. The winner, with 56.8 percent, was former pediatrician Jaime Lusinchi of AD. The nation's third largest electoral force was the Euro-Communist PCV splitoff MAS (Movement toward Socialism). Its presidential candidate, ex-guerrilla Teodoro Petkoff, garnered 4.2 percent of the vote, compared with 3.3 percent for ex-MAS member José Vicente Rangel of the PVC-backed and URD-supported electoral coalition Nueva Alternativa. AD was still the Venezuelan representative in the SI (West Europe-dominated Socialist International), but MAS was said to be receiving funds from Germany's Friedrich Ebert Foundation, a group allied to Willy Brandt's liberal wing of Germany's Social Democrats. MAS was still a minor, under-financed party, however, plagued by internal splits and an often vague populist Socialist ideology reminiscent of the early history of AD. Moreover, leftist parties were almost precluded from gaining power by the two-party system of "partidocracia" and "carnetocracia" (respected party membership cards useful in patronage and employment). Frustrated opponents of the system attempted guerrilla uprisings that were snuffed out in Cantaura in October 1982 and in Yumare in May 1986.

When Lusinchi took office, unemployment was running at 20 to 25 percent. He headed a party that in 1981 had officially disowned its traditional socialist pretensions by announcing it was no longer a working-class party but a polyclass one committed to working "within the mold of classical capitalism." President Lusinchi vowed to correct "unhealthy tendencies of waste, squandering and illicit profiteering," but ended up running one of the nation's most corrupt administrations since Pérez Jiménez, outdone only by its successor. To bolster private capital's confidence, Lusinchi liberalized the foreign investment code and implemented IMF-style economic austerity measures. He hiked domestic fuel prices by 20 percent. He also carried out partial devaluations of the bolívar, the nation's currency, bringing its decline in dollar value to fourfold since 1981. Despite grumbling from other OPEC governments, the Lusinchi administration increased Venezuelan investments in U.S. and European refineries and oil distribution agencies in order to protect or increase Venezuela's share of the oil buyers' market. Finally, Lusinchi occasionally hiked wages or selectively froze prices. Nonetheless, most families could buy less, not more, since the wage increments were too modest to keep up with the galloping rate of inflation (80 percent by 1989).

As the 1980s drew to a close, oil still accounted for over 75 percent of the nation's exports. Recent discoveries of bauxite had catapulted aluminum to its position as second leading export. The government relied on oil for more than 80 percent of its revenues, but oil revenues were only half what they had been in the mid-1970s. Foreign investors were holding back, and industry was operating at less than 59 percent capacity. An industrial work force of 650,000 faced repeated layoffs, and the construction trades were in a long slump. Unemployment surpassed 18 percent by official figures. Food still had to be imported in huge quantities. Nearly half the nation's exports were going toward annual debt payments. Even big business' Fedecámaras (Federation of Chambers of Commerce) agreed with organized labor's CTV that the government should reduce its debt service payments. The half-century period of "sowing the oil" had done little to diversify the economy so that it might survive the day when oil reserves ran out.

AD's Carlos Andrés Pérez won the December 1988 presidential elections with 55 percent of the vote. COPEI's Eduardo Fernández garnered 40 percent, and MAS's Petkoff again finished third. As a second-time president,

Pérez oversaw a very corrupt but pro-business administration that contrasted with his earlier "populist" policies of the mid-1970s. Pérez embraced the new neo-liberal economic orthodoxy, privatizing dozens of the nation's 430 state-owned companies, holding wages down, linking Venezuela to Mexico, Colombia, and Andean and Caribbean countries through incipient free trade agreements, and encouraging foreign investment in the oil sector. His "reforms" generated a brief economic recovery in terms of high economic growth rates and a modest reduction of the principal on the debt granted by foreign creditors. But the IMF austerity package hit the masses hard.

On "Black Monday," February 17, 1989, rioting broke out in the working-class suburb of Guarenas on the eastern outskirts of Caracas and soon spread throughout the nation. People were upset with shortages of basic foodstuffs like milk and the Pérez government's surrendering to IMF pressures to hike gasoline and public transportation prices to help pay off the debt. As stores were looted and torched, the army was called in to restore order. Soldiers killed innocent people in riot zones and shot into slum shacks (*ranchos*), causing an escalation in the spontaneous revolt. Next day, the disturbances continued as worker absenteeism reached 98 percent. A priest witnessing the events called it "an explosion . . . with no leadership."

By the time the upheaval simmered down, more than a thousand lay dead. Venezuela would never be the same. The long-cultivated Venezuelan dream was exploding into a nightmare. Food riots proliferated in the early 1990s.

The first signs of serious social conflict predated the food riots during the decade-long economic contraction and upsurge of Latin America's "new politics" (see Overview). In the countryside, where only 5 percent of arable land was being used, most of it in pasture, farm workers and holders of small land parcels clashed with large- and medium-scale producers. In the Orinoco Basin, Indians stepped up their demands for an end to human rights abuses by rubber gatherers and developers (see chapter 20). In the cities youth movements from all parties rallied against the government's making more concessions to the international banking community. On February 26, 1986, police fired pellets into a peaceful COPEI youth rally against the signing of a debt-refinancing agreement, leaving five wounded.

Most startling of all, the AD's corporativist stranglehold on organized labor's CTV began to loosen before the offensive of a new rank-and-file labor militancy. Troops had to be dispatched to break up labor protests. In the words of political scientist David Blank, the military "praetorian subsystem of Venezuela's politics increased in importance."

The armed forces numbered 100,000 well-trained, well-armed men. Since 1974 Venezuela had devoted half a billion dollars a year to military expenditures. The military ran a number of state armaments industries and had its own national war college and National Security and Defense Council. Since the 1960s the military had periodically held civilians in its prisons and tried them in its courts, including many leftist congressmen during the Betancourt government and a deputy from the MEP (People's Electoral movement, founded by former AD members) during the first Pérez administration. The Organic Law of Security and Defense permitted the military to impose "exceptional means" to preserve order. The law was used to break strikes, particularly in the iron and steel industrial hub of Ciudad Guayana–Ciudad Bolívar in eastern Venezuela and the camps housing the workers constructing the Raúl Leoni-Guri Dam.

The new labor militancy that the military was being asked to control surfaced most strongly in the public sector. It was a response to the exceptionally strong role of the state in the economy (60 percent of GDP) and in labor-management relations. Ever since the nation's first labor law in 1936 the state legally had intervened in collective bargaining and the internal affairs of labor unions. Parallel unionism (more than one union in an industry or a single firm) was allowed, and the union shop (requiring union membership for employment) was banned. Trilateral commissions of government, business, and labor representatives oversaw work conditions in much of industry.

By far and away the largest labor organization was the 1.1 million-member CTV, dominated by AD. COPEI ranked second in the CTV. Its own CODESA (Confederation of Autonomous Trade Unions) was a flop. Various AD dissidents and leftists formed the CUTV (Unified Confederation of Venezuelan Workers) in the 1960s with similar dismal results. Non-CTVs trade union confederations had fewer than 200,000 members. MAS preferred to work where the power was—inside the CTV.

CTV had over a billion dollars invested in forty enterprises. These investments and CTV's top-down corporativist method of operation lubricated widespread corruption in the top ranks of labor-union leadership—and discontent in the membership.

In 1977 trade unionists who were sympathetic to the left-wing political parties PCV, MIR, MEP, and MAS won an election in the nation's largest local union, the 16,000-strong SUTISS (Steel Workers and Allied Activities Union). They declared themselves the "classist tendency" of organized labor. Two years later independents, radicals, and union militants dissatisfied with "traditional" control over labor exerted by political parties, even if by left-wing parties, swept the SUTISS elections and sparked the development of an autonomous "new unionism" movement.

Both the classist tendency and the new unionism won numerous local union elections in the late 1970s. They showed their greatest strength in textiles. Ever since the government had taken over cotton lands and garment factories from the personal friends of Gómez after the tyrant's death in 1935, the textile sector had been a stormy area of labor-management relations. The state still controlled 40 percent of it. In 1977 the Left swept union elections. Over the next few years the state and other textile employers responded by laying off three thousand workers and bringing in Colombian women to do the work at less pay. The unions struck.

In 1980 textile workers and their sympathizers occupied Caracas's main cathedral to protest the layoffs. Another textile strike was called in 1981, one that the government ruled "illegal." On September 11, workers in every branch of industry in the major industrial state of Aragua honored a general strike in solidarity with the "illegal" textile strike. The government responded by conceding many of the striking textile workers' demands. When the "classists" of the left-wing parties held out for guarantees against future layoffs, however, the strike movement split and the package of agreements came apart. The strike was defeated.

Meanwhile the labor struggle heated up in iron and steel. The boomtown industrial city of Ciudad Guayana was in turmoil from the 1970s' influx of federal investments in the state steel enterprise SIDOR (Orinoco Steel Co.) and of migrants seeking employment. The population of Ciudad Guayana passed one-quarter of a million in the early 1980s. Unemployment there rose from 5,000 in 1979 to 30,000 in 1983. In 1981 CTV "intervened" the steel workers' SUTISS to reassert moderate control over the union. CTV later admitted it accepted a payoff of nearly half a billion dollars from SIDOR to resolve the labor conflict but defended its action as "completely normal." AD goon squads violently enforced labor discipline, leading to frequent public demonstrations demanding trade-union democracy. By the late 1980s, the new labor militancy was sweeping the nation. A new voice emerged from its iron and steel ranks: Causa R (Radical Cause), a militantly left-wing political party that soon challenged the survival of the AD-COPEI two-party system.

As in Mexico, the government sought to use foreign policy to "cool out" the unrest. During the Malvinas/Falklands war of May 1982 Venezuela sided with Argentina. The state oil firm PDVSA repatriated $2 billion of its international reserves being held in British banks. That same year Venezuela refused to renew a 1970 moratorium with Guyana on their border dispute and rejected Guyana's proposal to have the World Court arbitrate the issue. Finally, as the war in Central America heated up, Venezuela joined Panama, Mexico, and Colombia to form the "Contadora" peace-seeking group. Like most Latin Americans, Venezuelans saw the axis of conflict not as "East-West" but as "North-South" (see introduction to Part One).

The biggest problems in perhaps Latin America's richest, semi-industrialized nation were widespread poverty and government corruption. Few working people enjoyed more than one full meal a day. Venezuelans showed their disgust at the polls, starting with the December 1989 state elections when voters ousted AD governors in half the nation's twenty states. Previously, governors had been appointed by the president. Since the state governments are federally funded from Caracas, the contest had mainly symbolic value. Leftists fared very well—Causa R captured Bolívar state, while MAS won in Sucre. Even though voting remained mandatory in Venezuela, more than half the electorate abstained.

An even bigger sign of trouble for AD and COPEI occurred in February 1992, when disgruntled soldiers, many of them army paratroopers, launched a bloody and nearly successful armed revolt. Ten percent of the army participated. Public opinion polls ranked the jailed nationalist-populist leader of the uprising, Lieutenant Colonel Hugo Chávez Frías, as the nation's most popular political figure. Another aborted coup attempt, joined by the air force, occurred in November. Hundreds died in the coup attempts, and thousands were arrested. A further sign of voters' independent and leftist mood occurred in Caracas's December 1992 election of a new mayor. Causa R won the contest despite running a black candidate in a predominantly mestizo nation.

Then, in May 1993, President Pérez was impeached by the Senate and removed from office to be tried on charges of embezzling and misappropriating $17 million in government funds. Venezuelans mobilized in the streets for his impeachment and then celebrated.

The year 1993 witnessed a surge in anti-establishment political protest, including fourteen hundred street marches and a strike by 270,000 public administration workers demanding wage hikes. University students and faculty launched huge marches against the government's neo-liberal economic program. The interim president felt obliged to pardon some of the participants in the 1992 coup attempts. Three financiers from the Proclass Security Business Group were arrested on charges of terrorist bombings and stock market speculating aimed at destabilizing the government. Rumors of right-wing as well as Left-populist military coup plots abounded.

Not surprisingly, the December 1993 elections spelled the end of the AD's and COPEI's thirty-five-year-old stranglehold on Venezuelan governance. While 44 percent of the electorate abstained, more than half the votes went to candidates to the left of AD and COPEI. The predominantly left-of-center CN (National Convergence) coalition of MAS, a COPEI breakaway faction, and some fifteen other much smaller groups backed the winning independent candidate, seventy-eight-year-old former president Rafael Caldera. After bolting from the badly divided COPEI he originally had helped found, Caldera had campaigned as a leftist-populist against the AD government's neo-liberal "epidemic of privatizations," price hikes, national sales tax, and other IMF-type measures. Yet, once elected, Caldera announced he would follow a policy of "austerity." Congress gave him "special powers" to deal with the economic crisis in 1994.

In a frequently altered and disputed vote count, Caldera had been awarded 30 percent of the vote, followed in the initial tally by Causa R's candidate, thirty-nine-year-old former leader of the new labor militancy Andrés Velásquez, with nearly 25 percent. Later, Velásquez was demoted by the national electoral council to a close fourth after the AD and COPEI candidates— each one ending with around 22 percent of the presidential vote. Velásquez, like Cárdenas in Mexico's 1988 elections (see chapter 1), claimed he had actually won the elections. Some people shied away from voting for Causa R because of the military's threat to seize power should Velásquez be elected. The threat was sufficiently grave for President Clinton to warn of an end to "normal relations" should a military dictatorship be established. President-elect Caldera lacked a political party of his own and faced a Congress dominated by four parties, reading from left to right: Causa R, MAS, AD, and COPEI.

But with AD support, Caldera was able to suspend constitutional guarantees in June 1994 in order to deal with a run on the banks following the collapse of the nation's second largest bank. The Caldera government poured in some $7 billion to bail out the failing banks, in effect nationalizing them. (One constitutional guarantee suspended was the protection of private property against expropriation.) This sent conflicting signals to foreign investors, who earlier had smiled upon Caldera's pledge to privatize several state enterprises, including Ciudad Bolívar's gigantic steel and aluminum Venezuelan Corporation of Guayana. Foreign and domestic capital began pulling out of Venezuela, and the gross national product dropped by an estimated 8 percent in 1994.

South American's most shining example of relative democratic stability thus faced a cloudy future. Many areas lacked sewers, and Latin America's cholera epidemic reached the country in the early 1990s. Nearly a quarter of the populace lived in Caracas, half of them in slums. Mudslides regularly killed scores of people residing in half a million *ranchos* ringing the city— hillside shacks made of old billboards and tin. Street crime, illegal gambling, and prostitution were on the rise. The nation sported Latin America's highest rate of prison deaths and prison riots. As Colombia stepped up its war against drug lords, cocaine traffickers began using Venezuela as a major transshipment point. Drug-tainted corruption in government was public knowledge. The days of middle-class prosperity were a thing of the past, and Venezuelans were beginning to doubt that "God was a Venezuelan."

Selected Bibliography

Blank, David Eugene. *Venezuela: Politics in a Petroleum Republic*. New York: Praeger, 1984.

Ellner, Steve. *Organized Labor in Venezuela, 1958–1991*. Wilmington, DE: Scholarly Resources, 1993.

Hein, Wolfgang. "Oil and the Venezuelan State." In Petter Nore and Terisa Turner (eds.), *Oil and Class Struggle*. London: Zed Press, 1980.

Hellinger, Daniel C. *Venezuela: Tarnished Democracy*. Boulder, CO: Westview, 1991. Excellent backgrounder for 1992–1993 crisis.

Liss, Sheldon B. *Diplomacy and Dependency: Venezuela, the United States, and the Americas*. Salisbury, NC: Documentary Publications, 1978.

Martz, John D., and David J. Myers (eds.). *Venezuela: The Democratic Experience*. New York: Praeger, 1986. Informative collection.

Naim, Moises. *The Politics of Venezuela's Economic Reforms*. Washington, DC: Brookings Institution, 1993. Short, up-to-date.

North American Congress on Latin America (Nacla). "Venezuela: Rethinking Capitalist Democracy." *Nacla Report on the Americas*, 27(5)(March/April 1994).

Petras, James, Morris Morely, and Steven Smith. *The Nationalization of Venezuelan Oil*. New York: Praeger, 1977.

Ray, Talton F. *The Politics of the Barrios in Venezuela*. Berkeley: University of California Press, 1969.

Wright, Winthrop R. *Café con leche: Race, Class, and National Image in Venezuela*. Austin: University of Texas Press, 1992. Explodes myth of racial harmony.

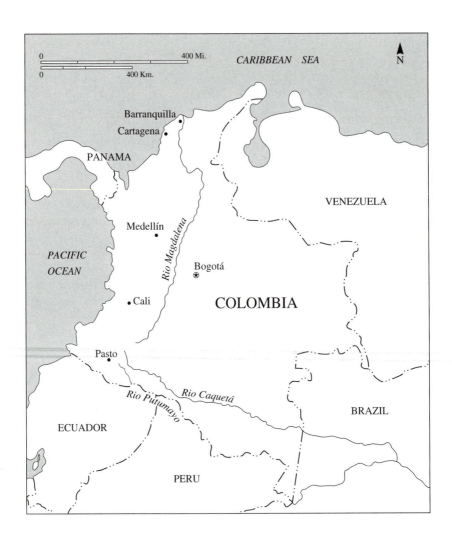

Colombia _____ 12

The "dependent republic" of Colombia will continue to obey the North Americans in order to destroy by blood and fire the "independent republics" (guerrilla-held areas) of independent Colombians. . . . I joined the Revolution out of love of my neighbor. —*Father Camilo Torres, 1965*

In Colombia, if you don't govern with the military, you won't be able to govern at all for very long.—*President Julio César Turbay Ayala, February 1982*

While the press is focused on drugs, Colombian "death squads" are getting away with murder. . . . Military and security forces . . . commit violent [human rights] abuses themselves and condone and support killings by paramilitary groups.—*Amnesty International, 1989 and 1990 reports*

November 6, 1985, was an overcast and crisp day in Bogotá, Colombia's capital, 8,600 feet high in a tilted plateau of the Andes. Office workers in the downtown area were taking their first coffee break when the news broke. Word spread instantly out past the Chapinero suburbs and to the outlying luxury homes and country clubs of the very rich.

Thousands of anxious relatives rushed to the massive four-story stone building. Troops cordoned them off from "the action." A few hundred of their loved ones were said to be still inside.

The M-19 guerrillas were demanding publication of the minutes of the cease-fire verification committee regarding the collapse of the previous year's truce between themselves and the administration of President Belisario Betancur. They wanted television time for a public trial on the government's peace policies to be conducted by the Supreme Court justices held hostage inside the building. They trusted the judges because the Court had convicted former Minister of Defense General Miguel Vega Uribe of torturing political prisoners. The guerrillas also sought the release of an alleged secret agreement reached in May between Betancur and the IMF (International Monetary Fund).

Observers began preparing for a long siege, perhaps a repeat of the M-19's two-month-long occupation of the Dominican Embassy five years earlier that had ended in a negotiated compromise.

Then, early that afternoon, armored cars mounted with 90-millimeter cannon rumbled forward and knocked down the building's tall, intricately carved wooden doors. Troops rushed in and seized the first two floors, as rebels retreated upstairs. Paratroopers seized the building's roof. Almost in unison the assembled spectators cried out: "For God's Sake, Don't Shoot, Negotiate!"

There followed twenty-four hours of anxious waiting, while politicians and prominent personalities pleaded with the president for "more time, more time." At 2:00 A.M. next morning army troops set the building on fire. Rockets, artillery, incendiary bombs, gases, and machine-gun fire raked every inch. Supreme Court President Alfonso Reyes telephoned President Betancur from inside the building, beseeching him to stop the attack. Instead, at 8:00 A.M. security forces set off twenty dynamite charges, and Reyes died in the explosion.

When the smoke cleared the national Palace of Justice lay gutted and in flames. For hours afterward stretcher-bearers brought out barely identifiable charred corpses and severed limbs. The more than one hundred dead included twelve Supreme Court justices, fifty Justice Department employees, thirty-five guerrillas, and thirty-five soldiers. Relatives of the slain judges boycotted religious ceremonies organized by the government.

Accepting responsibility for the armed forces' assault, President Betancur defended it as the only way to preserve democracy and combat terrorism. "Institutions are more important than individuals," he said. Many governments sent praise. "We endorse President Belisario Betancur's actions," announced U.S. State Department spokesman Bernard Kalb.

Colombia's on-again, off-again "peace process" seemed consumed in the ashes of its Palace of Justice. Liberal party Senator Emilio Urrea resigned from the official Peace Commission.

While Colombians were still trying to absorb the shock and magnitude of this latest of violent incidents in their long and bloodied heritage, on November 14 the centuries-dormant, 16,000-foot high Nevado de Ruíz volcano erupted in the nation's northwest coffee-producing area near Manizales. It unleashed floods and mudslides that buried the town of Armero and left at least 25,000 dead and many more homeless.

Gas emissions from the volcano had started almost a year earlier. Almost daily the town's twenty-six-year-old mayor had called state-level and federal authorities to ask for help in evacuating people while there was still time. In a country whose annual export earnings surpassed $7 billion (illegal drugs ranked first, far ahead of coffee) the mayor was informed that the

$60,000 needed to fund an evacuation could not be found. The few survivors of Armero flatly told reporters, "The government is to blame."

In the aftermath of these back-to-back tragedies, migrant-worker and middle-class Colombians by the hundreds of thousands in New York City, Caracas, and other foreign cities began collecting money and supplies to send home to the victims. In the dark of night, in the privacy of their small crowded apartments, they wondered what was becoming of their emerald nation of lush, green valleys, their beloved mix of Caribbean "cumbia" (dance with candles), highland Indian "*ruanas*" (woolen ponchos), and *llanero* (eastern plains) outdoor barbecues. Would "*la violencia*" never end?

"*La violencia*" was the household word for the violence that had wracked Colombia ever since the 1946 inauguration of a Conservative party government that had ordered thousands of killings of mostly peasant followers of the rival Liberal party. In its first decade, la violencia pitted Liberals against Conservatives in a civil war marked by decapitations, disembowelments, and the bayoneting of babies. One-quarter of a million people in a population of 10 million perished.

Over the years the violence became less party related and more socially based, pitting peasants against landlords, poor against rich. It eventually incorporated a medley of armed groups—from bandits, to guerrilla armies, to drug traffickers, to right-wing "death squads" linked to the Medellín and Cali drug cartels and to elements of the government.

Starting in the 1960s the nation's armed forces, backed by U.S. military aid programs that zipped past $111 million a year in 1990, carried out "scorched earth" sweeps of leftist guerrilla-controlled areas, killing tens of thousands of civilians. An April 1990 report of the U.S. Congress confirmed that much U.S. aid officially designated to fight "the drug war" instead focused on combatting guerrillas in non-drug producing areas. Militarized zones where the army ruled independently of civilian authorities covered one-quarter of the national territory. By the end of 1993, under the guise of combatting narco-trafficking, some 259 U.S. soldiers were active in Colombia's internal wars. From 1990 to 1993, Colombia was Latin America's largest recipient of U.S. military aid. According to almost all human rights groups, the government's armed forces, national police, and paramilitary groups accounted for about three-fourths of the political killings and disappearances that shook the nation.

Violence grew especially severe in the 1977–1993 period, as living conditions for most Colombians deteriorated and popular movements of the "new politics" (see Overview) took root. Narcotics-related corruption in the 200,000-strong military, 50,000-member national police force, and the civilian branches of government deepened. Political assassinations of leaders of the "popular movements," including their presidential candidates, became everyday occurrences. Well-armed "drug armies" murdered prominent politicians, judges, and journalists. Rival drug gangs fought one another as well. Urban office buildings were bombed, and many citizens feared for their lives.

Fueled by political violence and drug-related assault squads, including self-defense "popular militia" units in urban slums to ward off the druglords' sadistic *sicarios* (hired gunmen), the nation's already phenomenal homicide rate—four times the U.S. rate—passed 20,000 murders *a year*. Colombia sported one-quarter of a million private guards who protected the lives and properties of the wealthy. Bulletproof cars were everywhere.

The government eventually did negotiate political agreements with all but two of the major guerrilla armies in exchange for their disarming, but by the end of 1993, 10,000 guerrillas under the umbrella group Simón Bolívar National Guerrilla Coordinate were still active in the field.

In 1990, the small M-19 guerrilla army laid down its arms. Its first presidential candidate was murdered a month later. Its second won 13 percent of the presidential vote and became the new government's health minister. The disarmed M-19's political party, M-19/AD, went on to win 27 percent of the popular vote for a constituent assembly to draft the nation's new, more democratic national constitution of 1991 that formally ended the unpopular Liberal-Conservative alliance that had governed the nation for generations. The Constitution contained progressive provisions for human and social rights, including Indian rights and environmental protection. It set a framework for a more democratic politics and made unconstitutional much of the 1887 Concordat with the Vatican. But the Constitution also granted immunity from prosecution for all military and police personnel who act by "due obedience" (following orders).

In late 1992, the government implemented an "emergency state of siege" to declare a "total war" on the remaining guerrillas and the drug cartels. Colombians entered their fifth decade of living under repeated "states of siege" in Latin America's oldest and largest Spanish-speaking "democracy" that some labeled a "death-squad democracy." More citizens joined the swelling expatriate community in Venezuela (an estimated 3 million) and the United States (as many as a million).

The Colombian government's "total war" against the druglords faced three obvious obstacles. The first was the mind-boggling sum of money involved in the drug trade, a fabulous lubricant for government corruption and drug-army arms procurement. The second came from within the nation's ruling elites, known as "*la oligarquía,*" or oligarchy. Established politicians and financiers regularly negotiated powersharing with the extremely wealthy drug kingpins, with whom they rubbed shoulders in the nation's exclusive country clubs. For example, at one point Medellín drug czar Pablo Escobar, a known mass murderer, contributed to both the Liberals and the Conservatives and held an alternate seat in congress. With his millions he created public parks, brick housing, and other projects on behalf of the poor that some experts called more effective than the government's "development" projects. Escobar later cut a deal and was arrested. He was provided a luxurious "prison" from which he could continue to conduct "business." Then he escaped. Internationally embarrassed, the government finally went all out to nail him, offering multimillion dollar rewards for information leading to his capture. Escobar was finally found in December 1993, and soldiers and police gunned him down in a hail of bullets.

The third obstacle was the oldest and most stubborn: the central political and social clash in society, a Right-Left conflict pitting "narcofascists" in the upper ranks of the military, the Medellín and Cali drug cartels, and 137 death squads (by Interior Ministry count in 1987) against the ongoing threat of the popular movements' National Civic movement and the guerrillas-turned politicians, as well as the guerrillas remaining in the field (see Boxes 12.1 and 12.2).

There remained some dispute about alleged druglord-guerrilla alliances in Colombia, a charge first raised by Louis A Tambs in the 1980s when he served as American Ambassador to Colombia before opening up the "southern front" in Costa Rica for President Reagan's contras invasion against the Sandinista government of Nicaragua (see Introduction to Part One and chapters 5 and 6). Tambs, a history professor, was rabidly anti-Communist. Most of the evidence pointed against his allegation, including the guerrillas' practice of kidnapping druglord family members. But some of Colombia's leading intellectuals asserted in 1992 that the remaining guerrillas *were* receiving cartel financing. Alliances, real or otherwise, kept falling apart, as happened when some of Escobar's former henchmen claimed to have organized a terrorist hit squad of their own—the so-called "Pepes" (People Persecuted by Pablo Escobar)—to bomb Escobar properties and "rub out" his relatives and allies.

Informed observers agreed that the key "structural" causes of Colombia's violence were large-scale narcotics consumption in the United States and Western Europe and the abject living conditions and high rates of unemployment and underemployment in Colombia. By the *lowest* estimates, the top 5 percent of Colombia's population received 40 percent of the nation's total income.

In terms of amount of industrialization and gross national product Colombia ranked about fourth in Latin America after Brazil, Mexico, and Argentina. But, as a former finance minister observed, by the 1980s the country was "one step away from the point where four or five people [handled] the main controls of the economy." A handful of "financial groups" incorporating the "old wealth" of nineteenth-century miners, merchants, and coffee barons with the "new wealth" of twentieth-century financiers, industrialists, and select drug entrepreneurs ran the economy and funded the Liberal and Conservative parties. Prior to la violencia, about 350 persons—"*la oligarquía*"—accounted for 30 percent of the total personal income. Later they numbered more and received an even greater percentage.

Colombia's financial groups held overlapping investments with the government's IFI (Institute for the Support of Industry). The IFI and other state agencies made critical economic decisions, most of which favored big business, domestic and foreign. Colombia's steel and automotive industries, for instance, became "privatized" by means of the alliance between financial groups and the state.

The life-styles of Colombia's economic elites, like their income, were far removed from the middle classes of low-paid government employees, teachers, and lawyers—and light years from the universe of displaced peasants crowding the sprawling urban slums of Bogotá, Cali, Medellín, and Barranquilla. Seventy-five percent of Colombians lived in or around those four cities. One Bogotá slum area alone, greater Ciudad Bolívar, contained 1.3 million people, about 4 percent of the 1991 population of 34 million. Street people—so-called "discardables" (*desechables*)—slumped against downtown walls. A million *gamines* (orphaned children), some organized into "beggar gangs," wandered ragged and hungry on the nation's streets. Another half a million adults, according to the Central Bank, were self-employed street vendors. Three-quarters of a million were domestic servants, mostly women. A group of concerned businesspeople sponsored a study in the late 1970s that showed Colombians would have to work two hundred hours a week at the minimum wage just to cover their basic living expenses. A decade later 500,000 people—15 percent of the work force—were unemployed, and 43 percent of the populace lived in absolute poverty.

In the countryside violence was as Colombian as the corn-and-spittle home brew known as "chicha." Most peasants who were not simply laborers for owners of the big estates (*latifundistas*) growing coffee, bananas, sugar, and flowers for export remained holders of small parcels of land too small for feeding their own families (*minifundistas*). According to the World Bank, 3 percent of all landowners owned 70 percent of the arable land. One-quarter of a million peasants were landless. Advertisements for Colombian coffee shown on American television showed a happy and contented family farmer, "Juan Valdés," but in fact most family coffee farmers were tenant farmers. Often they were tenants on their own land, which they had been forced to rent or put up as collateral for credits and future purchases ultimately controlled by the coffee oligarchy's FNC (National Federation of Coffee Growers). Sharecropping on the *latifundio* was also common.

In 1982 (a presidential election year when one candidate, Betancur, campaigned on a peace platform of amnesty for the guerrillas), a bankers' association conducted a poll that showed 60 percent of those polled viewing "social inequities" as the greatest threat to peace. Only 11 percent saw subversive groups as a threat. Two-thirds thought the best way to solve the guerrilla problem was to combat unemployment and poverty. Only 5 percent favored a military solution. The proamnesty candidate, Betancur, won the election. But as the Palace of Justice shootout illustrated, his peace program failed, and the military remained the arbiter of the nation's destiny.

La violencia, poverty, politics, drug-related corruption, amnesties or special arrangements for guerrillas and druglords who turn themselves in, the power of economic elites and the military, U.S. military presence—all are interrelated issues. To understand how they reached their present constellation of crisis, it is first necessary to review Colombia's geography and history.

Background: From El Dorado to the Great Depression

Straddling the Afro-Caribbean and Indo-American worlds, Colombia was always marked by a set of separated communities having their own means of economic survival and sense of regional pride and custom. This regionalism was reinforced by three Andean mountain ranges that separated two broad valleys running south to north. To the east stretched the *llanos* (plains); to the north, the Atlantic–Caribbean coast; and to the west, the Pacific lowlands. The most densely inhabited areas were in the Andes and their valleys, home to three-fourths of today's Colombians.

The Spaniards developed the coastal city of Cartagena as a trans-Atlantic shipping point for the gold and silver they brought from the Viceroyalty of Peru. The city's encircling 60-foot-high battlement wall still stands. From the coast the *conquistadores* pushed up the Magadalena River and challenged the Andes' high peaks and the Chibcha Indians in quest of a fabled Kingdom of "El Dorado," the "Golden One." Fewer than one-fifth of the Spanish expedition—166 individuals—made it as far as Bogotá. Like the Incas before them, they found a tantalizing amount of gold, silver, emeralds, and salt and some people they could enslave, but not the abundance they found in Peru.

After the "first families" established their domination of the Indians and consolidated their ownership of *haciendas* (large estates) and mines there remained little for the next generation of Spaniards and colonists. Most of these "vecinos" (literally, neighbors) became peasants, some of whose descendants would form the twentieth-century backbone of a predominantly mestizo *minifundista* peasantry. Others became artisans.

After being militarily subdued the Indians were almost destroyed by new infectious diseases like malaria and yellow fever. Mine and *hacienda* owners imported African slaves to supplement the vanishing supply of Indian labor. Generations of miscegenation produced today's racially mixed population: an estimated 58 percent mestizo, 20 percent of unmixed European ancestry, 14 percent mulatto, 4 percent black, 3 percent zambo (mixture of Indian and black), and 1 percent Indian. Some estimates of blacks go as high as 30 percent.

Although many Colombians claimed their society was racially "integrated," elite families prided themselves on being of pure Spanish stock—*abolengo* (pedigree). In Bogotá they boasted of speaking the purest Castillian Spanish of the Americas.

A subtle racism against people of Indian or African ancestry persists to the present, giving rise to new empowerment movements among these two groups in the 1980s and 1990s. In the coastal urban centers of Barranquilla and Cartagena a special vocabulary marked race and class differences: "*moreno*" (brown-tinted) or "*claro*" (clear), "*trigueño*" (wheat-colored) or "*trigueño claro*" (light wheat), "*negro por el pelo*" (black by virtue of hair texture), and so on. Usually these creative descriptions implied no direct racial slur; they portrayed primarily a person's economic clout and/or status and only secondarily his or her physical traits. But the fact remained that the lighter skinned were usually better off economically.

Colombia's skewed colonial power structure meant that most people had to rely on the good will of patriarchs of the elite families. Generations of this system produced one of the world's strongest, most deeply rooted traditions of male-dominated personal patronage—what social scientists call "patron-client" relations. Daily life became stamped by *compadragco* (god-father-hood), extreme deference to authority, and loyalty to one's "patrón" (in Spanish, "boss")—whether he was a political party leader or *hacendado* (owner of a large estate). Often the patrón was both. During the nation's many civil wars the elite patrones called upon their clients to defend their property and political party. The fighting of the wars created fierce party loyalties among the peasantry. Beneath the thick layers of party loyalty, however, there lay a volcano of personal resentment toward the patrón—quick to erupt into violence.

In 1780 tobacco farmers and Creoles (Spaniards born in Colombia) sparked an uprising known as the "Comunero Revolt." It coincided with the Indian uprising of Tupac Amaru in Peru and Bolivia (see chapters 14 and 15). Initially it opposed colonial sales and head taxes and reflected discontent with Spanish rule. But slaves and Indians used the occasion to launch their own "revolt within a revolt" to demand freedom and the return of their ancestral lands. The combined Creole and lower-class rebels seized Bogotá, Spain's administrative center for Colombia and Ecuador, before eventually being driven back.

The only rivals in wealth and influence to the elite families were the Catholic Church and the Spanish Crown itself. Shortly after Napoleon's armies conquered Spain early in the nineteenth century these elite families divided on the issue of independence. Some favored it, seeing a chance to gain control over more land, industry, and trade, while others felt it would unleash too much popular revolution. Educated Creoles and artisan workers were among the first to pick up the democratic banners of the French and American revolutions, but who knew what would happen when the lower classes rallied to the same lofty ideals?

Aided by the British and Americans, proindependence elite-family Creoles financed and often led the armies that fought the Spaniards from 1810 to 1819. The foot soldiers were peasants, artisans, Indians, and *cimmarrones* (runaway slaves). By the time independence was won in 1819 at the Battle of Boyacá, the contours of race and class conflict were clear to see, as were the passions of the divided elites.

The self-proclaimed liberator, Venezuelan Simón Bolívar, called Colombia "a debating society." He favored a strong central government and advocated a life term for the president. Like-minded people became known as "Conservatives." The multination merger over which Bolívar presided, Gran Colombia (see chapter 11), fell apart in 1830. Bolívar's colleague at the Battle of Boyacá, Colombian Gen. Francisco de Paula Santander, became Colombia's first president in 1832. He favored a federal, decentralized system and opposed the power of the Roman Catholic Church. His followers became known as Liberals.

Because of the many decades of Liberal-Conservative civil wars, Colombians referred to their young nation as the *"patria boba,"* or foolish fatherland. The single most divisive issue was the role of the Church—the 1886 Constitution and 1887 Concordat with the Vatican almost made Colombia a theocracy like the earlier one of its southern neighbor, Ecuador (see chapter 13). The Liberals sought to develop Colombia by means of seizing the wealth of the Church and putting it to "better" use. Conservatives dominated some regions, such as Antioquia, site of today's industrial hub Medellín. Liberals controlled others, such as Santander and Boyacá north and east of Bogotá.

At least six civil wars occurred. The one involving the most significant issues for the future economic development of the country took place in 1854, at a time when gold production was in decline because of competition from California. The two parties' elites agreed that the nation must henceforth develop on the basis of agricultural exports and free trade. Over the next few decades first tobacco and then coffee emerged as major export crops. The 1854 decision in favor of an economic "monoculture" was not viewed favorably by artisans, underpaid army officers, and a dissident faction of the Liberal party (known as "Draconians") that advocated more emphasis on development of manufacturing industry. When a Draconian won the election to the presidency the elites united to paralyze his administration. Civil war erupted, pitting the lower classes against the dominant elites, who emerged the victors.

The other civil wars were classical Liberal-Conservative wars: intraelite squabbles fought by peasant followers. One occurred from 1860 to 1863 and was won by the Liberals. A more bloody encounter was the "Thousand Days War" from 1899 to 1902. It claimed 100,000 lives and was won by the Conservatives.

In actuality the two parties were not always at each other's throats. They often governed by means of an informal bipartisan coalition system. When the elites saw coffee export earnings rise in the 1880s, for instance, they united behind Liberal Rafael Nuñez who then turned the government over to the Conservatives. Both agreed on using the abundant coffee wealth to develop some industry protected by modest tariffs. Another coalition occurred in 1903 to mend the wounds of war and to confront the loss of Panama (see chapter 7). But from 1886 to 1930 the Conservatives prevailed.

In 1917–1918 a post–World War I depression hit Colombia hard, bringing a momentary end to the "coffee boom" of the previous decades. Workers' strikes forced the government to pass laws allowing the government to intervene in labor–capital relations. In 1922, still reeling from economic hard times, Colombia signed the Thompson–Urrutia Treaty acknowledging the independence of Panama. The United States paid Colombia a $25 million indemnity, described in both countries' presses as "conscience money" because of the way the United States had "stolen" Panama from Colombia. Shortly after the ink dried a U.S. banking mission headed by Princeton Professor E. W. Kemmerer proposed to Colombia's government a fiscally conservative program similar to those later proposed by the IMF. The government agreed to balance the budget and laid off scores of its employees, slashing the wages of those who remained. U.S. loans skyrocketed, equaling nearly half of total investment from 1925 to 1930.

During the 1920s Colombia's elites began to centralize their power around the coffee trade. In 1927 they founded the FNC, a wealthy combine of coffee barons and exporters. Four-fifths of the coffee crop came from small parcels, whose owners sold the picked coffee beans to the FNC for marketing. The FNC persuaded the government to create a National Coffee Fund, which became its own tool for apportioning coffee taxes, improving production techniques, and obtaining state subsidies that FNC members could then reinvest in other areas. The National Coffee Fund assured state funding for completion of the nation's transportation grid of roads, railroads, ports, and shipping arteries, mainly the Magdalena River.

Meanwhile foreign companies set up "export enclaves" for banana and oil production. In 1901, UFCO (United Fruit Company) set up shop in the Santa Marta region east of Barranquilla on the Caribbean coast. By the 1920s it was employing more than 30,000 workers. When some of these struck in 1924 against their inhuman work conditions the company claimed they were not really company employees since small labor contractors had hired them.

The next time UFCO's banana workers struck they were better organized. UFCO again said the workers were not their responsibility. The court
concurred. Then, on December 6, 1928, at Ciénaga, troops opened fire on workers and townspeople gathered in the village square. Here's how Colombia's
Nobel Prize-winning novelist Gabriel García Márquez wrote about it in one
of the world's most widely sold novels, *One Hundred Years of Solitude*:

> They were penned in, swirling about in a gigantic whirlwind that little by little
> was being reduced to its epicenter as the edges were systematically being cut off
> all around like an onion being peeled by the insatiable and methodical shears of
> the machine guns.

> "There must have been three thousand of them," said José.

> "What?"

> "The dead," he clarified. . . .

> The woman measured him with a pitying look. "There haven't been any dead
> here," she said.

> [José turned to the officers in command, who responded:] "You must have been
> dreaming. . . . Nothing has happened in Macondo [Ciénaga], nothing has ever
> happened, and nothing will ever happen. This is a happy town."

After the massacre authorities arrested Communist and Socialist leaders.
A similar policy, with fewer deaths, was implemented against striking transportation workers, who formed some of the nation's first trade unions. Oil
workers at the U.S.-owned Tropical Oil Company in Barrancabermeja on the
Magdalena River received similar treatment. Foreign petroleum firms, the
biggest being Standard Oil of New Jersey, had started investing in Colombia
in 1914 after the U.S. government had pressured Colombia's president to offer
a "favorable" investment climate.

The rise of militant trade unionism became an even more serious threat to
elite power when the Great Depression of 1930 took hold. The FNC and the government were suddenly hit with falling coffee prices and rising unemployment
and social unrest. New groups moved to center stage: trade unionists, unemployed workers, land-hungry peasants, and underpaid middle-class employees.

Labor's Challenge, La Violencia, the 1953 Coup, and the National Front

Throughout the 1930s the challenge to elite power presented by these new social forces shaped Colombia's politics. An unofficial popular front of Communists, Socialists, and Liberals gave rise to an attempt by the Liberal party to

introduce reforms. President Alfonso López Pumarejo (1934–1938) attempted a "new deal," similar to the one being launched by President Franklin D. Roosevelt in the United States. He amended the 1886 Constitution in 1936 to include a guarantee for labor of the "special protection of the state" and an income tax to finance social improvements. Colombia's Socialists reentered the Liberal party. Communists championed President López, whose efforts at reform were blocked by the Supreme Court and his own party's conservative faction. This faction obtained the presidency in 1938 and governed until 1942. The new deal was dead.

Two strong-willed politicians emerged during those turbulent times. One was a firebrand Liberal espousing anti-imperialism, Jorge Eliécer Gaitán, a self-made lawyer from an impoverished background who had become famous for his defense of workers while serving in congress during the late 1920s. He had formed a short-lived Socialist party and then rejoined the Liberal party. Gaitán advocated a populist nationalism that some thought smacked of communism.

The other was an equally outspoken Conservative advocating the Catholic faith and fascism, Laureano Gómez, publisher of the Conservative daily *El Siglo*. President López, reelected in 1942, had Gómez arrested in 1944 in solidarity with the United States and other Allies fighting World War II against fascism. On July 10, 1944, troops loyal to Gómez momentarily detained the president in the southern Conservative bastion of Pasto but lacked sufficient support to carry off a coup d'état.

López again found his reformist program blocked by the Supreme Court and the legislature. In 1945 he quit in disgust. His successor as provisional president was Alberto Lleras Camargo, an ex-supporter of his who had gone over to the conservative wing of the Liberal party. Lleras Camargo and Gómez would do much to shape Colombia's future.

In the 1946 presidential election a split among Liberals allowed the Conservative candidate, Mariano Ospina Pérez, to win with less than a majority of votes. Ospina garnered 523,000 votes, 200,000 fewer than his Liberal rivals, Gabriel Turbay (401,000) of the conservative wing and Jorge Eliécer Gaitán of the López wing (332,000). Turbay died a year later, and no one of sufficient stature could challenge Gaitán's growing hold over the Liberal party.

President Ospina, per a bipartisan "National Union" agreement worked out with Lleras Carmago and Gómez, appointed some conservative Liberals to his cabinet. Offering peace with one hand, he dealt war with the other. He unleashed the army and Conservative goon squads against Gaitanista Liberals. He founded the *policía política,* or political police, which terrorized Liberals.

The Liberals fought back, and la violencia was underway. The unaware traveler took chances in those days. A typical story told of well-armed Liberals stopping a train and ordering its passengers, students from a music conservatory, to identify themselves. As they started to say they were from the "conserva . . . ," the gunmen thought they were about to say "Conservative party." Blam!

For his part Gaitán addressed immense crowds pleading his cause of unity among Liberals and Conservatives and social peace through reform. Raising a white handkerchief as a symbol of peace high over his head, he commanded silence from hundreds of thousands of spellbound listeners. After the Liberals, most of them Gaitanistas, swept the 1947 congressional elections, no one doubted that Gaitán would win the 1950 presidential elections handsdown.

In April 1948 Foreign Minister Laureano Gómez called to order the Ninth Inter-American Conference, a diplomatic meeting following up on the 1947 Rio de Janeiro declaration of mutual defense (see Overview). President Ospina denied Gaitán a seat in the Colombian delegation and beefed up security measures for the Conference.

On April 9, 1948, Gaitán left his downtown office with four friends to go to lunch. On the crowded sidewalk a poorly dressed man with crazed eyes brushed past him. The man turned and fired four shots into Gaitán's neck and shoulders. A lottery-ticket vendor rushed the assassin. While Gaitán breathed his last, an angry mob beat the assassin to death and dragged his battered body through the streets to the presidential palace, shouting "Death to the assassin! Death to Gómez!" Within an hour all of Bogotá was aflame with rioting, burning, and looting.

The National Police sided with the rioters. Peasants honed their machetes on street corners. Troops gunned down mobs trying to assault the presidential palace and the cathedral. One witness later said that half of the "several thousand dead" he saw over the next few days had been shot by soldiers at close range, "a bullet through the forehead."

When the news of Gaitán's death spread, Liberal-controlled municipal juntas took over the cities of Barranquilla, Cali, and Ibagué. For two days the nation's capital was controlled not by the rich but by the poor. The arrival of military reinforcements, the rising death toll, and the exhaustion of the rioters led to restored calm.

For two years the military had been used by the government to kill Liberals. Now, after the "Bogotazo," as the April 1948 rioting was called, military assaults on Liberal strongholds intensified. So did Liberal resistance. Whole areas of the nation went over to the control of Liberal-Communist guerrillas, particularly in the eastern plains and southern Tolima. Colombia's "independent republics" were born.

In 1950 Gómez ran for president and the Liberals, convinced President Ospina would not allow an honest vote count, boycotted the elections. Gómez's attempts to achieve total victory over all Liberals disturbed some fellow Conservatives who thought his fanaticism would provoke more popular rebellion. Groups from both parties conspired with some generals in 1953 to bring about a military coup, led by former colonel Gustavo Rojas Pinilla.

Rojas governed from 1953 to 1957. He introduced some public programs in education, construction, and industrialization and began to develop his own popular following. He closed down the press, offered an amnesty to guerrillas that the army later failed to honor, and issued numerous populist appeals to the masses. His strong-armed rule alienated many initial followers, however. By 1956 the Church, students, and all the country's major political figures had turned against him. The mere appearance of the uniformed *policia política* at Bogotá's bullfight arena was greeted by high-pitched whistles, the public's way of denouncing them as *pájaros*—"[for the] birds." Even leaders of prospering new industries turned against him. In May of 1957 these and other big employers told their own workers to strike. Rojas packed his bags, turned over the government to an interim military junta, and flew off to the same place of exile used by Gómez: dictator Francisco Franco's Fascist Spain.

On July 20, 1957, Lleras Camargo as Liberal party leader met with Conservative party leader Gómez in Sitges, Spain, and drew up a constitutional reform known as the National Front (NF). It provided for sixteen years of parity between the two parties in all branches of government down to the levels of mayor and janitor. The Liberals and Conservatives would alternate the presidency.

The right to vote was extended to women, whose concern for peace was well known. A plebiscite ratified the NF agreement. The family elites had reestablished their political hegemony, but there remained the problems of armed "independent republics," peasant land rights, and labor unrest.

Roles of the Military, Alliance for Progress, Industrialization, and Drugs

While the politicians haggled over parity, Colombia's military gradually emerged as one of Latin America's foremost counterinsurgency forces. The NF political peace arrangement significantly reduced but never fully ended la violencia; the military often added fuel to the flames. Its sheer firepower and key role in combating resurgent guerrilla warfare helped make it a behind-the-scenes arbiter of the nation's destiny.

From an early date U.S. personnel helped train and supply Colombia's armed forces. Colombia was the only Latin American country to send troops to fight alongside U.S. soldiers in the Korean War. In 1952 it hosted the first U.S. military counterinsurgency training school in Latin America. One of the U.S. trainees was dictator Rojas Pinilla.

In the 1960s, Colombia became a "showcase" for the Alliance for Progress. Using Alliance for Progress aid, Colombia launched "Plan Lazo," a sophisticated combination of "civic action" reforms and military counterinsurgency aimed at crushing the "independent republics." While CIA-financed radio broadcasts promoted literacy and warned of "the dangers of communism," troops swept into guerrilla-controlled rural zones. In 1963–1964 some 7,000 soldiers destroyed the independent republic of Marquetalia. Each soldier had received U.S. training.

In congress Liberals and Conservatives gave each other hearty *abrazos* after approving an agrarian reform law required to qualify for Alliance for Progress aid. According to American adviser Ernest A. Duff, the law served to maintain the control of the *latifundistas*. Another American, longtime Colombian resident Lauchlin Currie, an economist, had proposed a more radical program of agrarian reform and industrialization known as the "Currie Plan." The elites rejected his plan as too great a threat to their landed estates, even though it guaranteed all "productive" private property.

From 1960 to 1975 U.S. aid in loans and grants to Colombia surpassed $1.5 billion. Usually "tied" to the purchase of U.S. goods, this aid facilitated a rapid integration of the economic interests of the nation's coffee barons, bankers, and industrialists with those of big U.S. corporations—and the state.

Colombian entry into the quasi-nationalist Andean Pact common market (see Overview and Introduction to Part Three) did not deter the trend. Like the 1968 constitutional reform that formally ended the unpopular NF parity agreement and authorized the government to retain general direction over the economy, it served to blunt the Left's popular outcry against foreign investors "looting" the nation. It sped up the creation of joint business ventures that served to make foreign capital's presence less visible. For foreign investors state approval meant the Left could shout all it wanted—their investments were safe. Seven-tenths of all foreign investment from 1950 to 1970 poured into Colombia *after* 1968, mostly in manufacturing.

Foreign companies soon accounted for more then one-third of industrial production, most of it in the fastest-growing sector, "intermediate goods." These goods were products and manufacturing "inputs" like basic chemicals, steel rods, tires, and fertilizers necessary to sustain other areas of production and distribution. Colgate Palmolive, Chrysler, Goodyear, Purina, Quaker, and others invested heavily in Colombia.

Meanwhile agricultural production for export received a shot in the arm from the "Green Revolution" (see chapter 1). New coffee tree varieties were introduced, along with irrigation and fertilization. Modernized coffee farms soon accounted for more than half of coffee production. As in other parts of Latin America, domestic food production fell by the wayside. A country that devoted 175,000 hectares to wheat production in 1948 planted only 30,000 hectares of wheat in 1975. Colombia began importing sugar, rice, salt, and other basic foods.

Peasants found it hard to make ends meet and migrated to the cities looking for jobs. As in Mexico, in the 1970s the World Bank responded with its "investment in the poor" strategy. Through provision of credits, fertilizers, and tools the Bank tied peasants to their land and gave them hope, making less likely their supporting leftist or guerrilla movements.

During the mid-1970s coffee prices rose sharply, as did the international demand for cocaine, leading to an export "boom" that flooded Colombia with dollars and drove up the rate of inflation. Banks and other financial institutions helped "launder" illegal drug monies. Their capital resources doubled, in spite of a 1975 government decree that had obligated foreign bank subsidiaries to sell 51 percent of their stock shares to Colombian nationals. Investors had a lot of dollars and began speculating in banking, real estate, and other financial markets. Little reinvestment occurred in industry. Soon the sea of dollars had major banks rising and falling overnight on a tidal wave of frenetic speculation. By October 1982, the government was budgeting $120 million to save failing banks.

The U.S. DEA (Drug Enforcement Administration) estimated that by the early 1980s some 80 percent of all cocaine and 70 percent of all marijuana entering the United States was being smuggled from Colombia. More than 50,000 families were said to make their living from marijuana production and trade based in the eastern *llanos*. Most were peasants who were unable to earn one-tenth the sum by growing other crops. Only half the cocaine processed in Colombia was grown there. The rest came from Bolivia and Peru.

With the drug trade came skyrocketing corruption. In the 1970s the press publicized numerous cases of drug trafficking among high officials of Colombia's DAS (Administrative Department of Security—a kind of militarized FBI). In 1979 former DAS boss General Jorge Ordóñez Valderrama was sentenced to seven and a half years for embezzlement. Up to 20 percent of the congress was said to be elected with drug funds. In the 1980s the press reported that relatives of Presidents Turbay and Betancur were linked to drug trafficking.

Colombia faced new economic difficulties when it stopped being an oil exporter in the late 1970s. Even though the state oil firm Ecopetrol owned half the nation's oil holdings, it was tied to fifty-two foreign oil concerns through "association contracts"—a series of technology, advertising, sales, marketing, and other agreements. One way Colombia "paid" for these services was to buy its own oil back from the foreign companies at a price up to five times higher than what the companies paid Ecopetrol. For thirteen months in 1992–1993 these high prices and power shortages caused prolonged blackouts which, with electricity rationing, cost the economy $3 billion. But discovery of a vast new oil field in Cusiana, east of Bogotá, said to have more than 3 billion barrels of recoverable crude, attracted the investments of British Petroleum Company and Ecopetrol. Gold, copper, lead, mercury, platinum, uranium, and zinc added to the nation's subsoil wealth.

Relatively good economic times followed by inflation, speculation, and higher energy costs for industry were accompanied by the *new politics* then sweeping Latin America (see Overview). In Colombia the theology of liberation started early. One of its most important theoreticians was a Colombian priest and prominent sociologist named Camilo Torres. After working at building a united front of political parties to break the NF monopoly on power, "Father Camilo," as he was affectionately called by the people, found his efforts blocked by the unyielding "oligarchy." Torres decided in 1965 to join the guerrilla's ELN (National Liberation Army—see Box 12.1). The ELN was a guerrilla army founded a few years earlier by students and others inspired by the examples of Fidel Castro and Ernesto "Ché" Guevara.

Box 12.1:   Colombia's Political Parties, Guerrillas, and Death Squads

ANAPO   National Popular Alliance, a populist coalition founded by ex-dictator Rojas Pinilla and his daughter in 1971; since split into many factions

CNGSB   Simón Bolívar National Guerrilla Coordinate, founded in 1987 to unite all guerrilla armies; by 1993, mainly ELN and FARC

Conservative party   Founded in 1840s, fought, but also shared power, with Liberal party until 1991. Split in 1974 between "Alvarista" faction led by Alvaro Gómez Hurtado and "Ospina-Pastranista" faction led by ex-President (1970–1974) Pastrana Borrero, but reunited in 1981–1982; renamed PSC (Social Conservative party) in 1987; split again in 1990

ELN   National Liberation army, run in 1960s by Maoists, Guevaraists, and radical priests like Torres; almost wiped out in 1973; rejected truce offers

EPL   People's Liberation army, founded in 1968, Maoist, third largest guerrilla army, oriented to urban actions; accepted 1991 truce and renamed Esperanza, Paz y Libertad (Hope, Peace and Freedom)

FARC   Revolutionary Armed Forces of Colombia, largest guerrilla army founded in 1966 by PCC after army destruction of Marquetalia

Liberal party   Founded in 1840s, fought, but also shared power, with Conservative party until 1991. Split in 1982 between New Liberals (centrists) backed by ex-President (1966–1970) Lleras Restrepo and "legitimista" faction (conservatives) led by ex-President (1974–1978) López Michelsen but reunited in 1986

M-19   April 19 movement, guerrilla army named after date of defeat of Rojas Pinilla in 1970 election; advocates vague populism and democracy; split in 1981 on amnesty issue; renamed M-19/AD party after disarming in 1990

(Continued on next page)

Box 12.1 *(Continued)*

MAO Workers' Self-Defense movement, founded in late 1970s, small Trotskyist guerrilla army, urban-based, accepted truce in 1984

MAS Death to Kidnappers, founded in 1981, one of many right-wing death squads linked to drug trade and armed forces

MCN National Civic movement, a broad coalition linking labor unions and "popular movements" of urban slum-dwellers, students, and peasants

MRN National Restoration Movement, founded in 1989, linked with right-wing "self-defense" forces; suspected of having Medellín drug cartel backing

NFD New Democratic Force, dissident Conservative party founded in 1991, led by former Bogotá mayor Andrés Pastrana Arango and favored by anti-Gómez Hurtado Conservatives

PCC Communist party of Colombia, founded in 1930, became semi-legal in 1957, took up guerrilla warfare in 1960s behind FARC; backed UDI in 1982, UP after

PSC See Conservative party

UDI Democratic Unity of the Left, founded in 1982 by PCC and smaller groups to contest presidential election

UP Patriotic Union, founded in 1985 as political arm of FARC; close to PCC

Camilo Torres died in battle, February 15, 1966. His example became an inspiration to others. Politically conservative Medellín became the site of the 1968 CELAM (General Conference of Latin American Bishops—see Overview) that honored Torres's memory and issued a hemispherewide call for Latin America's social transformation.

That same year, attempting to control the appeal of the new politics in the countryside, the government of President Carlos Lleras Restrepo (1966–1970), cousin of ex-president Lleras Camargo (1945–1946, 1958–1962), created the half-million-member ANUC (National Association of Peasant Users). The officially stated goals of ANUC were to promote peasant participation in state services and "collaboration in the massive application of agrarian reform." Peasant land claims and other grievances were too much for the state's technocrats to handle, however, and ANUC soon moved leftward, becoming a vigorous mass peasant movement opposed to government policies.

Since most voters were cynical about the two parties' NF and its post-1968 informal agreement to share government posts 50–50, they abstained from elections at rates of 65 percent and higher. In 1970 many rejected the two parties' official candidates and voted for ex-dictator Rojas Pinilla. During the ballot counting Rojas Pinilla was ahead when all radio reports were cut off. When the final results were announced, Rojas lost by 66,000 votes of 4 million cast. His supporters cried "Fraud!" Giving up on the electoral process, some of them founded the M-19 guerrilla band. Over the next decade the M-19 carried out a series of sensational actions, including kidnappings of government officials and U.S. business people, big ransom payoffs, bank holdups, and embassy takeovers.

Civic Strikes, States of Siege, and the Peace Process

Perhaps the most original and popular political method people used to express their grievances was the illegal "civic strikes" launched by coalitions of workers, slumdwellers, students, and peasants. On September 14, 1977, all four major labor confederations (Conservative, Liberal, Communist, and independent-leftist) backed the First National Civic Strike that brought the economy to a standstill (even though less than one-fifth of the work force belonged to trade unions). The leadership of the two major parties opposed the strike and realized that they no longer had control over "their" labor confederations. The government sent soldiers and police to attack the strikers. Fierce confrontations left fifty dead, hundreds injured, and thousands arrested.

The military used the occasion to acquire more legal power to occupy urban slum and working-class neighborhoods before more civic strikes could occur. In January 1978 congress passed a law exempting the military and police "from any legal responsibility for their actions against violence and drug trafficking." Known as "the license to kill" law, it was passed right after a hardline faction of officers consolidated their control over the army by forcing three top-ranking generals and two dozen other officers into early retirement.

Later that year Liberal President Julio César Turbay Ayala (1978–1982) reimposed the state of siege under which Colombians had been living for most of thirty years. Tens of thousands were arrested—68,000 in the first year alone. Human rights groups like Amnesty International and Americas Watch reported on cases of torture and disappearances. More than 16,000 peasants were arrested in the first four months of 1981 alone; 422 were killed.

President Turbay also established a peace commission to explore a possible cease-fire with the nation's guerrilla armies. It failed. Ex-president Lleras Restrepo, who headed the commission, said he was told that the proposals put forth by its civilian members "would demoralize the Armed Forces."

Events during and after the Turbay administration reflected the turbulence marking the peace-negotiating process (see Box 12.2).

Box 12.2: Chronology of Peace-Negotiating Process

1977	First National Civic Strike
1978	Law exempting military and police from legal action; state of siege declared; official peace commission created
1980	M-19 occupation of Dominican embassy
1981	Outlawing of Communists' labor-union confederation CSTC; break in relations with Cuba; M-19 shift to rural guerrilla warfare
1982	Betancur elected president on peace platform; state of siege lifted
1982, November	Cease-fire agreement with FARC and M-19; amnesty for political prisoners
1982, December	Creation of new peace commission to bring about cease-fire with all guerrillas
1982–1983	Breakdown of cease-fire process, each side blaming the other
1983	Increase in military budget to $2.6 billion
1983, February	Fifty-nine members of armed forces found active in right-wing death squad MAS
1983, March	Arrival of new American Ambassador Tambs, a militant right-winger
1983, November	FARC, M-19, and ELN political alliance
1984	IMF-imposed austerity program; U.S. military aid up to $25.3 million; increase in kidnappings
1984, February–March	Civic strikes
1984, April	Assassination of minister of justice; war on drug trade, extradition treaty with U.S.; state of siege
1984, May	One-year cease-fire with FARC
1984, August	Six-month cease-fire with M-19, EPL, and MAO
1984, September	Presidential speech charging military coup plot
1984, December	Army and air force attack on M-19 at Carinto
1985	Devaluation of peso by 54 percent
1985, May	Amnesty law for guerrillas
1985, June	General strike; M-19 pullout from cease-fire
1985, November	M-19 takeover of Palace of Justice followed by military assault claiming more than 100 lives
1985, December	Army assault on Cali slum of Siloe, killing seventeen
1986	Election of Barco Vargas; formation of a verification commission to monitor peace program; birth of united labor's CUT and its alignment with Movement for the Defense of Life; offer by drug bosses to pay off foreign debt
1986, December	Assassination of newspaper publisher Guillermo Cano

(Continued on next page)

Box 12.2 *(Continued)*

1987 Banana workers' strike protesting murders of union leaders; dozens more labor leaders assassinated; assassination of UP 1986 presidential candidate Jaime Pardo Leal; 1,500 political assassinations. Ministry of Interior acknowledges existence of 137 right-wing death squads

1988 Forty workers assassinated in front of women and children at Urabá banana plantations in region controlled by Army's Eleventh Brigade; U.S.-approved joint mobilization of Ecuador's and Venezuela's armies along borders during rise in popular protests

1989 Assassination of leading presidential candidate of Liberal party, Dr. Luis Carlos Galan Sarmiento, an opponent of drug cartels; armed forces' "dirty war" escalates; more murders of UP and labor union leaders

1990 M-19 acceptance of truce followed by assassination of its presidential candidate but success in elections to draft new constitution; murder of UP presidential candidate, Bernardo Jaramillo Ossa; party claims 3,000 members killed since 1985

1991 EPL accepts truce, then suffers over 100 assassinations of its members; new, more democratic Constitution promulgated

1992–94 Liberal government's "state of siege" and "total war" against the drug armies and the ELN, FARC, and an EPL splinter group of guerrillas; drug czar Pablo Escobar tracked down and killed; FARC starts armed actions in cities; calls for truce continue

---

In 1982 the majority Liberal party split. This opened the doors to a victory in the presidential election for the minority Conservative party. Both parties by then had become practically indistinguishable, and each contained nationalist factions that gained the upper hand from time to time. The Conservatives ran the nationalist Belisario Betancur, who focused his campaign on the need to hold talks with the guerrillas. Betancur had the backing of a small but vocal Christian Democratic party. He won with 46.8 percent of an exceptionally large vote.

Betancur came from a rural family that had lost seventeen of its twenty-two children to a disease he characterized as "underdevelopment." As early as 1965 he had condemned "the desires of Wall Street" behind the U.S. invasion of the Dominican Republic and the "imperialist behavior" of the IMF. His son Diego Betancur ran for congress in 1982 on the slate of the Maoist MOIR (Independent Revolutionary Workers' movement).

As president, Betancur initiated a vigorous attempt at an independent foreign policy by backing the Contadora peace process in Central America (see Introduction to Part One). He renewed diplomatic relations with Cuba and brought Colombia into the Non-Aligned movement. On the other hand, he swam against the main current of Latin American nationalism by condemning

Argentina and endorsing the U.S.–British position on the Falklands/Malvinas War (see chapter 18), a policy reversed by his successor.

Distressed by Betancur's leading role in Contadora, the Reagan administration appointed Professor Tambs as ambassador to Colombia. Under Tambs' pressure to beef up the strength of Colombia's military, President Betancur increased the armed forces' budget for 1983 to $2.6 billion, up from the 1970s' annual average of $200 million. U.S. military aid doubled, and Betancur agreed to implement an antilabor IMF-style austerity program.

These steps were being taken during the height of Betancur's attempts to negotiate a peace settlement with the guerrillas. In late 1982 he had achieved some cease-fires and granted an amnesty for political prisoners (see Box 12.2). Colombia's hardline generals, claiming the guerrillas were breaking their cease-fire promises, started giving orders to attack and talked publicly about being "victorious." Right-wing death squads also swung into action. In less than a year the cease-fires of 1982 broke down. Armed actions carried out by right-wing death squads and "protection armies" of drug traffickers sped the unraveling of the truce. The number of kidnappings rose into the hundreds by 1984.

The military was unwilling to discipline known cases of its members collaborating with right-wing death squads. In early 1983 a presidential inquiry confirmed that fifty-nine members of the armed forces, including a top officer attending a special course in Washington, were active in the right-wing death squad MAS (Death to Kidnappers), known to have links to the drug trade. The army high command, echoing Tambs' charge that some of the leftist guerrillas and drug armies had allied, ordered its officers to contribute a day's pay to the accused officers and soldiers for their legal defense. MAS was responsible for countless kidnappings and more than 500 murders by decapitation, mostly of peasants and left-wing leaders, including the nation's only Indian priest.

In response to these developments three guerrilla armies, the FARC, M-19, and ELN, agreed in November 1983 to form a political alliance. The tempo of civic strikes picked up. In February and March of 1984, general strikes paralyzed Nariño and Antioquia Departments, seriously hurting a depressed economy burdened by a foreign debt of $12 billion.

Then, on April 30, 1984, an alleged band of drug traffickers assassinated Minister of Justice Rodrigo Lara Bonilla. Announcing a war on the drug trade, President Betancur reimposed the state of siege, ending a twenty-three month hiatus.

Despite these setbacks to the peace process, the FARC renewed its cease-fire with the government for one year in May 1984. After signing, the FARC declared war on a breakaway group that refused to honor it, the Ricardo Franco front. In August 1984 the government signed a six-month cease-fire with M-19, EPL, and MAO (Workers' Self-Defense), leaving the small ELN as the only holdout. The agreement with M-19 included its call for a "national dialogue."

The military brass grew restless with all the truces. On September 24, 1984, President Betancur in a speech in Arauca charged that a military coup was being plotted. On December 16, 1984, the air force bombed an M-19 camp near Carinto, while the Army swept in with 7,500 elite troops. The Carinto attack was widely condemned as a grave violation of the cease-fire. Novelist García Márquez, whose grasp of the nation's psycho-history was without parallel, opined that the president was "a noble man" who seemed unable or unwilling to rein in the military.

In May 1985, congress passed an amnesty law allowing guerrillas to reintegrate with civilian life unless accused of kidnapping, extortion, or murder outside armed combat. The peace process was still alive.

The biggest general strike in the nation's history occurred on June 20, 1985. It was carried out by the MCN (National Civic movement). Strikers demanded salary increases, land reform, and a moratorium on foreign debt payments. Despite thousands of arrests, the illegal strike was reportedly 80 percent effective. The government said the strike was a failure and announced firings, heavy fines, and the loss of union charters for those who participated. The next day, the M-19 pulled out of the cease-fire agreement on the grounds of continued army violations. The following November, the Palace of Justice tragedy occurred, and the peace process lay in ashes.

In September 1986 the civic-strike movement received a big boost from the formation of a unified labor movement, the CUT (Single Workers' Central). It brought together all four of the nation's major trade-union confederations. The CUT announced it would break with the tradition of political party control over labor. It aligned itself with the "Movement for the Defense of Life," a loose-knit coalition of Indian, Christian, peasant, artist, and journalist communities.

During the 1986 election campaign the Liberal party reunited behind its presidential candidate Virgilio Barco Vargas, a sixty-four-year-old civil engineer and former World Bank director. Known as a cool-headed technocrat, Barco had been educated at MIT and was married to an American. He received 58.3 percent of the vote, leaving his Conservative opponent, Alvaro Gómez Hurtado, son of ex-president Laureano Gómez, with only 35.9 percent. Leftist Jaime Pardo Leal of the Communist-backed UP garnered 300,000 votes. President Barco formed a verification commission to monitor his peace program of "rehabilitation, normalization, and reconciliation." He also broke the skein of twenty-eight years of NF-style coalition government by announcing an all-Liberal cabinet.

The scope of the war shaking Colombia could be glimpsed from the official statistics for battlefield deaths in the first six months of 1986: more than a thousand, including 605 guerrillas, 168 policemen, 72 soldiers, and 272 peasants. Priests advocating liberation theology were being killed at the rate of one a month. National television showed peasants with modern weapons who said they were being paid by big landowners to police the countryside against rebel organizations. Death lists circulated. The FARC's political arm UP, founded in mid-1985, suffered especially heavy casualties.

The "dirty war" of the military and the dozens of death squads with which it cooperated nearly wiped out the noncombatant civilian UP. In October 1987 the 1986 UP presidential candidate Pardo Leal, a former judge who had fingered retired and active military officers as ringleaders of death squads, was machine-gunned and killed while driving near Bogotá with his wife and children. A one-day general strike protested the killing and shut down the country. Some 25,000 demonstrators in Bogotá cheered the unfurling of a banner of the CNGSB, a coalition of all major rebel organizations.

Barco declared a "democratic opening"—elections in March 1988 for 1,009 mayors, previously appointed. He also hiked the military's budget. The Liberals edged out the Conservatives in the mayorality contests, although losing Bogotá and Medellín. The UP and a smaller Maoist current swept fifteen towns and came close to winning a few cities.

During the rest of Barco's administration the power of the military and the drug armies rose to new violent heights. The military felt so sure of itself that it defied civilian authorities and conducted its own justice system. In its "dirty war" in guerrilla territories it rarely bothered to take prisoners, preferring summary executions. Labor organizing became more life-risking than ever, as scores of labor leaders and unarmed workers were assassinated. Army patrols were seen following death squad victims. The drug bosses grew so cocky that they offered to pay off the foreign debt in exchange for amnesty. Instead, the public and private sectors continued to cooperate with the IMF and foreign creditors. The Banco de Colombia renegotiated its one-third of a billion dollars foreign debt on condition that it hand over 51 percent of its stock as collateral to foreign creditors.

Even as the peace process picked up fresh momentum with promises of amnesty for guerrillas and an elected constituent assembly to draft a new constitution, the violence continued. In August 1989 Dr. Luis Carlos Galan Sarmiento, a severe critic of the drug cartels and the Liberals' leading presidential candidate, was assassinated. In March 1990 the very popular presidential candidate of the UP, Bernardo Jaramillo Ossa, was murdered. The nonviolent UP was all but wiped out, claiming that three thousand of its members had been killed since 1985, including one thousand "leaders," among them several members of congress and city councils. Observed the highly respected New York-based human rights group Americas Watch: "Since members of the FARC put down their arms and entered the Patriotic Union, peaceful political participation has proved to be more dangerous than armed struggle." The very next month, April 1990, the M-19/AD candidate was also gunned down. And after the demobilization of the EPL (People's Liberation army) in early 1991, more than one hundred of its members were murdered.

In the presidential elections of May 1990, Liberal César Gaviria defeated dissident Conservative Gómez Hurtado, third place finisher Antonio Navarro Wolff of M-19/AD, and an official Conservative candidate who trailed the pack. In the December 1990 election for the constituent assembly, M-19/AD finished a close second to the Liberals (only five fewer seats). After the new Constitution became official in July 1991, the Liberals won majorities in October's elections for both houses of congress and won fifteen of twenty-seven governorships. In the 1992 municipal elections, the Liberals again won the majority of contests, but the M-19/AD allied with the Conservative party to sweep the mayoral races in Cali and Medellín.

Colombia's economy was still on the ropes, despite renegotiated debts, oil discoveries, and the Liberal governments' privatization measures. Unemployment was above 11 percent and underemployment 30 percent. More and more people, despite the risks, were seeking jobs in the flourishing drug industry. A seven-day strike in 1992 by workers at the state-owned telephone company prevented its sale to private interests. But the government jailed strike leaders and allowed foreign investors to compete in the phone sector of the economy—a subtler way of strangling the state firm according to CUT. In 1993 the CUT threatened more general strikes to delay or modify further acts of privatization affecting areas like the state social security system.

President Gaviria pushed efforts by the Group of Three (Colombia, Venezuela, and Mexico) for a free trade and investment agreement with Central America and also pressed for Colombia's inclusion in the NAFTA (see Overview, chapter 1, Introduction to Part Three, and Conclusion). In 1992, Venezuela became Colombia's second-largest source of imports, after the United States. Gaviria also launched a three-year program called "Peaceful Revolution." It aimed to pull 4 million people out of poverty—one-fourth of the nation's poor. But World Bank studies showed that, in the past, indicators of Colombian poverty were deliberately selective in order to reduce the number of possible beneficiaries and to lower administrative costs.

Meanwhile, the violence continued, as it was almost bound to with all the money available from the drug trade. The Cali cartel had become the world's cocaine center, superseding Medellín even before Escobar's arrest and subsequent death. It also was said to be a pivot of the heroin trade. In the 1994 elections, losing Conservative presidential candidate Andrés Pastrana Arango accused the Liberal winner, Ernesto Samper Pizano, of accepting campaign funding from the Cali cartel.

In the first round of the 1994 elections, two-thirds of the voters abstained (the highest rate since 1930). M-19's Navarro Wolff garnered only 3.8 percent of the vote. Samper, a forty-three-year-old economist and lawyer, won the runoff against Pastrana with 50.4 percent of the vote. Pledging to maintain neo-Liberal economic policies, Samper nonetheless campaigned against "savage capitalism" and promised more emphasis on "social" programs.

In 1993, the FARC began operating in cities and not just its traditional rural strongholds. The other main guerrilla group, the ELN, claimed responsibility for several oil pipeline bombings that Ecopetrol asserted had cost $1.8 billion in the previous five years and ecological destruction from resultant spills. The already fat military budget had tripled since 1991, accounting for 8.5 percent of government spending. As army soldiers appeared everywhere and U.S. planes and ships patrolled Colombian airways, rivers, and coasts, many citizens were wondering, as the widely read monthly *Nacla Report on the Americas* once headlined, "Whose Country Is This, Anyway?"

Selected Bibliography

Carrigan, Ana. *The Palace of Justice: A Colombian Tragedy.* New York: Four Walls Eight Windows, 1993. On 1985 turning point.

Martz, John D. *Colombia: A Contemporary Political Survey.* Chapel Hill: University of North Carolina Press, 1962. Excellent background.

Nacla (North American Congress on Latin America). "Colombia Cracks Up." *Nacla Report on the Americas,* 23(6) (April 1990).

Osterling, Jorge Pablo. *Democracy in Colombia: Clientelistic Politics and Guerrilla Warfare.* New Brunswick, NJ: Transaction, 1989.

Pearce, Jenny. *Colombia: Inside the Labyrinth.* London: Latin America Bureau, 1990. Insightful on 1980s.

Rausch, Jane M. *The Llanos Frontier in Colombian History, 1830–1930.* Albuquerque: University of New Mexico Press, 1993. Insightful on violence.

Sharpless, Richard E. *Gaitán of Colombia.* Pittsburgh, PA: University of Pittsburgh Press, 1978.

Torres, Camilo. *Revolutionary Writings,* with Introduction, "Camilo's Colombia," by Maurice Zeitlin. New York: Harper Colophon Books, 1972.

Torres, Javier. *The Armed Forces of Colombia and the National Front.* Boulder, CO: Westview, 1989.

Wade, Peter. *Blackness and Race Mixture: The Dynamics of Racial Identity in Colombia.* Baltimore, MD: Johns Hopkins University Press, 1993.

Films

La Magia de lo Real. 60 minutes. Color video with García Márquez and archival footage of banana zone (Princeton Films for the Humanities).

Love, Women and Flowers. 1988. 58 minutes. Color. On women and environment in nation's third largest export industry (cut flowers).

Rodrigo D No Future. 1990. Award-winning film about Medellín's teenage culture in midst of drug-running urban poverty. Spanish with English subtitles.

PACIFIC
OCEAN

COLOMBIA

•Esmeraldas

Rio Putumayo

⊛ Quito

ECUADOR

•Riobamba

•Guayaquil

•Cuenca

PERU

N

| 0 | 50 | 100 Mi. |
| 0 | 50 | 100 Km. |

Ecuador 13

Give me a balcony and I will govern.—*Five-time president, José María Velasco Ibarra*

Welcome to Houston, Ecuador.—*1987 road sign put up by an American oil company in oil-rich Napo province*

In March 1987, earthquakes measuring above 7 on the Richter scale shook the tiny nation of Ecuador. They left 2,000 dead, 75,000 injured, and 20,000 homeless. The human toll would have been higher had they not occurred in the thinly populated *oriente*, or eastern region. *Oriente*'s forested tropics accounted for half the nation's territory but less than 3 percent of its 10 million population. Most *oriente* residents were Indians who scratched out a living from "slash-and-burn" farming and riverfishing. They included the Jívaros, once famous for their shrunken-head war trophies. A few Indians worked in construction in the oil fields of northeastern Napo province.

On the day of the first quake the Indians watched in silence as white men speaking foreign tongues dropped from the sky in noisy whirlibirds, looking for more petroleum and places to install African palm oil plantations. Then, in the distance, they heard the thunderous noise as the land trembled, opened, and gobbled up all around it. Down the swollen Napo River floated chunks of oil rigging and the corpses of fishermen, cows, and horses. Black liquid gushed from cracks in the pipeline running from Lago Agrio to Balao. Ecuador's lifeline—oil accounted for more than half of its exports—was ruptured. The government announced there would be no more payments on the foreign debt of

$8.5 billion and people would have to "sacrifice" for the sake of economic recovery. The nation's future was as bleak as it had always been when major exports suffered setbacks from natural disasters or unreliable foreign markets.

For most Ecuadoreans, though, life already was filled with sacrifice. A nation of stark contrasts and rugged geography, Ecuador had always been compared in its extremes of poverty to Bolivia or Honduras. Except for the earthquakes, the spring of 1987 was like any other: rainy season along the coast, pleasant days in the mountains, kidnappings and gunplay by the politicians, and, for the majority of the populace of 11 million a harsh struggle to survive.

Tropical rains lashed the Pacific lowlands and Andean foothills—the so-called *costa*, where more than half the population lived. The slum communities of the major *costa* cities, Guayaquil in the south and Esmeraldas in the north, suffered their usual floods and mudslides. A sweltering tropical port of 1.9 million people, Guayaquil traditionally had been the nation's economic heart. Through it had pumped the blood of imported manufactured goods and food supplies in exchange for cacao, bananas, fish, and other exported primary products that had kept the nation alive for as long as people could remember. Guayaquil's sloshy streets teemed with underpaid workers, sweating dockhands, noisy street hawkers, children with swollen bellies. Its slums were a traditional breeding ground for social unrest and the demagogic appeal of politicians. Since the days of its challenges to Spanish colonialism and defiance of conservative Catholic elite families who had taken over the country after independence, Guayaquil had long been marked by radical and liberal ideas. Wielding more clout than politicians, however, were Guayaquil's merchants, bankers, and occasional industrialists. They were what passed for Ecuador's "national bourgeoisie," a comprador bourgeoisie that had long catered to the interests of wealthier and stronger foreigners.

Esmeraldas, or "emeralds," named for the green jewelry the Spaniards found the Indians wearing during their first exploration of 1526, was a sleepy outpost recently brought to life by a new oil refinery and marine terminal. Its freshly bulldozed streets now bustled with activity day and night. In 1972 an oil pipeline running from the Amazonian petroleum fields had reached Esmeraldas. In the late 1980s Indians from greater Esmeraldas denounced the owners of African palm plantations for encroaching on their lands—one of several Indian protests that mushroomed into a nationwide *indigenista* movement by the 1990s.

In both Guayaquil and Esmeraldas poor people lived in rickety palm-thatched huts supported on wooden stilts to stay suspended above the swirling flood waters that came each spring. They had little or no sanitation or safe drinking water. From the popular bars and cantinas came the beats of Afro-Caribbean conga drums.

A different Ecuador lay high above the *costa* in the towering snow-capped Andes—the region known as the *sierra*. More than 40 percent of the population resided there. Half of them spoke Quechua or other Indian dialects.

Quito, the world's second highest capital after La Paz, Bolivia, sat in an intermont basin 9,250 feet above the Pacific not far from a monument marking the Equator, source of the nation's name. The spring of 1987 brought little change to this sleepy colonial capital with its wooden balconies leaning over narrow, hilly cobblestone streets. The Catholic Iglesia de la Compañía still symbolized the medieval past with its every altar, post, and beam made of gold—enough to house and shod the millions of Ecuadoreans without adequate homes or shoes. Quito experienced its usual crisp cool days of intermittent sunshine and cloudiness. A city of 1.4 million, its Indian and mestizo residents hawked their wares, treked to the textile mills and food-processing and pharmaceutical factories in the north, or entered the many government offices to go on with life as usual, scarcely noticing the shining peak of Chimborazo (20,577 feet high) that loomed over the city and its outlying villages.

The *sierra*'s popular bars had little music. The sounds from the distant mud-thatched, dirt-floor huts of the Andes were of crying, dying babies, echoed by the plaintive wails of homemade Indian wind instruments.

The politics of Ecuador was also typical in 1987: unstable. On January 16, air force commandos kidnapped the president, a millionaire industrialist-rancher named León Febres Cordero. They demanded the release of a popular colleague named Lieutenant General Frank Vargas Pazzos. Vargas had been detained for having led two uprisings the previous spring. The unicameral congress, led by a left-center coalition, had granted Vargas amnesty in September. President Febres, however, had refused to release him. Febres, who championed U.S. President Ronald Reagan's get-tough economic and foreign policies, cultivated the image of "lion of the Andes" (after his first name). He regularly slandered his opponents in a shocking gutter Spanish, sent the police to quell public unrest, and puffed out his chest at photograph-taking sessions.

For many months, then, Ecuador's politicians had fought over the destiny of Lieutenant General Vargas, whose popularity among the masses had grown with the length of his martyrdom. Meanwhile the commanding generals of the army had looked on, shaking their heads in amusement. They knew full well that the "lion" with the presidential sash was a pussycat whom they could cage at any time.

Even the troublesome air force could be kept under control, if need be. In mid-January, the army generals moved to settle matters swiftly. The kidnapped president was released after promising amnesty for his captors. His captors' air commando unit was disbanded, and the main kidnappers were locked up. Several small political parties of the center and Left hastily announced a "united front" behind Lieutenant General Vargas and then divided when they couldn't agree on whether or not to run him for president. Vargas founded his own party. Political matters returned to "normal"; that is, they continued unstable.

In the aftermath of the earthquakes students and labor leaders called for a twenty-four-hour general strike to protest President Febres's emergency price hikes on food, energy, and public transport. The country's universities suspended classes, and student and labor leaders were thrown in jail. On March 25 up to 90 percent of the employed work force honored the general strike.

Aware that a similar strike had almost toppled the center-right government of Osvaldo Hurtado Larea in 1982, the lion lashed back. He sent police to evict workers occupying factories in northern Quito. People rioted. In Esmeraldas demonstrators ransacked a warehouse belonging to an unpopular congressman. Guayaquil slumdwellers shouted slogans against the IMF (International Monetary Fund) and the Quito politicians. In scattered incidents troops opened fire. By the end of the day hundreds of protesters and innocent bystanders had been jailed or wounded. Reacting to subsequent press reports of these events, President Febres ordered a two-week shutdown of four radio stations. The labor minister resigned. Angry congressmen waved their pistols at one another during inflamed parliamentary debates.

Ever since the 1960s, Latin America's "new politics" (see Overview) had been making inroads in Ecuador. By the mid-1990s, occupations of government buildings and general strikes were an annual affair. They linked up students, workers, and the powerful *indigenista* movement—an unusually "broad alliance" in a nation 40 percent Indian, 40 percent mestizo, 10 percent black, and only 10 percent Caucasian. This "popular movement" made the "old politics" less relevant and the military more important than ever. To understand why, we must first look at the historical roots of Ecuador's "political game" played by squabbling elites, the exploitation of Indians and workers, and the easy rise of demagogues.

From Colonial Backwater to Velasquismo

As in Peru, the Spanish ways of power and corruption rapidly asserted themselves over the Inca civilization's *ayllu* (community) traditions of collective solidarity. In Ecuador's Indian highlands the Spanish colonial system lives on in today's tripartite authority structure of large landowner (*hacendado*), priest, and government-appointed *teniente político*—a kind of labor foreman and justice of the peace.

The original Spanish *hacendados* took over the best farmlands. Using the *encomienda* and *repartimiento* systems of labor recruitment, they virtually enslaved the Indian peasants (see chapters 1 and 14). A majority of the original population died from overwork and diseases brought by the Spaniards, causing African slaves to be imported before the end of the sixteenth century.

For maintenance of the surviving Indian labor force the *hacendados* introduced the *huasipungo*, immortalized in Jorge Icaza's *Huasipungo*, a famous novel describing the lives of Indian villagers. Still prominent today, the *huasipungo* is a tiny parcel of hacienda land "paid" the Indian laborer instead of cash. *Huasipungo* literally means "house-door," so close is the land parcel to the hut in which the Indian family lives. Part of the *huasipungo* system includes sending the Indian family's womenfolk, especially the young, to the master's house to satisfy every whim of its menfolk.

The introduction of first cacao and later coffee, rice, bananas, and sugar as cash-crop exports to finance imported tools and manufactured goods branded Ecuador's economy as a typical Latin American monoculture (see Overview). It kept Ecuador totally dependent on foreign markets for more than four centuries. Since most of the production and trading of these items was carried out in the coastal lowlands, a wealthier economy than the *sierra*'s emerged there. But whether for a highland Indian campesino or a coastal *mantuvio* (mixed-blood migrant peasant) or black, life was always short and wretched.

Spanish colonialism's administrative centers for Ecuador were first Lima, Peru, and then, after 1718, Bogotá, Colombia. Economically Ecuador lacked the mineral wealth of the other two countries. It was a colonial backwater. Quito, as the colonial seat of a judicial administrative unit called the *audiencia*, remained the center for political authority after independence.

The fight for independence was sparked by powerful merchants of Guayaquil in 1820, the monied group with the real clout. Independence was consummated in 1822 at the battle of Pichincha, outside Quito, won by Antonio José de Sucre, the loyal friend of the "liberator," Simón Bolívar. That same year Bolívar met with South America's other main liberator, Argentina's José de San Martín, in Guayaquil. The two men decided to incorporate Ecuador into the multination merger known as Gran Colombia (see chapter 11) and to have Bolívar direct the independence armies in their final liberation of Peru.

In 1830, when Gran Colombia fell apart, Ecuador became an independent republic. But it remained a backwater. Liberal-Conservative rivalries similar to Colombia's (see chapter 12) and the needs of regional *caudillos* to keep peasants from rebelling by recruiting them into "local defense" armies kept the nation politically unstable. To this day Ecuador has experienced on average a different government every few years and a new constitution every decade or so.

In the nineteenth century local *caudillos* rose to power and fell from grace as quickly as governments and constitutions. Civil war raged. Having inherited the seat of political power, Quito kept it in the hands of the Conservatives for most of the century. The Guayaquil-based Liberals wrested it away in 1895 and kept it until 1944. The Conservatives did not regain the presidency until 1956, holding it until 1960. The colonial heritage of personalism and corruption steadily deepened, giving rise to nepotism, bureaucratic inefficiency, and today's *palanqueo* (employment based on personal connections).

Border wars with Peru and Colombia added to the nation's instability. They also created a basis for Ecuadorean nationalism. In the 1830s Colombian troops began grabbing what is today's southern Colombia. In 1904 Brazil forced Ecuador to cede some of its lands in the *oriente*. In 1916 Colombia took over another chunk of disputed territory. Worse yet, in 1941 Peruvian troops invaded the *oriente*, seizing half the nation's land. Under U.S. pressure Ecuador signed a 1942 treaty known as the Rio de Janeiro Protocol that ceded Peru most of its claims. In 1960 popular protests caused Ecuador to reject the Protocol. Peru and Ecuador renewed their border war briefly in January 1981, but nothing was settled.

Political instability guaranteed that structural economic reforms would occur rarely, opportunistically, or not at all. Frequent government turnovers gave the wealthy (and those who sought to make their fortunes in politics) a chance to pilfer the national treasury, further cementing the country's maldistribution of wealth. As a textile worker in the *sierra* city of Cuenca once pointed out, "the musicians change, but the music remains the same."

An ideological extreme of the Conservatives' half-century of rule was achieved under Gabriel García Moreno (1860–1875). A fervent mystic, he established a theocratic state. The Concordat of 1863 granted the Vatican more privileges than it had enjoyed during colonial times. In 1873, García Moreno dedicated the Republic of Ecuador to the Jesuits' Sacred Heart of Jesus. He was assassinated in 1875. From his exile in Colombia the Christian Liberal poet and essayist Juan Montalvo boasted, "My pen killed him."

Montalvo's writings provided an ideological basis for two decades of Liberal revolts that finally ended the Conservatives' reign in 1895 and installed in power Eloy Alfaro, a "radical" Liberal. In Ecuador radical talk was a way of winning popular support—but it rarely produced any radical economic changes. The Liberals used their tenure in government to secularize education, legalize divorce, complete the laying of railroads, highways, and electrical and telecommunications grids, and extend their economic alliance with foreign capital. They squandered a lot of their funds on fighting the Roman Catholic Church and one another, but they also grew wealthy from their frequent backroom deals with foreign investors and looting the state treasury.

During the cacao-based "chocolate prosperity" of the 1910s the Liberals expanded the state bureaucracy, hoping it would be forever loyal to them. There emerged the first generation of student and middle-class political activists, as well as a nascent working class in rail and urban transport and electricity. In the wake of the 1920 Second National Congress of Workers in Guayaquil, Socialists and Communists organized new labor unions.

In 1920-1921 cacao prices plummeted fivefold and insect plagues swept the agricultural sector. Ecuador found itself in its usual crisis of overdependence upon foreign markets. Students and unionized workers sparked street demonstrations in Guayaquil. Disenfranchised rag-clad slumdwellers (illiterates were not given the vote until 1984) joined them. By late 1922 workers were disarming the police, students were fighting back, and troops had to be sent.

On November 15, 1922, in a massacre immortalized by Joaquín Gallegos Lara in his moving novel *Crosses over the Water*, soldiers attacked protesters and chased them through the streets and into homes, their rifles spitting fire. That night, trucks picked up the corpses and dumped them into the Guayas River. A year later dissatisfied peasants at Leyto hacienda were gunned down. Ecuador's political game had entered a new phase.

Now the military wanted more of the traditional economic benefits associated with a say in governmental affairs. Some of the army's junior officers became attracted to Socialist ideas being pushed by the nascent student and labor movements. In July 1925, these officers launched a coup d'état and initiated what became known as the "Julian Reform." They issued new labor laws regulating female and child labor. They spoke of the right to strike and agrarian reform. Shocked by such talk, the agromercantile bourgeoisie's Commercial and Agricultural Bank of Guayaquil cut back on loans for trade. When the government's funds ran low at the customs houses, the government caved in to the demands of the elites. Things returned to "normal."

The next big crisis was triggered by the worldwide Depression of the 1930s. This time, as government succeeded government, no political or military faction could meet the challenge. Student protests and worker and slumdwellers' demonstrations became more frequent. A wealthy Liberal was elected president, but with the treasury shy on export earnings he became very unpopular.

The *sierra* oligarchy and the Catholic Church cynically formed a movement called the National Worker Compact. Its militants were also known as the "dirty shirts," a distant echo of Europe's Fascist "brown shirts." The Quito oligarchy promoted to the leadership of congress' opposition one of their own, a forty-year-old Conservative named José María Velasco Ibarra (1893–1979). Velasco's impassioned speeches on behalf of "the shoeless ones" soon drew widespread public attention.

By 1933, almost every Ecuadorean was looking for a fresh way to handle the nation's rocky ride down the potholed road of economic monoculture and political instability. They were unable to find a solution. But consistent with the nation's past of strong *personalismo, caudillismo,* and lofty ideals, they were able to find an individual—Velasco.

Born in Quito in 1893, Velasco had grown up in the home of a mathematician-politician. On his mother's side he was descended from the hero Bolívar. A tall, very thin man, he was nicknamed "the skeleton." His very large head sat on a skinny neck. He had deep-set black eyes behind prescription dark glasses, and a thick moustache. If good looks were not his drawing card, economic probity was. Velasco prided himself on never having profited from holding public office, something practically unheard of in Ecuadorian history. "I do not even own a house," he later announced proudly.

Sierra loyalists, steadily losing power to the Guayaquil agromercantile bourgeoisie, welcomed a "native son" they had promoted. *Costa* elites were relieved to have found a proper *caudillo* to keep the masses under control. The urban and rural poor opened their arms to an uncorrupted politician who was willing to walk among them. Devout Catholics quickly recognized Velasco's frequent references to "good and evil." His fiery oratory mesmerized millions.

Like Argentina's elites in the case of Perón (see chapter 18), Ecuador's Conservatives and Liberals turned to Velasco whenever the going got tough. They jointly elected him president in 1933. Socialists, Communists, and priests jumped on his bandwagon in 1944. In 1960, when he won his largest popular mandate, Velasco defined the populist character of Velasquismo as "a liberal doctrine, a Christian doctrine, a socialist doctrine"—in other words, something for everyone, all things to all people. Unlike Perón's populism, however, Velasco's was launched in a nonidustrialized country with a minuscule working class. His appeal was addressed not to the "shirtless ones" of the industrial proletariat, but to the "shoeless ones" of the subproletariat and peasantry.

Since Ecuador's real problems could not be solved by a demagogue, however uncorruptible he might be, Velasco was repeatedly thrown out of office by the military. He would be elected president five times—in 1933, 1944, 1952, 1960, and, at age seventy-five, in 1968. The only time he completed a term was in the mid-1950s, at the height of the "banana prosperity," by which time he was already known as the "viejo loco" (the old madman). But mad or not, Velasco kept Ecuador's weak central government afloat in troubled waters for four decades. Velasquismo defined the parameters of every other politician's and army officer's public appeal.

After the military removed Velasco from power the first time (1934) Ecuador experienced a decade of growing repression overseen by Liberal presidents. When Velasco's 1940 electoral victory was denied him by a fraudulent stuffing of ballot boxes from the provinces, angry demonstrators filled the streets of Guayaquil. The Carabineros (police) and army troops once again opened fire. Velasco fled to Colombia.

As Ecuador's shoeless ones licked their wounds, the politicians seeking to control them split into three camps: middle-class Socialists versus agromer-cantile elite Liberals versus Conservative landed oligarchs and priests. Peru's military forces were able to grab half the nation's territory in 1941 (see chapter 14) for the simple reason that the ruling elites and generals were concerned more with keeping the army's attention focused on controlling Eucadoreans than with defending the nation.

In May of 1944 an insurrection erupted in Guayaquil. People burned down the Carabinero headquarters. They chased fleeing policemen and tore limb from limb the few they caught. Worried elites welcomed a military coup that brought Velasco home and installed him in the presidency. Crowds cheered his return. Meanwhile the cost of living tripled—Velasco's rhetoric could not put food on the table. The Left protested with a hunger march on Christmas Eve, 1945. The police savagely broke it up. Velasco turned against his former leftist allies with a wave of repressive laws and actions in the name of the "McCarthyist" anticommunism then sweeping the Western Hemisphere. A 1947 military coup forced Velasco once more into exile. This time he went to Argentina, where he found sympathizers among the Peronists. Few Ecuadoreans mourned his departure.

A boom in exports, particularly bananas, yielded Ecuador's only period of relative democracy and political stability, 1948–1960. Some of the landed oligarchy even "modernized," most notably, President Galo Plaza Lasso (1948–1952), an eloquent spokesman for "economic development." Plaza, the son of an earlier Liberal president, was a good friend of the United Fruit Company (UFCO). He even wrote a book praising UFCO, which controlled 90 percent of the nation's bananas. Ecuador became the world's largest producer of bananas.

All three presidents of the banana prosperity—Plaza, Velasco, and Conservative Camilo Ponce Enríquez (1956–1960)—championed "developmentalism," free enterprise, and foreign investment. The steady flow of banana-export income made it possible for the ruling elites to incorporate dissident middle-class elements into the expanding "developmentalist" bureaucracy. Even the Socialists sided with the established parties. The seeds of today's technocratic elite among state bureaucrats were planted in the developmentalism of the 1950s. Known as *kikuyus*, they are considered by some to be a "fourth branch of government."

But development depended on bananas. Central American competition, Panama Canal tolls, severe weather, and dependence on foreign markets spelled eventual disaster for Ecuador. Its banana boom went bust in 1959–1960. In 1959 the "shoeless ones" rioted in Guayaquil, troops opened fire, hundreds fell dead. Once more the elites had to turn to Velasco to pull their chestnuts out of the fire. It was time for "the Great Absentee," "the National Personification," to try again.

By then new revolutionary winds were sweeping the continent. Fidel Castro's youthful and colorful guerrillas had taken power in Cuba and were standing up to "Uncle Sam." A movement of "Fidelistas" had been launched by a new generation of students, calling themselves URJE (Revolutionary Union of Ecuadorean Youth). Velasco conveniently changed his ideological robes, campaigning in 1960 as a leftist reformer. He was swept into office. One of his first acts, cheered wildly by the people, was to renounce the Rio Protocol that Ecuador had signed in 1942 ceding half its territory Peru.

Ascent of Military and Politics New and Old

As an international guarantor of the Rio Protocol with Argentina, Brazil, and Chile, the U.S. government did not look kindly on Velasco's defiant act of nationalism. It saw Castros under every bed. It frowned upon a friendly visit to Moscow made by Velasco's vice-president, Carlos Julio Arosemena Monroy. The CIA set in motion a plot to destabilize Ecuador and reverse its "leftward" tangent.

The main group selected to confront the reformist threat was the military. Its officers, like those in the rest of Latin America, began getting more U.S. weapons and training. From now on the military would not only arbitrate the nation's politics, as it had frequently done in the past. If necessary, it would refuse to turn over the presidency to a civilian.

In 1960–61 coffee prices fell with banana prices and Velasco had to decree higher taxes. Consumer prices rose sharply. Workers struck. Once again, like clockwork, the military acted. In November of 1961 the air force spearheaded a coup d'état, Velasco departed for Argentina. Arosemena succeeded to the presidency, the military watching his every move.

With the military "stick" at his back, Arosemena jumped for the economic "carrot" of U.S. aid. In exchange he broke diplomatic relations with Cuba and fired his leftist cabinet ministers. But the United States was taking no chances. It got behind a rightist military coup, staged in July 1963.

The new military junta (1963–1966) outlawed the PCE (Ecuadorean Communist party) and jailed its leaders. In 1964 it passed an agrarian reform law. The nation's landed oligarchs first grimaced, then relaxed. The new law left 0.4 percent of landholders holding more than half the arable land in huge estates (*latifundia*) of more than a hundred hectares. Three-quarters of all landholdings remained *minifundia* of under 5 hectares. A 1970 report of the U.S. Agency for International Development described the law as leaving Ecuador in a "prereform period."

The junta arrested and tortured students and workers. It closed the Central University. It even detained Conservative ex-President Ponce. Nevertheless, student and worker strikes and riots forced it out in 1966. Subsequent interim governments were unable to right the ship of state, and so there was only one thing to do: bring back "The Great Absentee."

Velasco governed from 1968 to 1972 but did not finish his term. In December 1971 Cuban President Fidel Castro visited Ecuador and Velasco received him warmly. That same month Ecuador arrested several U.S. fishermen "poaching" inside the two hundred-mile maritime territorial limit long recognized by Ecuador but not by the United States. The United States retaliated with an aid cutoff.

Meanwhile a new popular figure had come forth to challenge the aging Velasco for the presidency in the 1972 elections. He was the frequently elected mayor of Guayaquil, Assad Bucaram, an up-and-coming self-educated son of Lebanese immigrants who knew the language of the streets. Velasco had exiled this potential rival to Panama in 1970. By then everyone knew that Ecuador was sitting on a sea of oil discovered in the late 1960s. In 1972 the military, fearful that Bucaram would be elected, carried out a coup.

Reflective of the "new politics" sweeping the continent, the 1972 coup managers included an army faction with nationalist aspirations. It admired the populism of Panama's General Torrijos and Peru's General Velasco Alvarado (see chapters 7 and 14). Another faction, however, advocated the repressive approach of Argentina's and Brazil's "gorilas" (see chapters 18 and 20). The new head of state was a U.S.-trained "centrist," General Guillermo Rodríquez Lara.

Although he welcomed foreign loans and investments to expand oil output, General Rodríquez Lara quickly earned his nickname "bombita" (little bomb). He expelled the U.S. military mission and announced he would "sow the petroleum" in reforms and economic development. He decreed an agrarian reform law. The new law affected less than 1 percent of arable land but obligated many *minifundistas* to form "cooperatives"—the only organizations with which the state would deal. Some 100,000 peasants joined co-ops. Now the *latifundistas* had to share their control of the peasantry with the state. In 1974 Rodríquez Lara suspended all political parties. He took back 4 million hectares of oil holdings from Texaco and Gulf, which had usurped one-third of Ecuador's territory during the previous decade. He led Ecuador into OPEC (Organization of Petroleum Exporting Countries—see chapter 11). He heated up the "tuna war" by detaining more U.S. fishermen.

At first the 1973 "oil prosperity" generated by OPEC's fourfold hike in oil prices made it possible for Rodríquez Lara's government to increase economic growth rates and to initiate reforms with impunity. Then, after the 1973–74 Arab oil boycott, which OPEC members Ecuador and Venezuela did not honor, the United States undertook to break up OPEC by focusing on its weakest link—Ecuador. The 1974 Foreign Trade Act denied OPEC members favorable treatment granted other nations. Texaco and Gulf ceased exploration, cut back on production, and forced Ecuador to slash its price on crude oil by 41 cents a barrel and to reduce oil taxes. With state revenues suddenly less than originally anticipated, the military government chose to continue investing in industry but to slow down its populist reforms.

The United States recognized Ecuador's maritime territorial claims and contributed to an increase in foreign investment, which reached $90 million in 1975. Three-quarters of it was in manufacturing. Many enterprises were "mixed," with Ecuadorean private capital and the state. As in the rest of South America, the military went "capitalist," gaining shares of various industries and creating its own commercial airline, merchant fleet, shipyards, and fleet of oil tankers.

Both the elites and the United States feared, however, that a military populism like Peru's, Panama's, or Ecuador's would move to the Left. Rightwingers in the military set about planning a coup. Their first attempt aborted in 1975, but by 1976 they succeeded. Even after their initial failure the government veered sharply rightward. For example, Ecuador joined Pinochet's Chile in rescinding the nationalist Decree 24 of the Andean Pact (see Overview and Introduction to Part Three). Ecuador also refused to honor OPEC price hikes on oil.

After the rightists' successful military coup of 1976 the IMF imposed its standard "austerity" package in support of private enterprise and reinforced Ecuador's export-dependent monoculture (now oil). The government agreed to a demand by United Brands (formerly United Fruit) not to join a cartel of banana exporting nations proposed by Panama's military reformer Torrijos.

In spite of its clear stance on behalf of foreign capital and private enterprise, the government projected a nationalist image by buying out scandal-ridden Gulf Oil (see chapter 15), while leaving Texaco untouched. The state enterprise CEPE (Ecuadorean Petroleum Company), founded in 1972, increased its control to 62 percent of the nation's oil. The nationalization provided Gulf excellent buyout terms. As in Venezuela, big oil corporations like Gulf and Standard were realizing that adjusting to nationalism could mean more reliable profits through state contracts for their technical assistance in producing, developing, and marketing the oil (see chapter 11).

In 1975 trade unions carried out a successful general strike. The urban poor began to mobilize for land and housing. Latin America's new politics began to take hold in tradition-bound Ecuador. The CIA backed AIFLD (American Institute for Free Labor Development—see Overview) stepped up its training of Ecuadorean workers. By 1975 10 percent of the labor force, including many oil workers, had received some kind of AIFLD-related education. In 1977 a hundred disgruntled workers were massacred at one of the nation's main sugar mills. There was another national strike and a work stoppage by teachers.

As peasants continued fleeing rural misery to seek work in the cities, food production slumped. Ecuador had to import greater amounts of food. Additional loans had to be taken out, driving the national debt up higher. The elite-family pillars of domestic economic power—owners of plantations, banks, foreign trade, and the mass media—were merely scratched by the economic turmoil. But peasants were hard hit. They organized a series of regional protests and, in the 1980s, held national congresses of the FENOC (National Federation of Peasant Organizations). Indians followed the FENOC example of bringing together people on a nationwide basis by founding the CONAIE (Confederation of Indigenous Nationalities of Ecuador). Both groups denounced the government's favoring of agribusiness at the expense of the small producer.

Latin America's new politics of broad-based popular movements in support of democracy took root in Ecuador, the first South American country to return to civilian rule after a long period of military governance. The "broad front" approach of uniting rival political parties succeeded in 1979 in returning the government to civilians and granting illiterates the right to vote. But few alliances stuck, and the democratic movement was rife with factionalism and mistrust.

In turning the government back to civilians, the military once again blocked the candidacy of popular Guayaquil mayor Bucaram, who died in 1981. Bucaram's fast-growing CFP (Concentration of Popular forces), with support from the Christian Democrats, won the 1979 presidential race against a conservative ticket.

At age thirty-eight the CFP candidate, a reformist named Jaime Roldós Aguilera (Bucaram's nephew), became Latin America's youngest president. He and his wife died in a plane crash in 1981, just when oil prices were beginning their big slump of the early and mid-1980s. Vice-President Osvaldo Hurtado, far more conservative, succeeded to power. Student and worker unrest led to several declarations of a state of emergency, before new elections in 1984 narrowly brought the ultra-conservative León Febres Cordero into the presidency.

The economic approach of the lion was based on the free-market theories of the "Chicago Boys" (see chapter 17). Febres's government signed agreements with the IMF in 1985 and 1986 so favorable to private capital that international bankers loaned Ecuador half a billion dollars. Meanwhile loans for peasants were cut back, whereas those for large farmers producing for export were increased. Agriculture still accounted for nearly half the nation's exports and employed over half the labor force. New export crops included strawberries, asparagus, quinoa, and flowers. Fishing and forestry exports were rising—Ecuador was the world's largest producer of balsawood.

President Febres removed state subsidies on basic foodstuffs and limited raises in the minimum wage, which lagged behind the usual rising cost of living. He virtually eliminated state controls over banking and foreign oil exploration. He broke diplomatic relations with the Sandinista government of Nicaragua. He also invited back the U.S.-based Summer Institute of Linguistics, a private Christian group engaged in translating the Bible into Indian dialects and widely accused in Latin America of having links to the CIA. The Roldós government had expelled the Institute.

All these policies provoked general strikes in 1986 and 1987. They were broken up by security forces. Charges of police beatings and use of electric shock, murders, and arbitrary arrests became widespread. Congress impeached the interior minister for human rights violations, but he remained at his post.

After the 1987 earthquakes Ecuador not only was out half a billion dollars in expected oil revenues, but also needed $300 million for oil pipeline repairs. The most severe economic crisis since the end of the banana boom of the 1950s faced the nation.

Ecuador's politics remained unstable. The nation's power blocs of the *costa*'s comprador bourgeoisie, the *sierra*'s landed oligarchs, a very reactionary Catholic Church, and the military seemed unlikely to be budged even by occasional challenges from within their own ranks. Only a few priests and the bishop of Riobamba spoke out for the theology of liberation (see Overview). Students, workers, and small leftist parties annually advocated "broad fronts" but rarely maintained unity for more than a few months. A guerrilla organization or two sprang up in the late 1970s but posed no real threat. The strongest one called itself *"Alfaro Vive, Carajo!"* ("Alfaro Lives, Damn It!"—after the 1895 Liberal President Eloy Alfaro). Under terms of a peace accord, most of its members laid down their arms in 1991.

But until then the government used the guerrilla presence to justify severe acts of repression against all dissenters. The majority of about two dozen political parties (see Box 13.1) contesting the 1988 presidential elections campaigned on platforms of enforcement of human rights and renewal of relations with Nicaragua, while the generals kept a wary eye on matters. The winner was fifty-two-year-old political science professor Rodrigo Borja of the ID (Democratic Left), a center-left affiliate of the West Europe-dominated Socialist International. In the runoff contest, Borja defeated sharp-tongued thirty-six-year-old populist Abdalá Bucaram of the PRE (Roldosista Party of Ecuador), an admirer of the "organizational genius" of Adolf Hitler. Bucaram had been mayor of Guayaquil in 1985 when he went into exile rather than face charges of slandering the armed forces. The election was Ecuador's third successive one on schedule but did not deter the rise of the popular movement.

Box 13.1: Ecuador's Main Political Parties and Labor Organizations

APRE Popular Revolutionary Ecuadorean Action, supported rebel officer Frank Vargas Pazzos in 1988 and 1992 presidential races

CEDOC Ecuadorean Confederation of Free Labor Organizations, founded in 1938 and said to have CIA funding. Split in 1976 between moderates and radicals

CEOSL Ecuadorean Central of Labor Union Organizations, founded in 1962, backed by AIFLD

CFP Concentration of Popular Forces, founded in 1946. Populist and center-right. Split in 1980 when pro-Roldós forces launched PRE. In 1984 CFP supported the conservative Febres government

CONAIE Confederation of Indigenous Nationalities of Ecuador, strong in 1980s and 1990s

CTE Communist-led Workers' Central, founded in 1944, part of FUT

DP Popular Democracy—Christian Democratic Union, affiliate of Christian Democratic International, founded in 1964, split into many factions since

FADI Front of the Left, founded in 1977 by Communists' PCE, PSR, Christian leftists, and Maoists. Joined in 1984 with centrists to form Progressive Democratic front

FENOC National Federation of Peasant Organizations

FRA Alfarista Radical front, founded in 1972, populist-centrist; supported the conservative Febres government after 1984

FUT Unified Workers front, largest labor union confederation

GL Liberty Group, an underground responsible for a wave of bombings starting in 1992

ID Izquierda Democrática, or Democratic Left, large center-left party, member of West Europe-dominated Socialist International; won presidency in 1988

MPD Popular Democratic party, Maoist Communist party, member of 1984 Progressive Democratic front

PC Conservative party, founded in 1855, governed until 1895, now much weaker; in 1984 supported conservative Febres government

PCE Ecuadorean Communist party, founded in 1926

PLR Radical Liberal party, founded in 1895 as new name for the Liberals; in 1984 supported conservative Febres government

PRE Roldosista party of Ecuador, founded in 1980 and officially recognized in 1982, centrist, named after late president (1979–1981) Jaime Roldós Aguilera

Progressive Democratic front Formed in 1984 by FADI, ID, MPD, PRE, and other Left and centrist forces as political alliance briefly controlling slim majority in Congress

PSC Partido Social Cristiano, or Social Christian party, conservative, founded in 1951 to back political ascent of President (1956–1960) Camilo Ponce Enríquez; its León Febres Cordero elected president in 1984 as part of center-right electoral alliance called National Reconstruction front

PSE Ecudorean Socialist party, allied with APRE

PSR Revolutionary Socialist party, founded in 1961 as PCE splitoff championing Cuban Revolution; part of FADI

PUR Republican Unity party, a PSC splinter led by President Durán Ballén

President Borja gradually implemented economic austerity measures insisted upon by the IMF and World Bank and removed constraints on foreign investment. He was rewarded by favorable terms on reduction of the nation's unpayable foreign debt. Although he nationalized oil operations to try to correct falling revenues, most of the oil business was done under contract to foreign firms anyway. In order to restrict union activity, Borja modified the 1938 labor code. Organized labor's FUT (Unified Workers front) responded by stepping up the pace of its general strikes. Less than 13 percent of the labor force was employed in manufacturing. There were 60,000 industrial workers but 150,000 bureaucrats. Most peasants and workers were a poorly paid, intermittently employed "subproletariat," much of which rallied to the popular movement.

In 1990 the Indians' CONAIE launched a national uprising, taking twelve military hostages. Church-mediated peace negotiations followed. When the government broke some of its promises, however, the CONAEI occupied Congress for two days in May 1991. Its demands were: local autonomy, amnesty, agrarian reform, human rights, assistance in combatting the cholera epidemic, defense against incursions by paramilitary groups in pay of big landowners, and Indian control over natural resources on Indian lands. A year later it achieved an agreement granting about 20,000 mostly Quechua-speaking Indians 3 million acres in a part of southeastern Ecuador that included a disputed border with Peru (the border dispute with Peru had flared up in 1981 and threatened to erupt again). Although not winning control over their natural resources, the nation's Indians did win the right to veto any forms of oil or other production that were ecologically damaging.

Meanwhile, Borja's ID party became a shadow of its former self. Borja's backers in the unicameral Congress became a minority as a result of the 1990 off-year elections. The leftwing MPD and FADI (see Box 13.1) voted with the majority as Congress impeached several cabinet members. Inflation galloped along at above 50 percent, families went hungry, and illiteracy rates remained at 30 percent or higher. In its last days, the Borja government arrested fifty-one people involved in narco-trafficking, including a few prominent police and military personnel.

For the 1992 presidential race, one of several pro-business candidates, seventy-year-old Sixto Durán Ballén, a U.S.-educated architect, was denied renomination by his PSC. He proceeded to organize the PUR (Republican Unity party). He and the PSC candidate won the first round of the presidential elections. Then Durán Ballén won the runoff contest. His PUR ranked only third in Congress, after the PSC and PRE, with the ID a distant fourth.

As president, Durán Ballén pulled Ecuador, out of OPEC, received a World Bank loan to spur his privatization of the state oil firm, and sped up Ecuador's entry into a refurbished "free trade" Andean common market (see

Introduction to Part Three). Introducing a program of radical economic neo-liberalism, he raised utility and gas prices, slashed public spending, froze public hiring, and let prices rise freely. The popular movement protested more loudly than ever. Troops occupied Guayaquil, showing where the ultimate armed power of political arbitration remained—at least for the moment. Those Ecuadorians who could afford the trip joined the 5 percent of the population living in the United States—about half a million.

Selected Bibliography

Agee, Philip. *Inside the Company: CIA Diary.* Harmondsworth, England: Penguin, 1975. Ex-CIA agent's inside story of CIA destabilization and 1963 coup.

Bromley, R. J. *Development Planning in Ecuador.* Sussex, England: Latin American Publications Fund, 1977. Its inadequacies and why.

Cubbit, David, and David Corkill. *Ecuador.* London: Latin America Bureau, 1988. Brief overview.

Cueva, Agustín. *The Process of Political Domination in Ecuador.* New Brunswick, NJ: Transaction Books, 1982. Short history; original analysis of Velasquismo.

Icaza, Jorge. *Huasipango.* Carbondale: Southern Illinois University Press, 1964. Famous novel about Indian villagers.

Martz, John D. *Politics and Petroleum in Ecuador.* New Brunswick, NJ: Transaction Books, 1987.

Needler, Martin C. *Anatomy of a Coup d'État: Ecuador 1963.* Washington, DC: Institute for the Comparative Study of Political Systems, 1964.

Schodt, David W. *Ecuador: An Andean Enigma.* Boulder, CO: Westview, 1987. Solid economic history.

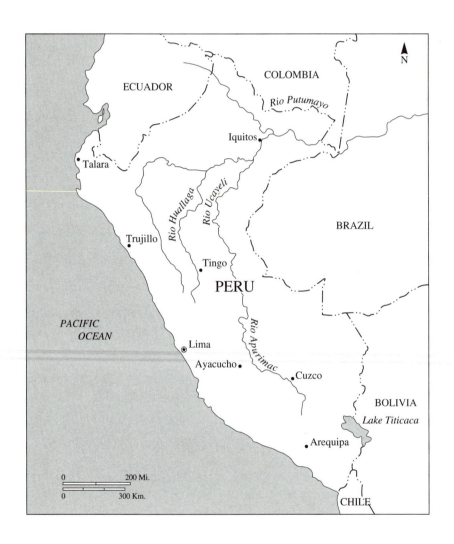

PACIFIC
OCEAN

ECUADOR

COLOMBIA

Rio Putumayo

Iquitos

Talara

Rio Huallaga

Rio Ucayeli

BRAZIL

Trujillo

Tingo

PERU

Rio Apurimac

Lima

Ayacucho

Cuzco

BOLIVIA

Lake Titicaca

Arequipa

CHILE

N

0   200 Mi.

0   300 Km.

Peru ___ 14

The time has come to dedicate our national energies to the transformation of the economic, social, and cultural structures of Peru.—*October 3, 1968, manifesto of Peru's new military government*

"The situation is very serious, poverty is growing deeper, and there are more and more undernourished children."—*Gustavo Gutiérrez, "father" of liberation theology, 1993*

On the morning of July 19, 1977, on the Central Highway a few miles from Peru's capital city of Lima, workers in the industrial zone of Vitarte gathered 10,000 strong and rolled huge boulders into street intersections. For weeks many of them had been occupying their textile factories to protest layoffs. In downtown Lima workers and students joined up in mammoth antigovernment demonstrations. Pickets blocked the three avenues linking Lima to the port city of Callao. To the north and south of Lima entire shantytown families swarmed into dusty unpaved streets to march to Avenida Tupac Amarú and Avenida Pachacutec, the new avenues used by buses to transport people to work.

Everyone linked arms and chanted "Down with the IMF (International Monetary Fund)" and "*No pasarán!*"—not a single bus would pass that day. No worker would be able to reach any part of greater Lima or Callao, the nation's industrial hub where 6 million people lived—nearly one-third of the populace. In the southern districts, for as far as the eye could see, there stretched row after row of sagging shacks of mud, wood, matted straw, cardboard, tin, occasional cement—one of the world's most extensive and water-scarce slums, the famed *barriadas* or shantytowns of Lima, once known as "the City of Kings." Only a distant "lake" ended the panorama of dusty squalor, and it was a heat-created mirage in the southern desert.

A year earlier, in mid-1976, foreign banks had refused new loans to Peru unless the debt-ridden military government accepted the IMF's "economic austerity cure." And what was the cure? Price hikes, wage limits, currency devaluations, federal budget cutbacks, in short, likely zero or negative economic growth in the name of "economic recovery" and "combatting inflation." Peruvians had refused to swallow that distasteful medicine more than once. They had launched strikes and street demonstrations and had fought police with rocks and clubs.

The government had given them a tough answer in 1976 that satisfied the international banking community, a "state of emergency" establishing a night-to-dawn curfew, outlawing strikes, and restricting collective bargaining. The new edict ordered the firing of workers who violated the "national emergency," allowed arrests and house searches without warrants, and suspended freedom of assembly and press. In the succeeding twelve months the government had implemented most of the IMF's recommendations, and thousands upon thousands of workers had been arbitrarily fired—10,000 in the fisherman's union alone. But the promised economic recovery had not materialized; matters had gotten worse. Now the government had again given in to fresh IMF demands.

At midday, marines from the very conservative 12,000-strong navy ordered a crowd in the district of Comas to disperse and allow traffic to flow on Avenida Tupac Amarú.

"*Nunca más!*" a distraught housewife cried out. "*No pasarán!*"

Others picked up the chant: "Never again! You shall not pass!"

The marines began firing their guns. There were screams as people raced to escape the bullets.

When the dust settled, five had been killed, countless wounded. Some seven hundred people had been hauled off to jail, including the heads of the major labor confederations. Nevertheless, the illegal strike held firm. On the next day, July 20, nothing moved, no one worked, production remained at a standstill.

The only sizable labor group to approve the government's actions was the one led by the military's main political ally, the APRA (American Popular Revolutionary Alliance). From the 1920s until the 1960s army officers had fought tooth-and-nail to prevent APRA from gaining the presidency, but during the past two decades an amicable working alliance between the old rivals had been worked out. Now both groups were losing public respect! Even APRA's iron-clad grip on the bus drivers was slipping. More and more of them were refusing to obey orders to break strikes.

452

The nine-year-old military government's much heralded "revolution," despite its agrarian reform and takeover of numerous subsidiaries of foreign corporations, had not fooled everyone. To a growing number of Peruvians, it seemed as fraudulent as APRA's similar promises. Even the PCP (Peruvian Communist party), which had lent its "critical support" to the "revolution" and had delayed supporting the 1977 general strike, was growing impatient with the military's post-1975 swing to the extreme Right.

The words of a street leaflet announcing the forty-eight-hour general strike reflected the feelings of most working Peruvians:

> We declare our firm rejection of the government's economic measures. Their only object is to unload the economic crisis onto the backs of workers and the Peruvian people. We announce the following Platform of Struggle.
>
> (1). For a general increase in salaries and wages commensurate with the rise in the cost of living and rejection of IMF austerity measures
> (2). For a price freeze on basic necessities
> (3). For respect of collective bargaining rights without limits on the number of employees or other restrictions
> (4). For full respect for job security
> (5). For reinstatement of sacked workers, freedom for political prisoners, and return of those deported because of their trade-union or social struggles
> (6). For unrestricted respect for democratic freedoms and no interference in the representative organizations of workers
> (7). For solution of the situation facing the fishermen
> (8). For cancelling the agrarian debt and for non-interference in peasant enterprises
> (9). For non-intervention in the universities

The July 1977 nationwide general strike radically altered the course of Peruvian politics. The impoverished millions of greater Lima's _barriadas_—today's 2,000 shantytowns housing half the city's 8 million residents—had developed a heightened political consciousness and become important participants in Latin America's "new politics" (see Overview). Peru's _barriada_ residents were the first to raise the cry of "Down with the IMF!"—leading some to characterize Peru as "the IMF's Vietnam." The 1977 events shattered the good reputation of the military government's "nationalist, anti-imperialist" revolution once and for all. The strike forced the regime to freeze prices in open defiance of the IMF. The military was obliged to lift the state of emergency and to promise a return to civilian rule by 1980.

The changes took place. The military brass stepped down and there was a "return to democracy." Every political party, above all the APRA, reformulated their programs to catch up with the altered consciousness of millions of Peruvians.

But IMF pressure and the onset of a deeper economic crisis in the 1980s made matters worse. Peru could not meet its debt-service payments and its economy faced near collapse. Illegal cocaine trafficking and everyday crime became major economic props for a growing number of people. Civilian administrations tolerated the military's Argentine-style "dirty war" against a spreading guerrilla movement launched in 1980 by a fanatical Maoist group called "Shining Path." Acts of terrorism spread across the land.

Peru, for all its democratic glitter, became a focus of international human rights protests. A new APRA government, the first since the party's founding in 1924, took power in 1985 but could not carry through on its populist promises. The U.S.-aided military's "dirty war" against the Shining Path and other guerrilla groups (see Box 14.1) was taking its toll: 30,000 lives by the end of 1993, plus the frequent destruction of electric power stations and other guerrilla "economic targets" in the cities. Peru's soldiers and policemen routinely raped girls and women. The United Nations, the U.S. Congress, and other groups rated Peru's security forces as among the world's worst violators of human rights. In 1990 a political outsider was elected president, but he destroyed Peru's shaky democracy two years later through a military coup that left him as nominal president and only gradually reopened the door to fair elections some time later.

Peru was a semi-industrialized, highly urbanized country of 23 million people torn by conflict between a white elite minority and an Indian and mestizo majority. During the 1950–1975 period manufacturing had overtaken agriculture as a share of national output and employment. Foreign capital had led the way, often in joint ventures with Peruvian private and state capital. As Lima sociologist Julio Cotler once observed, "U.S. capital provided the know-how, and Peruvian capital the know-whom." In addition to new industries in consumer durables like cars and industrial inputs like cement, Peru sported an unusually rich mix of important exports: oil, chemicals, metal products, copper, gold, silver, iron ore, lead, zinc, fish and fish products, cotton, sugar, and coffee.

Yet little of this wealth ever trickled down to the majority of Peruvians. Peru had the "vital statistics" of a sick and dying patient—more closely resembling Bolivia (see chapter 15). Its income distribution was one of the world's most unequal. Two-thirds of its people lacked electricity. Potable drinking water was a luxury. Latin America's cholera epidemic first broke out in Peru, claiming 3,000 lives in 1991. Spreading through impure drinking water systems, it made ill five hundred people *a day* and cost the economic infrastructure an estimated $25 billion. Peru's infant mortality rate was one of the Western Hemisphere's highest. Life expectancy was sixty-one years. By the mid-1990s, the number of Peruvians living below the poverty line of $40 a month had skyrocketed to 70 percent of the population. Nearly three-fourths of urban "employment" consisted of people working in the "informal" sector—making things at home, hawking their wares on the street, begging in the streets, trading with one another or dealing a few drugs—unable to find work in the "regular economy." Half the industrial work force of nearly a million had been laid off, and those remaining with jobs had seen their real wages plummet. Combined unemployment and underemployment stood at over 60 percent. Manufacturing firms hard hit by the economic crisis increasingly subcontracted out production and distribution of textiles, shoes, furniture, household utensils, and other goods to low-paid women and children.

Malnourishment affected 60 percent of Peruvians. Hunger was the main concern of most people. Neighborhood soup kitchens were everywhere. More than a million Peruvians chewed coca leaves mixed with lime in order to alleviate their hunger pangs, although fewer and fewer could afford the rising prices of that once inexpensive but now highly demanded "export." Peru was the world's largest supplier of coca for the production of cocaine, much of it based in Colombia (see chapter 12) and increasing amounts in Peru itself. Peru's coca/cocaine trade brought in a billion dollars a year, dwarfing all other exports.

Illiteracy rates surpassed 20 percent in Peru's cities, where 75 percent of the population resided. In the even poorer rural areas illiteracy was more widespread. Some 37,000 Peruvian children died of preventable diseases like tetanus and diarrhea in 1993. Historians agreed that even in the harsh and hierarchical world of the Inca Empire (ca. 1450–1530), a hard-working population estimated at between 5 and 25 million had been better fed and clothed than Peruvians in the 1980s and 1990s. Cholera and starvation stalked the ancient, suffering land of the Incas.

Geographical and Racial Factors

Peru's economic crisis was compounded by its unusual geography, climate, and ethnography. Less than 15 percent of its immense land area (South America's third largest) can produce crops. A thin strip of some of the world's driest desert lands stretches along the Pacific Ocean coastline from the northern border with Ecuador to the southern one with Chile. Some fifty-two rivers wind down from the towering Andes Mountains, ten of them continuously into the Pacific Ocean, to create oases of fertile coastal agriculture, largely sugar and cotton in the north. Thermal inversions are common, helping to make Lima one of the world's ten most polluted cities. More than half the population resides in the coastal cities and towns.

The "sierra" region of 20,000-foot-high Andean peaks and intermont basins and valleys that makes up more than one-quarter of the national territory is cold, impassable, mostly dry. With the exception of an occasional valley, land use in this "Altiplano," as it is known, is limited to potatoes, root crops, and rough grazing pasture for llama, alpaca, vicuña, sheep, and cattle—the sources of Peru's wool exports and textile and dairy industries. Some of the world's most copious mineral resources are found in the sierra, where 38 percent of Peruvians live. Many reside in the south-central region near Cuzco and Puno (Lake Titicaca), one of Latin America's most impoverished areas. A drought in this region and floods in northern Peru in 1983 contributed to an awesome 11 percent decline in GDP (gross domestic product) for the year.

More than half the nation's territory consists of jungles and tropical rain forests, inhabited by 11 percent of the population. These lands start in the *"ceja de la selva,"* or eyebrow of the forest as the sloping "montaña" region rich in coffee and coca production is called, and spread eastward into the sweltering lowlands. The "boom-town" coffee and cocaine city of Tingo María is the montaña's main commercial center, bustling with Italian and German immigrants. The only major city in the northern and eastern Amazonian rain forests into which flow most of the nation's rivers, is Iquitos, once a thriving rubber colony and now tied to the production and export of oil.

By far and away the most oppressed group, Peru's Indians, comprising almost half the population, speak mainly Quechua, although some Aymara is spoken near Lake Titicaca and dozens of Indian dialects survive in the jungles. Indians are not only economically the worst off, but they are also looked down upon when not romanticized by the whites (in Peru, known as *criollos*, 12 percent) and by the mestizos (known as *cholos*, 33 percent—or more if one counts Indians assimilated into the dominant culture). About 3 percent of Peruvians are black or mulatto, and another 3 percent are Chinese, Japanese, and "other."

Peru's cholos have higher levels of education than Peru's Indians because of their access to criollo-dominated urban environments. With roots or links to the Indian communities, they often have been the leaders of the sierra peasantry's land-occupying and unionizing efforts of the past four decades. (Criollos often have led the agrarian movements of the costa, where hardly any Indians lived until the 1960s.)

An immense geographical, linguistic, and cultural gap, then, divides Peru in half, separating the criollos, cholos, and Asians from the Indians. The only times Indian movements for revindication succeeded in Peru were when they came from within the Indian communities, about four thousand of which still exist in the sierra and another seven hundred in the jungle. Usually the leaders were the Indians themselves. When cholos led, they spoke Quechua and still did not have the complete trust of their followers. Not until 1975 was Quechua made an official language, to be taught in schools along with Spanish. Clearly, Peru cannot be understood without addressing the encounter between Indian and Western civilizations.

Inca Empire, Spanish Conquest, Tupac Amaru Revolt, and Independence

In the second half of the fifteenth century the Incas of Peru's Altiplano gained control over civilizations with thousands of years of history, including complex societies with monumental architecture 100 miles north of Lima as early as the time of Egypt's great pyramids and Sumeria's city-states. Only Chile's Auracanians successfully fought off the Incas' advance (as they did the Spaniards—see chapter 17).

Almost all the pre-Inca civilizations had amazingly advanced agricultural techniques—highly developed irrigation systems, the use of fertilizers, and the terracing of mountainous slopes for growing crops. They also excelled at weaving tapestries and making jewelry and vases, and in the case of Colombia's Chibchas, architecture and sculpting. The Spaniards discovered that the Incas, who understood the decimal system and counted on knotted rope cords called *quipus* still in use today, were sophisticated physicians and surgeons. They regularly extracted medicines from local plants; quinine, extracted from Peruvian *cinchona* bark, was the cure for malaria for centuries. Inca surgeons even dared to perform brain surgery!

The Incas combined centralized, sometimes brutal authoritarian rule with the winning over of local pre-Inca chieftains (called *kurakas*) who were given titles of Incaic nobility and leadership positions. Acceptance of Incaic rule was furthered when the Incas saw to it that the physical needs of the people were taken care of—hunger and acute hardship became relatively unknown. The Incas's usual punishment for acts of defiance or even petty thievery was death. But a man robbing out of need was provided for, and the officials responsible for his desperation were sentenced to death.

The peoples subjugated by the Incas provided labor to the Inca rulers, nobles, and priests as warriors, tillers, masons, weavers, construction gangs, domestic servants, and teams of relay runners bringing fresh fish to the sierra from the coast. The main social unit during Inca times was the ancient *ayllu*, a traditional kinship group or clan. While differences in wealth and power existed within an *ayllu*, group solidarity was the norm. The *kurakas* of clustered *ayllus* composed the nobility and were tied to the Inca, or ruler, who claimed descent from the sun-god. All land technically belonged to the Inca, but he parceled it out through his bureaucratic underlings—the gods, priests, and royal courts, with only a third ending up in the hands of the local *ayllu* communities.

The people planted and harvested communally—an *ayllu* tradition that still survives. A small class of semislaves known as *yanaconas* existed, and every year the Inca imposed a forced labor call-up, the *mita*, for the construction of roads and temples or other work. Traces of the Inca network of rope-cord suspension bridges and stone-paved foot paths lined with adobe walls can still be glimpsed in Peru's sierra and coastal lowlands. In Cuzco, a sierra city more than 11,000 feet high populated by 100,000 in Inca times, Spanish churches were built on foundations of old Inca walls composed of gigantic stones cut, angled, and joined so precisely that nothing can be seen between the joints.

In 1532 Francisco Pizarro, an illiterate swineherd from Extremadura considered by many to be Spain's most bloodthirsty *conquistador*, landed at Tumbes and commenced the slaughter of hundreds of thousands of Peru's Indians. He laid siege to an empire already in a state of disintegration. A devastating plague in the 1520s had taken many Inca lives and provoked a long civil war. This, plus the far superior military technology of Spanish cannon and horse cavalry, doomed the fading Inca Empire. Pizarro offered peace to Inca Atahualpa, lured him and his supporters into the plaza of the sierra valley city of Cajamarca, and ambushed them. Atahualpa bought his freedom by filling two rooms with gold and silver, but Pizarro betrayed him again. Taken prisoner, Atahualpa was first baptized and then strangled to death. In 1533 the Inca capital of Cuzco fell to the Spaniards.

Indian resistance continued for centuries. In 1536 forces led by Inca Manco defeated Pizarro's foot soldiers by tumbling boulders upon them and ambushing them with slingshots and javelins. Eventually Pizarro's troops drove the rebels back to Cuzco. There, the Indians took cover behind the cyclopean walls of Sacsayhuaman, an immense fort of stones weighing as much as 250 tons that had taken decades to build. During three days of savage fighting, as condors darkened the skies and swooped down to peck at the carnage, the Spaniards slaughtered thousands. Some survivors retreated 70 miles northward to the Machu Picchu fortress but also were conquered. Inca Manco fought from mountain strongholds until his death in 1545. The Spaniards, taking a page from the Inca book of *kuraka*-led empire, made Inca Manco's son, Sayri Tupac, the puppet sovereign of Spanish-ruled lands and labor.

The last of the Inca line, Tupac Amarú, resisted Spanish blandishments. From a fortress in the mountains northeast of Cuzco he launched periodic raids. He was not captured until 1571, when Viceroy Francisco de Toledo, famed for his administrative talents and humanitarian concerns, ordered his execution.

The Spaniards used the Indians as virtual slaves for the mining of silver at Potosí (see chapter 15) and of mercury (used in silver smelting) at Huancavelica. Overwork and European diseases like measles, smallpox, and influenza reduced the Indian population to 2 million by the year 1600. The silver and gold of the vice-royalty of Peru filled the coffers of northern European banking and merchant houses and governments, ultimately stimulating the rise of early capitalism.

Lima became the center of the South American branch of the Spanish

Empire and the seat of the Inquisition. The Roman Catholic Church hierarchy and Spanish settlers seized the best of the *ayllu* lands and converted them into haciendas and plantations. The *criollo* (white) oligarchs who used haciendas to produce crops and livestock for servicing the mining centers allotted minuscule parcels to Indian tenants and sharecroppers (*colonos*) whom they indebted to the haciendas' "company stores." At the mines work conditions were indescribably cruel. As more and more Indians perished from their travail, African slaves were imported to keep agricultural production going on the coast and sometimes to supplement the dwindling work force at the mines. Peru's hacienda owners, known as *gamonales*, led an easy life.

Some one hundred popular uprisings occurred between 1730 and 1814, but were usually localized and violently snuffed out. The most serious one came close to establishing Indian rule. It was led by a Cuzco *kuraka* baptized at birth in 1742 as José Gabriel Condorcanqui. Calling himself Tupac Amarú II, he beseeched royal administrators, to no avail, to end their mistreatment of the "castas," as the noncriollos were called.

In 1780, Tupac Amarú II recruited Indians into an army that swiftly grew to number 80,000 men; it included members from all the castas and even some poor whites. Tupac Amarú II hoped to create a new society of complete equality between whites and nonwhites. His uprising spread like wildfire over southern Peru, most of Bolivia, and northwestern Argentina. Spanish reinforcements from Buenos Aires and Lima finally captured him and forced him to witness the murder of his wife and family before having his tongue cut out and his body pulled asunder by horses tied to his legs and arms. To intimidate others, Spanish soldiers paraded through villages carrying bloody parts of his body on poles.

But this only fanned the fires of popular revolt. Attacks and counterattacks spread throughout the Andes, leaving 80,000 dead. Peru's criollos from that point on welcomed Spanish military garrisons to help them control the rebellious Indians and castas.

Peru's role as centerpiece of Spanish colonialism faded as the mines became less profitable and Argentine, Chilean, and Venezuelan ports gained prominence in international trade. Spain's so-called Bourbon reforms of 1765–1795 were intended to meet the challenge of British, Dutch, French, and U.S. trading companies by extracting more revenues from the colonies and permitting criollos and Spanish colonists to trade with nearby countries. Peru's colonial bureaucrats raised "head taxes" (Indian tribute) and levies on local merchandise. The criollo elites used the long-established *repartimiento de mercancias* technique of obliging peasants and workers to buy more goods at the company stores. Buried ever deeper in debt, field hands, miners, and textile factory workers put in even longer hours. Production shot up, and surplus goods were sold to neighboring countries. Spain gained some revenues for its commercial wars with other European powers, and the gap between the rich and the poor in Peru widened.

Napoleon's occupation of Spain early in the 1800s emboldened some merchants, intellectuals, and young military officers of Buenos Aires, Santiago-Valparaíso, and Caracas to consider declaring independence from Spain. Peru's criollo elites, however, feared an independence war might encourage another Indian uprising and sweep them away. Consequently, while popular rebellions of Indians and castas continued into the nineteenth century—the most successful being the 1814–15 Pumacahua revolt—the final liberation of Peru from Spanish rule awaited the intervention of outside forces.

The two great "liberators" of South America, Argentina's José de San Martín and Venezuela's Simón Bolívar, converged on Peru in the 1820s. San Martín seized Lima in 1821, driving the royalist forces into the Andes. Then, in 1824, Bolívar's nine-thousand-strong army of mostly Colombians commanded by Venezuelan Antonio José de Sucre smashed the royalist army in the sierra battles of Junín and Ayacucho.

Caudillos and Civilistas—Guano, Nitrates, and the War of the Pacific

A forty-year period of virtual political chaos in the newly independent Republic of Peru followed. Some thirty-four presidents briefly took office in Lima, twenty-seven of them officers from the Wars of Independence. These caudillos formed alliances with the provincial elites who claimed (usually falsely) to have opposed the royalist bureaucrats of Lima. Criollo landowners profiting from wool exports handled by British and French merchant houses helped form a federation of Peru and Bolivia in the 1830s, but it was broken up by a Chilean invasion in 1839, which assured Valparaíso's supremacy over Callao as South America's principal Pacific Ocean port (see chapter 17). Peru's regional caudillos continued to fight for control of Lima-Callao, while the economy, devastated by two wars in less than twenty years, barely sputtered along.

The first signs of economic recovery came in midcentury with a sudden rise in European demand for fertilizers to increase agricultural production for its fast-growing and industrializing population. Peru happened to be the world's best source of guano, the nitrogenous droppings of birds on the cliffs of coastal islands. Peru's government subcontracted the guano industry to British merchant houses, keeping 60 percent of profits for itself. Part of these earnings were spent on the foreign debt incurred after independence to get the new republic started. Another sizable chunk was spent on salaries for the army and the state bureaucracy. Still another part lined the pockets of merchants and bankers who handled the guano trade. This new group of guano profiteers helped found the "Civilista" party, which introduced a semblance of stable political rule in the mid-1860s.

Peru's elites imported some 100,000 indentured Chinese laborers to take the place of recently freed African slaves (1854). Many Chinese joined Indian workers on the guano islands, where they suffered burns and sometimes blindness from ammonia fumes. Others worked on the coastal sugar and cotton plantations. These agricultural exports further enriched Peru's elite families.

From 1868 to 1872 the government quadrupled its debt to finance the construction of two trans-Andean railroads, engineered by "the Yankee Pizarro," U.S. entrepreneur Henry Meiggs. Meiggs had made and lost a fortune in San Francisco during the "gold rush" and then had grown wealthy again by building bridges and railroads in Chile. Bribing Peruvian officials and importing Chinese "coolie" laborers and Chilean "rotos" (see chapter 17), Meiggs gained notoriety for his ability to manipulate Lima's Civilistas running the government.

Peru's government soon exhausted the guano deposits and faced bankruptcy. It hoped to resolve the crisis with profits from huge southern nitrate fields. By then sodium nitrate was considered superior to guano as a fertilizer and was also a constituent in gunpowder manufacture. But Chile's elites, some of them backed by the British, already were eyeing the nitrate bonanza. During the War of the Pacific (see chapter 17), the victorious Chilean navy and army overran the nitrate fields, and in 1881 seized Callao and Lima, occupying them until 1883.

This humiliating defeat left Peru's Civilistas in disgrace. Seven months of civil war and a decade of caudillo rule followed during which Peru signed the so-called Grace Contract with its foreign, mostly British, creditors. In exchange for cancellation of the debt Peru granted foreigners control over its railroads, guano, and some jungle lands, as well as annual payments of 80,000 British pounds for thirty-three years.

The Oligarchy, U.S. Investments, Mariátegui, and Haya de la Torre

Scandals like the Grace Contract gave the Civilistas the opening to regain political control in 1895. The next twenty-four years were called the "aristocratic republic"—governments democratically elected by a small male electorate based on literacy and property qualifications. Peru's so-called oligarchy of forty families consolidated its power. It was an informal alliance, sometimes cemented by intermarriage between the wealthiest of the sierra's *gamonales* and mine owners and the coastal sugar and cotton magnates, exporters, and bankers.

Accustomed to working with foreign capitalists, Peru's oligarchy welcomed an influx of U.S. investments during the aristocratic republic and the subsequent dictatorship (1919–1930) of ex-president (1908–1912) Augusto B. Leguía. U.S. loans poured in, accompanied by bribery, graft, and growing U.S.

control of the economy. Citibank paid Leguía's son $415,000 to persuade his father to accept the biggest of the loans.

U.S. corporations took over almost all of Peru's mining and oil industries. Cerro de Pasco Mining Company owned the best mines of the central sierra. Northern Peru Mining Company (a subsidiary of American Smelting and Refining Company) gained control of those in the northern sierra. The Vanadium Corporation held Peru's vanadium deposits, the world's largest. These three companies accounted for almost all of Peru's mineral exports. Standard Oil of New Jersey's subsidiary IPC (International Petroleum Company) bought out British and Peruvian oil firms in 1913 to control the lush oilfields near Talara in the northern desert.

U.S. firms also invested in agriculture. W. R. Grace and Company, a big U.S. chemical, shipping, agroindustrial firm today, got its start in Peruvian trading, textile manufacturing, sugar, and mining. Even the mining companies got into the agribusiness act. Cerro de Pasco, for instance, after starting its La Oroya smelter operation in 1922, refused to place filters over its smokestacks until after the arsenic, lead, and poisonous chemicals that belched forth had destroyed animals and crops for miles around. Then Cerro bought up the damaged lands, modified the smokestacks, and became a big *latifundista* with 1,000 square miles of Peru's best pasture lands (equivalent in size to Rhode Island) and a guaranteed labor supply of dispossessed peasants.

In 1927 Citibank's vice-president was able to conclude, "the vast majority of the principal sources of wealth in Peru . . . are controlled by foreign owners, and apart from wages and taxes, none of the value of production is retained in the country."

Recruiters called *enganchadores* for the U.S. mining firms lured peasants off their lands with "loans" to be worked off at the mines. Becoming further indebted to the *mercantiles* (company stores), the former peasants passed their debts on to their children, who also were forced into the mines to pay them off.

Labor protest against long hours, the company store, child labor, and foreign ownership started early in Peru. Workers struck in 1912–13 in Lima-Callao and the northern oil fields and sugar plantations, demanding the eight-hour day. By 1919 an anarchist-led general strike won a seldom enforced eight-hour-day law in Peru—nearly two decades ahead of the United States.

Peru's radical labor movement gave rise to two competing political currents: a revolutionary movement led by writer and journalist José Carlos Mariátegui (1895–1930) and a populist movement headed by former student leader Víctor Raúl Haya de la Torre (1895–1979). Both were influenced by Manuel González Prada (1848–1918), an anarchist teacher at Lima's University of San Marcos who renounced his aristocratic background to condemn what he called "the unholy alliance" of oligarchy, Church, military, and foreign capital. Initially Mariátegui and Haya de la Torre worked together, but they soon parted company.

From an impoverished background and in poor health, Mariátegui used Marxist methods to explain the situation in Peru and has been called "the father of Latin American Marxism." He envisioned a worker-peasant alliance, guided by a Socialist party, that would lead an anti-imperialist revolution to democratize and develop Peru. He founded the Socialist party in 1928 and the CGTP (General Confederation of Peruvian Workers) in 1929. His party changed its name to the PCP (Communist party of Peru) in 1930. The PCP later abandoned his emphasis on allying peasants and their collectivist traditions with the working class. Mariátegui's thesis, nonetheless, became widely accepted among Peruvian leftists during the 1970s and 1980s.

Haya de la Torre came from a completely different background. A son of the oligarchy born in Trujillo, in northern Peru, he had become a student leader at the University of San Marcos in Lima. Jailed and deported to Panama, he later became Minister of Education José Vasconcelos' secretary in Mexico. Vasoncelos' vague ideas about spreading the Mexican Revolution captivated Haya de la Torre, who founded the APRA (American Popular Revolutionary Alliance) in 1924 to reunite all of "Indo-America." APRA's other founding principles were anti-imperialism, nationalization of land and industry, internationalization of the Panama Canal, and solidarity with all oppressed peoples.

Although he shared Mariátegui's anti-imperialism, Haya de la Torre, like populists everywhere, envisioned a broad alliance of *all* social classes replacing the "feudal" oligarchy and foreign "imperialists" with a state-guided independent capitalism. APRA-type parties were organized in many Latin American countries over the next few decades. The strongest gained power in Costa Rica and Venezuela. Like APRA, as the threat of radical revolutions on their Left flanks grew, they developed extremely cordial relations with the United States (see chapters 6, 10, and 11).

In 1930 the Great Depression caused prices on Peru's exports to drop by more than two-thirds from 1929 to 1932. Half the work force at the mines and sugar plantations were laid off, as were 40,000 migrant cotton pickers. Haya de la Torre announced that APRA would run candidates in Peru's elections. Mariátegui's followers called for a revolution.

In August 1930 Colonel Luis Sánchez Cerro seized power in a coup. He sent police to kill miners and oil workers and banned the PCP and CGTP. In 1931 Haya de la Torre, back from exile, ran for president and lost in elections widely viewed as fraudulent. Many months of instability and near civil war followed. In July 1932 Aprista peasant followers seized and held the northern city of Trujillo for four days, killing some captured army officers. The army retook the city, captured six thousand Aprista prisoners, and hauled them off to the pre-Inca ruins of Chan Chan where they were forced to dig their own graves before they were executed.

The Aprista movement, which demanded complete loyalty to Haya de la Torre as its supreme leader, then spawned shock troops called "búfalos," who claimed credit for various retaliations against army slaughters of Apristas, including the assassination of Sánchez Cerro in 1933. During the dictatorship of pro-Fascist General Oscar Benavides (1933–1939), APRA formed disciplined cells that operated semiclandestinely.

Oil, APRA's move to the Right, Middle Classes, and Industrialization

In 1941–42 Peru won its first victory in a war when, in a border dispute, its army seized nearly half of Ecuador, mostly eastern jungle country. It was later announced Peru's new territory contained oil. Standard Oil's IPC was reputed to have been behind the original Peruvian invasion. Brushfire wars along the disputed border continued to simmer into the 1980s (see chapter 13), usually as a means for a weak government in either country to rally public support around the banner of nationalism.

In 1944, in the final year of Lima banker Manuel Prado's first of two presidencies (1939–1945, 1956–1962), APRA and the Communists were allowed to found a labor organization, CTP (Confederation of Peruvian Workers, eventually dominated by Apristas). President Prado was a conciliatory conservative, the son of the university mentor of Mariátegui and Haya de la Torre. He allowed Haya de la Torre to return from his second exile.

In 1945 mine workers gained legal recognition of their unions. Large street demonstrations demanding more reforms led to the election of an APRA-backed candidate as president. APRA leader Haya de la Torre by now was a confirmed anti-Communist who welcomed U.S. investments. Nonetheless, government concessions to workers' insistent wage demands generated calls from the oligarchy for military intervention. The situation remained unstable until 1948 when an Aprista uprising among sailors in Callao was crushed and General Manuel Odría staged a military coup.

General Odría's dictatorship (1948–1956) closely paralleled that of Venezuela's Marco Pérez Jiménez, which lasted three years longer. Both dictators came into power to reverse the growing influence of Aprista-type parties, and both cultivated close relationships with U.S. oil and mining firms. Both struck hard blows against organized labor and left-wing parties. Both sped up industrialization processes initiated by preceding governments, using state investments to build roads, dams, and other "economic infrastructure" while usually allowing foreigners to take out profits tax-free. Both were decorated by U.S. President Dwight D. Eisenhower for their "contributions to the free enterprise system." And after their departures from office in both countries students launched angry demonstrations against Eisenhower's touring vice-president Richard Nixon in 1958 (see chapter 11).

But there the parallels ended. In Peru, unlike Venezuela, the state remained thoroughly dominated by the traditional export-oriented so-called oligarchy of forty families. No industrialists championed a mass movement to topple Odría. No general strike or revolution in the streets toppled him. Odría called elections in 1956. After he failed to win them because APRA threw its support to Prado his followers carried on their politics in the halls of congress, blocking as many reforms as possible.

Meanwhile the oligarchy's and U.S. capital's stranglehold on the nation's scarce cultivable lands tightened. By 1961 more than half the nation's land consisted of gigantic haciendas averaging 1,338 hectares. Another 11 percent of the land was classified as "family units," mostly *minifundia* too small to support a family. The remainder—36 percent—were communal lands, largely rocky pasture and woodlands.

Not all Peru's *gamonales* were old-fashioned *latifundistas*. Half to three-fourths of the directors of the powerful SNA (National Agrarian Society) held large stock portfolios in banks, insurance companies, construction firms, real estate, commercial firms, and oil companies.

U.S. agribusiness moved into Peru on a large scale. In the southern province of Arequipa, starting in 1942, Carnation Milk built up a dairy industry that accounted for nearly 90 percent of Peru's canned evaporated milk. Some six thousand small peasant landholders tied to Carnation's credit and production schedules lost their autonomy as independent producers. As family farmers became agribusiness laborers, production of food for domestic consumption failed to keep up with the pace of population growth (Peru's population was doubling every thirty years). Peru had to import basic foods, often from some of the same agribusinesses dominant inside its own economy. In order to weaken strong unions, W. R. Grace mechanized its sugar estates and textile factories in the 1960s. Before it was nationalized in the early 1970s, Grace had fired three-fourths of its work force.

U.S. corporations increased their investments in Peru to more than $600 million by the mid-1960s, half in mining and smelting and $100 million in capital-intensive manufacturing. Standard Oil's IPC accounted for $208 million in oil and other activities. Mining production zoomed up with mechanization. The U.S.-owned SPCC (Southern Peru Copper Corporation) became the leading mining firm, taking out huge profits during a boom in mineral exports.

For the more skilled jobs, mining firms hired cholos, some of whom linked up with unskilled workers to lead trade-union struggles. The big mining companies quieted down labor's demands by granting some concessions— building housing for workers to rent and sending social workers to instruct housewives on nutrition and health. Many workers considered these reforms "paternalistic." Women organized their own "comités de damas," which later played an important role during strike waves in the 1960s.

The production of fishmeal, used for animal feed, became an important industry. Developed initially by small-scale Peruvian investors, it was also penetrated by foreign capital. By 1963 Peru had the world's largest fishing industry, as some 154 factories ground the abundant anchovy catch into fishmeal.

The predictable consequences of so much concentration of land and wealth in so few hands were increased social unrest and a rise in nationalism. Starting in the late 1950s, *comuneros*, members of Indian sierra communities, conducted hundreds of invasions of haciendas. In La Convención valley near Cuzco, peasant *colonos* began organizing unions, led by a cholo, Hugo Blanco, a young Trotskyist (see chapter 15) who spoke Quechua. Peasant combat with local landlords, the 30,000-strong Civil Guard (a uniformed constabulary), and the military evolved into a full-scale insurrection that the army crushed in the early 1960s. Blanco and more than a thousand peasant leaders were packed off to the offshore "Devil's Island" prison of El Frontón. An international human rights campaign to free the prisoners eventually gained the release of Blanco and others.

Other social groups also resented the oligarchy's continued political dominance. Women were given the right to vote in 1956, but neither they nor workers, Indians, and peasant migrants to urban slums had genuine access to political power. Peru's middle-class people and burgeoning industrialists joined the outcry against the oligarchy.

Since the days of Mariátegui, Peru's middle classes had been small but vocal. Relatively excluded from "legitimate" politics, their leaders had usually been left-wing or populist. But with industrialization their numbers increased, their politics diversified, and by the 1960s many were permitted to enter the "political mainstream," such as it was. A varied group, the middle classes included occasional well-off farmers, businesspeople, lawyers, and military officers. The overwhelming majority, however, were poorly paid tradesmen, independent craftsmen, professionals, technicians, and office workers.

New ideological groups emerged to match the challenge of the Marxists and populists. Composed of intellectuals, professionals, and businesspeople, they espoused Christian Democratic-type ideals and did not oppose private enterprise or castigate "imperialism." They supported conservative-populist parties like APRA (as it moved right), PDC (Christian Democratic party), and AP (Popular Action). Both the PDC and AP were founded in 1956 in the southern sierra provincial city of Arequipa, Peru's second largest. Because it had long felt neglected by the government in Lima, Arequipa had often spawned opposition movements.

Since most voters were middle class, the 1962 elections produced a close contest between APRA's Haya de la Torre and AP's Fernando Belaunde Terry, an architect from a leading Arequipa family. Amidst widespread cries of "fraud," Haya de la Torre won by a hair. Odría ran third. The U.S. State Department was satisfied—it had backed Haya de la Torre since the 1950s. Peru's military, however, had always been nervous about letting him have the presidency. It resolved the electoral dispute by a coup and called for new elections. Fearing Belaunde's and the PDC's populism much more than it did Haya de la Torre's politics, the pro-Odría wing of the officer corps formed a pact with APRA that lasted over the next several years—the so-called military-APRA _convivencia_ ("living together").

Despite APRA's agreement with the military, Haya de la Torre was defeated by Belaunde in the scheduled 1963 elections. During the campaign the issue of foreign domination of the economy moved to center stage. For half a century IPC had sent out massive profits and not until 1952 did it pay even a penny in taxes. Belaunde promised to end that practice. He formed an alliance with PDC and gained the backing of the PCP (Peruvian Communist party), winning by 2 percentage points.

President Belaunde (1963–1968) launched a modest agrarian reform. It legitimized earlier peasant land seizures by "allowing" the peasants to purchase legally the disputed parcels. In 1964 Belaunde became the first president not to farm out the collection of federal taxes to a private company. But other reformist measures were blocked or defeated by the Odría-APRA majority in congress—the same forces that applauded when the Belaunde government later sent troops to occupy the smelter town of La Oroya and to imprison union leaders.

Social protest turned violent. In 1959 a leftist section of APRA had adopted the ideas of the Cuban Revolution and broken with Haya de la Torre to form the MIR (Movement of the Revolutionary Left). The MIR set up four different guerrilla fronts in 1965. U.S. military advisers rushed to Peru, the IPC helped the military produce napalm, and the guerrillas soon found bombs and liquid fire raining down on their heads. Most were wiped out; a few accepted amnesty.

Belaunde's government welcomed foreign capital. By late 1968 foreign investors controlled three-fourth of Peru's mining, half of its manufacturing, two-thirds of its commercial banking, and one-third of its fishing.

But late in 1968 Belaunde signed an agreement with IPC that ceded the nearly exhausted oil fields at Talara to the state oil firm EPF. The IPC had already started to wind down its operations. A political scandal erupted when the agreement's "secret page 11" was made public by EPF's president. Page 11 obligated EPF to sell to IPC oil at a ridiculously low price, guaranteeing yet again the transfer of the bulk of oil profits to Standard Oil. Nonetheless, nationalization of a U.S. oil firm had occurred, and even this small dog barking caused the U.S. government to swing into immediate action.

Early on the morning of October 3, 1968, U.S. Sherman tanks surrounded the presidential palace. U.S.-trained commandos and troops evicted the pajama-clad president and deported him to Argentina. The civilian-military game of musical chairs seemed endless. Indeed, the new military regime eventually called elections in 1980 that returned the man it overthrew, Belaunde, to the presidency. But in the intervening *docenio militar* (twelve-year military rule), the military accomplished what lower-class and middle-class political movements had never been able to do on their own—break the oligarchy's iron grip on government.

Military Government and the New Politics

The new military government of Peru surprised everyone, including the people in Washington who had supported its coup. It soon gained a reputation of being "revolutionary."

With hindsight, however, analysts of Latin America concluded that it was "reformist," and in its later phrases "reactionary." Nonetheless, the officers who seized power in 1968, loudly proclaiming a social revolution, represented a new military politics in Latin America that soon spread to other countries (see chapters 7, 13, and 15).

Peru's officers and junior officers, trained at CAEM (Center for Advanced Military Studies), established in the 1950s to educate them about economic development, had learned about the import-substitution and "dependency" ideas of the United Nations' ECLA (Economic Commission on Latin America—see Overview). U.S. advisers like Luigi Einaudi of the Rand Corporation had taught them how to avoid a Cuba-type revolution by adding "civic action" components (reform projects involving local people) to standard counterinsurgency techniques such as those used to crush the MIR guerrillas.

Many officers involved in the 1968 coup were from the provincial lower middle classes and had no inherent love for the oligarchy. Coup leader General Juan Velasco Alvarado was himself a cholo with a lower-middle-class provincial upbringing. Like many Peruvians, the officers felt humiliated by the IPC scandal. Growing numbers inside the military wanted to reclaim national honor, deal with economic underdevelopment, and at the same time avoid the pitfalls of violent revolution and atheistic communism. Indeed, these officers reasoned, unrest from below could be better controlled by reform than by massacre.

To win popular support, their government introduced what Velasco called a "Socialist revolution." Starting out with a nationalist bang, it immediately expropriated Standard Oil's IPC. Washington began enforcing the 1963

Hickenlooper Amendment, which called for terminating foreign aid and trade with any country expropriating a U.S.-owned company without "just compensation." Peru's military junta rallied support by suggesting that fifty years of superprofits were *more than* just compensation. (It later indirectly paid off IPC and granted lucrative new concessions to Occidental Petroleum).

Despite his revolutionary rhetoric, Velasco wanted to make sure that the nationalization of IPC did not panic other leading domestic and foreign investors. He repeatedly guaranteed their rights even while decreeing reforms that seemed to threaten them. He liked to say his government was "neither Communist nor capitalist"—the slogan of populists all over the world and a household phrase in Peru ever since it had been introduced by the PDC and AP.

The decision makers who engineered the Velasco government's reform-minded program "Plan Inca" were select military officials who drew heavily on the advice of middle-class intellectuals, technocrats, and occasional businesspeople. Fishmeal millionaire Luis Banchero boasted of coauthoring an "industrial community" law intended to bring labor peace by making workers minority shareholders reluctant to strike against "their own interests." A similar "profit-sharing" law was also put into effect for newly created, state-run agrarian cooperatives. Social security and other benefits were financed by the profits, when profits occurred. Peru's regressive tax laws so lenient on the rich remained untouched.

After taking over the IPC, the government declared its independence in foreign policy. It recognized Cuba, joined the Non-Aligned Movement and the Andean Pact, and built political alliances with Allende's Chile and Torres's Bolivia (see chapters 15 and 17). For a short while it enforced the Andean Pact's Decision 24 (see Overview), which called for eventual 50 percent local ownership of all enterprises (rarely enforced after 1973—some two hundred foreign companies stayed in Peru). It seized U.S. tuna ships fishing inside the 200-nautical-mile limit recognized by Peru, Ecuador, and most other nations in the world. Peru's trade with the Soviet bloc increased.

In May 1969 the United States suspended arms sales. Peru responded by kicking out the local U.S. military mission. The United States slashed loans and "aid" programs and pressured other lenders, including the World Bank, to embargo Peru.

Although both the Peruvian and the U.S. governments engaged in highly publicized nationalist posturing, there was no foreign military intervention in Peru. For one thing the United States was mired down in an unpopular war in Vietnam; for another, U.S. policymakers were able to arrange behind-the-scenes terms of compensation for nationalized enterprises and conditions for future foreign investment. In 1974, for example, Peru agreed to pay $150 million in compensation for eleven expropriated firms, $22 million of which was channeled through the U.S. government to Standard Oil. Thus the IPC got "its just compensation."

State Department Peru watchers in Washington, D.C., realized that the military's new politics had no resemblance to what Guatemala's officer-turned-guerrilla Yon Sosa had set out to do in the mid-1960s (see chapter 2). Peru's military was as opposed as they were to a bottom-up revolution against the existing system. Rather, the new government was taking the authoritarian populist road of top-down reforms to foster capitalist development and to contain organized labor and social unrest.

Nevertheless, many corporate executives reacted to Velasco's pronouncements by curtailing production and holding back on new investments until they could receive more substantial assurances. As they cut back, the state increased its share of production. Industrial production doubled in the early 1970s, even as it had doubled during the 1960s. Under Velasco (1968–1975) the state's share of total production doubled to 21 percent and came to account for half of mining and one-fifth of industrial production. but this was before the newest and biggest mining operation—the U.S.-owned Cuajone project—reached full production. The state also assumed control over two-thirds of banking.

Politically the model of the military reformers resembled Mexico's corporativist system of separating and controlling different social groups through a series of populist appeals and the creation of new state-run "popular" organizations of peasants, workers, and other constituencies (see Box 14.1 and chapter 1). The most important new organization was SINAMOS (National System to Support Social Mobilization), formed in 1971 in response to a big land invasion by squatters in southern Lima. SINAMOS's local branches varied according to the political bent of their leaders, but their proclaimed goal was to rally public support, guide public works, and insure stability.

Box 14.1: Peru's Political Parties, Guerrillas, and Labor Organizations

AP	Popular Action, founded in 1956, populist-conservative, led by two-time president Belaunde; joined Fredemo in 1990
APRA	American Popular Revolutionary Alliance, populist social democratic, founded in 1924 by Haya de la Torre and followed rightist trajectory; split in 1980 (see MBH), won presidency in 1985, but then split again; consultative member of Socialist International
Cambio 90	Change 90, created by Fujimori for his 1990 election campaign
CCP	Peasant Confederation of Peru, founded in 1956, mainly sierra communities, VR-led
CD	Democratic Convergence, founded in 1985 as a rightist coalition of PPC and MBH

(Continued on next page)

Box 14.1 *(Continued)*

CDRF   Rodrigo Franco Democratic Command, right-wing terrorist group named after an APRA leader assassinated in 1987

CGPP   General Confederation of Slumdwellers of Peru, founded in 1980

CGTP   500,000-member General Confederation of Peruvian Workers, founded in 1968, led by PCP and other leftists

CNA   National Agrarian Confederation, formed by military government in 1974, mostly cooperatives created by agrarian reform, PSR-led, close to CCP

CNT   Christian Democrat-led National Workers Confederation, founded in 1971, later split; small

CS   Socialist Confluence, founded in 1991 as a new but small leftist alliance

CTP   110,000-member Confederation of Peruvian Workers, founded in 1944, APRA-controlled

CTRP   10,000-member Confederation of Workers of the Peruvian Revolution, founded in 1974 by military government, close to CTP

FLT   Tawantinsuyo Liberation front, founded in 1981 by Indian leaders from Bolivia, Ecuador, and Peru seeking new nation with boundaries of Peru-centered Inca empire ("Tawantinsuyo")

FNTC   National Front of Workers and Peasants, electoral coalition based in Puno highlands, won two congressional seats in 1985 and 1990 elections (also known as PIN—Nationalist Left party)

FNTMMP   40,000-member leftist National Federation of Peruvian Mining and Metallurgical Workers, critical of PCP but in CGTP

Fredemo   Democratic Front, 1990 presidential candidate Vargas Llosa's electoral alliance of AP, CD, PPC; disbanded after election (see PL)

Independent Unions   Emerged in mid-1970s in disagreement with CGTP support for military government and included FNTMMP and SUTEP

IS   Socialist Left, founded to back 1990 presidential bid of Lima's first Marxist mayor, Alfonso Barrantes

IU   United Left, founded in 1980 by wide range of Left Marxists, Social Democrats, and Christians, got 21.3 percent of 1985 presidential vote; split in 1987, with more moderate elements backing 1990 presidential bid of Lima's first Marxist mayor, Alfonso Barrantes (see IS)

MATA   Ayacucho Anti-Terrorist movement, right-wing death squad, founded in 1992

MBH   Hayista Bases movement, founded in 1981 as right-wing APRA splitoff; close to PPC (see CD)

MRTA   Tupac Amarú Revolutionary movement, guerrilla group founded in 1984, reportedly linked to military officers advocating Velasco-style reforms and Colombia's M-19; in late 1980s and early 1990s underwent several splits, as main group formed truce with government

(Continued on next page)

Box 14.1 *(Continued)*

New Majority party	A Fujimori "front" party, led by Fujimori's ex-minister of mining and energy, formed to run candidates for the 1992 interim congress elections
PCP	Peruvian Communist party, founded in 1928, strong in CGTP; in 1970s and 1980s, pro-Moscow; part of IU, although backed IS candidate in 1990
PDC	Christian Democratic party, founded in 1956 by Arequipa intellectuals, split in 1966 (see PPC); tiny
PL	Liberal party, founded by Vargas Llosa after 1990 election, an outgrowth of his Freedom movement (1988) and Fredemo (1990)
PPC	Popular Christian party, founded in 1956 as right-wing PDC splitoff (see CD)
PRT	Revolutionary Workers' party, founded in 1978, led by Trotskyist Hugo Blanco, close to IU
PSR	Revolutionary Socialist party, founded in 1976 by left-leaning social democratic military officers, part of IU
PUM	Unified Mariateguista party, founded in 1984 as coalition of VR and MIR (Movement of the Revolutionary Left, a Castroite APRA splinter), broke from IU endorsement of anti-insurgency decree powers for Fujimori in 1991
Sendero Luminoso	Shining Path, founded in 1970 by philosophy lecturer Abimael Guzmán Reinoso and PCP Maoist faction as "Communist party of Peru on the Shining Path of José Carlos Mariátegui"; became guerrilla army in 1980; spread from base in Ayacucho peasant communities to other provinces and cities; about 2,500 members; close to four other minuscule guerrilla groups; Guzmán, captured and jailed, called for peace in 1993
SUTEP	100,000-member, Maoist-led Single Society of Peruvian Educational Workers (teachers' union), in CGTP
Unir	Union of the Revolutionary Left, a pro-Beijing coalition founded in late 1970s; close to PUM
VR	Revolutionary Vanguard, founded in 1965 by intellectuals, former guerrillas, AP dissidents; Mariátegui-type Marxist ideology; strong in peasants' CCP; part of IU until 1991 (see PUM)

The logical consequence of a populist-style corporativism, it was expected, would be the demobilization of existing mass movements. The effort was not very successful. Many groups refused to fold, and the regime's new organizations failed to rally public enthusiasm. Slumdwellers burned local SINAMOS offices when promised improvements in their lives did not materialize. University students denounced the regime when it decreed an end to student-faculty control. The government's own peasant confederation, its biggest success story, moved leftward in 1974–75 and eventually allied itself with the radical CCP (Peasant Confederation of Peru).

The experienced trade-union movement was difficult to coopt. Although the government recognized organized labor's Communist-dominated CGTP in 1971, it repeatedly attacked the most radical labor unions, like those among the miners and schoolteachers. The military government arrested, killed, or deported their left-wing leaders.

Cerro de Pasco proposed selling its holdings to the government in December 1971. Two years later the "nationalization"/sale was completed on mutually agreed-on terms. Part of the agreement with Cerro was a giant concession to U.S. mining companies, led by the SPCC, to develop the open-pit copper mines of Cuajone, the most profitable venture since the sixteenth-century days of the Potosí silver mines. Foreign banks, including Citibank, Chase Manhattan, and Bank of America, financed the SPCC's Cuajone project, and helped the World Bank fund other select development programs. The government also borrowed to "nationalize" (with compensation) the subsidiaries of W. R. Grace, General Mills, Cargill, ITT, and Chase Manhattan.

This added to the military government's debt, already swollen from using borrowed money to purchase more arms. In the short run higher wages were paid to noisier sectors of the working class, but by 1978 Peru's debt stood at $8 billion. A new high in workers' real wages in 1972–73 was already in decline by 1975.

A growing gap between profits and wages provoked a rise in the number of strikes in the 1970s, sparked by about 200,000 workers employed by the country's largest firms producing three-fourths of the national product. These were also the workers most affected by the "industrial community" shareholding law; in 1977 worker shares averaged about 15 percent of the affected companies' stock. By 1978 the strike waves incorporated some 1.4 million workers, including a million in the general strike of May 22-23. The government attacked the strikers, who increasingly expressed political demands.

A new *clasista* (politically class-conscious) tendency in organized labor emerged, challenging the older, more cautious Communist and APRA leaders. By 1977 nearly 40 percent of the work force was unionized, two-thirds of it under leftist leadership. APRA's decline in union strength included its traditional stronghold of textiles, where *clasistas* made deep inroads in 1980's union elections.

The Velasco government had better results with agrarian reform. It and its successor distributed lands to 360,000 families, mostly in state-run cooperatives, effectively breaking the old structure of *gamonalismo* (bossism by hacienda and plantation owners). The reform modernized backward sectors of agriculture. Landowners were compensated by bonds that were redeemable if invested in industry, thus accelerating industrial development. The money came from the peasants, not from the government. All those who received land had to pay for it on the installment plan. Since most rural families were located on small landholdings outside the sierra haciendas and coastal plantations, less than one-third of Peruvian rural households benefited from the reform.

With so many favorable business deals being made behind the scenes in Peru and the more threatening election of Socialist Salvador Allende in Chile, the U.S. government cooled off its anti-Peruvian rhetoric. Nevertheless, the Peruvian government felt threatened when it saw how the United States participated in the 1973 overthrow of its ally, the Allende government (see chapter 17).

When Washington sold eighteen F-5s to dictator Pinochet's Chile but hesitated to meet Peru's requests for arms, the Peruvian government stepped up its purchases from the Soviet Union. In addition to several T-54 medium tanks already delivered, Peru obtained from the Soviet Union fifty-three MI-8 helicopters, one hundred SA-7 surface-to-air missiles, one hundred SA-3 surface-to-air missiles, thirty-six SU-22 Sukhoi fighter-bombers, and twelve MIG-21 fighters. This trend continued after the 1980 return to civilian rule. In 1983 Peru purchased sixteen Soviet MI-24 Hind-D helicopters. In addition, the Soviet Union accepted more than one thousand Peruvian students in its universities and helped to build fish-processing facilities in Paita and a hydroelectric power plant in Olmos in northern Peru.

Why didn't the U.S. government protest all this Soviet "intervention," as it did in the case of a much smaller Soviet arms package for Nicaragua's Sandinista government (see chapter 5)? Perhaps it was about to, but in a matter of months Peru's government entered an economic crisis and moved to the Right. First, in 1973 Peru's fishmeal industry collapsed. Cargill, a major distributor and producer of Peruvian fishmeal, had set up new feed and food-processing facilities in Argentina, El Salvador, and Guatemala in the late 1960s, where the atmosphere was less nationalistic. The government nationalized fishmeal companies in 1973 to save them from bankruptcy. A year later prices on other leading exports began dropping.

Then General Velasco fell ill and conservative elements in the military increased their power as the economic crisis worsened. By 1975, what was known as the hot "phase one" of the Peruvian revolution was over, and the frigid "thermidor" of "phase two" was underway.

On February 5, 1975, the army responded to a police strike by sending tanks against the country's largest garrison of police, killing several. APRA agitators and looting mobs rampaged through Lima's streets. Army tanks withdrew. Then, as crowds of onlookers gathered, the tanks returned, killing 150 looters and bystanders. General Velasco's reputation was tarnished beyond repair. A month later Velasco stepped aside, and a more "balanced" junta of all three armed services took over, led by General Francisco Morales Bermúdez.

The Morales Bermúdez government (1975–1980) purged the armed forces of Left-leaning officers, undid many of the earlier reforms, and cracked down even harder on labor. Some officers attempted a coup in July of 1976 but were repulsed and dismissed. After that, out-of-power Social Democratic officers founded the PSR (Revolutionary Socialist party). The government abolished the right to strike on August 13, 1976, and ruled under repeatedly declared states of emergency. It struck a series of IMF-type conditionality accords with foreign creditors for future loans.

In February 1978 a year after a general strike had forced the government to freeze prices and promise elections, the IMF declared Peru in violation of debt bail-out agreements. Its main complaint was the government's failure to turn more state enterprises back to private capital. The military brass had already reprivatized the fishing industry and sacked its striking workers but was counting on the remaining state enterprises for its own enrichment. It toed the IMF line by imposing its most austere "economic package" yet, doubling food, gasoline, and cooking oil prices.

These measures, taken in the wake of an inflation rate steaming toward 100 percent a year, provoked massive popular protests. SUTEP's schoolteachers struck for eighty-one days and, despite a newly declared state of siege, a general strike shut most of the nation down on May 22-23, 1978. The government broke the strikes, killing more than thirty people and deporting several left-wing leaders, including candidates for the June Constituent Assembly elections. Some union leaders disappeared, their corpses turning up later in roadside ditches.

Even though it had been driven underground and was badly divided, the Left won 30 percent of the vote in the 1978 elections. A coalition led by Trotskyist Hugo Blanco garnered 12 percent. APRA won thirty-seven of the one hundred Constituent Assembly seats, in part because AP decided to boycott the elections. AP believed the elections would not be fair since the military-APRA *convivencia* was back in the driver's seat. The right-wing PPC (Popular Christian party) won twenty-five seats.

The Left gained some of its demands in the Constituent Assembly, including the right for 2 million illiterates to vote and the abolition of the death penalty except in wartime. With peasants now enfranchised, the Left looked forward to doing well in 1980. Upon forming a broad, united coalition, its best vote-getter, Blanco, declared "If the Left didn't unite, the masses were prepared to send us to hell, and justly so."

The economy momentarily bounced back in 1979 and early 1980, when the trans-Andean oil pipeline began operating and Peru's cooper exports commanded better prices. The 1980 presidential elections were won by AP's Belaunde, who campaigned on the premise of "civilian government" and "a million new jobs." He got 45.4 percent of the vote. The united Left fell apart when Blanco pulled out of the new coalition and five different candidates entered the fray (Blanco's vote fell to 4.4 percent). APRA also fell into feuding camps and suffered from its identification with the preceding military dictatorship. The electorate symbolically sent both APRA and the fractionalized Left "to hell." Even though voting was mandatory, less than two-thirds of the electorate cast valid votes, hardly a "mandate" for Belaunde.

1980s and 1990s: Lurching from Crisis to Crisis

The Belaunde government (1980–1985) attempted a "Taiwanization" strategy of export-led development based on free-market ideas similar to those of the "Chicago Boys" being implemented next door in Pinochet's Chile (see chapter 17). Belaunde's team of economic advisers, known as the "Dyánamo," slashed tariffs on manufactured imports by as much as half. It cut back trade with the Soviet bloc by more than 50 percent and cultivated close relations with the United States. It lifted price controls, devalued the sol, and allowed the cost of living to rise 57 percent during Belaunde's first eight months in office. Its proposal to phase out the profit-sharing "industrial communities" was voted down by workers in 1982. The free market in land led to the collapse of many agrarian cooperatives unable to compete, and by 1984 one-third of them had been divided up.

Meanwhile the government doubled the maximum profit foreign companies were allowed to send home. Corruption in government, a traditional problem in Peru, grew rampant. The most successful domestic businesses during the second Belaunde presidency were those engaged in finance, agroindustry for export, and real estate. Typical of the "12 Apostles," as Peru's largest corporate-financial syndicates became known, was the Romero-Raffo group. Founded by ex-cotton *gamonales* in the 1970s, it gained control of the Banco de Crédito in 1979, Peru's largest commercial bank with one-third of the market.

The "Dyánamo's" policies produced a short-lived economic boom that went bust when the worldwide recession in 1982 tumbled Peru's export prices to their lowest levels since the 1930s. Belaunde's promised new jobs went out the window, as 900,000 workers were laid off. Inflation passed 100 percent in 1984. Peru then relived the cycle of IMF agreements of the 1960s and 1970s with the same results. Each major period of extreme austerity IMF-type economic packages throughout the 1980s led to more poverty and the loss of legitimacy of the government in power. President Belaunde's party got only 6.3 percent of the 1985 presidential vote.

Peru's civilian governments of the 1980s and early 1990s attempted to reduce drug trafficking in vain. A migrant worker could make more than $200 a month harvesting coca in the mid-1980s, far more than what jobs paid in Lima. In the Tingo María area land turned over to coca production increased twelvefold to 20,000 acres in the decade 1972–1982. A 1984 U.S.

government sponsored coca eradication and crop substitution campaign spent more than two-thirds of its $4.2 million budget in counterinsurgency training for Peruvian soldiers to fight the Shining Path guerrillas. The guerrillas in Peru's coca-rich upper Huallaga Valley were difficult to dislodge since they protected peasant coca leaf growers and charged narco-traffickers "war taxes" to purchase high-powered weaponry in return for providing the growers and traders armed protection from the police.

Sendero Luminoso was a fanatical group of "fundamentalist" Maoists opposed to almost every government in power in the world. With historical roots in the impoverished Ayacucho region of southern Peru, particularly the university there, the main reasons for its not being wiped out by the 70,000-strong army were twofold. First, its members spoke Quechua and understood peasant grievances. Second, the military and police searching for Sendero militants unleashed violent assaults on villages, turning people against the government. The military's policy was to take no prisoners. Sendero's policy was to kill "informers." The military relocated villagers, dragooning many into civil defense outfits known as _rondas campesinas_. Sendero withdrew from previously occupied zones, leaving the peasants to fend for themselves. Before long a medley of peasant groups were engulfed in retribution killings, some aimed against Senderistas for their "abandonment."

As Sendero bombings of electricity installations began blacking out Lima and other cities in the middle and late 1980s, feelings of fear and panic spread across Peru. The vast majority of the nation's leftists rejected Sendero as an extremist and terroristic blend of personality cultism (its leader was called "the fourth sword" next to Marx, Lenin, and Mao) and peasant millenarianism harking back to an imagined Inca utopia. Urban workers expressed disgust for Sendero, but some young slumdwellers and students sympathized with its proclamations for elementary justice. In addition to Sendero's alleged twenty-five hundred members, there emerged half a dozen other tiny, localized guerrilla groups.

The Belaunde government called in United States, Israeli, and Argentine counterinsurgency experts for assistance. In 1981 it issued a security law that authorized the military to arrest and hold incommunicado anyone even "contemplating" dissent or "suspected" of terrorism. The nation's conservative Catholic bishops noted that the law helped institutionalize torture. Priests advocating the theology of liberation (see Overview), schoolteachers, trade-union leaders, and peasant militants were swept up in a dragnet of arrests. More than two thousand were detained in Lima after one of Sendero's bombings in 1984. A police antiterrorist unit known as the "Sinchis" broke into a rural wedding party, shot the guests, and hauled survivors off to a gully where they machine-gunned them. More and more "mass graves" were discovered. State terrorism became a reality.

President Alan García Pérez (1985–1990) stepped up the by now traditional populist attempt at defusing the growing crisis. "We know," he proclaimed, "that to carry out a democratic revolution, we must be anti-imperialist and fight against hegemonism." He introduced an anti-inflation package, hiked wages, and vowed to restore agrarian reform and promote the interests of "the marginal 70 percent of the population." He appointed a peace commission similar to the one in Colombia (see chapter 12). Most of its members resigned because of lack of cooperation from government authorities; APRA loyalists took their place. The youthful, baby-faced president lectured the military, "To fight barbarism it is not appropriate to fall into barbarism." After sacking three top generals for their involvement in Ayacucho atrocities, he reportedly reached an agreement with the top brass that in return for their ceasing massacres and "disappearances," he would protect them from investigations of past human rights violations. The security forces' terrifying "dirty war" continued, scarcely skipping a beat.

In foreign policy, President García renewed relations with Cuba (broken in 1980 during the Mariel boatlift—see chapter 8). He helped create the "Lima group" of Argentina, Brazil, Peru, and Uruguay to support the Contadora peace-making process in Central America (see Introduction to Part One). Voters rewarded García with an APRA victory in the November 1986 municipal elections, as even the Marxist mayor of Lima (1983–1986) failed to be re-elected in a close race. It was a symbolic extension of the presidential "honeymoon," which soon ended, however.

García attempted to woo the noncombatant Left while cracking down on Sendero Luminoso. A prison revolt led by Sendero detainees in June 1986 was snuffed out by security forces, who murdered more than two hundred prisoners. Police raided five university campuses in February 1987, killing one student. As more anti-Sendero leftists were victimized during such roundups of suspected Sendero sympathizers, President García declared an "aperture," or "opening" to the Left. "The Left is not the problem," he proclaimed, "the Right is our main enemy; let the Left enter the struggle behind our leadership." He pardoned twenty-eight members of IU (United Left) accused of subversion in July 1987. IU and other leftists opposed to violence were the nation's second largest political force after APRA, a factor making it difficult for the military to mount a coup. But in mid-1988, García approved the concept of "intellectual responsibility" for terrorism, subjecting leftists to arrests for no concrete action. Security forces stepped up their hounding of the Left, and a resurgent Right activated more death squads. By the time of the 1990 elections the non-guerrilla Left was both subdued and divided, although it continued active, especially in the by-now traditional strike waves and "popular movements" of the poor. In 1990, the IU and its IS splinter remained among Peru's major electoral blocs, along with APRA, AP, and an ultra-conservative coalition known as CD (Democratic Convergence—see Box 14.1). The CD ran novelist Mario Vargas Llosa for president in 1990 under the banner of Fredemo, or Democratic Front.

García's administration started with a bang but ended with a whimper. Economically, despite the refusal of the IMF and foreign banks to extend it loans, its reforms helped trigger a 20 percent growth rate in the first two years. By limiting payments servicing Peru's $14 billion foreign debt to 10 percent of export earnings, García had irked the Reagan administration and the IMF. The U.S. government invoked the Brooke-Alexander Amendment, a Hickenlooper-type law suspending new aid for debt delinquents. On the other hand, President Reagan increased his request for military aid to Peru eightfold, seeing a "Soviet-Cuban" threat in the anti-Soviet, anti-Cuban Shining Path guerrillas.

García's unsuccessful attempt to nationalize private banks in 1987 elicited a storm of protest from the refashioned financial-industrial "oligarchy," in spite of his generous concessions to industrialists during "The Year of Investment." The banking community lashed back at the president with a public campaign for privatization of all state enterprises. Bankers' speculative activities and stashing of funds in safe overseas banking "havens" undermined Peru's currency and fueled a runaway inflation that, along with the stepped-up internal warfare, effectively crippled the economy.

García's attempts at reform initially provoked talk about the "Allendeization of Peru" (see chapter 17). But García was no Allende. Moreover, as became clear after he left office, García was corrupt. He had illegally deposited Peruvian public funds with the CIA/druglord/scandal-ridden BCCI bank (see introduction to Part One). By the early 1990s, García was in disgrace and being ejected from his APRA leadership post.

When the financial oligarchy's counteroffensive succeeded and the bottom fell out of the noncoca parts of the economy, the public heard rumors that President García invited the military to launch a coup. But the military knew it could not salvage the situation and preferred to let García take the heat. Peruvians seemed to give up on all the political parties. The Shining Path guerrillas' initial gains and growth in membership in greater Lima's _barriadas_ were undermined by their murdering of popular community woman leaders who disagreed with Sendero's "correct political line." The powerful noncombatant left-wing political party coalitions of the 1980s were suffering from the security forces' repression and seemed hopelessly divided. Ongoing army and right-wing death squad massacres of noncombatant civilians terrified the populace. The violence of Peru's drug armies and the druglords' shadowy but well-known alliances with police, military, and civilian officials further caused Peruvians to throw up their hands.

So in the 1990 presidential elections Peruvians did what other Latin

Americans were doing at the polls. In a two-man runoff election, they elected a political outsider, Alberto Keinya Fujimori of the hastily formed Cambio 90 (Change 90) movement. A U.S.-educated fifty-two-year-old son of Japanese immigrants, Fujimori edged out Vargas Llosa, another "outsider." In his campaign, Fujimori seemed less extremist in his economic neo-liberalism than Vargas Llosa and also spoke demagogically about helping the poor. Sympathizers of the Left voted for him as "the lesser evil." Peru's Protestant evangelicals who, unlike priests advocating liberation theology, were never arrested, backed Fujimori wholeheartedly (one of their leaders was elected second vice-president).

As president, Fujimori carried out IMF-type austerity policies even more extreme than those advocated by Vargas Llosa. An agricultural engineer who used to host a television talk show on the nation's social problems, Fujimori hoped new technologies, "hard work," and the free-market conversion of Peru into another Singapore or South Korea would save the nation. He introduced what the press called "Fujishock"—a neo-liberal economic program that initially let fuel costs rise by 3,000 percent and basic food and transportation costs by 200 to 300 percent. Thousands more workers were laid off. Fujishock "privatized" (sold off) state companies in oil, mining, industry, and finance and eventually slashed the 1990 annual inflation rate of 7,650 percent down to 40 percent by late 1993. The privatization scheme brought the government a billion dollars in 1993, an amount equal to Peru's annual coca income. Fujishock "freed the market" by reversing the previous twenty years' land redistribution programs and allowing peasants to sell their parcels. Once again, wealthy individuals accumulated huge tracts.

Fujimori formed alliances with key military commanders and did their bidding. He quadrupled the number of government-armed *rondas campesinas* and established similar "self-defense" patrols in urban areas (*rondas urbanas civiles*). The *rondas* were a way of dragooning hundreds of thousands of young men and unemployed youth into the "dirty war" against anyone suspected of supporting left-wing parties or the guerrillas. The new president evoked a certain sympathy among Peruvians long discontented with their failing institutions by arresting leaders of the political parties, launching corruption proceedings against seven hundred judges, and, in defiance of the Catholic Church, distributing free birth control information and devices. Fujimori irked Peruvian nationalists, however, when he made an agreement with the Bush administration to welcome U.S. military "trainers" to assist in "antiterrorist warfare" supposedly aimed at drug traffickers. Later, in 1993, he acknowledged that the strategy had failed. Coca production continued to increase, and the head of the U.S. Drug Enforcement Agency (DEA) announced that it would be pulling out its operatives from Peru (see Introduction to Part Three and Conclusion).

The social costs of "Fujishock" were immense. People protested in vain. A rash of strikes reminiscent of earlier general strikes swept the country, including ones by teachers, health workers, doctors, and university employees. The Fujimori government cracked down. For example, in one of the first strikes involving 150,000 workers, 6,000 strikers were arrested under Peru's renewed state of emergency; four were killed. The prisons filled to overflowing with labor leaders. In the early 1990s, by UN count, Peru's security forces achieved the world's highest number of "disappearances." States of emergency were decreed for 37 percent of Peru, and local elections were cancelled in 101 of 371 districts.

Then, sensing his growing popularity among the business and more affluent-white collar segments of the middle classes, Fujimori took a political gamble in April 1992—and won. He dissolved congress, suspended civil liberties, arrested opponents in congress and much of the judiciary, imposed censorship, and introduced rule by decree. Ex-President García fled to Colombia. Fujimori's *"auto-golpe"* (self-coup) against democracy, initially protested by the world community including the U.S. government, established a total military dictatorship with Fujimori as president. Many, including Vargas Llosa, viewed the coup as an indirect "cocaine coup" (see chapter 15), since congressional and press investigations of alleged military profit-sharing alliances with the druglords and human rights violations had begun to uncover damning evidence.

Starting in August 1992, the new dictatorship introduced military tribunals that dispensed summary justice by "faceless" judges. A "second coup" in April 1993 left Fujimori as president but the armed forces as firmly in command as ever. The army sent tanks into the streets to discourage popular attempts to locate and prosecute army officers and a secret death squad responsible for "disappearing" nine students and a professor and then covering the story up from investigators. A high-ranking general slated to become head of the army in 1995 fled to the U.S. embassy and then to Buenos Aires, accusing Fujimori's top security adviser and overseer of the government's intelligence network of operating a death squad of twenty to twenty-five officers. A mass grave with the students' and professor's bullet-riddled bodies was discovered at an army firing range in early 1994. The United States considered suspending aid to Peru as it had intermittently done in the past because of the security forces' grisly human rights violations. A military court convicted nine officers and enlisted men of the killing of the nine students and the professor but gave them light sentences.

The military's intensified counterinsurgency "dirty war" against the guerrillas, on the other hand, began to succeed. Bolstered in 1991 by a U.S. economic and military aid package of $95 million and a $845 million IMF loan, Peru's government offered rewards for information leading to the capture of guerrilla leaders and easy surrender terms. The policy led to the capture and jailing of top guerrilla leaders like Shining Path chief Guzmán in September 1992. Some fifteen hundred rebels surrendered in 1993. Guzmán, sentenced to life in prison, was calling for peace by the end of the year. The capture of Guzmán helped Fujimori's backers win a November 1992 election of an eighty-member interim congress to draft a new constitution. Because of the way Fujimori scrapped the old constitution in the *autogolpe*, however, Vargas Llosa and Peru's major political parties, including the IU, IS, APRA, and the rightist AP (Popular Action—see Box 14.1), refused to take part in the election.

In late 1993, voters narrowly approved the new constitution prepared by the Fujimori-dominated interim congress. Few bothered to read the constitution, which greatly strengthened the presidency, provided for elections in 1995, and allowed Fujimori to run for reelection and possibly rule for twelve more years. The constitution reintroduced the death penalty and codified "antiterrorist" ideology in a way that threatened civil liberties. It also eliminated distinctions between local and foreign capital and codified economic "neo-liberalism" (see overview), banning the government from businesses like mining, petroleum, banking and insurance.

Despite their widely condemned human rights record, Peru's military officers seemed to be secure in their power. If Fujimori used his new constitutional authority to make military promotions that countered the will of the top brass, the generals could always engineer a "third coup" to remove him. The real powers in Peru remained its domestic and foreign financiers and the military. The central conflict remained the one between the haves and the have-nots.

Selected Bibliography

Americas Watch. *Peru Under Fire: Human Rights since the Return to Democracy.* New Haven, CT: Yale University Press, 1992. Documents increased abuses.

Blanco, Hugo. *Land or Death: The Peasant Struggle in Peru.* New York: Pathfinder Press, 1972. By a Trotskyist leader.

Booth, D. and B. Sorj (eds). *Military Reformism and Social Classes: The Peruvian Experience.* New York: Macmillan, 1983.

Eco-Andes. *Women in Peru.* New York: Ecumenical Committee on the Andes, 1987. Samples of the new politics, with photos and testimonies.

Fitzgerald, E. V. K. *The Political Economy of Peru 1956–1978: Economic Development and the Restructuring of Capital.* Cambridge, England: Cambridge University Press, 1979. By a former economic adviser of Velasco government.

Graham, Carol. *Peru's APRA: Parties, Politics, and the Elusive Quest for Democracy.* Boulder, CO: Lynne Rienner, 1992.

Latin American Perspectives. "Peru," *Latin American Perspectives*, 4(32) (Summer 1977). Overview of major issues.

McClintock, Cynthia, and Abraham F. Lowenthal (eds.). _The Peruvian Experiment Reconsidered._ Princeton, NJ: Princeton University Press, 1983. On military.

Mariátegui, José Carlos. _Seven Interpretive Essays on Peruvian Reality._ Austin: University of Texas Press, 1971. By Peru's most influential thinker.

Nacla (North America Congress on Latin America). "Peru Today" and "Garcia's Peru," _Nacla Report on the Americas_, 14(6) (Nov./Dec. 1980) and 22(3) (June 1986).

Palmer, David Scott (ed.). _The Shining Path of Peru._ New York: St. Martin, 1992.

Poole, Deborah, and Gerardo Rénique. _Peru: Time of Fear._ New York: Monthly Review Press, 1992. The "dirty war" and "coca capitalism."

Quijano Obregón, Aníbal. _Nationalism and Capitalism in Peru._ New York: Monthly Review Press, 1971. Critique of military "radicals."

Stein, Steve. _Populism in Peru: The Emergence of the Masses and the Politics of Social Control._ Madison: University of Wisconsin Press, 1980.

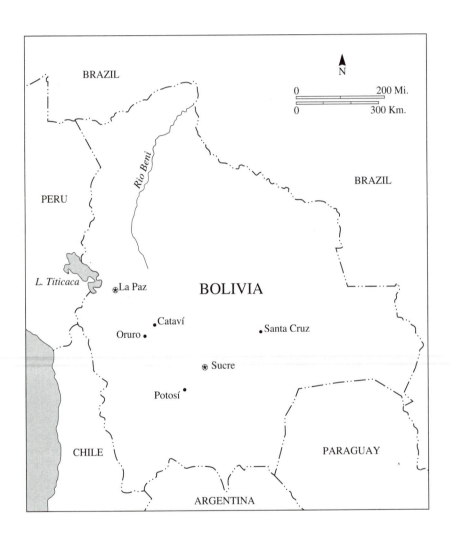

BRAZIL

N

0   200 Mi.

0   300 Km.

PERU

BRAZIL

Rio Beni

L. Titicaca

⊛ La Paz

BOLIVIA

• Cataví

Oruro •

• Santa Cruz

⊛ Sucre

Potosí •

CHILE

PARAGUAY

ARGENTINA

Bolivia   15

Well, my son died here and I'm going to die here too. . . . You keep on saying I'm a communist, that I'm this and that. If I get out alive, now I'll become one, now that I feel a greater and deeper hatred for all of you.—*Domitila Barrios de Chungara, a former Jehovah's Witness, to her military torturers in La Paz prison after being beaten hours before giving birth to a baby boy who died from the blows, 1967*

They are trying to dismantle the nationalized sectors of the economy and thrust us into the informal sector. We will not have any of the rights we have gained from years of struggle.—*Housewife from Huanuni, on mining community picket, 1986*

Indigenous peoples exemplify the rational use of natural resources in the face of ecological damage caused by exploitative business interests.—*Zulema Lehm of Beni regional development center, 1991*

On a bitterly cold September morning of 1965, a barefoot, rag-clad girl ran screaming into the Plaza del Minero fronting the mine workers' union head-quarters at the huge Siglo XX mining complex high in the Andes. People rushed from their one-room shacks and hovels, exclaiming and waving their arms.

The girl leaped onto the base of an immense statue that depicted a bare-chested miner pressing a pneumatic drill into the ground in one hand while raising a rifle with the other. The statue symbolized hard work and rebellion. In "the old days" workers had crawled naked through Siglo XX's 500 miles of tunnels to hack out one-sixth of the world's tin for a few centavos a day. Their attempts to win better pay and decent safety standards had repeatedly been crushed by the army. But in 1952 they had won a revolution, nationalization of the mines, and the right to "*co-gobierno*" or "workers' control"—a voice in management and effective veto power over decisions.

Raising her hands to hush the crowd, the girl announced breathlessly, "The soldiers are coming!"

Just then, the sound of a low-flying airplane grew louder. Inside the union headquarters, wives concerned about their husbands still inside the mine shafts asked Domitila Barrios de Chungara, newly elected secretary-general of the Housewives Committee, what to do. She later recalled what happened:

> The army came in planes to machine-gun us. For the first time, we could see how a plane flies, dips down or noses in, and how some little rays of light came from the inside of the plane and there were the bullets falling: pa! pa! pa! They fired on the Plaza del Minero, on Cataví (the mine office complex), on the rock pile. The bullets came toward us from everywhere, like rays of light. And not only that, but they also attacked the ambulances. . . .
> [Afterward] all of Siglo XX was declared a military zone. . . . It was worse than a concentration camp!
> Zacarias Plaza did all that. He was in charge . . . and he mocked us: "Why do you want to get into the dance if you can't dance? Okay, dance now if you want!" And he gave the order to massacre us. But in 1970 . . . Zacarias Plaza turned up dead . . . dead! They made a mess out of the guy. . . . And that was the fate which awaited all those who'd massacred the people.

That massacre happened in 1965, year two of an eighteen-year period of military dictatorship in Bolivia, South America's poorest, most illiterate, most rural, and most Indian country. In 1982, a catastrophic economic slump, combined with massive protest movements of the "new politics" (see Overview), helped force into exile the leaders of a 1980 "cocaine coup." Unable to deal with the disastrous economy and popular antimilitary sentiment, army officers turned the government over to civilians. Then, in 1985, the long-sagging market for tin, Bolivia's leading legal export, collapsed. The economy went into a free fall, inflation rising to 24,000 percent by the end of the year. At the local *mercado* bundles of pesos brought by Indian women in their traditional bowler hats often outweighed the items they were purchasing.

Natural gas replaced tin as a leading export, although tin still represented nearly half the nation's noncoca export earnings in 1992. Coca export revenues equalled those of all legal exports in 1987. With Peru (see chapter 14), Bolivia was the source for 90 percent of the world's coca. And as in Peru, coca leaves at the *mercado* were so expensive that Indians no longer could afford to chew the coca-lime mixture that produced a gastric secretion to ease hunger pangs. Despite extreme political instability, social unrest, and the occasional presence of U.S. troops, civilian presidents managed to govern for more than a dozen years—the longest period of civilian rule in Bolivian history. In 1985 Harvard economist Jeffrey Sachs laid out a severe neo-liberal economic plan like the one he would later introduce into the former Soviet Union—and with equally harsh results for the majority of citizens. The planning minister who implemented Sachs' plan was elected president in 1993. The IMF beamed its approval as inflation tapered off. But Bolivians still went hungry. Children's stomachs were bloated from protein deficiency. Cholera and yellow fever out-breaks occurred as early as 1991.

In the world's highest capital, La Paz, 12,000 feet above sea level, glit-tering mansions overlooked miserable slums. In the surrounding windswept, and "Altiplano" zone of Bolivia and Peru, Indian peasants speaking Quechua shivered and survived on little more than the potatoes they grew. From float-ing straw islands in the world's highest navigable lake, Lake Titicaca, Ay-mara-speaking Indians cast their nets for a few undersized fish. Three-fourths of today's 7.8 million Bolivians live in the Altiplano and its surrounding mountain valleys. Two-thirds of all Bolivians are Indian; one-fourth are mesti-zos or cholos (Indians adopting mestizo customs); 2 percent are of African descent; and 5 percent are white.

Bolivia had a reputation of being Latin America's most unstable coun-try. Since becoming an independent republic in 1825, it had gone through 189 changes in government, often by military coup. Yet it was the first Latin American nation after Mexico (1910–1920) to have a revolution based on pop-ular participation (1952). To know Bolivia is to know the roots of that revolu-tion; how it came about and was reversed; and how the United States, the army, cocaine drug lords, and a handful of wealthy elites came to dominate.

Centuries of Monoculture, Race-Class Conflict, and Regionalism

The roots of the Bolivian Revolution may be found in a history of economic overdependence on one commodity (monoculture), race/class conflict, and re-gionalism. Bolivia was not always poor. In 1545 the fabulous silver mountain "Cerro Rico" of Potosí was discovered, the richest concentration of silver ever known. With its silver wealth came greed, the exploitation of Indian workers and imported African slaves, and the growth of the southern mountain cities of Potosí and Sucre as regional centers of power.

From childhood to death silver workers dug out and minted the wealth that funded the Spanish Armada and greased the financial and commercial wheels of early European capitalism (see chapters 1, 11, 14, and 18). Working feverishly under the lash in thin, frigid air 14,000 feet above sea level, the min-ers often fell dead, their bodies cascading down the mountainside.

Ever since the 1530s, when the *conquistadores* destroyed the Inca empire, Spanish settlers had virtually enslaved Bolivia's Indians. They estab-lished the institutions and culture, dominated by the Catholic Church, that pro-duced a legacy of superstition and racism mixed with humane concern for Indians' rights to their traditional communal lands (see Overview). The Indi-ans took advantage of Spanish ignorance of their languages to preserve as much as possible the communal bonds of their clanlike *ayllus* (see chapter 14).

This was not easy in the face of overwork when the economy was booming and lack of work during economic depressions. A mid-seventeenth-century mining depression and an upsurge in Mexican mining in the eighteenth century left most Bolivians impoverished. A handful of owners of fading silver mines and immense tracts of land called *haciendas* dominated a society of Indian and mestizo peasant serfs and artisans.

Indian rebellions periodically flashed across the landscape. Tupac Amarú's 1780–1781 revolt (see chapter 14), which spread throughout the Altiplano, was the most serious. Thousands of Indians took over La Paz for 109 days before Spanish reinforcements arrived to drive them off. The momentarily successful Indian uprising left the Altiplano's whites and mestizos terrified.

Most mestizos were as bad off as the Indians, although some were better off city dwellers or landowners. A number of them became leaders in the anti-Spanish struggle that won Bolivia independence in 1825. Mestizo farmers grabbed Indian communal lands no longer "protected" by Spanish law; educated mestizos gained access to the government bureaucracy and even political power. Afterward they sometimes outdid the white elites in racist denunciations of "lazy, drunken" Indians. Some became generals, presidents, miners, merchants, wealthy landlords.

In post-1825 Bolivia military strongmen (caudillos) ran the country from regional strongholds. Their chaotic and violent rule reinforced a colonial tradition of clientelism—loyalty systems that tied people to more powerful individuals or institutions. The most notorious caudillo, Mariano Melgarejo (1862–1871), sold chunks of national territory to the highest bidder and dispossessed 100,000 Indians from their lands.

Renewed European demand for silver in the 1850s led to the rise of a new generation of "silver barons"—Bolivians assisted by more wealthy Chileans. The discovery of valuable nitrate fields near the Pacific Ocean in the Atacama Desert, then part of Bolivia and Peru, also attracted the interest of Chilean investors and traders. In what became known as the War of the Pacific (1879–1883), Chile invaded first Bolivia and then Peru in order to seize the nitrates—and, as it turned out, the world's richest copper deposits in Bolivia's Andes (see chapter 17). Stripped of its western lands facing the Pacific Ocean, Bolivia was landlocked. Not until the 1992 "treaty of friendship" with Peru did Bolivia again have access to the Pacific, via the treaty's permission to use two free zones at Ilo.

As silver prices declined and tin prices rose, tin replaced silver as Bolivia's new monoculture, gaining in relative importance at the turn of the century. A "Liberal-Conservative" civil war (see Overview) in 1898 was won by the Liberals. Liberal elite families hooked their dreams on the rising star of tin, while Conservatives clung to their silver wealth. There was a brief interlude of rubber monoculture, 1906–1913, but Malaya rubber outcompeted what Bolivians hacked out from their northeastern tropical forests.

Tin was a different story. by the mid-1920s, underpaid mestizo and Indian miners were producing nearly one-quarter of the world's supply. In 1927 tin and other "primary products" accounted for 94 percent of Bolivia's exports; manufactured goods accounted for 64 percent of its imports. The nation's capital shifted from Sucre to La Paz, which was closer to the more productive tin mines. The so-called Big 3 emerged as Bolivia's "tin barons": Bolivian-born Simón I. Patiño and Carlos Aramayo and European-born Mauricio Hochschild.

Because of financial deals the Big 3 made with foreign bankers and refinery owners, two-thirds of the tin industry fell under the control of foreigners. Bolivia had no foreign debt in 1908, but by the mid-1920s it owed $40 million. As security on its so-called American Loan, Bolivia pledged half its 1922 national revenue. Americans headed up Bolivia's mining and customs bureaus. Together with Chileans, British, Swiss, and Germans, they held the highest positions at the mine sites, often ordering the Bolivians around like slaves. The largest foreign owners of Bolivian mines were the Guggenheims' American Smelting and Refining and W. R. Grace's International Mining Company. The main refining of Bolivian tin shifted from England to Perth Amboy, New Jersey, and Brooklyn, New York. In 1924 Patiño established his corporate headquarters in Delaware and retired to New York City's Waldorf Astoria hotel, rarely visiting his home country.

Resenting the way they were treated by foreigners, some 27,000 tin miners, influenced by the ideas of socialism and anarcho-syndicalism, became the backbone of a leftist, "anti-imperialist" trade-union movement. There were few other industrial workers in Bolivia. In the cities typographers and transportation workers organized some trade unions. Women street hawkers founded the Women's Labor Federation in 1927. But it was the miners' unions, federated in 1923 into the forerunner of the later FSTMB (see Box 15.1), that became the focus of political conflict. Army massacres of protesting miners occurred as early as 1918, 1919, and 1923.

Box 15.1: Bolivia's Main Political Parties and Economic Organizations

ADN	Democratic Nationalist Alliance, founded in 1979 by ex-president (1971–1978) Banzer, ultrarightist-populist (see AP)
AP	Patriotic Accord, founded in 1989 as ADN-MIR-PDC unity pact; torn by factionalism
CEPB	Bolivian Confederation of Private Businessmen
COB	Bolivian Central Labor Confederation, organized labor
COMIBOL	Mining Corporation of Bolivia, once state-owned firm undergoing privatization
Condepa	Conscience of the Fatherland, populist party founded in 1988 by an ex-Communist and a radio talk show host; ran fourth in 1993 presidential contest

(Continued on next page)

Box 15.1 *(Continued)*

CSUTCB Unified Peasant League Federation of Bolivia, founded in 1983, independent of government

FPU United People's front, founded in 1985 by PCB, PRIN, and two dissident factions of MIR to run a presidential candidate

FRI Left Revolutionary Front, led by Maoists who left PCB

FSB Bolivian Socialist Falange, founded in 1937, right-wing party modeled after Falange that backed Franco's Fascist regime in Spain; main party in Banzer government of 1971–1978 (see ADN), it split, many backing 1980 "cocaine coup"

FSTMB Union Federation of Mine Workers of Bolivia, founded in 1944, heart of COB until its post-1985 decline

IU United Left, coalition of seven groups founded in late 1980s, often split

MIR Movement of the Revolutionary Left, founded in 1971 to defend Popular Assembly; left-of-center, joined AP in 1989 to gain presidency; led by ex-President Paz Zamora (1989–1993)

MIR-BL MIR-Free Bolivia, an MIR splinter formed in 1985, joined IU briefly

MNR Nationalist Revolutionary movement, founded in 1941, led 1952 revolution, split in 1979 into MNRI and MNRH

MNRH Nationalist Revolutionary movement-historic, center-right MNR splitoff led by four-time president Paz Estenssoro; its "renewalist" right-wing faction led by Sánchez de Lozada, elected president in 1993

MNRI National Revolutionary movement of the Left, center-left MNR splitoff led by two-time president Siles Suazo; split into many new groups after 1984

PCB Communist party of Bolivia, founded in 1950, split in 1965 when Maoists broke away, legalized in 1982, split into two factions in 1985

PDC Christian Democratic party, small fractionalized center-right party that joined AP in 1989

POR Workers' Revolutionary party, Trotskyist party influential in 1952 revolution but severely fractionalized since

PRA Authentic Revolutionary party, founded in 1960 as an MNR faction by presidential candidate Guevara Arce; close to MNRH

PRIN Revolutionary party of the National Left, founded in 1964 by organized labor's Lechin after his expulsion by MNR, left-wing

UCS Civic Solidarity Unity, populist party founded in 1988 by right-wing industrialist who ran third in 1993 presidential race

---

Depression, Chaco War, and World War II: Prelude to Revolution

The Great Depression caused tin prices and Bolivian exports to fall by 70 percent in the early 1930s. Unemployment and death haunted the land. Those not dying from hunger or disease perished in a long and bloody war Bolivia fought with its eastern neighbor, Paraguay (1932–1935). Known as the "Chaco War," it threw onto the swampy, insect-infested battlefields of the eastern lowlands thousands of unemployed workers and starving Indians and peasants from both nations.

The slaughter in hand-to-hand combat was great in what commentators called "the war of the naked soldiers" and "the petroleum war." Rival U.S. and British oil companies wanted total control over supposedly oil-rich lands in the eastern borderland region known as the Chaco Boreal. Standard Oil of New Jersey, awarded concessions in 1922, backed Bolivia, while Royal Dutch Shell supported Paraguay. Bolivia lost 20,000 square miles of its territory. A negotiating commission headed by Standard's Spruille Braden (later famous for his intervention in Argentina, see chapter 18) retained for Bolivia a big chunk of land that turned out to be the richest in oil.

The Depression and Chaco War brought to a head new tendencies shaping Bolivia's destiny. On the one hand, use of the government to break the trade-union movement intensified. The government of Daniel Salamanca (1931–1934) outlawed unions. On the other hand, political parties tried their hand at coopting organized labor, issuing populist-style appeals to win its support and bring it under control.

The attempt to coopt labor peaked in the late 1930s. Returning war veterans organized the "Veterans of the Chaco" and allied themselves with urban trade unionists and miners. This broad-based movement carried off a general strike in 1936 that toppled the government. Two military officers ruled for the next three years: David Toro (1936–1937) and Germán Busch (1937–1939).

Toro and Busch sought to bring organized labor under government control by endorsing its Socialist platform and creating state-corporativist forms of organization (see Overview). Labor, dominated by Marxist and anarchist leaders, supported reforms but resisted top-down control during this so-called period of "military socialism." The government's attempts at cooptation and reform failed. But the government nationalized the properties of Standard Oil in 1937 and issued a liberal constitution in 1938 reminiscent of the Mexican Constitution of 1917 (see chapter 1). In 1939 Busch committed suicide—or was murdered—and conservative army elements loyal to the ruling elites reassumed power.

The right-wing government of General Enrique Peñaranda (1940–1943) paid Standard Oil $1.5 million for unsettled claims and developed very friendly relations with the United States. The outbreak of World War II stimulated demand for Bolivia's tin and a measure of prosperity.

People from the small but rapidly growing urban middle classes had long been trying to muscle their way into the political arena by joining or creating the many new political parties that proliferated in the late 1930s and early 1940s. The well-being of middle-class people often depended on clientelism and job patronage. With suffrage denied illiterates, then a majority of the population, the middle classes carried significant political weight at election time.

In 1941 middle-class intellectuals and lawyers founded the MNR (Nationalist Revolutionary movement). An APRA-type populist party with a radical program (see chapter 14), the MNR encompassed a mixed bag of dissidents ranging from the neo-Fascist Right to the Socialist Left.

In December of 1942 tin miners noted the good price on the international market fetched by the fruits of their labor and demanded a wage hike. The Big 3 said no. The workers laid down their tools in protest. General Peñaranda sent troops to massacre them at the Siglo XX/Cataví mines. The Cataví massacre rallied popular opposition behind the left-wing parties and the MNR.

In 1943 an army-MNR coalition engineered a coup that installed Major Gualberto Villarroel in power. The following year tin miners founded the FSTMB (Union Federation of Mine Workers of Bolivia), headed for the next forty-two years by Juan Lechín of the MNR's Socialist wing. Miners began arming themselves in anticipation of a possible repeat massacre.

In 1945–1946, because of the end of World War II, the tin market "boom" collapsed. Villarroel's government failed to do anything about it, and Villarroel was overthrown in July 1946. An angry mob lynched him and draped his body over a lamppost in front of the national palace. An unstable coalition of army officers and Left-populist and Right-Fascist political parties took over. The rightists gained the upper hand over the next five years, killing students and workers while foiling attempted coups by the MNR and a growing number of followers it was recruiting inside the military.

In November 1946 delegates to the Fourth Miners' Congress of the FSTMB, held at Pulacayo, endorsed the famous "Tesis de Pulacayo," written by Guillermo Lora, leader of the Trotskyists' POR (Workers' Revolutionary party). The "Thesis" echoed the ideas of Leon Trotsky, the late leader with Lenin of the Russian Revolution of 1917, who lost the power struggle to Stalin after Lenin's death and founded the Fourth International with branches in many countries. It declared that since Bolivia was a "backward" and "imperialist-dominated" land, there wasn't a "national bourgeoisie" capable of achieving the democratic goals of a bourgeois revolution or of building a viable capitalist economy. The workers would have to win democracy and create socialism. The Trotskyists opposed top-down bureaucratic socialism. They advocated a nationalist revolution built on alliances with parties like the MNR and groups like the peasantry, guided by a workers' "vanguard" party. The goal would be "workers' control" and the creation of a bottom-up democratic socialism. To avoid isolation and economic strangulation by capitalist powers, such a revolution would have to spread to other countries—so-called permanent revolution.

The tin miners' acceptance of the Tesis de Pulacayo accelerated revolutionary pressures for change. In 1949 the Big 3 called in the Army once more to massacre protesting miners. As the 1951 elections approached, the anti-government forces of the middle classes and the lower classes needed each other's support. The "roscas"—a derogatory term used to describe the oligarchy and its lawyer or military administrators—hoped to divide and defeat them both. The MNR leadership was in exile but its followers were confident of victory at the polls. The cost of living index had risen from 100 in 1938 to nearly 1,000 by 1951, and people wanted a change. The FSTMB, dominated by MNR's Lechín and the Trotskyists and fearful of another massacre, needed alliances with the MNR and with the university-based student movement.

MNR's presidential candidate Víctor Paz Estenssoro won the 1951 elections on a platform of nationalizing the mines and agrarian reform. But the army refused to hand power over to him and ruled by force over the next eleven months. Then, in April 1952, workers, students, and political dissidents, backed by the *carabineros* (national police), launched a revolt in La Paz. The uprising was carefully planned by the MNR. In three days of bloody fighting during which three thousand people were killed, neither the government nor the rebels had won.

Then, with the bodies of their fallen *compañeros* stacking up behind street barricades, the rebels took heart: well-armed tin miners arrived from the outlying mining regions. A mighty cheer went up. The tide of battle turned, as soldiers fled the advancing miners or joined them. On April 9, 1952, the Bolivian Revolution toppled the *ancien regime*.

The 1952 Revolution and the U.S. Role in Its Reversal

Bolivia's MNR revolutionaries faced an economy that was completely impoverished. The tin industry was so antiquated that it cost (as it still does today) more to produce tin than what the international market was willing to pay for it. Inflation was out of hand. Frightened elites were sending their savings abroad. Many middle-class people soon began blaming the miners and peasants for their increased cost of living, pointing to the expenses incurred by the revolution's reforms.

Paz Estenssoro served as president of the Bolivian Revolution's first government (1952–1956). His regime introduced universal suffrage and eliminated literacy requirements, quintupling the size of the electorate. It dismissed officers and enlisted men from the coup-addicted army and distributed their weapons to civilian militia units. It nationalized the tin mines of the Big 3, creating the state mining corporation COMIBOL. And it introduced agrarian reform.

While MNR's largely middle-class leadership undertook these measures as a means of carrying out a bourgeois-democratic nationalist revolution against the "roscas," the party's Left-oriented labor base sought more radical changes. Lechín and labor advocated central state planning leading to socialism rather than state-sponsored capitalist economic development. Influential in the first years of the revolution was the Trotskyists' POR. These differences and personal conflicts eventually led to a split in the MNR between its four main leaders: Paz Estenssoro, Lechín, Hernán Siles Suazo (president, 1956–1960), and Walter Guevara Arze (founder in 1960 of the PRA, Authentic Revolutionary party). Lechín founded the PRIN (Revolutionary party of the National Left) after Paz Estenssoro expelled him from the MNR in 1964.

The tin miners welcomed nationalization of the mines but objected to the government's indemnifying the Big 3. They believed the money for indemnity might better be used to upgrade the mines and to create refining foundries in Bolivia in order to sever dependence on foreign firms. The workers lost on that issue but won "co-gobierno," or "workers' control," including a veto over COMIBOL decisions and a "worker controller" at each mine empowered to block implementation of unwanted measures. They also gained the right to form armed militias nominally subject to MNR control but actually commanded by trade-union militants. Similar forms of representation were granted organized labor's COB (Bolivian Central Labor Confederation) inside the government and the MNR. A mixed pattern of "co-gobierno" and cooptation soon developed, the COB sometimes acting like a "government within the government," and yet the MNR bringing growing numbers of workers and other groups, especially peasants, under its tutelage.

Most Bolivians lived in the countryside, and two-thirds still do today. The 1953 agrarian reform provided peasants greater access to land and there were few job opportunities elsewhere. All told, the agrarian reform distributed more than 10 million hectares to nearly 200,000 rural heads of household between 1953 and 1972. The main beneficiaries were the *colonos*, who were suddenly freed from their unpaid labor obligation to the *hacendados*. The *colono* gained legal title to his tiny *sayana* or *pegujal* plot of land the landlord had assigned him in exchange for his labor (in Ecuador, it was called the *huasipungo* and still exists). The *colono*'s labor obligation was annulled. Most of the *hacendados'* estates were broken up and reassigned to the categories of small or medium-sized properties. Many *latifundistas* manipulated these categories to reconsolidate their monopoly on land, while others left the country.

Although statistical compilations by the government were extremely rough, they provided a good overview of land distribution after the land reform. By 1963 the *latifundistas* still held about 70 percent of the land, a decrease from 95 percent in 1950. Smallholders—those with plots of land from 5 to 20 hectares in size—accounted for another 12 percent of the land. Holders of plots less than 5 hectares in size (*minifundistas*) accounted for only 8 percent of land but made up nearly three-fourths of the peasantry.

The main accomplishment of the agrarian reform was to give peasants a dignity long denied them. They were able not only to get a piece of land, however small, but also to organize themselves into peasant leagues (*sindicatos*). They were freed from tribute labor. Yet only a handful of smallholders ever succeeded. Most peasants remained poor subsistence farmers. A 1992 UN study found 97 percent of Bolivia's rural people living in poverty, the worst in the world. A 1994 World Bank book spoke of the "gap between promise and reality." Some peasants seasonally migrated to northern Argentina for the sugarcane and cotton harvests or to the Santa Cruz eastern lowlands or Beni's northeastern coca fields to look for work there. By 1994, half a million Bolivians lived and worked in Argentina.

Peasants sold their crops and handicrafts in the market economy, where they often became indebted to middlemen known as *comerciantes* or *rescatadores*. Government loans went largely to medium and large producers in the semitropical Yungas and the Beni and Santa Cruz frontier areas being developed for export agroindustry (coffee, sugar, and cotton). Roughly one-third of the lands distributed between 1952 and 1972 were public lands on the Santa Cruz and Beni River frontiers, emergent centers of Bolivia's export-oriented "economic development."

Poverty and politics served to atomize the peasantry. Often, as in 1956 and 1963, the government mobilized and armed peasants to help put down labor protests in the mines. Rival peasant organizations sprang up during the 1964 elections, and open warfare developed over conflicting land claims. The military governments that ran Bolivia after 1964 engaged in outright repression of peasant leagues and the resubmission of peasant groups to leaders assigned or bought off by the military through "government/peasant pacts" similar to those initiated by the MNR.

The Bolivian Revolution's radical reforms in mining appeared to be too little too late. A number of private mines remained, employing half the mining labor force, estimated at 70,000 in the mid-1970s. Dust-induced silicosis and related lung diseases remained common: the average life span of a miner was thirty-five years. Those workers laid off because they were in the last stages of silicosis often became *veneristas* (veiners), digging their own tunnels to find ore to sell to the companies. Despite receiving some long overdue pay hikes, most miners earned under a dollar a day. Some of the worse-paid, besides the *veneristas*, were the *locatarios* (scavengers of slag piles) and *lameros* (panners).

The government's COMIBOL retained many of the practices of the "tin barons," such as company stores that victimized the work force; limited water, bathing, and sanitation facilities; or sparse housing that forced many families, known as *agregados* ("additional tenants"), to move in with others. The MNR set up spies in the mines to report on left-wing dissidents. It sent "barzolas"— women armed with knives and whips—to attack peaceful demonstrations launched by the Housewives' Committee, founded in 1961.

In 1963 the Siglo XX/Cataví mining community suffered a flu epidemic. It was told that COMIBOL did not have enough funds to send medicines. The miners took as hostage for medicines a performing troupe sent by "Moral Rearmament," a private but U.S.-backed international anti-Communist crusade then active in Latin America. COMIBOL sent the medicines, and the hostages were released.

That same year progovernment thugs kidnapped some mine union leaders whom the government threw in jail. Miners retaliated by seizing a U.S. labor attaché and several other Americans attending a COMIBOL meeting. The Housewives Committee guarded this prestigious human cargo. MNR's Lechín asked the Committee leaders to release the Americans. The women folded their arms and refused. Lechín puzzled out loud, "How is it possible for me to come to an agreement with 10,000 mine workers and here, with ten women, I can't get anywhere?" The jailed miners then asked the Committee to release the Americans, and the women reluctantly agreed to do so. They did not get their union leaders out of jail until 1964, when people took advantage of the turbulence of a military coup to rush the prison and release them.

Both the manifest failure of the MNR to satisfy people's revolutionary expectations and the rising tide of anti-Americanism were connected to the dismal state of Bolivia's economy. As historian Herbert Klein later observed, "The net result of this economic crisis was that the MNR leadership decided to turn to North American aid on a massive scale to support themselves in power while reconstructing the economy . . . but they had to pay a heavy price for it." That price included conservative monetary policies inimical to the interests of labor; the opening of the oil fields to foreign companies; demobilization of armed peasants and workers; and the reconsolidation and modernization of the military, trained and supplied by the United States. U.S. aid, mostly loans, totaled nearly half a billion dollars from the mid-1950s to 1970, a foundation for Bolivia's later unpayable foreign debt and its largely U.S. and IMF-imposed "privatization" campaigns of the 1980s and 1990s.

The administration of Siles Suazo (1956–1960) implemented a monetary stabilization program drafted by U.S. adviser George Eder. The second administration of President Paz Estenssoro (1960–1964) introduced the "Triangular Plan" to rehabilitate mining. The "triangle" consisted of the plan's sponsors, the U.S. and West German governments and the World Bank. The plan laid off workers, froze wages, suppressed workers' veto powers over COMIBOL decisions, and extended government control over the trade unions. Its harsh and undemocratic character provoked widespread protests and strikes. Many middle-class elements not yet economically wiped out by earlier inflation closed ranks with the antilabor "nuevos ricos"—as MNR bureaucrats and politicians who grew wealthy from U.S. aid programs and government corruption became known. Small private miners, merchants, and a handful of industrialists also lined up against labor.

Confident of his support among the middle and upper classes, President Paz Estenssoro fully implemented the Triangular Plan. He sent the rebuilt military to put down strikes and rallies by trade unions, dissident peasant leagues, and student groups. Troops killed several students at Oruro in 1964 and repressed workers in La Paz.

Paz Estenssoro's efforts succeeded to his own detriment, splitting the MNR and making the Army arbiter of the nation's politics. On November 4, 1964, a military coup d'état overthrew him. He and other MNR leaders fled for their lives. General René Barrientos emerged as the nation's military strongman (1964–1969). Lechín's PRIN and the COB initially backed Barrientos, but they too were soon harshly repressed. A tin miner summed things up in 1966: "When the MNR came to power in 1952, we felt it was a workers' party and things would be different. But then the MNR politicians organized a secret police and filled their pockets. They rebuilt the Army which we had destroyed, and when it got big enough the Army threw them out. Now the Army has new weapons which we cannot match."

Military Rule versus the New Politics, 1964–1982

The 1964 coup ended the MNR's twelve-year reign and introduced an eighteen-year period of uninterrupted, usually violent, military rule. The military officers who ran Bolivia's governments after 1964 were all U.S.-trained. Defenders of the U.S. aid programs pointed to the construction of roads and homes, while detractors noted that the roads facilitated military transport to strike-plagued mine sites and the homes were too few and too expensive for most Bolivians.

There were three attempts to change military rule: a guerrilla war launched in 1966 by Cuba's Ernesto "Ché" Guevara and Inti Peredo, Bolivian chief of the ELN (National Liberation Army); a "People's Assembly" in 1971 spearheaded by the trade unions, the Left, and populist military officers; and an eventually successful "democratic transition" in 1982, engineered by the same forces of popular mobilization and reformist officers but led by old-time MNR politicians like ex-presidents Siles Suazo and Paz Estenssoro who were allowed back into the country after many years of exile.

Barrientos liked to fly his own airplane around the country to visit with workers and peasants, making demagogic promises of a better life to come. He told miners he was taking half their wages to help put COMIBOL back on its feet economically but would return their wages to normal "in a year." He never did. Instead, he outlawed workers' control, disarmed the MNR's militias, and prevented labor's COB from functioning. He set up a secret police, DIC (Department of Criminal Investigations), and created his own political party, the Popular Christian movement.

Predictably, the people protested, and in May 1965 Barrientos declared a state of siege. He arrested mine union leaders and deported PRIN leader Lechín to Paraguay. His troops evicted wives of deportees from their COMIBOL-provided homes, leased to the miners so long as they worked.

Barrientos sent troops to enforce two kinds of massacres, what the miners called "blood massacres" (killings) and "white massacres" (worker layoffs). In 1965 and 1967 the military carried out two blood massacres reminiscent of those in 1942 and 1949. Some four hundred widows of miners killed in the 1965 massacre tried to survive by becoming *palliris*—picking at the rocks accumulated in huge slag mountains, some of which still had traces of ore. Each day their fingers became bloodied, and the amount of ore they found sold at a pittance. The 1970–1971 government of General Juan José Torres banned the practice and set up a pension fund. After the overthrow of Torres, the widows lost their pensions and returned to the slag heaps.

The June 24, 1967, massacre at Silgo XX of hundreds of men, women, and children happened at daybreak, when many were still in bed. The government believed the mining communities were about to furnish reinforcements to the guerrillas of the ELN, then fighting in the jungles south of Santa Cruz, the main city of the eastern lowlands. The ELN was engaging the Bolivian Rangers, a crack counterinsurgency regiment trained by U.S. soldiers at a camp just north of Santa Cruz.

Ernesto "Ché" Guevara, the Argentine-born revolutionist and former Cuban minister of industries, had renounced his Cuban citizenship before going to Bolivia to fight with Inti Peredo and the ELN in November 1966. His presence heated up Bolivian politics, where the "new politics" of the theology of liberation was just getting a start (see Overview). Although she did not participate in the ELN and knew little about Ché Guevara, Domitila Barrios de Chungara, head of the Siglo XX Housewives Committee and a former Jehovah's Witness, used her religious background to win over the conservative Christian Family movement to the miners' Socialist cause. Barrientos's repressive acts had stimulated the radicalization of Christian students and youth, many of whom became inspired by Colombia's guerrilla-priest Camilo Torres (see chapter 12). Up to one-third of the recruits into the guerrillas' ELN were Christian radicals.

Ché Guevara's self-declared mission was to spread revolution and create "two, three, many Vietnams." His ideas were not so different from those of Bolivia's Trotskyists at the time, but his main Bolivian links were through the

Bolivian Communist party. He broke with the party's leadership a month after his arrival, however, noting in his diary that "The party is now taking up [ideological] arms against us." There was little political work done among Bolivia's peasantry to gain support for Guevara.

Guevara wrote in his diary that he could not understand why each time his group outmarched and lost "the enemy," it would quite suddenly be on his tail again. He had no way of knowing that researchers at the University of Michigan had perfected the use of infrared photographic "sensors" that detected human body heat from long distances. "The enemy," used these sensors in its airplanes and knew where Guevara was all the time!

After eleven months, on October 7, 1967, Guevara was cornered, wounded, and captured. The next day he was taken to a schoolroom in La Higuera, near the Vallegrande military base. There he was executed. His corpse was transported to Vallegrande, where it was displayed to the press. Controversy raged on the exact circumstances of his death, but most believed that an obscure Bolivian soldier fired the shots into his neck on orders from Barrientos or the CIA or both. A small airplane flew his body out from Vallegrande a day later. No one yet knows where Guevara's remains are. But ever since, Bolivian peasants, some of whom had been won over to his cause, lit candles at crosses marking the places where he had camped. Some called him "Saint Ché."

Many months later Bolivia's Interior Minister Antonio Arguedas Mendieta gave the Cuban government Ché Guevara's diary, stating that he had received it from the CIA in whose pay he had been for many years. According to a *New York Times* summary of Arguedas' revelations, August 25, 1968, "The declarations he made, if true, would indicate that the Bolivian Government for the past three years has been little more than a mouthpiece for the United States, notably the CIA." The revelations rocked Bolivia and gave new life to the ELN, which fought on until finally defeated in late 1970. In 1993, a top Bolivian general said he had ordered Guevara's execution on orders from Barrientos and that those who knew where the corpse was buried were all dead now.

In 1969 Barrientos, ruling under a state of siege declared earlier in the year, was killed in a helicopter crash that some attributed to groundfire mounted by men in the military wishing to cover up their involvement in an international arms racket linked to the CIA. Hearing of Barrientos's death, people rushed into the streets, clamoring for another revolution, this time a real one. Barrientos's successor ignored them, but in September Army chief of staff General Alfredo Ovando Candia led a popular and successful coup.

Taking a page from the populist book of General Velasco in neighboring Peru (see chapter 14), Ovando allowed labor's COB to function again, declared a new "government/peasant pact," and nationalized the oil holdings of Gulf Oil Corporation. Five years later U.S. congressional hearings revealed that Gulf had bribed several officials in past Bolivian governments.

The military-reformist dimension of Latin America's new politics (see Overview) now showed its face in Bolivia, but its roots were in the militancy of the old labor movement and the military socialism of the 1930s. With Lechín still in exile and barred from political activity, the Trotskyists' POR regained strength inside the FSTMB and called for revolutionary changes. Ovando's populist rhetoric and the growing militancy of organized labor and the student movement stimulated a regroupment by right-wing officers, who attempted a coup in October 1970.

A countercoup squashed it. The countercoup was led by Left-leaning General Torres and backed by organized labor's COB, the rapidly growing student movement, and the PRIN, POR, and other left-wing parties. The Torres government released political prisoners, including French journalist Regis Debray who had been captured when he was covering Ché Guevara's guerrilla force. It assisted ELN guerrillas in gaining safe transit to the border with Chile. It expelled the Peace Corps and nationalized the Matilde mining complex, partly owned by U.S. Steel Corporation.

In November 1970, the Nineteenth National University Convention of the CUB (Bolivian University Confederation) condemned the murder of Ché Guevara and of subsequent student recruits to the ELN by "the Army and the CIA." It proclaimed "armed struggle" as "the only way to liberate the country."

Then the Right attempted another coup, led by Colonel Hugo Banzer of the army's "pro-Brazilian and Argentinian sectors" (so named because of the alliances they built with repressive generals, or "gorilas," running Brazil's and Argentina's dictatorships). Workers and students rushed to defend the Torres government, and Banzer was forced to flee to Argentina.

All of these events pushed Bolivia to the brink of revolution. By early 1971 the trade-union and leftist forces had established a unified "Political Command." It convoked a Popular Assembly on May Day, the international workers' holiday. The Popular Assembly included most of the MNR and was probably Latin American's most radical "broad front"—a new type of alliance among former rivals and a hallmark of the *new politics* shaking the continent. Combining legislative and executive powers, the Popular Assembly voted to defend the Torres government, bring it under popular control, and introduce socialism.

But the assembly spent more time debating fine political points than expanding the armed militias its members had been organizing since coming to Torres's defense in 1970. It also spent little time building peasant support. Consequently, when Banzer returned from exile and mobilized the army's tank and artillery corps in August 1971, to crush the burgeoning revolution, the assembly's militias were outgunned.

Banzer's coup had the backing of MNR ex-president Paz Estenssoro and the extreme Right's Socialist Falange. It introduced the savage seven-year wave of repression known as the "Banzerato" (1971–1978). On November 9,

1974, in the name of national security against the "Red menace," Banzer ordered the dissolution of political parties and trade unions. His regime machine-gunned students and stationed troops at the mines. Agents of its DOP (Department of Public Order) terrorized the populace. General Torres was assassinated in Argentina. Army officers silenced conscripts who refused orders. After bludgeoning to death ten Indian draftees at Uncia, the army brass explained the men had died in a "collective drowning at the swimming pool because Indians don't know how to swim."

Banzer organized another "government-peasant pact." He strengthened his alliance with Brazil's military officers, providing Brazil the rights to oil and iron at El Mutun in the eastern lowlands. The modern new city of Santa Cruz in the east was Banzer's hometown. Drawing on nearby oil, natural gas, cocaine, and agroindustrial resources, Santa Cruz emerged as Bolivia's newest regional power center, challenging the authority of La Paz.

The strength of the popular movement in the face of Banzer's repression led to instability in the ranks of the military and a series of unsuccessful coup attempts. During this time two groups increased their presence in the opposition—women and peasants. In 1973, for example, five thousand women demonstrated against the government's IMF-style "austerity" programs, known as _paquetes económicos_—"economic packages." They demanded more job openings. Peasants also protested the economic packages and organized against land taxes and high prices on necessities. In January 1974 they set up roadblocks at Tolata in the Cochabamba Valley. Troops opened fire on them, killing hundreds. Some peasants, having ignored the ELN in the 1960s, launched their own guerrilla warfare in the eastern lowlands.

For a while during the "Banzerato" the economy perked up because of higher prices for mineral exports, but actual production continued to stagnate. The government borrowed heavily to pay for the federal budget, the officer corps, highly speculative investments, and imports of luxury items and food. Some of the loan money ended up in Swiss banks, part of "flight capital." Individuals grew rich by means of personal favors granted them by Banzer. When the worldwide recession reached Bolivia in the late 1970s the bottom fell out of its already fragile economy. The foreign debt zoomed past $3 billion.

"Democratic Transition One" Blocked by
Cocaine Coup and Nazi Connection

The intensely repressive character of Banzer's rule alienated the rest of society and caused the U.S. government, during the first flush of President Jimmy Carter's human rights pronouncements, to distance itself from Banzer. It was time for a "democratic transition." Banzer called for elections in 1978, confident he could arrange his own victory. But other military factions forced him to accept the candidacy of a different general. The MNR formed two rival political coalitions, one backed by ex-president Siles Suazo and most of the Left, and another led by ex-President Paz Estenssoro and a portion of the Right.

The 1978 election process was riddled with fraud, and before the courts could make a ruling on its outcome, the military candidate mounted a coup. He was overthrown by officers wishing to hold another national election. In the next election, July 1979, Siles Suazo edged out Paz Estenssoro with Banzer running a distant third. Since no one had a majority, congress had to decide the winner. Too fractionalized to reach a decision (Bolivia by then had close to seventy political parties and factions), congress appointed an interim president who was overthrown in another coup.

When workers resisted the coup in pitched battles with troops, the military brass and congress agreed that another interim civilian president would hold office until new elections could be held in June 1980. Siles Suazo increased his plurality in those elections, but congress again had to decide. Before it could act, Bolivia's drug barons got together with a clique of military officers and, on July 17, 1980, General Luis García Meza launched what became known as the "cocaine coup."

The next twenty-six months of military dictatorship revealed three things: (1) all the civilian politicking was a sideshow to the main action, which was still inside the military; (2) the military establishment was riddled with factions based more on greed than on principle; and (3) the big money was in cocaine—the cocaine billionaires were deciding which group of military kleptocrats would run the show. In 1981 Bolivia became the first Latin American nation not to meet service payments on its foreign debt. The cocaine coup government also brought to a climax Bolivia's "Nazi connection," known as the "Barbie affair."

In some ways Bolivia, by tradition and geography, was a logical place for a military strong-armed government run on behalf of cocaine traffickers allied with Nazi war criminals. Coca leaf production flourished on the traditional *latifundista* plantations in the humid semitropical Yungas; on the small peasant landholdings of the Chapare tropical rain forest settled by migrants from the Cochabamba region; and in the northeastern Beni lowlands, where coca paste labs were set up in sheds and drug czar Roberto Suárez was praised by the locals for his "community work."

Whether dealing with peasants, generals, or presidents, Suárez, the son of a prosperous cattle rancher descended from a long line of diplomats and senators, was a master of the "soft cop/hard cop" routine. While building public parks and offering to pay off the nation's whopping foreign debt, Suárez used his private security squad to intimidate uncooperative peasants or high state officials. Suárez's "cop force" was a private death squad, the "Fiances of Death." Suárez had bankrolled Nazi war criminal Klaus Barbie to use his old-time Fascist connections to recruit these right-wing terrorists, one of whom was Italy's Pier Luigi Pagliai, wanted for the 1980 bombing of a Bologna train station that killed eighty-five people. As part of their "protection" of Suárez's drug empire, the "Fiances of Death" attacked Bolivia's left-wing labor leaders.

Suárez helped finance the "cocaine coup" of 1980. General García Meza's minister of interior, Colonel Luis Arce Gómez, was Suárez's cousin. He was popularly known as the "Minister of Cocaine" and was later indicted by U.S. grand juries and extradited to Miami in 1989 to face charges of cocaine dealing. Another friend of Suárez in the Bolivian military was Colonel Lara, an officer in the elite Rangers Regiment used to combat Ché Guevara. The 1980–1982 cocaine coup government was widely viewed as the most violent and undemocratic ever in Bolivia. One of its first acts was to murder nine members of the political directorate of the coalition that had backed Siles Suazo's presidential candidacy.

Klaus Barbie had served as Adolf Hitler's Gestapo chief in German-occupied France during World War II. He was known as "the Butcher of Lyon"—because of his killing and deporting to Hitler's gas ovens thousands of French resistance fighters and Jews from that city. After the war, the U.S. Army brought Barbie to the United States. CIA and U.S. military intelligence personnel wanted to use him to help identify Europe's anti-Fascist resistance activists as part of the anti-Communist campaign being carried out against Europe's large Left-leaning trade-union movement in the late 1940s. In 1951 Barbie was smuggled into Bolivia, where he assumed the name of Klaus Altmann and lived in plush comfort. Not until 1983 was Barbie finally expelled to France and brought to justice. A French jury convicted him in 1987 of mass murder. There being no death penalty, he was sentenced to life in prison. During the trial a former deputy interior minister of Bolivia testified that Barbie had been a lieutenant colonel in the Bolivian Army, had helped set up concentration camps, and had been one of those responsible for imprisoning, torturing, and killing opponents of Bolivia's 1964–1982 military rule. Barbie had also set up arms sales to a ring of international drug traffickers.

1982–1993 "Democratic Transition Two": Civilian-Military Pact, Drugs, IMF, and U.S. Troops

Bolivia became a pariah nation, its military a target of international reproach. People were willing to risk their lives to topple the ruling generals. Organized labor's COB mounted a general strike in 1982. The country's business elites and politicians discussed how to "restore democracy." The officer corps, aware it had to lower its drug-contaminated profile, worked out a deal that allowed congress to approve Siles Suazo as the winner of the 1980 election. García Meza and Arce Gómez fled to Argentina, overnight millionaires.

Siles Suazo assumed the presidency on October 2, 1982, and formed a coalition government. The main partner in his coalition was the left-of-center MIR (Movement of the Revolutionary Left), whose leader Jaime Paz Zamorra (Paz Estenssoro's nephew) was vice-president. Siles Suazo and COB worked out a renewal of workers' co-gobierno with the state at COMIBOL. The government attempted six successive IMF-recommended "*paquetes económicos*"; organized labor resisted each one with strikes. The MIR abandoned the sinking ship of the Siles Suazo government in 1983. Inflation was running out of control and the economy was in an even worse shambles than before.

The traditional government-peasant pact approach no longer worked. The peasants reorganized their *sindicatos*, forming a national organization with the unpronounceable acronym CSUTCB (Unified Peasant League Federation of Bolivia). Thousands of them engaged in eighteen major roadblocks in 1983–1984. Increasingly their protest actions were undertaken in solidarity with dissatisfied miners.

In 1984 a longtime aide and friend of Siles Suazo accused the president of having instructed him to negotiate with drug baron Suárez. In the face of this scandal and the declining economy, Siles Suazo was pressured to announce he would not finish his term but would hold new elections in 1985.

In March 1985 the COB pulled off the fifth general strike in three years, calling for economic relief. The government was unsympathetic: it hiked bread prices 75 percent in May. Labor's COB viewed the upcoming presidential election as a no-choice, no-win situation. The three candidates— President Siles Suazo, three-time president Paz Estenssoro, and former dictator Banzer—were all antilabor, and any one of them was acceptable to the military.

In the voting no one won a majority, but Banzer outpolled Paz Estenssoro by 37,000 votes, whereas Siles Suazo finished a distant third. The choice of a winner once more fell in the lap of congress, where leftist parties threw their support to Paz Estenssoro as "less evil" than Banzer. For the first time in history, on August 5, 1985, congress declared the loser the winner: Paz Estenssoro.

The seventy-seven-year-old landowner's son and former professor of economics and history started his fourth term facing falling tin prices, an inflation rate of 30,000 percent, and a foreign debt of $4.8 billion on which the government had not been able to pay a cent for more than a year. His solution? An economic austerity program more severe than any known before. It aimed to break organized labor, privatize the nationalized mines, and sell off the oil and natural gas fields—in sum, to open up the economy to "market forces."

In late September 1985 labor responded with another general strike. Paz Estenssoro declared a state of siege that lasted three months. The government arrested most of labor's leaders, including Lechín, banishing them to internal exile in remote areas or to prison.

On October 16, 1985, Paz Estenssoro entered into an antilabor "pact in support of democracy" that linked his MNRH party to Banzers' ultra-rightist ADN (see Box 15.1). It committed both groups to cooperation in congress and to unflinching support for an austerity program even harsher than ADN's earlier proposals. The ADN would be phased into control over various municipal governments and eventually a number of state agencies. The pact, reminiscent of Colombia's National front 50-50 power-sharing arrangement between Liberals and Conservatives (see chapter 12), gained the momentary backing of the military. It led to the passing of a law diminishing the power of the many small leftist parties that together had commanded so many of Bolivia's votes (and seats in congress) in the past.

The MNRH-ADN unity's economic austerity program became known as the NEP (New Economic Policy). It was prepared by Harvard's Jeffrey Sachs and started bringing inflation under a semblance of control. But the collapse of the tin market in 1985 made it impossible for Bolivia to recover. President Paz Estenssoro's 1986 budget allocated 36.5 percent of expenditures to the foreign debt and 22.3 percent to defense. In April 1986 the IMF rewarded Bolivia with a $56 million standby loan. Wage and salaried workers faced harder times, and even public employees began to protest. Sachs later cynically commented: "I always told the Bolivians . . . if you are gutsy, if you do everything right, you will end up with a miserable, poor economy with stable prices."

During the economic hard times many Bolivians began forming new community organizations to maintain their households. Women played a central role. Inside the unified peasant leagues' CSUTCB, women peasants formed their own section with its own national committee. The miners' Housewives Committees became voting members of the FSTMB.

Meanwhile miners protested the privatization of COMIBOL and forced the government to organize a large mining cooperative. Because of inadequate technology and funding, however, the cooperative amounted to "self-exploitation" by co-op members, many of them women who for the first time went down into the mine shafts since their husbands had migrated to the Santa Cruz lowlands or Argentina looking for work.

Cocaine was still the only industry showing robust life signs in Bolivia's dying economy. Coca leaf cultivation and coca paste production represented one-quarter of Bolivia's GNP. Numerous peasants and underemployed migrant workers, including laid-off tin miners, depended on it for their survival. In January 1986, 17,000 coca farmers surrounded an antidrug police camp demanding an end to harassment. More than four hundred murders related to the drug trade were reported that year.

Back in August of 1983 Bolivia had signed four treaties with the United States aimed at reducing coca production to a level commensurate with the needs of Indians for the alleviation of hunger pangs. One treaty provided for the creation of a U.S.-trained mobile paramilitary unit, the Leopards. Former Air Force Major Clarence Edgar Merwin, a one-time CIA operative and ex-director of the Air Force's Special Operations school, was assigned by the U.S. State Department's Bureau of International Narcotics Matters (INM) to oversee the Leopards' training.

After completing his assignment, Merwin issued his final report, "Our current level of effort is largely a waste of time and money." Every director of Bolivia's Narcotics Police was "on the take." One Leopard commander, Germán Linares, when leading his troops in an attempted kidnapping of President Siles Suazo, was caught, exiled, and later returned to his command post.

In July 1986 some 160 U.S. marines and six Blackhawk helicopters arrived in Bolivia to carry out a widely publicized drug raid known as "Operation Blast Furnace." U.S. troops did not leave until the end of the year. Together with the Leopards, they destroyed a few empty processing labs and frightened some peasants. The drug lords withdrew their operations for a while, creating a shortage of dollars and causing a run on the Bolivian Central Bank. But according to the U.S. State Department's INM Strategy Report of 1987, "Bolivia's coca cultivation expanded during 1986 by at least 10 percent." In mid-1988 Suárez was arrested, tried on drug charges, and sentenced to fifteen years.

The U.S. military presence coincided with the peaking of federal budgetary cutbacks on education and social services and popular mobilizations denouncing the government's subservience to the IMF. Some 15,000 mine workers were being laid off. They, together with the civic committees of Oruro and Potosí Departments, teachers, farmers, and factory workers, launched in late July 1986, a "March for Life and Peace." The Bolivian Army broke it up on July 28. Then, during the last week of August, a longer, more arduous "March for Life and Bread" took place. As thousands of marchers converged forty miles outside La Paz, they were met by tanks, troops, and fighter planes. By now their demands included not only the saving of the mines, farms, jobs, and wage scales, but also the removal of U.S. troops. They were dispersed. The women followed up with hunger strikes.

In September 1986 the government imposed another state of siege and arrested 162, including the remaining leaders of the labor Left. In a move reminiscent of the Banzerato, it banned all trade-union and political activity. It dismissed two-thirds of the miners of COMIBOL but promised to keep the mines open. Then it gradually closed down state mines. The miners' trade union movement lost much of its clout; peasant organizations made up the majority of COB. Lechín retired as COB head, and his place was taken by a member of the communists' PCB.

Shortly afterward the United States delivered a loan of $100 million, and the IMF cleared another $128 million in credits. By 1987 business was back to usual and, because of Operation Blast Furnace, druglords had placed a $400,000 bounty price on President Paz Estenssoro's head.

From 1988 to 1991, U.S. Ambassador Robert Gelbard, fresh from his work with the State Department's Elliott Abrams in the contra war against Nicaragua's revolution (see the introduction to Part One and chapters 2 and 5), oversaw the stepped-up militarization of Bolivian drug policy as part of "Operation Snowcap," a U.S. program to assist Peru and Bolivia in the war on drugs. A $35.9 million military aid package for Bolivia in 1990 led to the sending of fifty-six U.S. Special Forces (Green Berets) in mid-1991 and widespread popular demands for Gelbard's removal. A brief appointment as head of Bolivia's antidrug forces of a former intelligence chief for the García Meza cocaine-coup dictatorship was reversed by popular outcry in February 1991. A labor union leader dubbed Gelbard "Bolivia's alternative president." Later in 1991 Gelbard became President Bush's assistant secretary for inter-American affairs.

U.S. aid to fight the drug war in Bolivia jumped to $140 million in 1992. Popular protests continued when a U.S.-DEA employee shot a Bolivian in a barroom brawl. The government announced it was withdrawing special police and army units from the drug war. A 1993 AID study claimed that the size of Bolivia's coca/cocaine industry was halved in 1992, but many observers doubted its accuracy. The Supreme Court sentenced cocaine-coup multimillionaire García Meza and fifty-four associates in 1993 to long prison terms. Others had taken their place in the cocaine trade.

All political activity remained illegal except during suspensions of the state of siege. Elections for municipal officials occurred for the first time in thirty-nine years in December 1987. The presidential elections of 1989 resulted in another deadlock broken by a new "unity pact for democracy" known as AP (Patriotic Accord)—this time between Banzer's ADN and Paz Zamora's MIR. Top vote getter (23.1 percent) Gonzalo Sánchez de Lozada of the "renewalist" faction of the MNRH was thereby denied the presidency, awarded to third-place finisher (after Banzer) Paz Zamora. Paz Zamora continued the NEP's drastic austerity measures. The major political parties agreed to introduce several constitutional reforms, including: defining Bolivia as a "multi-ethnic and pluri-cultural state"; guarantees for the rights of Indian peoples; lowering the voting age to eighteen and eliminating any qualifications for enfranchisement; and possible presidential reelection. While the politicians dickered in the late 1980s and early 1990s, the popular mobilizations continued to advocate prioritizing people instead of superprofits.

Leadership during the popular protests increasingly came from the bottom-up. The old "political class" (see Overview) was being pushed aside, in a pattern typical of Latin America's new politics. In May 1988, however, labor leaders still commanded enough respect to be able to persuade 10,000 workers and students to lift a hunger strike during a visit by Pope John Paul II. The Pope called for a more just society and sipped local tea made from coca leaves.

The popular movements were largely based in shantytowns and among organizations of women, students, teachers, and Indians. Bolivia's street vendors union grew to 800,000 affiliates. In early 1993, a twenty-four-day series of hunger strikes, industrial actions, and street protests won a temporary concession from the government that privatization would proceed through joint ventures with private capital but without transferring "ownership" to the private sector.

Popular protest had a new environmentalist twist too. For years big lumber companies had been stripping the mahogany forests on Indian lands on the Beni frontier. Huge tractors had been cutting down trees to clear land around Santa Cruz to make way for land speculators and Mennonite farmers who planted soybeans for export. Bolivia became one of the first nations to conclude a "debt-for-nature" swap when it used New York's giant bank Citicorp as its financial agent for a $100,000 grant to buy $650,000 in Bolivian debt and help preserve the Beni Biosphere Reserve, home of thirteen endangered species and the nomadic Chimane Indians. Nonetheless, deforestation and abuse of Indians' human rights proceeded almost as rapidly as in neighboring Brazil (see chapter 20). The Indians protested as they saw the destruction of the delicate ecological balances on which their way of life depended. In a 1990 march "For Territory and Dignity," some eight hundred of them treked for thirty-three days from the Beni tropical lowlands to La Paz where they conducted an historic meeting with highland Indians. Besides human rights and ecological concerns, a universal complaint of all Bolivia's indigenous peoples was the way they were being driven by cheap imports and U.S. food aid to abandon their farms and look for work elsewhere. Economists agreed that in the absence of the rapid expansion of the "informal" economy in petty trade and manufacture Bolivian unemployment rates would have soared to 35 percent.

In 1993 a few neo-liberalism advocates hailed Bolivia as a privatization success story because its annual inflation rate had dropped to 10 percent and economic growth rates had chugged along at 2 to 3 percent for several years. Moreover, the foreign debt had been partially forgiven and renegotiated down to $1.9 billion. Yet a World Bank mission in 1991 found that consumption per capita had been steadily falling since 1986, private investment had declined by 6 percent, and the economy was stagnating. Transport, retail trade, construction, and financial services jointly accounted for 40 percent of GDP (gross domestic product) by 1993, and there was talk of new oil and gas discoveries in the eastern lowlands. The neo-liberals envisioned running a natural gas pipeline to Brazil's industrial area of São Paulo. Many in Bolivia's business classes hoped to integrate the nation with the Mercosur common market but found Bolivian membership in the Andean Pact an impediment (see Introduction to Part Three).

The 1993 presidential elections were again won by MNRH's Sánchez de Lozada, a millionaire mining entrepreneur popularly known as "the gringo" because he spoke Spanish with an American accent (he was raised in the United States). This time second-place finisher Banzer, whose AP running mate was Paz Zamora's nephew, a former guerrilla fighter, gave the nod to Sánchez de Lozada. President Sánchez de Lozada's vice-president was Víctor Hugo Cárdenas, an Aymara-speaking intellectual and leader of an indigenous-based party allied with the MNRH. Populist self-made millionaire beer magnate Max Fernández, known for his public works projects in poor areas and alleged ties to drug traffickers, finished third on his UCS (Civic Solidarity Unity) ticket. Another "political outsider" populist, radio talk show host Carlos Palenque of CONDEPA (Patriotic Conscience), came in fourth.

The NEP marched onward, while in the wings at least four military factions rattled their sabres. Major military discontent came from middle-level and lower-level officers discontented with reduced military budgets, government corruption, and U.S. interventionism. A few were right-wing but most were left-populist. Most senior officers, however, for the moment at least, were marching in step with the new president and the NEP.

One thing was certain: the Bolivian Revolution was dead, even if its traditions and goals were not. The ruling elites, generals, and politicians continued to look nervously over their shoulders at the popular organizations led from the bottom-up.

Selected Bibliography

Barrios de Chungara, Domitila. _Let Me Speak! Testimony of Domitila, a Woman of the Bolivian Mines_. New York: Monthly Review Press, 1978. A moving book popular with students.

Crabtree, John. _The Great Tin Crash: Bolivia and the World Tin Market_. London, England: Latin America Bureau, 1987.

Dunkerley, James. _Rebellion in the Veins: Political Struggle in Bolivia, 1952–1982_. Thetford, England: Thetford Press, 1984.

Kelley, Jonathan, and Herbert S. Klein. _Revolution and the Rebirth of Inequality_. Berkeley: University of California Press, 1981.

Malloy, James M., and Eduardo Gamarra. _Revolution and Reaction: Bolivia 1964–1985_. New Brunswick, NJ: Transaction, 1988. Places events in larger regional context of southern cone.

Mitchell, Christopher. _The Legacy of Populism in Bolivia: From the MNR to Military Rule_. New York: Praeger, 1977.

Nash, June. *We Eat the Mines and the Mines Eat Us*. New York: Colombia University Press, 1979.

North American Congress on Latin America (Nacla). "Bolivia: The Poverty of Progress." *Nacla Report on the Americas,* 25(1) (July 1991).

Queiser Morales, Waltraud. *Bolivia: Land of Struggle*. Boulder, CO: Westview, 1989.

Films

Blood of the Condor. 1970. 95 minutes. Black and white film by Jorge Sanjinés on Indian and Western cultures in conflict.

Courage of the People. 1972. 95 minutes. Color film by Jorge Sanjinés on popular movements.

Cry of the People. 1972. 65 minutes. Color film by Humberto Ríos covering twentieth century history.

Hell to Pay. 1988. 52 minutes. Insightful, moving color film on debt crisis as seen through eyes of women. English subtitles.

Hotel Terminus: The Life and Times of Klaus Barbie. 1988. 4 hours, 29 minutes. Feature documentary directed by award-winning Marcel Ophuls; spellbinding; English subtitles.

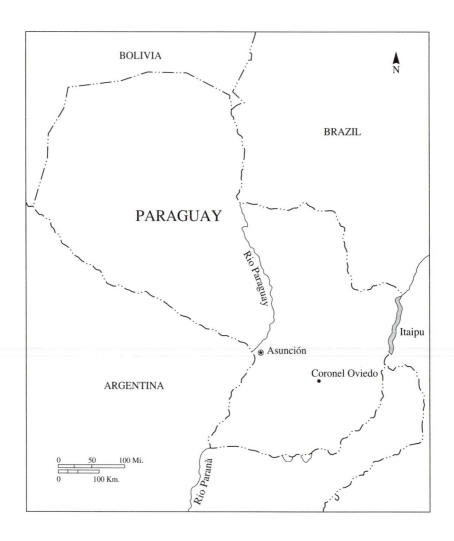

BOLIVIA

BRAZIL

N

PARAGUAY

Rio Paraguay

Itaipu

⊛ Asunción

Coronel Oviedo

ARGENTINA

0   50   100 Mi.

0   100 Km.

Rio Paranà

512

Paraguay _____ 16

Here we respect human rights. Human rights are for the well-behaved people, for the workers.—President Alfredo Stroessner, 1980

In early September 1987 moderate opposition leaders were holding a public meeting in the local church of the town of Coronel Oviedo, eighty miles east of landlocked Paraguay's capital city of Asunción. Witnesses later said the atmosphere was subdued, tense. Out of long custom, people expected a police attack and spoke almost in whispers.

Suddenly a group of parapolice thugs shouting "Long live Stroessner!" and "Death to Communists!" stormed into the church, wielding whips and clubs. They beat up people, including the leaders of the PLRA (Authentic Radical Liberal party), the PRF (February Revolutionary party), the MPCC (Popular Colorado Movement for Unity), and the journalists' trade union (see Box 16.1). Several persons had to be hospitalized.

The ruling Colorado party's Ramón Aquino, self-styled national "commander of the Colorado Assault Regiment," announced, "There will be wholesale beatings, we will beat them all up if they try to disrupt the peace, stability, and tranquility of the Paraguayan people." Seventy-four-year-old dictator-President Alfredo Stroessner, completing his thirty-third year in office, gave Aquino a hardy *abrazo*, having earlier praised him as the "moderator" of the

Catholic University, that is, the man in charge of silencing dissident students. Justice Minister Eugenio Jacquet, an ideologue of the fascistic GAA (Anti-Communist Action Groups), lauded the attack as "a sign that we Colorados are walking tall."

Later in the month defiant opposition activists were on their way to a rally organized by the PLRA in Tebicuarymi, sixty miles southeast of Asunción. Police detained dozens of them, including Domingo Laino, head of the PLRA who had recently returned from exile, and Miguel Angel Casabianca, president of MOPOCO (a 1959 Colorado splitoff). All the detainees were later released, but the atmosphere remained unusually tense.

Many of Paraguay's 4.5 million people, most of whom spoke both Spanish and the Indian language of Guaraní, knew nothing about these or other political events. They had lived under an almost continuous state of siege ever since the military coup that brought General Stroessner and the army to power in 1954. Among the politically knowledgeable, though, fear of kidnapping, torture, or death was a daily reality. Opposition activists tried to inform other Paraguayans of past events and convince them to act.

Leaflets, whether or not read, were quickly thrown away. To be caught with such material could mean arrest. The leaflets mentioned incidents like the following:

In January 1985 police arrested fourteen people attending a PLRA meeting in Itapua. Six of them, including a young girl, were tortured.

In March 1980 army patrols in the economically booming frontier area of eastern Paraguay near the Brazilian border arrested three hundred peasant members of the "peasant agrarian leagues." The army killed several of the detainees, including a popular peasant leader.

In April-May 1974 police arrested two thousand peasants and two hundred students alleged to be members of the short-lived OPM (Political-Military Organization). Twenty of them, including two OPM leaders, died while in police custody. Seven Jesuit priests were expelled for their presumed support of OPM.

In late 1975 and early 1976 some seventy people alleged to be members of the outlawed PCP (Paraguayan Communist party) were detained. The party secretary-general, two central committee members, and even pregnant women and children died from torture.

In late 1974 authorities arrested one thousand people accused of being involved with guerrillas of Argentina's ERP (see chapter 18) in a plot to kill Stroessner. Scores were deported and later disappeared in the neighboring military dictatorships of Argentina and Brazil; most were said to be members of MOPOCO (see Box 16.1).

Box 16.1: Paraguay's Political Parties and Other Organizations in the Stroessner Era

AN   National Accord, founded in 1979, centrist opposition coalition of MOPOCO, PDC, PLRA, and PRF

APCT   Permanent Assembly of Landless Peasants, founded in 1986

CCT   Christian Federation of Workers, outlawed peasant leagues organized by PDC

Colorado party   Ruling *stronista* party, founded in 1877 and taken over by Stroessner in 1959 (see MOPOCO); split in 1987 between "*militantes*" and the expelled "traditionalists" and "*éticos*"; affiliated with World Anti-Communist League

CPT   Paraguayan Workers Federation; government-controlled labor organization inactive between 1958 and 1980

DIPC   Police Investigations Department, with an interrogation center staffed by fifty experienced torturers

DT   semiautonomous Technical Division for the Repression of Communism, said to be close to Asunción CIA station; most of staff U.S.-trained

FEUP   Paraguayan Federation of University Students, founded in 1986 as alternative to government-controlled groups

GAA   Anti-Communist Action Groups, ultrarightist denunciators of "subversives"; linked to World Anti-Communist League

G-2   Intelligence division of armed forces

MCP   Paraguayan Peasant movement, founded in 1986 to unite landless peasants with Commission of Relatives of Disappeared and Murdered Persons

MIT   Inter-union Workers' movement, founded in 1984, independent trade unionists

MOPOCO   Popular Colorado movement, founded in 1959 by dissident Colorados, centrist; member of AN

MPCC   Popular Colorado movement for Unity, opposition group founded in 1987

PCP   Paraguayan Communist party, founded in 1929; illegal except briefly in 1936 and 1946; two very small, mostly exiled PCPs since the 1967 China/USSR split

PDC   Christian Democratic party, founded in 1960, without legal status; member of AN and Christian Democratic International

PL   Liberal party, founded in 1961, very anti-Communist, a legal opposition party; lost most members to PLRA in 1978

PLR   Liberal Radical party, moderate right-wing, legal opposition party founded in 1961 as a splitoff from PL; lost most members to PLRA; walked out of congress in 1987

PLRA   Authentic Radical Liberal party, founded in 1978 by PLR and PL majorities, centrist; largest of opposition liberal groups, but without legal status; member of AN

PRF   February Revolutionary party, founded in 1936, small Aprista-type party (see chapter 14); purged of leftist members; has legal status; member of AN and Socialist International

Those old enough to remember whispered about the one-month lifting of the state of siege in 1959 that had led to MOPOCO's founding. The army had opened fire on street demonstrators, and when the dictator's Congress protested, Stroessner closed it down, imprisoning and exiling hundreds of his party's dissident members. Ever since, up to half of all Paraguayans had lived in exile. Three-quarters of a million of them were peasants working in Argentina. A common saying was, "The slums of Paraguay are to be found in Argentina."

The main reason for the unusual tension of late 1987, however, was not merely that opposition movements were being subjected to severe repression. After all, that was not new. Rather, recent economic changes in Paraguay had generated energetic new social movements. The nation was in the throes of a full-scale political crisis. Ruling Colorado circles were divided on how to handle the situation. And Stroessner's days were numbered.

Background: From Independence to the Chaco War and Stroessner

Because of its remoteness from major trade routes and its lack of gold and silver, Paraguay did not attract immediate Spanish or Portuguese settlement. The first Spanish colonists, fleeing Indian attacks in Argentina, settled today's capital city of Asunción in 1537. Intermarriage between seminomadic Guaraní Indians and the Spanish created Latin America's most homogeneous population—95 percent mestizo.

The Spanish Crown and Jesuit priests fought for control over Guaraní labor needed for the production of yerba mate, a popular tea in the Plata River countries of South America. The Jesuits combined religious conversion with military defense of more than 100,000 Guaranís fleeing Spanish conquest in Asunción and slave hunters from Portuguese Brazil. By the eighteenth century there were thirty economically self-sufficient Jesuit colonies.

One of the first major, although unsuccessful, rebellions against Spain in the New World shook Paraguay from 1721 to 1735. Known as the "Comunero Revolt," it pitted mestizos and Indian sympathizers against both Spanish troops and the Jesuits. The Crown scapegoated the Jesuits for these and later popular uprisings that shook its Latin American colonies, expelling the Jesuits in 1767.

When Argentina declared independence from Spain in 1810, Paraguayan mestizo militias repelled Argentine attacks. They wanted neither Argentine nor Spanish domination. Leery of the mestizos' freshly proven strength, Spanish officers in Asunción sought assistance from Portuguese troops in (today's) Brazil. The mestizos felt they could manage the country without the Portuguese as well.

On October 12, 1812, Paraguay became Latin America's first independent republic, threatened from both the south and north. To the south Buenos Aires controlled Paraguay's access to the sea. The Paraná-Paraguay river system flowed to Argentina through the Río de la Plata. To the north Portuguese forces occupied half of Paraguay's territory. From its birth as an independent nation, then, Paraguay faced powerful neighbors with the potential to absorb it. This led to a feisty nationalism among its people.

To defend the young nation, theologian-lawyer José Gaspar Rodríguez de Francia established a strong, authoritarian central government, founded upon an alliance with peasants, artisans, small tradesmen, professionals, and the urban poor. Declared ruler for life in 1816, Francia ruled with an iron hand. He reduced the potential political threat from local elites by confiscating their lands. Allowing peasant squatters to farm state lands, he built up a state-run livestock industry.

After Francia's death in 1840, other strong rulers used the state to develop Paraguay into an economically self-reliant nation. In 1846 the state took over all yerba mate and timber resources, allowing individuals to run state concessions. It pursued similar policies in other areas, stimulating the formation of a small business class in agriculture and industry. By 1854 Paraguay had a modern iron foundry. Two years later it built Latin America's first ship with metal hulls. By 1861 Paraguay had an array of rail and telegraph services, printing presses, armaments factories, roads, canals, and public schools and health services. Its population increased fivefold from 1810 to 1865, reaching more than half a million—and there were nearly as many cattle. Back then Paraguayans had enough to eat. Today Paraguay is notorious for gross inequalities that make four-fifths of its 4.5 million people extremely poor.

Greed and war undid these accomplishments. Wealthy merchants, coffee interests, and foreign capitalists saw prosperous Paraguay as an economic plum for the plucking. In 1865 Paraguay's neighbors—Uruguay, Brazil, and Argentina—signed a secret pact known as the Treaty of the Triple Alliance. British bankers backed the treaty, which first became public in the British parliament. In 1864 Paraguayan dictator Francisco Solano López declared war against Brazil, ostensibly to turn back a Brazil-inspired coup in Uruguay but with the real aim of defending and extending Paraguay's northeastern border. The savage "War of the Triple Alliance" (1864–1870) cost Paraguay nearly two-thirds of its population and left only 29,000 male Paraguayans alive. Paraguay surrendered one-quarter of its territory to Argentina and Brazil.

Afterward Paraguay fell under the sway of regional caudillos (military chieftains), many of whom allied themselves with foreign interlopers. Argentine and British citizens bought off the bulk of state-owned acreage between 1883 and 1898. Thousands of immigrants from Italy, Spain, Germany, and Argentina helped develop the livestock, agricultural, and forest industries. Some five thousand pacifist Mennonites set up agrarian colonies. Ninety percent of Paraguayans worked for a pittance on the lands of others and were illiterate.

For half a century two Paraguayan political parties, the Colorados and the Liberals, ruled in the midst of their own internal factionalism and frequent popular revolts and military coups. Both parties championed liberal ideas of free trade, but the Colorados were more conservative and more caudillo-dominated. Backed by Brazilian interests, the Colorados governed until 1904. The Liberals, supported by Anglo-Argentine capital, ruled from 1904 until 1940. Both parties defended the dominant system of *latifundismo* (large landholdings). In the mid-1940s, twenty-five foreign companies owned one-third of Paraguay's land area; two of these accounted for 13 percent.

The Chaco War of 1932–1935 with Bolivia, also known as "the petroleum war" (see chapter 15), expanded Paraguayan territory westward. Some 100,000 men from the two nations perished in hand-to-hand combat in the deserts and swamplands of the vast Chaco lowlands.

After the war, veterans and unemployed workers teamed up with students and professionals to demand economic and political reforms in Paraguay. Popular war hero Colonel Rafael Franco spearheaded a coup, February 17, 1936, for which the PRF (February Revolutionary party, or Febreristas) was named.

The PRF-Franco government enacted a more democratic constitution. It approved a progressive labor code and implemented an agrarian reform that gave several thousand families titles to 180,000 hectares of expropriated lands. The Franco government was unable to bring emergent peasant organizations and labor unions under sufficiently firm state control to satisfy its conservative big business and Liberal party critics, however. Therefore it began jailing labor leaders, shutting down leftist newspapers, and curtailing the agrarian reform.

Meanwhile, Standard Oil of New Jersey's Spruille Braden headed up a peace-negotiating commission to draw the final boundaries resulting from the Chaco War. Seeking to retain known and suspected oil lands inside Bolivia's prewar borders for Standard's benefit, Braden believed the peace conference could "upset the Franco regime" that is, lead to its overthrow, and bring to power "other politicians who would be willing to compromise and effect a settlement."

Disgruntled Paraguayan elites and politicians mounted a coup against the Febreristas and Franco, installing another Liberal government in August 1937 and ending the most serious attempt at democratic reform in the nation's history. Paraguay's new conservative government signed the Chaco Peace Treaty of July 21, 1938, granting to Bolivia oil-rich lands Paraguay had conquered during the war. Standard's Braden went on to meddle in Argentina's politics (see chapter 18).

General Higinio Morínigo consolidated a personal dictatorship from 1940 to 1948, based on the army's support, which he won by assigning half the state budget to the military. He banned political parties, jailed opponents, muzzled the press, silenced labor unions. Although he favored German economic interests and acted like a Fascist, he took the Allies' side during World War II in exchange for U.S. loans and gifts of arms and planes.

After the war some of the military joined a rising popular movement against Morínigo's tyranny and forced him to accept a Febrerista-Colorado coalition government. It fell apart, however, and a civil war erupted in 1947 pitting the Colorados against Febreristas, Liberals, and Communists. The Colorados won, banned all other political parties, and ruled by the force of the Army and the police. They soon split between the ultrarightist "Guión Rojo" faction and the more moderate "democráticos."

Paraguay was a predominantly rural country, and the Colorados still based their strength on regional caudillos who controlled a large, politically passive peasantry on behalf of big landowners (_latifundistas_). Most peasants were small landholders (_minifundistas_) or had no land at all; they generally worked private or state lands as sharecroppers or tenant farmers. Colorado thugs known as "Py-Nandu" (silent feet) terrorized spokesmen of other parties or occasional dissident peasants. They were reactivated whenever needed, such as during the early 1960s and in the 1980s.

In Asunción wealthy _latifundistas_ and their sons had set up lucrative business interests in banking, commerce, and small manufactures. Their enterprises were linked to powerful foreign companies, mainly Anglo-Argentine and U.S. These companies owned cattle ranches and forest reserves. They produced meat, lumber, yerba mate, and tannin for export. They also owned, or controlled through the credit system, the manufacturing sector, which employed around 20,000 workers, half of them in the meat processing and chemical-dye (tannin) industries. Paraguayan moneylenders and tradesmen were overshadowed by banks such as the Bank of London and South America, Banco de la Nación Argentina, Banco Brasil, and after 1958, City Bank.

The 1947 civil war and its aftermath left Paraguay's politics in a state of factionalism and instability. Rival caudillos representing different landed and business interests of the triumphant Colorados could not agree on how to govern. People in Paraguay's tiny middle and working classes sought political democracy, better living conditions, and the right to organize—serious threats to traditional ways. The peasantry, although large, was too weak and passive to effect any change. It could be used by any Colorado faction gaining the upper hand as an ideological and organizational base for stable rule.

But since no faction could assert its hegemony, only one force remained to step into the resulting political vacuum: the Army. A thirty-five-year-old veteran of the Chaco War, Alfredo Stroessner, recognized this. He mounted a successful coup d'état on May 4, 1954, less than a year after visiting the United States as the guest of Secretary of the Army Robert Stephens. His long reign guaranteed foreign economic interests in Paraguay and stopped in its tracks the often-repressed democratic movement of the middle and working classes.

"Preventive Repression" and Stronismo

Son of a German father and a Paraguayan mother, Stroessner started his military career at age sixteen and knew little more than barracks life. Order and discipline were the values he championed, values deeply ingrained in Paraguayan culture. During the political upheavals after World War II he sided with dictator Morínigo, who stepped down in 1948, and the victorious Colorados. In October 1951 he was appointed commander-in-chief of the armed forces under the government of President Federico Chávez (1950–1954), a Colorado dictator in the Morínigo tradition whom he over-threw.

Although best known for his rule by terror, Stroessner differed from most other Latin American dictators in that he had a semblance of an orga-nized, popular base, through the Colorado party. He used this base effectively throughout his long reign, subordinating it to the Army that he controlled (he also brought the police under army control, in 1956). Traditional forms of *caudillismo, patrón* (boss)-peasant clientelism, and political patronage flour-ished under Stroessner, the supreme "Caudillo."

Stroessner used Paraguay's traditions of a strong state by peddling state recognition, favors, and business contracts in a manner so thorough that few Paraguayans escaped his influence. Public employees, teachers, doctors, and most students had to affiliate with the Colorado party. Those that objected too strenuously he imprisoned, deported, tortured, or killed. Two common torture techniques were immersion in the *pileta* (a bathtub of excrement) and electric shock to sex organs by the *picana elétrica* (electric poker). Stroessner also ruled by dividing his opponents, currying favor with some while repressing others.

In the cities and bigger towns his Colorado followers built up the GU (Urban Guard) to terrorize dissidents and break up political meetings. They were augmented by secret police known by the Guaraní word of *pyragues* ("people with hairy feet"). Above all, Stroessner provided his army with mod-ern weapons and lucrative land and industry handouts, hoping to assure its loyalty for as long as he lived.

After exiling his chief Colorado opponent in 1956, Stroessner imple-mented an IMF (International Monetary Fund)-proposed economic austerity program (see Overview) that drove real wages down and provoked a general strike two years later. Some 300 trade-union leaders were arrested, but social discontent did not go away.

In 1959 Stroessner had to lift the state of siege briefly as a concession to his opposition. After troops and police attacked dissident Colorados demanding more democracy Stroessner responded to congressional charges of police brutality by dissolving congress and arresting or exiling all remaining or suspected "dissidents" inside the ruling Colorado party. These numbered in the hundreds. From that point froward Stroessner did not even bother with the façade of democracy.

Stroessner's method of prolonging his rule became known as "preventive repression" and was publicly revealed at a 1972 Inter-American Defense Board meeting of U.S. and Latin American military brass. It was adopted by other dictators in the southern cone of South America, who coordinated in one another's countries. Preventive repression involved "nipping in the bud" any signs of unrest by every conceivable means. As a result, Paraguay gained the reputation of having a "culture of fear" deeper than any other in Latin America, even though it clearly had rivals in each of its bordering countries and in El Salvador and Guatemala.

Brazilian and U.S. Investments:
Economic Growth, ITAIPU, and Ethnocide

Stroessner's dictatorship established stable political conditions and a government-controlled labor force that attracted foreign investors. Brazil and the United States supplanted Argentina as the leading economic powers in Paraguay.

Construction of the world's largest hydroelectric project, the Itaipu dam on the eastern border with Brazil, sparked impressive economic growth rates in the 1970s—and controversy about Stroessner's giving in to Brazilian aggression. In 1964 Brazilian troops had occupied the Guaira Falls, the world's biggest waterfalls, today under water as part of the Itaipu dam. Paraguay had long claimed the falls as part of its territory. Nonetheless, Stroessner signed the Act of Iguazú with Brazil on June 22, 1966, which became finalized as the Treaty of Itaipu on April 26, 1973.

The treaty provided for construction of the Itaipu dam with a capacity of 12,600 megawatts, six times greater than Egypt's famed Aswan dam. The two nations would share the resultant hydroelectric power 50–50. Paraguay would sell unused parts of its share to Brazil at a price fixed for the next fifty years at a level below international rates. For some time to come Paraguay's "sales" to Brazil would in fact be repayments of loans taken from Brazil to finance the $20 billion construction of the dam. Most of the construction contracts went to Brazil.

The two nations' armed forces policed the falls area, prohibiting anyone from seeing the conditions under which 25,000 workers labored eleven-hour shifts six days a week to complete the dam by 1991. Official figures showed that forty-three workers had died on the job by 1987, but most people believed the number of deaths was far higher. Wildcat strikes were put down, and in March 1978, three thousand workers rioted. Roads linking Paraguay to the Brazilian ports of Santos and Paranaguá were completed, breaking Paraguay's dependence on Argentina for its land and river trade routes.

New cities sprang up in the area around the falls, as the population quadrupled to more than 600,000. The great Itaipu region in eastern Paraguay was colonized initially in the 1960s by the IBR (Rural Welfare Institute), with the backing of the World Bank and IDB (Inter-American Development Bank). The IBR sent politicized peasants who had been claiming lands near Asunción to the eastern forests. There, they cleared lands for which they had no permanent title. They were followed in the 1970s by more than one-third of a million Brazilian colonists, mostly peasants, who received much more favored treatment from the IBR, as well as financial backing from Brazil. Germans, Koreans, and eight thousand Japanese also established farming communities in eastern Paraguay. With the new colonists came foreign industrialists, bankers, agribusinesses, and timber companies, mostly from Brazil and the United States.

Brazilian land companies bought up much of the land of eastern Paraguay, and the Brazilian "frontier" moved from the original eastern border deep into Paraguay halfway to Asunción. Portuguese became the area's prevalent language and the Brazilian cruzeiro its most commonly used currency. Paraguayan nationalist dissenters were ruthlessly subdued, leading Bishop Claudio Silvero of Caaguazú Department (just west of Itaipu) to declare, "Too many have died, deaths have been concealed, and a climate of terror reigns."

To make way for the forces of "modernization" (see Overview), the ranks of bee-keeping and hunting and fishing Indian tribes were decimated. Less than 5 percent of Paraguay's population was Indian, but much of it faced ethnocide. Nobel Prize winner Elie Wiesel wrote, "Until now, I always forbade myself to compare the Holocaust of European Judaism to events which are foreign to it. And yet, I read the stories of the suffering and death of the Ache tribe in Paraguay and recognize familiar signs." Widespread destruction of the environment and the displacement of 30,000 peasants on both sides of the shifting border helped generate a desperate and aggressive independent peasant movement that contributed to the growth of a broad political movement to topple Stroessner in the 1980s.

Business favoritism from the top—the arrangement of land sales and contracts by Stroessner and his friends in the military—was how the game was played throughout Paraguay. State investment went to infrastructure: the Itaipu dam, the Yacireta dam, the Trans-Chaco highway, telecommunications, river shipping. According to Riordan Roett, a member of the influential U.S. policy-advising Council on Foreign Relations, Paraguay's economy underwent "increasing denationalization."

Stoessner's government encouraged foreign investment in agroindustry and energy-intensive industries, including cattle-breeding, soybean production, fertilizers, and aluminum smelting. Three dollars left the country in profits and other payments for every one dollar that entered. Paraguay became the world's fifth largest exporter of soybeans, and World Bank president Robert McNamara described its eastern area as "the future bread basket of the southern cone." Cotton, soybeans, and timber, in that order, surpassed meat products as the nation's leading exports. Paraguay's traditional "hidden economy" of smuggling boomed, particularly in timber (mostly Brazilian-controlled), agricultural products, whisky, cigarettes, and narcotics.

Among U.S. firms investing in Paraguay were Coca-Cola, Exxon, Firestone, Florida Peach Corporation, Levi, and the "Big Three" of world banking— Citibank, Chase Manhattan, and Bank of America. Typical investment terms were those granted Gulf & Western in 1970 for 60,000 hectares of soybeans and wheat: all profits could be remitted to Gulf & Western's home offices tax-free.

Stimulated by the Itaipu project, Paraguay's annual GDP (gross domestic product) growth rate averaged 6 percent during the 1970s. With growth came government claims of improvements, including an "official" literacy rate of 92 percent and an increase in life expectancy from fifty-six years in 1960 to sixty-eight years in 1987. Few believed all the government's claims, however, since poverty remained extreme. For example, even by government figures, less than 7 percent of Paraguayans had sewage service and only 18 percent had indoor water supplies.

Itaipu's heating up of the economy generated runaway inflation, which officially stood at 32 percent in 1986 (44 percent in foodstuffs) and was said to be two or three times higher. The purchasing power of the average wage dropped by one-third in the 1970s and even more in the 1980s. Unemployment soared, although the official figure was only 12 percent. Paraguay's terms of trade declined during the 1976–1986 decade, and the foreign debt tripled to $1.8 billion, equivalent to half the GDP. Interest payments still were under 11 percent of export earnings, low by Latin American standards. According to the IDB, industry stagnated in the 1980s because of a lack of internal demand for goods, contraband competition, and insufficient credits.

Politics: Strong Foreign Influences, Weak Opposition

U.S. military aid increased during the 1960s and 1970s, helping to convert the army into an efficient "high-tech" force. In 1965 the U.S. House of Representatives passed the "Selden resolution" authorizing the dispatch of U.S. troops to Paraguay in case of a threat of "international communism, directly or indirectly." More than 1,000 members of Paraguay's armed forces received U.S. training in either the Panama Canal Zone or the United States.

The United States backed Stroessner economically as well, despite U.S. criticisms of some of his government's practices (heroin smuggling, child prostitution, and human rights violations). Prior to 1970 U.S. official aid amounted to $146 million. Larger amounts began to flow through international bodies like the World Bank and the IDB—half a billion dollars between 1961 and 1978.

Opposition to Stroessner's dictatorship initially came from banned political parties, the Church, and students. The most effective was the Church, which went so far as to excommunicate government officials accused of corruption or torture. All other groups were easily infiltrated by the one-million-member Colorado party or the government's intelligence agencies (see Box 16.1).

Liberal party elements launched unsuccessful guerrilla actions in late 1959, and Communists also failed with guerrilla warfare in 1960. Stroessner ordered that no prisoners be taken alive. Christian Democrats and radical priests practicing the theology of liberation (see Overview) organized peasant leagues. Troops and landlords' "hired guns" attacked them in the 1960s, when entire peasant communities were wiped out. In 1965 an independent student movement was formed but it too was crushed.

Paraguay's two universities, the National University of Asunción and the Catholic University, with 10,000 students, were centers of dissent monitored by Stroessner's secret agents. Throughout most of the 1970s, preventive repression did its job effectively.

The human rights proclamations of the Carter administration (1977–1981) stirred new waves of opposition in Paraguay. Stroessner made only one concession to the pressure from Washington, however. He released some political prisoners who had been held for twenty years.

Then, in late 1977, Stroessner closed down the headquarters of the "loyal opposition" PLR (Radical Liberal party) and froze its bank account. Most party members founded the illegal PLRA a year later. Stroessner also broke up newly emergent peasant leagues, organized by Christian Democrats. In 1978 the OAS (Organization of American States) condemned the Stroessner regime for its human rights violations.

Despite the repression, Stroessner's opponents formed the tiny opposition coalition AN (National Accord) in 1979. Of its four parties, only the illegal PDC (Christian Democratic party) went beyond middle-class demands for political rights to call for social and economic rights for the peasantry (nearly 60 percent of the population).

Stroessner resembled Chile's General Pinochet in his disdain for U.S.

pressures on the human rights issue. Both men prided themselves on having cleansed their nations of all Communists (see chapter 17). Unlike Pinochet, however, Stroessner used a traditional political party (the Colorados) to legitimize his reign.

In 1979 Paraguay hosted the twelfth congress of the WACL (World Anti-Communist League), a fanatical ultraright organization known for its anti-Semitism and recruitment of Fascists, including former members of Hitler's SS and Gestapo. The WACL congress called Asunción the "capital of freedom and anticommunism" and elected the head of Paraguay's IBR as WACL president. Other Paraguayan members of the WACL included the heads of the major branches of Stroessner's internal intelligence apparatuses —the G-2, DIPC, DT, and GAA (see Box 16.1). Three other WACL members were a person who acted as Stroessner's ideological representative in repressing the prodemocracy wing of the Catholic Church, Stroessner's press secretary, and the former longtime head of the inactive CPT (Paraguayan Workers Federation). The president of the U.S. branch of WACL was John Singlaub, later famed for his role in the Iran-contragate affair (see Introduction to Part One).

Stroessner cultivated close relations with the white minority government of South Africa and provided political refuge for former Nazis such as Dr. Joseph Mengele, the "Angel of Death" at Auschwitz concentration camp. Paraguay's "Horror Files" (see Introduction to Part Three) revealed that SS Captain Eduard Roschmann, the "Butcher of Riga" (where 40,000 Jews were murdered during World War II), died of a heart attack in 1977 in Asunción. Other Nazis were prominent in Stroessner's military and police intelligence operations, which maintained tight relations with the CIA, the FBI, or the U.S. military and became infamous for their tortures and murders of suspected dissidents. Italian Fascists and right-wing terrorists also found refuge in Paraguay. To train his personal bodyguard, the "Escolta Batallion," Stroessner hired Croatian extremists (anti-Yugoslavian refugees). He also had his personal pilot fly Nicaragua's toppled dictator Somoza into Paraguay to set him up in a mansion that once had served as the South African Embassy. Somoza was later murdered by gunmen believed to be Argentine leftist guerrillas, leading to jubilant celebrations in Nicaragua (see chapter 5).

The completion of most of the Itaipu dam project and ensuing economic downturn emboldened Paraguayans opposed to the dictatorship. The mid-1980s witnessed a rising tide of street protests, strikes, and peasant land occupations sparked by the newly created peasant and labor organizations APCT, MCP, and MIT (see Box 16.1). All of these groups acted independently of the ineffective opposition parties.

The nation's Roman Catholic Bishops Conference publicly endorsed peasant land occupations and urged Stroessner to engage in a "national dialogue." Even big business' president of the Union industrial association stated,

"All of us believe that democracy is best for free enterprise." But business groups, like labor groups, were weak, subject to either government favoritism or repression.

The government, refusing to dialogue with an opposition it described as "subversive," "Communist," or "terrorist," responded with the largest number of arrests in many years. In March 1984 it shut down the nation's biggest circulating newspaper, *ABC Color*, whose publisher, Aldo Zuccolillo, had been a longtime friend of Stroessner and ran a financial empire in ranching and department stores. The paper had published an interview with a MOPOCO leader who had been one of twenty prominent party members to be allowed back in the country after two decades in exile. The paper had also criticized "corruption in high places," a daring act in a *stronista* system that thrived on the parceling out of lucrative moneymaking opportunities. *ABC Color*'s journalists regrouped and launched in 1986 the opposition magazine *Nuestro Tiempo*, directed by Bishop Mariot Melanio Medina.

One frequently arrested leader of the growing independent social movement was twenty-seven-year-old Dr. Carlos Filizzola, president of the Association of Physicians, the most popular labor leader in years. Striking hospital workers were able to mobilize bigger rallies than all the opposition parties combined. One problem the political parties and the Roman Catholic Church seemed unaware of, according to Dr. Filizzola, was that "You can't dialogue with a dictatorship."

Even the conservative Reagan government in Washington publicly expressed concern over Stroessner's escalating political repression. In 1985 a career diplomat named Clyde Taylor was appointed ambassador to Paraguay. Taylor established contact with the tiny opposition coalition AN. Younger rank-and-file AN members urged the older leadership to remain independent of U.S. influence. The leadership, however, cleansed the AN's youth ranks of "leftist influences," thereby losing many of its younger members and cutting the AN off from larger social movements being spurred by the younger generation. In 1986 the United States suspended Paraguay's trade benefits under the Generalized System of Preferences because of the Stroessner regime's abusive treatment of labor.

In early 1987 Stroessner lifted the state of siege to allow the return of more political exiles. One who had returned earlier only to be beaten up by the police was Domingo Laino, an economist exiled for having written a book about Stroessner's friend Somoza. Laino was the leader of the AN's largest party, the PLRA. He liked to compare himself to the Philippines' assassinated moderate anti-Marcos leader Aquino, who was killed when he returned from exile but whose widow became president after a mass popular uprising. On June 21, 1987, Laino was allowed to speak at a public rally attended by 30,000—the biggest crowd in decades.

But most opposition activity was restricted, and meetings were repeatedly broken up in the style of the September 1987 Colonel Oviedo incident described in this chapter's opening scene. In February 1987, police even lobbed tear gas at three hundred "guests" seeking to enter a party being held for Ambassador Taylor, seen by the government as a symbol of the opposition because of his critiques of press censorship. The guests had come to declare their support for Taylor and had been organized by "Women for Democracy." In March the government silenced the independent Radio Nanduti; *ABC Color* also remained closed.

After so many years of banishment the opposition parties lacked a popular base. Laino endorsed the Church's call for a "national dialogue" and acknowledged that the opposition parties would play little, if any, role in a "democratic transition." The key actors, he said, would be the Church and military officers.

This was borne out in October 1987, when Archbishop Ismael Rolón, of Asunción, called for a protest campaign against "government-inspired violence." A Church-sponsored "silent march against repression" drew 40,000 citizens on October 30.

In response to the escalation of protests, both domestic and foreign, the ruling Colorado party divided sharply—a kind of falling out among thieves. The triumphant "militantes," led by Interior Minister Sabino Augusto Montanaro who controlled the expanding political intelligence services once monopolized by the army's "G-2," expelled the "traditionalists" in August 1987. Both groups refused to criticize Stroessner. Also kicked out was a much smaller "*ético*" or "moralist" faction, which had called for someone other than Stroessner to run for the presidency in 1988. Stroessner's ruling coalition further disintegrated in late 1987 when Liberal radicals walked out of congress. They even ran a candidate in the February 1988 election, predictably won by Stroessner in his eighth reelection.

As public protests grew, military factions scrambled to maintain political power. Stroessner's eldest son, forty-four-year-old Air Force Colonel Gustavo, was expected by some to succeed his father. He reputedly had the backing of the militante Colorado faction. But it was an anti-militante, the youngest son Alfredo's father-in-law, army commander General Andrés Rodríguez, who seized control in a palace coup, February 3, 1989, ousting the seventy-six-year-old multimillionaire caudillo. Fear of continuing repression limited the street celebrations that followed. Up to two hundred were killed during the coup. Over the next few years, peasants clamoring for land were repressed, even though the Rodríguez government's agrarian reform commission acknowledged that 120,000 families were without land and that 15 million acres had been given to Stroessner and his cronies during the preceding dictatorship.

Rodríguez, like most of the military, reputedly had strong ties to drug traffickers. He had been known as the czar of the smuggling business in the Itaipú region's Puerto Stroessner. His son-in-law, Alfredo Stroessner, Jr., was addicted to cocaine and, according to some, mistreated Rodríguez's daughter, leading to tensions between Rodríguez and the caudillo. A Colorado long reputed to be Stroessner's "main man," Rodríguez wished to maintain army intelligence supremacy. After the coup, he avoided criticizing Stroessner, promised democracy, and had himself elected president in May 1989. Runner-up presidential candidate Laino (20 percent of the vote) cautioned against prosecuting human rights violators, since "The length of the dictatorship makes the transition difficult."

Under continuing popular pressure, the government permitted opposition parties a growing degree of freedom to organize. In May 1991, the independent "Constitution for All" movement gained a solid electoral majority in Asunción; Dr. Filizzola won the mayoralty on an independent slate. Nationally, less than half the electorate voted as the Colorados swept the election for the assembly that wrote the nation's most democratic constitution ever.

The new 1992 constitution allowed military personnel already in a political party (usually the Colorados) to stay there but prohibited new military entrants into parties. A president could not be immediately re-elected. The military was protected from civilian oversight. Labor won the right to organize and strike, but continued to be repressed.

Meanwhile, from his heavily guarded exile home in Brasilia, Brazil, Stroessner sought a political comeback. In 1991, the Rodríguez government expelled the deposed dictator's twenty-year-old grandson for political conspiracy with diehard Stroessner loyalists. It also unsuccessfully sought the extradition from Brazil of Colonel Gustavo Stroessner on charges of illegal enrichment.

Economically, post-Stroessner Paraguay was again awarded U.S. trade preferences and began receiving substantial U.S. aid. It joined MERCOSUR, the regional common market phasing out tariffs between itself, Argentina, Brazil, and Uruguay. All the leading presidential candidates favored privatization of the military-dominated state sector and more free trade.

On the eve of general elections in May 1993, General Rodríguez threatened to rule jointly with the election's winner. A massive pro-democracy march of 150,000 squelched that option. The military then made it clear it would brook only a Colorado victory. According to an election observer team sent by the prestigious Latin American Studies Association (LASA), the Colorados "were both judge and jury of the entire electoral process." The Colorado candidate, wealthy businessman and engineer Juan Carlos Wasmosy, who had headed a consortium that helped build Itaipú, was declared the winner of the twelve-candidate presidential contest with 39.9 percent. The

PLRA's Laino finished second with 32.1 percent. National Encounter coalition candidate, rancher and textile manufacture millionaire Guillermo Caballero Vargas, came in third at 23.1 percent. Although the vote count was disputed and delayed, many agreed Wasmosy had the edge. At the borders, soldiers blocked Paraguayan workers from returning from Argentina, Brazil, and Uruguay to vote, since it was known they supported the opposition. The _New York Times_ editorialized about Paraguay's "dirty democracy."

In October 1993, when the opposition-controlled congress proposed a law to force soldiers to leave the Colorado party, hundreds of promilitary goons beat up congressmen and blocked their entry into Congress. Paraguay still faced a heavy military hand as it attempted to create a democratic system to replace nearly a half century of military/Colorado tyranny.

Selected Bibliography

Arens, Richard. _Genocide in Paraguay_. Philadelphia, PA: Temple University Press, 1976.

Grow, Michael. _The Good Neighbor Policy and Authoritanism in Paraguay_. Lawrence: The Regents Press of Kansas, 1981.

Latin American Bureau. _Paraguay Power Game_. Nottingham, England: Latin American Bureau, 1980.

Lewis, Paul H. _Socialism, Liberalism, and Dictatorship in Paraguay_. New York: Praeger, 1982.

Miranda, Carlos R. _The Stroessner Era: Authoritarian Rule in Paraguay_. Boulder, CO: Westview, 1990.

Rout, Leslie, B., Jr. _Politics of the Chaco Peace Conference, 1935–1939_. Austin: University of Texas Press, 1970.

PERU

BOLIVIA

Iquique

PARAGUAY

PACIFIC
OCEAN

CHILE

La Serena

Valparaíso • Santiago ARGENTINA
Rio Maule

Concepción

Puerto Montt

ATLANTIC
OCEAN

Strait of Magellan

Beagle Channel

N

0   400 Mi.
0   200 Km.

Chile   17

I don't see why we need to stand by and watch a country go Communist due to the irresponsibility of its own people.—*Henry Kissinger, head of NSC (National Security Council), at White House meeting of "Committee of 40" in June 1970, discussing possible election of Socialist Salvador Allende in Chile's elections*

This [Republican] administration overthrew an elected government and helped establish a military dictatorship [in Chile].—*Presidential candidate Jimmy Carter in 1976 campaign debate with Republican candidate President Gerald Ford*

Our problem isn't one law more or one law less, it's much more profound: it's the entire economic, cultural, and political system that has tried to asphyxiate us with weapons such as fear and coercion. . . . We have reached the moment to stand up and say: Enough!
—*"Vow of El Salvador Miners," calling for May 11, 1983 national strike, first "National Day of Protest"*

In early May of 1986, concerned citizens, trying to overcome the silence of the censored press about recent events, went to the office of the Conference of Bishops in Santiago, the capital of Chile. There, they were handed a news bulletin issued by the human rights organization CODEPU (Committee to Defend the Rights of People, founded in 1981). The bulletin stated:

On the first of May 1986—while the sound of ricocheting bullets continued to be heard in the streets of Santiago—the *pobladores* (shantytown people) gathered at Santa Julia to celebrate a Mass. Hundreds prayed "that this would never happen again." The arms of many still showed the bright stamp "secret" that had been printed on them during their detention.

During the previous 48 hours, armed soldiers had surrounded the shantytowns . . . of San Miguel. They had cut off the telephone service and the electricity. Then, the *Carabineros* (national police) and the CNI (secret police) had gone house to house and grabbed all men ages 14 to 60. They used methods reminiscent of the way Hitler's Gestapo rounded up Jews in Europe.

Thousands of persons were hauled off to the stadium. Each one was registered, beaten, insulted, humiliated. Many were later freed, but officials said 118 were still detained. Each and every one of them was subjected to the stamp that was printed on the arm. All remembered that the Nazis too marked their Jewish prisoners in this manner. . . .

The only reason, as it has always been, was to try to terrorize the population on the eve of May Day. It was a part of the continuing strategy of the military government to contain the growing mobilizations in favor of democracy and an end to the dictatorship. The Secretary General of the Bishops Conference, Sergio Contreras, summed up the roundups in one phrase: "It is barbaric," he said.

Finding out what was going on in Chile had been difficult ever since September 11, 1973, when the thousand-day-old government of President Salvador Allende was overthrown by a U.S.-backed military coup. Estimates of those killed during the month of the coup ranged from 5,000 (U.S. Embassy) to 30,000.

After the violence of the coup a "long, dark night" of arrests, torture, murder, censorship, secrecy, and silence settled over Chile. During the Allende regime (1970–1973) information was widely available. The Chilean press, TV, and radio presented an extensive range of facts and points of view, as Chileans became caught up in an intense public debate about reform, revolution, and counterrevolution.

Allende had been elected fairly and democratically, but he was suspect in U.S. government circles for his Socialist ideas. The administration of President Richard Nixon described Allende as a controversial "Marxist" and "revolutionary." In fact he had entered public life as a self-proclaimed Marxist and had spent three decades as a highly respected parliamentary Socialist campaigning for peaceful change. The mass media presented an image to Americans of an incompetent and undemocratic Chilean president who was unpopular among his own people. From this informal "smear" campaign originated the concept "disinformation."

The truth emerged in March 1972, when columnist Jack Anderson leaked the "ITT Papers" that revealed joint U.S. and private corporation plans for destabilizing and toppling Chile's elected government. Then the Watergate scandal broke and Congress passed the Freedom of Information Act. More of the truth came out. Several congressional investigations in the mid-1970s revealed that the U.S. government, acting in concert with private groups, had started laying the groundwork for the 1973 coup as soon as Allende was elected and even before he became president.

Hearings into CIA covert activities conducted by the Senate Select Committee to Study Governmental Operations in Respect to Intelligence Activities (the "Church Committee," named after its chairman the late Senator Frank Church) revealed how CIA and private corporation funding of the presidential campaigns of Allende's opponents dated back to the 1950s. "Project

Camelot," an intelligence-gathering and contingency plan for a coup against a leftist government, had been developed in the early 1960s by the U.S. Department of the Army and a team of U.S. university professors. It had called for the coordinated buildup of civilian and military forces inside Chile, with U.S. support, into a force capable of overthrowing any elected left-coalition government.

Hearings in the Senate and House went on to reveal a full-scale plan to prevent Allende's taking office in November of 1970 by means of a coup and, if that failed, to destabilize his regime until a coup could succeed. The plan was managed from the White House by the so-called Committee of 40, headed by NSC (National Security Council) director Henry Kissinger.

Prior to the September 11, 1973 coup, Chile had been the Latin American country holding the record for longevity of constitutions and democratic rule. The United States received a diplomatic "black eye" for its complicity in the Chile coup, especially in Europe. The coup triggered international protests involving millions. French dockworkers refused to load repair parts for French Mirage jets being used by Chile's Air Force. An AFL-CIO national convention condemned Chilean fascism and the military junta's destruction of organized labor's CUT (Single Workers Central). The prestigious U.S. academic organization LASA (Latin American Studies Association) condemned the coup and went on to oppose U.S. interventionism anywhere else in Latin America.

Because of the coup's impact, "Chile 1973" replaced "Guatemala 1954" as the "textbook" case for understanding the explosive political dynamic of Latin America and U.S. policies in the region. Yet Chile had its own special characteristics. Propelled by mass street demonstrations of the "new politics" (see Overview), Chile's people were able to dislodge military dictator General Augusto Pincochet from the presidency in 1989 and introduce a limited democracy more promising than Guatemala's. While many Chileans championed the free-market neo-liberalism of both Pinochet and his civilian successors as an economic success story (10 percent economic growth in 1989 and again in 1992), others disagreed—a debate typically Chilean. But the majority clearly rejected Pinochet as their leader, even though he tenaciously held on to his power as chief of the powerful, 60,000-strong army after voters roundly defeated him in a 1988 plebiscite and his candidates in presidential elections of 1989 and 1993.

Geographical, Demographic, and Early Historical Background

From the outset Chile's varied geography contributed to the formation of its political culture. Chile is a narrow strip of land, with a 2,600-mile-long Pacific coastline, averaging 110 miles in width. The northern fifth of the country is one of the world's driest regions, rich in copper and sodium nitrate deposits. South of the desert there are 400 miles of semiarid lands fit for farming and enriched by iron ore deposits. Then, starting in La Serena and running between a coastal mountain range and the snow-capped Andes through the capital of Santiago and on to Concepción there unfolds the fertile, lush, green Central Valley, where nine-tenths of Chileans live. From Concepción to Puerto Montt there are coal mines, forests, lakes, rivers, and a half-year-long rainy season (the area's timber and forest account for 10 percent of Chile's export earnings). After Puerto Montt, a thousand miles of mostly uninhabited mountains, glaciers, and islands unfold.

About one-fourth of Chile's 13.6 million people are of European descent, but the vast majority are mestizo (70 percent). There are some Indians (3 percent) and a smattering of Arabs, Asians, Jews, and other minorities (2 percent). Ethnic distinctions become visible in economic categories. For the most part, the economic elites and even many of the top echelons of the middle classes have European names and lighter skin than those beneath them.

The Spanish conquest of the Incas in 1533 included today's northern Chile. Pedro de Valdivia founded Santiago in 1541. He could not defeat the Araucanian Indians south of the Maulé River, however. Led by a young chief named Lautaro, they captured Valdivia and cut off his head.

During the seventeenth century Spanish colonists, by then largely mestizo, signed a treaty allowing the Araucanians to retain the southern half of Chile. The colonists then broke the treaty and drove the Araucanians further south. By the end of the nineteenth century German immigrants had set up permanent homesites in the Valdivia–Puerto Montt area, and the Araucanians were finally confined to southern forested reservations. Their descendants, today's Mapuches (named after the Araucanian language), number half a million and were cruelly treated by the post-Allende military government.

In early colonial times gold and silver mining developed. Then, in the 1600s wheat, grape vines, and cattle brought by the Europeans flourished, and agricultural production on large estates called *fundos* was consolidated. The *fundo* owners and their labor foremen imposed harsh work conditions upon tenant laborers and sharecroppers called *inquilinos*. The *fundo* chapel of the Catholic Church demanded its "tithe" of 10 percent. The *fundo* store gouged the tenants. To get married, *inquilinos* needed the consent of the owners, who often were godfathers to their children. Much of this tradition remains today, but most *fundo* owners are now large-scale capitalist farmers.

British and French pirates infested the coasts during the seventeenth century. The monarchy's "Bourbon reforms" in the late eighteenth century allowed Chileans to trade directly with Spain, weakening the hold of the viceroyalty of Peru over the colony (see chapter 14). Imports of British manufactured goods soon began to undercut Chile's home-grown spinning mills, textile mills, tanneries, metal shops, boat-building, and other nascent industries. By 1838 Chile was the second most important market for British goods, and British businesspeople dominated commerce in Santiago and Valparaíso.

Independence, Expansionist Wars, Nitrates, and Copper

Chileans declared independence from Spain in 1810 and won it in 1817. General José de San Martín led an army from Argentina across the Andes to assist General Bernardo O'Higgins in achieving final victory. O'Higgins became Chile's first president (1818–1823).

Blue-eyed and fair-skinned, O'Higgins was an illegitimate son of a Creole mother and an Irish father, Ambrosio O'Higgins, at one time a viceroy of Peru. The new president's liberal, anticlerical ideas and willingness to distribute land to small farmers brought about his ouster in 1823 by the *pelucones* (bigwigs, as the Central Valley's landed oligarchs were called). They were backed by the Roman Catholic Church. The *pelucon*/Church alliance pitted Conservatives against anticlerical Liberals (known as *pipiólos*, pipsqueaks or novices) in a civil war in 1829. The Conservatives triumphed and ruled until 1861. Liberals governed until 1891. Both ideological camps included *fundo* owners and rich merchants and miners who championed Chilean territorial expansion, first against the Indians to the south and then against the Bolivians and Peruvians to the north.

Behind-the-scenes dictator Diego Portales (1830–1837) was a Conservative merchant from Valparaíso who liked to say "the people must be given both bread and blows." His strong-arm rule led to victorious wars with Bolivia and Peru (1836–1839). Portales was assassinated in 1837, but Chileans won the war and Valparaíso replaced Callao, Peru, as the principal port of South America's west coast.

Over the next fifty years there occurred two unsuccessful attempts to "modernize" Chile by breaking the political power of the Central Valley's allied landowning oligarchs, merchants, and church, the first in the 1850s and the second in 1891 (on "modernization," see Overview). A loose alliance of northern silver and copper mine owners and southern coal mine owners, grist mill owners, and farmers made the first attempt. These groups controlled the economy's most dynamic sectors but were deprived of some of their profits by the workings of the credit network controlled by the Central Valley's merchants and large landholders, many of whom in turn were indebted to British bankers and traders. The modernizers called for land reform—anathema for the big landowners! The reformers failed.

The second attempt, in the 1890s, occurred under quite different circumstances. A couple of decades earlier agricultural chemists had discovered that fertilizers could be produced from sodium nitrate; the world's largest deposits lay in the Atacama Desert of today's northern Chile (then Bolivia and Peru). Europe needed fertilizers to increase food production for a rapidly growing population. As during the guano era in Peru (see chapter 14), the rise of nitrates as Chile's leading export generated a foreign-dominated economy, but unlike guano, the nitrates had more linkages to the rest of the economy and expanded the ranks of both workers and capitalists.

At first many of the nitrate field owners were Chilean. They were hurt by a worldwide depression in the mid-1870s. They fumed at Bolivia's imposition of steep taxes on them and resented Peru's 1875 expropriation of the *salitreras* (nitrate fields) with payment in bonds. The Chilean army invaded the nitrate fields, starting the so-called War of the Pacific (1879–1883). It overran Bolivia, leaving that country without a port on the Pacific coast. Part of Bolivia's lost territory in the Andes included what later became famed for containing the world's largest deposit of low-grade ore, the copper mines of Chuquicamata. Backed by a superior navy, Chile's army swept on to seize the Peruvian capital of Lima and its port of Callao.

When the War of the Pacific broke out, nitrate sales brought in less than 5 percent of the Chilean government's income. A decade later they accounted for more than half the income. During the war the more Peru retreated, the more its bonds declined in value. British businesspeople, using credits from the Chilean-owned Bank of Valparaíso, bought the bonds at bargain rates. Two years before war's end the Chilean government ordered the return of the nitrate fields to "their legitimate owners"—by then, mostly British!

Overnight British adventurer John Thomas North became the world's most famous nitrate millionaire. While he danced in a London mansion in his Henry VIII costume, Chilean nitrate workers labored sixteen hours a day, seven days a week. North's labor foremen paid them in script redeemable at the company store at inflated prices. By the early 1890s Chile was more commercially dependent on England than even India.

British domination of nitrates irritated wealthy Liberal José Manuel Balmaceda, who ran for president on a platform that promised to nationalize them. Balmaceda's presidency (1886–1891) was the second attempt to modernize Chile. It led to a civil war that pitted Balmaceda and his supporters against Chile's generally conservative elites. Chilean workers did not support Balmaceda because he sent police to break their strikes. The British were divided. Several backed North against Balmaceda, but others resented North's concentration of economic power and supported Balmaceda.

Economically, Balmaceda planned to upgrade Chile's infrastructure in order to facilitate more rapid and diversified development of capitalist production. His programs of industrialization, public works, sanitation, health services, and schools for everyone, including the *rotos* (or "broken ones," as the poor were called), made the oligarchy, the Church, and nitrate magnate North uneasy. They counted on congress for help. Some British businesspeople privately boasted that Chilean congressmen were easily "purchased."

Alleging that Balmaceda was a "dictator," congress voted to replace him with a provisional president, Captain Jorge Montt of the navy. Balmaceda refused to step down. Then, as British Ambassador Kennedy wrote North's attorney, "The fleet seceded suddenly. . . . If only they could have waited the army which had been mainly bought would have risen and then all was easy." Instead, Balmaceda rallied a minority of the army to his side and over the next eight months, 10,000 Chileans perished in a civil war. Montt's naval forces, supplied by the British and soon joined by regiments from the "bought" army, triumphed. Balmaceda took refuge in the Argentine Embassy, where he committed suicide.

The 1891–1920 period became known as the age of the "Parliamentary Republic." It was marked by much political debate and vote-taking, but little real change. Voting in elections, then and later, was limited to literate propertied males. As historian Frederick Pike observed in 1963, "What we have praised as democracy in Chile since 1920 has amounted to little more than a system in which a small privileged class has been gentlemanly determining, through very limited electoral processes, which of its members would rule the country." Women could not vote until 1952; political parties controlled voter registration until the early 1960s; and it was only after electoral sentiment turned decisively to the Christian Democrats, Socialists, and Communists in the 1960s that suffrage was finally extended to all men and women eighteen years and older, including illiterates.

In 1914 a German chemist discovered that nitrates could be produced by fixing nitrogen from the air. The so-called Haber process, applied broadly after the end of World War I, spelled the end of Chile's nitrate-based prosperity for *fundo* and mine owners, merchants, and congressmen.

Copper gradually became Chile's leading export, and the United States replaced Britain as the dominant economic power. U.S. economic penetration of Chile had begun in the 1850s and 1860s when William Wheelwright and Henry Meiggs (see chapter 14) had made their fortunes building Chile's bridges and railroads. U.S. investors built up a portfolio worth an estimated $15 million by 1912, largely in nitrates and copper. By 1928 U.S. investments totaled $451 million. From 1910 to 1960 U.S. investors remitted $4 billion to their accounts back home on a Chilean investment of under $1 billion. U.S. copper companies dominated Chile's economy for half a century until Allende nationalized them.

Early Rise of Labor and the Middle Classes

Meanwhile new political alliances began to take shape. Returning veterans of the War of the Pacific, often unemployed, began to link their complaints to those of overworked, underpaid laborers. They turned to the new ideas of anarchism, socialism, and syndicalism sweeping Europe, the United States, and Latin America (syndicalism advocated a general strike to launch a revolution).

During the 1890s Chile's workers carried out three hundred strikes. Soldiers were used to repress their movement. In 1907, at Iquique, prostrike demonstrators refused an army order to disperse. Officers then ordered their troops to open fire; two thousand men, women, and children fell dead. In 1909 typesetter Luis Emilio Recabarren helped organize the Workers' Federation of Chile, the base for what in 1919 became Chile's PC (Communist party).

Expanding middle classes in the government bureaucracy and the professions demanded representation and contributed to the growing political importance of the Radical party, founded in 1861. Schoolteachers conducted Chile's first white-collar strike in 1918. The following year some 100,000 persons rallied in Santiago to call for economic relief from high prices and low wages. Workers struck, troops opened fire, students protested. By 1920 the country was on the verge of a revolution. Coal miners in the south carried out an eighty-three-day strike.

Arturo Alessandri Palma, backed by the middle classes and labor, won the 1920 presidential elections on a platform of a strengthened executive branch of government and social reform. But he failed to get a majority of the ballots. Chilean law decreed that when a candidate did not win by a majority, congress had to decide on the winner. Noting the growing social unrest, the *pelucones* in congress prudently decided to ratify Alessandri's election.

The chunky "Lion of Tarapacá," as Alessandri was called, was the well-off lawyer son of an Italian immigrant. He had earned large fees representing the nitrate corporations. Like Balmaceda, he found his reforms blocked in parliament. The army was divided and included officers who argued that since massacres had not ended unrest, it was time for some reforms. Officers and soldiers alike needed pay raises. The high command put pressure on congress in 1924 to approve a labor code that included child-labor laws, recognition of trade unions, collective bargaining, and boosts in army salaries. Then, when congress returned to its old ways, the army ousted Alessandri and took power for itself.

Viewing the coup as politically untenable, Colonel Carlos Ibáñez del Campo and other reform-minded officers led another coup in 1925 that brought Alessandri back. This time Alessandri secured a new constitution that lasted until the anti-Allende coup of 1973. The 1925 Constitution strengthened the presidency and assured the separation of Church and State. But Alessandri

538

resigned when he could not get Ibáñez to step down as minister of war, and Ibáñez remained an effective ruler until 1931.

Ibáñez governed like a dictator. His spending on public works, financed with foreign loans, reduced opposition until the Great Depression of the 1930s. Then Chile's export earnings dropped from $277.4 million in 1929 to $34.1 million in 1932. The government defaulted on its bonds, the unemployed rioted, students demanded Ibáñez's ouster. Some of the old elites called for a return to the days of their ruling through parliament. The oligarchy funded Fascistic youths who wore blue shirts to fight against Ibáñez's soldiers. Disgruntled leftists also fought the army. Finally a general strike forced Ibáñez to flee to Argentina in 1931.

In the subsequent chaos a new coup, June 4, 1932, backed by Air Force chief Mármaduke Grove and supported by the student and labor movements, introduced a "Socialist Republic." It lasted only ten days but gave birth to the PS (Socialist party of Chile). Another military coup ended the "Socialist Republic," new elections were called, and Alessandri, now running on a more conservative platform, won the presidency again.

Alessandri, like Ibáñez before him, acted like a populist—offering a little for everyone but not enough for anyone. The extreme Right viewed the "Lion" as a pussycat, soft on communism. It sought a strong leader like Germany's Adolf Hitler, Italy's Benito Mussolini, or Spain's Francisco Franco, Europe's rising Fascist luminaries about to plunge humanity into World War II. Hitler's Nazi ideology of "national socialism" was well received among some of Chile's small shopkeepers, German-descended farmers and businesspeople, unemployed, and military and _Carabineros_ (national police). Alessandri beat back an attempted Nazi coup, ordering sixty-three young Nazis executed. He also attacked the growing left-center movement, suppressing strikes and suspending civil liberties. The Radical party saw him as without popular support and in 1936 joined a Popular Front with the Communists' PC. A year later the Socialists' PS became a member of the Popular Front.

Popular Front and Dominance of Radical Party, 1938–1952

The Popular Front won the 1938 elections behind a Radical candidate, wealthy winegrower Pedro Aguirre Cerda. Although not a majority party, the Radicals were able to control the presidency until 1952. They drew money and support largely from small businesspeople, lawyers, schoolteachers, other professionals and public employees, and traditional liberals belonging to the Freemasons (a secular fraternal organization with significant influence in nineteenth-century Latin America). The Radicals also were funded by occasional elite families interested in modernizing Chile. The elites' economic interests had suffered from the retraction in world trade brought on by the Depression.

Some had turned to manufacturing activities and therefore accepted the re-formist tendencies of the Radicals, such as the creation of the Chilean Devel-opment Corporation (CORFO) to help stimulate industry.

Aguirre Cerda died in 1941. His successor, elected in 1942, was a color-less Radical businessman who died in 1946. A special election was called. The winner was Gabriel González Videla, another Radical backed by the Popular Front, who governed from 1946 to 1952.

President González Videla had promised the Communist party three ministries, but when Communists backed a coalminers' strike in the south and refused to support a settlement arranged by a government arbiter, he balked. Supported by the PS, he sent troops to break the strike. He banned the PC and threw its militants into a concentration camp at Pisagua in the northern desert. He did this under the 1948 Law of Defense of Democracy, a witch-hunting "Red-baiting" device. One of the world's greatest poets, Pablo Neruda of the PC, was deprived of the seat he won in the Senate. U.S. copper executives were delighted by the "Red scare." It helped defang the labor movement.

Copper exports had boomed during World War II, since copper was a strategic metal used in airplane and munition manufacturing and Chile had 30 percent of the world's known copper reserves. During the Korean War of the early 1950s copper production again expanded and there was a continuing at-tempt to diversify the economy in the direction of manufacturing activity. Many saw agriculture, with its backward technology and concentration of ownership in a few hands, as an obstacle to balanced economic growth. Infla-tion continued to plague the nation: by 1958, calculated on the 1940 base index of 100, it zipped past 4,900. This cut into people's "share" of the eco-nomic surplus and accelerated political and social strife.

Economic Problems and Renewed Challenge of the Left, 1952–1964

Ibáñez, now an aging general but still a populist, won the 1952 election by promising Chileans honesty and strength in government. Middle-class voters were tired of the political factionalism that had brought them unreliable mate-rial progress and a higher cost of living. Copper prices took a tumble after the end of the Korean War. Chile's inflation rates became the world's highest, workers struck, people rioted.

Most labor unions, which had federated in 1953 to create the CUT (Sin-gle Workers Central), urged Ibáñez to raise wages to keep up with the rate of inflation. Instead, he took the advice of the Washington, D.C.-based firm of Klein-Saks. It recommended an antilabor austerity program, along lines then being developed by the IMF (International Monetary Fund—see Overview). CUT, representing about 15 percent of the work force and concentrated mainly in mining and big industry, fought back with a series of general strikes.

Ibáñez's only concession was his last reformist measure in 1958; repeal of the 1948 Law of Defense of Democracy and legalization of the PC.

The former Popular Front, now called the FRAP (Popular Action Front), reunited Communists, Socialists, and other leftists to run a fifty-year-old doctor, Salvador Allende Gossens, in the 1958 presidential elections. In a four-cornered race Allende came within 30,000 votes of winning against the victorious right-wing candidate Jorge Alessandri, nephew of the "Lion of Tarapacá." In the 1961 midterm election FRAP outvoted all other parties and coalitions.

The government of banker-industrialist Alessandri (1958–1964) imposed IMF-style austerity measures that reduced inflation; but unemployment rose to 18 percent. Chile accepted large foreign loans to keep the economy afloat. Workers launched bigger, more militant strikes. Alessandri's supporters in congress were repeatedly outvoted by the FRAP and PDC (Christian Democratic party). In 1961 the Radicals threw their support to Alessandri, but by then the Radicals' confused reformist politics had been eclipsed by the promises of the Christian Democrats' PDC, founded in the 1950s.

The PDC espoused a kind of centrist populism that rejected both socialism and capitalism. Its corporativist approach sought to reorganize Chile's economy and politics by channeling social unrest through "interest groups," preserving powerful economic interests and yet modernizing Chile. The PDC brought together old-timers from the 1930s' splitoff factions of the Conservative party and younger recruits championing agrarian and other reforms in the name of "Christian humanism."

The Christian Democrats in Power and U.S. Influence, 1964–1970

Given the failures of Ibáñez-type populism and Radical party-type reformism, no one doubted that either the PDC or FRAP would win the 1964 elections. Noting labor's growing militancy, the Liberals and Conservatives threw their support to Eduardo Frei, presidential candidate from the PDC's older conservative leadership. Frei conducted a "Red-baiting" campaign that portrayed a future FRAP government as one that would violate the sanctity of home, church, and family. The CIA financed over half the costs of his campaign, spending $20 million to elect him over Allende by an unprecedented landslide. First National City Bank's John M. Hennessy helped funnel the CIA monies and later joined the Nixon administration to assist it in destabilizing Allende's Chile.

The U.S.-financed Alliance for Progress heralded Frei's 1964–1970 administration as a showcase of democratic reformism. During the mid-1960s Chile received more U.S. aid (loans) per capita than any other Latin American country. When Allende won the presidency in 1970, Chile's per capita foreign debt was one of the world's highest.

With the Alliance for Progress carrot came the counterinsurgency stick. U.S. aid beefed up Chile's military and *Carabineros*, whose combined strength doubled to 90,000 men. More than 4,387 Chilean soldiers received U.S. training in "domestic counterinsurgency." Each member of the military junta that ruled Chile after the overthrow of Frei's successor, Allende, had been to the United States at least once. From 1950 to 1970 Chile received $175.8 million in U.S. military aid, more than any other Latin American country except Brazil.

U.S. aid programs sought to reverse the Left's rising strength in labor and the peasantry. The AIFLD (American Institute for Free Labor Development—see Overview), after failing to divide the CUT, created the CNT (National Confederation of Workers). By 1970 AIFLD training courses had graduated 10,000 persons. Most of these AIFLD graduates helped destabilize Allende's 1970–1973 government. An AIFLD executive board veteran, William Thayer, became labor minister in the Frei government and supported the rural oligarchy's National Society of Agriculture that violently resisted the agrarian reforms of both Frei and Allende and then became a mouthpiece for the Pinochet dictatorship. In the countryside the CIA-funded International Development Fund formed the CNC (National Peasant Confederation).

Frei's agrarian reform distributed lands to only 21,105 families. Peasants reacted by unionizing. More than 110,000 peasant workers, or one-third of the rural salaried work force, organized 488 trade unions. Much of the impetus came from one of Frei's agrarian reform spokesmen, Jacques Chonchol, who represented some of the younger, more radical members of the PDC. Chonchol objected to Frei's allowing big landholders to form armed "defense" squads to beat back the agrarian reform. He took his followers out of the PDC in 1968–1969 (the PDC experienced other splits as well).

Chonchol and Christian Democrats advocating the emergent theology of liberation (see Overview) founded the MAPU (United Popular Action movement). It joined the Left's reconstituted FRAP, the six-party UP (Popular Unity). Pro-MAPU peasants composed almost half of the newly unionized rural work force, while the Marxist-led confederation "Ranquil" accounted for more than one-quarter. Together they spearheaded an historic nationwide general strike of peasants in 1970 that demanded a thorough-going agrarian reform.

Confident that Frei's "revolution in liberty" would take the wind out of the sails of popular revolution, U.S. corporations increased their Chilean investments to more than a billion dollars. Their expansion into Chile peaked during the late 1960s, a decade that saw foreign investments triple. Of Chile's eighteen largest nonbanking corporations, all but two heavily involved foreign capital. Twenty-four of the top thirty U.S.-based TNCs (transnational corporations) operated in Chile, including Standard Oil of New Jersey, Ford, GM, Dow, Dupont, ITT, and First National City Bank.

Their investments did not bring the economy out of stagnation, causing a certain public disillusionment with the Christian Democrats' promised prosperity. The 1967–1970 height of foreign capital influx was accompanied by a negative per capita rate of economic growth and unemployment rates of 20 to 25 percent. In fact TNCs took out huge sums of money in the form of profits, charges on foreign licenses, patents, and "know-how" agreements, and debt and service payments to foreign creditors.

Foreign economic influence contributed to a "denationalization" of Chile's elites, in the sense of their often serving foreign interests rather than those of national development. Based on data about the boards of directors of the fifty largest nonfinancial corporations in Chile, Rutgers University's Chile Research group found that two-thirds of Chile's top corporate officials had either personal or close family ties to foreign interests. An example was the Rockefellers' IBEC (International Basic Economy Corporation), which penetrated thirteen of Chile's largest twenty-five corporations. IBEC relied on business associates like banker Agustín Edwards, whose family owned the prestigious conservative newspaper *El Mercurio* (circulation 300,000).

Top echelons of the middle classes employed in the professions or the state and corporate bureaucracies saw themselves as benefiting from the informal alliance with foreign capital. They subscribed to the ideology of anticommunism, and in general voted for the conservative National party (1966 merger of Liberals and Conservatives) or the PDC. Together with the denationalized elites, they later became the main civilian supporters of the 1973 anti-Allende military coup.

Frei's program of purchasing a 51 percent share in foreign copper enterprises ("Chileanization") backfired among the electorate, as became obvious in 1970 when the PDC candidate Radomiro Tomic agreed with Allende that copper companies should be nationalized. By 1971 no one in congress dared vote against Allende's nationalization law.

In Frei's time as president the state, as part owner, had a vested interest in higher copper profits for the companies. Frei's government reduced taxes on the copper industry, broke its labor strikes (killing some of the workers), and kept costs to a minimum. The foreign copper firms increased their profits. They also obtained more than half a billion dollars in new credits that added to the $3 billion foreign debt inherited by Allende from the Frei administration. When they learned of the Allende government's decision to nationalize copper, they left the mines in general disrepair.

In 1970 the National party, noting the popular disenchantment with the Christian Democrats, decided to make a run at the presidency for itself. This split the votes of rightists from centrists and opened the way to a leftist victory for the UP's Allende.

Allende's Presidency and Political Polarization, 1970–1973

In his fourth consecutive bid for the presidency on September 4, 1970, Allende garnered more than a million votes (36.3 percent), a plurality in a three-way race against the runner-up National party's Jorge Alessandri (34.9 percent) and the somewhat discredited PDC's Tomic (27.8 percent). Voter turnout was heavy—83 percent of the electorate. Allende did particularly well among industrial workers and unionized peasants.

The son of a lawyer, Allende had earned a medical degree at the University of Chile in 1932, had helped found the PS, and had served as minister of health under Aguirre Cerda (1939–1941). A parliamentary Socialist and Freemason, he had repeatedly been elected to the Senate. His colleagues had chosen him to preside over the Senate as its president during the Frei administration.

According to Chilean law, when no candidate won a majority, congress had to decide the winner. In the past congress had always ratified as president the leading vote-getter. Alessandri's National party proposed a deal with the PDC: vote in congress for Alessandri and he would resign the presidency to call for new elections in which his party would back Frei.

Meanwhile, as the Church Committee of the U.S. Senate later reported, President Nixon had "instructed the CIA to play a direct role in organizing a military coup d'état in Chile to prevent Allende's accession to the Presidency." Among CIA Director Richard Helm's scribbled notes about his meeting with Nixon and NSC chief Kissinger was the subsequently enacted economic destabilization strategy, "Make the economy scream." Chile depended on U.S. loans for 78.4 percent of all short-term credit.

Blocking the road to a military coup prior to the Chilean congress's vote was the "constitutionalist" Army Chief of Staff René Schneider. The CIA decided to remove Schneider. After two muffed CIA attempts at kidnapping him, right-wing extremists associated with the National party succeeded. They assassinated Schneider on October 22, 1970, and blamed it on the far Left. Then the true plotters were uncovered.

Most Chileans reacted with outrage. On October 24, PDC and UP congressmen voted for Allende, confirming him as president. In an unprecedented move Allende's opponents legislated conditions on his ratification. They passed a constitutional reform guaranteeing noninterference by the new government in freedom of expression, education, and worship. They barred Allende from tampering with the country's security forces by placing limits on the traditional presidential authority to appoint commanding officers. Moreover, Allende was obligated to preserve the jobs of the previous administration's state functionaries.

When Allende assumed office on November 3, 1970, he controlled only the executive branch of government—and even that power had these unprecedented limits set upon it. For the next thousand days he lacked a majority in congress; the Supreme Court disallowed many of his reforms; and the military prepared to intervene.

In his first year as president Allende began implementing the UP's "anti-imperialist" platform of building socialism within a democratic framework. He nationalized (with compensation) public utilities, banks, and several basic industries, starting with the U.S. copper firms. He raised workers' wages, reduced unemployment to under 5 percent, and undertook a land redistribution program that began breaking up the oligarchy's *fundos*. Food production and consumption rose.

On July 16, 1971, congress unanimously approved nationalization of copper, source of three-fourths of the country's foreign exchange. Iron ore, steel, and nitrates were also nationalized. The parliament passed a constitutional amendment requiring compensation for the copper companies but allowing the government to make deductions from the book value of their properties based on faulty equipment, disrepair, or excess profits (calculated on a formula estimating normal profits). Anaconda and Kennecott later were found to have pocketed $774 million in excess profits during the previous fifteen years.

In November-December 1971, Cuban premier Fidel Castro toured Chile, often accompanied by Allende. Castro drew large crowds, but Chile's rightists accused him of helping Allende set up intelligence operations.

After columnist Jack Anderson leaked the "ITT Papers" revealing plots to overthrow Allende, the government nationalized ITT. In size of U.S. firms' investments in Chile ITT's subsidiaries in communications, electricity, hotels, and related areas ranked second to Anaconda Copper. Its nationalization increased the size of the "socialized" (or state) sector of the still capitalist economy. A "mixed" sector of joint state-private enterprises also expanded.

Many employers reacted by getting behind a campaign similar to ITT's to destabilize the Allende government. They funded violent acts of sabotage, such as bombings of state plants carried out by right-wing terrorist squads. They also engaged in nonviolent sabotage of the economy: production cutbacks, worker layoffs, and sending their savings abroad. Two-thirds of the press, owned by members of Chile's elite families, openly applauded the sabotage and advocated a military coup and other forms of sedition. Edward's *El Mercurio* accepted $1.5 million in CIA monies to print this kind of antigovernment propaganda, much as Nicaragua's *La Prensa* did a decade later (see chapter 5).

To the surprise of many employers, the workers, some of whom had been deferentially obedient for one or more generations, reacted to this so-called right-wing offensive by seizing factories and farms and running them themselves. Even during strikes by private truckers and lockouts by employers in October 1972, and much of 1973, many areas run by workers not only successfully distributed basic necessities but actually *increased* production. Neighborhood-run "JAPs" (price and distribution committees) angered small shopkeepers who feared a loss of business.

A U.S.-sponsored attempt to limit loans and credits to Allende's Chile, or what became known as "the invisible blockade," moved into high gear in 1971. That year the IDB (Inter-American Development Bank) got so tight-fisted that it denied emergency relief for victims of an earthquake. In 1972 Kennecott Copper started embargoing Chilean copper. In early 1973 President Nixon proposed that the U.S. Congress legislate the release of U.S. copper stockpiles. This caused the international price of copper to plummet. As CIA Director Helms' 1970 notes had prophesied, Chile's economy began to "scream."

Allende's opponents accused his government of ruining Chile's economy. In late 1972 and 1973 basic goods and repair parts became scarce. People began hoarding, a black market thrived, and inflation, initially reduced by Allende's price-regulating programs, zipped past 300 percent—fueled by an ever-increasing government deficit. The right-wing opposition and even occasional leftists working at the grassroots level pinned the blame on management mistakes made by state bureaucrats. Mismanagement, of course, was not unusual in a country where government incompetence in dealing with economic stagnation and runaway inflation had prevailed for two decades. The "invisible blockade" and cooper embargo made matters worse, since the economy depended on U.S. credits, U.S. repair parts, and copper sales.

Yet overall, comparing Allende's first two years in office (1971–1972) to those of Alessandri (1959–1960) and Frei (1965–1966), his administration scored the highest in improved employment statistics and GNP (gross national product) growth rates. Only the transportation, commerce, banking, and real-estate sectors compared less favorably. Much of Allende's success owed to income redistributive policies such as an agrarian reform, improvements in systems of social security, education, and healthcare, and state subsidies for small and medium-sized industrial and agricultural producers.

While public debate raged about the economy, the only sure way Chileans could get a reading on which way the political winds of change might be blowing was, as tradition dictated, at the ballot box. In the 1971 municipal elections the pro-Allende UP garnered about half the vote. Then, in the March 4, 1973, midterm congressional election, pro-Allende candidates received 8 percent more of the popular vote than Allende had polled in 1970, an unprecedented gain for a midterm election.

Employers closed more doors, inflation got out of hand, and the Christian Democrats broke off talks with Allende for a compromise. The United States pulled out of bilateral debt negotiations, declaring them "a waste of time." The conservative press called for a well-organized coup.

Military plots by "golpistas" (coup advocates) initially failed because of opposition from "constitutionalist" officers and a failure to unite the three armed forces and the national police (*Carabineros*). But they provided lessons used for the September coup. For instance, on June 29, 1973, an armored regiment seized the plaza fronting the presidential palace, La Moneda. Tanks attacked the palace. Troops loyal to constitutionalist Army chief of Staff General Carlos Prats, who had been appointed minister of the interior in late 1972 in exchange for the ending of a truckers' strike, forced them to surrender. During the coup attempt few officers lent support to Prats. Some, like General Pinochet, claimed they were not involved—but they carefully noted which officials and soldiers balked at joining the golpistas.

A number of Allende supporters believed that men like Pinochet would conform to constitutionalist traditions. Pinochet had said in 1971, "I hope the Army won't have to come out, because if it does, it will be to kill." The Communist party newspaper *El Siglo* wrote laudatory articles about the military. Other backers of Allende advised the president to "purge" the military of anti-constitutionalist elements and to replace the top leadership, including Pinochet. But Allende's hands were tied by the terms of congress' ratification of his election to the presidency: no meddling in military affairs. Knowing that many soldiers held PS and PC membership cards, he apparently feared a bloody civil war would erupt if he encouraged a "worker-soldier alliance" or challenged the castelike officer corps.

Military purges did occur. They were carried out by procoup officers against known constitutionalist officers. A particularly publicized incident was the July 27 murder by unidentified gunmen of President Allende's naval aide-de-camp. During the next two weeks several navy units were purged of leftist elements; some navy recruits were tortured. Then, on August 23, General Prats resigned, stating that he was forced to do so by a "sector of army officers." His position as army commander-in-chief was assumed by Pinochet.

During and after the June 29 coup attempt workers seized more factories. Peasants grabbed more lands, bringing their control over former *fundos* to some 40 percent of farmable lands. Many Chileans began calling for "poder popular" ("people power") and "arms for the people."

On July 26 the "right-wing offensive" moved into high gear with a renewed strike by private truckers calling for spare parts promised by the government. Acts of sabotage against government installations increased—five hundred in late July and early August alone. A dozen private business and professional associations announced on August 1 that they had formed a "civic front" to overthrow the Allende government. A main force behind this move was the Confederation of Chilean Professionals, founded in May 1971. About one hundred of its members had been trained by the CIA-backed AIFLD at Port Royal, Virginia.

Pressured by the Left and Right, President Allende made a series of concessions to his right-wing critics. He approved evictions of workers from illegally occupied workplaces. In the months after March 1973 the military, using a gun control law, had begun to surround and search factories and neighborhoods favorable to the Left. In August troops attacked numerous worker-occupied factories at some cost of life. On August 9, while workers carried out a twenty-four-hour general strike to display their discipline and power, Allende gave in to opposition demands that he appoint the commanders of the three armed forces and the *Carabineros* to his cabinet. In effect, he legitimized the military's becoming the arbiter of the nation's politics. Indeed, he had done this earlier in November 1972 when he had first invited the military into his cabinet.

Bewildered and demoralized by Allende's incapacity to control the military, progovernment activists launched less frequent and less militant demonstrations in the streets. Workers occupied another one hundred factories, bringing the total to three hundred being run by workers' councils. Lower-class Chileans and their revolutionary supporters from the middle classes were creating a skillfully mobilized, highly participatory organizational network of power, parallel to but relatively independent of the government. Some of these groups, particularly those led by the left wing of the PS and by the MIR (Movement of the Revolutionary Left, not a member of the UP), were storing arms and, in vain, asking the president for more.

Allende continued to negotiate behind the scenes with the nation's leading generals and politicians. Throughout his administration, he refused to give the rank-and-file military the vote or in any other way go "over the head" of the established political institutions to rally the people. Events were passing him by, however.

The rising revolutionary threat of "workers' control" caused the military's "golpistas" to move faster than they might otherwise have been inclined to do. They staged a carefully prepared bloody coup on September 11, 1973. A week before that historic date, on the third anniversary of Allende's election, more than three-quarters of a million Chileans marched through downtown Santiago chanting "Allende, Allende, the people will defend you!"

The Coup

On the morning of September 11, the armed forces cut off Chile's communications with the outside world and demanded President Allende's resignation by noon. Government radio stations were bombed. Allende responded on one of the last state radio stations to be heard, "I am ready to resist by any means, even at the cost of my own life, so this will serve as a lesson in the ignominious history of those who have strength but not reason." He headed for the presidential palace. The military was so confident of its plans that no soldier or policeman interfered with his trip to La Moneda.

Upon arrival at the palace, the president ordered it evacuated. Then he and a few aides remained, as two Hawker Hunter jets swooped overhead and released a pair of rockets each. Smoke and flames belched from the palace. Allende shouldered a bazooka and scored a direct hit on an advancing tank. He reportedly said, "This is how the first page of this story is written. My people and all of America will write the rest." By 2:00 P.M. the palace was a bombed-out, smoldering shell. Allende was dead, allegedly by suicide. Concluded his wife Hortensia Bussi de Allende in June 1990 upon her return from sixteen years in exile, "Whether it was homicide or whether it was suicide, his was, by all means, an heroic death."

A leaflet justifying the coup said "Marxists and foreigners have come to kill Chileans." This was a reference to as many as 10,000 Latin Americans who had found political refuge in Allende's Chile from the dictatorships of Brazil, Argentina, Uruguay, and Bolivia. With the assistance of intelligence personnel from these military regimes (see Introduction to Part Three), Chile's security forces swiftly rounded up as many of the refugees as possible and deported them "back home" to likely imprisonment or death.

South America's dictatorships backed the coup in more ways than one. At Santa Cruz, Bolivia, half a year earlier, Brazilian and Bolivian soldiers who had been trained at U.S. Army schools in the Panama Canal Zone instructed two hundred fifty Chileans in the techniques of terrorism. Brazil's government committed $62 million in aid to Chile's newly installed junta, composed of the chief of each military service and the head of the Carabineros. Argentina sent $35 million.

Chile's coup was no ordinary one. It was a "high-tech" coup—one based on the firing power of sophisticated weaponry more than mass infantry support. Very few persons were foolish enough to try to resist the well-armed armed forces and *Carabineros*. If they did, they were shot on the spot. Only an occasional dissident soldier or armed leftist engaged in sniper fire. The night before the coup the "golpistas" had ordered several hundred "constitutionalist" officers shot. Armed battles between constitutionalist military units and the coup's supporters lasted only a few hours. Many soldiers stayed in their barracks. In the streets troops shot down, or hauled off for later torture, thousands of "suspects." Suspects even included women in slacks and long-haired men.

The coup lived up to its code name, "Plan Djakarta," after the 1965 coup in Indonesia that killed more than 300,000 alleged "Communists." The armed forces unleashed tanks, bazookas, rockets, bombs, and napalm against leftist strongholds. Several factories, trade-union headquarters, shantytowns, newspaper offices, and schools went up in flames. Bodies and severed limbs floated down Santiago's Mapocho River, where the waters turned reddish-brown. Wild-eyed militants of the Fascistic, anti-Semitic Patria y Libertad (Fatherland and Liberty) torched piles of "subversive" books at street intersections. Top government and UP officials were hauled from their homes with black hoods over their heads and thrown into army trucks. Later they were packed off to concentration camps or exile.

While PDC leader Frei welcomed the military coup on the grounds that it was "saving Chile from a Marxist dictatorship," the army and police were herding 10,000 citizens into Santiago's National Stadium, converting it into a prison camp and torture chamber. There, arrested popular folksinger-guitarist Victor Jara tried to lift the spirits of the detainees with his songs. Officials reportedly smashed his guitar and broke his hands before beating him to death. A few days later Nobel Prize-winning poet Pablo Neruda died of cancer. At risk of death, thousands attended his funeral.

While the news about Jara and Neruda gained worldwide attention, the suffering of the people their songs and poems honored—thousands of nameless workers and peasants—went practically unnoticed. But the nameless people were the main target of the coup.

Billows of smoke rose throughout the first week from Santiago's *cordones*. These were factory and residential areas having their own workplace and neighborhood *comandos comunales*, or popularly elected councils. Also devastated were the *campamentos*—self-governed, militant slum settlements where one party often had a majority (MIR, PS, PC, MAPU, or even PDC). Peasant co-ops and "collectives" were likewise bombed, burned, searched, destroyed. All these grassroots organizations had been viewed by Chile's elites as even more threatening than Allende's cautious "parliamentary socialism."

Those suspect areas that were not wiped out were subjected to roundups of their residents and their "disappearance." Sometimes, as the October 8, 1973, issue of *Newsweek* pointed out, people were simply lined up and shot. Bodies at the Santiago morgue were stacked in piles. *Newsweek* correspondent John Barnes reported they had been "shot at close range . . . some machine-gunned. . . . Most of their heads had been crushed." Up to one-quarter of the work force was fired for political reasons, and the junta canceled scheduled wage increments.

Ultimately the coup plotters aimed not just to eradicate Chilean democracy. By the military's own statements, their fundamental goal was nothing less than "to change the mentality of the people." As coup leader General Pinochet stated in 1974, "Democracy is the best pot for growing Marxism. . . . [all government opponents] will be crushed and made to disappear." Manuel Valdés, head of the landed oligarchy's National Society of Agriculture, stated, "The masses have to suffer more pain, hunger and misery before they will understand the need for an intelligent elite to have control over their lives."

The military outlawed or recessed all democratic institutions—elections, parliament, local governments, organized labor's CUT, political parties, a free press. Chile's elites, faced with the failure of their own democratic institutions to guarantee their privileged positions, had opted for their destruction.

U.S. Role

During the first month of military rule the U.S. press blacked out most of the junta's crimes and generally whitewashed the new regime. For example, the *New York Times* editorialized that the coup had the backing of the majority of Chileans, whom the *Times* called "middle class." (In fact no authority on Chile placed the "middle classes" at more than 30 percent of the populace.) The *Times* said that Chile's armed forces were not "political" and that the United States was not involved in the making of the coup.

Yet the U.S. role in helping to create the conditions for a successful coup was evident to all. The perceived threat was not to U.S. national security. In 1970 a high-level interdepartmental group of the Nixon administration, agreeing with a CIA intelligence memorandum of the same year, concluded that the United States had no vital strategic interests in Chile and that Allende was not a threat to the peace of the region. Again, as during the early days of the Cuban and Nicaraguan revolutions, the threat perceived by Washington was economic—an example of successful reforms and tougher terms for foreign investment that might be imitated by other countries. The threat was also viewed as political. An ex-aide on the staff of NSC director Henry Kissinger later noted that "Henry thought Allende might lead an anti-U.S. movement in Latin America more effectively than Castro, just because it was the democratic path to power." On September 16, 1970, Kissinger told a group of editors that Allende's Chile could become a "contagious example" that "would infect" NATO allies in southern Europe.

At first, President Nixon's advisers could not agree on how to bring about Allende's overthrow. Meeting as the White House "Committee of 40" to coordinate all Chile policy, they worked in close consultation with the CIA and executive officers from ITT, Kennecott, and other corporations. Once it became clear a quick coup was impossible, they opted for destabilization of Chile, followed by a "hard" coup—one that would not allow any democratic institutions to survive. Internal ITT memoranda that later were made public revealed a lot of what went on "behind the scenes."

ITT director John McCone was the former head of the CIA. He had called his CIA friends to offer $1 million in ITT funds for the anti-Allende effort in the 1970 election campaign. An ITT memo dated September 14, 1970, offered further financial assistance and disclosed that "undercover efforts" were being made to bring about "a run on banks and the closure of some factories" that would create "massive unemployment and unrest." The result would be "enough violence to force the military to move." In September 1971, various U.S. corporate officials met with Secretary of State William Rogers and agreed to an economic destabilization of Chile. In October 1971, President Nixon appointed Nathaniel Davis as ambassador to Chile. From 1968 to 1971, Davis had been ambassador to Guatemala where he had helped coordinate the "pacification" program that killed at least 20,000 people (see chapter 2). His career crossed paths with that of E. Howard Hunt (of Watergate fame), whose "White House plumbers" staged a raid on the Chilean Embassy in Washington in May 1972.

The CIA set up a "coup team" at the American Embassy in Santiago. Nearly half its operatives had been involved in either the 1954 Guatemalan coup or the 1965 U.S. invasion of the Dominican Republic (see chapters 2 and 10). The CIA poured millions of dollars into the campaign to destabilize Allende's government. One of its first publicized actions was a December 1971 demonstration by upper-class housewives banging pots and pans and shouting about a lack of food in Allende's Chile. Ironically the government had just introduced free milk programs for schoolchildren.

Even though U.S. intelligence reports showed Allende respecting freedom of the press and other democratic norms, the CIA contributed to a smear campaign portraying Allende as a subverter of democracy. CIA monies flowed into special funds to disrupt copper production and transportation through sabotage and work stoppages. Private networks helped funnel the money to striking truckers in 1972–1973, whose actions partially paralyzed Chile's economy. CIA money also funded the pro-Nazi terrorist group Patria y Libertad, whose members engaged in countless terrorist attacks from 1970 to September 1973, and then became key leaders and torturers during the "mopping up" operations in the aftermath of the coup.

U.S. aid to Chile, including IDB loans, dropped from over $100 million a year in the late 1960s to under $20 million a year under Allende, nearly all of it for Chile's military or for AIFLD labor affiliates. During the first months of the new military regime the IMF, World Bank, IDB, private U.S. banks, and the U.S. government sent half a billion dollars in credits and aid to Chile. Even after U.S. congressional bans on aid because of human rights violations, U.S. aid during the presidency of Jimmy Carter averaged $200 million a year (it was channeled through multilateral development banks). The Reagan presidency sent Chile higher sums by innovating a further way to bypass congressional bans: credit guarantees by the Commodity Credit Corporation and the Export-Import Bank.

During the months preceding the September 1973 coup an estimated one hundred U.S. military personnel were working with the Chilean officer corps. A few days before the coup, while Ambassador Davis returned to Washington to consult with Kissinger, U.S. warships undertook "joint U.S.-Chilean naval maneuvers" in the Valparaíso area where Chile's Navy initiated the coup. Jack Kubisch, an assistant secretary of state, told a news briefing the day after the coup that "the highest levels" of the U.S. government knew of the coup and its approximate date before it happened.

On the eve of the coup foreign observers, including a young American journalist named Charles Horman, said they were puzzled by what looked like a heightened presence of U.S. military and civilian personnel. Horman worked for the two-year-old news service "Fin" (North American Information Service) that sent factual reports back home to counter the anti-Allende campaign in the U.S. press. Shortly after the coup Horman's colleagues noted that "Charlie" was missing.

For several weeks the U.S. Embassy and Consulate in Santiago pledged their cooperation with Horman's wife and friends while covering up his whereabouts. Chile's military had seized Horman the day after the coup, not long after he had visited the embassy to ask for protection. The embassy had refused to assist him and, through its contacts in the military, had found out in just a few days that Horman's body lay in the city morgue. A friend of Horman's, Frank Teruggi, Jr., of Chicago, was also arrested and killed in September. Years later the 1982 Costa Gravas film *Missing* appeared, providing a fictionalized account of the Horman family tragedy and the U.S. Embassy's unsavory role.

Criticisms of Allende and the "Peaceful Road"

Although he was clearly a popular man, Allende was criticized by Chileans from a wide range of views. Broadly speaking, their sympathy for Allende depended on their position in society. The elites viewed him at best as a bungling democrat who would open the doors to revolutionary chaos or at worst as a dangerous revolutionary. The middle classes were divided, but by mid-1973 the majority of them were critical. Most workers, peasants, and urban slum-dwellers welcomed the new opportunities being created by Allende's administration, while also criticizing its failures to satisfy their expectations.

Within the UP and among UP sympathizers overseas, criticism of Allende was widespread. The UP's minority left-wing agreed with MIR's criticisms of Allende for going "too slow" in carrying out reforms and "too fast" in surrendering to opposition demands. Intense polemics revolved around the issue of the "peaceful road to socialism" (PC and PS) versus "armed road" (MIR and left wing of PS). As one member of the minority leftist branch of the PS stated, "Of course, we all want a peaceful change—but no ruling class in the whole of history has ever given up its power without a fight with no holds barred."

Few could deny that the 1973 coup left the "peaceful road" thesis in tatters. Yet armed struggle was not easy either in the Chile of 1970-1973. Even the MIR, learning from its unsuccessful urban guerrilla warfare of the late 1960s, realized that more than armed struggle was needed to make construction of a Socialist democracy possible. Some of its members became bodyguards for President Allende, some joined the PS, and all advocated infiltrating the military, arming the people, and pushing the government to the Left through more workers' takeovers of factories and farms.

Few Chileans believed that, in the short run, the armed forces could be defeated in the event of a showdown. Nonetheless, many felt that had Allende formed popular militia units of armed civilians when nationalist feelings against U.S. plotting were running strong (e.g., after the March 1972 "ITT Papers" scandal or when worker and peasant takeovers were escalating after the aborted coup of June 1973), then at least the military would not have been able to kill at random and the chances for victorious worker-soldier alliances would have become a real possibility. Chile's leftists and democrats also severely criticized themselves for lack of unity.

In Pinochet's concentration camps and prisons former ideological enemies often came to new agreements. Later, in the early 1980s, the MIR and PC agreed that armed revolution should be used as well as other forms of struggle to overthrow the dictatorship. Most activists who were not in prison were dead or overseas—some 200,000 exiles (one out of every fifty-five Chileans) scattered to the four winds. But their debates continued to rage.

Pinochet Dictatorship and Crises of the 1980s and 1990s

General Pinochet emerged as the junta's leading figure, assuming the presidency in December 1974. His long dictatorship ruled by brute force under first a state of siege (1973–1978), then a state of emergency until 1984, and then renewed states of siege until 1989. Pinochet boasted in 1986: "The only country in the world to get rid of the Communists is us." Apparently convinced he should trust no one, Pinochet recruited tens of thousands of informants known as *soplones* (whisperers) to infiltrate government offices. The postcoup height of the Pinochet government's repression prior to the mid-1980s occurred in 1975–76, when disappearances averaged at least thirty a month. Internal banishment to the northern desert or the isolated southern Straits of Magellan continued, as did deportation of suspected foreign leftists.

A national secret police called DINA was organized with U.S. technical assistance. It reportedly numbered in the thousands. DINA rubbed out opponents at home and abroad. In Buenos Aires General Prats was assassinated. In Rome PDC leader Bernardo Leighton was wounded. In Washington, D.C., Allende's former ambassador to the United States, Socialist Orlando Letelier, was literally blown up.

On September 21, 1976, a booby-trapped car exploded, killing Letelier and his assistant, twenty-five-year-old Ronni Moffitt. Moffitt's husband survived the explosion. Five anti-Castro Cubans and an American living in Chile were found to have been involved in the crime, but the chain of command reached to the top of the Chilean government. A U.S. grand jury indicted DINA boss General Manuel Contreras, who was forced to step down. Eleven years after the car bombing a DINA officer involved in effectuating it implicated three of his superiors, including Pinochet, who maintained his position that the entire affair was the CIA's doing. Naturally, U.S. relations with the Pinochet government grew tense over the "Letelier affair," leading to intermittent aid cutoffs. In 1990 one of the Cuban Americans pleaded guilty in a Federal District Court to having plotted to detonate the car bomb. In 1992, an international commission ruled that Chile must pay $1.2 million in "uncontestable" damages to the Letelier family and $815,000 to the Moffitt family.

A new "bigger and better" secret police, the CNI, replaced the discredited DINA in 1977, incorporating most of its members. CNI torture techniques refined those of DINA and terrified the citizenry.

The Pinochet government's repression facilitated implementation of an antilabor economic program drawn up by U.S.-trained economists. It left the poorer sectors of the population with half the annual income they had been getting before the coup. When unemployment passed a million in 1983, compared to 145,000 at the time of the coup, many housewives found feeding the family an almost impossible task. Pinochet and his wife Lucía Hiriart de Pinochet referred to Chile's women as "Our women" and praised their "staying at home and raising their families."

A group of Chilean economists called "the Chicago Boys" concocted and implemented Pinochet's economic program. They had received their training at the University of Chicago's conservative economics department under an exchange program financed by the U.S. government from 1955 to 1963. Prior to the 1973 coup, the Chicago Boys had met regularly with a shadowy group of right-wing businesspeople known as the "Monday Club" (because it met on Mondays). One club member described its role as destabilizing

Allende's regime by "distributing money, much of which came from abroad."

The Chicago Boys' mentor was Nobel Prize winner Milton Friedman, a champion of the "free-market economy." When the Chicago Boys split in 1975 on the need to implement a draconian economic "shock treatment," Friedman visited Chile and recommended that it be implemented immediately. The "shock" went beyond standard IMF austerity formulas by reducing tariffs to under 10 percent, freezing or cutting back wages, transferring the entire tax burden onto consumers through a value-added tax, and allowing foreign investors to take out profits tax-free. Aimed at slashing Chile's 600 percent rate of inflation (1974), it deliberately induced a recession by cutting back the money supply and forcing weaker firms into bankruptcy. The GNP dropped 13 percent in 1975, and by the end of 1976 nearly half the nation's productive capacity lay idle. On the other hand, inflation dropped to under 200 percent, and by 1984 it stood at 27 percent.

During the 1976–1982 period foreigners invested in Chile and the income of some middle-class people went up. Speculation replaced industry as the heart of Chile's economy. International bankers—many using oil-money deposits that flowed in after the 1973–1974 hikes in world oil prices—invested an average of $6 million a day in Chile's real estate and credit markets. Some $14 billion in foreign loans propped up an economy that showed a very unfavorable balance of trade in the Chicago Boys' "free marketplace." The 1982 worldwide recession depressed Chile's economy, and by 1984 Chile was spending three-fourths of its export earnings just to service its $18 billion foreign debt.

The Chicago Boys' economic program significantly deindustrialized Chile and left the heart of the economy at the mercy of foreign bankers and twelve domestic conglomerates. Some called the conglomerates "financial groups"; others nicknamed them "piranhas," "crocodiles," and "sharks." In agriculture the government returned peasants' agrarian reform land holdings to *fundo* owners, who then replaced basic food crops with grapes, peaches, and pears for export. Chile had to import most of its grains and other basic foods.

Part of the Chicago Boys' plan was to "privatize" the state sector of the economy. By the early 1980s only a dozen firms remained under state control. Only half the nation's copper mines were privatized under Pinochet since the military depended on copper revenues for its own vastly improved economic situation. The Pinochet government eliminated most social welfare programs and turned one of Latin America's most advanced social security and employee pension systems over to a handful of the financial groups. They in turn reduced employer contributions to near zero. Workers' social security and pension deductions became the largest single source of investment capital in Chile—roughly a third of the GDP (gross domestic product).

Pinochet's regime restructured not only the economy but also the educational and trade-union systems. Outlawing the teaching of sociology and other social sciences, it fired two thousand professors. It reduced student enrollments in the University of Chile from 80,000 to 25,000.

The government disbanded CUT and issued new laws that, directly or indirectly, made strikes illegal. Not daring to ban unions altogether, since membership had reached 1.8 million or 45 percent of the work force by 1973, the government forbade collective bargaining except at the plant level and permitted unions to meet only with police permission and for informational purposes. It prohibited former union leaders from ever becoming union officials again.

The government unveiled a new constitution in 1980, claiming it provided for a gradual "transition to democracy." Voters ratified the document in a plebiscite where voting was mandatory. Some genuinely approved of Pinochet because the economy was on an upswing. Others felt that opposing the constitution might lead to recriminations. Still others believed that voting for it might make possible later changes. Several exiles began returning to Chile in the 1980s.

The 1980 Constitution institutionalized most of Pinochet's policies, making it next-to-impossible for the Left to operate. It assured Pinochet's presidency until 1989 (when elections would be called) and perhaps beyond. In 1989 the armed forces would nominate the single presidential candidate and the elections would not be competitive. One-third of the Senate would be subject to executive appointment instead of democratic election. Article 8 outlawed any group or person advocating ideas that were "based on the notion of class conflict" or that threatened "the family." Other articles authorized the president to name all Supreme Court and Appelate court judges and town mayors.

Under military rule the only legal body through which dissent could be channeled was the Roman Catholic Church. Officially 89 percent Catholic and 11 percent Protestant, Chile under Pinochet experienced a well-financed "offensive" by U.S.-based Evangelicals, who today have followers among 10 to 15 percent of the population. Although welcoming the coup at first, the Catholic church soon found itself pressured to investigate concentration camps, torture, and more than seven hundred disappearances. A month after the coup, the Roman Catholic clergy joined Jewish and Protestant clergy in sponsoring the human rights Peace Committee. In late 1975 the government arrested nine Peace Committee leaders, accusing them of protecting "Marxist elements." The Church established the Vicariate of Solidarity a month later, and the government continued to harass it. The Vicariate documented eight "mass graves" discovered by citizens. It trained young union leaders. Its activities brought leftists, devout Christians, and trade-union members into a working relationship at a time when things looked gloomiest for Pinochet's opponents.

Chile's failure to recover from the 1982 recession may have contributed to the unexpected outbreak of popular protest a year later. In 1982 Chile's GNP (gross national product) dropped 15 percent. The country held an estimated 23 percent of the world's known reserves of copper, but copper exports revenues declined as world prices fell. Chile had to import 75 percent of its energy needs and most of its capital goods. Large oil deposits were subsequently discovered in the southern tip of the country. Oil wealth augured long-run economic relief, as did rising copper prices in the late 1980s.

But most Chileans were not concerned with the long run. A new younger generation was coming of political age with little knowledge of Allende's Chile. They formed the spark of a political revival that caught Pinochet's government by surprise.

On March 25, 1983, hundreds of young *pobladores* (shantytown dwellers) rushed into Santiago's streets chanting "work, bread, justice, liberty." Four weeks later, working with the million-member CNS (National Trade Union Coordinating Committee), the 22,000-strong Copper Workers Confederation, led by a young Christian Democrat named Rodolfo Seguel, voted to strike against the government's economic program. CNS bureaucrats, their progovernment role meaningless in the absence of collective bargaining, went along. The strike became Chile's first "National Day of Protest" (May 12), followed by others on a monthly basis.

By August 1983 some 18,000 army troops were patrolling the streets to "maintain order." The soldiers shot and killed twenty-four demonstrators. Labor leader Seguel was eventually stripped of his position and arrested, but the Christian Democrats built up their UDT (Democratic Workers Union, founded in 1981) to forty-nine unions and more than half a million members.

Signs of disunity in the military began to appear. In October 1983 air force commander and junta member General Fernando Matthei said he was willing to negotiate with the PC because "the Marxists are a reality in this country and I prefer to face reality." Back in 1970 Chile's PC had been the non-Communist world's third largest Communist party after those of France and Italy. Apparently it still had some followers.

As popular protests spontaneously spread to shanytowns, schools, and working-class neighborhoods, Chile's outlawed political parties tried to create an organizational network for a transition to democracy. Two broad camps emerged, each racked by internal divisions. One was the moderates' AD (Democratic Alliance) that included the PDC and the right-wing National party (once a Pinochet supporter). The other was the radicals' MDP (Popular Democratic movement) that included the MIR, the PC, and a minority wing of the PS. The AD wished to dialogue with Pinochet and to obtain his resignation and a return to democracy that would leave the military unscathed. The MDP called for a provisional government, the dismantling of repressive state agencies, the restructuring of the armed forces, and economic revindications for the poor and working class. MAPU and IC (Christian Left) elements joined both the AD and the MDP.

An additional opposition group, composed of lawyers and professionals, called itself the Democratic Intransigence and opposed negotiating with the military. It called for massive civil disobedience to bring Pinochet down.

In October 1984 the regime arrested several AD and MDP leaders. On October 30 a work stoppage reached levels of a general strike in Santiago and elsewhere. Pinochet reinstalled the state of siege in November and gave the go-ahead to almost daily operations by death squads. Arrests, tortures, and other forms of repression recalled the postcoup days of September 1973.

On March 3, 1985, an earthquake rocked Santiago and central Chile, causing serious damage in urban slums. That same month three people—a teachers' union leader, an artist, and a staff member of the Roman Catholic Church's human rights office—were abducted in broad daylight. Their bodies were dumped on the airport road with their throats slashed. Fifteen thousand people showed up for their funeral. Few Chileans believed *Carabinero* denials of involvement in the atrocity. When a courageous special prosecutor confirmed *Carabinero* complicity, the *Carabinero* representative in the governing junta had to resign. The prosecution of the guilty, however, could not succeed in the face of police noncooperation.

World public opinion reacted in outrage to the escalation in human rights violations, and the United States began to distance itself from Pinochet. At one point President Reagan called Chile's government "an entrenched military dictatorship."

In June 1985 Chile ended its state of siege and returned to a state of emergency. The opposition responded with some of its largest demonstrations, again calling them "National Days of Protest." In August the moderate coalition AD divided on whether to back the very moderate "National Accord" proposed by the Catholic Church to bring more right-wing groups into the alliance and demonstrate Pinochet's complete isolation from former supporters. The AD majority signed the Accord, even though it would base Pinochet's departure on the document that institutionalized much of his program, the 1980 Constitution. The National Accord promised the military none of its people would be prosecuted for human rights violations. It guaranteed private property and rejected groups advocating "violence," including the nation's second largest party, the PC.

The U.S. State Department described the National Accord as "pragmatic" and "forward-looking." President Reagan replaced the pro-Pinochet American Ambassador James Theberge with a career diplomat, Harry Barnes, who broadened the American Embassy's contacts with the opposition.

The year 1986 witnessed startling events that continued, yet slowed, the momentum of the opposition movement. In July the "Civic Assembly," a network of forty-seven grassroots organizations, including the private truckers who had struck against Allende, carried out a two-day national strike. Attacks on strikers by security forces left six dead and fifty wounded. Pinochet stated he expected to continue as president *beyond* 1989. That same month soldiers seized, beat, and burned two young people, one of whom, Rodrigo Rojas de Negri, a nineteen-year-old Chilean resident of Washington, D.C., died. The other, an eighteen-year-old girl named Carmen Gloria Quintana, recovered but remained scarred for life.

Divisions in the military became more public. Within the junta, all but the Army representative let it be known that they would not support Pinochet beyond 1989 and were conducting private meetings with opposition leaders. Their goal was to make sure the Communists and the Left would not be represented in any future government.

In September 1986, National Accord supporters signed the Pact of Governability, accepting the 1980 Constitution as the point of departure for a transition process. On the eve of what was to be a massive demonstration in early September, some people opened fire on Pinochet's motorcade and escaped. When the dust settled, several of the dictator's bodyguards were dead; Pinochet was only slightly wounded. Some doubters suggested he might have "prearranged" the event. But most observers concurred that an independent guerrilla unit said to have links to the PC—the FPMR (Patriotic Manuel Rodríguez front)—had carried out the action. The FPMR divided in late 1987, when a majority denounced the PC for its newly announced political stance, which was critical of guerrilla violence. (The other major leftist guerrilla force in Chile was the MIR's FARP—Fuerzas Armadas de la Resistencia Popular, founded in 1984).

After the September 1986 attempt on his life, Pinochet reimposed the state of siege. All the national leadership of the predominantly leftist MDP was arrested. Repression again became severe: house-to-house searches in the shantytowns, hundreds of arrests, soldiers at street corners with machine guns and faces painted black.

On the eve of a papal visit in March 1987, during which immense antigovernment demonstrations occurred, the five-man permanent committee of the Chilean Bishops' Conference denounced the government's record of violations of human, economic, and political rights. Nonetheless, the Pope met with Pinochet.

Meanwhile the United States had voted for a large World Bank loan to Chile, and in 1987 the economy rebounded with a 5.4 percent GNP growth rate. The foreign debt approximated $20 billion. With the real minimum wage of $38 a month leaving most Chileans excluded from the benefits of economic growth, several business leaders called for a fairer distribution of productivity gains. Then the United States abstained from a fresh vote continuing the World Bank loan and suspended Chile's status as a trade beneficiary of the U.S. Generalized System of Preferences (GSP).

As death squads ran rampant, threatening the lives of eighty prominent artists and actors, students launched a successful strike in October 1987 against the appointment of an ultrarightist as president of the university. That same month the CNT (National Labor Command) conducted an effective one-day general strike. In November a mass rally called by the Civic Assembly drew an estimated 200,000. CNT leader Manuel Bustos pleaded with the divided opposition parties to unite behind a single strategy to confront the 1988 one-candidate-only plebiscite being called by Pinochet.

On the Right much of the faction-ridden RN (National Renovation) supported the plebiscite and its candidate, Pinochet. The National party was lukewarm. In the opposition camp the PFC and a minority of IU (Left Unity) groups called for a "no" vote in the plebiscite. The majority of IU groups, including the PC, rejected the plebiscite until mid-1988 when they joined the "Command for the No," a bloc of sixteen groups from right-center to left. Organized labor's CUT resurrected itself in August.

Public opinion polls showed 85 percent of the population opposing the Pinochet government and wanting a return to democracy. And the government response? A proposed new law, yes, to allow political parties to exist with one big "but"—they could only exist if they "share the same political doctrine of the government." On October 5, 1988, Chile's electorate responded with a majority "No" vote in the one-candidate plebiscite. Demonstrations for democracy grew in intensity, as did military and police violence in dispersing crowds. But the people would not be denied. Another plebiscite was held July 30, 1989, to reform Pinochet's 1980 constitution. The electorate voted to replace the ban on Marxist parties with a "true and responsible political pluralism." They also voted to reduce the presidential term to four years, to increase the number of directly elected senators, and to return to direct elections for mayors in 1992.

Then, in presidential elections held in December 1989, people rejected the rightist RN and ultra-rightist UDI (Independent Democratic Union). In a three-man race, Pinochet's candidate was decisively defeated by seventy-one-year-old Christian Democrat Patricio Aylwin Azócar, the former head of the Senate who had initially backed the coup against Allende. Now supported by a seventeen-member Coalition of Parties for Democracy (CPD) that included most of the Socialists, the Communists, the MIR, and a newly formed ecology-oriented party called the Humanist party, Alywn received 53.8 percent of the vote.

The "transition to democracy" was, however, limited. General Pinochet refused to relinquish his military command post or permit civilian control over the Armed Forces. A 1992 scandal involving military spying on politicians left civilian authorities unable to interfere with the army's handling of its highly professionalized intelligence services. Moreover, Pinochet had imposed an amnesty law barring prosecution of earlier human rights violators. Several mass graves of suspected leftists tortured and executed after the 1973 coup were discovered in the early 1990s, causing a national outcry. As a means of ending court investigations of soldiers for crimes committed during the seventeen-year dictatorship, army troops were called up and placed on alert in May 1993. Earlier, in December 1991, the military had decreed a "coordinated exercise" in response to a congressional investigation of army checks paid to a son of Pinochet. The investigation had faded away.

In sum, the threat of another military coup sufficed to keep investigators from going too far. Torture victims in a small country like Chile sometimes had the offensive experience of seeing their torturers on the street or at the local grocery store.

As the political parties took increasing charge of the "democratic transition's" negotiations with Pinochet, many of the popular organizations were shunted aside. This especially affected women's groups favoring less hierarchical and more local organization, since Chile's political parties' leadership councils were largely national in scope and male. But the *"poder popular"* (people's power) movement of urban slum dwellers kept up the pressure on the new civilian government, called by some "co-gobierno" between Aylwin and the military.

In 1990 the Socialist party reunited its Left and moderate factions and received six of twenty cabinet posts (ten went to Christian Democrats). The Communist party and the MIR renounced armed resistance; most of the FPMR and FARP disbanded. After the fall of the Soviet Union, Chile's Communists declared Marxism-Leninism a "narrow formula" and rebaptized their coalition with the MIR and other groups the MIDA (Movement of the Allende Democratic Left). In the 1992 municipal elections, the Right opposition faded to 28.9 percent of the vote and the Communists' MIDA to 7 percent, while the Christian Democrat/Socialist CPD governing coalition swept most offices with 53.4 percent. In 1993 the MIDA ran a priest for president. He was promptly excommunicated by the Church.

In the 1993 contest, the Christian Democrat/Socialist-dominated CPD, now reduced to eight parties, ran fifty-two-year-old Eduardo Frei Ruiz-Tagle, son of the 1960s' president. He won 58 percent of the votes, easily defeating Arturo Alessandri, grandson of the former president and candidate of the right-wing coalition Union for Progress (National party, RN, UDI, and UCC— Union of the Center-Center), who obtained 24 percent. The MIDA priest trailed with 4.6 percent, just under the percentages received by two others, an independent conservative and a candidate of the newly formed Ecology party, but well ahead of the candidate of the Green Humanist party. The CPD did not obtain enough seats in Congress to pass constitutional reforms limiting Pinochet's and the Armed Forces' power. The seventy-eight-year-old Pinochet's term extended until 1988. President Frei's six-year term ran until 2000.

Under President Aylwin's CPD coalition government (1990–1994), Chile maintained the free-market "neo-liberal" policies of Pinochet. Despite the worldwide recession, foreign capitalists invested more than $3 billion in Chile in 1990–1991, largely in mining, energy, construction, and financial services. Business investment rose to 22 percent of GDP, much above the average during Pinochet's rule. With one-quarter of the world's known copper reserves, Chile still depended on copper for at least 40 percent of its export revenues. It began expanding all mining production, especially copper and gold. Aylwin further liberalized mining codes to grant foreigners property rights over mining concessions. Giant multinationals like Chevron and Shell/Billiton rushed to Chile. Environmental problems plagued the mining sector, and the government vowed to require environmental impact studies and to introduce sound environmental standards. Little was provided for enforcement, however. The main environmental measure taken was to require catalytic converters in all new cars in order to reduce the choking fumes of mountain-encircled Santiago.

The Bush administration restored the GSP trading privileges for Chile and signed a framework agreement that augured eventual free trade between the two nations. Hoping to benefit from the North American Free Trade Agreement (see Overview and Conclusion), Chile signed a free trade pact with Mexico that would phase out bilateral tariffs by 1996. Chile also started an economic integration process with Argentina in hopes of benefitting from MERCOSUR (see Introduction to Part Three). It settled twenty-two border disputes with Argentina, receiving three islands in the Beagle Channel north of Cape Horn in exchange for conceding all Atlantic Ocean rights. In 1994 Chile joined the Asia Pacific Economic Cooperation Forum (APEC).

The Aylwin government moderately hiked taxes in order to invest in social programs, and unemployment dipped in early 1992 to under 5 percent. The government later claimed to have pulled a million Chileans out of poverty. That still left 4 million in poverty, nearly a third of the population— and, according to poverty studies published by the World Bank in 1994, they were worse off than before. In the 1973–1993 period, for example, the few gains in infant mortality rates were largely a result of inexpensive steps like capping open sewers rather than improvement in calorie intake or good nutrition. The Bank's researchers found that rural Chile's impressive growth of production of fruits for export resulted mainly from pricing policies without adequate "investment in social service infrastructure." About 40 percent of

Chileans consumed only three-fourths of the calories they needed daily. Pinochet's reversal of Allende's agrarian reform had led to half of the reform's beneficiaries selling their land parcels and sinking into poverty. A "new class of medium-size [100-acre], structurally stable, capitalized farms" emerged. Larger farms (*fundos*) increased their share of cultivated land from 3 to 25 or 30 percent. Nationally, the Bank concluded, income was redistributed upward.

Within the middle classes, the same income patterns emerged, with the majority, including educators and some other professionals, suffering a severe "economic squeeze." Teachers and health workers launched angry strikes in late 1993. Chile's minimum wage remained lower than what it had been in 1974. Chile's "economic miracle" and "transition to democracy" faced an uncertain future.

Selected Bibliography

Constable, Pamela, and Arturo Valenzuela. *A Nation of Enemies: Chile under Pinochet.* New York: Norton, 1991.

Davis, Nathaniel. *The Last Two Years of Salvador Allende.* Ithaca, NY: Cornell University Press, 1985. By former U.S. ambassador.

de Vylder, Stefan. *Allende's Chile: The Political Economy of the Rise and Fall of the Unidad Popular.* New York: Cambridge University Press, 1976. Strong on economy under Allende.

Drake, Paul W. *Socialism and Populism in Chile, 1932–1952.* Urbana: University of Illinois Press, 1978.

Garza, Hedda. *Allende.* New York: Chelsea House, 1989. Excellent account with photos—students read this in one sitting.

Gatica Barros, Jaime. *Deindustrialization in Chile.* Boulder, CO: Westview, 1988. Documents absolute reduction of manufacturing jobs and productive capacity, 1974-1982.

Johnson, Dale L. (ed.). *The Chilean Road to Socialism.* New York: Anchor, 1973. Includes Chile Research Group data.

Leggett, John C., et al. *Allende: His Exit and Our Times.* New Brunswick, NJ: New Brunswick Cooperative Press (Rutgers, Sociology), 1978. Pioneering study of "disinformation" in U.S. press.

Lomnitz, Larissa, and Ana Melnick. *Chile's Middle Class: A Struggle for Survival in the Face of Neoliberalism.* Boulder, CO: Lynne Rienner, 1991. Short study of Chilean educators and "squeeze" on middle classes.

Loveman, Brian. *Chile: The Legacy of Hispanic Capitalism.* New York: Oxford University Press, 1979. Includes excellent bibliographic essay.

"Military Rule and the Struggle for Democracy in Chile." *Latin American Perspectives,* 18:1 (Winter 1991).

Nacla (North American Congress on Latin America). "Chile: Beyond the Darkest Decade" and "Pinochet's Plebiscite: Choice with No Options," *Nacla Report on the Americas,* 17(5) (Sept./Oct. 1983) and 22(2)(March/April 1988).

Oppenheim, Lois Hecht. *Politics in Chile: Democracy, Authoritarianism, and the Search for Development.* Boulder, CO: Westview, 1993.

Petras, James, et al. *Democracy and Poverty in Chile.* Boulder, CO: Westview, 1994.

Roxborough, Ian, et al. *Chile: The State and Revolution.* New York: Holmes & Meier, 1977.

Sigmund, Paul E. *The United States and Democracy in Chile.* Baltimore, MD: Johns Hopkins University Press, 1993. Critical of Allende; informed about his overthrow and later events.

Winn, Peter. *Weavers of Revolution: The Yarur Workers and Chile's Road to Socialism.* New York: Oxford University Press, 1986. Based on 200 interviews with workers who took over largest cotton mill; view of 1970–1973 events from bottom up.

Films

Chile: Hasta Cuando? 1987. 60 minutes. Color film documentary by award-winning Australian director David Bradbury covering a Chilean music festival. Reveals dramatic events of 1985–1986 and interviews pro- and anti-Pinochet individuals.

Chile, I Don't Take Your Name in Vain. 1984. 55 minutes. Color video on 1983 mass protests, from Icarus Films.

Interview with President Salvador Allende. 1971. 31 minutes. Color film directed by Saul Landau and Haskell Wexler.

Missing. 1982. 122 minutes. Color film by prize-winning director Costa Gravas on kidnap and murder of U.S. journalist Charles Horman after 1973 coup.

Argentina   18

I have some traits in common with Hitler, such as the wish to save mankind and to fight against the Communists.—General Ramón Camps, former Chief of Police after boasting about the murder of five thousand Argentines, including twenty-one children, to Madrid's daily El Tiempo, *1983*

I can never forgive those murderers.—Mother whose children were kidnapped and disappeared, 1983

First we will kill the subversives, then their collaborators, after that their sympathizers, then the indifferent, and finally the timorous.—General Ibérico Saint-Jean, in 1976 speech.

They were also giving electric shock treatment to Fatima. . . . When they saw me moving the hood, they nearly lynched me with a cord around my neck. . . . Life at police headquarters is one continuous hell, with Swastika crosses painted on the passages. —Father Patrick Rice, in Amnesty International Report, 1976

While General (President) Videla governs, I kill.—Slogan of General Benjamín Menéndez, commander of Army III Corps in area of Córdoba concentration camps, 1976

The prisoners' corpses were piled up and later dismembered. . . . The odor was unbearable. . . . My daughter's hands were in that jar.—Dr. Laura Bonaparte, professor of psychology who's entire family disappeared, in letter to U.S. Congressman Donald Fraser, 1977

It's curious. . . . Our generals listen to the Pentagon. They learn the ideology of National Security and commit all these crimes. Then the same people who gave us this gift come and ask, "How did this terrible thing happen?"—President Raúl Alfonsín, 1984

The year was 1977. In the historic Plaza de Mayo of Buenos Aires, Argentina, site of the presidential Casa Rosada (Pink House), the Cabildo (Town Hall), and the Metropolitan Cathedral, the women's sudden appearance was scarcely noticed by anyone except the secret police. They were only a handful of women, and they looked scared. Then, as the weeks went by they numbered more than two dozen, then fifty and one hundred. Eventually, with the passing of months and years, there were more than a thousand. Tourists stopped taking pictures and began asking questions.

Walking in plain flat shoes and wearing kerchiefs over their heads, they said they were mothers and grandmothers. On their chests photographs of missing family members were pinned. They had only one question, "Where were their children and loved ones, including husbands, pregnant daughters, newborn infants?" Because vocal dissent was tantamount to arrest, torture, or death, the silence of their weekly processions spoke volumes.

These women dared to challenge the legitimacy of the 1976–1983 military dictatorship. The regime was guilty of directing the disappearances or murder of about 30,000 citizens and the detention and torture of countless more.

The mothers' visits to high authorities in the Catholic Church yielded no results. "The complicity of the church is unspeakable," one woman told reporters. Her son had recognized the ring on the hand of a cardinal who had been present at his torture session. Her story was not published.

As the years went by these women became known as the "*Madres y Abuelas de la Plaza de Mayo*"—the "Mothers and Grandmothers of the May Plaza." From every social class, most were housewives "thrown into the street," as one explained, "to fight the Armed Forces, the politicians, the clergy, the press, the trade unions, to find our children. Well, we started to grow. I was born through my children."

Their steadfast weekly appearance inspired hope in some and curiosity, followed by moral outrage, around the world. While Argentina's president honored the nation's 1978 World Cup soccer championship team, the Mothers and Grandmothers of the May Plaza lined up eight blocks deep to give testimony before a visiting human rights commission of the OAS (Organization of American States). As junior-high school students, whipped into a Fascistic frenzy by the progovernment mass media, heckled them, they bore witness to crimes against humanity perpetrated by what many observers described as Latin America's most vicious state-terrorist regime, comparable only to Hitler's Germany.

In fact Argentina had harbored Nazi war criminals like genocide administrator Adolf Eichmann (kidnapped by Israel, tried, and executed in the early 1960s), SS Captain Eduard Roschmann ("Butcher of Riga"), and Josef Mengele, Auschwitz's "Doctor of Death," who drowned in Brazil in 1979 (see chapter 16). Newly opened military and diplomatic files in 1992–1993 revealed that Argentina had harbored many hundreds more Nazi war criminals, including perhaps Martin Bormann, Hitler's deputy. The files further displayed Argentine military officers' deep admiration for Hitler's use of internal violence as a way of guaranteeing obedience. Some believed that the Argentine government opened the files not only in response to world pressure but also to divert attention from demands to open military and intelligence files assembled during the military dictatorship's 1976–1983 "dirty war."

Against Latin America's largest Jewish community (400,000), the Argentine dictatorship unleashed a full-scale terror campaign, marked by the same tactics used against the rest of the citizenry but with special venom. Slogans on city walls read, "Be a patriot, kill a Jew" (a variation on El Salvador's death-squad slogan, "Be a patriot, kill a priest"—see chapter 3). Jewish schools, businesses, and synagogues were firebombed. Even the Jewish publisher of the moderate newspaper *La Opinión*, Jácobo Timerman, who in the 1970s wrote editorials advocating military intervention to crush left-wing terrorism, was hauled off to a torture chamber by the generals' thugs.

Dissident Catholic clergymen were also targeted, while the powerful Catholic Church hierarchy looked the other way. Carlos Múgica, a founder of Argentina's Third World Priests' movement, was machine-gunned to death near his parish in a Buenos Aires slum in 1974. Two years later Bishop Enrique Angelelli died in a suspicious car accident. In 1976–1977 some seventeen Catholic priests and nuns were killed.

The steak-wine-and-tango veneer of civilization in one of Latin America's most European (85 percent white—15 percent mestizo, Indian, and other nonwhite groups), most literate, most urban, least religious, and best-fed nations was stripped away. Students, professors, and journalists were silenced. Doctors' and lawyers' organizations were disbanded. No one was safe from the "reign of terror" unleashed by the military dictatorship. As the Jesuit magazine *Mensaje* reported, "Anyone who was not a trusted ally . . . had to be destroyed or neutralized."

Some 14,000 political refugees from Bolivia, Brazil, Chile, Uruguay, and Paraguay were also hunted down and thrown in jail or killed in torture chambers. Bolivia's and Chile's former "constitutionalist" army commanders, Generals Torres and Prats, were assassinated in Argentina (see chapters 15 and 17). Uruguayan congressmen and Paraguayan dissidents fleeing their military dictatorships (see chapters 16 and 19) were kidnapped and killed. Argentine dissenters were given similar welcomes by neighboring dictatorships. A "body brigade" shipped corpses back and forth across the Río de la Plata separating Argentina from Uruguay.

In 1980 the Argentine human rights movement picked up steam with the awarding of the Nobel Peace Prize to Christian humanist Adolfo Pérez Esquivel. In 1981 unemployed and low-paid workers started a movement to protest inadequate housing and high local taxes. These "vecinazos" sparked a series of occupations of vacant lots, organized by "neighbors' commissions." At heavily attended pop music concerts, young people caught up in the new wave of "national rock" chanted "The military dictatorship is going to end."

Then, in February 1982, a most unusual thing happened. A column of trade unionists marched into the Plaza de Mayo. The mothers' and grandmothers' five-year-long silent protest had found a powerful ally. One nervous young worker, a third-generation Italian immigrant, raised a banner that read "Peace, Bread, Work." Then another, an old-timer Spanish immigrant who had been around in the 1940s during the first administration of President Juan Domingo Perón (after whom the suppressed "Peronist" workers' movement drew its name), cried out "The military dictatorship is going to end!"

Workers began organizing to remove reactionary union leaders known to be allies of the military. Housewives launched Thursday shopping boycotts to protest the high cost of living. In the bloodied shadows of a thorough-going military police state Latin America's "new politics" surfaced—human rights activism, a spreading women's movement, urban slumdwellers' protests, young people's awakening, a new labor militancy (see Overview).

On March 20, 1982, the Buenos Aires daily *La Nación* published a remarkably candid statement by retired Admiral Emilio Massera, a founding member of the 1976 junta who had graduated from the Inter-American Defense College at Washington, D.C.'s Fort McNair and had established a terrorist network in Buenos Aires. "If there is not a revolution by those in power," Massera stated, "then it will come from the streets below . . . a social explosion in which not only the working class and urban or rural businessmen take part, but also the middle class."

The military regime made a desperate move to save itself by currying patriotic sentiments against Argentina's longstanding "foreign occupier," Great Britain. In early April 1982 it dispatched Argentine soldiers to seize the bleak and distant Malvinas/Falkland islands, claimed and administered by England since 1832. Located in the Atlantic Ocean northeast of the Antarctic, the Malvinas were populated by lots of sheep but fewer than two thousand longtime British residents. Argentina's dictatorship won a very short-lived moment of reprieve with this nationalistic move that gained the backing of most of the rest of Latin America.

Facing political and economic problems of her own, British Prime Minister Margaret Thatcher, with U.S. support, set out to prove her reputation as "the iron lady." Ruling out negotiations and demanding complete surrender, she sent an overwhelming defense force across the Atlantic that killed one thousand Argentines defending the Malvinas. A report was leaked to the press that showed the Argentine military had acted hastily and without careful preparation for conducting a war. This evoked further charges of military corruption, indifference to human life, and lying to the citizenry.

By June 1982 Argentina's military brass was humiliated in war and faced a full-scale political and economic crisis. The officers decided to hand power over to civilians, but under specific conditions protecting their own interests. They sought an agreement to continue their self-proclaimed "dirty war" against "terrorism" and to maintain the military's "constitutional presence" in any future government. However, a huge rally of citizens in December 1982 answered with a resounding "No!" Unconditional national elections were the only solution that were acceptable to most Argentines.

The following year, 1983, the military issued an unpopular decree granting itself amnesty from previous human rights violations. Then it allowed elections for a new civilian government. Raúl Alfonsín of the moderate Radical party was elected president. Himself a critic of the military's human rights violations, President Alfonsín welcomed the 1984 publication of the revealing documentary book "Nunca Más" ("Never Again") by the state-appointed CONADEP (Commission on the Disappearance of Persons). Some nine thousand people testified before CONADEP. Tens of thousands of relatives were unaccounted for and presumed dead or too terrified to testify. Two million exiles headed for home.

At first not one of the murderers or torturers was brought to justice. The Mothers and Grandmothers of the May Plaza renewed their marches, joined by 50,000 Argentines in March 1985. They forced Alfonsín to shift the trials of accused military officers from military courts to civilian ones. By the end of the year five top officers were actually convicted of their crimes. Two—Admiral Massera and General Jorge Rafael Videla, the president during the 1976–1979 phase of the dirty war—were sentenced to life in prison. Receiving lesser sentences were former president Roberto Eduardo Viola and junta members Admiral Armando Lambruschini and Air Force Brigadier General Orlando Agosti. Former Chief of Police Ramón Camps was convicted of torture and imprisoned. Later, a new president, Carlos Saúl Menem (1989–), pardoned these criminals in the name of "national reconciliation."

Nonetheless, even momentarily punishing murderous tyrants without an accompanying revolution was a unique thing in Latin American history and reflected the strength of an aroused public opinion. But the military's power base was still in place. Its security and intelligence apparatuses were fully staffed, and the officer corps controlled the technology for making enriched uranium, the fuel for nuclear explosives. Nonetheless, in 1991 Argentina signed an agreement with Brazil on nuclear-weapons inspection and nonproliferation and a year later agreed to comply with the Tlatelolco Treaty banning nuclear weapons in Latin America. Still, Argentines had good reason to worry about how long the process of democratic reform could continue.

In May 1986 there was a rumored attempt on Alfonsín's life during a presidential visit to a military base. By the end of the year congress, fearing a new military coup, passed a "punto final" ("final stop") law to end any additional prosecution of hundreds of well-known torturers and murderers who had been recognized by their victims on city streets.

Then several distrustful military officers close to those implicated in the dirty war launched a nearly successful "Easter coup" in April 1987. Before President Alfonsín or the political parties could decide on a response, nearly a million Argentines poured into the Plaza de Mayo to chant "democracy yes, dictatorship no!" and "No negotiations with the murderers!" Alfonsín appeared on the balcony of the Casa Rosada to assure the throng there would be "no negotiations." The coup lost steam and collapsed, but only after the president broke his promise and negotiated with military commanders.

Apparently in exchange for their help, President Alfonsín granted amnesty to all but fifty officers still charged with human rights violations, dismissing charges against anyone who was simply "following orders." The next day a newly appointed army chief of staff demanded additional concessions to calm the fears of the military. Terrorist bombings of fifteen Radical party headquarters and the assassination of a leftist in Buenos Aires soon followed—a pattern reminiscent of the dirty war.

Frightened politicians in congress approved in June 1987 the law of "just following orders" (*obediencia debida*), exempting officers from lieutenant colonel on down from being tried for human rights violations. In effect, this exempted the entire active-duty officer corps from future trials since they had held lower ranks during the dirty war. An incensed public dealt Alfonsín's Radical party a sharp rebuff in the September 1987 elections.

Then, in mid-January 1988, another military coup attempt occurred. It was led by Lieutenant Colonel Aldo Rico, a former army commando leader trained by the U.S. Special Forces and the same officer who had led the frustrated Easter coup. He recently had been released from prison by the Supreme Court, his case having been transferred to military courts. This time the army's chief of staff, General José Dante Caridi, moved swiftly to squash the coup, thereby strengthening his own hand. Like other senior officers, Dante Caridi wanted official approval for the military's role in ridding the country of "subversive" guerrilla groups in the 1970s.

The mothers and grandmothers of the May Plaza mobilized yet again. One of their founding members announced, "More than ever before, the consolidation of democracy requires that no concessions be made to appease the military." Yet more coup attempts and government concessions to the military would be forthcoming. And by 1994, in their seventeenth year, the mothers and grandmothers were still trying to find or reclaim 217 children, some of whom had been born in prison and sold by military personnel responsible for their parents' deaths. To understand this troubling drama affecting the passions of 33.1 million Argentines, it is necessary to review an unusual history of authoritarianism.

From Colonialism to Independence, Civil Wars, and Oligarchic Rule

From the time the first Spanish settlers arrived in 1516 the country experienced a series of strong-arm rulers who were reluctant to brook dissent. Democratic interludes were short-lived, swiftly corrupted, and always dependent on the collaboration or consent of outside powers or the military.

Because they noticed some Indians using silver objects, the Spaniards called Argentina the "Plata" (silver) region. They soon realized there was little mineral wealth, however, and Argentina remained relatively unimportant in Europe's eyes until the eighteenth century. The population did not reach half a million until the end of the colonial period, by which time the majority were white Creoles (Argentine-born Spaniards) and the minority were *castas* (mixed races). There were also some Indians, African slaves, and other nationalities.

Settlers from today's Chile, Peru, Bolivia, and Paraguay moved into northwestern Argentina in the second half of the sixteenth century. To provide for the work force at the lavish silver mines of Potosí (in today's Bolivia) they produced textiles, food, and draft animals in towns like Mendoza, Tucumán, and Córdoba. Wineries controlled by a royal monopoly also flourished. Settlers from Spain occupied the Río de la Plata estatuary and founded Buenos Aires in 1580. The Europe-oriented *porteños* (port dwellers) had little contact with the northwestern provinces except through the exporting of Potosí silver to Europe. But both regions of Argentina developed standard colonial practices of elitism, paternalism, patriarchy, patron-client social relations, and bureaucratic malfeasance.

In 1776 Spain dispatched a viceroy to Buenos Aires to thwart Portuguese occupation of Uruguay and Brazil's southerly expansion to the Río de la Plata. The Bourbon reforms (see chapters 1 and 11) freed up Spanish trade and gave Buenos Aires control over the export of silver. Because of the stepped-up economic activity, Buenos Aires' population doubled by 1810.

In the decades leading up to Argentina's independence English merchants and financiers gained economic influence over Buenos Aires. Many Creole merchants collaborated with them and thereby increased their fortunes. Ambitious individuals from the *castas* also began to prosper, "making it" in real estate and commerce. Argentina's Creoles looked down upon them, however, as vulgar latecomers who lacked the purity of manners associated with white skin and the finery of British and French clothing. Both to fend off this *casta* challenge from below and to counter Spain's strengthened bureaucratic control, the Creoles began to contemplate more economic and political independence.

After defeating the Spanish in the naval wars of 1796–1801 and 1804–1808, the English "ruled the seas." They occupied Buenos Aires in 1806. A patriot militia commanded by Creoles drove them out. As a result, the Creoles felt a new sense of power that conceivably could make them rulers of all of Spain's tottering colonies in South America. In May 1810 Buenos Aires held an open town meeting (*cabildo abierto*). Imitating the example of independent rule being established in Spanish cities after Napoleon and the French had taken King Ferdinand VII prisoner, the delegates deposed the viceroy and elected a municipal junta that pledged its loyalty to Ferdinand. They opened the port of Buenos Aires to unrestricted trade.

The Wars of Independence in South America got their start in the trading centers of Buenos Aires and Caracas. Not surprisingly, the two main "liberators"—José de San Martín and Simón Bolívar—came from Argentina and Venezuela and looked to the English for help. Son of a prominent Spanish official, San Martín had received a military education and become a lieutenant colonel by his thirtieth birthday in 1808. His military genius guided the liberation of Chile and Peru (see chapters 14 and 17). But unlike the more flamboyant Bolívar (see chapter 11), San Martín rarely held power for more than a short time. After having his attempts at reform rebuffed by the Creole oligarchy, he sailed for France in 1823 with his only daughter to complete her education and retire from the turbulence of the countries he had helped liberate.

Dreaming of riding the new wave of British trade to endless prosperity, the merchants of Buenos Aires initially sent their victorious armies northward under San Martín's leadership to what are today's Uruguay, Paraguay, Bolivia, Peru, and Ecuador. In 1816 a congress of provincial delegates in Tucumán proclaimed the independence of the United Provinces of the Río de la Plata. They were not so "united," however, as events in neighboring Paraguay and Uruguay were showing (see chapters 16 and 19).

Meanwhile a modernizing of livestock and hide production was occurring for the benefit of Argentina's free-trade-oriented merchants and landed oligarchs. In 1816 an arsenic-based method for preserving hides expanded the livestock business of the fertile coastal plains and the Buenos Aires slaughterhouses. To assure a subservient labor force, an 1815 decree declared every propertyless person a servant who had to carry a card that would be checked by the "master" every three months. Buenos Aires' merchants shipped salted meat, hides, tallow, and bones to Brazil, the Caribbean, Africa, Europe. They imported Manchester gowns, Flanders lace, and Hamburg cigars. From England came silks and knives, spurs and bits, camp kettles and ponchos, as British manufactures flooded Argentina and undermined the craft industries of the interior provinces.

Argentina's landed and merchant elites had many interests in common. For example, throughout the nineteenth century they kept pushing the nation's frontier southward, slaying the Indians as they went and expanding the lucrative farmlands so critical for the trade in livestock and grains. State policies of land grants, whether or not offered with the intent to foment creation of a small farmer class, led to the expansion of the wealthy landed oligarchy known as *estancieros* (large estate owners).

But despite their common interests, Argentina's elites failed to create a unified nation and system of government until 1862. Buenos Aires' leading families of merchants, slaughterhouse owners, and intellectuals favored free trade, modernized production techniques, and a strong centralized state. These _porteños_ were known as _unitarios_ (centrists). Most of the landed oligarchs, _gauchos_ (cowboys and ranch foremen), and owners of wineries and small industries in the rest of Argentina's provinces preferred local autonomy. They were known as _federales_ (federalists). They opposed free trade because cheaper and superior European goods imported through Buenos Aires outcompeted the products they produced.

Backed by fellow beef and hide ranchers of Buenos Aires Province, Juan Manuel de Rosas, the so-called "blue-eyed _gaucho_," became its governor in 1829. By 1835 in the name of federalism, he imposed by force a centralized order that gave Buenos Aires merchants a monopoly on the Río de la Plata area's trade while granting regional caudillos (strongmen) autonomy so long as they did not rebel. Rosas censored the press and stubbornly defended ultimate Buenos Aires hegemony. His secret, tight-knit organization _Mazorca_ (literally, ear of corn) beat up or murdered his opponents.

The "tyrant," as the foreign press and domestic opponents called Rosas, embroiled Argentina in numerous wars. He sent troops into Bolivia in 1837 and almost gained control over Uruguay in 1842. An earlier war with Brazil in the mid-1820s had engulfed Argentina in an endless trade and political squabble with its neighbors and with England and France. In the 1830s England seized the Malvinas/Falkland Islands and France invaded the Río de la Plata area. Rosas stood up to both foreign aggressions as much as possible, establishing the roots of today's feisty Argentine nationalism.

Rosas's government dissolved the National Bank, an institution serving English traders. It imposed protective tariffs that favored a hundred burgeoning industries, mainly in textiles, shoes, cigars, shipbuilding, and wine and brandy distilleries. The free-trade nations of England and France responded by imposing a naval blockade of the La Plata estuary from 1845 to 1848. Rosas's armies fought off the foreign invaders, but Argentina's industries could not prosper during the blockade and war. Nor could they easily survive once free trade was restored, bringing a new flood of superior European manufactured goods.

In 1852 Rosas was sent packing to English exile by an alliance of provincial landed oligarchs, liberal exiles, and regional _caudillos_ led by General Justo José de Urquiza and aided by Brazil and Uruguay. Urquiza was a modernizing federalist who moved the capital to Paraná in his home Province of Entre Ríos, northwest of Buenos Aires. He called a constitutional convention. The periodically modified U.S.-style constitution of 1853 became the nation's banner until 1949 and was utilized for the restoration of democratic rule in 1983.

Civil wars between the Paraná government and Buenos Aires Province erupted in 1858 and 1861. The conflict focused on how the customs revenues of Buenos Aires should be divided. The *porteño* Bartolomé Mitre, a voluminous writer of poetry and history, an able soldier, and the founder of the major newspaper *La Nación*, finally led a successful centrist counterattack against the *federales* of Paraná, defeating them in 1861. Buenos Aires became the capital of a new Federal Republic of the Argentine in 1862. The *porteños* conceded to the *federales* nationalization of the Buenos Aires customshouse, finally unifying the nation.

Mitre was succeeded in the presidency by a very influential statesman-essayist, Domingo Faustino Sarmiento (1868–1874). A *porteño*, Sarmiento looked down upon the *gaucho* culture of the *pampas* (fertile flatlands of central Argentina located between Buenos Aires and the Andes) as bucolic "barbarism." Sarmiento believed Europe held the secret to "civilizing" Argentina, both through the higher culture of its industrialist-financiers and the industriousness of its impoverished work force, particularly those in southern Europe. He envisioned the economic development of the nation by means of the exchange of primary products for European manufactures. As he wrote in his much read book *Facundo*, "We are neither industrialists nor navigators and Europe will provide us for many centuries with its artifacts in exchange for our raw materials."

Argentina needed cheap labor to expand its agricultural production, then in great demand in Europe, and Sarmiento encouraged throwing open Argentina's doors to poor European immigrants. He also advocated the liberal educational ideals of U.S. pedagogue Horace Mann, about which he learned during his stint as Argentine minister in Washington.

The administrations of Mitre, Sarmiento, and their successors placed Argentina on the road to becoming a major Latin American economic power, tied to British interests. They built railroads and telegraphs, docks and shipyards, schools and postal services, slaughterhouses and the National Bank. They cracked down on their rivals among the *gauchos* and regional caudillos. Sarmiento wrote President Mitre in 1861, "Don't try to economize on *gaucho* blood, it's all they have that is human—it is a fertilizer that must be made useful to the nation."

The *gauchos* and peons of the interior often joined rebel bands known as *montoneros* to repel the armies sent by Buenos Aires to subdue them. The last of the *montonero* rebel leaders, Felipe Varela, led an unsuccessful uprising in the 1860s and died in 1870 of tuberculosis and poverty. A sentimental folksong lamented that for the *gaucho* there remained only "grim prisons, the right of a wooden churchbell, the right of the poor."

The "liberal" policies of free-trade advocates like Mitre and Sarmiento and the extension of the nation's railroads and highways into the interior spelled economic doom for craft and artisan centers like La Rioja in the northwest. Rebels under General Angel Vicente Peñaloza, also known as "El Chacho," made the northwest's last stand against Buenos Aires. Peñaloza's head was cut off and prominently displayed in the Plaza de Olta. Commented Sarmiento, governor of La Rioja at the time, "If the head of that inveterate rogue had not been cut off and displayed, the rabble wouldn't have quieted down in six months." La Rioja's ruined craftsmen and small farmers headed for Buenos Aires, where they moved into the *villas miserias*—slums on the city's outskirts.

In the 1865–1870 War of the Triple Alliance (see chapters 16 and 20) Argentina teamed up with Brazil and Uruguay to seize immense chunks of prosperous Paraguay. On the eve of the war President Sarmiento inaugurated a new British rail line with the words, "What is the force driving this progress? Gentlemen, it is British capital!" The Bank of London, Baring Brothers, and the Rothschild bank extended high-interest loans to Argentina and Brazil to finance the war. The ensuing slaughter of most of Paraguay's male population yielded for Argentina the Misiones and Chaco areas of Paraguay and a staggering foreign debt.

In 1880 a grab for total power by a group of *porteños* was crushed by government forces and provincial leaders. Buenos Aires Province was federalized to make the city a federal district like Washington, D.C., and the nation's capital. The provincial capital was moved to nearby La Plata.

Starting with the government of Tucumán native Julio Roca that year Argentina entered a new period of economic dynamism. Agricultural production and trade increased rapidly, converting the nation into a meat and wheat basket for Europe. From 1862 to 1914 nearly 20,000 miles of railroad were laid. The area of cultivated land grew from 200,000 acres to 60 million, mostly in the lush *pampas*. Sheep and cattle pasturelands extended everywhere. Argentina achieved some of the highest GDP (gross domestic product) growth rates in the world. On the eve of World War I it was exporting 350,000 tons of beef and 5 million tons of cereals a year. Wool and mutton exports were also voluminous. More schools were built and illiteracy dropped to under 35 percent.

Foreign investors did extremely well. English and U.S. firms owned or managed most of the *frigoríficos* (meat-packing plants). British financiers dominated shipping, utilities, and other key areas of production. British Foreign Minister George Canning's dream of the 1820s became a living reality in Argentina: Latin America was the farm for industrial Europe (see chapter 20). From 1900 to 1929 Argentina accounted for more than 30 percent of British foreign investment. Foreign financiers bought up bonds sold by the Argentine government to finance the construction of railroads and public works.

Debt payments and the return of profits to foreign countries cost Argentina then, as now, up to half the foreign exchange it received for its exports. Argentina's governments worried about the potential dangers of their mounting debts. The nationalist Drago Doctrine of 1902 was a direct result of the dispatch of British, German, and Italian gunboats to Venezuela's shores to collect unpaid debts there (see chapter 11). Argentine Foreign Minister Luis María Drago wrote the Argentine minister in Washington, "The public debt cannot occasion armed intervention, nor even the actual occupation of the territory of American nations by a European power." Ironically, Drago's specific reference to Europe gave weight to the Monroe Doctrine then beginning to flourish (see Overview).

Argentina's economic dynamism was based on the hard labor of everyone from impoverished craftsmen and *gauchos* to millions of newly arriving Italian and Spanish immigrants. The groups that gained most were the *estancieros* and the owners of trading firms and *frigoríficos*, whose families often intermarried and became known as "the oligarchy." Local industrialists by 1914 were supplying a big share of the internal market.

Promised a chance to become independent family farmers, European immigrants flocked to Argentina. Half were from Italy, one quarter from Spain, and the rest from France, Germany, England, Switzerland, and Eastern Europe. The Italian accents of Argentine Spanish date from this time. The number of new immigrants peaked at 200,000 a year in the late 1880s and again in the early 1900s, dropping dramatically after 1913 before rising to more than 100,000 a year again in the 1920s. Few immigrants made it as family farmers, however, since inflation drove up land prices and the credit system favored the *estancieros*. Many immigrants became sharecroppers, tenant farmers, or ranch hands. The majority ended up in the *villas miserias* of Buenos Aires, Rosario, and La Plata, joined later by Paraguayan migrant workers.

Argentina's population increased sixfold from 1870 to 1910, reaching 8 million people. Some 1.25 million resided in Buenos Aires, which became a bustling cosmopolitan city indistinguishable from many European capitals. There, the immigrants worked as artisans, traders, and peddlers or in meat packing and other industries. They contributed numbers to the nation's expanding middle classes. The anarchists among them also led the first major strike actions in the 1880s and 1890s, which climaxed in 1902 with a ruthlessly repressed general strike.

Argentina's wealthy merchants and landowners consolidated their privileged positions during this period. They established the so-called *unicato*, or one-party rule by Conservatives (National Autonomist party). Prohibiting the immigrant population from voting, they centralized power in the executive branch of government and engaged in widespread corruption, electoral fraud, and suppression of dissent. Enjoying their sumptuous parties at Buenos Aires' Jockey Club, many of the elites advocated positivism, or "order and progress," the philosophy then spreading from industrializing Europe to Mexico, Brazil, and other parts of Latin America (see chapters 1 and 20). Profoundly conservative and ingrown as a group, some of them were nonetheless sufficiently "modern" to incorporate the liberal ideas of secular public education and separation of church and state.

Challenges of Radicals, Workers, Students, and Officers, 1890–1930

The rule of the oligarchs was harsh on the rest of the population. The expensive importation of luxury goods for the nation's elites contributed to a deteriorating balance of trade and the exhaustion of foreign exchange reserves (gold). New paper monies were issued, leading to runaway inflation. People had to pay more for basic necessities, but the oligarchs lost nothing since the market values of their properties rose dramatically.

Yet long-run political and financial stability was not to be theirs. In 1890 a stock market collapse triggered a chain of bankruptcies and the resignation of the cabinet. These events coincided with the founding of the Radical party, then called the UC (Civic Union). It was organized by discontented urban politicians, Catholics, new landowners, old aristocrats, and others whose only commonality was the demand for universal suffrage and a more representative political system.

Ex-president Mitre first joined the UC, then abandoned it when its Radical leaders launched an unsuccessful revolt in 1890. The Radicals then regrouped into the UCR (Radical Civic Union). Juan B. Justo took a left-wing segment of the UCR into the Socialist party that he founded in 1894. Justo advocated parliamentary socialism. The UCR and the Socialists developed a following among small traders, artisans, and professionals, many of them the offspring of immigrants who were anxious to obtain positions in government, an area long dominated by Creole elites.

Finding some but not enough support in the army, the Radicals launched unsuccessful revolts in 1890, 1893, and 1905. Their slogan was "Revolutionary Intransigence," which meant using the tactics of revolt until honest elections with universal suffrage could be held. Their appeal was to the masses but their economic power base was among large landowners and middle-class professionals. Both these groups depended on the import-export economy for their well-being—the professionals through customs revenues that paid for their government and other jobs. The Radicals' democratic ideology was vague, populist, and infused with high-blown rhetoric that fired the imaginations of millions.

A movement for improvements in the deteriorating wage structure and abysmal working conditions of Buenos Aires emerged in the ranks of labor. Socialist and syndicalists (advocates of one big general strike to introduce workers' control and the abolition of the state) joined anarchists in sponsoring a series of strikes between 1902 and 1910. Fearing that these strikes and rising political agitation would fuel a popular revolution, the Conservatives opted for opening the electoral system by passing the Sáenz Peña Law of 1912. It granted minority representation in congress and "free, secret, and obligatory" suffrage to all males over eighteen years of age. Argentina's outspoken feminists, most of whom came from the anarchist and labor movements, cried "foul."

Under the Sáenz Peña Law, the Conservatives did not anticipate ever becoming a minority, but by 1916 they were one. A harvest failure in 1913 followed by a three-year depression gravely undermined their power. In the nation's first honest elections the UCR's main leader, Hipólito Irigoyen, an inarticulate man of mystery said to have a past in shady business deals, became president. The Radicals won subsequent elections and governed from 1916 to 1930, establishing a system of government patronage and corruption not unlike the one that had sustained earlier colonial and postcolonial traditions.

Irigoyen and the Radicals introduced some modest social legislation but eventually gave up their efforts to win over labor. An economic upswing stimulated by the outbreak of World War I failed to compensate for worker poverty. President Irigoyen sent troops to crush strikes. He sought to keep student radicals from linking up with labor militants by granting them a stronger voice in running the universities and by creating new campuses where he hoped to confine their political agitation. A decade of student strikes came to an end with the 1918 Córdoba University Reform. It simplified entrance requirements and, more importantly, gave the students input into university governance ("co-gobierno")—the inspiration for university "autonomy" in the rest of Latin America in subsequent decades. Irigoyen's reforms in education helped the Radicals to consolidate their backing among students and the middle classes.

Almost all Argentine political groups courted the powerful military, whose strength came from its actual participation in "nationalist" wars in the nineteenth century and its rapid "modernization" at the turn of the century. In 1900, German officers arrived to direct and staff a newly created War College for Argentina's officer corps. Conscription began soon afterward. Up to half of the military's higher-ranking officers were trained in Germany over the next two decades, and the ranks became infused with a Prussianistic spirit of discipline and superiority.

Despite this, by 1916 a new group of junior officers was openly expressing its sympathy for the Radicals. This helped assure the inauguration of Irigoyen as president (1916–1922). The Conservatives also turned to the military to establish their return to power in 1930. With no more foreign wars to fight, the officer corps readily defined its role as serving as political kingmaker and "saviour of the nation." Generals and admirals founded military lodges modeled after secret societies like the Freemasons, a traditional form of political participation in Latin America dating back to the early nineteenth century.

Ironically, the officers asserted their political voice most strongly during Argentina's first and longest democratic period (1916–1930), when their own isolation from the common citizenry was increasing. Officers and their families were moving into new neighborhoods and building clubs for their exclusive use. Their growing self-definition as a privileged caste above the rest of society made them distrustful of workers and civilian politicians, especially reformers. Using their newly acquired modern weapons and Prussianistic sense of national order, they swung into action against striking workers whom they viewed as "subversives" intent upon breaking down authority.

Labor unrest persisted during the wartime boom and the postwar 1921 depression. From 1914 to 1926 unemployment in Buenos Aires reached 15 percent or higher every year (30 percent in 1917). A wave of strikes swept the nation between 1916 and 1919, as workers demanded higher wages to offset declines in their purchasing power caused by inflation.

In January 1919 police and army repression produced a bloodbath known as "la semana trágica" or "tragic week." Police first shot and killed striking workers, then opened fire on a crowd attending their funeral. Workers' riots spread across the nation. The number of those killed by troops and police rose into the hundreds, perhaps even the thousands. Communists, anarchists, syndicalists, Russian Jewish immigrants, and Catalans were particularly targeted. Those not killed became the victims of an anti-Communist witch-hunt similar to the "Palmer Raids" that shook the United States that same year. The militant backbone of organized labor was broken, and the dominant economic interests had their way for most of the 1920s.

Depression, Coup, and Conservative Restoration, 1930–1943

Argentina's economic "boom" went bust in 1929, as the world entered the Great Depression. The Radicals, already divided among themselves, lost whatever popular backing they had gained. In 1930, as congress prepared to nationalize Argentina's abundant oil resources, General José Félix Uriburu, backed by foreign oil executives, oligarchs, reactionary "nationalist" intellectuals, and, for a brief time, Socialist and anti-Radical liberals, led a military coup d'état against newly elected President Irigoyen (1928–1930). Uriburu and his followers advocated a mishmash of Fascistic, anti-Semitic, and pro-church ideas that called for a strong corporative state modeled after Mussolini's Italy.

They stood behind the "Conservative Restoration" of 1930–1943, also known as "the infamous decade." It was marked by widespread gangsterism, political opportunism among the divided Radicals, and an ironhanded rule by the Conservatives (or Nationalists) on behalf of the oligarchy. They were backed by large factions among the Radicals in a corrupt arrangement known as the "Concordancia."

The Conservative Restoration repressed labor, eliminated democracy, and then set up a constitutional regime guaranteeing Conservative power through electoral fraud. It also gradually led Argentina out of the Depression. It secured the British market for Argentine exports through the Roca-Runciman Treaty of 1933. It reformed the banking and foreign-exchange systems, paid much of the foreign debt, and balanced the budget. It introduced public works projects and "import-substitution" programs (see Overview) to help develop local manufactures and put people back to work. It threw open the doors to foreign investment which had soared to $2.5 billion. Foreigners introduced new areas of industry and dominated the meat-packing, electrical, petroleum, pharmaceutical, and metallurgical sectors. British investors accounted for 60 percent of foreign investment and Americans for 20 percent.

For its part, the military vastly increased its strength. The officer corps doubled in size. The number of troops it commanded nearly tripled. In 1941 officers oversaw the creation of the General Directorate of Military Factories, a complex of modern industry that grew more powerful in subsequent decades. This established the principle of military-run industrial enterprises. It also provided the military caste a relatively independent economic base.

Meanwhile the labor movement gradually reemerged. In 1930 moderate remnants of the repressed Socialists and syndicalists founded the CGT (General Confederation of Labor), mainly as a defensive measure. By the late 1930s, however, the Communists and others had organized many new trade unions, and by 1943 close to half a million workers were unionized. This, together with the outbreak of World War II and the rising strength of new Argentine civilian and military industrialists who were anxious to replace the landed oligarchy in power, set the stage for the rise of a new movement known as "Peronism."

Peronist "Revolution," 1943–1955: Populism and Corporativism

Rising labor unrest and political protests against the domination of the oligarchy set the stage for another military intervention to restore order and "save the nation." On June 4, 1943, General Arturo Rawson and thirteen colonels of the GOU (Group of United Officers, founded in 1941) threw out the Conservatives and set up a new "revolutionary" military government. Much of the leadership was Fascist. It proscribed political parties, jailed its opponents, banned Jewish and leftist newspapers, outlawed organized labor's Marxist-dominated CGT, and packed labor leaders into concentration camps. It restricted strikes, cutting their number to a paltry twenty-seven in all of 1944. In light of this, the powerful Unión Industrial Argentina, a confederation of big industry, expressed its backing of the new regime.

But the military's iron-handed rule could not conceal internal factionalism. After three days Rawson was replaced by General Pedro Ramírez, who vowed to keep Argentina neutral during World War II—thus backing the Latin American trend of siding with the Western democracies and the Soviet Union. Washington responded by freezing Argentine gold reserves in the United States, recalling the American ambassador, and restricting shipping to Argentine ports. By early 1944 the U.S. pressure worked. Argentina broke relations with the Axis powers (Germany, Italy, and Japan) and Ramírez resigned.

On March 2, 1944, Vice-President General Edelmiro J. Farrell was sworn in as acting president. By then the original 1943 coup leaders were in disarray and a shrewd forty-eight-year-old six-footer of the GOU, Colonel Juan Domingo Perón, the minister of labor and welfare and newly appointed interim war minister, was emerging as the regime's strong man.

Like many other officers, Perón came from a humble middle-class background. He was the farm-family son of immigrant, Creole parents. He had entered the military college at age sixteen and had gradually risen through the ranks. He had lived in Europe and admired the "orderly" successes of Nazi Germany and Fascist Italy. Perón and other colonels in his clique aspired to free the nation from the control of British and U.S. economic interests. They had little patience for either the old-guard oligarchy that had dominated the nation for most of the last eighty years or the quarreling pro-middle-class politicians of the Radicals and other parties.

Major civilian groups were too weak to counter Perón. The oligarchs were more unpopular than ever; the new industrialists and middle classes could not unite. Perón recognized what recent events had made obvious; a new social group, the working class, many of them recent arrivals to the factory and *figorífico* zones of Buenos Aires, was ready to enter the political arena. In September 1943 the Communist-dominated, outlawed meat workers' union led a general strike that was lifted in October only after Perón negotiated with its leaders. Argentina's unions sought government recognition, collective bargaining, higher wages, and a better deal for labor. Communist labor leaders agreed to lift the September general strike in part because they welcomed the renewal of meat shipments to the Allies fighting fascism in Europe.

Perón was deeply anti-Marxist. In late November 1943 the government upgraded the labor department to create the Labor and Welfare Ministry under Perón's leadership. It renewed arrests of leftist labor leaders, including Communists. Perón began forging an alliance with strike militants and independent unionists who had opposed the Communists' agreement to lift the general strike. He drew his initial mass labor support from the railroad unions, headed up by his personal friend Colonel Domingo A. Mercante. The railroads were

British-owned and unpopular, so granting their workers big benefits did not particularly worry domestic industrialists.

Anxious not to alienate big business, Perón was at first slow to grant many of labor's economic demands. By April of 1944, however, many unions, independents, and leftists were preparing for a huge antigovernment May Day rally to protest its antilabor policies. This forced Perón to step up his wooing of labor. By granting unions loyal to him official government recognition and delivering wage hikes and social welfare benefits to workers, Perón was able to forge a mass base among Argentina's "descamisados," or "shirtless ones" as he and his companion Eva Duarte liked to call them.

The May Day rally was called off, and the government began enforcing labor laws and collective bargaining, leading to a huge rise in the number of contracts signed. Real wages among unskilled workers jumped by 17 percent between 1943 and 1945. Perón's "tilt" to labor alienated big business' Unión Industrial Argentina, which by the end of 1944 joined sides with the landed elites' Sociedad Rural to oppose him.

Also in late 1944, Nelson Rockefeller became U. S. assistant secretary of state in charge of Latin American affairs. He advocated a more conciliatory posture toward Argentina, since it had finally declared war against the Axis powers and the United States would need friends in Argentina to counter Perón's further radicalization. Rockefeller helped to bring about Argentina's inclusion in the United Nations at sessions held in San Francisco in 1945.

By mid-1945 Argentine society was polarized on the issues of Perón's concessions to labor, his attempts to change rural tenancy regulations and help the downtrodden, his nationalist and independent foreign policy, and continued military rule. The United States shifted its policy once more—to a position of hostility toward Perón's government symbolized by the appointment of Spruille Braden as ambassador. Son of copper magnate William Braden (whose interests later became part of Kennecott Copper), Braden was a veteran troubleshooter for U.S. corporations in Latin America, including Rockefeller's Standard Oil (see chapters 15 and 16).

On October 9, 1945, Perón's rivals in the military and his civilian opponents, including Socialists, Radicals, and oligarchs, mounted a coup, arrested Perón, and jailed him in a military hospital. During the next week tens of thousands of the descamisados took over Buenos Aires, facing down police and defying soldiers. Judging from recent scholarship, their spontaneous protest had little coordinated leadership from Peronist leaders.

The protesters were joined by contingents of workers from Rosario and other cities, who jammed the Plaza de Mayo on October 17, one-quarter of a million strong. Their chants for Perón's release reverberated into the night. Finally, Perón was released to appear on the balcony of the Casa Rosada and to wave a victory salutation to the roaring masses. The CGT then launched a general strike in favor of Perón, whose military opponents were arrested as Perón loyalists danced in the streets.

By the end of October Perón's followers had organized the Labor party and Perón had made up his mind to run for the presidency in February 1946. Ambassador Braden was recalled to become assistant secretary of state for Latin American Affairs and to direct the anti-Perón campaign from Washington. Braden's outspoken denunciations of Perón contributed to a nationalist swell of support for Perón.

On the eve of the 1946 elections the U.S. State Department published a "Blue Book" charging Perón with pro-Nazi activities. Perón countered with a Blue and White Book (Argentina's national colors) critical of "Yankee imperialism." His campaign slogan was "Braden or Perón?" Argentines answered by electing Perón president by the commanding margin of 300,000 votes. Braden went on to serve as United Fruit's public relations director and pointman for attacking the democratically elected reformist government of Arbenz in Guatemala (see chapter 2). He also became a founder of the ultrarightist John Birch Society in the United States.

As a popularly elected president, Perón was able to practice a broad-based corporativist populism (see Overview), appealing to both big business and organized labor. He had a rare opportunity granted him by Argentina's large foreign currency and gold reserves accumulated during World War II. From 1945 to 1948 real wages rose another 20 percent. Industrialists' profits multiplied, as industrial production increased by one-third and domestic consumption expanded because of the wage hikes. Despite subsequent signs of an economic decline, Perón was easily reelected president in 1951.

Perón's operative style was consistent with his corporativist and personalist ideology of bringing conflicting groups under the tutelage of a strong state and his ultimate individual leadership. His anticommunism pleased big business, even though it initially opposed him in 1945–1946. While controversy rages about what Perón's ideology and intents were—he said many conflicting things in the course of his life (1895–1974)—his practices were clearly anti-Communist, procapitalist, corporativist, populist, and often nationalist. He gained the backing of the Roman Catholic Church by promising to block legal divorce and to protect Church schools and by marrying his companion Eva Duarte.

Perón nationalized many leading foreign firms, including the railroads, urban transport, ports, and utilities companies. He established state enterprises in steel, shipping, insurance, and banking. He set up rent controls and worker pension funds. He brought nationalized German companies into a state manufacturing complex and also expanded the military-industrial conglomerate Military Factories. He created a state trading board to control foreign trade and an industrial credit bank to support the growing group of Argentine industrialists, large and small.

Foreign exchange from agricultural exports helped fund the importation of equipment needed for industrialization. Throughout the 1940s the lot of many Argentine businesspeople and workers improved notably. But when the costs of capital goods imports rose and severe draughts and drops in world prices for wheat and other grains occurred in the early 1950s, the initial successes of Peronist populism and nationalism were undermined by economic hardship. Workers continued their militant demands for economic relief, trusting that Perón would aid them again.

Perón's immense popularity with Argentine workers was based on his having brought them into the political arena and advanced their living standards. Between 1943 and 1949 labor's share of national income rose from 45 to 59 percent. The workers' own mobilizations and militancy kept the heat on Perón in case he wavered. From 1946 to 1948 the meat-packing unions continued to disrupt production to demand compliance with earlier agreements and recognition of many leaders who were independent and not Peronist. Perón jailed his opponents in labor and consolidated a bureaucratic ruling bloc inside the rapidly expanding unions, whose membership quintupled to 2.5 million. Even after the bulk of workers' gains had been made, rank-and-file union militants had to pressure the Peronist bureaucratic leadership to maintain their benefits.

Many workers looked to Perón's flamboyant actress-wife, Eva Duarte de Perón, for help. "Evita," as they affectionately called her, oversaw charity projects that provided benefits to the working poor. She herself had been raised in poverty, an illegitimate child scorned by society. The ranks of the poor were expanded by a new influx of immigrants—160,000 a year from 1948 to 1950—needed to staff Argentina's expanding industries and services. "Evita" gained a reputation in worker circles as an "untiring defender of our union interests." She advocated women's suffrage, and in 1947 women got the vote. Together, Evita and Juan Perón could rally huge buoyant crowds. When Evita died of cancer in 1952 the nation mourned. She remained a symbol for the working poor.

In reality, President Perón's concessions to labor could not be sustained in the face of obstacles presented by declining export prices in the 1950s and a deepening recession combined with inflation ("stagflation"). To combat the economic crisis, Perón encouraged foreign investment, took out a big U.S. loan, and struck a deal with Standard Oil of California. He offered price incentives for rural landowners and coddled big business. He had the CGT order workers to restrain their wage demands and to increase their productivity. An entrenched bureaucratic caste in the trade unions increasingly cast its lot with big industrialists, domestic and foreign. As labor historian Charles Bergquist later noted, "wages fell behind the rise of living costs for long periods of time" and leaders of both the independent and pro-Peronist unions tended to become "passive instruments obedient to the dictates of Perón." They substituted "mystical loyalty" to Perón "for the radical reformism of a class-conscious proletariat."

By 1955 most Argentine industrialists had turned against Perón. Like Perón, they looked to foreign capital for help, even if it meant making them "junior partners" of better-off U.S. and European investors. Other former allies also turned against Perón, including the Church and many people from the middle classes. Students were fed up with Peronist "goons" sent to their campuses to control their political life. The moment was opportune for the most reactionary forces of the landed oligarchy to ally themselves with other dissidents and turn the clock back.

Military Interventionism and Popular Resistance, 1955–1973

Once again Argentina's contending social and political forces were entering a political stalemate that invited military intervention. This time, however, the nation was more industrialized. Under Perón, manufacturing's share of GNP (gross national product) surpassed agriculture's. A newly enfranchised urban working class, aware of its having made recent gains through militant political action, stood in the way of turning the clock all the way back.

The tensions between reaction and progress, dictatorship and democracy, were soon stretched to their ultimate limits. For the next three decades or more the shadow of Perón hovered over the nation's attempts to extricate itself from relative economic stagnation and what Argentine sociologist Juan Corradi once called its "stalemated pluralism" pregnant with "civil war."

As throughout its history, Argentina's military intervened to "restore order" and "save the nation" in 1955—and again in 1962, 1966, and 1976—by initially ruling with an iron hand and for the benefit of itself and Conservative oligarchic interests and increasingly foreign industrial-financial groups. The officers that overthrew Perón and forced him into exile in 1955 typified the pattern.

The 1955 coup leaders crushed an ineffective general strike, eliminated price controls on basic foodstuffs, abolished wage contracts, and jailed Peronist military officers. Taking over the CGT, they froze wages and vainly tried to purge the unions of Peronist leadership. In mid-1957 the CGT split into the "62 Organizations" loyal to Perón and the "32" liberal trade unions opposed to Perón. The military government also eliminated Perón's powerful state trade agency and reduced financing for the state-run industrial credit bank he had created. It encouraged the sale of state firms and turned to U.S. and foreign institutions for loans.

Throughout the late 1950s and on into the 1960s, Argentina's economy suffered a series of ups and downs that tied it increasingly to the dictates of powerful TNCs (transnational corporations) and the IMF (International Monetary Fund). U.S. investments in Argentina skyrocketed from $161 million in 1960 to $1.2 billion in 1968. In the process a number of Argentine firms were "denationalized," as U.S. and other foreign investors set up a booming business in automotive, pharmaceuticals, machinery, chemicals, cigarettes, and banking. The new firms were capital-intensive and failed to generate enough jobs to keep all Argentines employed.

Argentine's foreign debt, all but eliminated under Perón, rose to $1 billion by 1958 and $3 billion by 1963. Later the 1976–1983 military dictatorship built up nearly *fifteen* times that amount in foreign-debt obligations, in effect pauperizing the nation. The intervening decades of alternating military and civilian governments witnessed an up-down cycle of inflationary bursts of government spending and IMF-imposed deflationary currency devaluations, all of which helped channel income into the hands of oligarchic landowners, agricultural exporters, and, increasingly, bankers, real-estate speculators, and foreign investors and creditors.

Perón, after fleeing to Paraguay and then to Panama where he met his future and third wife, María Estela Martínez, known as Isabel, went on to Caracas and Santo Domingo exile before settling in Madrid in 1960. He sent orders to an underground command structure he had left behind in Argentina.

Most workers remained "Peronist," in the sense of calling for Perón's return and, so the hope went, with him the "golden era" of the 1940s. But the landed and industrial-financial oligarchy, most of the civilian politicians, and the military were dead set against letting Perón return or the Peronist political party function after the scare of worker insurgency they had received during his decade in power.

One moderate Radical politician, Arturo Frondizi, president from 1958 to 1962, recognized that Peronism was alive and well. He struck a deal with Perón to get some 2 million Peronist votes for his presidential candidacy. In return, as president, Frondizi normalized the CGT in 1961 and legalized the Peronist political party in 1962. He desperately needed Peronist support in the midst of 1962's economic recession during which one-third of the labor force was unemployed. Representing a momentary ascendancy of middle-class elements, including owners of small and medium-scale enterprises and liberal technocrats, Frondizi advocated the developmentalist goals of the UNs Economic Commission on Latin America and the Alliance for Progress (see Overview).

Frondizi's negotiations with Perón, an example that almost every major political group followed behind the scenes to one degree or another, proved too "radical" for the tastes of the nation's big industrialists and financiers, who got behind the 1962 military coup and the "counterrevolution" of President Arturo Illia (1963–1966). Illia, a more conservative Radical, was elected president in 1963, but the generals (or "*gorilas*"—apes—as many Argentines called them) were the power behind his short-lived presidency.

Argentina's "pluralism" was becoming ever more restricted. Growing threats from a "new Left" inspired by the Cuban Revolution and a reinvigorated Peronism were polarizing political options. During the 1960s students and young workers became inspired by the romantic guerrilla image of Argentine-born Ernesto "Ché" Guevara, whose achievements and writings underwent such close scrutiny in Washington (see chapters 10 and 15). Guerrilla "focos" formed in the mountains of the northwest as early as 1959 but were snuffed out by the military. Stronger guerrilla bands emerged in the early 1960s, but most of them were crushed by the end of Illia's second year in office, 1964.

The Peronist Youth, founded in 1958, were not immune to the new ideas and tactics advocated by the Guevarists. Increasingly, radical students and intellectuals infused Peronism with Marxist terminology. The concepts of the "theology of liberation" (see Overview) also caught fire, especially in the interior of the nation. Many revolutionary activists were from the first generation of sons and daughters of those industrial workers who had helped bring Perón to power in 1945–1946. When appealing to older workers, they realized how much Perón was idolized. Revolutionary "left Peronism" originated in the 1960s.

The strengthening of Peronism's right wing, or "right Peronism," also occurred at that time. The Socialist and "workers' control" demands of the new Left frightened Peronist labor bureaucrats, who increasingly sided with the military. The mid-1960s witnessed several splits in the CGT leadership, as a powerful Conservative wing inside the "62" lined up with the officer caste. Death squads supported by the military and Peronist right-wingers swung into action to eliminate suspected leftists.

Even so, neither Illia nor the generals could stem Peronism's appeal. In those occasional elections in which Peronists were allowed to be on the ballot from 1957 through 1966 their vote was always large. In 1966, in fact, the Peronists were fully expected to win the scheduled March 1967 congressional elections.

Therefore the military launched a "preventive strike" that booted Illia out, dissolved all political institutions, jammed the prisons with political detainees, set up concentration camps, and initiated naked military rule by force (1966–1973).

The policies of the 1966–1973 dictatorship foreshadowed those of the more infamous 1976–1983 dictatorship. It repeatedly broke strikes and occupied workplaces. Like its civilian predecessors, it imposed wage freezes and followed an IMF-style program of austerity and "stabilization" that ended by driving several small and medium-scale producers into bankruptcy and increasing the economic power of big industrialists, foreign and domestic. Its harsh measures created intense opposition to its rule, particularly among workers, the middle classes (including small business owners), and youth.

In 1969 in the interior industrial city of Córdoba, the most momentous revolutionary event since October 17, 1945, occurred—the so-called Cordobazo. A student-worker insurrection seized the entire city and issued a call for Socialist revolution. Many middle-class people supported it. The big foreign-owned automotive plants and other factories fell into the hands of the revolutionists. Ever since the 1918 "Córdoba Reform" of the university, student revolutionism had enjoyed a strong base in Córdoba. Responding to the calls emanating from Córdoba, students and workers in Rosario, Tucumán, Mendoza, and other cities rose up. All these uprisings were crushed by the military. In Córdoba full-scale war erupted before "order" was restored.

Argentina's officer caste saw itself as in a "state of war" against the forces of "internal subversion," that is, Marxists, left-wing and moderate Peronists, Communists, and Zionists. The high command cast its repressive net wide, and a steady flow of even apolitical artists and intellectuals began arriving from Argentina in the cosmopolitan cities of Mexico City, New York, Paris, and Rome. Later the flow would become a flood.

A year before the Cordobazo, Peronist Youth elements had revived guerrilla warfare under the banner of the FAP (Peronist Armed Forces). The Cordobazo and military wave of terror that it unleashed stimulated the founding of three additional guerrilla organizations.

The most powerful one was known as "the Montoneros," an urban guerrilla operation influenced by both Guevaraism and the ideals of Father Camilo Torres, the martyred Colombian guerrilla-priest (see chapter 12). The Montoneros were soon joined by Peronist commandos. The FAR (Revolutionary Armed Forces) was a Guevarist guerrilla organization that merged with Peronism in 1970. The ERP (People's Revolutionary Army) was launched in 1970 by advocates of Trotskyism (see chapter 15). The guerrillas, particularly the Montoneros, engaged in spectacular bank robberies, political assassinations, and kidnappings of foreign corporate executives to rally public resistance to the dictatorship.

The warlike situation of the early 1970s pitted a strong popular movement against a repressive state security apparatus that had been modernized with the help of $352 million in U.S. military credits from 1950 to 1976. Since room for political maneuver and a "return to democracy" was clearly disappearing before the advance of the military juggernaut, most major proscribed political parties, including the Peronists, as early as November 1970 formed a nationwide coalition to pressure the military government to call new elections.

By then, however, the armed forces' *gorilas* were having none of it. They tightened the screws of repression and torture. In March 1974 the second so-called Cordobazo of strikes and factory takeovers erupted. Again the military swept through, killing and arresting.

Nonetheless, the persistence of popular resistance evidenced by the second Cordobazo, together with stepped-up pressure from the political parties, caused another change at the top of the military government. The new man in charge, General Alejandro A. Lanusse, legalized most of the political parties in July 1971. As Lanusse later explained in his 1977 memoirs, the top brass realized that "a total erosion of Perón" could create a "grave problem if the active groups impregnated with leftism—the youth formations and the combative union groups—came to predominate."

The parties, illegal for five years, quickly began reorganizing their ranks, while the military stepped up its terroristic methods against leftists. In August 1972 the "Trelew massacre" occurred. Sixteen political prisoners belonging to the Montoneros, ERP, and FAR were tortured and executed at the Trelew concentration camp. Later investigations would reveal how widespread this type of activity was even prior to the grisly 1976–1983 dirty war dictatorship. Leftist labor leaders were hounded. Organized labor, even in the unions controlled by right-wing Peronists, could not stand idly by while wages tailed far behind rising prices. Strikes, although made difficult, were common.

By 1972 even the dominant industrialists, oligarchs, and military brass were looking for a way out of the nation's "stalemated pluralism." In one of history's greatest ironies they turned to the one man they had long fought so hard to keep out of the country—Perón! On November 17, 1972, the armed forces agreed it was all right for Perón to return but that he would not be permitted to run in presidential elections called for March 1973.

Crisis of Peronism and Coup by Quotas, 1973–1976

In March 1973, the Peronist FREJULI (Justicialista Front of Liberation) swept national elections with half the vote. Héctor Cámpora, a Peronist, was elected president. Crowds filled the streets calling for democracy, socialism, and Perón. Human rights teams began arriving to look into the prison massacres and concentration camps. Suddenly, in its mass mobilizations for revolutionary change, Argentina resembled next-door Chile, where an elected Socialist president (Allende) presided and immense mass mobilizations in favor of changing the social structure were underway (see chapter 17). The Chile example struck fear in the hearts of Argentina's gorilas and industrial-financial oligarchy.

President Cámpora immediately invited Perón back from Madrid. Exiled in semidisgrace in 1955, Perón, an aging and sick man, now returned to a hero's welcome. Large contingents of Montoneros marched through down-town Buenos Aires chanting "Mon-to-ne-ros," their chants reverberating off the stone buildings' walls. Perón smiled and waved his hand to them. On his arm was his third wife, Isabel Martínez de Perón, whom he had sent to his homeland on earlier political missions to lend approval to the use of armed vi-olence against the dictatorship. In the eyes of the masses Isabelita was no match for Evita.

Once again Argentina's military bureaucracy that had held power back in the 1940s and reclaimed it fully in 1966 was forced to share it with Perón, this time with the Peronist labor and political bureaucracy. But unlike the situ-ation in the 1940s, the military was antinationalist and anti-Peronist. It was al-lied to the oligarchy, big business, and the TNCs. Its antilabor policies defied the base in organized labor of the Peronist wing of the government bureau-cracy. This gap, although visible even in the 1940s, was now far too wide to bridge.

Perón's honeymoon with the Left was unstable. Pressure from the right-wing of Peronism forced Cámpora to resign in July 1973. He was replaced by provisional President Raúl Lastiri who oversaw new presidential elections in September, in which Perón was allowed to run. Not surprisingly, Perón for the third time was elected president. He garnered 60 percent of the vote. Isabel Perón, now known as Isabelita, won the vice-presidency. With this mandate, Perón launched a campaign of "ideological purification" against the very Marxist "infiltrators" he had encouraged earlier.

In response the Montoneros merged with the FAR and sought to reorga-nize the Peronist Youth movement, in alliance with older left-wing Peronists of the APA (Association of Authentic Peronism). They became "movemen-tist," that is, committed to working within the Peronist movement and using their guns solely to defend the government against a coup. A "classist" sector of Peronism's Left, led by the FAP, labor militants, and the PB (Peronism of the Bases), opted for cooperating with non-Peronist guerrilla groups and fight-ing on until the establishment of a "Socialist Fatherland." This sector formal-ized its rupture with Perón's government in February 1974 and was widely viewed as "ultraleftist."

On July 1, 1974, Perón died of heart disease at the age of seventy-eight. Throngs turned out for his funeral, Isabelita succeeded to the presidency, be-coming Latin America's first female president in a country renowned for its virulent male chauvinism and where homosexuality is illegal. Her personal secretary and main adviser was José López Rega, a notorious ex-policeman believed to be in charge of the ultraright AAA death squad (Argentine Anti-Communist Alliance). The AAA was allegedly responsible for two thousand political murders from June to October 1974. In September the Montonero-led movementists, suffering heavy casualties, denounced the government of Isabel Perón and went underground to wage war against her government.

Two months later the government declared a state of siege, giving free hand to the Federal Police to combat the guerrillas. In February of 1975 it authorized the military to undertake full-scale war on the guerrillas. It then replaced a top general for refusing to send troops against 25,000 striking workers at Villa Constitución, the nation's main steelworks. Big business's APEGE (Permanent Assembly of Employers' Guild Entities, founded in 1974 after Juan Perón's death) stepped up its campaign for strict enforcement of economic austerity programs and direct military interventionism in politics.

Even though President Isabel Perón was formally "in charge," the military had a free hand to conduct its war and gradually carry out what political analyst Donald Hodges later called a "coup by quotas" (a phase-by-phase creeping coup). The economic situation contributed to the 1976 coup's success. The worldwide 1973–1974 recession worsened "stagflation." Prices went through the roof, government corruption went unchecked, and investors began stashing their funds in overseas banks.

As a result, the military bureaucracy was able to marshall some public support for its impending 1976 coup. Public apathy, confusion, and fear pro-, vided ideal conditions for increasing state terror in the name of national security. This time, however, unlike the 1940s, civilian support for military rule came not from the workers or lower middle classes but from frightened businesspeople, foreign investors, government technocrats, high-level professionals, and many middle-class people who feared the militancy of the left-wing of Peronism in the midst of a collapsing economy.

The Argentine military's national security doctrine was much more spontaneous and hysterical than Brazil's (see chapter 20). Journalist Jácobo Timerman later wrote that his military interrogators thought World War III had already started, but _not_ as a struggle between "democracy" and "communism." Rather, they thought it was a war of the entire world against "left-wing terrorism" and "Zionism"! This irrational assessment may have reflected the officer caste's decade-long frustration at failing to corner the urban guerrillas or to erase the appeal of Peronism to the nation's workers.

In June 1975 President Isabel Perón implemented an IMF-style "shock treatment" austerity program. It granted organized labor only half the level of its requested wage hikes. Again, labor leaders called out their forces for a twenty-four hour "general strike."

Finally, in July 1975, the main split within anti-Left Peronism was acted out, pitting the moderate Right that controlled the CGT "62 Organizations" against the ultrarightists led by López Rega. A two-day general strike in July left López Rega in a weakened position. Both the CGT moderates and the military blocked his bid for total power and forced him into exile on July 19. It was the first major public act of direct military intervention since the return of Perón—the first phase of the "coup by quotas."

Next, on August 27, 1975, the army's top brass openly defied President Isabel Perón by forcing out the army commander-in-chief who had favored a military appointment to a Peronist cabinet. The new chief of staff was Jorge Videla, eventual head of the first military government after the 1976 coup. His appointment in 1975 was, in retrospect, the first of a series of "minicoups."

He set up a high-tech, centralized command structure to coordinate the antiguerrilla war and announced he was drafting a National Defense Law providing for military tribunals and the death penalty. Isabel Perón was a mere figurehead. From September 13 to October 13 she took an extended sick leave. She was replaced by Italo Luder, head of the moderate Peronist bloc in the Senate.

From December 18 to 22, 1975, rebels at an air force base in Morón demanded that Videla lead a coup. The CGT and Peronist response to this second minicoup was belated, divided, and weak. Videla chose to bomb the rebels as a symbol of his constitutionalist posture. Meanwhile he gained the backing of opposition parties and dissident Peronists ("Work Group") for achieving the coup's aims through other means. They pressured Isabelita to take a second, more extended leave of absence. When she refused, they encouraged impeachment proceedings based on graft in her government. These proceedings became bogged down in congress in early 1976.

On February 2, 1976, the commanders-in-chief of the armed forces imposed an army tank commander as chief of the Federal police. They then personally moved and approved the appointment of a new minister of economics and his IMF-style austerity program. President Perón, her hand weakened by recent exposures of graft in her government, did not object to the military's increased role. There was talk of her overseeing a gradual coup, along the lines of President Juan María Bordaberry's support for the June 1973 coup in neighboring Uruguay (see chapter 19). General Videla reportedly reached a consensus with more "hardline" generals in setting a coup deadline for a time prior to labor's organizing an active response to a new austerity program due to take effect in March 1976.

In early March the austerity program took effect. Prices were hiked by 50 to 60 percent on basic foodstuffs and more on gasoline and public transportation fares. In protest, workers again struck, idling 70 percent of productive capacity by March 10. Shopkeepers and retailers called for shutdowns a week later, and every sector of society clamored for Isabel Perón's removal.

Night of the Generals: Dirty War Dictatorship, 1976–1982

On March 23, 1976, the well-coordinated coup occurred. The military took President Isabel Perón prisoner, shut down congress, dismissed Supreme

Court justices, and scrapped all the preceding political structures of Argentina. Troops rounded up and threw in jail leaders and members of the Peronist movement, including the moderate CGT 62 Organizations. An "interventor" was appointed to the CGT. The military junta proscribed strikes and collective bargaining. Martial law was introduced, and military courts swung into action. In less than a month 10,000 people were arrested, mostly workers, leftists, and young people. Many top political and labor bureaucrats escaped by boat across the Río de la Plata into Uruguay, from where they sought more secure places of exile.

The coup's leaders saw themselves as creating "order" by winning the war against "subversion." To stabilize the political situation and provide a basis for eventual "economic recovery" in the mid-1970s, however, they felt they had to eliminate the political participation of not only workers and farmers, but also of landed oligarchs, businesspeople, industrialists, and intellectuals. They allowed the Church to retain some traditional authority, but only after it concurred with their drastic measures. Dissenting bishops, worker-priests, and nuns working in the slums were killed or silenced.

Unlike their Brazilian counterparts (see chapter 20), Argentina's new military rulers did not have an advance plan for "developing" the economy while providing for "national security." They removed tariff protections for local industry and opened the market further to international interests. Their freeing up of currency exchange controls, raising of interest rates to check inflation, and deregulation of banking favored those investors engaged in finance markets, real-estate, and other speculative activities rather than industry. Big landowners and industrialists were scarcely consulted, and financial speculators and "friends" of the military benefited.

The result of these policies was the relative deindustrialization of Argentina and many businesspeople's disenchantment with military government. The percentage of the nonagricultural work force engaged in industrial production dropped from 32.4 percent in 1974 to 24.2 percent in 1981. Even foreign capital preferred investing in finance, trade, and agribusiness to investing in industry. On the other hand, it stepped in to take over portions of the state sector of the economy being privatized and denationalized.

As early as 1978, workers' wages had plummeted to one-third of what they had been just four years earlier. Firms shut down in unprecedented numbers. Huge foreign loans fueled the military's budget and an economy of increasing speculative activity. By the early 1980s unemployment was widespread and most of the urban working class was active in the services sector of the economy or a plethora of small, unsuccessful businesses (street vending, and so on).

Three months after the 1976 coup, according to American Ambassador Robert Hill, U.S. Secretary of State Henry Kissinger gave the green light to

Argentina's coup leaders to continue their dirty war. Hill, who greeted the coup, later became disturbed by the military's grand-scale violations of human rights. His criticism of Kissinger carried weight since he could not be accused of being a liberal. A former director of the United Fruit Company, Hill had helped plan the coup that overthrew the elected government of Jácobo Arbenz in Guatemala (see chapter 2).

In 1978 the Carter administration placed an embargo on U.S. military sales and assistance to Argentina. Doing so in the name of "human rights," it was also troubled by Argentina's growing commercial ties to the Soviet Union. The Carter government, however, looked the other way when Argentina sent military assistance to Guatemala, a country for which Carter also ceased military aid (see chapter 2).

By the late 1970s U.S. training and aid programs had long since beefed up Argentina's military and police as one of Latin America's strongest counterinsurgency forces (see Overview). Some 3,676 members of Argentina's armed forces, including the head of the secret service, had received U.S. training. The Argentine armed forces had 130,000 well-equipped personnel, including a 32,000-strong navy. After the return of civilian rule in 1983, U.S. military assistance was renewed.

The chief of the Federal Police and eighty other Argentine policemen had received U.S. training in the Panama Canal Zone. After the 1974 congressional ban on the police-training program of AID (Agency for International Development) because of its involvement in the training of torturers (see Overview and chapters 19 and 20), aid for Argentina's police arrived through antinarcotics programs of the State Department and DEA (Drug Enforcement Administration). Once more the Federal Police, hotbed of Argentine torture, were the main beneficiaries.

Argentina's military and police justified their self-proclaimed dirty war as "a defense of tradition, the family, and property against subversion." They created 340 detention centers. Later human rights investigators found 50,000 pages of documents on the tortures and killings in these centers. These papers showed that the military constructed several concentration camps and dumped the corpses of its thousands of victims in the ocean, secret mass graves, and numerous cemeteries.

The dirty war was by no means limited to eliminating urban guerrillas who by 1974 no longer posed a serious threat. The dirty war was a way to guarantee stability for the implementation of an economic program favorable to those Argentine and foreign businesspeople who had an intersectoral "spread" of interests and near-monopolistic control over the economy. The junta's finance minister José Alfredo Martínez de Hoz explained that with "the economic stability the armed forces guarantee us" the IMF-style economic austerity program "can be fulfilled despite its lack of popular support."

Even so, not every policy of the generals favored foreign capital. The IMF's prescriptions for privatizing the state sector of the economy, for instance, eventually ran up against the obstacles of military officers' heavy investments there. Consequently, the IMF's limits on public sector expenditures affected social welfare but not military items. By 1983, military spending stood at 8 percent of GDP (gross domestic product) compared to less than 3 percent under prior administrations. When the officers handed the government back to civilians in December 1983, they could retire as millionaires.

Military-Constrained "Democratic Transition," 1980s and 1990s

Argentina's prolonged economic stagnation, triggered by the military's "supply-side economics with machine guns" (as political scientist James Petras dubbed the junta's policies), gave way to total collapse by the early 1980s. Industrialists, farmers, salaried professionals, workers, and peasants found themselves worse off than they had been before the coup. The result was an upsurge in protest movements and illegal strikes, a call for "return to democracy," and a strategic retreat by the military.

But before retreating, the generals and admirals, proud of the "success" of their dirty war, decided to instruct others. They agreed with the conservative Reagan administration in Washington to train the contras for an invasion from Honduras against the Sandinista government in Nicaragua. The U.S. government allocated $15 million to fund the program, and Nicaraguan "trainees" soon arrived in Buenos Aires. Trained in Argentina were major contra leaders Enrique Bermúdez and Ricardo Lau, as well as the future Honduran president, Colonel Gustavo Alvarez Martínez. These men learned their dirty war lessons well (see chapters 4 and 5 and Introduction to Part One). A CIA-financed Argentine training mission was dispatched to Honduras.

International protest movements, combined with the military's defeat in the 1982 Malvinas/Falklands War and Argentina's perception of a "U.S. doublecross" in that war, led to the official termination of the U.S.-funded Argentine training missions for contras in 1983. The Malvinas fiasco made the military's "strategic retreat" both swift and chaotic.

The top brass agreed to hold elections on condition that they be granted amnesty from prosecution for human rights violations. They strove to control the nationwide elections of October 30, 1983, obstructing the participation of Peronists wherever possible. They censored the press, closed down newspapers, and claimed that the Montoneros, most of whom were dead or in exile, would kill centrists and right-wing Peronists in the event of a Peronist victory. In May 1983 two Peronist leaders were gunned down by unknown assassins. It proved difficult for the Peronists to mount a campaign with the resources and access to the media enjoyed by the more conservative Radicals of the UCR.

Eleven political parties (see box 18.1), many of them regional, participated in the 1983 elections. In the contest for delegates to the electoral college that named the president, the UCR won 51.8 percent of the vote and the Peronists' PJ (Justicialista party) garnered 40.2 percent. More than 14 million Argentines went to the polls, an exceptional turnout by any standards. Some claims of fraud occurred because it seemed odd that the Radicals won when they had only 1.5 million registered voters, compared with the Peronists' 3 million.

The election to the presidency of the UCR's Raúl Alfonsín, a human rights activist, led many to believe that, unlike other militaries in the region, Argentina's might in fact be punished for its crimes. Alfonsín promised in his campaign to bring all human rights violators to justice. More than two-thirds of the highest-ranking army officers resigned or retired, all in disgrace but with their pockets full. New enlistments almost stopped, and the number of men in the army dropped to less than 25,000 by 1986.

Yet under Alfonsín, the military retained most of its privileges and suffered only tokenistic punishment for its crimes. The new president slashed the list of scheduled trials from two thousand to four hundred. As late as 1984 his government was selling $2.5 million in arms to Honduras that were earmarked for Nicaragua's contras. In September 1985 he promoted officers involved in the dirty war. He continued Argentina's arms buildup, replacing equipment lost in the Malvinas war. He retained military appointees in almost all the top posts of the armed forces and in the judiciary. On the other hand, Alfonsín allied Argentina with other new South American democracies in forming a "support group" for the Contadora peace process in Central America (see Introductions to Parts One and Three).

The military did not dismantle its terror network. Human rights activist and Nobel laureate Adolfo Pérez Esquivel noted 215 abductions by right-wing paramilitary groups in 1984. The armed forces thus remained a constraining influence on Argentine democracy.

Alfonsín came into office on an electoral platform of slashing the military's budget by 20 percent and increasing real wages. He did precious little of either. Unemployment rose in manufacturing, where the portion of workers earning less than 90 percent of the minimum wage rose to one-fourth by early 1985. Hard hit by foreign competition and runaway inflation, garments and other manufacturers laid off workers in droves. Alfonsín went along with the old policies of slashing state social expenditures and favoring agricultural exports in an effort to service the $52 billion foreign debt (higher per capita than Mexico's or Brazil's). Interest payments on the debt absorbed more than half of export earnings and by 1988 could not be met.

To govern, Alfonsín had to fashion a broad alliance with the Peronists and several other parties. In June 1984 they agreed to the "Acta de Coin ciden-

---

Box 18.1: Argentina's Political Parties and Organizations

Broad Front
(Frente Grande)   Center-left successor to FRAL and IU that became nation's third political force in 1994

FRAL   Broad Liberation front, electoral alliance of small leftist groups including PCA and a PDC splitoff formed in mid-1980s, joined IU in 1989

IU   United Left, an expanded FRAL whose candidate got 2.4 percent of 1989 presidential vote

MAS   Movement Toward Socialism, founded in 1982; Peronist-Trotskyist

MDS   See URC

MID   Integration and Development movement, founded in 1963 by UCR dissidents; centrist; led by former president Frondizi and economist Rogelio Frigerio; backed Menem in 1989

Montoneros   Left-wing Peronist guerrilla movement, founded in 1969, largely wiped out by 1980; leader Mario Eduardo Firmenich extradited from Brazil in 1984, jailed on a thirty-year sentence, pardoned by President Menem in 1990

MTP   All for the Country movement, founded in 1987 by human rights activists and left-wing clergy and based on neigbhorhood-level "Committees to Defend Democracy"

PCA   Communist party of Argentina, founded in 1918, banned in 1966, semilegalized in 1973, suspended in 1976, legalized in 1983; orthodox, pro-Soviet; see FRAL and IU

PDC   Christian Democratic party, allied with Peronists' "Renewal" faction; affiliated with Christian Democratic International

PI   Intransigent party, small Socialist party founded in 1980 as UCR splitoff; backed Menem in 1989

PJ   Justicialista party, multifactioned Peronist party, founded in 1949; often formed agreements with UCR and military; led by "Renewal" faction member, President Menem

Provincial Blocs   Unsually centrist or rightist coalitions based at the provincial level in most of the twenty-two provinces

Radicals   See UCR

UCD (UCeDe)   Union of the Democratic Center, right-wing descendant of oligarchy's Conservative party, founded in 1980 and later called UCeDe; led by Alvaro Alsogaray, former finance minister for military dictatorship and Presidet Menem

UCR   Radical Civil Union, founded in 1890 (also known as Radical party, or Radicals); moderate; main factions ex-President Alfonsín's "Renovation and Change" (later MDS, or Movement for Social Democracy) and ex-Vice-President Víctor Martínez's "Córdoba Line" (center-right provincial faction)

---

cias," a sixteen-point program to stabilize the political and economic situation. A year later Alfonsín caved into IMF demands for more economic austerity. He announced the "Austral Plan" to replace the peso with a new currency called the "austral" (1 austral = 1,000 pesos). The plan was meant to adjust the economy to the reality of 1,000 percent annual inflation and a veritable collapse in the peso's value.

In one respect the Austral Plan ran counter to standard IMF practice: it froze prices. But in other respects it favored private capital. It cut real wages by 30 percent and reduced public spending by 12 percent. The IMF reciprocated with $1.2 billion in credits. By the end of 1985 manufacturing production was still declining and unemployment was up by 7.7 percent.

In 1986 a bill permitting civil divorce passed the lower house of congress. Some bishops threatened to deny communion to those who voted for the proposal. Right-wing demonstrators joined the Catholic Church's calls for "profamily" demonstrations. The Mothers and Grandmothers of the May Plaza shouted "hypocrites." Priests encouraged military school graduates to take up arms to defend Christian values, and the graduates responded by chanting *"Mucho más!"*—meaning "Many more" disappearances—counter to the human rights slogan of *"Nunca más"* ("Never again"). The 1987 Easter coup attempt and its January 1988 repeat try showed that the military was by no means "staying in the barracks." The U.S.-based human rights organization Americas Watch opined that "the officers who are gaining influence in the armed forces today are, if anything, more totalitarian and fanatic than the generation that took over the country in 1976."

Argentine voters expressed their dismay with Alfonsín's policies in the September 1987 elections. The Peronists' PJ obtained 41.6 percent of the vote and swept the governorships of Buenos Aires and most of the provinces. The UCR's vote plummeted to 37 percent. The Peronists, as in the past, feuded within their own ranks. The "Renewal" faction led by Governor-elect Antonio Cafiero of Buenos Aires Province won internal party elections in November 1987. Many "orthodox" leaders refused to accept the results. The Peronists' labor base in the CGT divided three ways.

In late 1987, the "Austral II Plan" was introduced to meet the demands of foreign creditors and combat inflation. More than Austral I, it favored private capital. It deregulated key state enterprises in petroleum, communications, the military's defense industries, and the provision of public services, opening them to private ownership. Foreign lending agencies drew up another $4 billion worth of credit packages to help bail out Argentina. A 1988 discovery of large gas and oil reserves off Tierra del Fuego caused some cautious optimism, despite renewed inflation of over 300 percent for 1988 and a foreign debt of $55 billion.

On November 4, 1987, organized labor responded to the economic crisis with its ninth general strike since Alfonsín's taking of office. The CGT used these strikes as a bargaining weapon in emergency meetings among itself, the business community, and the government. The CGT leadership was also striving to retain control over the rank and file, since workers in banking, rails, foodstuffs, construction, and the postal service conducted unauthorized protests against rising prices and inadequate wages. The continued drawing off of all available economic surplus from those least able to pay—the working people—in order to meet Argentina's debt obligations provided a dismal climate for democracy's survival.

A poll by _La Nación_ in late 1987 showed 45 percent of army officers supporting the Peronists, 25 percent the Radicals, and 20 percent smaller conservative parties. But supporting Peronists no longer meant anything very nationalist or radical, as history had shown. Peronist Governor Cafiero was a self-described Christian Democrat who reputedly had links to the right-wing Roman Catholic secret society Opus Dei. He was upset in the July 1988 Peronist primary for the presidential nomination by Carlos Saúl Menem, who also favored restructuring the party but had closer ties to labor leaders.

Menem won the May 1989 presidential contest against the Radicals' Eduardo César Angelos, a firm believer in free enterprise. Once in power, Menem proved to be more "neo-Liberal" in his economic policies than Angelos had promised to be. His economics ministers, especially Harvard-trained economist Domingo Cavallo appointed in January 1991, offered all of the state sector of the economy for sale, bringing more than $7 billion dollars of payments from Argentine, Chilean, U.S., Spanish, and French purchasers into federal and military coffers. Foreign investment capital poured into the country at the rate of $8 billion a year in 1992–93, when economic growth rates reached 8 percent and manufacturing activities increased by 12 percent. The state's majority shares in oil were privatized through "joint ventures" that allowed foreign firms up to 90 percent ownership. One-third of the nation's territory was opened up to foreign oil companies for exploration activity.

The Menem government also removed the state monopoly over social security, unemployment insurance, and retirement plans. It reduced the austral to one-thousandth of its 1985 value and then replaced it with a peso pegged one-to-one with the U.S. dollar, helping to bring inflation under control. It renegotiated the $65 billion foreign debt downward by nearly $10 billion and transferred another $13 billion of debt to private purchasers of state firms. It lifted price controls and freed up trade. Argentina joined with Brazil, Uruguay, and Paraguay to launch the Southern Cone's common market MERCOSUR (see introduction to Part Three).

When Menem took office in 1989 the economy was in such a shambles that the date of his inauguration had to be moved up by five months—a sudden upsurge in commodity prices had led to massive food riots and the declaration of a state of siege. In February 1990 Menem authorized the military to intervene in civilian affairs to control social unrest. A wave of strikes against privatization of the state sector led to his restricting the right to strike among public sector employees. Tens of thousands of workers were laid off. The government bowed to demands by the IMF and other creditors to freeze salaries and pensions. As early as 1991 the IMF announced new standby credits of over a billion dollars. There took place several marches of 70,000 or more to protest the anti-labor economic policies, including the failure of a minimum wage hike to cover more than two-fifths of a family's basic necessities. Organized labor's first general strike against the Menem government occurred in 1992.

The majority of army officers stood by the new Peronist government, even while defending the 1976–1983 dirty war as having "saved the nation." In December 1990, the military's *"Carapintadas"* (painted faces) faction launched their fourth aborted coup attempt in three years. Troops loyal to Menem crushed it.

Despite several corruption scandals rocking his administration, Menem gradually recovered his initial popularity among the electorate. With inflation under control, voters rewarded his PJ party with additional seats in congress and retention of Peronist governorships in 1991's midterm elections.

Shortly after the electoral sweep and another aborted military coup attempt, Menem pardoned and freed the leaders of the 1976–1983 dirty war. Some 50,000 people protested in vain. A few of the leaders of the several aborted coups, however, were given long prison terms. In June 1992 Buenos Aires voters cast half their votes for the Radical candidate for a Senate seat but only 32 percent for the Peronist candidate. The press interpreted the result as a rebuke of the Menem government's numerous corruption scandals and its leniency on "dirty war" criminals.

Besides establishing good relations with its neighbors and the United States, President Menem renewed diplomatic relations with Great Britain. On the tenth aniversary of the Malvinas/Falklands War, however, he said Argentina would recover the Malvinas Islands by the end of the century—albeit by diplomatic means rather than force. Despite British protests, the United States agreed in 1994 to sell Argentina thirty-six A4M Skyhawk jet attack planes with advanced radar technology. U.S.-Argentine relations were extremely cordial, mainly because of Argentina's economic policies but also because Argentina dismantled its intercontinental ballistic missile project and militarily supported U.S. troops in the Persian Gulf war and UN forces in the former Yugoslavia. Menem also approved of the U.S. hard line on Cuba and sent a negotiator to try to resolve the Haiti problem (see chapter 8 and Introduction to Part Two). Argentina resolved twenty-two border disputes with Chile (see chapter 17).

Of Syrian-Muslim extraction, Menem sought a role for Argentina in Middle Eastern affairs. He allowed the PLO to open a Buenos Aires office in November 1989. In 1992, however, a car bomb destroyed the Israeli Embassy in Buenos Aires and killed thirty persons. From Beirut, a Lebanese Shiite group, the Islamic Jihad, claimed responsibility. Two years later, a truck bomb killed more than a hundred persons and destroyed the main Jewish community center in Buenos Aires. No one took responsibility, and some suspected a domestic connection to neo-Nazi elements.

In October 1993 the Peronists swept congressional elections with 42.3 percent of the vote to the Radicals' 30 percent. This set the stage for an agreement signed in December by Menem and Radical leader Alfonsín (the president before Menem) to reform the 1853 Constitution so that Menem could run for reelection in 1995. In exchange, the Radicals were assured of having some executive powers transferred to Congress.

Only days later thousands of government employees in the northwestern province of Santiago del Estero rebelled, sacking governmnet buildings and burning government vehicles. They demanded an end to layoffs and the delivery of long-delayed paychecks for those dismissed. The revolt spread to neighboring cities and towns before a "federal interventor" and security forces restored order by the use of force and the promise of new elections in five months. Defending the rebels' cause, organized labor's Peronist CGT declared that "democracy will be a fragile artifice if it is not invigorated with a clear social content."

President Menem's PJ handily defeated the UCR in the April 1994 Constituent Assembly elections, with the big surprise being the emergence of the center-left coalition Broad Front (*Frente Grande*) as the nation's third political force. Campaigning against the high social costs of Menem's neo-liberalism, the front finished in first place in Buenos Aires.

As the politicking for the 1995 elections got underway, Argentina faced declining social conditions, including rising unemployment, and outbreaks of meningitis in greater Buenos Aires. The dirty war had pretty much destroyed the Left. The bottom-up popular movements against the earlier dictatorship had lost momentum—most of their militants were trying to survive economically or engaging in the activies of the nation's reemergent political parties. The long, dark night of military terror was over, but the dirty war's sponsors were free and the repressive apparatus was still in place. Journalists complained of physical assaults on them whenever their investigations of corruption got too close to Menem or his government. Organized labor was on a tight Peronist leash. Argentina's last "democratic" period had lasted only three years. The one initiated in 1983 surpassed that record, but for how long remained to be seen.

Selected Bibliography

Corradi, Juan E. *The Fitful Republic: Economy, Society, and Politics in Argentina*. Boulder, CO: Westview, 1985. Brief, insightful overview by Argentine sociologist.

Crassweller, Robert. *Perón and the Enigmas of Argentina*. New York: Norton, 1987. By former ITT General Counsel for Latin America.

Dabat, Alejandro, and Luis Lorenzano. *Argentina: The Malvinas and the End of Military Rule*. New York: Routledge-Verso Editions, 1984.

Fraser, Nicholas, and Marysa Navarro. *Eva Perón*. New York: Norton, 1980.

Hodges, Donald. *Argentina 1943–1976: The National Revolution and Resistance*. Albuquerque: University of New Mexico Press, 1976. An inside look at Peronism using primary sources.

———. *Argentina's "Dirty War": An Intellectual Biography*. Austin: University of Texas Press, 1991. " . . . will remain the standard resource on Argentina's modern era"—*Choice* magazine.

O'Donnell, Guillermo A. *Modernization and Bureaucratic Authoritarianism*. Berkeley: University of California Press, 1973. Early influential attempt to explain military state.

Poneman, Daniel. *Argentina Democracy on Trial*. New York: Paragon House, 1987.

Potash, Robert A. *The Army and Politics in Argentina 1928–1945, Yrigoyen to Perón*. Stanford, CA: Stanford University Press, 1969.

———. *The Army and Politics in Argentina, 1945–1962*. Stanford, CA: Stanford University Press, 1980.

Rock, David. *Authoritarian Argentina: The Nationalist Movement, Its History and Its Impact*. Berkeley: University of California Press, 1993.

Smith, Wayne S. (ed.). *Toward Resolution? The Falklands/Malvinas Dispute*. Boulder, CO: Lynne Rienner, 1991.

Timerman, Jácobo. *Prisoner Without a Name, Cell Without a Number*. New York: Knopf, 1981. By prominent Jewish victim of military regime's terror.

Walter, Richard J. *Politics and Urban Growth in Buenos Aires, 1910–1942*. New York: Cambridge University Press, 1993.

Films

Funny Little Dirty War (No habrá más pena ni olvido). 1987. 80 minutes. Color film by Héctor Olivera; English subtitles.

The Hour of the Furnaces. 1968. Award-winning three-part documentary directed by Solanas and Getino; excellent historical footage on Peronism and Argentina's wealthy elites.

Las Madres: The Mothers of the Plaza de Mayo. 1985. 60 minutes. Documentary directed by Susana Muñoz and Lourdes Portillo.

Man Facing Southeast. 1985. 105 minutes. Award-winning parable about the human condition; English subtitles.

The Official Story. 1985. 110 minutes. Oscar-winning film dramatizing Argentine elites' attempts at cover-up of complicity in military regime's reign of terror.

Only Emptiness Remains. 1984. 60 minutes. TV documentary of "Mothers and Grandmothers of the May Plaza," directed by award-winning Rodolfo Kuhn.

Perón and Evita. 1958. 25 minutes. Black and white film in CBS Twentieth Century Series.

Rio Uruguay

N

0   40 Mi.

0   40 Km.

BRAZIL

ARGENTINA

URUGUAY

Isla Martín García
(Claimed by Argentina
and Uruguay)

Rio de la Plata

Montevideo

Punta del
Este

ATLANTIC
OCEAN

Uruguay _____ 19

Few can doubt that today the Third World War is being waged.—*President Juan María Bordaberry (1972–1976)*

The market economy requires of the entrepreneur the willingness to run risks and the survival and development of the fittest. It is something similar to the "natural selection" of the Darwinian process in the biological evolution of the species.—*Minister of Economics (1974–1976) Alejandro Vegh Villegas*

In Uruguay . . . [there are] wholesale violations of human rights, including arbitrary arrest, torture, and murder of political prisoners.—*Inter-American Commission on Human Rights of the OAS, 1978*

We are the only country of our America to have slapped the face of neo-liberalism and stopped it.—*Frente Amplia's General Liber Seregni Mosquera referring to December 1992 plebiscite's 72 percent vote against privatization*

On a sunny and warm day in downtown Montevideo, Uruguay, in December 1987 there was a buzz of activity. Shirt-sleeved civil service employees, students in blue jeans, cigar-smoking shopkeepers, and scores of housewives scurried from corner to corner, shop to shop, office to office, bus stop to bus stop, sweatshop to sweatshop. Each one carried a clipboard with a petition on it.

The petitioners were on their last big push of a year-long campaign to gather enough signatures to force a public plebiscite on whether or not amnesty should be granted military personnel accused of torture and other violations of human rights. In 1986 the elected civilian government had promulgated amnesty for all military personnel before any trials even could get started. With some 600,000 signatures already obtained in earlier door-to-door canvassing, they had more than the required minimum of one-fourth of the electorate. On this day, however, they set themselves a quota to obtain one final additional "surplus" in case any signatures were invalidated by the authorities. Crowds gathered. "Sign it if you haven't, sign it!" the petitioners urged. Well-dressed bosses and senior staff members in the offices and floor managers in the sweatshops complained about "disturbing the peace." Several employees nevertheless scribbled their signatures. At the bus stops and in the crowded shopping *mercados* more people signed.

By late afternoon a huge crowd of clipboard carriers and their supporters gathered at the foot of Montevideo's Obelisk. After a half hour of agitated whispering and muttering over the stack of papers, one of the woman organizers yelled out above the noise of the cars joining the rush-hour traffic for the suburbs: "We've done it! We've met the quota!" The crowd roared its approval. Like a chain reaction, automobile horns began blaring. Street urchins set off firecrackers.

For returning exiles, Uruguay's new democracy resembled a delicate yet resilient plant. The so-called Switzerland of South America, Uruguay had boasted for most of the twentieth century of strong democratic traditions and a small, nonintervening army. But in the 1960s it had undergone militarization, and in 1973 it had fallen under the iron heel of military dictatorship. One returned exile, prominent author Eduardo Galeano, was puzzled by the public's reference to the dictatorship as "the Process." "The language," he wrote, "was, and perhaps still is, sick from fear; they have lost the healthy custom of calling a spade a spade." After the declaration of the 1986 amnesty for the very officers and soldiers who had forced him and up to one-fifth of all Uruguayans into exile, Galeano concluded:

> A responsible government is an immobilized government; its duty is to keep the latifundios and the repressive machinery intact, to forget the dictatorship's crimes and to pay punctually the interest on the foreign debt. The officers left the country in ruins, and in ruins it remains. In the village, the old people water flowers among the tombs.

On that bright summer day in 1987 there was evidence of the public's determination to never again return to the Process. Yet by the time the plebiscite was held in April of 1989 a slim majority approved the amnesty. Many feared that to revoke it might bring the military down on their heads with even greater ferocity than before. How Uruguay came to its present uncertain situation has much to do with both its history as a weak buffer state for more powerful nations and its early vigorous development of a "Swiss-style" democracy.

From Buffer State to "Swiss Democracy"

As in Argentina (see chapter 18), the conquering Spaniards found little mineral wealth in the riverlands or plains (*pampas*) of the "Eastern Shore" (*Banda Oriental*)—as tiny Uruguay was known in colonial times. Cattle were introduced in the late 1500s, and the land's grassy, rolling hills of rich black soils and a mild, damp climate early established Uruguay as a pastoral country. The Charrua Indians fought the foreign intruders in vain. Portuguese slave raids on Jesuit and Franciscan missions and eventual colonization of parts of Uruguay in the late seventeenth century forced the Spaniards to firm up their own claims by founding Montevideo, today's capital, in 1726. Fifty years later Spain sent a viceroy to Buenos Aires to check Portugal's southerly expansion from today's Brazil.

The Spanish colonial administration encouraged large private landholdings and opened Montevideo to trade in 1778. This furthered the growth of a landowner/merchant oligarchy similar to the more powerful one in neighboring Argentina. Four contending powers fought for control over the greater Río de la Plata region that incorporates today's Uruguay: the Spaniards; the Portuguese; the ascendant British mercantile-financial elite and powerful navy; and the first relatively independent regime of Latin America, the Buenos Aires municipal junta established in 1810.

Buenos Aires' ambitious Creole merchants dreamed of controlling all South America. The Uruguayans, under the leadership of a rough and brilliant *gaucho* (cowboy-cattleman) named José Gervasio Artigas, fought to establish their own self-governing autonomous nation in a loose confederation with Buenos Aires. Artigas fought the Portuguese in 1811 and then, in 1814, evicted the Buenos Aires junta from Montevideo. He proclaimed the Autonomous Government of the Eastern Provinces in 1815.

Artigas's regime began implementing an agrarian reform that distributed lands to the landless. On the principle that "the most unfortunate will be the most privileged," it favored the few remaining Indians, the *castas* (mixed races), the poor white *gauchos,* and the freed slaves (blacks today are 5 percent of the population). Artigas sought to unite all the provinces of the Río de la Plata region and to introduce protective tariffs to help local industry. Calling his soldiers "Americans," he was eventually defeated by a combination of big landowner/merchant, British, and Portuguese forces. He fled Uruguay in 1820 and died in Paraguay in 1847, a poor and lonely exile.

Portugal seized Uruguay in 1817. A group of exiled patriots in Argentina known as the "33 Orientales" returned to Uruguay in 1825 to launch the final battles for independence. They had Argentine backing. Their military victories against troops from newly independent Brazil led to Uruguayan independence in 1828. The Uruguayans owed their success also to the efforts of British mediator Lord Ponsonby, who got Brazil and Argentina to renounce their claims.

Lord Ponsonby noted Uruguay's usefulness as a buffer state. "The *Banda Oriental* contains the key," he wrote, and the British must "perpetuate a geographical division of states which would benefit England." Uruguay's first constitution was issued in 1830.

During the early years of the new republic Italian and Spanish immigrants settled the farming belts near Montevideo. Foreign powers meddled as before, while rival *caudillos* (local chieftains) launched a forty-five-year struggle for control under the banners of the Colorados (Reds) and Blancos (Whites), the names of Uruguay's two major political parties ever since. The Colorados espoused anticlericalism and a vague liberalism, but the conflicts were often more regional and personalist than ideological. In fact members of prosperous landed and merchant families often intermarried, creating a contentious but interrelated set of elites.

English, French, and Italians intervened in a raging civil war in the 1840s and early 1850s and some twenty governments came and went before the Colorados prevailed over the Blancos in 1865. They dominated the nation's politics for the next ninety-three years. In actuality, factionalism *within* each party, regionalism, and *caudillismo* prevailed during all the nineteenth and most of the twentieth centuries, whether in periods of instability or stability.

Blatant foreign interference peaked when British financiers bankrolled the 1865–1870 "War of the Triple Alliance" during which Uruguay allied with Argentina and Brazil to defeat South America's most independently prosperous nation, Paraguay (see chapters 16, 18, and 20). Uruguay's main benefit from the costly war was the preservation of its own nationhood through its alliance with stronger nations that otherwise threatened to seize its territory or run its politics.

After the war Uruguayan politics entered a new phase with the consolidation of the strong central state. Colonel Latorre put an end to much of the regional squabbling in 1876 when he seized power with the backing of the landed oligarchy's Rural Association (founded in 1871). European demand for Uruguayan wool and meat was stimulating a rapid "modernization" of the country's agroproductive and transportation facilities. A rural code sanctified private property relations, and fields were fenced. English rail and telegraph companies laid a communications grid. Technical innovations like refrigeration stimulated a massive export of Uruguayan meat. English loans flowed, and by 1900 Uruguay had South America's highest per capita debt.

Uruguay was a nation of immigrants. By 1875 more than one-quarter of the population had been born outside the country. Then European immigration escalated, bring tens of thousands of skilled and unskilled workers into the work force to help expand production. By 1889 almost half of Montevideo's population consisted of immigrants, mostly Italian and Spanish. A census in 1908 counted more than a million Uruguayans, nearly one-third of whom resided in Montevideo. Many Uruguayans spoke Spanish with an Italian (or, from earlier times, Portuguese) accent.

As in Argentina (see chapter 18), the European immigrants proved to be hard workers. Some became small-scale manufacturers and helped found the Industrial League in 1879 that by 1888 succeeded in restoring protective tariffs eliminated more than a decade earlier. Other immigrants, preaching anarchist and syndicalist ideas, launched the first strikes and later, in 1905, founded the Workers' Federation of Uruguay. Still others gained employment in the expanding banking and state bureaucracies, contributing to the growth of a proportionately large middle class and a nascent feminist movement.

By the early 1900s many Uruguayans were eating, dressing, and living better. The prosperity of Uruguay's landed and merchant elites brought about by the British-dominated trade had begun to "trickle down." These changes lent energy for political movements advocating full economic and political democracy—an equitable share of wealth and power for the nation's majority of working and middle-class people.

In 1903 a liberal-minded visionary Colorado party leader named José Batlle y Ordóñez was elected president. He crushed a rebellion by a group of Blancos who feared a Colorado monopoly of power and then, in his second presidency (1911–1915), cemented the bases for a new power-sharing system of government that would weaken the executive and make the nation a parliamentary democracy. An electoral law legislated in 1910 introduced Uruguay's unusual *lema* system, assuring that party factionalization would not rip the nation apart. The voter in national elections chose one of the two parties and at the same time a candidate of one of the party's factions—in U.S. terms, *simultaneous* primaries and final elections. The winner was the most popular candidate of the party gaining the most votes.

After a visit to Switzerland where Batlle was impressed by the collegiate system of governance he proposed eliminating the presidency. Opposition from the Blancos, the Rural Federation (established in 1915), and conservative Colorados blocked his efforts, viewed by some as a means of perpetuating *Batllismo*. The compromise solution, rooted in earlier traditions of caudillo and regional compromises and the 1910 *lema* law, was biparty government with a weakened presidency. The president would oversee foreign policy and security matters, while the nation would be governed by a strong nine-member Council (*colegiado*), one-third of whom would be from the minority party. The 1917 Constitution became the basis of Uruguay's collegiate "Swiss-style" democracy.

More notable than this political experiment was the semiwelfare statism of social reform and state intervention in the private economy introduced by Batlle and his followers. Nationalization of foreign banks, utilities, and other firms gave the state new powers and Uruguayans a sense of national pride. State enterprises sprang up in meat-packing, alcohol manufacturing, petroleum refining, telephone and port systems, insurance, and banking. Protective tariffs and easy credit terms were provided for private manufacturers, whose industrial firms multiplied tenfold from 1901 to 1930. The eight-hour day was legislated in 1915. Workers' pension funds were created, along with paid holidays and accident and unemployment compensation. The Roman Catholic Church was disestablished, and divorce was legalized. Women's suffrage was proposed in 1917 and enacted in 1932. Paid maternity leaves were established in 1934.

Over the years Uruguayans became Latin America's least religious people with the lowest rates of illiteracy, birth, and infant mortality and highest levels of social security and life expectancy. By the mid–1950s they enjoyed the highest per capita income in Latin America.

Symptomatic of the idealism behind these changes that in fact helped stabilize Uruguay was the famed literary work *Ariel,* penned in 1900 by one of Latin America's most influential writers, José Enrique Rodó (1872–1917). Rodó contrasted the lofty idealism of Ariel (Latin America) with the crass materialism of Caliban (the United States).

Strong middle-class and industrialist backing for Batlle's economic and political reforms, together with increased revenues provided by surging exports of meat, wool, and hides, helped make the reforms work until 1930. While some of the economic surplus was being transferred to the nonrural sector of the economy, the landed oligarchy's huge estates remained untouched; most peasants and rural laborers continued to live in squalor. Although opposed to Batlle's reforms, the conservative rural oligarchy could live with them since they provided social peace and left their privileges intact.

Economic Crises and the End of the "Swiss" Model of Democracy, 1930–1967

Uruguay's "Swiss" collegiate system of governance could not stave off problems created by changes in the international economy like the 1930s Depression. Nor could it cope with the costs incurred by an expensive "spoils system" of machine politics and patronage and an old-fashioned agricultural system.

A military coup in 1933 generated a new constitution in 1934 and restored the single executive. Backed by the landed oligarchy, it brought to power Gabriel Terra of a conservative faction of the Colorados. It only momentarily interrupted the course of Uruguayan political compromise, however. In 1942 a new constitution brought back outlawed factions of the two parties. A decade later not only was the collegiate system reinstituted, but the presidency was eliminated altogether (1952–1966).

Starting with the Depression and World War II, Uruguay, like most other Latin American countries, introduced import substitution in an effort to industrialize (see Overview). On the issue of the war, Blanco leader Luis Alberto Herrera supported the Fascists, whereas Colorado President Alfredo Baldomir (1938–1942) did not. In 1941 Baldomir allowed the United States to build naval and air bases in Uruguay. In 1942 he broke relations with the Axis. The United States reciprocated with generous loans that helped Uruguay stave off renewed Argentine expansionist aims being expressed during the revolutionary ferment of Juan Perón's ascent to power (see chapter 18). By 1952 the number of industrial firms in Uruguay had increased fourfold and the number of workers they employed threefold (141,000). Industry's share of GDP (gross domestic product) rose from 12.5 to 20.3 percent.

A new *Batllista*-style populism emerged after World War II under the leadership of Batlle's nephew, Luis Batlle Berres (president, 1947–1951, and head of the *colegiado,* 1955–1956). Uruguay's greatest industrialization and urbanization occurred during those years. Middle-class and worker support for "the system" was assured through ongoing state welfare benefits. The countryside was nearly depopulated, as young people rushed to Montevideo and other cities in quest of employment in industry or services. Today Uruguay is 80 percent urban.

To sustain industrialization, Uruguay had to augment its spending on expensive technology imports. During the 1950s a dropoff in state revenues caused by declining world prices and stagnated production of agricultural exports made this unfeasible. Further draining government resources was the unchecked growth in the state bureaucracy to about 170,000 employees (up threefold since 1938).

After 1955 industrial production slowed, inflation rose. Space for either economic transformation or political compromise—by then traditional Uruguayan ideals and practices—suddenly shrank.

Some Uruguayans, especially prominent landholders, bankers, and industrialists, blamed the nation's economic decline on excessive welfare statism. They proposed privatizing the economy. Other Uruguayans noted that during the 1950s the value of the peso had dropped fivefold and the value of the private sector's exports had dropped by half, making *any* economic improvement hard to imagine. Growing numbers, particularly after the revolutionary changes brought about in Fidel Castro's Cuba in 1959–1960 (see chapter 8), spoke of the need for an agrarian reform and a Socialist revolution to restructure the nation's failing political economy.

In 1958 the Blanco party won its first election in nearly a century. The Blanco government rewrote foreign exchange regulations to favor big landowners and signed an agreement with the IMF (International Monetary Fund) to favor the private sector. Nonetheless, the economy continued to stagnate. A more moderate wing of the Blancos won the 1962 elections but proved unable to cope with the faltering economy.

Political unrest accompanied Uruguay's prolonged economic downturn. Strong leftist currents emerged, especially among students, intellectuals, white-collar professionals, bank employees, and frustrated peasants and workers. In 1964 the nation's trade unions merged into the powerful CNT (National Labor Convention). Strikes became more frequent.

From 1962 to 1967 private investors sent one-quarter of a billion dollars in flight capital to overseas banks. Industrial production dropped to 50 percent of capacity. The agrarian sector continued to stagnate with failure to replenish stock, technify production, or distribute lands to the landless. Eduardo Galeano believed Uruguay suffered too great a concentration of economic power: "Five hundred families controlled half of all the land and three-quarters of the capital invested in industry and banking."

The collegiate system of biparty government also received much of the blame for Uruguay's woes. In 1966 voters restored the presidential system, turned out the Blancos, and returned a conservative wing of the Colorados to power. But economic problems remained deep-set. Workers' wages could buy only three-quarters of what they had bought a decade earlier and the annual inflation rate reached a record 125 percent in 1968. One-third of the population was living on state pensions.

The nation was entering a full-scale political crisis. Both major parties had shifted to the Right. Economic hardship had spread. Classes and groups had polarized. Many youth were calling for revolution. In the eyes of the dominant elites, the "Swiss" model of a two-party collegiate democracy had apparently outlived its usefulness.

Transition to Military Dictatorship, 1967–1973

The conservative Colorado presidency of Jorge Pacheco Areco (1967–1972) served as a transition from representative democracy to military dictatorship. In 1968 Pacheco signed a new agreement with the IMF and froze wages and prices. Labor's response was to carry out some seven thousand strikes that paralyzed the country. That same year Pacheco introduced "emergency security measures" to censor the press, ban strikes, and crack down on leftists. These antilabor measures contributed to a brief economic upturn in 1968–1970, during which foreign capital took over many bank resources. By 1972, however, new currency devaluations and increased speculation had renewed galloping inflation and plunged wages to pre-1950 levels.

During the same period numerous people suspected of harboring "subversives" or advocating labor strikes were rounded up and thrown in jail. In 1970 a bipartisan congressional commission observed that "The application of tortures in different forms is a normal, frequent, and habitual occurrence."

Left-wing guerrilla activity became a serious problem during this time. In 1967 Raúl Sendic of Uruguay's small Socialist party, frustrated by government repression of his organizing endeavors among sugarcane workers, founded the MLN (National Liberation movement), or Tupamaro urban guer-rillas. In raids on business, government, and foreign embassy offices the "Tupas," as they became known, captured documents that exposed widespread corruption among businesspeople and politicians. The Tupas' spectacular bank robberies and kidnappings of high officials, including the British ambas-sador, evoked counterattacks from the military, the police, and ultra-rightist "death squads." Almost overnight, Uruguay's "stable" peaceful democracy re-sembled a wartorn urban battlefield.

The Tupamaros were composed mostly of middle-class young adults en-amored of the Cuban Revolution and Marxist ideas, including numerous Christian radicals advocating the "theology of liberation" (see Overview). Lacking a social base in the nation's ongoing workers' movements, they were not able to withstand the intense government offensive.

Most radical workers, students, intellectuals, parties, and even factions of the two main parties opted for the electoral road to power by forming the Broad Front (Frente Amplia) to contest the 1971 elections. The Broad Front challenged the two-party *lema* system by bringing together ideologically di-verse currents, including Christian Democrats, Socialists, and Communists. The Left got around the problem of not having an established party with its own *lema* by having Broad Front candidates run on lists under the banner of the "moderate" Christian Democratic party. Far more inclusive than Chile's newly elected left-wing Popular Unity alliance, the Broad Front shared its op-timistic spirit of a new politics (see Overview and chapter 17). On the other hand, it resembled the Blancos and Colorados in the catchall, multiclass, mul-tifactioned character of its membership.

Prior to the 1971 elections the Tupamaros publicly issued a cease-fire and declared their conditional support for the Broad Front. In the elections the Broad Front had a smaller campaign chest and less chance for media attention than did the traditional parties. Nonetheless, its presidential candidate, former Colorado General Liber Seregni Mosquera, obtained an impressive one-fifth of the vote, making it the nation's third largest political formation. Cattle-rancher Juan María Bordaberry, an ultrarightist Colorado, was declared the victor by a slim margin over Blanco candidate Wilson Ferreira Aldunate, a populist who campaigned for agrarian reform and nationalization of banking. Most observers viewed the vote count as fraudulent.

A contingency plan of the Brazilian military dictatorship known as "Thirty-Hour Operation" was shelved. It called for a Brazil-backed military coup in case of a Broad Front victory. Brazilian generals kept a heavy hand in Uruguayan affairs throughout the early 1970s, advising Uruguayan officers on their 1973 military coup. Afterward the Bank of Brazil expanded its role in Uruguay's economy, while Brazilian landowners bought up chunks of prime Uruguayan farmland.

In 1972 several general strikes and mass mobilizations protested the stepped-up militarization of society. Although weakened and in decline, the Tupamaros carried out further actions. Except for the Broad Front representatives, congress voted a "State of Internal War" in April 1972. This act granted the military unlimited powers, in effect turning the government over to the officers. Public protest, nonetheless, continued, as did military and police repression. By early 1973 the armed forces were able to declare the Tupamaros "completely destroyed."

The military brass was opposed not only to "Communist subversion," but also to liberal democracy. As thousands of frightened Uruguayans raced for exile, the officers completed their gradual coup with President Bordaberry's support. In June 1973 they made their year-long rule official by dismissing the congress. They banned left-wing organizations, declared the Colorado and Blanco parties "in recess," closed the National University, and instituted press censorship. With the aid of its Brazilian allies, the Uruguayan military crushed a general strike called to protest the 1973 coup.

There were no reported strikes for the next decade. Free-trade unions were smashed and the CNT was banned. Leaders of workers in education, construction, commerce, transportation, banking, public services, and industry were jailed or forced into exile. Public employees were classified "A," "B," or "C," according to their views; many were fired. Teachers were dismissed wholesale.

The post-1973 military regime stripped major political leaders of their rights. It jailed Broad Front presidential candidate Seregni, released him in 1974, reimprisoned him in 1978, and did not release him again until 1984. Blanco presidential aspirant Ferreira escaped to exile, returned in 1984, and then was jailed until after the holding of the 1984 elections.

Military Dictatorship, 1973–1985, and the Role of U.S. Aid

The 1973 coup initiated a twelve–year military dictatorship and the bloodiest political persecution in the nation's history (although not so violent as that in Chile or Argentina). Bordaberry remained president for three years, ruling by decree on behalf of the military.

In 1976 Bordaberry proposed eliminating Uruguay's parties and establishing a permanent corporativist system of government. This proposal elicited little support in the military, whose officers recognized that most Uruguayans were too accustomed to voting to surrender all hopes of ever going to the polls again.

The military ousted Bordaberry in a coup and appointed a figurehead president. In a series of "Institutional Acts" reminiscent of those following the 1964 Brazilian coup (see chapter 20) it banned all political parties, prohibited

15,000 former politicians from political activity for up to fifteen years, stripped the judiciary of its independent powers, and reorganized public education and the welfare system. But the military still spoke of an eventual return to an elected "representative" government. At the time, according to the respected human rights organization Amnesty International, Uruguay had more political prisoners per capita than any other nation.

U.S. economic aid to Uruguay was never great and U.S. private investments were only about 1 percent of the total in the rest of Latin America. Nonetheless, U.S. aid increased dramatically under the right-wing presidencies of Pacheco and Bordaberry (1967–1976). The United States had at least an indirect role in making the military takeover possible. The "Nixon Doctrine" of strengthening "regional influentials" to police neighboring countries (see Overview) was implemented in Uruguay's 1973 coup via the Brazilian military dictatorship's collaboration. Also, while U.S. economic aid helped sustain IMF-style programs favorable to private banking and industry, U.S. military aid significantly expanded Uruguay's small armed forces that until the late 1960s had rarely intervened directly in political affairs.

Totalling $137 million for the 1962–1977 period, U.S. economic aid jumped from $6.5 million in 1971 to $10 million in 1974. An IMF loan that year reportedly saved the military regime from bankruptcy. More than 2,800 Uruguayan military personnel were trained under U.S. programs from 1950 to 1977, U.S. military assistance, which approximated $50 million from 1962 to 1977, radically increased in 1972, the year of the final offensive against the Tupamaros. The sale of U.S. military equipment increased seventeenfold in the early 1970s, compared to the annual averages of the 1950s and 1960s, reaching an annual peak of $8.2 million in 1975.

The influence of CIA operatives in Uruguay's increasing loss of democracy and emergent "long, dark night" of state terrorism (see Overview) later became public knowledge through unshredded state documents and former agents' memoirs like Philip Agee's _Inside the Company_. Some CIA agents were close to President Bordaberry.

The role of U.S. officials like Dan Mitrione, a police officer employed by the AID (Agency for International Development), who trained torturers in Brazil (see chapter 20) and Uruguay, became known as early as 1970 when the Tupamaros captured and executed him (subject of the widely heralded Costa Gavras film _State of Siege_). A police photographer seized by the Tupamaros in 1972 also provided evidence of U.S. complicity in torture, fingering William Cantrell, a U.S. public safety advisor whom he had often accompanied to police installations. Like ex-CIA operative Agee, the police photographer noted that Uruguayan police and military officers routinely ordered murders and bombings in order to create public fear and to make it appear as though the Tupamaros were responsible.

The U.S. Congress was sufficiently shocked by such revelations to terminate the AID public safety, police-training program in 1974 and military aid to Uruguay in 1977. Military aid was partially restored in 1979 and more fully renewed during the 1980s under President Ronald Reagan. Numerous first-hand testimonies revealed a complex but fairly well-coordinated web of intelligence and international terrorist work conducted out of the offices of the CIA, the U.S. embassies in Montevideo and Buenos Aires, and the governments of all the "southern cone" nations of South America. Typical of the international "cooperation" was the 1976 kidnapping and murder in Buenos Aires, Argentina, of Uruguayan ex-senator Zelmar Michelini and ex-president of the Chamber of Deputies Héctor Gutiérrez Ruiz, a widely investigated event that caused world outrage.

Uruguay's military had 45,000 members in 1976, or 3 percent of the economically active population (the police numbered about 20,000). Known as "milicos," military personnel lacked prestige. Low salaries and the absence of conscription meant that most who chose a military career were unable to complete a university education and came from lower- or middle-class families.

Governing behind a civilian façade, the "fourteen generals" of the army who effectively ruled Uruguay from 1973 to 1985 had few differences other than the degrees of their right-wing extremism and personal ambition. They lacked the full-blown economic development plans of Brazil's more sophisticated and powerful officer corps and instead echoed the national security hysteria of Generals Videla of Argentina and Pinochet of Chile (see chapters 17, 18, and 20) in their statements about—to use President Bordaberry's formulation—the "Third World War" against subversion. Like their civilian predecessors, Uruguay's officers fattened at the public trough, some retiring as millionaires. Firing state employees suspected of leftism, the generals established their own patronage system of loyal followers. They doubled the armed forces' salaries and increased the military's share of the national budget from about 8 percent in the 1960s to more than 50 percent in the late 1970s, or about 8 percent of GDP (gross domestic product).

In the course of the twelve-year dictatorship one of every fifty Uruguayans was detained at least once. People were arrested for raising their voices when singing the "tyrants tremble" portion of the national anthem. Some spent up to eight years in jail without a trial.

The cruelty of Uruguay's dictatorship elicited worldwide condemnation. Among the most commonly used torture techniques were "the stake" (hooded prisoner kept standing); "the telephone" (striking of ears with palms of hand); "electrification" (shock to parts of body); "the submarine" (submerging of head in tanks of foul water); "the horse" (a variation on the medieval rack); "hanging" (by the wrists with metal wire); "mock execution"; "rape" (by torturers, sticks, fists); and "the grill" (binding of prisoner to barbecue grill). Relatives of suspected "subversives," especially women and children, were also submitted to torture, kidnappings, and "disappearances."

Favored targets of the fourteen generals were intellectuals and journalists. Cultural repression reached shocking heights in a nation known for its contributions to world literature, art, and music. More than half a million books were burned. The works of Freud, Marx, Chilean poet Pablo Neruda, and Uruguayan literary giants like Mario Benedetti were proscribed. Well-known novelist Juan Carlos Onetti was placed in an insane asylum. The contemporary songs of Daniel Viglietti and other renowned Uruguayan folksingers were banned. Thirty newspapers were shut down. Magazines read throughout Latin America, like Montevideo's *Marcha,* were closed down. Journalists were jailed or exiled. The national university was purged of most of its faculty, not only in the social sciences and humanities, but also in the physical sciences, including engineering, mathematics, and agronomy. Primary and secondary school students had to write essays on subjects like "My parents' opinions."

Worsening Economic Conditions, New Politics, and Elections

Living conditions deteriorated under military rule. As a result of the IMF-fostered "free-market" policies and loss of trade-union rights, income was redistributed upward. By 1979 some 13 percent of the population received 40 percent of total income. Real wages had plummeted 44 percent since 1971. Industrial accidents averaged 76 per five hundred workers, and some 57 percent of workers in Montevideo were working more than twelve hours a day. Rent controls were abolished, and a three-bedroom apartment sold at more than $150,000. Foreign banks accounted for more than three-fourths of the nation's banking resources.

Uruguayan industrial exports of finished leather and wool products (shoes and textiles) rose impressively in the late 1970s, when the nation experienced annual GDP growth rates of 5 percent, but the worldwide recession in the early 1980s hit Uruguay hard. Argentine investors withdrew their dollars from the lavish real-estate construction boom in the beach-resort city of Punta del Este. Uruguay's GDP plummeted by nearly 20 percent from 1981 to 1983. Unemployment in 1984 stood at an estimated 15 percent of the work force. The foreign debt zipped past $5 billion, or five times the nation's export earnings—an immense sum for a population of 3.1 million, nearly half of whom resided in Montevideo. In 1988, Uruguay's creditors granted a six-year grace period on one-third of the debt.

The 1980s also witnessed a series of sharp reversals for the powerful dictatorship and a reinvigoration of the "new politics" that had surfaced in

Uruguay in the 1960s prior to the dictatorship. New organizations of students, trade-union leaders, and housing cooperatives began to emerge. A medical society was founded to investigate doctors' collaboration with torture. Most Uruguayan youth had been raised under total dictatorship and knew little of earlier times. They were not so active as older Uruguayans who eagerly collaborated with the different political parties and leaders to move the country back to some form of democracy.

In November of 1980 the military received a startling setback. On very short notice it sought to cement its rule by holding a plebiscite on a new constitution. The document provided for a transition to a civilian government in which there would be only one presidential candidate and real power would remain in the hands of a National Security Council and military courts. Despite the military's $20 million publicity campaign for a "yes" vote in the plebiscite, people voted "no" by a 57 to 43 percent margin. Then, in 1981, the regime was rocked by a scandal involving kickbacks and gambling.

In 1982 the military allowed primary elections within the Blanco and Colorado parties but prohibited left-wing parties from participating. Voter turnout was low. Three-fourths of the votes went to candidates opposed to any form of continued military rule.

The year 1983 witnessed several bold illegal strikes and demonstrations against the government. In August the government banned media coverage of all political activities. Later in the year, hundreds of thousands marched in Montevideo to demand democratic elections and the release of political prisoners. The rally was organized by the "Interpartidaria," a new alliance incorporating the major parties (see Box 19.1) and the still illegal Left.

Repression reescalated, yet in January 1984 the newly founded PIT (Inter-Union Workers' Plenary), a confederation of 150 trade unions, organized the nation's first general strike since the coup. The government dissolved PIT. Public protest continued, as Uruguayans took hope from Argentina's "return to democracy" (see chapter 18).

In May 1984 the Broad Front's leader General Seregni was released from prison. The following month, Blanco populist leader Wilson Ferreira Aldunate and his son returned from exile and were arrested. On June 27, 1984, the eleventh anniversary of the military coup, a general strike paralyzed the nation.

In July and August 1984 the Blancos, resenting Ferreira's imprisonment, abstained from negotiations of a new agreement to return Uruguay to some form of elected government. The so-called Naval Club Accords, negotiated by the military, the Colorados, and most of the Broad Front, provided for a return to democracy without the military-proposed National Security Council. Financial elites, fearing the populism of the Blancos' Ferreira, threw their support to the Colorados. Elections for a president and a congress were called for November.

In November 1984 Julio María Sanguinetti of the Colorados was elected president, with a vote count that resembled the last democratic election of 1971. This time, however, the more moderate and progressive factions of the Colorados had gained the upper hand over the right-wing of the party, which ran former president Pacheco for the presidency. President-elect Sanguinetti had served in the cabinets of both Pacheco and Bordaberry.

Broad Front leader Seregni, Blanco leader Ferreira, and Communists were not allowed to participate in the 1984 elections, although their parties (the Communists inside the Broad Front) were. The Broad Front garnered 20.4 percent of the vote, compared to the Blancos' 32.9 percent, the Colorados' 38.6 percent, and the Civic Union's (a right-wing splitoff faction from the Christian Democratic party) 2.3 percent. After the elections Ferreira was re-leased from jail. He called for the maintenance of "governability" in Uruguay, warning against any return to military rule and yet expressing his willingness to compromise.

The Broad Front echoed his sentiments. It had improved its vote count over 1971 and, in the eyes of some observers, was emerging as a more centrist "loyal opposition." Because of the Broad Front's remarkable perseverance and vote-getting abilities, Uruguay's two-party system had become a three-party system. The 1984 election showed an immense support for democratic institu-

---

Box 19.1: Uruguay's Political Parties

Frente Amplio	Broad Front, founded in 1971, left-wing alliance of a dozen groups, including Christian Democrats, Communists, Socialists, former Tupamaros, and Blanco and Colorado factions
MLN	National Liberation movement (Tupamaros), left-wing urban guerrilla movement, founded in 1967, defeated 1972–1973, renounced armed struggle 1985 to become legal political party
Partido Blanco	Blanco party, founded 1836, Conservative, multifactioned; moved to Left-center under Wilson Ferreira Aldunate, who died in 1988, then to Right-center under President Lacalle; also called National party
Partido Colorado	Colorado party, founded 1836, liberal, multifactioned; moved to Right in 1970s–1990s
PCU	Communist party of Uruguay, founded in 1920, made illegal in 1973, legalized in 1985; strong in unions, part of Broad Front, but divided between orthodox and reformist wings
PDC	Christian Democratic party, founded in 1962, left-center; part of Broad Front
PSU	Socialist party of Uruguay, founded in 1910, elected Tabaré Vázquez Montevideo mayor in 1989, major partner in Broad Front in 1990s
UC	Civic Union, Christian Democrat splitoff, right-wing, founded in 1971

tions—part of the new politics in Latin America of citizens of diverse ideological persuasion stating a firm belief in democratic rule as opposed to military state-terror rule.

After the military warned that it would stage another coup if the new government proved unable to control the country, President Sanguinetti was allowed to take office on March 1, 1985. Public pressure obligated him to restore diplomatic relations with Cuba and to legalize outlawed organizations and permit a free press, fulfilling the main points of the opposition's demands for a full return to the 1967 Constitution. Uruguay signed an IMF agreement in 1986, and a year later the IMF praised the nation's progress.

The military dictatorship had broken the old welfare system, and one-quarter of all Uruguayans depended on pensions only a fraction of their former worth. Inflation remained at better than 60 percent a year. In mid-1988 organized labor's PIT-CNT (Inter-Union Workers' Plenary-National Labor Convention) launched its sixth twenty-four-hour general strike since Sanguinetti took office.

During the late 1980s Uruguay's Left reemerged as the major force inside student and worker organizations, contested only by Blanco populists, whose leader Ferreira died of cancer in March 1988. The ruling Colorado party sought to depoliticize the scene. Reports of a meeting in May 1987 between the president and the army alleged that the generals had ruled out letting the Broad Front take power by electoral means.

In 1989's national elections, the Blancos' right-center candidate, forty-eight-year-old senator Luis Alberto Lacalle, won the presidency. His party garnered 38 percent of the vote. The Broad Front finished a not-so-distant third behind the Colorados, improving by two points its 1984 vote percentage. Voters swept into office the Front's candidate for mayor of Montevideo, Dr. Tabaré Vázquez, a popular forty-nine-year-old cancer specialist and moderate Socialist.

Lacking a majority in congress, President Lacalle formed a short-lived coalition government with the Colorados. Although he had campaigned as a pragmatist who would preserve much of the emasculated social welfare system, he introduced a neo-liberal economic program of privatization, favorable conditions for foreign investment, and renegotiation of the $6.5 billion foreign debt. The IMF, World Bank, and other foreign creditors poured in loans to help finance debt relief. Annual GDP growth rates rose from around 1 percent in 1989 to 7 percent in 1992, but then dropped back to under 2 percent in 1993 and 1994. The more than 50 percent inflation rate caused real wages to drop. Organized labor's PIT-CNT responded with five more general strikes. Angry Uruguayans demanded a referendum on Lacalle's economic program. In a 1992 plebiscite they voted by nearly three-to-one against privatization. By 1993 Lacalle had the support only of his own faction of the

Blanco party and the right-wing Colorado faction led by ex-President Pacheco Areco, who in the early 1970s had eased the military's way into power.

In foreign policy, President Lacalle cooperated with the United States on antinarcotics legal assistance programs but did not modify Uruguay's financial secrecy laws that made the nation's banks notorious for their laundering of dollars from the drug trade. Pushing free trade, Lacalle took Uruguay into the Southern Cone's incipient common market MERCOSUR, where it faced growing trade deficits with the more powerful and productive Argentina and Brazil. The president also backed the Paraná-Paraguay Waterway project (see the introduction to Part Three) and approved a privately owned free-trade zone for Montevideo.

The "Operation Condor" scandal (see Introduction to Part Three) escalated tensions with Chile and undermined people's belief in Uruguay's having truly moved out from under the military's control over its partially restored democracy. The Broad Front showed its wariness by claiming it would be satisfied to win only the Montevideo mayoralty in the November 1994 national elections, which it did. In August, police opened fire on PIT-CNT demonstrators, killing two and wounding dozens. In a three-way photo-finish, former President Julio Sanguinetti of the Colorados won the national election by barely one percentage point over the Blancos' National party and the Broad Front's "Encuentro Progresista" (Progessive Meeting). Uruguay's underlying problems still demanded solutions.

Selected Bibliography

Fitzgibbon, Russell H. *Uruguay, Portrait of a Democracy.* New Brunswick, NJ: Rutgers University Press, 1954.

Fynch, Martin H. J. *A Political Economy of Uruguay Since 1970.* New York: St. Martin, 1981.

Kaufman, Edy. *Uruguay in Transition: From Civilian to Military Rule.* New Brunswick, NJ: Transaction, 1979.

Latin American Bureau. *Uruguay Generals Rule.* London, England: LAB, 1980.

Latin American Review of Books. *Generals and Tupamaros.* London, England: LARB, 1974.

Servicio Paz y Justicia—Uruguay. *Uruguay Nunca Más: Human Rights Violations 1972–1985.* Trans. by Elizabeth Hampsten. Philadelphia, PA: Temple University Press, 1993.

Street, John. *Artigas and the Emancipation of Uruguay. Cambridge, MA:* Harvard University Press, 1969.

Vanger, Milton I. *José Batlle y Ordóñez, The Creator of His Times, 1902–1907.* Cambridge, MA: Harvard University Press, 1963.

Weinstein, Martin. *Uruguay: Democracy at the Crossroads.* Boulder, CO: Westview, 1988.

Films

Eduardo Uruguayo. 1983. 45 minutes. Color video from Icarus Films showing a family's life
　　since early 1970s.
State of Siege. 1973 Costa Gavras film about Tupamaros and AID torture-trainer Mitrione.
Welcome to Uruguay. 1982. 25 minutes. Color video from Icarus Films on human rights.

Brazil 20

They cleared the forest and invaded the Indian land. We used to be 700 Indians; now we are a little over 400.—*Suruí Indian, 1974*

Organized soon after the 1964 coup, the Death Squad began by assassinating delinquents and "marginalized" people, whose bodies were left in the streets with notices and slogans aimed at terrorizing those who saw them. A one-year-old baby was given electric shocks in the presence of her father. The father threw himself at the torturer and was immediately killed.—*Bertrand Russell II, Tribunal on Latin America, 1974*

It is necessary to defeat capitalism, for this is the greatest evil. What's needed is the social ownership of the means of production, the factories, the land, the businesses and the banks.—*"Marginalization of a People" proclamation signed by Archbishop of Goiás and Bishops of the Midwest, 1974*

They have the capacity to laugh. They're alive, they're oppressed, and they're sometimes massacred, but they're not dead.—*Jorge Amado, seventy-five-year-old dean of Brazilian novelists, on Brazil's people, 1988*

Without Fear of Being Happy.—*Campaign slogan of popular leftist presidential candidate "Lula," 1989*

My life is like the wind. Nothing can stop it blowing away.—*Rusty, one of Brazil's 10 million street children, 1990*

At around ten o'clock one evening in 1965 a typical middle-class apartment's living room in Mexico City filled up with about fifty people sipping everything from South American yerba mate tea to Caribbean rum. They spoke a babel of tongues—mostly Brazilian Portuguese, but also Spanish, French, and English. Some wore the collar of the Catholic Church, some wore Indian ponchos, but most looked like students, teachers, and workers gathering after a day's work. Except for the Mexicans, all were political refugees from Latin America's military dictatorships. They were in a state of obvious excitement.

In the middle of the hubbub someone cried out that the two guests of honor had just pulled up in a taxi from the airport. The two needed no introduction. They had gained fame as successful organizers of peasants and slumdwellers in Brazil's northeast, one of the most impoverished areas in the world. As the result of an international campaign, they had both just been released from the prisons of South America's first of a fresh wave of military dictatorships and allowed to fly to safe refuge in Mexico. One was known simply as "Julião," a Marxist lawyer, the other as "Padre Lage," a priest.

People made space for the two men to sit in two cushioned chairs at the center of the room. Then, refusing offers of drinks but asking for "just water, thanks," they sat down.

There was a long silence. The two men gazed out over the crowd, which gaped back. Julião was short and gaunt. Padre Lage was large and plump. Julião nervously moved his hands, puffed a cigarette, darted his head to the left and right to survey the room. Padre Lage folded his hands and bowed his head.

Finally a young Brazilian student broke the silence by asking them if they were all right, if they needed anything.

Speaking simultaneously, they gave fulsome expressions of thanks but added "No, no, no." Padre Lage added, "Please give us just a minute to absorb this moment of new life."

Nervous laughter, sighs, silence.

Then, Julião and Padre Lage asked the crowd: "Well, how would you like to proceed?"

Someone shouted "Tell us about conditions in the prisons!"

Simultaneously, they shook their heads "No, oh no, not that, please."

Then, in low intense voices, they said they'd rather talk about the situation in Brazil and Latin America.

There was visible disappointment on the faces of some of the Brazilian students who still had friends languishing in the year-old dictatorship's jails, rumored to be "high-tech" torture chambers, but people politely said "Yes," "Of course."

The two men's analysis that followed was spellbinding in its originality and passion. Not much whispered simultaneous translating of their Portuguese was necessary. At one point the lawyer and priest began to exchange glances of surprise at what they were hearing one another say.

Julião, the Marxist, was sketching the hunger and misery of Brazil's poor. He was describing how the government and big landholders violently kicked millions of peasant squatters and smallholders off their lands and how they had to migrate to the cities. There, they crammed into unsanitary *favelas* (hillside shacks) and *cortisos* (downtown high-rise tenements). Julião's words resembled a sermon, poetically pleading for what he insisted was "a necessary option for the poor"—a paraphrase of the famous Vatican doctrine behind Latin America's nascent "theology of liberation" (see Overview).

For his part, Padre Lage was describing the international economy. He warned his audience that "In the capital flows and new loans that turn us into debtor nations and surplus labor pools, we see the future of our America." Backing up his exegesis on political economy with facts and figures about

U.S., European, and Japanese "transnational corporations" and the World Bank, the priest used phrases like "the dialectic," "the new industrial proletariat," and "imperialism." Not a trace of catechism or even sermonizing could be detected in his words. The few priests present strained to follow the flow of his statistics and class analysis. A veteran Marxist labor organizer from Mexico yawned.

A number of people in the room were beginning to whisper, when Julião interrupted Padre Lage to snap:

"Hey! Wait a minute! Who's the Marxist here, you or me?"

The room broke into laughter and applause.

The good-natured priest snapped back:

"And you? Who do you think you are anyway? A priest?"

Amidst cascades of laughter, the two men embraced.

There followed countless questions and answers. As people said their "good nights" and filed out of the apartment, they shook their heads and whispered, "Something new is going on here in our America, something different . . ."

The world's seventh largest economy and fifth largest country, Brazil was the first South American nation to experience the iron heel of military dictatorship (1964) that ushered in the region's "long dark night" of state-sponsored terror (see Overview)—and the last to replace it with an elected civilian government (1985). Sporting natural resources like iron ore, bauxite, gold, silver, uranium, copper, nickel, niobium, chromium, manganese, quartz, and newly discovered petroleum, Brazil had Latin America's largest population—an estimated 157 million by 1993, nearly twice Mexico's. During the early 1970s the military regime's high economic growth rates were trumpeted as a "miracle." In the 1980s and early 1990s, however, because of a $114 billion foreign debt (the Third World's highest), galloping inflation approaching 5,000 percent a year, unemployment of more than 15 percent, and two world recessions, the miracle was rebaptized a "crisis."

The government acknowledged that for three-fifths of Brazilians the wage of the main family breadwinner averaged less than $100 *a year* even though annual *per capita* income was over $2,000. These families lived in "absolute misery," their children usually out of school wandering the streets. Three-fourths of Brazilians were malnourished. In 1992–93 there were food riots in the biggest central and southern cities as well as the more rural Northeast, hard hit by a drought. Yet Brazil produced more than enough grains to meet the entire population's nutritional needs. Nearly a third of Brazilians were illiterate. Only 50 percent of Brazilian households had electricity and 29 percent home plumbing. Seven percent of infants died before their first birthday, an infant mortality rate double that of Mexico. More than one-third of the adult population suffered from tuberculosis and more than 40 million Brazilians had parasitic diseases. One study indicated that the income of the wealthiest 1 percent of Brazilians equaled that of the poorest 50 percent.

Internal World Bank reports stated that most health, education, housing, and other "social benefits" went to the better-off people. Homelessness was widespread; squatters were routinely driven away from unused lots or buildings. In some agricultural areas, debt peonage tantamount to slavery was common. Government programs to correct the imbalance were failing. According to World Bank internal reports, even recent tax reforms left the system "regressive." Government corruption was so widespread that in 1992 the nation's president was impeached and a year later several dozen congressmen faced possible dismissal. A University of São Paulo researcher concluded: "If policy changes were introduced at the highest levels of decision making in Brazil, then many changes would follow at the level of [social] programs, both in their design and management."

The bottom-up popular resistance movement that toppled the dictatorship in the early 1980s was a fulfillment of the type of cross-class, cross-ideological alliance being passionately discussed in that Mexico City living room back in 1965. It incorporated major currents of Latin America's "new politics"—the "new labor militancy," the theology of liberation, the disenchanted middle classes, and the increasing political activism of women, Indians, and the urban poor.

Even though the military outlawed every basic right, slum dwellers along the edges of the southern industrial hub of São Paulo, aided by lawyers and priests, set up neighborhood committees in 1976–1977 to demand legal title to the homes they had built on lands owned by real-estate developers. Half of São Paulo's 11 million people lived there. Then, from 1978 to 1980, illegal trade unions sparked a series of strikes that involved millions. As more and more people took courage from the bold job actions of metallurgical and automotive workers in São Paulo, a two-fisted political alliance took shape. Broad, informal, sometimes confused but always disciplined, it brought together secular leftists and liberals, on the one hand, and politicized religious people, on the other. Together, their ranks filled by citizens from all walks of life, they marshaled the largest peaceful street demonstrations seen anywhere in the world in recent years (see photo).

In cities and towns throughout the land, millions chanted one simple slogan, "*directas já!*"—direct democratic elections instead of the limited democracy being offered by the military and, after 1985, its successor civilian regime. To understand both the successes and the limitations of this popular movement, however, one must first examine Brazil's authoritarian legacies from earlier times.

Authoritarian Traditions: Colony, Independence, and Empire

From its discovery in 1500 by Portugal's Pedro Alvares Cabral, Brazil became a Portuguese variant of Iberian colonialism. Most of its authoritarian traditions resembled South America's (see chapters 1, 14, and 18). These included governmental corruption and patronage; patriarchical family structures; *compadrio* (godfathership); paternalistic and personalistic patron-client forms of social interaction; the power of regional *caudilhos* (bosses); and state organizing and regulating of entire groups (corporativism).

Brazil too developed an export-oriented monoculture—timber and dye-woods in the sixteenth century; sugar in the seventeenth century; and sugar, cotton, gold, and diamonds in the eighteenth century. Its colonists too killed or enslaved the Indians. Brazil too developed a landholding oligarchy, known as *fazendeiros* (owners of large estates). Its colonial authorities too expelled the Jesuits after they formed colonies to defend fleeing Indians, oppose slave-runners, and harness local labor (see chapter 16). And Brazil also imported African slaves—two-thirds of its nearly 4 million people by 1822.

Because of the harsh treatment they received, slaves lived an average of only seven years after arriving in Brazil. Like Cuba, Brazil had a tradition of runaway slaves who set up their own communities (*quilombos*). The most famous of these, Palmares, was destroyed by Portuguese troops at the end of the seventeenth century.

Brazil also experienced pirate attacks and the consequences of shifting foreign power balances. The Dutch seized Pernambuco in 1630 and extended their growing control over Brazilian sugar trade. Since Portugal was bogged down in the intra-Iberian conflict of reclaiming its independence from Spain (1640), it was the Brazilian settlers who led the pro-Catholic, anti-Protestant guerrilla campaigns that eventually expelled the Dutch (1654). These victories of the settlers, like their conquest of Brazil's western frontier lands, laid lasting roots for nationalism and popular culture.

By 1700 the English were captains of the seas and anxious to dictate Brazil's future. By then, Brazil's *bandeirantes*—frontiersmen of mixed white/African/Indian stock—had pushed inland and discovered gold, diamonds, and other mineral wealth in the hills of Minas Gerais, Goiás, and Mato Grosso. From 1700 to 1800 Brazil became the world's top gold and diamond producer.

Brazil also experienced "precursor revolts" against the "mother country," although not so many as in Spanish America—partly because of the huge distances separating Brazilian settlements and the milder rule of Portugal. Brazil's regionally based plantation, mining, and trading elites held immense power over the rest of the population. When slaves, peasants, or workers rose up, they were quickly subdued or packed off to new "colonies" in the interior, a tactic still in use.

The most serious popular revolt occurred in 1788 in the central mining area of Minas Gerais. Its jack-of-all-trades leader was known as "Tiradentes" (tooth-puller—one of his several trades), but his actual name was Joaquim José da Silva Xavier. The quickly crushed "Revolt of Tiradentes" incorporated armed miners and tradesmen and called for the abolition of slavery, the creation of a university, the building of factories, and national independence.

Brazil's colonist elite feared revolt from below the same way elites did throughout Latin America. They also resented royal taxes and recognized the greater profits to be made from "free trade" with Europe's emergent industrial giant, Great Britain. The nascent middle classes of intellectuals, professionals, and tradesmen in the cities and bigger towns shared the elites' disdain for *os massas* (the masses) and increasingly expressed anticolonialist sentiments.

When independence did come to Brazil, it was bloodless and much less turbulent than the devastating wars that shook the rest of Latin America. After Napoleon's armies invaded Portugal in 1807 the Brazil fleet escorted Prince Regent Dom João VI from Lisbon to Rio de Janeiro, establishing Rio as the seat of Portugal's empire. Britain consolidated its influence in Brazil with a treaty signed in 1810 that granted it tariff rates lower than Portugal's. João VI and his royal entourage soon built new schools and military defense installations. In 1816 João VI was crowned ruler of "the United Kingdom of Portugal, Brazil, and the Algarves." When liberal parliamentarians seized power in Lisbon in 1820 Britain advised João VI to rush home and save his throne. He left behind as regent his twenty-three-year-old son Pedro with the sage counsel, "If Brazil demands independence, grant it, but put the crown upon your own head."

Brazil's conservative elites and nationalist intellectuals, led by Prince Pedro's Minister of Interior José Bonifácio de Andrada e Silva, preferred independence to governance by Lisbon's liberal parliament. So did Pedro, whose powers were rapidly being usurped by Lisbon. On September 7, 1822, Pedro stood on the banks of the Ypiranga River and, ripping the Portuguese flag, declared "Independence or Death!" Portuguese troops resisted in Bahia, but proindependence Brazilians, backed by British ships under the command of Lord Cochrane, defeated them.

An independent Brazil became Latin America's only hereditary constitutional monarchy. Pedro was crowned Pedro I, Emperor of Brazil, December 1, 1822, and a constitution was promulgated in 1824. It conferred upon the monarch the *poder moderador,* or "moderating power." This proved to be an authoritarian way of controlling conflicts among the legislative, judicial, and executive branches of government and an early precedent for centralized, corporatist rule that subsequent twentieth-century governments refined to a fine art. The real moderating power turned out to be the military—first during the empire, then the oligarchic republic (1891–1930), then the Vargas era (1930–1954), then the final years of populism (1955–1964), and finally the "national security state" (1964–1985) and its successor, the "nova republica" (new republic), initiated in 1985.

Brazil's 1824–1889 constitutional monarchy, like later forms of the state, served elite interests well. During the late 1840s, for example, it violently broke up utopian-Socialist communities set up by rebellious artisans and workers in Pernambuco. It also crushed republican movements against centralized authority in 1817 and 1831–1835. Although some plantation and mine owners backed regional revolts, they soon settled for the rotation in power of the two political parties they and other elites controlled, the Liberals and the Conservatives.

Brazil's central government grew more powerful in the 1840s when a coffee "boom" furnished monies to beef up the armed forces. Brazilian coffee accounted for half the world market in 1850 and three-fourths of it by 1900. Coffee revenues helped provide military security for vested landholding, mining, and merchant interests against potential lower-class revolt.

Brazil's elite families enjoyed the free-trade benefits of exporting sugar, cotton, coffee, hides, cacao, tobacco, rubber, and other primary products to Europe and North America in exchange for finished manufactures and luxury goods. The main foreign beneficiary was Great Britain. Foreign Secretary George Canning's vision of the 1820s for Latin America could well be applied to Brazil, "England will be the world's workshop, and Latin America its farm."

The extremely bloody 1865–1870 "War of the Triple Alliance," provoked by a series of Brazilian military raids into Uruguay dating from the 1850s that worried the rulers of prosperous Paraguay, expanded Brazil's frontiers deep into Paraguay but cost Brazil 50,000 lives and $300 million (see chapter 16). Funded by English loans, the war left the nation in debt and created new contenders for political power, including a victorious military "establishment" wanting more pay and status.

The Roman Catholic Church also had grievances against the emperor, Pedro II (1840–1889), who had jailed two bishops for enforcing an 1865 papal ban on Freemasonry. The Church in Brazil, unlike the rest of Latin America, had rarely clashed with the secret order of Freemasonry, some of whose members were clergymen.

An antislavery abolitionist movement also grew stronger after the war. Many desperate coffee growers opted for the successful abolition bill of 1888, hoping to stem the flight of their slaves to the cities and to create a more secure wage-labor force of field hands. Urban artisans and intellectuals called for more democracy. Miners and tradesmen demanded fairer treatment.

Oligarchic *fazendeiros* viewed the entire scene with dismay and contemplated replacing the monarchy with a more decentralized political system. Since social discontent was on the rise and the emperor had no male heir, the time was ripe for a change in the political system.

Oligarchic First Republic and Personalist Politics, 1891–1930

Military officers decided they should step in as the *poder moderador*. They seized power in 1889, exiled Pedro II, disbanded the two political parties, and eventually allowed a new constitution to be drafted creating the First Republic (also known as "the old Republic"). The authoritarian and hopeful slogan of the new system was emblazoned on the national flag: *"Ordem a Progresso,"* or Order and Progress. This reflected the "positivist" ideology that for decades had been spreading from Europe into all of Latin America. The main idea of positivism was that progress would inevitably come as a result of a rationally ordered world—a notion consonant with the free-trade/industrialization economic doctrines prevalent at the time.

Brazil's 1891 Constitution spoke a modern, republican language, as opposed to a traditionalist, monarchical one. It perpetuated authoritarianism while updating it. It eliminated the moderating power clause so crucial for preserving the monarchy and opened the way to political domination by the actual economic powers, the regional oligarchies.

After a shaky start during which warships from Great Britain, the United States, France, Italy, and Portugal patrolled offshore, the First Republic eventually stabilized, rotating the presidency between natives of São Paulo and Minas Gerais. The coffee barons of São Paulo and the cattle ranchers and mine owners of Minas Gerais had long since superseded the slave-dependent sugar, cotton, tobacco, and cacao *fazendeiros* of the Northeast.

Thus commenced the oligarchic republic known as "the period of the governors," 1891–1930. It was dominated by state-level regional parties that set up federal patronage systems, increased the power of the *fazendeiros* and the agroexport oligarchy, and ruled through "democratic" elections in which less than 3 percent of Brazilians were allowed to vote. Personalist traditions of political power were reinforced by local political bosses known as *coroneis* (colonels), who were the heads of rural landowning clans and often officers in state militias. Their *jaguncos* (hired gunmen) kept peasants in a state of near-feudal bondage. The *coroneis* allied themselves with state governors who in turn had connections with federal officials. Some states grew so autonomous that they took out foreign loans and built up militias stronger even than local army posts. Ever since, Brazil's states financed and administered numerous social and economic programs.

In 1898 Brazil's government, recognizing the power of foreign bankers, renegotiated its foreign debt in London. Foreign investors rushed into Brazil the way they did elsewhere in Latin America. In the case of the rubber barons they left behind South America's most incongruously ornate opera house in the sweltering inland Amazon River city of Manaus. Brazil's fabulous rubber boom collapsed when world production shifted to Malaysia and the East Indies during the 1910s.

U.S. economic influence gradually surpassed England's, accounting for half of Brazil's imports during World War I. U.S. loans increased during the 1920s, shifting the weight of foreign banking from London to New York. Some of the local oligarchies, particularly São Paulo's, took an interest in industrialization. They intermarried with European investors and imported foreign labor and "know-how." Believing that white Europeans were superior to the "ignorant and rebellious dark masses," Brazil's elites sought to "whiten" the nation. Both the monarchy and the First Republic paid for the importation of millions of Europeans, a third of them Italians. The famed 1897 massacre of the rural religious settlement of Canudos in the northeast backlands flowed logically from the elites' insistence on maintaining both economic and racial "supremacy." In the massacre, the military slaughtered as many as 35,000 devout and independent-minded people of mixed-race descent. The killing of darker skinned people unwilling to do the elites' bidding runs like a blood-red thread through the fabric of Brazilian history to the present. In the early 1990s there even surfaced a white secessionist movement to create the Republic of the Pampas in the lush southern farmlands of Santa Cruz do Sul, settled by German immigrants a century earlier.

The huge influx of immigrants, peaking in 1913, contributed to Brazil's diverse ethnic composition—about 52 percent European; 40 percent mixed European, Indian, and African; 6 percent black; and 2 percent "other," including over a million Japanese, whose descendants were recruited to replace slave labor on the coffee plantations and went on, like some of the Germans, to become efficient small farmers for urban food-processing plants. Most newcomers were Roman Catholic, leaving the Church in a strong position of having many "souls" despite the permeation of society by African religious customs. Spiritism, or the belief in spirit mediums, often having a surprisingly "rational" scientific approach of its own, still affects significant numbers of Brazilian intellectuals and politicians. Culturally, spiritist sects like Candomblé influence half the populace and dominate Brazil's annual Lenten three-day "Carnaval" of dance and song.

Other factors besides immigration contributed to Brazil's early attempts at industrializing. These included the nation's conversion to wage labor after the end of slavery; the consolidation of local industries like salted beef and textiles; and the momentary suspension of imported manufactures during World War I, forcing the country to fall back upon its own resources.

Paradoxically, expanded coffee production did not decrease the Brazilian government's drive toward industrialization. Plummeting international coffee prices during the 1890–1910 period caused the Paulistas (as people from São Paulo were called) to welcome state intervention to shore up their interests through the purchasing and warehousing of coffee at inflated prices. This strengthened the state's hand in the economy. At the same time Brazil's currency declined in value, a fact that made manufactured imports more costly and thus encouraged the development of Brazilian industries.

Brazil's agroexport oligarchy, with overlapping interests in local manufactures, refused to tolerate labor unions. General strikes in 1917 and 1919 were crushed; their anarchist and Socialist leaders were jailed or deported. Accustomed to near-total power, the oligarchs resisted demands for greater political representation coming from several labor organizers, junior military officers, urban professionals, and new industrialists.

Consequently, during the 1920s social movements for change erupted. In the mid-1920s, junior officers sparked several revolts, the last of which was commanded by Luis Carlos Prestes. He led a long guerrilla march across mountains and jungles to Bolivia, spreading the ideals of universal suffrage, labor unionism, antiforeigner nationalism, and Socialist-type reforms. The military snuffed out this "lieutenants" or *tenentes* movement, but its ideals gained widespread approval in the 1930s.

When the Great Depression hit Brazil in 1929–30 the oligarchs found their economic power undercut by a collapse in the coffee market. Hungry tenant farmers and sharecroppers joined unemployed workers to demand federal relief. The opportunity for a successful political coalition of industrialists, trade unionists, junior officers, and middle-class nationalists was at hand.

Corporativism and Populism: The Vargas Era, 1930–1954

A civilian-military coalition toppled the "old Republic" and introduced an authoritarian system that eliminated elections most Brazilians viewed as fraudulent to begin with. The new system was led by Getúlio Vargas, a short, bespectacled man from a southern ranching family who spoke poorly and made sardonic jokes. Vargas started his career in the army, got a law degree, and became a state governor in the late 1920s. As Brazil's new president, he gather around him a group of liberal intellectuals and dedicated reformers, including survivors of the *tenentes* movement.

Because of the many reforms he introduced, Vargas was popular. He was even able to walk the streets without bodyguards. People called him simply "Getúlio." His reforms included the vote for eighteen-year-olds and working women (but not illiterates, the majority of the population); social security; an eight-hour workday; a minimum wage; legality for trade unions and the right to strike; construction of schools; and a career civil service based on merit.

When not coopting opposition movements by bringing their leaders or their programs into the government, Vargas and the military put them down. Thus in 1932 he swiftly ended a revolt by Paulista oligarchs. A big landowner himself, Vargas wanted Brazil to industrialize. In 1935 he crushed an uprising by a popular front of Socialists, former *tenentes,* and Communists. He arrested 15,000 and jailed the popular Prestes, by then a member of the PCB (Brazilian Communist party, founded in 1922). Prestes was not released until 1945. Several leftist prisoners died under torture. In 1938 Vargas personally opened fire on Fascists attacking the presidential palace. They were a handful of fanatics from the outlawed Integralist movement sponsored by Hitler's Nazi Germany and some of the oligarchy.

Vargas moved erratically between reformism and repression, elections and coups, finally consolidating his power in 1937 by creating the "Estado Novo," or New State. It curtailed "states' rights" that had favored the regional oligarchies. It banned strikes and lockouts. Vargas's centralized, authoritarian system of governance, like Perón's in Argentina (see chapter 18), was classically populist and corporativist (see Overview). In the name of "class harmony" and "the nation" it promised something for everyone and incorporated the two main groups of society—employers and workers—into "sindicatos" under state regulation and tutelage. By claiming to place national above regional or class-based interests, Vargas was able to steer Brazil down the road of industrialization without seriously disrupting existing power relationships.

Vargas and his successors increased the state's role in the economy. Compared with foreign investors, Brazil's oligarchs and industrialists were too cautious or too weak to lead the way. As foreign capitalists turned their attention to resolving the Depression and producing for World War II, Brazil expanded its manufacturing industry for the internal market. By 1941 the number of manufacturing plants was triple the number in 1920 and employed nearly a million workers. Vargas, although he spoke like a nationalist, welcomed foreign investment. In 1940 foreign capital still accounted for nearly half of Brazil's stockholdings.

Internationally, Vargas expanded trade with Germany and then told the United States that Germany was anxious to set up a steel industry in Brazil. In this way he obtained a U.S. loan to help finance construction of the National Steel Company (1941). He also took the U.S. side in World War II, during which U.S. training and arms shipments helped convert Brazil's armed forces into a powerful military machine. Vargas set up government enterprises to produce engines, trucks, materials for the chemical industry, armaments, ships.

After World War II Brazilians in the trade unions, private industry, and the middle classes clamored for their democratic rights. Proclaiming an amnesty for political prisoners, Vargas called national elections. Then he threatened to expropriate "national or foreign enterprises known to be connected with associations, trusts, or cartels." U.S. Ambassador Adolph A. Berle, Jr., later to become a prominent voice in President John F. Kennedy's Alliance for Progress, reacted by proclaiming U.S. interest in an end to Vargas's "*Estado Novo*" and a return to parliamentary democracy.

On October 29, 1945, conservative military officers ousted Vargas and set up national elections for a parliamentary system. General Eurico Dutra, a coup leader, won the elections and served as president from 1945 to 1951. Dutra's government broke relations with the Soviet Union, outlawed the PCB, purged the military of nationalist elements, and launched a witch hunt against reformers and leftists. It sent "interventors" to take over trade unions. It squandered Brazil's foreign exchange reserves that were accumulated during the war by allowing unchecked imports of consumer and luxury goods. It threw open the doors to foreign capital. Direct U.S. investments tripled to nearly a billion dollars in 1951.

In the 1950 elections Vargas, as popular as ever, won the presidency. He ran as the candidate of the PTB (Brazilian Labor party) and had the backing of most workers, some industrialists, and many from the intermediate classes. During his second presidency (1950–1954) Vargas renewed his campaign to have the state lead Brazil to the modern industrial age. He established the National Economic Development Bank (1952) and state oil company Petrobras (1953). But his every move was watched suspiciously by the conservative military and Brazil's free-enterprise elites. The right-wing press lambasted him as a "dictator."

According to Gilberto Freyre, a prominent Brazilian intellectual known for his anti-Vargas positions, Vargas asked him in 1954 to help map out an agrarian reform that would expropriate the big estates of the *fazendeiros*. That may have been Vargas's final undoing.

On August 24, 1954, the military told the seventy-two-year-old Vargas he must resign or be deposed. Vargas chose suicide instead. He left behind a note denouncing foreign capital's "looting of Brazil."

Populism's Last Gasp, 1954–1964

In some ways Getúlio Vargas' personalist populism, known as *Getulismo,* had more impact after his death than before. Vargas left behind a more industrialized Brazil and a powerful legacy of political appeal to *os massas.* To obtain votes, politicians had to "measure up" to his standards and take stands on the issues of nationalism and reform.

Numerous parties with populist-tinted, confused programs contested the 1955 elections. The PTB-backed ticket of Juscelino Kubitschek for president and João Goulart for vice-president won. Because of his having favored the trade unions and better wages during his short stint as labor minister in 1953, Goulart received many more votes than Kubitschek.

President Kubitschek (1956–1961) launched an ambitious industrialization program based on extremely favorable terms for new foreign investments, which poured into Brazil. U.S. investments reached $1.5 billion by 1960. Foreign capital accounted for more than two-thirds of the largest thirty-four companies. Those Brazilian industrialists who could not compete dropped by the wayside. Most became junior partners, or "associates," of the more powerful foreign capitalists. Kubitschek shifted Brazil's capital from Rio de Janeiro to the newly created interior city of Brasilia. He was a "big spender" who left behind a burdensome foreign debt and runaway inflation amidst charges of widespread corruption.

In the 1960 elections conservatives backed a flamboyant former governor of São Paulo, Jânio da Silva Quadros, whose banner was a broom to sweep the thieves out of government. He won and took office in 1961. Goulart was easily reelected vice-president. President Quadros played his populist cards. He renewed diplomatic relations with the Soviet Union and opposed the U.S.-backed Bay of Pigs invasion of Cuba. On the other hand, like Kubitschek, he favored U.S. investment and did little to satisfy the needs of the lower classes. Nonetheless, his conservative backers began to view him as unreliable and used their power in parliament to block any hint of reform. One reason conservatives were so nervous was that the model of the Cuban Revolution posed a challenge to populism and corporativism. Cuba's leaders actually carried through on their promises of "delivering the goods" to the lower classes. Their arming of the people made Brazil's military shudder.

Unable to deal with Brazil's turbulent situation, President Quadros resigned in August 1961 with a declaration that echoed Vargas's condemnation of powerful foreign interests. His successor, Vice-President Goulart, was a centrist millionaire rancher thought to be influenced by his more radical brother-in-law, engineer Leonel Brizola. As governor of the southern state of Rio Grande do Sul, Brizola had expropriated an ITT phone company. Conservatives agreed to Goulart's succession to the vacated presidency only after passing a constitutional amendment limiting the powers of the executive.

During the 1961–1964 period of Goulart's presidency the influential UNE (National Union of Students, founded in 1938) broke its corporativist bonds and moved far to the Left of Goulart. Landless and smallholding peasants of the Northeast organized more than two-thousand "peasant leagues" with one-quarter of a million members. Rank-and-file workers responded to declines in their purchasing power by striking. Trade-union bureaucrats had to drive harder economic bargains with populist politicians.

In 1962 the CIA spent $20 million on the electoral campaigns of "anti-Communist" candidates for state offices and congress. Goulart found himself hamstrung by the constitutional amendment limiting his powers. A stronger executive would be able to decree some of the reforms he contemplated, such as agrarian reform, nationalization of select industries, and legalization of the Communists' PCB.

Hoping to marshall popular support for a 1963 plebiscite renewing a strong executive, Goulart encouraged protest marches in the streets. He apparently assumed he could keep them under state-corporativist control. In 1962 his party, the PTB, together with the Communists, founded the CGT (General Confederation of Labor). The CGT soon incorporated most of the Northeast's "peasant leagues." Ever since the Vargas era Brazil's trade unions had depended on partial government financing. They had been required to register with the state and submit to state intervention in union affairs. The CGT perpetuated this corporativist tradition, serving both to mobilize popular support for Goulart and to keep rank-and-file militants under state control.

Inflation and an economic recession placed Goulart in a perilous situation. The elites' opposition and U.S. pressures to "go slow" only compounded his difficulties as a centrist politician in a polarizing society. Even though he proclaimed his opposition to the Castro regime in Cuba, Goulart was viewed by many in the military officer corps as a firebrand radical populist like Brizola, a "dangerous leftist." The officers used their considerable power to limit the ability of striking workers to win economic demands, breaking strikes here, forcing unfavorable settlements there (and, on one occasion, forcing an employer to grant workers handsome wage increments). Independent or non-Communist leftists, radical prolabor Catholics, and many "Fidelista" youth—as those caught up in the new radicalism emanating from Havana were called—saw Goulart as a typical populist politician who had to be forced to carry through on his reform promises.

The end result of all these irreconcilable conflicts was that under Goulart Brazilian populism exhausted its possibilities. On January 1, 1963, Goulart won the plebiscite strengthening the executive. Soon thereafter the U.S. government cut off economic aid. Businesspeople sent their capital overseas.

When the CGT supported Left-oriented dissenters in the army in early 1964 the officers stepped in with a carefully prepared military coup. The rumbling of tanks and the prompt arrest of 40,000 moderates and nationalists, including more than eighty congressmen, spelled doom for the vaguely defined "political center" of Brazilian populism.

The 1964 Coup, U.S. Role, and National Security State

At first the military coup of April 1, 1964, elicited little popular resistance. Since the military had been acting as "the moderating power" for generations, many Brazilians assumed it would return the government to civilians after a short time.

But the top brass had no such intention. It aimed to eliminate "internal subversion" once and for all. In the name of a "revolution" for democracy it imposed press censorship, shut down left-wing publications, and prohibited the innovative teaching techniques introduced by Paulo Freyre in his internationally renowned book, *Pedagogy of the Oppressed*. It banned almost all political activity, outlawing the old parties and creating two new ones: the ARENA (National Renovation Alliance) and the MDB (Brazilian Democratic movement). In this way it created a democratic façade of a two-party system. The ARENA masqueraded as the government party and the MDB as the "loyal opposition." Regular elections were conducted in which only these two parties could field candidates. For the next fifteen years the top two-hundred military officers named the ARENA's candidate for the presidency.

Some Brazilians endorsed the coup wholeheartedly. Industrialists welcomed an end to strikes. Technocrats anticipated having a greater say-so in a more stable and efficient system. Well-off urban residents frightened by the street mobilizations and the sight of poor people getting organized gave a collective sigh of relief. Many shared the anti-Communist hysteria trumpeted by the conservative mass media. The powerful *Globo* media empire of Roberto Marinho, which got its start through Time-Life subsidies, became the unofficial "voice" of the military dictatorship. Today it is a mega-company controlling much of the media, including the highly popular television soap operas ("novelas") that dramatize modern themes with a conservative slant. *Globo* empresario and octogenarian Marinho is viewed by some as Brazil's "power behind the scenes" since he routinely makes "pacts" with military officers, presidents, senators, and deputies.

Brazil's well-armed military easily abolished more than half of the peasant leagues and sent "interventors" to take over the rest. It expelled the majority of elected trade-union officials and replaced them with interventors. Workers lost their rights to bargain collectively or to call strikes.

Foreign investors saw the coup as a good thing. In 1964 Goulart was on the verge of gaining Supreme Court approval for expropriating Hanna Mining Company's iron ore mines in Minas Gerais. The U.S. business magazine *Fortune* observed in 1965 that for Hanna the military coup resembled "a last minute rescue by the 1st Cavalry."

The influential U.S. role in the 1964 Brazilian coup, hotly disputed at the time, became documented when researchers delved into the presidential libraries and archives of the Kennedy and Johnson presidencies. The CIA, Pentagon, and State Department coordinated a "destabilization" campaign and preparation of a civilian/military base for the coup. U.S. military attaché Vernon Walters, a CIA veteran troubleshooter and later President Ronald Reagan's UN ambassador, coordinated matters with the Brazilian military. Coup plotters received assurances of U.S. troop intervention "if needed." U.S. battleships and aircraft carriers stood offshore, awaiting orders from U.S. Ambassador Lincoln Gordon. The head of the U.S.-funded AIFLD (American Institute for Free Labor Development—see Overview) told the U.S. Senate Foreign Relations Committee in 1968 that the coup "was planned months in advance" and that "many of the trade-union leaders" involved in the coup "were actually trained in our institute."

During the first eight years of Brazil's military dictatorship the U.S. government and U.S.-dominated international lending agencies extended almost $5 billion in aid to Brazil. Most top U.S. policymakers viewed the Brazilian coup of 1964 and its aftermath as an unfortunate but necessary continentwide break with the reformist option of the Alliance for Progress and a firmer commitment to military counterinsurgency, repression and stable conditions for foreign investment (see Overview).

U.S. techniques first implemented in Brazil were later perfected in the destabilization of other South American populist or reformist governments—most notably, Chile (see chapter 17). The U.S. government also knew about and condoned the Brazilian military government's introduction of "high-tech" torture techniques against its political opponents. Surviving victims of torture testified to the presence of U.S. civilian and military advisers at their torture sessions, not only in Brazil but in other countries, such as Uruguay (see chapter 19). A São Paulo dentist recalled in 1972: "[I] was made to sit in the 'dragon's chair,' on a metal plate, with hands and feet tied and electric wires connected to my body touching my tongue, ears, eyes, wrists, breasts and genital organs."

Brazil's coup marked a new stage in Latin America history, even as the Cuban Revolution did. Its "dirty war" against its opponents became one of many dirty wars spreading across the continent's landscape. In the 1970s Brazil provided logistical and financial support to the military coups in Bolivia, Uruguay, Chile, and Argentina. Brazil's military trained other countries' intelligence units and cooperated in the detention of exiled "subversives" (see chapters 15 through 19 and Introduction to Part Three).

The key figures in the "Brazilian national security state model," as it became known, were officers from the ESG (Superior War College), founded in 1949 with the assistance of U.S. and French advisers. ESG graduates staffed almost all the important posts of Brazil's post-1964 military regime. The regime's slogan of "security with development" reflected the ESG doctrine of economically developing Brazil by means of associating Brazilian private and state capital with foreign capital while maintaining internal security from the "enemy within" (supposedly communism).

General Golbery do Couto e Silva, a president of a Brazilian subsidiary of Dow Chemical (in the late 1960s widely censured for its production of na-palm for the Vietnam War) and a key spokesman for the military regime, often talked of a "master plan." This blueprint, he said, had a "manifest destiny" component that viewed Brazil as a geographically expanding power. Indeed, the government's "moving frontiers" doctrine led to indirect military interventions in Uruguay (see chapter 19) and the sending of troops into the greater Amazon region and neighboring Paraguay (see chapter 16).

Besides the army's standing on constant alert to repress the first signs of social unrest or political dissent, death squads swung into action to instill an atmosphere of terror. The most famous was the Esquadrão da Morte (Death Squad), founded in 1964 by policemen and said to have assassinated more than one thousand "undesirables" in the late 1960s. Criminal elements prospered under the new system. São Paulo Police Chief Sergio Fleury oversaw a death squad and a narcotics ring. Rio de Janeiro's Nova Iguacu suburb was run by organized crime.

The 1964 coup provoked deep splits in Brazil's Left, many of whose members suffered the regime's tortures. The PCB divided into squabbling factions (see Box 20.1). A few daring urban guerrilla groups sprang up, the most significant of which was led by Carlos Marighela, a former member of the PCB. His group kidnapped an American ambassador in September 1969 and exchanged him for fifteen political prisoners. Marighela was shot and killed by police in late 1969. After that the military snuffed out the remnants of urban guerrilla warfare.

Box 20.1: Brazil's Political Parties, Labor, and Other Organizations

ARENA	National Renovation Alliance, one of two parties created by military dictatorship; progovernment, became PDS in 1980
CGT	General Confederation of Labor, founded in 1962, dominated by PTB and PCB; a moderate trade-union body, strong in utilities, transport, and, since 1987, metallurgy
CNCT	National Coordinating Body of Working Classes, a PMDB-led trade-union movement
CONTAG	Federation of Agricultural Unions; CGT-dominated; 6.8 million members
CUT	United Confederation of Workers, created in 1983 by independent trade unions, close to PT
Esquadrão da Morte	Death squad, founded in 1964 by policemen
Green party	Small environmentalist party, formed in 1989, led by Professor and Deputy Fernando Gabeira
Mao Branca	White Hand, right-wing death squad
MDB	Brazilian Democratic movement, one of two parties created by military dictatorship; the "loyal opposition"; dissolved in 1980 mostly into PMDB

(Continued on next page)

643

Box 20.1 *(Continued)*

MNC	National Constituent movement, founded in 1985 by representatives of Catholic church, PDT, PMDB, PT, and student and trade unions to press for a democratic constitution
Movemento Brasil S.A.	Brazil Movement Inc., founded in 1992 by 1,200 big industrialists; proprivatization
PCB	Brazilian Communist party, founded in 1922, banned most of its life; its longtime leader Prestes expelled in 1984 as too leftist; Euro-Communist and pro-Soviet Union, it rejected Stalinism in 1991
PC do B	Communist party of Brazil, founded in 1961 as Maoist splitoff from PCB; banned; first pro-Chinese, then pro-Albanian; won five seats in Chamber of Deputies 1990
PDS	Democratic/Social party, created by government in 1980 to replace ARENA; far Right; split in 1984, losing key members to PFL
PDT	Democratic Labor party, founded in 1980 as heir to PTB, centrist and Social Democratic, led by Brizola who won Rio de Janeiro governorship in 1990
PFL	Liberal Front party, founded in 1984, right-of-center, led by ex-PDS leader President José Sarney (1985–1990); largest progovernment group in Chamber of Deputies early 1992
PMDB	Party of the Brazilian Democratic movement, founded in 1980 by centrist members of MDB and later joined by ex-members of ARENA, including 1985 president-elect Neves; wide range of ideologies, including leftist MUP (Movement of Progressive Unity); won congressional majority in 1986, plurality 1990
PRN	National Reconstruction party, created in 1989 as campaign vehicle for victorious presidential candidate Collor de Mello, won 8 percent of congressional seats 1990
PSDB	Party of Brazilian Social Democracy, formed in 1988 by center-left congressional deputies from PMDB, including (1993) Finance Minister Fernando Henrique Cardoso, plus others from PDS, PFL, PTB, and small PSB (Brazilian Socialist party); Cardoso became center-right candidate for presidency in 1994
PTB	Brazilian Labor party, founded in 1945; held presidency, 1961–1964; small after founding of PT and PDT
PT	Workers' party, independent party founded in 1978 by ex-members of PTB and leaders of CUT; left-reformist, often repressed; led by "Lula," who almost won 1989 election; with ten major factions and 600,000 members, it opted in 1991 for cooperation with both Socialists and non-Socialists and in 1994 ran Lula on a centrist platform
Running Horses	Death squad of two former military policemen from Congress and dozens of other military policemen behind 1993 Rio slum massacres
UNE	National Union of Students, founded in 1938, shut down in 1964, reorganized in late 1970s

Economic "Miracle" and Social Changes

Brazil's business community no longer ruled through civilian politicians. It did not even have much input into the military government. Its right to govern had been reduced to its right to make money. And make money it did!

The military's economic "master plan" imposed an IMF-style "stabilization" program that had the effect of redistributing income upward to the wealthy elites and better-paid segments of the middle classes, mostly administrators and technocrats. It froze wages and outlawed strikes. Less than half the labor force earned the minimum wage, which in turn lagged behind inflation. The government revoked job security and safety laws and allowed the rotation of workers through frequent hirings and firings. Car companies and other producers of durable consumer goods simply exchanged one another's workers, starting each new group at the minimum wage. Workplace injuries were five times the rate in the United States.

Annual GNP (gross national product) growth rates approached 10 percent from 1968 to 1973. The government boasted of an "economic miracle." The nation became a semi-industrial giant capable of exporting manufactured goods. Brazil led Latin America in the production of automobiles, chemicals, computers, and steel. It started up its own space satellite program. It became the world's fifth largest arms seller—$2 billion worth in 1985—falling to tenth in 1989 ($1.5 billion, or less than 3 percent of U.S. arms sales).

As a result of the nation's stepped-up pace of industrialization, Brazil's blue-collar working class grew by leaps and bounds, soon accounting for one-quarter of the work force. In the industrial hub of São Paulo, counting the so-called ABC factory-zone suburbs, there were 600,000 metalworkers alone—80,000 of them employed by Ford, Volkswagen, and Mercedes-Benz. The majority of São Paulo's expanded working class were first-or-second-generation migrants, recognizable by their brown faces typical of the nation's impoverished Northeast.

In 1987 less than 30 percent of the population remained rural. One-fourth of all workers in agriculture and industry were unionized, many by dint of their own persistent efforts. Most remained under the firm control of government interventors and employers. Women made up 27 percent of the paid labor force—a majority of them in domestic service. An estimated one-fourth of adult women were unpaid agricultural workers.

The military's economic policies were based on making land distribution even more lopsided than before in order to encourage large-scale production of export crops and to "release" peasants from the countryside to supply the cities with a growing pool of laborers. From this pool employers could draw desperate people willing to work for a pittance to help the nation industrialize.

The SUDENE (Regional Development Superintendency for the Northeast) granted 40 percent of its tax incentive to *foreign* corporations, claiming that some 28 million underfed people in the region would benefit. Instead, land concentration worsened, agribusiness boomed, and desperate people flocked from the Northeast's semiarid *sertão* to the cities. While the majority of its citizens went barefoot, malnourished, and dressed in rags, Brazil exported shoes (mostly to the United States), orange juice, and textiles. It became the world's second largest agricultural exporter and the leading producer of coffee and sugarcane.

In the southern soya and coffee states of São Paulo, Paraná, and Rio Grande do Sul, where 80 percent of the nation's tractors operated, most peasants and small farmers became wage workers. There still existed *posseiros* (landless peasants, land squatters, and colonists), *colonos* (tenant farmers), and *meeiros* (sharecroppers), especially in the Northeast, West, and center of the country. Even there the trend was conversion to rural wage labor, often debt peonage.

The first military president, General Humberto Castello Branco, implemented an agrarian reform program that sought to create a more modern agriculture. It was not unlike a land reform ex-president Goulart had decreed three weeks prior to the 1964 coup. At its peak, 1967–1969, some two thousand families received land. Tax incentives and loans at low or negative interest rates served to create "rural enterprises" and expand the *fazendeiros'* holdings. In the 1970s development of fuel based on sugar-derived alcohol proved profitable for sugar plantation owners.

The old landed oligarchy either modernized or lost out to modern agribusinesses. Foreigners took over Brazil's food-processing industry and much of its agricultural production for export, including the marketing of soybeans, orange juice, and meat. Exported to feed Japanese and European livestock, soybeans became Brazil's leading export as coffee fell to 6.6 percent by 1988. According to the Brazilian Institute of Economics and U.S. Department of Agriculture, hunger spread from one-third to two-thirds of Brazil's population. Landowners and animals fattened while people grew thinner. In order to produce for export to foreign markets, farmers stopped planting traditional food crops like black beans, manioc, and potatoes. They still planted corn, a traditional food, because it was for export. Black beans, the protein-laden staple of the Brazilian diet, became so scarce that in 1976, during municipal elections, Rio de Janeiro voters cast 200,000 write-in ballots for "Black Beans." With the world's fourth largest cattle herd, most Brazilians could not afford to eat meat.

The military dictatorship facilitated the penetration of Brazil by foreign-based TNCs (transnational corporations) and the relative "denationalization" of Brazil's economy. The finance ministry's declared policy of "constructive bankruptcy" forced local companies to sell to foreign investors or go broke. Among the largest twenty TNCs investing in Brazil were the U.S. firms of Alcoa, Anderson Clayton, Atlantic Richfield, Ford, General Electric, General Motors, Johnson & Johnson, Union Carbide, and U.S. Steel. Germany was also heavily represented.

By 1971 foreign corporations controlled the heights of industry and fourteen of the twenty-seven largest firms in Brazil; the state owned eight and private Brazilian capital five. During the preceding seven years, for every dollar invested foreign investors took out of Brazil $3.50 in profit remittances and royalty, interest, "intellectual property rights," and other payments. By 1979, according to a government financial agency in charge of acquiring heavy machinery, 57 percent of all industry was controlled by TNCs, 22 percent by private Brazilian firms, and 21 percent by state enterprises.

A U.S. scholar called this tripartite control of the economy a "triple alliance" dominated by foreign capital. Brazilians called it "a tripod." One Brazilian analyst claimed that the government's economic policies were guided by a "globalist" faction of the "state bourgeoisie"—the tiny techno-bureaucracy involved in managing state corporate investments and the federal budget. Members of this globalist faction were anxious to share in the TNCs' benefits from an increasingly internationalized system of production of which state investments were a part.

The state, while usually favoring foreign capital, also defended its own economic interests when necessary. For example, the government refused a request by Alcan to mine and export bauxite deposits in the Trombetas River area of the Amazon Basin, opting instead for a "joint venture" with Alcan (19 percent) and private Brazilian capital. It also played one foreign power off against another, as in the case of its 1975 nuclear-energy contracts with West Germany that drew U.S. criticism. In the 1970s Brazil imported more from the Soviet bloc than any other Latin American country except Cuba. Because of U.S. criticisms of its human rights record, in 1977 the dictatorship canceled Brazil's 1952 military assistance treaty with the United States. In early 1984, President Reagan signed a new military cooperation agreement.

Broad Opposition and the New Politics

The breadth and depth of the military regime's political repression made it almost impossible to organize a popular opposition movement. Nonetheless, there soon appeared signs of popular discontent, often, as in neighboring Uruguay (see chapter 19), subtly expressed in the lyrics of songs and intonations of voices. In 1966 a group of newly elected MDB deputies formed a caucus favoring democratization. Castelo Branco's successor, Marshal Arthur da Costa e Silva (1967–1969), promised to restore democratic rule within the parameters of authoritarian constitutions (1967, 1969) and the artificial two-party system. Opposition grew bolder and more widespread after that. It surfaced spontaneously from the ranks of civilian politicians, students, workers, and the Catholic Church.

In 1967 two former state governors who had played a central role in the plotting of the coup against Goulart and then objected to the military's restrictions on their own political activities helped organize the "Frente Amplia," or Broad Front. They gained the support of former presidents Kubitschek and Goulart. The government banned the Broad Front in April 1968.

The students' outlawed UNE held secret meetings. They organized public rallies to protest the government's wholesale firings of professors and to denounce the military's "university reform" being implemented under a 1966 agreement with the U.S. AID (Agency for International Development). These rallies evoked the wrath of the military police. A sixteen-year-old high school student fell dead from police machine-gun fire on March 28, 1968. Some 30,000 attended the student's funeral mass on April 4 at Rio de Janeiro's Candelaria Cathedral. Mounted police assaulted the crowd at the cathedral steps.

The Catholic Church condemned these attacks. Growing numbers of bishops, priests, and nuns joined a rising chorus of moral indignation. The Archbishop of Recife and Olinda, Helder Camara, denounced the dictatorship. Churches throughout Brazil opened their doors for meetings of dissident students and workers.

Labor protests erupted. In 1967 dissident workers won a union election in the Metalworker's Union of Contagem, Minas Gerais. Small factory-level committees sprang up to oppose limits placed on union elections in the automobile and metallurgical workers' unions of São Paulo, most notably at Cobrasma and Osasco. Strikes followed.

In 1968 the military crushed the labor movement, jailing, beating, and torturing scores of workers and exiling union leaders. On June 25, 1968, after troops attacked a series of public demonstrations, elements from all the opposition held an impressive rally in front of the Candelaria Cathedral in Rio known as "the March of the 100,000."

The events of 1967–68 stimulated splits in the officer corps between "hardliners," who favored smashing the nascent opposition, and "softliners," who advocated liberal treatment of opponents and less favorable terms for foreign investors. These divisions lasted for the remainder of the military's twenty-one-year direct rule.

In congress the MDB opposition caucus won a decisive debate condemning the military's attempt to lift the immunity of one of its members who had spoken out against the brutal repression. One day later, on December 13, 1968, the "hardline" faction inside the military emerged triumphant. It decreed Institutional Act No. 5, the main legal document of what became known as "the coup within the coup." It dissolved congress and permanently suspended the 1967 constitution. The hardliners held the upper hand for the next decade.

After President Costa e Silva was incapacitated by a stroke in 1969 the former head of the secret police, Garrastazu Medici, assumed the presidency, holding it until 1974. He was succeeded by General Ernesto Geisel (1974–1978). Because the opposition regrouped and kept up its pressures for democratization, President Geisel had to agree in 1974 to a "controlled decompression" of the dictatorship's prohibition against dissent.

An economic downturn following the 1973 hike in international oil prices contributed to growing opposition from many quarters. Latin America's explosive "theology of liberation" movement (see Overview) developed its biggest base in Brazil. Some 80,000 "Christian base communities" sprang up, helping to make up for the shortage of priests, spread the Bible, and bring opposition elements together.

In 1973 three archbishops, ten bishops, and the heads of five religious orders in the Northeast were prohibited from making public a statement condemning "injustice and oppression which stem from a capitalism dependent on international power centers." Bishops from the east-central regions were not allowed to publish a similar statement. In 1974 Brazil's Catholic Church published "Church and Politics"—a direct criticism of the government's authoritarian policies and human rights violations.

In 1975 Cardinal Paulo Evaristo Arns of São Paulo emerged as a leading advocate of grassroots Christian socialism, sparking increased organizing among the city's millions of slumdwellers. Numerous clergy underwent arrests, tortures, deportations. By the early 1980s the Vatican was prohibiting some of its Brazilian critics from conducting religious functions. One of these, Friar Boff, had written a book, "Church: Charisma and Power," that likened the Church to a capitalist institution in which bishops and priests produce religious values to be consumed by believers.

Although free political expression was denied, the military knew it was in trouble when its own "loyal opposition" party, the MDB, won more votes than the ARENA did in the 1974 and 1978 elections. MDB was emerging as a genuine opposition party, even electing representatives of the independent trade-union movement and of a burgeoning women's rights movement to Congress. The military decided to have one-third of the Senate virtually appointed instead of elected. The new senators quickly got nicknamed "bionic."

Brazil's "economic miracle" gradually evolved into a full-scale economic crisis. Starting in 1973 the country faced a severe deterioration in its balance-of-payments, as the costs of imports outpaced export earnings. Many companies, confronted with higher costs of production and shortages in heavy equipment, cut back on their plans to expand. The state tried to solve the problem by investing in the machine-goods sector and taking out more foreign loans. Brazil's foreign debt skyrocketed from $6 billion in 1973 to $50 billion in 1980 to more than $100 billion in 1985. High oil prices and rising interest rates compounded the problem.

The prior smooth alliances among Brazilian and foreign investors and the dictatorship showed strains. TNC executives and their Brazilian "junior partners" complained of too much state intervention in the economy, including the state's attempt to develop the production of machine goods. Some Brazilian businesspeople backed the state more strongly, hoping to profit from associating with it in machinery production.

Still other businesspeople—and their numbers were large—relied more on producing for the internal market of wage earners. They wanted protection from foreign capital and more state involvement in light industry instead of machine goods. They became advocates of a "return to democracy." Dusting off the cobwebbed formulas of Brazilian populism, they appealed to *os massas* and helped organize the emergent political parties of 1979–1985.

Finally there were factory owners who relied on low-cost labor in garment and other more traditional industries who complained about the government's "softness" in dealing with labor strikes in 1978. No single business group was able to assert clear-cut hegemony in the face of the growing crisis, aggravating divisions inside the military.

The "New Syndicalism" and "Democratic Opening"

A number of factors forced Brazil's military to agree to "a democratic opening." The expanded organizing of São Paulo slumdwellers in the mid-1970s and the first of a series of militant strikes by metallurgical workers in greater São Paulo in 1978 were critical. So were growing pressures from the Church and student and professional groups. As in Chile (see chapter 17), many middle-class people who first welcomed military rule grew disenchanted and actively opposed it.

Brazil's illegal strike wave started when one hundred workers at a bus and truck factory owned by Saab-Scania in São Paulo's industrial suburb of São Bernardo do Campo sat in front of their machines and crossed their arms. The "arms crossed, machines stopped" action spread in less than nine weeks to incorporate nearly one-quarter of a million workers. The main demands were a wage hike and the right to collective bargaining.

Because the strike movement was spontaneous, massive, and from the bottom-up against established union leaders, it was completely new in Brazil, earning it the name of "the new syndicalism." As in Mexico (see chapter 1), this new labor militancy emerged among the best-paid segments of the workforce—those employed in the most advanced industrial sectors. Engines and cars produced by these workers were exported to the United States and Europe.

With so much at stake, employers tried to nip the movement in the bud. They agreed to staggered wage increases for metalworkers, who returned to work. Nonetheless, by the end of 1978 more than half a million workers had engaged in strike activities, including doctors, bank employees, teachers, and agricultural workers. The new syndicalism was spreading.

Employers shifted tactics. They "locked out" workers and encouraged the government to return to its usual standards of harsh repression of independent labor activity. The government complied. Pickets and union offices were violently attacked; meetings were forbidden; jails filled up. Workers held meetings in soccer stadiums but were violently dispersed. The Catholic Church provided the Cathedral of São Bernardo do Campo as a union headquarters. Troops invaded local churches to break up meetings. A Catholic union leader was shot and killed in front of a factory's gates. Striking workers were dismissed. Police and death squads stepped up their searches and attacks in urban slums and working-class neighborhoods.

Yet, despite all this, 3.2 million workers struck in 1979. Indeed, the strikes spread to less-advanced sectors of the industrial and agricultural economy, incorporating millions of workers from all walks of life. In October, for instance, 100,000 sugarcane cutters struck in the Northeast. In 1980 one-quarter of a million sugarcane workers walked out. About one-fourth of the unionized portions of Brazil's labor force committed themselves to the mushrooming rank-and-file independent labor movement. Its hallmark was a radical break with Brazil's corporativist past of control from either the government or a political party or both.

The small urban "middle" or "intermediate" classes of state employees, teachers, professionals, bank employees, and other nonmanagerial white-collar workers jumped into the fray. Their numbers had grown somewhat with industrialization and an increase in educational facilities. From 1964 to 1980 university enrollments jumped from 138,000 to 1.4 million, whereas those in secondary and vocational schools rose from 1.8 to 2.8 million. The collapse of the economic "miracle" meant that many of the new graduates found their job chances reduced. The middle classes were politically significant because they voted in elections and often contributed leaders to popular protest movements.

To deal with the political crisis, President Geisel rescinded Institutional Act No. 5 in mid-1978. He sidestepped hardline generals to name a retired four-star general as his successor, João Baptista Figueiredo, former head of the SNI (National Security Intelligence). The SNI was the dictatorship's main secret police institution, the apex of what Brazilians called a "security community." The "community" numbered one-quarter of a million military and police agents sprinkled through all the agencies of national, state, and local government.

President Figueiredo (1979–1985) was considered a "centrist" among the military's hardliners and softliners. He extended Geisel's "limited liberalization" by promising to hand over the reigns of government to a civilian president in 1985. In response to "human rights" proclamations of the Carter administration in Washington and mushrooming opposition at home, the Geisel and Figueiredo governments eased up on censorship and promised to stop the tortures. The officer corps of the 165,000-strong army reacted nervously when they compared Brazil's strikes and street demonstrations to those in Iran that toppled the world's fifth mightiest military machine in January 1979.

The officers approved two bills in 1979 that sought to satisfy some of the demands of the rapidly growing opposition and to bring it under government control: the Amnesty Bill and the Party Reform Bill. The Amnesty Bill led to the release of political prisoners, the return of exiles, and the regaining of political rights for past political leaders. Significantly, it also pardoned *all* alleged or actual torturers.

The Party Reform Bill legitimized many previously outlawed political parties and abolished the unpopular ARENA, which regrouped as the PDS, and the MDB, which regrouped as the PMDB (see Box 20.1). The bill favored conservative parties by prohibiting "the use of a term that elicits an affiliation by appealing to religious beliefs"—directed at the Christian Democrats—"or feelings of class or race"—referring to labor, Communist or Socialist parties. This was meant to hamper not just the PCB, but the larger grassroots PT (Workers' party), then in its initial phases with both Marxist and Catholic leadership.

The most popular PT leader was the leader of the metalworkers' "new syndicalism," Luis Inácio da Silva, known simply as "Lula." The PT grew in strength despite the many obstacles put in its way. Lula was thrown in jail in 1981 for his role in the São Paulo strikes and barred from further trade-union activity, but this only furthered his popularity.

With censorship eased, though by no means eliminated, students and others began reading Marxist and Christian Socialist tracts. Courageous journalists began writing exposés of corruption and torture "in high places." Brazil's best-selling book in 1985 was *Brasil: Nunca Mais* ("Brazil: Never Again"), a shocking and irrefutable documentation of the regime's tortures based on military court records. It showed that Brazil's judges had full knowledge about the systematic use of such high-tech tortures as the electric-shock "dragon's chair." They routinely accepted as valid evidence testimony obtained under torture. The book also mentioned the role of U.S. officials like Dan Mitrione, a police officer employed by the AID (Agency for International

Development). Mitrione, the book noted, "took beggars off the streets and tortured them in classrooms, so that the local police would learn the various ways of creating, in the prisoner, the supreme contradiction between body and the mind by striking blows to vulnerable points of the body." Mitrione was later transferred to Uruguay, where he was killed by the Tupamaro guerrillas (see chapter 19).

A severe economic recession in 1981–82 took a lot of the steam out of the labor movement. Strike actions were limited to demanding the rehiring of fired employees. Job security became a more important issue than decent wages. Rank-and-file labor activists shifted their emphasis to the strengthening of opposition parties and the democratization of the workplace through factory-level committees.

For the first time the military regime called for direct elections in 1982 for state governors, most mayoralities, state assemblies, and most of the congress. It made registration as a party so complex and difficult a task that again the established conservative parties were favored. Retention of the "bionic" senators and a presidential electoral college (composed of congressional members plus delegates from state assemblies and city councils) seemingly assured continuation of PDS's rule.

Again, the government was surprised by the strength of its opposition. The 1982 elections produced victories for antigovernment candidates in governorship races affecting 58 percent of the population and more than 70 percent of the nation's "tax base." PDT candidate Leonel Brizola swept Rio de Janeiro by a 200,000 vote margin, provoking subsequent right-wing terrorist attacks and concern among hard-line generals.

End of Direct Military Rule: The New Republic

The failure of Brazil's economy to recover in the mid-1980s and the pressure of mobilized social discontent sealed the doom of Brazil's tottering dictatorship. More feminist groups, a "United Black Movement," and gay and lesbian rights organizations joined the broadening movement for change. Polls showed 90 percent of Brazilians favored direct elections for the presidency.

On April 10, 1984, a million people marched down Rio's Avenida President Vargas demanding "diretas já"—direct elections now. Six days later, 1.5 million paraded in an almost carnival atmosphere under the same banner in São Paulo. By then the U.S. government, the international banking community, and many in the military itself were more anxious to see a return to civilian governance.

However, the military brass was careful to maintain as much of its power as possible during the "transition to civilian rule." Brazil's military personnel remained immune from persecution for human rights violations. Despite military pressure, congress voted unanimously that the president after the one to be elected in 1985 would be chosen by direct elections. It also voted to permit new political parties to be formed without restrictions after 1985.

To come up with a presidential candidate the people would accept, the military had to turn to Tancredo de Almeida Neves, one of its critics inside the PMDB. In early 1985 the electoral college elected Neves as the next president and the little-known José Sarney of the small conservative PFL (Liberal Front party) as vice-president. At the time, the PMDB and PFL were allies in the Aliança Democrática.

Neves died before he could take office. At the moment many feared that the military would resume direct rule. But in a spontaneous show of strength and discipline, Brazil's by then experienced street demonstrators turned out in huge numbers for a silent march at Neves's funeral, showing their support for both the late Neves and his less popular running mate. They were making it clear that they would not accept a coup. Congress and the military agreed to let Sarney assume the presidency. Sarney became president on April 22, 1985. He appointed numerous military figures to his cabinet.

Whether at graveyards, downtown streets, or workplaces, it was the ongoing mass movement that created opportunities for further changes in "the system." The implied threat of massive street demonstrations guaranteed that congress, acting as a constituent assembly, would draft a new constitution and define the length of Sarney's presidency and the future character of Brazil's nascent "nova republica" (new republic). The PMDB had the most votes in congress, and by now it included in its ranks everything from known Communists to extreme rightists. It therefore could be influenced, although by no means swayed, by the tide of public opinion or mass protest.

It was also the mass movement that provoked old-style populist and nationalist measures on President Sarney's part. He helped organize an eight-nation "support group" for the Contadora peace process in Central America and called for Cuba's reincorporation into the OAS (see Introductions to Parts One and Three). Responding to public pressure for wage hikes, agrarian reform, and social welfare programs, he introduced the short-lived but dramatic "Cruzado Plan" in late February 1986. It forestalled further devaluations of the cruzeiro by creating a new currency called the cruzado (worth 1,000 cruzeiros). It set limits on prices and wages. Contrary to an IMF-inspired 1983 law making it illegal for wages to match the rate of inflation, it indexed wage increments to inflation whenever prices rose more than 20 percent a month.

In May 1986 President Sarney tried to implement a modest agrarian reform program. Landowners delayed and sabotaged it, while the Brazilian National Bishops Council denounced it as not thorough enough. Police summarily executed peasants involved in land disputes with absentee owners.

Organized labor complained that the Cruzado Plan "freezes our misery," but Sarney gave frequent speeches addressing the public as "workers of Brazil" and promising to "continue social programs so as to end hunger and poverty." The November 1986 elections were the first in which illiterates were allowed to vote. Sarney campaigned as "the president of the poor."

The pro-Sarney PMDB-PFL coalition (Aliança Democrática) won an impressive victory at the polls, sweeping all twenty-three governorships and obtaining an absolute majority in the Senate and Chamber of Deputies. Brizola's PDT and Lula's PT lost ground compared to their showings in the 1985 municipal elections. The far Right PDS suffered severe reverses.

Right after this victory at the polls, Sarney announced the end of the Cruzado Plan's price freeze. Prices on gasoline, alcohol fuel, utilities, sugar, bread, milk and other basic items shot up between 25 and 60 percent. People again took to the streets, protesting that Sarney had deceived them.

In mid-June 1987 the government caved in to IMF proposals without formally accepting them. It eliminated the Cruzado Plan's inflation-linked "trigger" for automatic wage adjustments. Claiming that workers' purchasing power was down by 38 percent since the start of the Cruzado Plan, organized labor called another one-day general strike for August.

Tens of thousands of army troops and police patrolled Brazil's major cities during the August 1987 general strike. Soldiers ejected three hundred workers occupying the National Steel Company at Volta Redonda. Public sector workers struck in September and won impressive wage hikes.

The debates in congress on the draft constitution grew intense. Labor kept up the pressure for reform with an average of nearly two thousand strikes a year affecting 50 million workers during the 1986–1988 period. President Sarney insisted on not weakening the executive branch of government or granting labor too much. A leftist faction in the PMDB added its voice to Brizola's PDT and "Lula's" PT to insist upon direct elections and greater economic democracy. The center-right PMDB-PFL Aliança Democrática came apart, as Sarney's PFL bolted.

The end result was the fairly progressive 1988 Constitution. It provided for direct presidential elections in 1989 and a plebiscite in 1993 on whether the government should be a monarchy, a system of parliamentary rule, or a presidential republic (voters opted to continue with the presidential republic). The new constitution called for a forty-hour work week, minimum wages, health and pension benefits, the right to strike, and greater labor autonomy. State recognition and regulation of unions was still required but with a more autonomous judiciary instead of the Labor Ministry. The constitution granted the legislature a little more power. It also provided for possible referenda or "popular vetoes" on proposed or enacted legislation. A nationalistic document, it restricted foreign investment in mining and limited oil exploration to the state oil firm Petrobrás. It guaranteed job security for the 1.6 million government work force.

Not long after promulgation of the new constitution, Brazil's creditors agreed to a refinancing of the huge foreign debt on which payments had been suspended for nearly two years. Leftists made strong gains in the November 1988 municipal elections. The PT's Luiza Erundina de Souza was elected mayor of São Paulo. Echoing several features of the new politics, she publicly described herself as "a Marxist," "a devotee of Mary, the Mother of God," and a person who recognized the need for "armed struggle."

Brazil's military remained powerful. It crushed a November 1988 steel-workers' strike at Volta Redonda, killing three workers. The strike had spread to much of modern industry, the oil sector, and the Northeast's 250,000 sugar-cane cutters. The Gestapo-type military intelligence agency SNI called the "*furia grevista*" ("strike frenzy") a threat to "economic recovery." Federal deputy and PT leader Lula of the powerful independent unions' CUT (United Confederation of Workers) urged workers to return to their jobs, which they did. But first the steelworkers won most of their demands, including reinstate-ment of dismissed strikers. An ironworkers' strike in March 1989 spread to other industries and represented the most comprehensive work stoppage of the 1980s.

In November 1989's presidential elections the PT and PDT candidates Lula and Brizola finished second and third. Their combined vote was greater than the plurality received by an obscure political newcomer, forty-year-old Fernando Collor de Mello, who earlier had held political posts under the mili-tary dictatorship. Collor was a wealthy scion of a conservative political family whose economic empire included a *Globo* affiliate. In the December runoff against the Socialist Lula, the telegenic Collor campaigned as a champion of honest democratic government and as a free-enterprise populist. Although provided unprecedented campaign funding by big business and backed by *Globo*'s powerful media conglomerate, Collor barely won by six percentage points.

When Collor took office in 1990, the economy was in a shambles. Con-sumer prices had risen 2, 750 percent in 1989. Debt payments had been sus-pended again. Private banks held two-thirds of the foreign debt; bankings' "Big Three" alone—Citicorp, Chase Manhattan, and BankAmerica—held nearly one-quarter of it. U.S. bank regulators told the banks in mid-1990 to write off a fifth of their loans to Brazil. Meanwhile, Collor continued Sarney's policy of debt-for-equity swaps and privatization of the remaining 188 state enterprises.

With the 1989 elections over, the popular mass movements entered a phase of demobilization. Families scrambled to survive the economic crunch. Collor carried out an extreme IMF-style economic shock treatment similar to

Peru's "Fujishock" (see chapter 14). He froze wages and hiked utility prices. He momentarily froze individual savings accounts, causing a minority of businessmen to call him a "class traitor." But most remembered the old Brazilian custom dating back to colonial times—"*jeitinho.*" It means "there's always a way to get around the law [or obstacle]"—if you are powerful. Many middle-class Brazilians saw their savings wiped out as Collor replaced the cruzado with a free floating cruzeiro currency.

Promising an era of free trade and teaming up with Argentina's President Menem to form the southern Cone's four-nation common market MER-COSUR (see the introduction to Part Three), President Collor slashed tariffs and lifted import bans on many consumer goods. Rather than increase development of Brazilian research in science and technology (only 0.6 percent of GDP compared with 2 or 3 percent in more industrialized nations), Collor offered protection to foreigners of their "intellectual property rights" (see Documents). This helped resolve longstanding trade disputes with U.S. computer and pharmaceutical companies. Foreign-based TNCs controlled 87 percent of Brazil's pharmaceutical market.

President Collor gave his neoliberal free market economic program a name: "New Brazil" (*Brasil Nuevo*). Its main instrument was the PND (National Destatization Program). It amounted to subsidizing the private sector through selling off state firms at bargain prices. Through various means, the PND transformed the internal public debt into shares of privatized firms—mostly industrial and financial conglomerates with strong ties to foreign capital. Export-oriented manufacturing firms were favored. The IMF responded with new loans, including a $2.1 billion standby credit in early 1992. Collor's neo-liberal PND seemed secure, even though it faced opposition in congress and among the public. The nation's 298 bishops attacked PND as "recessive." They turned out to be right.

Environment, Ethnocide, and Earth Summit 1992

President Collor had to cope with more than the economy. There was a growing world concern about the destruction of the Amazonian rainforests and its heavy toll in Indian lives (ethnocide). In tune with the World Bank's "poles of development" strategy, the military dictatorship had encouraged foreign firms and land speculators to "open up" the Amazon, the world's largest tropical forest and river system with vast iron, gold, and other mineral reserves. The world's rainforest plant species—most of them still unknown and only 1 percent of the known ones having been tested for medical applications—provided ingredients for 25 percent of modern medicines. One-fifth of the world's fresh water flowed through the Amazon.

The military government undertook construction of a 3,400 mile Trans-

Amazonian Highway. The government's SUDAM (Superintendency of Amazon Development) envisioned a "moving frontier" that would create new homesites for 30 million people. Brazil's landless *posseiros* "homesteaded" the "new frontier," often clearing tracts of land only to lose it later to unscrupulous speculators protected by hired guns, the local police or military, or the SUDAM.

The remaining 200,000 Indians of the Amazon were systematically uprooted or killed, causing anthropologists to warn that in less than a dozen years there would be no more Indians. By 1978 their numbers were already under 100,000. Among foreign firms that grabbed off Indians lands were King Ranch of Texas, Swift Armour (a subsidiary of the Canadian conglomerate BRASCAN), and Volkswagen.

The Italian conglomerate Liquigas gained the most publicity for its nefarious deeds against Amazonian Indians. Henning Albert Boilensen, director of Liquigas's Brazilian partner, Associgas, was gunned down by urban guerrillas, some of whose friends had seen him at their torture sessions—leading to the name "Boilensen pianola" for one of the electric-shock devices used against political prisoners.

Despite international protest, destruction of the Amazon proceeded rapidly. Giant bulldozers stripped closed to 10 percent of the area's virgin forest for timber, mining, and ranching interests. Heavy rains washed the precious topsoils far out into the Atlantic Ocean. U.S. mining firms like Hanna, Kaiser Industries, Alcoa Aluminum, Reynolds Metals, U.S. Steel, and Gulf & Western, as well as European, Canadian, and Japanese companies, obtained huge mineral and land concessions. Só did agribusinesses, especially livestock enterprises. The clearing of 250 million acres for new pasturelands produced quick profits while leading to more erosion. One minister of agriculture quit in disgust, declaring that the Amazonian projects hurt the majority of the population "to the advantage of transnational corporations."

Deforestation threatened to reduce the oxygen coming from the Amazon region—up to one-fifth of the world's supply. Since the trees also acted as a check against global warming by absorbing carbon dioxide (the main gas depleting the ozone layer), their continued removal could increase the carbon dioxide in the earth's atmosphere by as much as 10 percent—enough to raise the earth's temperature 7 degrees, leading to a meltdown of polar ice caps and a 100-foot rise in sea levels. Satellite photographs in the early 1990s indicated that the amount of deforestation in the Amazon was slightly less than originally thought. More than twice the deforested area, however, was discovered to have suffered biological disturbance—and possible loss of largely unmapped species and gene pools.

In the 1980s, Brazil launched the world's largest mining project—"Grande Carajás" in eastern Amazonia. A joint enterprise of state and foreign private interests like the Anglo American Corporation of South Africa, it aimed to produce 10 percent of the world's iron ore. It incorporated up to one-sixth of Brazil's portion of the Amazon basin. Megaprojects like Carajás and the world's largest dams to harness energy, such as Itaipu (see chapter 16) or the subsequent hydroelectric dams started on Brazil's tributaries of the Amazon, led to widespread flooding, deforestation, desertification, and displacement of indigenous peoples or destruction of the conditions of their existence. According to the Brazilian magazine *Veja,* 83 percent of the cultivable land in Rondonia State had lost its fertility by 1989.

Representatives of forty tribal nations organized the Alliance of the Peoples of the Forest to block further dam construction and to defend the environment. One Alliance leader, forty-four-year-old Francisco "Chico" Alves Mendes Filho of the National Council of Rubber Tappers, was assassinated in 1988. A member of the CUT national council and a PT activist, he had been awarded the UN Global 500 Prize for his years of active defense of the environment.

Besides the hydroelectric projects, smaller endeavors for billion-dollar stakes, such as those of the 45,000 *garimpeiros* (freelance gold-diggers), also threatened Indian survival. The *garimpeiros* drove 9,000 Yanomamis off their Amazonian lands. Fifteen percent of the Yanomami population died from diseases introduced by the gold miners. Mercury contamination downriver and mercury vapors released into the global atmosphere had serious ecological consequences. Yanomami and international protests on the eve of the UN Conference on Environment and Development—the so-called Earth Summit held in Rio de Janeiro in 1992—led to momentary government demarcation and protection of a Yanomami land reserve. Venezuela created a reserve for 14,000 Yanomamis living there. The Venezuelan military attacked Brazilian gold miners encroaching on the reserve in 1992, but Brazil's government did not join in the clashes on either side of the border. In August 1993 Brazilian gold miners brutally massacred several men, women, and children in two border area Yanomami lodges.

This seemed to indicate that the 1988 Constitution's progressive provisions for environmental protection and indigenous peoples' rights were not being implemented. As the daily *Jornal do Brasil* pointed out in 1990, special decrees had placed the government's environmental agencies far from public view under the Secretariat of Strategic Affairs, an outgrowth of the despised and dissolved military intelligence network SNI. Moreover, President Collor's Environment Secretary José Lutzenberger protested that the government's environmental authorities "accepted company bribes . . . and acted as if they were employed by the landowners." Collor dismissed Lutzenberger in March 1992. Meanwhile, plans went ahead for a new petrochemical "pole of development" in Rio de Janeiro, where pulp and paper companies would double their production capacity by 1996. The planned Paraná-Paraguay River seaway (see the introduction to Part Three) augured further ecological havoc.

Earth Summit 1992 brought together most of the world's leaders to pass resolutions in defense of the environment. President Bush initially refused to attend but then backed down. His top environmental aide, EPA chief William K. Reilly, later criticized the United States for its weak positions at the summit. The main bones of contention revolved not around the "Earth Charter" document so much as the "Agenda 21" plan for development of less industrialized nations. Brazil and most Third World countries harbored fears of "eco-imperialism" and wanted more favorable conditions for technology transfer and the sharing of "intellectual property rights" or their benefits (for a fuller account of the controversy, see Overview, Conclusion, and especially Documents).

Crisis of the State

In the end, the Collor policies of economic neoliberalism failed much as earlier IMF-style remedies had done. The world recession of the early 1990s and higher oil prices during the Persian Gulf War (Brazil imports half its oil), combined with government corruption and feuding between the executive and congress, contributed to the perpetuation of Brazil's economic crisis. Annual economic growth rates went from -1 percent in 1990 to 1 percent in 1991 and then back to -1 percent in 1992, while inflation skyrocketed. Unemployment rose to 15 percent in prosperous São Paulo and higher elsewhere. The monthly minimum wage of $88 could not meet the minimal basic food needs for a family of four.

As no single class or group proved able to assert political hegemony or accomplish an economic recovery, the state entered into a new crisis, this one triggered by its own corruption. In May 1992 President Collor's brother accused his 1989 campaign manager Paulo Cesar Farias of graft. A three-month-long congressional investigation revealed a multi-billion-dollar Farias-run influence peddling ring, kickback schemes, tax evasion, and drug racketeering that had delivered huge sums of money to Collor, Farias, and their friends in construction and big business. Cocaine traffickers had stepped up business in Brazil, which had become a prominent grower of coca leaf in the Amazon region and manufacturer of chemicals for processing cocaine. The president denied the corruption charges, but most Brazilians did not believe him. They knew of his lavish estates and high-priced life-style in the "fast lane." They watched transfixed as he allocated hundreds of millions of their tax dollars to governors and mayors in a desperate effort to shore up his fading political fortunes. The presidential spending spree further fueled inflation.

Once more the new politics surfaced, as more than a million incensed citizens took to the streets in August and September 1992 to demand Collor's impeachment. Collor's political allies jumped the sinking presidential ship. As the end neared, Lula met with *Globo* television's owner Marinho and persuaded the old man to televise September's street mobilizations, which assumed an almost festive air of celebration. In late September the Chamber of Deputies voted to impeach. The majority of the electorate voted for the PMDB and PT in October's municipal elections. Only minutes after the senate impeachment trial began on December 19, 1992, Collor resigned. Vice-President Itamar Franco, a former PMDB senator known for his honesty, nationalism, and reservations about Collor's extreme neo-liberalism, assumed the presidency until the expiration of Collor's term in January 1995. In April 1993 the Supreme Court indicted Collor for his theft of state monies, and in December it ratified the Senate's suspension of Collor's political rights until the year 2001. Brazil's attorney general presented a claim of $17 billion against Collor, his personal secretary, and Farias for reimbursement of stolen state funds. Farias, who had fled to Thailand, was extradited back to Brazil for trial.

As people's living standards continued to decline, Brazilians were shocked to learn in late 1993 about yet another corruption scandal—a congressional payoff scheme involving millions of dollars. The scandal implicated more than one hundred of the nation's 584 legislators.

Throughout the crisis of the late 1980s and early 1990s, the military rattled its sabres. Retired officers talked nostalgically of the need for another coup to "save the nation" from corrupt politicians. The armed forces numbered 350,000 men and women. After initial grousing about SNI's replacement by the Secretariat of Strategic Affairs and reductions in the military's share of the budget from a high of 23 percent in 1971 to 2.2 percent in 1990, the officer corps had responded to each fresh political crisis with murmurs of intervention sufficient to produce substantial military wage hikes. Further officer grievances included the privatizing of state industries they had once helped manage and Brazil's signing the nuclear nonproliferation agreement with Argentina (see chapter 18). Moves toward a nuclear power industry were stalled because of the "Brazilian Chernobyl" in Goiânia in late 1987.

Incidents of military terrorism persisted. In 1990 President Collor removed an air force base commander when it was discovered that a soldier had been tortured by electric shock in the commander's office. Worse yet, the London-based human rights body Amnesty International reported the systematic torture and murder of "street children" by death squads involving military police. Nearly five thousand children were killed in 1988–1990, most of them black, male, and poor. Massacres of homeless children sleeping on sidewalks and Church steps in Rio escalated in 1993. Blamed for some of the most grisly slaughters were the "Running Horses," a death squad made up of two state congressmen (ex-policemen) and several military policemen.

In the countryside the murder of union leaders and peasant activists escalated. In the Northeast, for example, Amnesty International reported two thousand killings of protesting peasants since 1985. In 1991, one day after the New York-based Americas Watch called for his protection from assassins, the leader of the Rural Workers Union of Rio Maria in Pará State was murdered. Americas Watch found that "the hired guns of powerful landowners" operated with "impunity." Even punished killers went free. In 1993 the convicted assassins of trade unionist-environmentalist Chico Mendes walked out of their jail and disappeared.

There were other problems too. A World Bank report warned that low literacy rates and high disease and malnutrition rates threatened to deprive Brazil's economy of "a skilled and productive labor force." An AIDS epidemic placed Brazil second to the United States in cases reported. Cholera cases were reported in the Northeast.

It was in this atmosphere of multiple crises that Brazil prepared for its October 1994 general elections. The initial presidential favorite was the 1989 runner-up, PT's Lula. At its 1991 party congress, the 600,000-member PT had committed itself to a mixed economy while retaining a process of defining socialism as inseparable from democracy and pledging coexistence or cooperation with non-Socialists. Delegates had voted that 30 percent of the party's "directive" positions should go to women. Lula ran on a centrist platform.

Even though it played in the arena of the old politics and engaged in some of the same personalist and populist practices, the PT retained the appeal of the "new politics." Lula's main opponent was former Finance Minister Fernando Henrique Cardoso, whose very well funded center-right campaign had the backing of the leaders of Brazil's business community. Brazil's foreign creditor banks slashed the nation's debt, reduced interest rates on it, and extended new loans. Inflation radically tapered off, and Cardoso overtook Lula in the opinion polls. As expected, *O Globo* opposed Lula, who complained that the "Mexicanized" electoral process amounted to a "setup"—big business and foreign investors were getting behind a single candidate to defeat him, much as had happened in 1989. Cardoso won the election with 54 percent of the vote. Lula garnered only 26 percent..

Big business's backing of Cardoso paid off, as the former dependence theoretician turned practical politician swept to victory with no need for a runoff election. In his first months in office, President Cardoso introduced constitutional amendments that would permit foreign investment in joint ventures with the state oil, telecommunications, and electricity companies. It remained to be seen if the young *"nova republica"* would suffer "infanticide" or endure, but optimistic observers insisted the clock could never be turned back. Everyone agreed that with or without direct military intervention Brazil's state crisis was by no means over.

Selected Bibliography

(See also Bibliographies to Overview, Introduction to Part Three, and Conclusion.)

Alvarez, Sonia E. _Engendering Democracy in Brazil: Women's Movements in Transition Politics._ Princeton, NJ: Princeton University Press, 1990.

Alves, María Helena Moreira. _State and Opposition in Military Brazil._ Austin: University of Texas Press, 1985. Insightful account of 1964–1984 period.

Archdiocese of São Paulo. _Torture in Brazil._ New York: Vintage Books, 1986. Translation of best-seller _Brasil: Nunca Mais,_ based on military court records.

Ayer de O. Santos, Leinad, and Lucia M. M. de Andrade (eds.). _Hydroelectric Dams on Brazil's Xingu River and Indigenous Peoples._ Cambridge, MA: Cultural Survival, 1990.

"Brazil: Capitalist Crisis and Workers' Challenge" _Latin American Perspectives._ 6(4) (Fall 1979). Includes interview with union leader "Lula."

"Brazil in Transition: Democratization, Privatization, and Working-Class Resistance." _Latin American Perspectives,_ 21:1 (Winter 1994).

Burdick, John. _Looking for God in Brazil: The Progressive Catholic Church in Urban Brazil's Religious Arena._ Berkeley: University of California Press, 1993.

Caipora Women's Group. _Women in Brazil._ London, England: Latin American Bureau, 1993. Poverty and the new women's movements.

Dean, Warren. _Brazil and the Struggle for Rubber: A Study in Environmental History._ New York: Cambridge University Press, 1987.

Dimenstein, Gilberto. _Brazil: War on Children._ London: Latin American Bureau, 1991. Short, well-documented look at death squads, crime, and street children's fears.

dos Santos, Theotonio. _The Political Economy of Brazil._ Boulder, CO: Westview, 1994.

Erickson, Kenneth Paul. _The Brazilian Corporative State and Working Class Politics._ Berkeley: University of California Press, 1977.

Evans, Peter. _Dependent Development: The Alliance of Multinational, State and Local Capital in Brazil._ Princeton, NJ: Princeton University Press, 1979.

French, John D. _The Brazilian Workers' ABC: Class Conflict and Alliances in Modern São Paulo._ Chapel Hill: University of North Carolina Press, 1992.

Guimaraes, Roberto P. _The Ecopolitics of Development in the Third World: Politics and Environment in Brazil._ Boulder, CO: Lynne Rienner, 1991. "Enthusiastically recommended for upper-division students"—_Choice_ magazine.

Hess, David J. _Spirits and Scientists: Ideology, Spiritism, and Brazilian Culture._ University Park: Pennsylvania State University Press, 1991. How Spiritism affects both politics and daily life.

Keck, Margaret E. _The Workers' Party and Democratization in Brazil._ New Haven, CT: Yale University Press, 1992. Award-winning study.

Skidmore, Thomas E. _The Politics of Military Rule in Brazil, 1964–1985._ New York: Oxford University Press, 1988.

Stepan, Alfred. _Rethinking Military Politics: Brazil and the Southern Cone._ Princeton, NJ: Princeton University Press, 1988. Sees political parties as failing to check military's capacity to intervene.

Films

Barravento (The Turning Wind). 1962. 76 minutes. Film on Bahia Christian-African mixture, macumba rituals, plight of the fishermen, old and new, first of "Cinema Novo" films by Glauber Rocha acclaimed abroad.

663

Barren Lives. 1983. 115 minutes. Black and white film by Nelson Pereira on peasant life in Northeast *sertão,* based on Graciliano Ramos's famous novel.

Brazilian Dreams: Visiting Points of Resistance. 1991. 54 minutes. Travel video on nationwide political struggle; by Caitlin Manning.

Bye Bye Brazil. 1980. 110 minutes. Feature film directed by Carlos Diegues about a carnival troupe touring Brazil.

Chico Mendes: Voice of the Amazon. 1989. 57 minutes. Award-winning color video includes Mendes' last filmed interview.

Kiss of the Spider Woman. 1986. Academy Award best actor William Hurt on Brazilian political prisoners.

Pixote. 1980. 127 minutes. Internationally heralded feature film about teenagers living in crime-ridden slums.

The Burning Season. 1994. A U.S.-made-for-television film about Chico Mendes.

Conclusion: Learning from the Past—Challenge for Policymakers

> You are looking at an individual that is the last one in the world that would ever want to put American troops into Latin America, because the memory of the great colossus of the North is so widespread in Latin America we would lose all our friends if we did anything of that kind. And we have not been asked.—*President Reagan, press interview, 1986*

> Soon the Communists' prediction of a "revolutionary fire" sweeping across all of Central America could come true. . . . I do not intend to leave such a crisis for the next American president.—*President Reagan, television address, 1987*

The two contradictory statements of President Reagan (above) exemplified the limited parameters of U.S. foreign policy in Latin America for several decades. President Reagan's 1986 recognition of Latin America's perception of the United States as "the colossus of the North" did nothing to change past policies of U.S. overt and covert interventionism against the forces of reform and revolution, as the "Iran-contragate" affair and invasion of Panama revealed (see introductions to Part One and chapter 7).

This left an awesome challenge for U.S. policymakers. What lessons could be learned? The main "lesson"—that U.S. military and CIA actions were counterproductive—was largely ignored, although many political analysts both in the United States and in Latin America knew that in the long run military muscle and political intrigue never resolved the sinews of social conflict. It was clear to them that U.S. armed interventions only complicated economic, social, and political problems that perpetuated Latin America's historical instability, lack of democracy, and ongoing attempts at reform or revolution.

Nevertheless, both the Alliance for Progress and the Kissinger Commission Report seemed to be unaware of this lesson by emphasizing a double-barreled economic/military aid approach to the region. This "carrot and stick" approach prevailed throughout the 1960s, 1970s, and 1980s. Yet, except for short periods, it did not generate either economic stability, political democracy, or friendlier feelings for the United States in Latin America. On the contrary, it fueled the introduction of the long, dark night of state-sponsored terrorism. By eliminating democracy and stripping organized labor of any meaningful voice, it set the stage for neo-liberalism's privatization schemes. It ballooned Latin America's foreign debt, thereby making the governments even more vulnerable to privatization. It left the majority of Latin Americans poorer and hungrier than before.

In fact these policies served to convince some Latin Americans that peaceful reform was impossible and violent revolution the only remaining option. To some, dissolution of reactionary armies and the formation of "people's militias" seemed necessary in the face of U.S.-backed military coups and contra-style invasions. They pointed to frustrations and defeats of the "revolutions" in Mexico (1911–1940), Bolivia and Guatemala (1950s), the Dominican Republic (1965), and Chile and Peru (1970s).

Defenders of the carrot-and-stick approach agreed that it had failed but differed in their explanations of its failure. Some believed the United States had not applied the stick strongly enough—the "Bay of Pigs" invasion of Cuba was the prime example. The Kissinger Commission Report, despite a minority dissent, reflected that estimate. It maintained that more, not less, military aid and even (if necessary) direct U.S. intervention had to be implemented to turn back "communism," that is, popular reform and revolution (see Overview). Others believed just the opposite: because the stick of counterinsurgency programs was "too big" and the carrot "too little," U.S. policy militarized Latin America, facilitating "the long, dark night of state terror" and making more enemies than friends among the area's major political groups and prodemocracy forces. But neither viewpoint contemplated a total change in the original policy.

First President Carter and then President Reagan spoke of the need for the United States to defend "human rights" and "democracy" against "tyranny in whatever form, whether of the left or the right" (in Reagan's formulation of March 1986). They differed only on how to force Latin American regimes to maintain some respect for human rights even while using the "stick." The debates were centered around tactical, rather than strategic, differences over whether and to what extent the U.S. government should curtail military aid to dictatorships (or vote against loans for them in international bodies). President Carter preferred open public criticism of dictatorships and occasional aid cutoffs versus Reagan's behind-the-scenes "quiet diplomacy" and rare or no aid cutoffs. The basic carrot-stick approach remained the same and, for the most part, violations of human rights continued along with U.S. aid (sometimes indirectly, via Israeli and Argentine arms and trainers in Central America—see the introduction to Part One and chapters 2 and 18).

But several analysts questioned the entire premise of U.S. policy in twentieth-century Latin America. They declared that U.S. policy was based on the belief that both full-scale revolutions and even reforms that went beyond cosmetic changes hurt U.S. investment interests. They said it was simplistic to ignore the differences among Socialists, Communists, and leftist and reformers of whatever stripe, calling anyone who championed changes that tampered with the status quo a "Communist." After the Cuban Revolution of 1959, the Washington view of Latin America increasingly had become one of an ongoing (or inevitable) "East-West" conflict. Despite the Communist world's post–World War II "polycentrism" that produced border clashes between China and the Soviet Union and a broad range of Communist systems from Yugoslavia's to Cuba's, the view of communism as monolithic prevailed in Washington's view of Latin America. The simplistic equation of revolution equals communism governed policy decisions. The same oversimplification was evidenced with the collapse of the "Soviet empire"—when it was almost assumed that the economic systems or political leaders of Cuba, North Korea, Vietnam, and China would soon fall too.

The view from Latin America was different, of course. There, a kind of "second revolution for independence" was being advocated—this time not the political one against colonialism, but the one for economic independence to meet human needs. Latin Americans viewed the central axis of conflict not as East-West but as North-South, wealthy nations versus poor ones (see Overview).

By the 1980s Latin America's "second revolution" had distinctive human, political, and ideological settings. The human setting was one in which millions of people lived from hand to mouth in wretched poverty. The political setting was marked by popular resentment at two decades of military rule (or civilian rule backed up by guns) and a hunger for genuine participatory democracy. The ideological setting was one in which moderates and radicals formed tentative alliances to rid their country of hated dictatorships, as in all South America's "southern cone" and most of Central America.

Many groups and ideologies sought to lead Latin America's "second revolution." Whatever their differences, they had one thing in common: the goal of greater economic autonomy, an improved standard of living for the people, and a more beneficial and balanced industrialization—in brief, a more equitable distribution of wealth, privilege, and power. The second revolution's nationalistic emotions momentarily bridged gaps between political groups.

Latin America's revolution for economic independence found itself navigating new waters fraught with tricky undercurrents. But overall it was the stark whitecaps of poverty and the undertow of the long, dark night of right-wing dictatorships that gave height and depth to the region's second revolutionary tide. More and more Latin Americas were beginning to realize that all the "free elections" in the world were meaningless if families could not be fed and "death squads," "informers," and torturers were given official tolerance or encouragement. They were tired of elections that left them hungry, underpaid, or unemployed.

The practitioners of the region's "new politics" realized this and vowed to do something about it. The Reagan administration, however, seemed insensitive to the area's new politics. Far from encouraging the democratic forces as it claimed, it hastened to reassure the forces of repression by issuing official statements not long before the popular overthrows of Marcos in the Philippines and Duvalier in Haiti that it had "no intention of destabilizing right-wing, pro-American dictatorships in Asia or Latin America." As events unfolded, however, it modified its stance in both Haiti and the Philippines. It often applied the simple formula of labeling those Latin Americans who criticized U.S.-supported policies in their homelands "Communists." The targets of this label were often nationalist reformers, even at times established presidents or ministers of government intent upon advancing Latin America's second revolution for independence. (In a similar "red-baiting" vein, several members of the U.S. Congress accused congressional opponents of Reagan's Central America policy of being leftists or liberals and therefore pro-Communist.)

This simplistic U.S. equation of reform with communism stamped Latin America's revolutionary surge with the imprint of anti-Americanism. People of diverse backgrounds perceived the Reagan administration's blustery "Ramboism" and anticommunism as a new interventionism reminiscent of the days of "Gunboat Diplomacy." Unlike the time of Teddy Roosevelt and the "Big Stick," however, now the ships come by air and sea, bearing land and harbor mines, "smart bombs," rockets, rotating machine guns. In Latin America distrust and resentment of the colossus of the north were not only the legacy of the distant past, as President Reagan recognized; they were also the legacy of his own presidency.

Latin Americans did not always distrust the United States. On the contrary, during their first revolutionary storm period, the nineteenth-century era of political independence, they turned to the United States for weapons and other forms of aid. But then the revolution was against colonialism, the dominant powers were European, and the United States was the Western Hemisphere's first country to achieve political independence. It was natural for Latin Americans to find inspiration in the U.S. Declaration of Independence and Bill of Rights and North Americans to sympathize with their cause.

Now, however, Latin America's second revolution of independence was against the excess of economic power in the hands of TNCs (transnational corporations) and U.S.-dominated institutions like the World Bank and the IMF (International Monetary Fund). The debt crisis was threatening to explode in the faces of these institutions, but their "expert advisers" failed to recognize that the economic problems, like Latin America's second revolution itself, were rooted in the failures of economic development models of the past forty years (see Overview). These problems could not be solved, critics of the simplistic reform-equals-communism policies declared, by continued opposition to Latin America's "second revolution."

It was time, they said, to recognize new economic and political realities: the United States could no longer so easily determine events in Latin America. Moreover, the interests of the people of the United States were perhaps not that different from those of Latin Americans. The late twentieth-century trends in "the North" of worker layoffs, stagflation, increased use of immigrant labor, rising long-term unemployment, and slowed economic growth, combined with rising public and private borrowing worldwide, had generated a kind of global debt economy marked by ever-deepening recession periods. Facing its own growing debt, weakened manufacturing base, federal budget deficit, and trade imbalance, the United States could no longer successfully serve as the world economy's regulator of last resort.

By 1980 the United States had slipped to the rank of eleventh in per-capita gross domestic production (total output of goods and services before expense deductions and tax payments). In 1984 it had the most unequal distribution of income among industrialized countries, with the exception of France. Real wages had dropped 14 percent since 1973.

Whether inside or outside national boundaries, the debt crisis had led to an economic skewing between the rich and the poor, with investors pouring most of their funds into speculative ventures rather than into the production of new goods. In describing this trend in the United States, *Business Week* entitled the cover story of its September 16, 1985, issue "The Casino Society." The near "crash" of Wall Street in late 1987 brought home to the U.S. public the gravity of the situation. "Instability," it seemed, might not be solely a Third World problem. The 1992 rioting or "rebellion" in Los Angeles and other cities further underscored the point. The United States had come to resemble a two-tiered society dominated by a relatively small number of well-off, mostly white people cut off from the rest of the population. The "great middle class" had skewed between a few who achieved economic security and growing numbers who did not. The lower tier of the poor mushroomed. Numerous African Americans, Latinos, women, and children had long since fallen into the lower tier and were now rapidly being joined there by millions of laid-off white workers and newly arriving immigrants. Economic hardship and scapegoating "the other" had created an incendiary brew.

Latin America's staggering debt of nearly half a trillion dollars was only one-sixth that of the United States. Paradoxically, some observers noted, debt strangulation, shrinking markets, and economic stagnation in both the North and South could offer the United States and Latin America unique opportunities for new adjustments that might prove mutually beneficial instead of destructive. For example, instead of resisting or paying lip service to Latin America's quest for more diversified international relations, the United States might actually support it and benefit from the potential redirecting of capital flows back from Japan, Western Europe, and North America into a more stable, democratic Latin America marked by economic recovery and peace instead of depression and war.

The political hegemony of the United States in Latin America clearly faced new challenges from European and Japan and Latin America itself. For example, the OAS (Organization of American States) was no longer a rubber stamp for U.S. intervention. This became evident as early as 1979 when the Nicaraguans' popular uprising was toppling the Somoza dynasty. Unlike the 1965 intervention in the Dominican Republic, even the usually pro-U.S. military dictatorships of Latin America (except for Argentina's) opposed a U.S. proposal to send a "peacekeeping" mission to Nicaragua (see chapters 5 and 10). Similarly, U.S. hostility toward Nicaragua's revolution in the 1980s was criticized by both Japan and Western Europe, as well as by almost all of Latin America's democratic governments. Canada joined the OAS in 1990 and became a peace-making force in El Salvador. And the United Nations established its presence as the major peace mediator in Central America (once upon a time viewed as the "U.S. backyard").

Inside and outside official U.S. policy-making circles there were louder calls for new analyses and radical policy changes. They questioned not only the wisdom of intervention in campaigns, but the interrelationships of foreign policy and TNCs, "runaway shops," and the decline in economic opportunity at home (where 94 percent of the 23 million people in the United States added to the nonagricultural payrolls from 1970 to 1984 worked in the service-producing sectors at an average hourly wage of $7.52). When the wage plus benefits per hour in Brazil remained one-thirteenth what they were in the United States (and even less in Central America), U.S. manufacturers found it difficult to compete. U.S. industrial output slowed (or firms "ran away" to set up shop in Latin America and other nations offering cheaper labor pools and better tax breaks), exports suffered, real wages declined, purchasing power lagged, and job security and public services deteriorated. In brief, most U.S. citizens faced a declining standard of living.

A growing number of AFL-CIO leaders criticized earlier AIFLD-style collaborationist policies with the TNCs. They began pointing out that when Latin American workers fought back and won the right to unionize or received higher wages, U.S. companies were less likely to "run away" to Latin America. "American jobs" could be saved if labor's conditions in Latin America were not abysmal. Logically, they said, when Latin American nations began to regulate the conditions for TNC investment, it would benefit American workers. The best interests of the American people were not necessarily served by blind defense of the immediate interests of the TNCs, they said.

Some North Americans, particularly among religious people, Latinos, organized labor, educators, and students, began mobilizing independently of the two political parties to bring about changes in U.S. policy. Demonstrations in Washington, D.C., Los Angeles, and other cities repeatedly stayed the hand of U.S. interventionism in the 1980s (see Overview and Introduction to Part One). Lobbying efforts in Washington exceeded those of the anti–Vietnam War movement.

Nonintervention groups also had policy differences. Some believed change could be best wrought by centering their efforts on elections and lobbying of those in office. They said that supporting one or another political candidate on the basis of their foreign policy votes could have immediate impact. The defenders of the "independence mass mobilization" strategy countered that nearly a decade of lobbying and electoral politics had produced little change while the country had edged closer to the brink of war in Central America. They claimed that any major policy change, from the women's suffrage movement to the winning of civil rights and the ending of the Vietnam War, had come about ultimately as a result of independent mass mobilizations (see Documents).

Although each anti-interventionist approach varied on its preferred technique or emphasis, the policy changes they recommended had much in common. Advocates of changing course from the traditional paths of "small carrot and big stick" in Latin America agreed that the government eventually would have to introduce several concrete steps, any one of which would represent a break with the past. The most commonly offered recommendations by 1988 were the following:

1. Restore diplomatic and economic relations with Cuba.
2. Cut off all aid to the contras, end the economic embargo of Nicaragua, and enter into direct negotiations with the Sandinista government.
3. Withdraw all troops from Grenada and Honduras and warships from the coasts of Haiti and Nicaragua as a sign that Uncle Sam would no longer make anyone "cry uncle" and was genuinely committed to a peaceful settlement of disputes.
4. Arrange for a debt moratorium that would help allow the "democratic transition" in Latin America to grow and prosper.

5. Change the 1986 Immigration Reform and Control Act or its implementation in at least two ways: (a) to prevent the massive internment or deportation of Mexicans and other Latin Americans through expansion or extension of the law's amnesty and political refugee provisions and (b) to honor the 1980 Refugee Act that obligated the United States to use UN criteria for defining a political refugee. (Every day this 1980 law of the land was being violated by the INS when it deported Guatemalans and Salvadorans, sending them back to an uncertain fate in their wartorn home countries.)

6. Restructure all U.S. aid and loan policies to demilitarize them and send the aid directly to the people involved, channeling it through existing governmental structures but giving grassroots people an effective oversight and veto power on the aid's delivery and application.

7. Provide Latin America with fairer, more stable terms of trade.

8. Address the narcotics problem at home in order to "dry up" the demand that fostered production and processing in Latin America; reach global agreements through international bodies on how to police the transnational trafficking.

9. Place conditions on "runaway shops" that would protect jobs in the United States and lead to more favorable work conditions for Latin Americans employed by U.S.-based TNCs.

10. Regulate U.S. corporations' and others' pollution of Latin America, including the dumping of toxic waste in Latin America, and recognize the international character of environmental problems.

Perhaps the most significant lobbying group advocating changes like these was the Washington, D.C.-based PACCA (Policy Alternatives for the Caribbean and Central America). PACCA was an association of policymakers and scholars "dedicated to promoting a humane and democratic alternative to present U.S. policies toward the region." PACCA's eighty-one-page 1984 booklet *Changing Course* was heralded as an alternative to the Kissinger Commission Report. It advocated nonintervention, respect for self-determination, collective self-defense, peaceful settlement of disputes, respect for human rights, and support for democratic development and values.

Another organization close to PACCA was PLAN (Progressive Latin Americanist Network), a group of Latin American scholars who put forth most of the anti-interventionist resolutions passed every eighteen months at the plenary meetings of the national organization of professional Latin Americanists LASA (Latin American Studies Association). At its 1986 Boston meeting,

PLAN voted to support the "independent mass mobilization" strategy, thus distinguishing its emphasis from the electoral/lobby emphasis of PACCA.

Voices like those of PACCA and PLAN argued that a majority of U.S. citizens would welcome a policy that, instead of backing militaristic regimes that ruled out democracy, jailed trade unionists, and made any kind of organizing difficult, got behind progressive governments and movements that encouraged trade unionism and other forms of organization for improving Latin Americans' standard of living.

Since ultimately only an improved standard of living would deny TNCs the lure to run away, there were material and not just idealistic grounds for the U.S. public's backing a "change in course." It would not be the first time North Americans welcomed promises of peaceful change. Millions had rallied to President Kennedy's call for a "Peace Corps" and advocacy of reform in Latin America. Even Fidel Castro had started out with a folk-hero image in much of the United States. But those bright early days of hope had soon been blacked out by Latin America's long, dark night.

Change advocates in the United States claimed that their proposals were totally feasible. Adjustments on the debt issue had already been made, a dialogue with Cuba had commenced and been cut short many times, a bill had been introduced in Congress to protect Salvadoran refugees (and temporary refuge was finally granted them in 1991), the Congress had repeatedly voted against aid to the contras, U.S. trade barriers to select Mexico products had been relaxed, and so on.

In order to concretize what a future U.S.–Latin American relationship might look like, advocates of change pointed to a number of realities and possibilities. An official alliance between more forward-looking U.S. policymakers with Latin America's younger technocratic elites and entrepreneurs, leaders of the widespread popular mobilizations, and representatives of the new ideological amalgams of the theology of liberation, Marxism, and nationalism, would give the United States a new and favorable image. In turn, by breaking the old, bankrupt alliance with outmoded elites, terroristic "national security states," aging gangster-style labor leaders, and corrupt bureaucrats, costly military adventures could be avoided and long-run peace and stability could be achieved.

This fresh U.S. alliance with the forces of the "second Latin America revolution" would bring more economic independence to Latin America, they said. Stagnation and mass unemployment would be replaced by a regional vigor offering the conditions for new international arrangements linking local, regional, and international economies. Traditional U.S. economic dominance, perceived by Latin Americans as, in the words of the Kissinger Commission Report, "economic imperialism," would be replaced by greater fairness of eco-

673

nomic exchange—and with it, greater productivity, dynamism, and economic growth.

Genuinely humanitarian and economic aid, they argued, would have to replace military aid instead of mask it. As it was, less than one-third of 1 percent of the U.S. GNP (gross national product) was spent on foreign aid, and 69 percent of foreign aid authorizations in the 1986 budget were for "security assistance." The U.S. "security" problem in Latin America was not a military one, they said, since "our southern neighbors" had neither the military means nor the political ambition to invade the United States. On the contrary, Latin Americans had ample reason to fear another U.S. invasion of one of their lands—as happened in Panama in 1989 and Haiti in 1994.

But there *was* a national security issue, they said, and that was an economic one. What was at stake was the U.S. standard of living, presently being undermined by TNCs that "knew no flag," repeatedly laid off workers, and yet strongly influenced the U.S. government to follow ill-advised policies in Latin America.

It would be either naive or duplicitous, change advocates suggested, to think that steps toward a new basis of friendship with Latin America could be taken short of fully endorsing its second revolution for economic independence. This endorsement might entail some strong measures to curb uncouth behavior by U.S. corporations, or to improve people's living standards. It might mean having to live and trade with some forms of socialism, at least in the case of Cuba. (This was already being done vis-à-vis China.) In the long run, however, it was the only way to avoid a veritable tidal wave of anti-Americanism, to check and reverse the sorry record of U.S. interventionism on the side of hated dictators, and to reenergize the economies of both the North and South.

The alternatives to a policy rooted not just in word but in deed to traditional American values of humanitarianism and democracy seemed a dark one. Its outlines could be detected in the clouds of war billowing up from Central America. It was never too late to change.

For a new U.S. aid policy to succeed, these voices acknowledged, there would have to be significant input from organized groups representative of the public interest. Safe and fair implementation and oversight of U.S. aid programs would have to be introduced at both ends of the exchange, rooted in democracy "bottom-up" processes like "town meetings," neighborhood or workplace councils, and "watchdog" committees elected by the people who were affected by each aid sector. To avoid corruption, they would have to have a voice in how the money would be spent as well as access to the account books to make sure actual decisions were implemented. They would have to have the right to immediate popular recall of those judged inadequate, corrupt, or negligent in carrying out their roles in the aid programs.

Examples from agriculture, health care, industry, and trade illustrated how such a new policy might work. In agriculture, instead of channeling machinery, fertilizers, and know-how into the export sector dominated by large landholders and forcing small farmers and peasants off the land into urban slums, U.S. aid would foment agrarian reform providing land for the landless and support of family farms and farm cooperatives. The goal in Latin America would be self-sufficiency in food production prior to export expansion, with profits from agricultural exports invested in the development of each nation's economy. The U.S. agricultural aid program could even be accompanied by a similar one at home to maintain and reinvigorate hundreds of thousands of failing U.S. family farms.

In Latin American health care the focus would be on the creation and staffing of clinics geared toward preventative medicine and local treatment. Money and training for corps of doctors, paramedics, and nurses would be increased. Instead of high-tech military equipment arriving in Latin America, high-tech medical diagnostic and therapeutic equipment would arrive, making it possible to lure back some of the "brain-drain" professionals who left Latin America every year for the United States or Western Europe.

In industry, instead of the irrationality, instability, and anarchy of current practices, such as production moving suddenly from one country to another or razor blades being produced in Puerto Rico, exported to the United States, and then being imported back to Puerto Rico at twice the price, indigenous profitable enterprises would be encouraged. Reliable payment of decent wages in order to stimulate both the production and consumption ends of the internal Latin American market would be fomented. Planning and regulation would take place. The aim would be to bring into progressive convergence domestic demand and production with indigenous technology and resources to meet community needs. Limits would be placed on the percentage of profits allowed to be sent abroad, forcing foreign investors to reinvest in the expansion of local economies from which they drew their labor and profits. Provisions would be made in all future labor contracts assuring minimum periods of job security and guaranteed retraining or reemployment for those laid off in case of bankruptcy or plant relocation or closure (a measure U.S. workers were already beginning to demand).

The shoe industry could be used to illustrate this type of rational industrial scheme. Brazil had the natural resources and trained labor force able to create a shoe industry that could shod all its people, millions of whom went barefoot. Instead, foreign companies hired Brazil's underpaid work force to produce footwear for export. These shoe exports in turn lead to U.S. manufacturers' closing down plants in Ohio and elsewhere, since they could make more money by producing in Brazil. A rational plan would provide start-up funds for locally owned shoe factories with decent minimum wage provisos.

As the wage gap between Brazil and the United States closed, the price gap would get smaller. It would not take long for competition to shift to the arena of quality and appearance. U.S. companies would be permitted to produce shoes anywhere so long as they paid workers a decent wage and allowed labor unions. If they closed down U.S. plants, they would be responsible for financing retraining programs for their laid-off workers. Such retraining programs would provide skills required in government-encouraged plans to rebuild the United States' deteriorating cities and economic infrastructure.

In trade, instead of debating free trade versus protectionism, people would concern themselves with providing guarantees of job security like those just mentioned. Tax and tariff policies making it attractive and easy for corporations to move production offshore would be eliminated. The criterion would be: let enterprises compete, but compete fairly. The present setup, as the Brazil-Ohio shoe example illustrated, was hurting producers and consumers everywhere.

Change advocates put forward creative versions of a North American Free Trade Agreement (NAFTA) that would give it a "human face"—as Mexico's "Group of 100" prominent intellectuals and former government officials suggested (see chapter 1). The version most popular among opponents of the actual NAFTA text was a continental development program first put forward by Mexico presidential candidate Cárdenas. It called for ironclad guarantees of environmental protection across borders, human rights, and "upward harmonization of wages" instead of "downward harmonization of wages." It, like the plans put forward by the pro-NAFTA "human facers," emphasized that the human rights of Mexican immigrant workers would have to be emphasized so that the abuses of the past would never be repeated.

Undoubtedly, public pressure would have to be mounted to bring about any real changes. In the case of trade, a grass roots movement linked up concerned citizens and groups in Mexico, the United States, and Canada— the "citizen diplomats" discussed in chapter 1. Objecting to the secretive and undemocratic manner in which NAFTA was drafted, this international movement came close to defeating NAFTA and won environment and labor "side agreements" in 1993. Since NAFTA's side agreements were not binding, the grass roots movement continued to push for change after NAFTA went into effect.

Many change advocates were convinced that if new policies vis-à-vis Latin America did not come about in the near future, advocates of current policies in Washington might find themselves engulfed by the maelstrom developing on the U.S. southern flank. More imaginative approaches to U.S. policy were not forthcoming during the Bush administration or the first years of the Clinton presidency. With the end of the Cold War and the momentary victory of peace advocates in Central America, change advocates had hoped for something more imaginative than the old nineteenth-century formula of "free enterprise, free trade." Yet Clinton embraced Bush's 1990 "Enterprise for the Americas" and free-trade/privatization initiative. In the 1992 presidential campaign Clinton was the first to embrace the tightening of the economic embargo against Cuba, and he stuck by his position even after some Reaganite conservatives in early 1994 called for lifting the embargo "immediately" (see Documents). Both Bush and Clinton championed an eventual hemispheric "common market."

Then, as president, Clinton wavered in his support for democracy in Haiti and tightened the rules against admitting Haitian refugees, some of whose predecessors still languished in barbed-wire detention camps (see the introduction to Part Two). U.S. pro-democracy proclamations, backed by an economic embargo against Haiti's military dictatorship, contradicted U.S. tolerance of a military regime that repeatedly broke its promises. As the reign of terror against Aristide supporters in Haiti intensified in 1993–94, Clinton finally decided to send in the Marines—not long after the crisis over Cuban refugees (see chapter 8). Even then the Clinton administration's stated aim of "restoring democracy" (where none had ever been permitted to exist more than a short time) was contradicted by the amnesty granted Haiti's military and police goons and the U.S. "training" programs to "modernize" Haiti's armed forces "to maintain law and order." Many observers believed the real aim of U.S. policymakers was to prevent Aristide's reforms from ever occurring, to crush the ongoing popular attempt at a "second revolution" in Haiti, and to preserve or create a Haitian military apparatus capable of continuing business as usual for Haiti's elites and TNCs. Some suspected that the 1994 Haitian invasion represented a bargaining chip or "threat" against Cuba, even as the 1989 Panama invasion had been used to threaten Nicaragua's Sandinistas (see chapters 5 and 7).

President Clinton's proposed health-care plan did not cover millions of Latin American immigrants, who did not qualify because they still were not citizens or lacked sufficient documentation. Unfortunately, germs do not distinguish between citizens and non citizens. A decade-old jingoistic anti-immigrant hysteria continued to plague the nation's largest emergent ethnic minority—Latinos (or "Hispanics," as the U.S. Census Bureau officially designated them). Change advocates called for implementing a multicultural education program from kindergarten through grade twelve and college. They won its mandating in most major states of the union, although the funds for its effective implementation were lacking. Multiculturalism's modest success represented an important first step in recognizing the links between Latin American history, politics, and culture and daily life in the United States (see entries under Cockcroft and Garza in Bibliography). The once "invisible minority"—the nation's Hispanic population—was becoming visible at last.

Multiculturalism reflected a growing awareness of the global character of all problems affecting U.S.–Latin America relations. The "global economy" touched everyone. The worldwide move toward less regulated market economies, even in still-socialist systems like Cuba's and China's, was not, however, necessarily so much a "free trade" trend as it was one of "free trade wars."

The competition between the EEC (European Economic Community), Japan, and the United States underlay the launching of NAFTA. Similar regional trade blocs within Latin America (MERCOSUR, Andean Pact, etc.) replicated the scramble to "defend one's area markets." Japan's encouraging of the APEC (Asia Pacific Economic Cooperation forum), although incorporating U.S., Mexican, and Chilean participation, could also be viewed as one more move on the trade-war chessboard.

If there was ever any doubt about how regional "free trade" blocs argued protectionism (against other blocs), then the breakdown in trade talks between the United States and Japan in early 1994 put that doubt to rest. Moreover, the free trade framework agreements signed by the United States with Chile and other Latin American countries were aimed at assuring favorable investment conditions for U.S.-based TNCs and—through "local content" clauses similar to those in NAFTA—at placing Japanese and European companies at a disadvantage in the U.S. "backyard." The "free trade wars" were, in effect, undemocratic since they tended to be carried out by small circles of elites without input from working people whose wages and living standards the elites were so willing to sacrifice in order to "make the nation competitive."

During the second half of the 1980s, Europe had replaced the United States as leader in new direct foreign investment in Latin America, with Japan a very close third. Likewise, both Europe and Japan fared better with the Latin Americans than the United States did at the Earth Summit 1992 in Brazil, agreeing to sign the biodiversity convention opposed by the United States (for details on that issue and the all-important conflict over "intellectual property rights," see chapter 20 and Documents). In early 1993, Japan extended Brazil a $840 million environmental cleanup loan. Japan also played a greater role in debt relief schemes for Latin America.

In part because of the new "free trade" agreements of the early 1990s and the world recession's reaching Europe and Japan, U.S. exports to Latin America surpassed U.S. exports to either Germany or Japan in 1992. Regaining export "competitiveness" became a major U.S. goal.

The Latin American Economic System (SELA), a UN body, warned in October 1993 that the monopolization of technological transformations by twelve industries involving more than a thousand competing TNCs threatened to leave Latin America behind. So did the December 1993 final conclusion of the "Uruguay Round" of GATT (General Agreement on Tariffs and Trade). Its assurance of favorable state subsidies to farmers in Europe and the United

States (a "no-no" in Latin America because of the privatization "free trade" doctrine of neo-liberalism) undercut Latin America's competitive position. On the other hand, several more Latin American countries applied for full membership in GATT, there being "no other game in town."

Neo-liberalism's major claim to success in Latin America was a return of foreign investment to the region and renewed economic "growth" in some countries (whose preceding negative growth rates made some improvement almost inevitable). However, the high social costs of neo-liberalism and an accompanying political backlash threatened to cut short its apparent ideological hegemony. Many Latin American governments were feeling popular pressure "from below" to drop the neo-liberal approach. Yet what new strategy might replace it was not immediately clear. The World Bank strategy on "investing in the poor," introduced in the 1970s as a means of confronting the bottom-up new politics, was not eliminating poverty in the long run (see Lipton entry in Bibliography). It was, however, linking small "independent" producers to international lenders and markets, such as the 40,000 women who worked as seasonal gatherers of roseships in Chile, whose low-wage labors yielded $5 million a year to export companies dealing with Europe and Japan.

Moreover, there was a *"crisis of the state"* that made government less able to meet the needs of the masses. Even though privatization schemes brought millions of dollars into state treasuries, thereby preventing complete state collapse, most of the new monies went back to the private sector through debt repayments and state subsidies, or to individuals and private firms through corruption. This circular flow of riches did not resolve the crisis of the state. Constrained state budgets in the face of pressing demands for urban and agrarian reforms left the hands of incumbent presidents tied. While promising more, they were able to deliver less. Typical results were food riots and the military's opening fire on people (see, for example, chapters 11 and 20 on Venezuela and Brazil).

State-based corruption related both to the crisis of the state and to a lack of clear-cut hegemony by any one set of elites or military officers or political party. Consequently, every party and competing interest escalated its efforts to tarnish the others' reputations with charges of corruption. Since corruption was so widespread in Latin America, just as it was in the United States or other parts of the world, some of the charges stuck! Brazilian sociologist Theotonio dos Santos maintained that both in amount of money transferred and in the harm done to "the masses," corruption was ultimately less costly or detrimental than "state subsidies to the oligarchy and the private sector."

As for the masses, many of them led not just by well-paid industrial workers but also by the most oppressed (women and Indians), they seemed to be following a strategy of fighting for control over economic production at the workplace and neighborhood levels instead of control over the bankrupt state.

Indians also moved to the forefront of the fight to defend the environment, and the United Nations declared 1993 as the International Year of the World's Indigenous Peoples. Many of Latin America's poor were female, leading to the concept "feminization of poverty." Women helped organize various forms of neighborhood cooperatives. Urban-based advocates of the "new politics," when not co-opted or absorbed into the struggle for control of crisis-ridden governments, dedicated themselves to this popular struggle from below.

The four limitations on the new politics described in the Overview grew more formidable with time, however. Especially limiting were two factors: first, the demoralization and exhaustion caused by economic hard times and by the failure of the new civilian presidents to carry through on their populist promises; and second, the lack of a cohesive organizational network to bring together the diverse mobilized groups. But the hope for some was in the stubborn persistence of the new politics and its proven willingness to learn from mistakes and experiment with new approaches.

Latin America's limited "democratic transition" was shorting out in several countries. Conservative political scientist Howard Wiarda warned in 1990 (see entry in Overview Bibliography) of a "pervasive ethnocentrism" in U.S. policy that led policymakers to expect elections to work in Latin America the way they did in the United States. Venezuela's voters, among others, rejected the U.S.-style two-party model in the early 1990s (see chapter 11). Wiarda continued to back the NED (National Endowment for Democracy) if it operated on a nonpartisan basis, which it had not done in the past (see Overview). The U.S. House of Representatives, under pressure from the anti-intervention movement, repeatedly refused to continue funding NED in the early 1990s. Wiarda asserted that without economic recovery in Latin America there would likely occur the demise of "an entire framework, model, and system of more or less moderate, more or less centrist, and more or less democratic rule." But Wiarda and others found hope in a "new consensus in Washington ... on a strong democracy/human rights agenda" for Latin America. That consensus had yet to be carried out in practice.

One requisite for a serious policy reassessment was the need to recognize the great differences between Latin American nations and the importance of geography. There were, of course, "haves" and "have nots" in every nation, but just as importantly there were "have" and "have not" *countries*. Nicaragua was no Brazil! Ironically, the U.S. policy conflicts that traditionally attracted the most attention involved the "have not" countries, yet the economic action was overwhelmingly with the semi-industrialized giants (Mexico, Brazil, and others—see Overview).

Ultimately, the challenge for U.S. policymakers was to become part of the solution instead of part of the problem. The unilateral and multilateral military intervention approach clearly was not working. Moreover, the ongoing militaristic approach to problems that are economic and political in character contradicted the pressures brought by some U.S. ambassadors to "democratize" militarized regimes or to prevent the radical Right from taking total power (Chile, Paraguay, El Salvador, Haiti). At a November 1987 meeting of the U.S. and Latin American army commanders in Argentina, a reported fifteen secret agreements were approved—all designed to prevent "Communists" and "revolutionaries" from taking power. With the end of the Cold War, the main military shift was—except for the case of Cuba—in fighting reformers and revolutionaries in the name of conducting a war against "terrorists" and "drug traffickers" instead of "Communists" (see various chapters, e.g., chapter 14).

But by the mid-1990s the Clinton administration was publicly stating that the "drug war" was a failure, so that excuse was wearing thin. Coca production kept rising in the Andes. The yearly $150 billion made from drug trafficking dwarfed traditional "exports" like coffee, sugar, oil, and so on. Anthropologists compared the role of coca, heroin, and marijuana to the role of gold and silver more than four centuries earlier. It served as a kind of "gold rush" (pun intended). Policymakers began talking of a "world court" for drug lords. But there remained knotty problems of extradition, "kidnapping" suspects in Latin America for trial in the United States (approved by the U.S. Supreme Court, lending legitimacy to the capture and trial of Panama's Noriega), and "going to the source"—in Latin Americans' eyes the huge market created by U.S. consumers, in Washington's eyes Latin America's countryside. U.S. critics of the "war on drugs" and its militarization advocated spending more on treatment and education programs and less on law enforcement and "interdiction."

According to some advocates of change, democratizing Latin America might best start at home by democratizing the United States. The early 1990s witnessed new revelations of the secret and undemocratic character of the U.S. government when it came to policy-making, including the long-term existence of a secret intelligence agency (see the introduction to Part One). Other revelations included ones about radiation testing on humans and widespread radioactive fallout in secret Cold War weapon tests, as well as proof of U.S. direct training of Salvadorans tied to death squads. The promised opening of CIA files might reveal more—especially on secret operations in Cuba and Guatemala—although some suspected the files might be "too laundered."

In light of past U.S. policy failures and intolerances of reform-oriented governments (Guatemala, 1954: Cuba, 1959; Dominican Republic, 1965; Chile, 1973; Nicaragua, 1980s; Grenada, 1983; Panama; 1989), it became incumbent upon policymakers to initiate new, more imaginative, even experimental policies to tap Latin America's potential for social peace and a broader opening to economic and political democracy—the only lasting source of stability. In the long run, the challenge in Washington was to adjust not just to the rise of one or another "Perón," "Castro," "Lula," or "Cárdenas" but also to the concrete demands of the mass movements that made their rise possible. In other words, the dilemma for policymakers was how to embrace the new politics instead of remaining part of the problem the new politics was confronting. This was the challenge, as well as the hope, of Latin America's new politics— and of those concerned citizens in the United States who wanted to see a genuine change of course in Washington.

Selected Bibliography

See also bibliographies to Overview, Introductions to Parts One, Two, and Three, and chapters 1 and 20.

Biodiversity: Social and Ecological Consequences. London, England: Zed Press, 1992.

Brown, Lester R., *et al. State of the World 1994.* Worldwatch Institute. New York: Norton, 1994. Annual environmental report.

Browne, Harry, and Beth Sims. *Runaway America: U.S. Jobs and Factories on the Move.* Albuquerque, NM: Inter-Hemispheric Education Resource Center, 1993.

Carr, Barry, and Steve Ellner (eds). *The Latin American Left: From the Fall of Allende to Perestroika.* Boulder, CO: Westview, 1993.

Clay, Jason W. *Indigenous People and Tropical Forests: Models of Land Use and Management from Latin America.* Cambridge, MA: Cultural Survival, 1990.

Cleary, Edward L., and Hannah Stewart-Gambino (eds.). *Conflict and Competition: The Latin America Church in a Changing Environment.* Boulder, CO: Lynne Rienner, 1992. New limits on theology of liberation social movements.

Cockcroft, James D. *Outlaws in the Promised Land.* New York: Grove Press, 1988. On political refugee issue, 1986 Immigration Act, detention camps, and U.S. "two-tiered" economy.

———. *Hispanics in the Struggle for Social Justice.* New York: Franklin Watts, 1994.

———. *Latinos in the Making of the United States.* New York: Franklin Watts, 1995.

"The Conquest of Nature, 1492–1992." *Nacla Report on the Americas,* 25 (Sept. 1991).

Cowell, Adrian. *The Decade of Destruction: The Crusade to Save the Amazon Rain Forest.* New York: Holt, 1990.

"Disposable Children: The Hazards of Growing Up Poor in Latin America." *Nacla Report on the Americas,* 27(6) (May/June 1994).

"Ecological Crisis of Latin America." *Latin American Perspectives,* 19:1 (Winter 1992).

Garza, Hedda. *Latinas: Hispanic Women in the United States.* New York: Franklin Watts, 1994. The only short synthesis; pioneering.

Goodman, David, and Michael Redclift (eds.). *Environment and Development in Latin America: The Politics of Sustainability.* Manchester, England: Manchester University Press, 1991.

Haar, Jerry, and Edgar J. Dosman (eds.). *A Dynamic Partnership: Canada's Changing Role in the Americas.* Miami, FL: University of Miami, North-South Center, 1993.

Hartlyn, Jonathan, Lars Schoultz, and Augusto Varas. *The United States and Latin America in the 1990s.* Chapel Hill: University of North Carolina Press, 1993. Post–Cold War assessment.

Hecht, S. B., and A. Cockburn. *The Fate of the Forest: Developers, Destroyers, and Defenders of the Amazon.* New York: Routledge, 1989.

Inter-American Development Bank. *Economic and Social Progress in Latin America, 1988 Report;* Special Section: *Science and Technology.* Washington, DC: IADB, 1988.

Jonas, Susanne, and Edward J. McCaughan (eds.). *Latin America Faces the Twenty-First Century.* Boulder, CO: Westview, 1994.

Landau, Saul. *The Dangerous Doctrine: National Security and U.S. Foreign Policy.* Boulder, CO: Westview, 1988.

Lappé, Frances Moore, and Joseph Collins. *World Hunger: Twelve Myths.* New York: Grove Press, 1986. Most eye-opening book for students—short, well researched.

Latin America Bureau (LAB). *The European Challenge: Europe's New Role in Latin America.* London, England: LAB, 1982.

"The Latin American Left: A Painful Rebirth." *Nacla Report on the Americas,* 25(5)(May 1992).

Lipton, Michael, and Jacques van der Gaag. *Including the Poor.* Washington, DC: World Bank, 1994. Much data from internal World Bank reports indicating favoring of vested interests over the poor.

Lowenthal, Abraham. *Partners in Conflict: The United States and Latin America in the 1990s.* Baltimore, MD: Johns Hopkins University Press, 1990. Calls for shifting focus from Central America to Mexico, Brazil, and Caribbean Basin.

Martz, John D. (Ed.). *United States Policy in Latin America: A Quarter Century of Crisis and Challenge, 1961–1986.* Lincoln: University of Nebraska Press, 1988.

Mower, Jr., Glenn. *The European Community and Latin America: A Case Study in Global Role Expansion.* Boulder, CO: Westview, 1981.

Muñoz, Heraldo. *Environment and Diplomacy in the Americas.* Boulder, CO: Lynne Rienner, 1992. Useful documents sections.

"Neoliberalism and 'Democratization' in Latin America." *Latin American Perspectives,* 21:4 (Fall 1994).

"The New Gospel: North American Free Trade." *Nacla Report on the Americas,* 24(6)(May 1991).

Pastor, Robert A. (ed.). *Democracy in the Americas: Stopping the Pendulum.* New York: Holmes and Meier, 1989. Policy recommendations by U.S. "experts" and some leading Latin American politicians.

Plant, Christopher, and Judith Plant. *Green Business: Hope or Hoax?* Philadelphia, PA: New Society Publishers, 1991. On leaving environmental cleanup and protection to the private sector.

Plant Shutdowns Monitor. Oakland, CA: Data Center, N.d. Only source tracking U.S. plant closures and worker layoffs (464 19th St., Oakland, CA 94612).

"The Politics of Corruption and the Corruption of Politics." *Nacla Report on the Americas,* 27(3)(Nov./Dec. 1993).

Purcell, Susan Kaufman, and Robert M. Immerman (eds.). *Japan and Latin America in the New Global Order.* Boulder, CO: Lynne Rienner, 1992. Policy-oriented.

Raghavan, Chakravarthi. *Recolonization: GATT, the Uruguay Round and the Third World.* London, England: Zed Books, 1990. Insightful on the free trade wars.

Randall, Margaret. *Gathering Rage: The Failure of Twentieth Century Revolutions to Develop a Feminist Agenda.* New York: Monthly Review Press, 1992.

Rich, Bruce. *The World Bank, Environmental Impoverishment, and the Crisis of Development.* Boston, MA: Beacon Press, 1994.

Sims, Beth. *Workers of the World Undermined: American Labor's Role in U.S. Foreign Policy.* Boston, MA: South End Press, 1992. Need to build long-absent international labor solidarity inside AFL-CIO.

Smith, Peter (ed.). *Drug Policy in the Americas.* Boulder, CO: Westview, 1992.

"Social Movements and Political Change in Latin America," *Latin American Perspectives,* 21:2 and 3 (Spring and Summer 1994).

Stallings, Barbara, and Gabriel Székely (eds.). *Japan, the United States, and Latin America*. Baltimore, MD: John Hopkins University Press, 1993.

United Nations. *Agenda 21: Rio Declaration and Forest Principles Post-Rio Edition*. New York: United Nations Publications, 1993. Official version of key document and proposed implementation steps coming out of Earth Summit 1992 (see chapter 20).

Wiarda, Howard J. *In Search of Policy: The United States and Latin America*. Washington, DC: American Enterprise Institute, 1984. Conservative "think tank" book.

Yoffie, David (ed.). *Beyond Free Trade: Firms, Governments and Global Competion*. Boston, MA: Harvard Business School Press, 1993.

Zagorski, Paul W. *Democracy vs. National Security: Civil-Military Relations in Latin America*. Boulder, CO: Lynne Rienner, 1991. South American case studies reveal limits to "democratic transition."

Films

The Amazon: A Vanishing Rainforest. 1988. 29 minutes. Color video.

The Politics of Food. 1988. 120 minutes. PBS color video—a real eye-opener for students and teachers alike.

___ Appendix: Documents _____

Note: In some documents only select portions are presented and ellipses are used sparingly in order to avoid overuse.

Contents

I. Official U.S. Policy Documents

Document I.1: President Reagan's May 1, 1985, Executive Order and Message to Congress Placing Economic Embargo on Nicaragua

Executive Order

By the authority vested in me as President by the Constitution and laws of the United States of America, including the International Emergency Economic Powers Act (50 U.S.C. 1701 et seq.), the National Emergencies Act (50 U.S.C. 1601 et seq.), Chapter 12 of Title 50 of the United States Code (50 U.S.C. 191 et seq.), and Section 301 of Title 3 of the United States Code,

I, Ronald Reagan, President of the United States of America, find that the policies and actions of the government of Nicaragua constitute an unusual and extraordinary threat to the national security and foreign policy of the United States and hereby declare a national emergency to deal with that threat.

I hereby prohibit all imports into the United States of goods and services of Nicaraguan origin; all exports from the United States of goods to or destined for Nicaragua, except those destined for the organized democratic resistance, and transactions relating thereto.

I hereby prohibit Nicaraguan air carriers from engaging in air transportation to or from points in the United States, and transactions relating thereto.

In addition, I hereby prohibit vessels of Nicaraguan registry from entering into United States ports, and transactions relating thereto.

The Secretary of the Treasury is delegated and authorized to employ all powers granted to me by the International Emergency Economic Powers Act to carry out the purposes of this order.

The prohibitions set forth in this order shall be effective as of 12:01 A.M., Eastern daylight time, May 7, 1985, and shall be transmitted to the Congress and published in the Federal Register.

Message to Congress

1. I have authorized these steps in response to the emergency situation created by the Nicaraguan government's aggressive activities in Central America. Nicaragua's continuing efforts to subvert its neighbors, its rapid and destabilizing military buildup, its close military and security ties to Cuba and the Soviet Union, and its imposition of Communist totalitarian internal rule have been described fully in the past several weeks. The current visit by

Source: From Executive Order and Message to Congress by Ronald Reagan on May 1, 1985, placing an economic embargo on Nicaragua.

Nicaraguan President Ortega to Moscow underscores this disturbing trend. The recent rejection by Nicaragua of my peace initiative, viewed in the light of the constantly rising pressure that Nicaragua's military buildup places on the democratic nations of the region, makes clear the urgent threat that Nicaragua's activities represent to the security of the region and, therefore, to the security and foreign policy of the United States. The activities of Nicaragua, supported by the Soviet Union and its allies, are incompatible with normal commercial relations.

2. In taking these steps, I note that during this month's debate on U.S. policy toward Nicaragua, many members of Congress, both supporters and opponents of my proposals, called for the early application of economic sanctions.

3. I have long made clear that changes in Sandinista behavior must occur if peace is to be achieved in Central America. At this time, I again call on the government of Nicaragua:

- To halt its export of armed insurrection, terrorism, and subversion in neighboring countries;
- To end its extensive military relationship with Cuba and the Soviet bloc and remove their military and security personnel;
- To stop its massive arms buildup and help restore the regional military balance; and
- To respect, in law and in practice, democratic pluralism and observance of full political and human rights in Nicaragua.

4. U.S. application of these sanctions should be seen by the government of Nicaragua, and by those who abet it, as unmistakable evidence that we take seriously the obligation to protect our security interests and those of our friends. I ask the government of Nicaragua to address seriously the concerns of its neighbors and its own opposition and to honor its solemn commitments to noninterference, nonalignment, respect for democracy, and peace. Failure to do so will only diminish the prospects for a peaceful settlement in Central America.

II.   Official Investigative or Judicial Findings on U.S. Policies

Document II.1: World Court Decision, June 26, 1986

The Court

(1) by eleven votes to four,

Decides that in adjudicating the dispute brought before it by the Application filed by the Republic of Nicaragua on 9 April 1984, the Court is required to apply the "multilateral treaty reservation" contained in proviso *(c)* to the declaration of acceptance of jurisdiction made under Article 36, paragraph 2. of the Statute of the Court by the Government of the United States of America deposited on 26 August 1946;

(2) By twelve votes to three,

Rejects the justification of collective self-defence maintained by the United States of America in connection with the military and paramilitary activities in and against Nicaragua, the subject of this case;

(3) By twelve votes to three,

Decides that the United States of America, by training, arming, equipping, financing and supplying the *contra* forces or otherwise encouraging, supporting and aiding military and paramilitary activities in and against Nicaragua, has acted, against the Republic of Nicaragua, in breach of its obligation under customary international law not to intervene in the affairs of another State;

(4) By twelve votes to three,

Decides that the United States of America, by certain attacks on Nicaraguan territory in 1983–1984, namely attacks on Puerto Sandino on 13 September and 14 October 1983; an attack on Corinto on 10 October 1983; an attack on Potosi Naval Base on 4/5 January 1984; an attack on San Juan del Sur on 7 March 1984; attacks on patrol boats at Puerto Sandino on 28 and 30 March 1984; and an attack on San Juan del Norte on 9 April 1984; and further by those acts of intervention referred to in subparagraph (3) hereof which involve the use of force, has acted, against the Republic of Nicaragua, in breach of its obligation under customary international law not to use force against another State;

Source: From decision made on June 26, 1986, by World Court on application filed on April 9, 1984, by the Republic of Nicaragua in dispute with United States. Issued by the World Court at The Hague, Netherlands, June 1986.

(5) By twelve votes to three,

Decides that the United States of America, by directing or authorizing overflights of Nicaragua territory, and by acts imputable to the United States referred to in subparagraph (4) hereof, has acted, against the Republic of Nicaragua, in breach of its obligation under customary international law not to violate the sovereignty of another State;

(6) By twelve votes to three,

Decides that, by laying mines in the internal or territorial waters of the Republic of Nicaragua during the first months of 1984, the United States of America has acted, against the Republic of Nicaragua, in breach of its obligations under customary international law not to use force against another State, not to intervene in its affairs, not to violate its sovereignty and not to interrupt peaceful maritime commerce:

(7) By fourteen votes to one,

Decides that, by the acts referred to in subparagraph (6) hereof, the United States of America has acted, against the Republic of Nicaragua, in breach of its obligations under Article XIX of the Treaty of Friendship, Commerce and Navigation between the United States of America and the Republic of Nicaragua signed at Managua on 21 January 1956;

(8) By fourteen votes to one,

Decides that the United States of America, by failing to make known the existence and location of the mines laid by it, referred to in subparagraph (6) hereof, has acted in breach of its obligations under customary international law in this respect;

(9) By fourteen votes to one,

Finds that the United States of America, by producing in 1983 a manual entitled *Operaciones sicológicas en guerra de guerrillas,* and disseminating it to *contra* forces, has encouraged the commission by them of acts contrary to general principles of humanitarian law; but does not find a basis for concluding that any such acts which may have been committed are imputable to the United States of America as acts of the United States of America;

(10) By twelve votes to three,

Decides that the United States of America, by the attacks on Nicaraguan territory referred to in subparagraph (4) hereof, and by declaring a general embargo on trade with Nicaragua on 1 May 1985, has committed acts calculated to deprive of its object and purpose the Treaty of Friendship, Commerce and Navigation between the Parties signed at Managua on 21 January 1956;

(11) By twelve votes to three,

Decides that the United States of America, by the attacks on Nicaraguan territory referred to in subparagraph (4) hereof, and by declaring a general embargo on trade with Nicaragua on 1 May 1985, has acted in breach of its obligations under Article XIX of the Treaty of Friendship, Commerce and Navigation between the Parties signed at Managua on 21 January 1956;

(12) By twelve votes to three,

Decides that the United States of America is under a duty immediately to cease and to refrain from all such acts as may constitute breaches of the foregoing legal obligations;

(13) By twelve votes to three,

Decides that the United States of America is under an obligation to make reparation to the Republic of Nicaragua for all injury caused to Nicaragua by the breaches of obligations under customary international law enumerated above;

(14) By fourteen votes to one,

Decides that the United States of America is under an obligation to make reparation to the Republic of Nicaragua for all injury caused to Nicaragua by the breaches of the Treaty of Friendship, Commerce and Navigation between the Parties signed at Managua on 21 January 1956;

(15) By fourteen votes to one,

Decides that the form and amount of such reparation, failing agreement between the Parties, will be settled by the Court, and reserves for this purpose the subsequent procedure in the case;

(16) Unanimously

Recalls to both Parties their obligation to seek a solution to their disputes by peaceful means in accordance with international law.

Document II.2: Iran-Contragate Congressional Hearings Executive Summary Report, 1987 (selections)

The Coverup

Indeed, the Administration went to considerable lengths to avoid notifying Congress. On learning that the President had authorized the Attorney General to gather the relevant facts, North and Poindexter shredded and altered official documents on November 21, 1986, and later that weekend . . . North testified that he assured Poindexter that he had destroyed all documents relating to the diversion. The diversion nevertheless was discovered on November 22, 1986, when a Justice Department official, assisting the Attorney General's fact-finding inquiry, found a "diversion memorandum" that had escaped the shredder.

The Attorney General then announced at his November 25 press conference that the diversion had occurred and that the President did not know of it. But he made several incorrect statements about his own investigation. . . .

In light of the destruction of material evidence by Poindexter and North and the death of Casey, all of the facts may never be known.

Findings and Conclusions

The common ingredients of the Iran and Contra policies were secrecy, deception, and disdain for the law. A small group of senior officials believed that they alone knew what was right. They viewed knowledge of their actions by others in the Government as a threat to their objectives. They told neither the Secretary of State, the Congress nor the American people of their actions. When exposure was threatened, they destroyed official documents and lied to Cabinet officials, to the public, and to elected representatives in Congress. They testified that they even withheld key facts from the President. . . .

Policy Contradictions and Failures. The Administration's departure from democratic processes created the conditions for policy failure, and led to contradictions which undermined the credibility of the United States.

The United States simultaneously pursued two contradictory foreign policies—a public one and a secret one:

The public policy was not to make any concessions for the release of hostages lest such concessions encourage more hostage-taking. At the same

Source: Selections from Executive Summary Report of the Iran-Contragate Congressional Hearings, prepared by U.S. House of Representatives Select Committee to Investigate Covert Arms Transactions with Iran and U.S. Senate select Committee on Secret Military Assistance to Iran and the Nicaraguan Opposition, December 1987.

time, the United States was secretly trading weapons to get the hostages back.

The public policy was to observe the "letter and spirit" of the Boland Amendment's proscriptions against military or paramilitary assistance to the Contras. At the same time, the NSC staff was secretly assuming the direction and funding of the Contras' military effort.

These contradictions in policy inevitably resulted in policy failure:

The United States armed Iran, including its most radical elements, but attained neither a new relationship with that hostile regime nor a reduction in the number of American hostages.

The United States opened itself to blackmail by adversaries who might reveal the secret arms sales. . . .

The United States undermined its credibility with friends and allies.

Dishonesty and Secrecy. The Iran-Contra Affair was characterized by pervasive dishonesty and inordinate secrecy.

North admitted that he and other officials lied repeatedly to Congress and to the American people about the Contra covert action and Iran arms sales, and that he altered and destroyed official documents.

Secrecy became an obsession. Congress was never informed of the Iran or the Contra covert actions, notwithstanding the requirement in the law that Congress be notified of all covert actions in a "timely fashion." . . .

. . . The lies, omission, shreddings, attempts to rewrite history—all continued, even after the President authorized the Attorney General to find out the facts . . .

As with Iran, Congress was misled about the NSC staff's support for the Contras during the period of the Boland Amendment, although the role of the NSC staff was no secret to others. North testified that his operation was well-known to the press in the Soviet Union, Cuba, and Nicaragua. . . .

Privatization. The NSC staff turned to private parties and third countries to do the Government's business.

Moreover, under the Constitution only Congress can provide funds for the Executive branch. The Framers intended Congress's "power of the purse" to be one of the principal checks on Executive action. It was designed, among other things, to prevent the Executive from involving this country unilaterally in a foreign conflict. . . .

Lack of Accountability. The confusion, deception, and privatization which marked the Iran-Contra Affair were the inevitable products of an attempt to avoid accountability. Congress, the Cabinet, and the Joint Chiefs of Staff were denied information and excluded from the decision-making process. Democratic procedures were disregarded.

Officials who make public policy must be accountable to the public. But the public cannot hold officials accountable for polices of which the public is unaware. Policies that are known can be subjected to the test of reason, and mistakes can be corrected after consultation with the Congress and deliberation within the Executive branch itself. Policies that are secret become the private preserve of the few, mistakes are inevitably perpetuated, and the public loses control over Government. That is what happened in the Iran-Contra Affair.

Congress was told almost nothing—and what it was told was false.

Deniability replaced accountability. Thus, Poindexter justified his decision not to inform the President of the diversion on the ground that he wanted to give the president "deniability." Poindexter said he wanted to shield the president from political embarrassment if the diversion became public.

This kind of thinking is inconsistent with democratic governance . . .

The very premise of democracy is that "we the people" are entitled to make our own choices on fundamental policies. But freedom of choice is illusory if policies are kept, not only from the public, but from its elected representatives. . . .

Intelligence Abuses. Covert Operations. Covert actions should be consistent with publicly defined U.S. foreign policy goals. Because covert operations are secret by definition, they are of course not openly debated or publicly approved. So long as the policies which they further are known, and so long as they are conducted in accordance with law, covert operations are acceptable. . . . These were not covert actions, they were covert policies; and covert policies are incompatible with democracy. . . .

In the Iran-Contra Affair, secrecy was used to justify lies to Congress. . . . It was used not as a shield against our adversaries, but as a weapon against our own democratic institutions.

The NSC was created to provide candid and comprehensive advice to the President. It is the judgment of these Committees that the NSC staff should never again engage in covert operations.

Disdain for Law. In the Iran-Contra Affair, officials viewed the law not as setting boundaries for their actions, but raising impediments to their goals. When the goals and the law collided, the law gave way:

The covert program of support for the Contras evaded the Constitution's most significant check on Executive power: the President can spend funds on a program only if he can convince Congress to appropriate the money.

The NSC ultimately developed and directed a private network that conducted, in North's words, a "full service covert operation" in support of the Contras.

This could not have been more contrary to the intent of the Boland legislation.

Numerous other laws were disregarded:

North's full-service covert operation was a "significant anticipated intelligence activity" required to be disclosed to the Intelligence Committees of Congress under Section 501 of the National Security Act. No such disclosure was made.

False statements to Congress are felonies if made with knowledge and intent. Several administration officials gave statements denying NSC staff activities in support of the Contras which North later described in his testimony as "false," and "misleading, evasive and wrong."

The application of proceeds from U.S. arms sales for the benefit of the Contra war effort violated the Boland Amendment.

The U.S. Government's approval of the pre-Finding 1985 sales by Israel of arms to the Government of Iran was inconsistent with the Government's obligations under the Arms Export Control Act.

The testimony to Congress in November 1986 that the U.S. Government had no contemporaneous knowledge of the Israeli shipments, and the shredding of documents relating to the shipments while a Congressional inquiry into those shipments was pending, obstructed Congressional investigations.

Congress and the President. . . . The Policies of the United States cannot succeed unless the president and the Congress work together.

Yet, in the Iran-Contra Affair, Administration officials holding no elected office repeatedly evidenced disrespect for Congress' efforts to perform its Constitutional oversight role in foreign policy: Numerous officials made false statements to, and misled, the Congress.

Who Was Responsible?

Who was responsible for the Iran-Contra Affair? Part of our mandate was to answer that question, not in a legal sense (which is the responsibility of the Independent Counsel), but in order to reaffirm that those who serve the Government are accountable for their actions. Based on our investigations, we reach the following conclusions.

At the operational level, the central figure in the Iran-Contra Affair was Lt. Col. North, who coordinated all of the activities and was involved in all aspects of the secret operations. North, however, did not act alone.

North's conduct had the express approval of Admiral John Poindexter, first as Deputy National Security Adviser, and then as National Security Adviser. North also had at least the tacit support of Robert McFarlane, who served as National Security Adviser until December 1985.

In addition, for reasons cited earlier, we believe that the late Director of Central Intelligence, William Casey, encouraged North, gave him direction, and promoted the concept of an extra-legal covert organization . . . The Attorney General learned of the diversion memorandum, yet he . . . waited too long to seal North's offices. These lapses placed a cloud over the Attorney General's investigation.

There is no evidence that the Vice President was aware of the diversion. The Vice President attended several meetings on the Iran initiative, but none of the participants could recall his views.

The central remaining question is the role of the President in the Iran-Contra Affair. On this critical point, the shredding of documents by Poindexter, North, and others, and the death of Casey, leave the record incomplete.

Nevertheless, the ultimate responsibility for the events in the Iran-Contra Affair must rest with the President. If the President did not know what his National Security Advisers were doing, he should have.

Members of the NSC staff appeared to believe that their actions were consistent with the President's desires. It was the President's policy—not an isolated decision by North or Poindexter—to sell arms secretly to Iran and to maintain the Contras "body and soul," the Boland Amendment notwithstanding. To the NSC staff, implementation of these policies became the overriding concern.

The President himself told the public that the U.S. Government had no connection to the Hasenfus airplane. He told the public that early reports of arms sales for hostages had "no foundation." He told the public that the United States had not traded arms for hostages. He told the public that the United States had not condoned the arms sales by Israel to Iran, when in fact he had approved them and signed a Finding, later destroyed by Poindexter, recording his approval. All of these statements by the President were wrong.

Conclusions

Out of necessity, covert activities are conducted, and nearly all approved and monitored, in secret. Because they are not subject to public debate and scrutiny, they must be examined carefully within the practical constraints imposed by the need for operational security. It has been the United States' historic achievement to develop a system of law, using statutes, executive orders, regulations, notification procedures, that provides this scrutiny and protection. The Committees conclude:

(a) Covert operations are a necessary component of our Nation's foreign policy. They can supplement, not replace, diplomacy and normal instruments of foreign policy. As National Security Adviser Robert McFarlane testified, "it is clearly unwise to rely on covert action as the core of our policy." The government must be able to gain and sustain popular support for its foreign policy through open, public debate.

(b) Covert operations are compatible with democratic government if they are conducted in an accountable manner and in accordance with law. Laws mandate reporting and prior notice to Congress.

(c) As the Church Committee [on U.S. intervention in Chile, 1973] wrote more than a dozen years ago, "covert actions should be consistent with publicly defined United States foreign policy goals." But the policies themselves cannot be secret.

(d) All Government operations, including covert action operations, must be funded from appropriated monies or from funds known to the appropriate committees of the Congress and subject to Congressional control. This principle is at the heart of our constitutional system of checks and balances.

(e) The intelligence agencies must deal in a spirit of good faith with the Congress.

(f) Congress must have the will to exercise oversight over covert operations.

(g) The Congress also has a responsibility to ensure that sensitive information from the executive branch remains secure.

(h) The gathering, analysis, and reporting of intelligence should be done in such a way that there can be no question that the conclusions are driven by the actual facts, rather than by what a policy advocate hopes these facts will be.

III. Environment Documents

Document III.1: Proposed Biodiversity Convention, Rio de Janeiro "Earth Summit," 1992

Outline of the Convention

Note: • *indicates a summary of an element which has a wide degree of support*
  ➤ *indicates a summary of an element which is more controversial*

Chapter I: Preamble/Objectives

- objective: to conserve biodiversity for the benefit of present and future generations
- ➤ objective: to establish an equitable system of measures for conservation and sustainable use and to acknowledge the special situation of developing countries
- identifies habitat destruction, pollution and "unsound management" as the major causes of biodiversity loss
- recognizes national sovereignty and the role of local peoples

Chapter III: Fundamental Principles

- ➤ "common heritage" or "common interest"
- ➤ free access or access restricted by states
- addresses conservation and utilization
- equitable sharing of costs and benefits

Chapter IV: General Obligations

- duty to take appropriate conservation measures
- duty to refrain from actions harmful to biodiversity in other states or beyond national jurisdiction
- duty to promote public/community awareness
- mutual assistance

Source: World Rainforest Movement, Penang, Malaysia.

698

Chapter V: Measures for Conservation and Sustainable Use (at National Level)

In Situ and Ex Situ Conservation
- surveys, information gathering, identification of important areas
- protection of important areas
- establish centres for *ex situ* conservation
- recovery and rehabilitation of threatened species, habitats and ecosystems
- reduction of pollution

Sustainable Use of Wild Resources
- support land use activities compatible with the maintenance of biodiversity
- recognition of the important role of biotechnology and of its potential dangers
- need to recognize and maintain local information on biodiversity and to reward and sustain informal innovation by local people
- integrate conservation into national development plans, ensure utilization does not have adverse impacts
- ➤ need for environmental impact assessments for proposed developments

Research, Training and Education
- train taxonomists, ethnobotanists, specialists in sustainable agriculture and ecosystem function
- promote research in all these areas
- formal and non-formal education of public and of local populations
- capacity building in research institutions of developing countries
- strengthen information exchange between governmental and non-governmental agencies

Chapter VI: Availability of Technology and Access to Biological Diversity

- guarantee availability and access to biological diversity for research, training, surveying and monitoring
- ➤ guarantee availability and access to biological diversity for other purposes
- ➤ preferential treatment for countries of origin
- ➤ guarantee availability and access to technology and information
- ➤ rules for patents and property rights on genetic resources

Chapter VII: Technology Transfer

- ➤ obligation on industrial states to promote
- ➤ technology transfer on a non-commercial or preferential basis
- ➤ undertaking for legislation for obligations on private companies

699

➤ promote exchange of information
• scientific cooperation and cooperation in training of experts
• promote joint ventures in biotechnology
• funding to facilitate technology transfer
• a clearing house mechanism to facilitate technology transfer

Chapter VIII: Technical Assistance

• obligation to provide reasonable levels of technical assistance
• a clearing house mechanism to facilitate provision of technical assistance

Chapter IX: Financial Mechanisms

• need for genuine additional resources
• mechanisms to be elaborated
➤ create new fund or adapt existing funds
➤ explore Montreal Protocol and World Bank's GEF as models

Chapter X: Relationship with Other Agreements

• not to replace other agreements
• other agreements to be supported
• other agreements eligible to become protocols

Chapter XI: Institutional Measures at the National Level

• obligation to legislate to set up specialised institutions at the national level

Chapter XII: International Cooperation

• promote international cooperation

Notes

1. Chapter II contains definitions; Chapter XIII—institutional arrangements for the Convention; Chapter XIV—dispute settlement mechanisms; Chapter XV will deal with annexes, protocols and amendments
2. It has been proposed that the structure of the convention be reorganized with chapters V and XI forming a new chapter on measures at the national level, and chapters VI–VIII and XII forming a new chapter on international mechanisms.

Document III.2: Summary of Critiques of 1992 Biodiversity Convention

The United States delayed signing the biodiversity convention because it believed that its "intellectual property rights"—for example, patents not only on technology but also on plants, animals, and their genetic components—might be undermined by Chapter VI. On the other hand, Chapter X can be interpreted as guaranteeing at least existing patents and other intellectual property rights. Some 160 states signed the convention, leaving the United States isolated.

Further at issue are _future_ discoveries, particularly in the immense gene and specie pools of tropical rainforests, sometimes called "gene banks," "green gold," or "pharmacies." What about "intellectual property rights" to them? In the age of biotechnology, U.S.-based pharmaceutical and biotechnology companies are especially interested in not just scientific and medical discoveries but potential profits from these gene pools as well.

Many Latin Americans point out that the more industrialized nations accuse poorer countries of engaging in "unfair trade practices" if they do not adopt U.S. and other patent laws which allow quasi-monopoly "intellectual property rights" over life or genetic forms. "Royalties" (a form of payment or profit) on use of this "green gold" typically go to the holders of the "intellectual property rights." Any profits derived from the use of the plants or genes rarely return to the country where they originated. Some Latin Americans believe that they should not have to pay royalties to foreign companies (TNCs) for hi-tech seeds derived from wild plants found in Latin America.

Typically, environmentalists from Latin America and other developing parts of the world fear "Western" imposition of control over "their" rainforests in manners detrimental to ecological balance and free flowing, low-cost technology transfer. They cite the history of the Green Revolution (see chapter 1), which replaced genetically diverse agricultural systems with "genetically uniform monocultures" to the detriment of the environment and indigenous cultures. They fear an unregulated, runaway commercialization of biological diversity for "free market" purposes. They note that today's "biobattles" are already being fought out in the trade wars of GATT and NAFTA.

Some Latin American governments complain that they are urged to engage in strict conservation but that the United States is not urged to reduce its levels of consumerism, waste, or dumping of toxic wastes in Latin America. A biodiversity program must be "global and fair" in scope, they maintain. They envision a fair system as one that allows more-equal access to genetic resources and any profits or other benefits derived from their use; more-equitable technology transfer; support for local communities; and prevention (or at

Source: Lecture notes of Professor James D. Cockcroft from a course on environment he taught at Rensselaer Polytechnic Institute's Department of Science and Technology Studies, 1993. See also chapter 20, the section on "Environment, Ethnocide, and Earth Summit 1992."

least regulation) of biotechnology companies' creation of substitutes for farm products traditionally exported from less developed countries. If biotechnology continues to be a near monopoly of industrialized nations, they claim, the technological gap between North and South will only widen.

In early 1993 the Clinton administration announced that the United States would sign the Biodiversity Convention. It can be presumed that the disputes over intellectual property rights, however, will continue. Disputes will likely be resolved either by international agreements or by rulings on individual cases through existing courts and trade bodies. An additional voice in the debate is the increasingly internationalist environmental movement led by nongovernmental organizations, concerned individuals, and environmentalist groups.

IV. Alternative U.S. Policy Recommendations

Document IV.1: Emergency National Council Against U.S. Intervention in Central America and the Caribbean, "Why Mass Action: A Strategy for Stopping the U.S. War Against Nicaragua and Ending U.S. Intervention in Central America and the Caribbean," November 1986 (selections)

. . . The Reagan administration has poured over $1 billion into El Salvador to maintain in power repressive regimes. And it has persecuted Americans (including religious figures) who are actively engaged in providing "sanctuary" for Salvadorans and Guatemalans fleeing the bombs and death squads.

In the last six years, El Salvador's military, security, and death-squad forces have murdered more than 60,000 unarmed civilians. Trade unionists and peasants have been prime targets for death, torture, and imprisonment. So have church leaders. . . .

Clear evidence exists that ties the death squads to high government officials in El Salvador, military leaders, and right-wing businessmen in Miami. The U.S. could put an end to the atrocities by cutting off military aid.

But Reagan claims that El Salvador is becoming a model of Central American democracy because of elections held there in 1984. The elections, an all-right-wing affair held at gunpoint, were for U.S. television viewers more than for the Salvadoran people.

Why Is It Happening?

The U.S. government supports dictatorships and other regimes in Central America that protect U.S. corporate investments. The story is an old one.

U.S.-backed regimes guarantee U.S. corporate investors high profit rates and a "safe" environment, often free of labor unions or strikes. That is why the auto workers' UAW and other mainline American labor unions have come out against U.S. policy in Central America.

In modern times, big U.S. corporations moved into Nicaragua and other Central American countries to run them like fiefdoms, from the days of United Fruit to those of American Cyanamid and Bank of America.

The word "runaway shop" is now understood by everyone. The corporations openly threaten their American employees with going overseas to cheap-labor areas like Central America or the Caribbean if they do not accept the employers' terms on contract renewals. And wages are inhuman in those countries.

When Central America and Caribbean Basin workers attempt to union-

Source: Selections from "Why Mass Action: A Strategy for Stopping the U.S. War Against Nicaragua and Ending U.S. Intervention in Central America and the Caribbean," Emergency National Council Against U.S. Intervention in Central America/The Caribbean (ENC), November 1986. Reprinted by permission of ENC, P.O. Box 21672, Cleveland, OH 44121.

The Risk of a Wider War [1986]

In a century-old fight between haves and have-nots, the entire region was at risk of exploding into war.

CUBA

President Reagan said he would not honor the Kennedy-Khrushchev accord that ended the 1962 Cuban Missile Crisis by which the U.S. promised not to invade Cuba in exchange for Soviet withdrawal of missiles. U.S. base remains at Guantánamo.

PUERTO RICO

U.S. military bases for staging armed interventions in the Dominican Republic (1965) and Grenada (1983).

GRENADA

Occupied by U.S. troops in 1983. U.S. military staged exercise "chasing Marxists in the mountains" in May 1986.

PANAMA

U.S. Southern Command headquarters, with many bases and training centers used in coordinating AWAC overflights, fleet movements off both Nicaraguan coasts, and sophisticated radar equipment.

COSTA RICA

U.S. built military influence. In February 1986, President-elect Oscar Arias announced agreement with Nicaragua to set up a bilateral border vigilance commission. Then, 186 U.S. Army engineers arrived to renovate border airstrips.

NICARAGUA

Thousands killed by U.S.-supported contras who sought to overthrow Sandinista government. Some Soviet-built helicopters here, plus anti-aircraft guns, ground-to-air missiles and tanks that U.S. State Dept. and Pentagon officials privately admit were defensive.

MEXICO

Since the late 1970s, the U.S. government has declared Mexico's oil fields vital to U.S. "national security." With oil reserves second only to Saudi Arabia and with billions of dollars of U.S. investments, Mexico is the target of concentrated U.S. attention to prevent popular uprising.

GUATEMALA

A newly elected civilian president admitted in 1986 that he cannot control the armed forces that have killed more than 100,000 since the CIA-sponsored 1954 coup that led to the military's assumption of real power. In spite of congressional bans, Reagan maneuvered to sell Guatemala more military equipment.

EL SALVADOR

Reagan aid programs poured $1 billion into a losing war against the have-nots. Meanwhile, the popular forces controlled nearly half the territory. The U.S.-backed government's death squads and saturation bombings of civilians made a third of the population homeless refugees.

HONDURAS

Six U.S. airbases and thousands of U.S. troops. Staging area for invasion of Nicaragua by contra army of 18,000 former supporters of dictator Somoza. U.S. "advisors" trained Salvadorans and contras.

ize and raise their wage levels, troops occupy their workplaces to "restore order." If the workers rebel and seek to establish a government that will put controls on the transnational corporations—or take them over—the U.S. government calls this "communism" and funds contras to defeat the revolutionary movement.

How We Can Stop It: Mass Action

The strategy that has worked most effectively in the past to end or reverse bad government policies has been the continuous mobilization of thousands of people in the streets protesting in an organized and disciplined manner.

That is how working people won the right to have unions and to strike.

That is how the system of legalized segregation was broken in the U.S.

That is how the women's rights movement won significant victories.

And that is how the nightmare of the Vietnam War was ended.

Post-Vietnam revelations by government officials as to why they acted as they did during the war and disclosures in the Pentagon Papers make clear that the mass anti-war movement played a decisive role in restraining U.S. military action in Vietnam and ultimately ending its military intervention in Southeast Asia. For example, in 1966, when urged to bomb Hanoi and Haiphong to dust, President Johnson said, "'I have one more problem for your computer—how long will it take five hundred thousand angry Americans to climb that White House wall out there and lynch their president if he does something like that?" And it is well to remember that the Vietnam War was ended under the presidencies of Nixon and Ford who, despite their commitment to the South Vietnam dictatorship, were forced by mass anti-war actions to pull U.S. troops out of Indochina. This showed that in many situations masses marching in the streets can be more decisive than which president is sitting in the White House.

Those who rule the United States and direct its wars fear the mass protest movement. That is why they did not invade and overthrow the Sandinista government years ago. Instead, they conduct their war against the government through surrogates, while constantly testing the waters of public opinion to determine whether they can take more direct action, as they did in Grenada.

The anti-intervention movement's most powerful method for countering U.S. government policies is through building united mass demonstrations in the streets. These demonstrations show the extent of the movement's support and reflect the determination of its participants that the anti-intervention demands be implemented.

Such demonstrations also provide a vehicle for mobilizing the largest number of people at a given time and place. They enable all sectors of the movement to come together, regardless of differences on other issues. They give the movement the visibility it must have and they send a message to the government and to people throughout the country and the world that there is deeply felt and widespread opposition to U.S. policies.

United actions help in building the movement and expanding its activist core. People who participate in a demonstration often become inspired by the event. They learn from the speakers and from other marchers, and they gain motivation to convince others and bring them into the movement. This is an important part of a process by which successive demonstrations can become progressively larger and have greater impact.

Mass demonstrations are not one-day events. A well-planned action takes months to prepare and build. It provides a vehicle for going to unions, the Black community, Latinos, other oppressed minorities, women's rights organizations, students and other youth, farmers, the unemployed, and religious groups, asking for their endorsement of the demonstration and participation in it. This provides opportunities to speak to groups on the issues involved, to distribute literature, to educate.

By relating U.S. intervention in Central America and the Caribbean to the critical economic and social problems facing the American people, demonstration organizers help people to understand their stake in opposing U.S. interventionist policies. They see that union-busting, plant closings, high unemployment and discrimination against minorities and women go hand-in-hand with U.S. foreign policies that deny to peoples in other lands the right to decide for themselves what kind of society they wish to build.

Most important, people who become convinced that U.S. policies are wrong have a way to do something about it: take to the streets with thousands of others as part of a protest demonstration.

Shortly after the New York City demonstration by 100,000 people on June 14, 1986, the House of Representatives passed a resolution calling for strong sanctions against South Africa. Mass pressure can force Congress to enact comprehensive sanctions.

The anti-intervention movement should give its all-out support to the anti-apartheid cause. The more these two great social movements are united, the stronger each will be. The best place for them to join is in the streets in demonstrations demanding "Boycott South Africa, Not Nicaragua!" and "U.S. Out of Central America and South Africa!"

Mass anti-intervention demonstrations do not materialize out of thin air. Someone has to call them. That "someone" should be a broad, all-embracing non-exclusionary national coalition made up of all anti-intervention forces. Such a coalition must be non-partisan so that people of diverse political persuasions can unite against U.S. intervention in Central America and the Caribbean.

The creation of such a coalition and the unification of the U.S. anti-intervention and anti-apartheid movements for ongoing and ever larger mass actions must be top priorities if the U.S. wars against the people of Central America are to be halted and if U.S. support for South Africa's apartheid government is to be ended.

Document IV.2: "Arias Peace Plan," August 7, 1987 (Central American Peace Accord)

As read by His Excellency the President of the Republic of Costa Rica, Dr. Oscar Arias Sánchez.

The Presidents of the Republics of Guatemala, El Salvador, Honduras, Nicaragua, and Costa Rica . . . have agreed to fully take up the historic challenge of forging a destiny of peace for Central America. We ask for international treatment which would guarantee [our] development so that the peace we seek will be a lasting peace. We firmly reaffirm that peace and development are inseparable.

The following is the text of the Agreement signed by the five leaders:

Procedure for the Establishment of a Strong and Lasting Peace in Central America

1. National Reconciliation

(a) *Dialogue*

To urgently carry out, in those cases where deep divisions have resulted within society, steps for national reconciliation which would allow for popular participation with full guarantees in authentic political processes of a democractic nature based on justice, freedom, and democracy. Towards this end, to create those mechanisms which, in accordance with the law, would allow for dialogue with opposition groups.

(b) *Amnesty*

In each Central America country, except those where the International Commission of Verification and Follow Up determines that such a measure is not necessary, an Amnesty decree will be issued containing all the provisions for the guarantee of the inviolability of life; as well as freedom in all its forms, property, and the security of the persons to whom these decrees apply. Simultaneous with the issuing of the Amnesty decree by the government, the irregular forces of the respective country will place in freedom all persons in their power.

Source: From widely published "Arias Peace Plan," agreed to by Presidents of Republics of Guatemala, El Salvador, Honduras, Nicaragua, and Costa Rica, and presented by Dr. Oscar Arias Sánchez, August 1987.

(c) *National Reconciliation Commission*

In order to verify the compliance with the commitments that the five Central America governments subscribed to by the signing of this document, concerning amnesty, cease fire, democratization, and free elections, a National Reconciliation Commission will be established whose duties will be to verify the actual carrying out in practice of the national reconciliation process, as well as the full exercise of all civil and political rights of Central American citizens guaranteed in this document.

The National Reconciliation Commission will be comprised of a delegate and an alternative delegate from the Executive Branch; a Bishop delegate and an alternate Bishop delegate recommended by the Episcopal Conference and chosen by the government from a list of three candidates which should be presented [by the Episcopal Conference] within a period of fifteen days upon receipt of a formal invitation. This invitation will be made by the government within five working days from the signing of this document.

The same procedure using a list of three candidates will be used to select a delegate and alternate delegate from the legally registered political opposition parties. The said list of three [candidates] should be presented within the same above mentioned period.

In addition, each Central American government will choose an outstanding citizen, who does not hold public office or belong to the governing party, and his respective alternate to be part of this Commission.

2. Exhortation for the Cessation of Hostilities. The governments make a vehement appeal so that in the States of the area, currently suffering from the activity of irregular or insurgent groups, a cessation of hostilities be arranged. The governments of these States commit themselves to undertake all the necessary steps for achieving an effective ceasefire within the constitutional framework.

3. Democratization. The governments commit themselves to promote an authentic democratic, pluralist, and participatory process that includes the promotion of social justice, respect for Human Rights, [state] sovereignty, the territorial integrity of States, and the right of all nations to freely determine, without outside interference of any kind, its economic, political, and social model, and to carry out in a verifiable manner those measures leading to the establishment, or in their instances, the improvement of representative and pluralist democratic systems which would provide guarantees for the organization of political parties, effective popular participation in the decision-making process, and to ensure free access to different currents of opinion to honest electoral processes and newspapers based on the full exercise of citizens' rights.

For the purpose of verifying the good faith in the development of this democratization process, it will be understood that:

(a) There shall exist complete freedom of press, television, and radio. This complete freedom will include the opening and maintaining in operation of communications media for all ideological groups, and the operation of this media without prior censorship. .

(b) Complete political pluralism should be manifest. In this regard, political groupings shall have broad access to communications media, full exercise of the right of association and the right to manifest publicly the exercise of their right to free speech, be it oral, written, or televised, as well as freedom of movement by members of political parties in order to proselytize.

(c) Likewise, those governments of Central America, which have in effect a state of exception, siege, or emergency shall terminate that state, and reestablish the full exercise of all constitutional guarantees.

4. Free Elections. Once the conditions inherent to every democracy are established, free, pluralist, and honest elections shall be held. As a joint expression of the Central American States to seek reconciliation and lasting peace for its people, elections will be held for a Central American Parliament, whose founding was proposed in the Esquipulas Declaration of May 25, 1986 . . .

These elections will take place simultaneously in all the countries throughout Central America in the first half of 1988, on a date mutually agreed to by the Presidents of the Central American states. These elections will be subject to vigilance by the appropriate electoral bodies. The respective governments commit themselves to extend an invitation to the Organization of American States and to the United Nations, as well as to the governments of third states, to send observers who shall bear witness that the electoral processes have been held in accordance with the strictest norms of equal access of all political parties to the media, as well as full guarantees for public demonstrations and other kinds of proselytizing propaganda.

The appropriate Founding Treaty shall be submitted for approval or ratification in the five countries so that the elections for the Central American Parliament can be held within the period indicated in this section.

After the elections for the Central American Parliament have been held, equally free and democractic elections shall be held with international observers and the same guarantees in each country, to name popular representatives to municipalities, congresses and legislative assemblies, and the presidencies of the Republics. These elections will be held according to the proposed calendars and within the periods established in the current political constitutions.

5. Cessation of Assistance to Irregular Forces or Insurrectionist Movements. The governments of the five Central American States shall request the governments of the region, and the extra-regional governments which openly or covertly provide military, logistical, financial, propagandistic aid in manpower, armaments, munitions and equipment to irregular forces or insurrectionist movements to cease this aid, as an indispensable element for achieving a stable and lasting peace in the region.

The above does not include assistance for repatriation, or in lieu thereof, the relocation of and assistance necessary for those persons having belonged to these groups or forces to become reintegrated into normal life. Likewise, striving for a true Latin American spirit, the irregular forces or insurgent groups who operate in Central America will be asked to abstain from receiving such assistance.

These petitions will be made in accordance with the provisions of the Document of Objectives regarding the elimination of arms traffic, whether it be inter-regional or extra-regional, intended for persons, organizations, or groups attempting to destabilize the governments of the Central American countries.

6. The Non-Use of Territory to Attack Other States. The five countries which signed this document, reaffirm their commitment to prevent the use of their own territory, and to neither render nor permit military or logistical support to persons, organizations, or groups attempting to destabilize the governments of the Central American countries.

7. Negotiations on Matters Relating to Security, Verification, Control and Limitation of Armaments. The governments of the five Central American States, with the participation of the Contadora Group in exercise of its role as mediator, will continue negotiations on the points still pending in the Contadora Treaty Proposal for Peace and Cooperation in Central America concerning "Security, Verification and Control."

In addition, these negotiations will entail measures for the disarmament of the irregular forces who are willing to accept the amnesty decrees.

8. Refugees and Displaced Persons. The governments of Central America commit themselves to give urgent attention to the flow of refugees and displaced persons brought about by the regional crisis, through protection and assistance, particularly in areas of education, health, work, and security and whenever voluntary, and individually expressed, to facilitate in the repatriation, resettlement, and relocation [of these persons]. They also commit themselves to request assistance for Central American refugees and displaced persons from the International Community. . . .

9. Cooperation, Democracy, and Freedom for Peace and Development. In the climate of freedom guaranteed by democracy, the Central American countries will adopt agreements permitting for the intensification of development in order to achieve more egalitarian and poverty-free societies. Consolidation of democracy presupposes the creation of a system of economic and social justice and well-being. To achieve these objectives the governments will jointly seek special economic support from the international community.

10. International Verification and Follow-Up

(a) *International Verification and Follow-Up Commission*

An International Verification and Follow-Up Commission will be established, comprised of the Secretary Generals of the Organization of American States and the United Nations or their representatives, as well as the Foreign Ministers of Central America, of the Contadora Group and the Support Group. This Commission will have the duties of verifying and following up the compliance with the commitments undertaken in this document.

(b) *Support and Facilities Given to the Mechanisms for Reconciliation and Verification and Follow-Up*

The five governments shall offer all the necessary facilities for full compliance . . .

11. Calendar for the Implementation of Agreements. Within a period of 15 days from the signing of this document, the Foreign Ministers of Central America will meet as the Executive Committee to regulate, promote, and make feasible compliance with the agreements contained herein, and to organize the working commission so that, henceforth, the processes leading to compliance with the contracted commitments may be initiated within the stipulated periods by means of consultations, undertakings, and other mechanisms deemed necessary. Ninety days from the signing of this document, the commitments pertaining to amnesty, cease fire, democratization, cessation of assistance to irregular forces or insurrectionist movements, and the non-use of territory to attack other states, will enter into force simultaneously and publicly as defined herein.

One hundred and twenty days from the signing of this document, the International Commission for Verification and Follow-Up will analyze the progress [made] in the compliance with the agreements provided for herein.

After 150 days, the five Central American Presidents will meet and receive a report from the International Commission of Verification and Follow-Up and they will make the pertinent decisions.

Final Provisions. The points included in this document form part of a harmonious and indivisible whole. . . .

We, the Presidents of the five States of Central America, with the political will to respond to the longings for peace of our peoples, sign [this document] in the City of Guatemala, on the seventh day of August of 1987.

> Oscar Arias Sánchez
> José Azcona Hoyo
> Vinicio Cerezo Arévalo
> José Napoleón Duarte
> Daniel Ortega Saavedra

Document IV.3: Policy Alternatives for the Caribbean and Central America (PACCA), "An Alternative U.S. Policy Toward Cuba," 1988 (selections)

An Alternative U.S. Policy Toward Cuba

Note: Policy Alternatives for the Caribbean and Central America (PACCA) is an association of scholars, development specialists, and policymakers with long-term experience in the region.

I. Restore relations and negotiate bilateral issues.

Begin negotiations to settle U.S. claims for compensation for expropriated property and Cuban claims for damage as a result of U.S. actions.

Resume trade and economic relations between the two countries.

Negotiate bilateral issues, including radio interference problems, medium wave broadcasts from one country to the other, maritime border disputes, violations of air space, handling of acts of sabotage and hijacking, and security and sovereignty concerns related to the U.S. Guantanamo Bay military base in Cuba.

The United States already has an enormous military presence in the Caribbean with bases in Florida and Puerto Rico. The Guantanamo base is now used mainly for training and most analysts do not consider it important to U.S. security. Talks over the base would help remove a major irritant in relations between the two countries. Some observers have urged "creative solutions" such as using the base for an international hospital or some other humanitarian facility.

II. Work to resolve regional and global security issues.

Open discussions on mutual security concerns. . . . Open exploratory discussions with Cuba on mutual commitment to, and compliance with, the provisions of the Central American Peace agreement forbidding foreign aid to irregular forces and the use of one Central American nation as a base for waging war on another.

Open discussions with Cuba with the aim of reintegrating it into inter-American forums such as the Organization of American States; seek Cuba's inclusion in regional development efforts for the Caribbean. . . .

III. Work for reconciliation between the United States and Cuba.

Lift economic sanctions against Cuba that have the effect of denying U.S. citizens the right to free trade in ideas, including restrictions on travel and the free flow of information.

Permanently halt . . . [denial of] visas to Cuban citizens who wish to participate in educational and cultural exchanges in the United States.

Foster the development of educational, cultural and tourist exchange programs between the United States and Cuba. . . .

Initiate discussions with Cuba on the rights of communication and travel for Cuban-Americans and Cubans wishing to visit their relatives for family and humanitarian reasons. Work to improve telephone services and establish direct mail service.

Document IV.4: Robert G. Torricelli, Letter to the *New York Times*, January 5, 1994

To the Editor:

"U.S. Companies Use Affiliates Abroad to Skirt Sanctions," your Dec. 27 front-page report on Cuba and Libya, misleads your readers to believe that the case regarding Cargill Inc.'s sale of Cuban sugar shows how American corporations seize on "porous laws" to use foreign subsidiaries and circumvent the United States embargo on Cuba. This is not the case.

The 1988–89 Cargill case involves the Trading With the Enemy Act and took place three years before enactment of the Cuban Democracy Act, which I sponsored and which became law on Oct. 23, 1992.

The Cuban Democracy Act prohibited such trade. The results speak for themselves: United States trade through foreign subsidiaries fell from $718 million in 1991 to only $1.6 million last year. What remains covers con-

Source: Letter by House Representatives member Robert G. Torricelli (Dem., NJ) to the *New York Times,* Jan. 5, 1994.

tracts in effect when the Cuban Democracy Act became law because United States laws are not applied retroactively. The Cargill case discussed in the article involves the possible involvement by Cargill United States in the 1989 financing of sugar, which had already been sold by Cuba to Venezuela. The case is an enforcement action under the Trading With the Enemy Act, and it is continuing.

I have expressed my outrage about this case to Attorney General Janet Reno and underscored that if the allegations are true and if Cargill is found guilty, both the corporate officers involved and the company should be prosecuted.

Contrary, however, to your article's assertion that "the trading involved here raises questions about the effectiveness of one of the most visible tools of United States foreign policy," the Cuban Democracy Act, passed four years after this case, definitely answers questions about the effectiveness of the embargo. United States trade through foreign subsidiaries has ground to a halt.

While your article's investigative reporting is valuable, your analysis of the United States embargo must be put into context. The Cuban economy, particularly without its Soviet benefactor, is crumbling; Fidel Castro's own family wants out, and the final period of President Castro's dictatorship is here.

The embargo has had its effect, and the day when the United States will trade with a free Cuba is near.

In the meantime, it is important to correct the impression that is given by the article, that United States laws regarding trade with Cuba are lax. That is simply wrong, and it is a dangerous impression because United States trade with Cuba, directly or indirectly, without a license is illegal, and violators will surely be prosecuted to the full extent of the law.

(Rep.) ROBERT G. TORRICELLI
Chairman, Subcommitte
on Western Hemisphere Affairs
Washington, Dec. 28, 1993

Document IV.5: Cuban American Committee for Peace president, Letter to the *New York Times*, January 20, 1994

To the Editor:

I write you as president of the Cuban American Committee for Peace, which has a membership of more than 17,000 Cubans residing in the United States, South America, Spain and Canada. All of us still have family in Cuba.

I was appalled by Representative Robert G. Torricelli's Jan. 5 letter, in which he brags of the effects his Cuban "Democracy" Act has had on the Cuban economy. He did not address the effect the decrease of United States subsidiary trade has had in human terms. Of the $718 million in subsidiary trade eliminated by Mr. Torricelli's law, 75 percent has been for food and medicine.

I visit Cuba regularly and have seen a significant change in my family's nutritional status since this law's enactment in 1992. I recently visited my 18-year-old son in Havana, and was disturbed at how thin he and the rest of my relatives have become.

Recently a United States subsidiary based in Canada sought to sell baby food to Cuba. It could not because of the Cuban Democracy Act, which states no United States subsidiary can trade with Canada. This is what Mr. Torricelli is proud of? We are talking about food for infants, not military weapons. This law is a policy of genocide that seeks to create a Somalia in Cuba.

Mr. Torricelli speaks of democracy's coming to Cuba any day. About a year ago he predicted the Cuban Government would fall in three months.

Average Cubans do not blame their Government for the food and medicine shortages. Rather, they blame the United States embargo. Even human rights dissidents in Cuba like Elizardo Sanchez have spoken out against the Torricelli law. In Cuba, there are 3.5 million children. They are the victims of the Torricelli law.

Mr. Torricelli and other politicians need to start hearing that the climate in the United States is changing. Cuban-Americans are beginning to state that we will no longer allow opportunistic Congressmen like Mr. Torricelli to use a small group of rich, reactionary, Cuban exiles like Jorge Mas Canosa and his Cuban American National Foundation to pursue a policy that brings suffering to our families living in Cuba.

Mr. Torricelli and Mr. Mas Canosa talk of bringing democracy to Cuba, yet the foundation and reactionary groups like Alpha 66 use political harassment and intimidation to silence those who disagree with them. I have received death threats for expressing my belief that the United States should normalize relations with Cuba.

Source: Letter from president of Cuban American Committee for Peace to the *New York Times*, Jan. 20, 1994.

New voices besides ours are being raised in the Cuban-American community—for instance, Cambio Cubano and the Cuban Committee for Democracy. All of them seek a new policy of dialogue between our two countries. These are the groups to whom Mr. Torricelli should listen.

It is time for this cruel and inhumane embargo to end and for men like Mr. Torricelli to realize that laws like the Cuban Democracy Act are not something of which they should be proud.

RAYMUNDO DEL TORO
Linden, NJ., Jan. 12, 1994

Document IV.6: William Ratliff and Roger Fontaine, *New York Times*, Op-Ed, February 17, 1994

Conservatives, Lead the Way
By William Ratliff and Roger Fontaine

STANFORD, Calif.

Nowhere has President Clinton been so true to his campaign promises as in his support for the 1992 Cuban Democracy Act, which tightened the 1962 U.S. economic embargo of Cuba. But for the good of the United States and the vast majority of Cubans, we should repeal the 1992 law and lift the embargo now. And the conservatives who have most vigorously opposed Fidel Castro should lead the movement for this change.

We supported the embargo in the past because it put pressure on a Soviet ally that aided anti-U.S. insurgencies and terrorism around the world. But such arguments no longer hold. The embargo is now both out of date—particularly in view of our opening to Vietnam—and contrary to our security interests.

The 1992 law is a policy of impoverishing Cubans at the behest of the most militant conservative groups in the émigré community. It is polarizing Cuba—driving many anti-Castro Cubans back into Mr. Castro's camp, since they fear a takeover (and reprisals) by Cubans returning from Miami—and enhancing his reputation as a fearless fighter of Yankee capitalism. All of this increases the likelihood of a civil war that could drag in the United States and abort the transition to stable democracy in Cuba.

Perhaps Mr. Clinton really believes the squeeze is the best policy. But we suspect that this is a case of domestic politics dictating foreign policy. President George Bush opposed tightening the embargo—as did President Ronald Reagan a decade earlier—until Mr. Clinton endorsed it in Florida during the 1992 campaign.

Now the President and some members of Congress fear losing votes and

Source: William Ratliff (senior research fellow Hoover Institution) and Roger Fontaine (former national security aide in Reagan administration), *New York Times,* Op-Ed, February 17, 1994.

financial support from Cuban-Americans if they lift the embargo, though more and more émigrés with families still in Cuba are turning against the embargo (if not always publicly). In any event, this "political" argument is an excuse for doing nothing.

It is no sign of moral strength or principled consistency to make Cubans suffer in order to force them to rise up against Mr. Castro, or to make them live in greater misery in apparent punishment for failing to do so. If we drop the embargo without negotiations or demands, he will have no credibility when he accuses the United States of interfering in Cuban affairs. His propaganda assaults will be exposed for the outdated cold war bombast they surely are. We will be saying he has become as irrelevant as the socialist creed he still professes.

If Mr. Castro is irrelevant, so is the embargo. Worse, it is a scapegoat for the economic malaise and repression he himself has brought on. All Americans should join forces in killing that scapegoat.

Index

___ Credits _____

Picture Gallery

Page 3 top: Godfrey Harris/The America's Group
bottom: Bill Gentile/Sipa Press
Page 4 top: © Lewy Moraes/Nexus, DDB Stock Photo
middle: © Alyx Kellington, DDB Stock Photo
bottom: Chip and Rosa Maria Peterson
Page 5 top: © Bill Gentile/Zuma
bottom: © Bill Gentile/Zuma
Page 6 top: © Jean-Marie Simon/Visions
bottom: © Alex Webb/Magnum
Page 7 top: © Chip and Rosa Maria Peterson
middle: © Ricardo Teles/DDB Stock Photo
bottom: © Tony Suarez/Zuma Images
Page 8 top: © Michael Moody/DDB Stock Photo
middle: © Bill Gentile/ZUMA
bottom: © Montecino/Zuma Images

A Nelson-Hall
Quality Paperback

LATIN AMERICA
History, Politics, and
U.S. Policy/Second Edition

James D. Cockcroft

ISBN 0-8304-1398-7

90000>

9 780830 413980